Economics Principles of Political Economy

Economics Principles of Political Economy

Daniel R. Fusfeld

University of Michigan

Scott, Foresman and Company   **Glenview, Illinois**

Dallas, Tex.   **Oakland, N.J.**   **Palo Alto, Calif.**   **Tucker, Ga.**   **London, England**

Cover photograph: Robert Frerck

Library of Congress Cataloging in Publication Data

Fusfeld, Daniel Roland, 1922-
   Economics, principles of political economy.

   Includes index.
   1. Economics.   I. Title
HB171.5.F87   330   81-21260
ISBN 0-673-15350-9   AACR2

123456-KPF-878685848382

Figure 28-5 (p. 500) from Robert J. Lampman, *The
Share of Top Wealth-Holders in National Wealth*, 1922-56,
p. 202. Copyright © 1962 by National Bureau of
Economic Research, Inc.

Figure 28-6 (p. 505) from William Fellner, et al., *Ten
Economic Studies in the Tradition of Irving Fisher*, p.
241. Copyright © 1967 John Wiley & Sons, Inc.

Preface

This text is an introduction to economics for those who have had little or no previous training in economics. This analysis of the political economy of modern capitalism focuses on the relationships among economic forces, the changing institutional structure of the economy, the sources and uses of economic power, and the conflicts inherent in and generated by the private-enterprise economy. Theories of exchange and the level of economic activity are explained and used as part of a political-economic-institutional analysis.

The Introduction and first three chapters form Part 1, which is an overview of the functions, limitations, and conflicts of the modern economy. Parts 2 and 3 (Chapters 4-14) cover macroeconomics. Parts 4, 5, 6, and 7 constitute the microeconomics presentation. Part 8 on socialism and Part 9 on the international economy are optional sections; either could be taught immediately after the macroeconomics parts. For those instructors who wish to do so, the microeconomics portion (Parts 4 through 7) can be taught before the macroeconomics (Parts 2 and 3). Various appendices appear throughout the text and either cover topics in greater depth or present material of optional interest. The appendices can be assigned at the discretion of the instructor.

The book aids student understanding and stimulates student interest by setting off key concepts and definitions in color, by ending each chapter with a summary, a list of key terms, and discussion questions, and by boxing off examples and other items of interest.

The theoretical and conceptual framework of the book includes the following specific elements:

1. The macroeconomic analysis uses a flexible-price post-Keynesian model rather than the fixed-price Keynesian model, which enables cost and supply-side considerations to be built into both the basic theory and the analysis of inflation.

2. This book uses the concept of money as the connecting link between the present and future in a time-consuming economic process rather than the monetarist concept of an autonomous money supply.

3. The macroeconomic analysis emphasizes the instability of the economy rather than equilibrium. It also shows that changes in aggregate demand and aggregate supply affect the level of prices as well as output and employment.

4. A partial-equilibrium analysis, rather than neo-Walrasian general-equilibrium theory, is used to explain the market adjustment process. The analysis focuses on the producer rather than on the consumer to emphasize the proposition that prices are determined by costs of production in the long-run adjustment of competitive markets.

5. Major attention is given to administered prices in the oligopolistic sector of the economy and to institutional factors, such as industry structure, corporate goals, price leadership, the kinked demand curve, and markup pricing.

6. The dual nature of the U.S. economy is stressed throughout, including the contrasts between competitive and monopoloid sectors in product markets and between primary and secondary sectors in the labor market.

7. Five full chapters in Part 6 are devoted to the distribution of income and wealth, bringing together market forces, institutional structures, economic power and collective bargaining, Marxist exploitation theory, and unearned incomes.

8. Alternatives to private-enterprise capitalism are discussed in Part 8 on socialism, in Chapter 39 on economic development in the third world, and in Chapter 23 on big business and public policy.

9. Economic power, institutional factors, and market forces receive equal emphasis in chapters dealing with the role of government (Chapters 29 and 30), war and defense (Chapter 31), pollution and the environment (Chapter 32), energy (Chapter 33), and the international economy (Chapters 37 and 38).

10. A continuing theme is the tendency in modern capitalism for economic power and wealth to become more highly concentrated in the hands of a few large corporate units. An alliance of this concentrated economic power with the political and military power of big government creates the political environment for economic activity.

The basic thrust of the book is that the functioning of the modern economy can best be understood by examining the forces of production, social relations of production, and market forces. This book expands and enriches the mainstream analysis of market forces to include the social relations of production and gives increased attention to the forces of production.

Daniel R. Fusfeld
Ann Arbor, Michigan

Acknowledgments

I am grateful for the suggestions and contributions of numerous colleagues across the country who reviewed this manuscript in various stages of its development:

Jose Alberro	University of Illinois, Chicago Circle
Raford Boddy	San Diego State University
Donald Bowles	American University
Paul Bush	California State University, Fresno
Robert Chernomas	University of Miami
Ken Cochrane	West Hills College
Brian Coghlan	University of Vermont
John Dahlquist	College of Alameda
Ken East	Delaware Technical and Community College
John Hardesty	San Diego State University
James Kahn	State University of New York, Binghamton
Martin Melkonian	Hofstra University
Robert Minick	California State University, Fresno
Joseph Morreale	Bard College
Ned Pearlstein	Laney Junior College
Joe Persky	University of Illinois, Chicago Circle
Michael Podgursky	University of Massachusetts, Amherst
Sam Rosenberg	Roosevelt University
Steve Smith	Oscar Rose Junior College
Ron Stanfield	Colorado State University
Edward Starshak	College of Lake County
Wade Thomas	Northeast Louisiana University
Michael Vaughan	Weber State College
Myles Wallace	Clemson University
Vivian Walsh	New School for Social Research
Dale Warnke	College of Lake County
Jim Weaver	American University
Richard Wolff	University of Massachusetts, Amherst
Anthony Yezer	George Washington University

Contents

Part 3
The Monetary System   168

Part 4
Competitive Markets   260

Part 5
Monopoloid Markets

Part 7
Government and the
Economy   516

Introduction

Any economic system uses material things to produce the goods and services people want. People, productive resources, and technologies are the raw materials that are organized to produce what is needed to reproduce the social order and provide for its growth. They are the *forces of production*. Relationships between people are also involved, including social classes and economic interest groups, and the structure of power. These are the *social relations of production*. In the modern world the forces and relations of production are embedded in a network of interrelated markets, which provides the *institutional framework* that distinguishes the modern economy from those that came before. Patterns of motivation and ideologies, or belief systems, may be included in the institutional framework. These three dimensions define the area of inquiry of political economy. A brief definition:

- **Political economy** is the study of the forces and relations of production in their institutional framework, their relationship, and how they change.

Political economy is simultaneously the newest as well as the oldest approach to understanding how the economy functions. It is new as a reaction against the narrow and restricted view of the nature of economies that came to dominate the field in the three decades following the Second World War in the United States and Western Europe. It is old in that it goes back to the broadly based classics of economics for its orientation and emphasis, to economists who were social philosophers as well as theoreticians, such as Adam Smith, Thomas R. Malthus, John Stuart Mill, Karl Marx, Thorstein Veblen, and John M. Keynes. These names include political conservatives, liberal reformers, and one revolutionary radical. However, they all shared two beliefs that are at the heart of the new political economy:

1. No economic system is static. The forces of change are an integral part of economic activity, and economic analysis must deal with them.

2. Economic activity is intimately interrelated with social classes and economic interests, the organization and locus of power, and belief systems or ideologies.

Modern political economy uses these principles to understand how the economy functions, the nature of its difficulties, and why it changes. If these issues can be understood, we should be in a position to resolve some of our pressing economic problems.

The approach to economics that preceded the rise of the new political economy is much narrower in scope. A typical definition is:

- **Economics** is a social science that examines the problems of scarcity and choice. It is the study of the production and distribution of goods and services in a world of scarce resources.

In this context people are seen in a situation in which they must choose between A and B, with both A and B limited in amount, in an effort to maximize their benefits. But concentration on the pure logic of choice loses sight of the fact that choices are made within the context of a particular organization of society, structure of power, and system of beliefs at a given point in historical time and within a continually changing, uncertain, and imperfect world. At its worst, this approach to economics becomes an exercise in the logic of rational action, cut off from reality in the metaphysics of a disembodied world.

At its best, however, the logic of rational action helps us to understand some important aspects of the modern market economy. Within this framework consumers make choices about how to spend their limited incomes and producers make choices about how to use their limited resources. The two come together in markets in which prices are attached to their alternatives. These are important aspects of the modern economy, which is largely organized as a system of interrelated markets. We can learn a good deal about how the economy functions from the traditional analysis of individual behavior in a market economy.

In modern political economy, people are viewed as more than maximizers of satisfaction in a constrained environment. People are seen as both independent units acting independently in their own interest and as members of a social system that requires cooperation in producing goods and satisfying wants. The forms cooper-ation takes, in a factory for example, define the place of the individual in a system of social classes and economic interests. Ownership and control of the means of production are particularly important, determining whether an individual is an owner or manager, wage earner, or salaried employee. Positions in the system of production, distribution, and exchange largely define the economic classes and economic interest groups of the economy, which are often embroiled in conflicts. The interactions of groups, classes, and economic interests are therefore vital in understanding the choices made in the complex modern economy, the direction and speed of economic growth, the level of economic activity, and the allocation of resources to alternative uses. The logic of rational choice must be modified by the insights of political economy.

A Brief History of Political Economy

A key issue in political economy is the relative merit of various ways of organizing economic life. The debate began in the eighteenth century, and focused on the advantages and disadvantages of the developing private enterprise economy of the time.

In the early days the great treatise by Adam Smith, *An Inquiry into the Nature and Causes of the Wealth of Nations* (1776), made the case for private enterprise and free markets. It remains, over two hundred years later, the classic statement of that position. Smith argued that a "system of natural liberty," in which each person was free to advance his own interests, would bring the most rapid advance of national wealth. A free market economy involves exchanges in which both buyer and seller maximize their gains, and this would result in the maximization of social benefits as well. Furthermore, it would lead to the most rapid accumulation of capital and expansion of the means of production. Free markets were essential to these results, and Smith strongly opposed both government intervention in the economy and monopolies that enabled business interests to control markets. Smith saw government and economic privilege as natural political-economic allies and wanted to eliminate their influence over the free operation of the economy. He was suspicious of both the political power that accrued to great wealth and the economic power that strong governments could exercise.

A generation later, during the political turmoil unleashed by the French Revolution, Thomas R. Malthus modified Smith's defense of the private enterprise economy to answer demands for reform and social change. His *Principle of Population* (1797) argued that there was no natural limit to population except poverty. Economic growth and increased output would cause population to increase, leaving workers at the subsistence level. Aid to the poor was futile, for it only enabled more poor to survive while reducing the resources available for capital accumulation and economic growth. The solution to poverty lay not in redistribution of income, government aid programs, or changing the economic system, but in voluntary limitation of the size of families by the poor themselves. The poor had only themselves to blame for their poverty. This argument, or variations of it, has comforted the wealthy ever since.

But Malthus did not give capitalism a clean bill of health. His *Principles of Political Economy* (1820) argued that a private enterprise economy was inherently unstable, for the capacity to produce tended to increase more rapidly than the ability of consumers to buy, resulting in unemployment and wasted production capacity. Malthus recommended that, during poor times, it was appropriate for government to increase its spending and reduce taxes. His chief emphasis, however, was on the idea that the luxury spending of the wealthy helped to stabilize the economy because it added to "effectual demand" and helped overcome the tendency of production to outrun demand. Malthus was the darling of the rich.

Other political economists did not agree that a capitalist economy was inherently unstable. A French popularizer of Adam Smith's theories, Jean-Baptiste Say, formulated the classic counterargument in his *Treaties on Political Economy* (1803). "Say's law of markets" argued that production of goods created the incomes necessary for consumers to buy them. Production requires payment of wages, interest, and rent, and creates a profit. These payments provide income for consumers. Despite temporary economic difficulties and depression in individual industries, in the long run the process of production produced the purchasing power required to sustain full use of productive capacity and full employment of the labor force. There could be no "general glut" of commodities.

A more subtle response to Malthus' criticism was provided by David Ricardo, whose *Principles of Political Economy* (1817) emphasized the importance of capital accumulation as the chief source of economic growth. Savings were the source of the capital necessary for expansion of production and should be encouraged as much as possible. But wouldn't saving reduce buying and bring on bad times? Ricardo said "No." Merely holding savings brought no benefit to the saver, while spending for consumption did. One would save only if the savings were invested to return a profit that the saver desired more than the benefits of consumption. It was inevitable, Ricardo argued, that the incomes created by production would be spent either on consumption goods or investment goods, and there could be no interruption of the flow of spending necessary to sustain high levels of economic activity. Ricardo's book appeared at the end of the first period of rapid industrialization in England. It helped to allay fears that machines would displace people from employment and bring hard times instead of prosperity—at the start of a quarter century of relative economic stagnation that culminated in the great depression of the 1840s.

The chief elements of capitalist ideology were now in place. An economy based on private enterprise in freely functioning markets would achieve the most rapid economic growth and highest possible level of affluence. There was a general tendency to use fully the productive resources available, including both capital and labor. It might not be possible to eliminate poverty, but the poor were responsible for their own poverty and attempts to ameliorate their condition would only worsen matters. These early political economists were strong supporters of the emerging industrial capitalism of their day and the class structure that went with it.

There were many critics, however, with a variety of approaches. John Stuart Mill is typical of the liberal reformers of the last century, and his *Principles of Political Economy* (1848) is the classic statement of that point of view. Mill was trained in the classical political economy of Smith, Malthus, Ricardo, and Say and accepted their basic propositions that the natural laws of production and exchange would generate full employment, economic growth, and affluence. But what about the laws of income distribution? They were manmade, argued Mill, and could be modified by measures designed to redistribute wealth and income to create greater equality. Land reform, tax reform, and government spending to alleviate poverty could improve the condition of the poor in ways that would not interfere with economic growth and capital accumulation and could even enhance growth by improving the productivity of the working class. In particular, Mill stressed education as the best way to improve the distribution of income. Mill was called a socialist in his day because he favored breaking up large estates, taxing large inheritances, fostering cooperatives of consumers and producers, and educating the children of the poor!

Karl Marx was the great radical thinker (and active revolutionary) of that era. His *Capital* (1867) stands with Smith's *Wealth of Nations* in the depth and breadth of its analysis of private enterprise capitalism, but from the opposite end of the ideological spectrum. Marx saw industrial capitalism as the most recent manifestation of two great patterns of conflict. The first involved people and the natural environment: faced with limited resources, both natural and technological, societies sought to improve the human condition by producing more and creating affluence and ease. Economic growth was seen as the path toward freedom from poverty, and capital accumulation and technological change were the instruments through which this aspect of human freedom was to be achieved. On this point Marx agreed with the conservative political economists.

The second great conflict was among people: one group could achieve greater affluence by subjugating and exploiting another. This type of conflict led to the appearance of social classes, dominance and subservience, wealth and poverty, and class conflict that, in all previous societies, made it impossible to continue the process of economic growth.

Capitalism was only the most recent social formation in the great sweep of history. It was the most efficient yet devised for the purposes of capital accumulation and the growth of affluence, far more so than the preceding feudal society. But it, too, was divided into antagonistic social classes—capital and labor—and the exploitation of labor by capital created an escalating complex of conflicts and contradictions that increasingly nullified capitalism's function as an engine of growth. But unlike its predecessors, capitalism would give way to a social formation free from destructive internal conflicts, releasing tremendous forces for further betterment of the human condition. Marx felt that this future society would be socialist—equalitarian, without class conflict, and democratic.

The Marxist critique of capitalism began with a major point borrowed from the earlier political economists: labor was the source of value. The earlier political economists had argued that labor created capital, and hence all the benefits from capital accumulation. Human progress was the result of human effort. But Marx argued that in a capitalist economy the profit going to capitalists prevents labor from being paid a wage equal to the value it creates, hence exploitation, inadequate purchasing power, and all the conflicts and contradictions of capitalism. Marx had taken the argument for capitalism, stood it on its head, and turned it into an argument against capitalism.

There was an almost immediate reaction, and out of it modern economics was born. Within fifteen years a new theoretical foundation for the ideology of capitalism rose to dominance, and the name "political economy" was dropped. The labor theory of value disappeared in favor of a theory of utility based on individual preferences. Analysis of social classes was relegated to sociology. The great political issues of classic political economy became side issues, set aside for an analysis of how consumers endowed with preferences and producers endowed with resources, meeting in the marketplace, create an equilibrium of forces that determines price, output, allocation of resources, and incomes. Market exchange under conditions of perfect competition and full employment was the subject analyzed. Individuals, not social classes, were the units considered. The market equilibrium of balanced forces assured the absence of conflict. Exploitation was not possible, since all transactions were voluntary and the equilibrium of market forces guaranteed that both labor and capital would be paid an amount just equal to their contributions to total output or total value. This great metaphysical scheme has been described as "the most elaborate philosophical system ever devised."

It did not accord well with reality, however, as the American economist, Thorstein Veblen, pointed out with devastating sarcasm in two books at the turn of the century, *The Theory of the Leisure Class* (1899) and *The Theory of Business Enterprise* (1904). The new econom-

ics ignored history and the processes of institutional change, Veblen argued. Consumers and producers did not act in the real world as the theory postulated but in response to their desire for status and power. The entire analysis was merely a giant apologetic for an essentially irrational and destructive system. The rise of big business, which Veblen felt was central to an understanding of the modern economy, would probably lead to an alliance of big business and big government to create a militaristic, authoritarian regime. Socialism was the only possible alternative, but Veblen did not think that likely.

Most of the new breed of economists thought of Veblen as a wildman, but his criticisms sparked investigations into big business and financial concentration, business cycles, labor unions, and other aspects of the modern economic world. The main line of development in economics, however, was still the pure theory of competitive markets under conditions of full employment.

The Great Depression of the 1930s revealed the inadequacy of that type of economic theory. It also marked the appearance of another great political economist, John M. Keynes, whose book *The General Theory of Employment, Interest and Money* (1936) returned to the great traditions of the older political economy. Keynes dropped the assumption of full employment and its theoretical foundation, Say's law of markets. He took up again the ideas of Malthus and Marx on the problem of production capacity outrunning the ability to consume. He argued that a private enterprise economy was inherently unstable and that government action was required to keep it on an even keel. This analysis of the economy has now become part of conventional wisdom in a modified and watered-down form.

After World War II, there was a slow but persistent trend in economics to leave the unstable world of Keynes and go back to the stable equilibria of the theory of competitive markets. The depression was over, the economy was growing rapidly, and all seemed well with the economic system. In this era of euphoria, the theory of market equilibrium was revived in a much more elaborate form, and the dynamic Keynesian theory was modified to fit in as a subsystem. All would be well if government budgets and monetary policies were used to maintain full employment. The private enterprise system could provide an efficient allocation of resources to meet consumer wants, while economic growth would provide an annual surplus to raise living standards, reduce and ultimately end poverty, aid the less-developed countries to do the same, and provide the military power to neutralize the threat of the Soviet Union and prevent the spread of socialism.

It was not to be. These illusions were shattered by growing unemployment, escalating inflation, the cynical use of U.S. military power in southeast Asia, and the onset of a new era of relative economic stagnation in the 1970s. The new political economy, which has not yet produced its grand treatise, was born out of these issues.

This book is in that new tradition. It draws on a good deal of the best from the economic analysis of markets, both competitive and monopolistic; it returns to the ideas of Keynes himself to understand the issues of unemployment and inflation; it derives from Marx and Veblen a framework of continuing conflict and institutional change in an economy of social classes and economic interests; it emphasizes the role of big business and big government; and it focuses on that great issue of classical political economy: what type of economic system is most desirable for improving the human condition.

Key Concepts

political economy   **economics**

PART 1

THE ECONOMIC SYSTEM

We start with an introduction to the economic system that prevails in the United States. It is a capitalist economy based on private ownership of resources and capital, and on the presence of a free labor force that works for wages. Production and distribution in such an economy are carried out within the framework of interrelated markets where all the inputs into the production system are available for purchase and where outputs are sold.

The next three chapters analyze the interplay between economic institutions such as private property and the market system, production as a means for satisfying human wants on a growing scale, and the social classes and economic interests that participate in economic life and struggle among themselves for wealth and power. Three themes are introduced that will dominate the remainder of the book: how the economy functions, its limitations and problems, and the conflicts inherent in it. Chapter 1 discusses the market economy with emphasis on how markets allocate resources in a society in which the means for satisfying wants are scarce relative to the wants to be satisfied. This chapter indicates some of the limitations of a market economy and introduces the chief topics that comprise the core of economic analysis of market systems.

Chapter 2 goes beyond exchange to introduce the forces that affect the production of goods available to satisfy wants. It emphasizes the process of economic growth and its relationship to capital accumulation, technological change and human effort in a private enterprise economy, and the barriers to increased affluence that must be overcome.

Chapter 3 explores the social relations of production: capital and labor, bureaucracy and the economic elite, the role of government, and the belief system or ideology characteristic of a market economy organized around private property.

Chapter 1

The Market Economy

Most people think of an economy like that of the United States as a private-enterprise or capitalist economy. Such phrases stress both the legal basis of the economy and the fact that the means of production are privately owned. These phrases also imply a contrast between capitalism and other economic systems such as socialism.

When we look at how the American economy *functions*, however, a different emphasis emerges. The economy appears as a gigantic system of interrelated markets within which vast quantities of commodities and services are exchanged. Joe Stack, for example, goes to work every day at an automobile assembly plant in Detroit. He earns wages that he and his family spend to buy all the things they use. At the factory he works on an assembly line that is fed with parts and components purchased from other companies or produced in the plant from materials and parts bought elsewhere. The finished automobile is then sold to a retailer, who in turn sells it to a customer. The customer probably pays for the automobile with money he has borrowed from a bank and will repay out of earnings from his own job. He may be Joe Stack's next-door neighbor, or he may live thousands of miles away. But the wages paid to Joe Stack ultimately come from the buyer by way of the interrelated market transactions of the economy, and the automobile finds its way to the buyer by the same route.

Every unit in the economic system, whether it is a business firm or an individual, is continually engaged in buying and selling.

Self-Adjusting Markets

A *market* for a commodity or service is defined by the price that prevails in it. Perhaps the best definition was given as early as 1838 by the French mathematician and economist Augustin Cournot (1801–1877). He defined a market as "the whole of any region in which buyers and sellers are in such free intercourse with one another that the prices of the same goods tend to equality easily and quickly." Some markets have a central location and are easily identified, such as the stock exchanges in New York and London or the wheat pit and corn exchange in Chicago. Others, such as the market for iron ore mined in the Great Lakes region, have no central location. That market is defined by the boundaries of the area in which the iron ore is bought and sold, at the price established by the large producers and published annually in Cleveland. Thus, the market for Great Lakes iron ore extends east to Johnstown, Pennsylvania, where it competes with imported ore, but not as far as Baltimore, Maryland, where imported ore is used.

Markets may be wide or narrow. A standardized product that is both in wide demand and easily described and transported, such as a particular type and grade of wheat, will have a market that extends over a large area. Other markets of this sort include stock exchange securities and precious metals. In these markets, buyers and sellers from all parts of the world compete with each other. At the other extreme are secluded local markets in which competition from outside is absent, although even there the effect of competition from outside may be felt indirectly. Between these extremes lie most of the markets with which the average person is familiar.

The price-making function of the modern market can, of course, be modified by governments, as exemplified in public utility regulation, or price controls during periods of inflation. It can also be modified by large corporations able to use their economic power to influence or control the prices of what they sell. Even these controlled or administered markets are influenced by the market forces of demand and supply, however, especially over long periods of time. Monopolies are continually threatened by potential competitors. And efforts of governments to hold prices at levels significantly different from normal market prices have seldom succeeded for any length of time.

The price-making function of markets is an integral part of their *allocative function*. Prices provide signals to buyers, indicating the relative costs of the various alternatives open to them. In response, buyers will allocate their purchases among the available alternatives in an effort to maximize their benefits. If relative prices change, we can expect buyers to shift their purchases and reallocate their expenditures.

Producers, in turn, are influenced by the prices they must pay for labor and materials, as well as the prices of what they sell. Producers channel their efforts into those lines of activity in which they expect the highest profits, and in doing so will draw labor, capital, and materials with them. Presumably, the most profitable activities will be those in which there is large demand from buyers. In this way, "as if by an invisible hand" to quote Adam Smith, resources are allocated to meet consumer wants.

Prices are a means by which scarce goods and resources are rationed. For example, if there is a shortage of gasoline at existing prices, a price increase will limit buying to those who are willing and able to pay the higher price. Conversely, a surplus of gasoline that brings the price down will make the supplies available to a larger group. In both cases the price is part of a self-adjusting rationing process that allocates goods and resources among the potential users.

When consumers and producers operate within the framework of a system of price-making, allocative markets, they tend to orient their thinking and their decisions toward maximizing their gains. Consumers spend their incomes in ways that give them the greatest satisfaction. Sellers and producers, in turn, tend to maximize the difference between their revenues and their costs. Relative prices in the market provide an easily measured standard for these decisions. The motive of economic gain becomes the driving force behind the operation of markets.

● A **market** is an economic institution in which buyers and sellers come together for the purpose of exchanging commodities.

The Adjustment Mechanism: General Equilibrium

In a market economy unfettered by private or public control over prices or production, there is a strong and continuing tendency for prices and quantities of output to adjust automatically to two powerful forces: consumers' incomes and preferences and producers' costs. The continual effort on the part of rational consumers to maximize their satisfactions creates the demand on which profits are based. Producers, meanwhile, trying to maximize their profits, have to supply the things consumers want. A seller who does so will prosper, while one who does not will fail. At the same time, the returns to producers must cover their costs and provide a profit if production is to continue. The profit itself is limited by competition among sellers. The result is a pattern of prices and output that enables consumers to maximize their welfare, limited by the constraint that producers must cover their full costs. A highly complex set of relationships is involved, in which an *equilibrium* between these contrary forces is continually being automatically sought, much as water seeks to find its level. When the equilibrium is broken, the market system will try to find another that is consistent with the new situation. This adjustment process is continually at work, and an understanding of it is fundamental to the science of economics.

- **A general equilibrium** is a situation in which no buyer or seller can improve his position by making a change. The conditions of equilibrium are: (1) consumer welfare cannot be increased by altering the pattern of consumption or the allocation of resources; (2) no unit of any factor of production can earn more in any alternative way.

Let us take, as an example, an economy that produces just two commodities, milk and whiskey. Consumers spend all of their incomes on either or both of these products, and all workers and other productive resources are employed in either dairies or distilleries or their related industries. It is a competitive economy: no producer or seller is large enough to influence prices in the markets in which his product is sold or his resources are bought. Let us assume further that the two industries have arrived at a long-run equilibrium condition: profits are at a level just large enough to support the existing producers, and profits on the last investments made in each industry are equal. This last point is important, for as we shall see, profits are a key to the adjustments a market economy makes.

We want to base our hypothetical case on a situation in which producers have incentives to continue their present operations unchanged, without expanding, contracting, or shifting to production of something else. Two basic conditions define the economic equilibrium in which the economy finds itself. First, output is adjusted to the demands of buyers in such a way that no consumer can shift his purchases to one more bottle of whiskey and one less bottle of milk, or vice versa, without making himself worse off. Consumers are maximizing their welfare at the existing ratio between consumption of milk and consumption of whiskey. Second, owners of productive resources are maximizing their incomes. No unit of labor, capital, or land could earn more by shifting to any other use or employment.

These two conditions of equilibrium are, of course, just as hypothetical as the simplified two-commodity economy. But note this very real principle: Where consumers and producers act rationally there should be a constant tendency for a market economy to approach equilibrium conditions. When something occurs that shifts the economy away from equilibrium, a process of readjustment will be set in motion that starts the economy back toward it. It is this process of self-adjustment that is the key to understanding how a market economy functions.

At any rate, into our economic Eden of full employment, adequate profits, and firms producing just what consumers want, we shall introduce a change in consumer tastes, and see what happens. Let us assume that a substantial shift in preferences toward drinking more whiskey and less milk occurs. We don't have to know why the change takes place, or whether or not it is desirable. But we do know that the pattern of production will change to match it, and that the process of change is an intricate one.

The first effects will be felt by the sellers of milk and whiskey. Milk producers will find that their sales have fallen, and the price of milk will start to decline. Supplies of milk coming into the market initially will continue at the same level, because no one knows yet that consumer preferences have changed; but reduced demand for milk, followed by reduced sales, will cause prices to sag and will bring down the profits of milk producers. They will then start to reduce their output. Whiskey sellers, on the other hand, will notice an increase in demand, will have difficulties in maintaining their inventories at the desired level, and will take advantage of the growing shortage of alcoholic beverages by raising their prices. The price of whiskey will rise, and so will the profits of the producers, who will then increase their output to take advantage of the favorable conditions in the market. Note carefully the exact sequence of events. A change in demand causes prices to change, which is reflected in the profits made by sellers, who then change their production decisions.

These, then, are the first effects of the shift in demand. The price and output of milk will fall, along with the profits of dairies, while the price and output of whiskey will rise, along with the profits of distilleries. Already the pattern of production has begun to change to match the new pattern of demand.

But more is yet to come. Profits in the two industries will no longer be equal. Some of the more astute dairy farmers will quickly see that they can increase their incomes by shifting their efforts from dairying to whiskey manufacturing. Enterprising new businessmen will enter the whiskey business and leave milk production and distribution alone. The resources of the economy will begin a slow shift from milk to whiskey production, with the following results:

1. Workers laid off in dairying will discover that jobs are opening up in distilleries.

2. Corn will be fed into stills rather than cows.

3. The least productive cows will be sent to the glue factory (to make glue to paste labels on whiskey bottles).

4. Banks will be eager to lend money to profitable distilleries, replacing their former loans to now struggling dairies.

All of these changes will affect the markets for whiskey and milk, this time from the supply side. As resources shift out of dairying, the supply of milk regularly coming into the market will fall. This, in turn, will cause prices to stop declining and start rising back toward their former levels. As this happens, the incentive of producers to shift out of dairying will gradually decrease, the decline in output will taper off, and the industry will begin to approach stability once more. Just the opposite pattern will occur in the whiskey business. As more resources are devoted to whiskey production, the supply of whiskey coming into the market will increase. This, in turn, will bring prices and profits down from their former high levels. As profits start falling, the incentive to expand whiskey output will diminish, its expansion will slow down, and this industry, too, will begin to approach stability.

These trends in the two industries can be expected to continue until profits in the two are equalized. At that point the economy will be back in equilibrium, for then there will no longer be any incentive to shift productive resources out of the one and into the other. But notice what will have happened in the meantime: output of whiskey will have expanded to new high levels and will be sustained there, and a larger proportion of the economy's resources will be used in whiskey production. Conversely, output of milk will be lower and will require a smaller proportion of the economy's resources. This is exactly the change the economy will need to make to accommodate to the shift in consumer preferences from milk to whiskey.

All factors of production are affected by the adjustment process. As the whiskey industry expands and the dairy industry contracts, opportunities for profitable employment of land and capital will begin to differ in the two industries, becoming better in whiskey than in milk. With the owners of resources presumably seeking the most profitable use for their assets —whether the labor time of the worker, the land of the farmer, or the money of the investor—resources will shift from milk to whiskey production. The growing whiskey industry will bid them away from the declining dairy industry until at the final equilibrium position the amounts paid to the factors of production will be equalized from one industry to the next. This does not mean that unskilled labor will be paid the same amount as skilled labor. But it does mean that skilled labor employed in dairying will earn the same amount as labor of comparable quality in the whiskey industry. The same conditions will prevail for all types and grades of labor, land and managerial skills, as well as capital. The economy will be back in equilibrium once more.

Throughout the adjustment process, consumers allocated their expenditures so as to maximize their welfare. Indeed, it was a shift in consumer preferences that started the whole process of adjustment originally. The adjustment began on the demand side of the market and shifted to the supply side, and ultimately the interactions between the two brought about a new equilibrium in which no producer or owner of a factor of production could better his position. The result was a pattern of production and consumption in which consumers maximized their satisfactions and welfare, subject to the constraint of paying incomes to the factors of production just necessary to draw forth their use in the patterns and proportions established by consumer preferences.

The Adjustment Mechanism in Individual Markets: Demand, Supply, and Price

A better understanding of how the system of markets adjusts itself will be provided by a close look at the adjustment mechanism in individual markets. There are two basic principles involved, the so-called "laws" of demand and supply.

- The **law of demand** describes consumer behavior. Everything else remaining the same, consumers will be willing to buy more of a product when its price is low and less when its price is high.
- The **law of supply** describes sellers' behavior. Everything else remaining the same, sellers will be willing to sell more of a product when its price is high, less when its price is low.

There are exceptions to these laws, and in real life everything seldom remains the same. But as generalizations these laws are two of the fundamental facts of life in a market economy. The interaction of the two laws determines the equilibrium price in any specific market. For example, as the price of one commodity rises in response to an increase in demand, while other prices remain the same, sellers will be induced to produce and sell more. At some point the willingness of consumers to buy and of sellers to sell will exactly match each other, and *at that price* the market will be in equilibrium. That is, there will be no unsatisfied buyers or sellers at the existing price, and there will therefore be no tendency for the price either to rise or to fall. To get a better view of this market equilibrium, we can go back to our hypothetical whiskey-milk economy and examine the demand for whiskey, its supply, and how these factors interact.

The Demand Schedule and the Demand Curve

A hypothetical schedule of the demand for whiskey is depicted in Figure 1–1. According to this demand schedule, we find that consumers will buy larger quantities of whiskey at lower prices than they will at higher prices, assuming that all other influences on consumer choices except the price of whiskey are held constant. This *demand schedule* can be readily transferred to a graph, providing a visual representation of the *demand curve*.

In real life, of course, the numbers are never rounded off, the demand curve is never smooth, and the observed data are scattered around the curve (which is a trend line or average) rather than falling on it. But since we are dealing with a hypothetical case to illustrate a general principle, estimates can be made so that everything comes out exactly right. To simplify matters, the demand "curve" has been drawn as a straight line. The essential point is that the demand curve slopes downward to the right.

- A **demand schedule** shows the quantities that buyers would be willing to purchase at alternative prices. It is shown graphically as a demand curve. The amount consumers would buy at a given price is the *quantity demanded*.

The Supply Schedule and the Supply Curve

Similarly, the amounts of whiskey that sellers would be willing to sell can be illustrated through a hypothetical *supply schedule* and *supply curve*, shown in Figure 1–2. In the case of the supply curve the trend is just the opposite of the demand curve. The higher the price, the larger the quantity that sellers will be

Figure 1–1
Demand for Whiskey

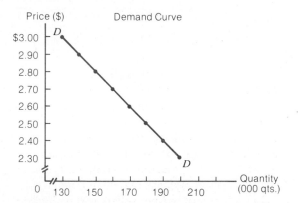

Demand Schedule

Price per Quart	Quarts Purchased per Day
$3.00	130,000
2.90	140,000
2.80	150,000
2.70	160,000
2.60	170,000
2.50	180,000
2.40	190,000
2.30	200,000

Data from the demand schedule are pictured above, showing that larger quantities will be bought at lower prices. Note the broken lines of the horizontal and vertical axes. This is often done to save space while showing substantial distances.

Figure 1-2
Supply of Whiskey

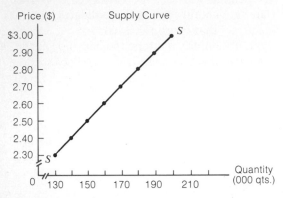

Supply Schedule	
Price per Quart	Quantity Sellers Will Supply (qts.)
$3.00	200,000
2.90	190,000
2.80	180,000
2.70	170,000
2.60	160,000
2.50	150,000
2.40	140,000
2.30	130,000

A graphic representation of the supply schedule shows that sellers will supply larger quantities at higher prices.

willing to sell. The supply curve slopes upward to the right.

- A **supply schedule** shows the quantities that sellers would be willing to sell at alternative prices. It is shown graphically as a supply curve. The amount sellers would supply at a given price is the *quantity supplied*.

Determination of Price
Prices in the market are determined by the interaction of buyers and sellers, of the forces of demand and supply. In the case of our hypothetical whiskey market, putting the demand and supply curves on the same diagram will indicate the price that will prevail under market equilibrium (Figure 1–3). Under the assumed demand and supply conditions, the normal price of whiskey would be $2.65 per quart and 165,000 quarts would be exchanged between sellers and buyers. At that point the amount that buyers wish to buy will be just equal to the amount sellers wish to sell. There will be no unsatisfied buyers or sellers at the existing price. *The market will be cleared.*

- **Clearing the market** occurs when the amount

suppliers are willing to sell equals the amount buyers are willing to buy at the existing price. The price at which the market is cleared is often called the *equilibrium price*.

No other price could long prevail under the existing market conditions. Suppose, for example, the price were $2.70 per quart. At that price, according to the demand schedule and

Figure 1-3
Demand, Supply, and the Price of Whiskey

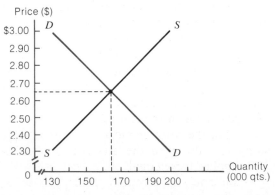

At a price of $2.65 per quart, buyers will be willing to take the same amount sellers wish to sell, 165,000 quarts.

Figure 1-4
Markets in Disequilibrium

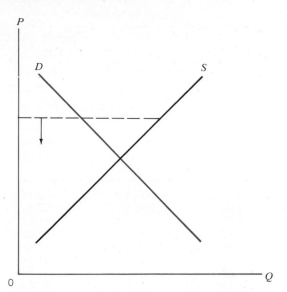

A. Price will fall when *S* exceeds *D* at the prevailing price.

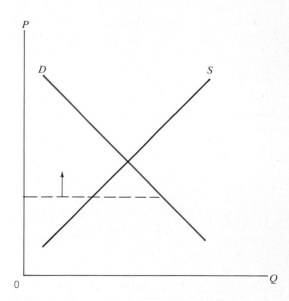

B. Price will rise when *D* exceeds *S* at the prevailing price.

curve, buyers would take only 160,000 quarts while sellers would like to sell 170,000. Competition among sellers for the limited number of customers would quickly start the price moving down toward $2.65, and it would continue moving down as long as the amount demanded remained less than the amount sellers wanted to sell. Only when the price reached $2.65 per quart and the amount demanded equaled the amount supplied, would the price stop falling. Conversely, if the price were to fall below the equilibrium level, say to $2.50 per quart, the amount of whiskey demanded would exceed the quantity sellers were willing to supply at that price, sellers would raise their prices to take advantage of the favorable market conditions, and the price would rise toward $2.65, stopping only when the amounts demanded and supplied were equal.

When prices in competitive markets differ from the equilibrium price, market forces themselves push the price either up or down

toward equilibrium. Prices higher than the equilibrium price fall as sellers compete with each other for sales. Prices lower than the equilibrium rise as buyers compete for scarce supplies. Some prices may be sluggish and move slowly, while others may react almost instantaneously, but the pressure to move toward equilibrium is present. Figure 1–4 illustrates the principle.

Under conditions of perfect competition, the market mechanism is effective. It automatically adjusts prices and quantities to the market conditions created by buyers and sellers. If at any time the existing price leaves some buyers unsatisfied, the price tends to rise as they bid for the amounts they want. If, on the other hand, some sellers want to sell more at the existing price but cannot find buyers, the price tends to fall. When the desire to buy and sell is satisfied for everyone in the market at the existing price, then and only then does the normal or equilibrium price prevail.

Figure 1-5
Increase in the Demand for Whiskey

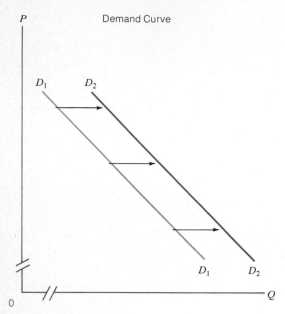

When demand increases, the entire demand curve shifts to the right.

	Demand Schedule	
	Quarts Purchased per Day	
Price per Quart	*Before Increase in Demand* (D_1)	*After Increase in Demand* (D_2)
$3.00	130,000	140,000
2.90	140,000	150,000
2.80	150,000	160,000
2.70	160,000	170,000
2.60	170,000	180,000
2.50	180,000	190,000
2.40	190,000	200,000
2.30	200,000	210,000

Changes in Demand and Supply

In our hypothetical whiskey-milk economy, the market adjustment process began with a *change in demand:* an increase in the demand for whiskey and a decline in the demand for milk. Let's see how that works out in the market for whiskey. Figure 1–5 shows the increase in demand and Figure 1–6 shows what happens to the price and quantity sold.

- A **change in demand** means that, at all prices, the amount that consumers will buy is larger or smaller than before, and on the diagram the demand curve shifts to the right or left. This must be distinguished from a shift along the curve, which shows how consumers react to a change in the market price of the commodity.

Quantities in the demand schedule are greater all down the line, and on the diagram the demand curve shifts to the right. The effect of an increase in demand on the market is to increase both the market price and the amount exchanged. In the case of our hypothetical whiskey market, the price rises to $2.70, and 170,000 quarts of whiskey will be sold after the increase in demand has occurred.

Just the opposite effect occurs when demand decreases. The price of the commodity falls and the amount sold declines (see Figure 1–7). This is just what happened in our whiskey-milk economy at the initial stages of the adjustment when consumer tastes shifted away from milk.

In the market adjustment process the changes seldom stop with a single market. As we saw in our hypothetical whiskey-milk economy, the increase in demand for whiskey and the decrease in demand for milk changed the relationship between the market prices of the two commodities. This, in turn, changed the

Figure 1–6
Effect of an Increase in Demand on Price of
Whiskey and the Quantity Exchanged

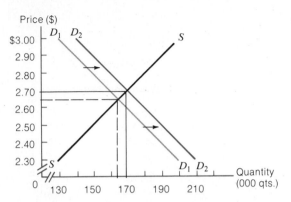

An increase in demand brings increases in both price and
quantity sold.

prospects for profits in two industries, including a shift in resource use that resulted in the *change in supply* schedules. The supply of whiskey coming into the market was increased, and the supply of milk declined.

- A **change in supply** is a shift in the entire supply schedule. It appears graphically as a movement of the supply or demand curve. It must be distinguished from a shift along the curve, which shows how sellers react to a change in the price of the commodity they sell.

These shifts in the supply schedules and supply curves can also be shown graphically in much the same way that changes in demand are shown (see Figure 1–8).

At this point you should be well equipped to go through the simple analysis of the market adjustment process, starting with changes on either the demand or supply side of the market and following through with the many-sided reactions that change at one point in the system induces in the other parts. For example, in the whiskey-milk economy, the increase in demand for whiskey pulled its price up. This, in turn, triggered an increase in supplies brought to the

market, which resulted in a decline in prices and profits back toward their former levels. This sequence of events is illustrated in Figure 1–9 by use of demand and supply curves.

At the final equilibrium in Figure 1–9 we showed the new equilibrium price as identical to the price in the original equilibrium. That would be the case if there were no changes in the cost of production, that is, if the resources moving into this expanding industry could be hired away from their former employment at the same costs as before. If the new resources had to be paid more to get them to move, or if diminishing returns or exhaustible resources were involved, production costs would rise from the first to the third stage in the adjustment, and p_3 would be greater than p_1. On the other hand, an expanded industry might have lower costs than one with a smaller output, and in this case p_3 would be lower than p_1. But whatever the situation, whether it be one of

Figure 1–7
Decrease in Demand

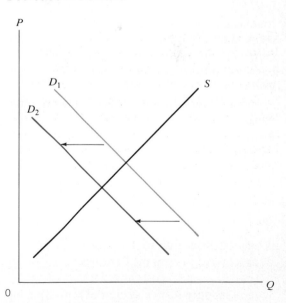

The demand curve shifts from D_1 to D_2 in response to
changes in consumer preferences.

Figure 1-8
Change in Supply

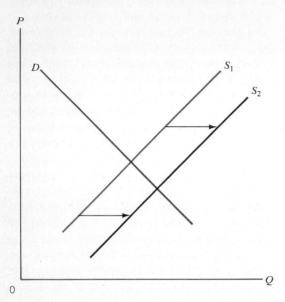

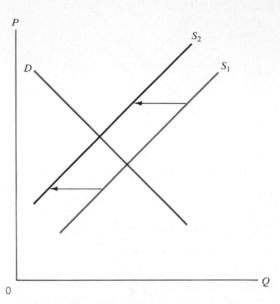

A. Increase in Supply   An increase in supply means that at all prices the amounts sellers wish to sell will be greater. The supply curve shifts to the right.

B. Decrease in Supply   A decrease in supply means that at all prices the amounts sellers wish to sell will be less. The supply curve shifts to the left.

increasing costs, constant costs, or decreasing costs, a new equilibrium price would be established at which profits in the industry would be equated to those in other sectors of the economy.

While these adjustments are going on in the whiskey industry, just the opposite is happening in milk production. Work out the three steps for yourself, with diagrams showing the original equilibrium, the initial effects of the *decrease* in demand, and the final equilibrium after the *decrease* in supply.

The Significance of the Market Adjustment Process

Seen in its pure form a system of self-adjusting markets seems able to create order out of the apparent chaos of an individualistic society.

Even when each person seeks his or her own goals, and does so without the imposition of political authority, welfare-maximizing positions can result for both producer and consumer, based on the existing distribution of income and property ownership. Producers and consumers must be satisfied with the result or else the adjustment process will continue until they are. The beauties of the system have led social philosophers from Adam Smith to mid-twentieth-century libertarians like Ayn Rand to eulogize the market economy as the economic foundation of individual freedom.

The market mechanism is indeed a powerful instrument for achieving individual goals. Alternatives open to the individual as a consumer or as a producer have a price or payoff that is stated in terms of money and can be compared with other alternatives. The choice is up to the individual and the outcome is the result of his

Figure 1-9 Moving to a New Equilibrium

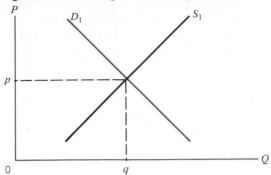

Stage 1: The Original Equilibrium

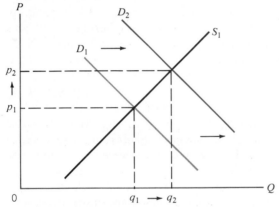

Stage 2: Demand Increases An increase in demand for whiskey causes price and quantity purchased to rise.

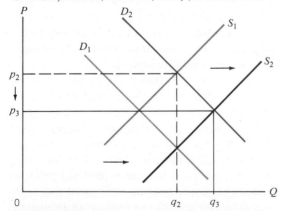

Stage 3: Supply Responds The rise in price (p_2) and quantity sold (q_2) increases profits of suppliers. New firms are attracted to the industry, production of whiskey is increased (q_3), and the increase in supply brings prices down again (p_3).

or her own decision. It is an environment in which individualism can flourish.

Yet the interests of others are not ignored. People are driven by self-interest to produce the things others want. If one wants to eat or to achieve "success," it is necessary to sell either efforts or products in the market. This means producing what others are willing to buy, that is, producing the things that enable others to maximize their own economic positions. In this sense, the welfare of one is tied inextricably to the welfare of all in a general system of relationships in which each serves the ends of everyone else while pursuing his or her own goals.

Ideally, it is a marvelous scheme for resolving the conflicts inherent in the meeting of buyer and seller in an exchange situation. Each person tries to make the best possible bargain, but each has the opportunity to buy or sell only at the going market price. Business manager and customer, worker and employer, borrower and lender must all submit their differences to the arbitration of the market price.

Limitations of the Self-Adjusting Market

Nevertheless, the market economy has several very serious limitations that have prevented modern nations from relying fully upon it in making economic decisions.

Full Employment
The most serious limitation of the free market has been its inability to maintain consistent full employment. In Chapters 4 and 5 we take a close look at economic fluctuation and the flow of spending and show in broad outline why instability seems to be one of the inherent characteristics of an uncontrolled market economy. At this point it is sufficient to note such instability and point out that the theory of welfare maximization through the free market *assumes* that the adjustments take place under

conditions of full employment. Indeed, the maintenance of full employment may be taken as a necessary precondition for the effective operation of the market adjustment process we have described.

Competition and Monopoly

Many of the advantages of the self-adjusting market system depend on the maintenance of competition. Monopoly interferes with the adjustment process and prevents the achievement of a welfare-maximizing equilibrium. For example, a monopolist may be able to prevent or seriously delay the entry of new firms into an expanding industry, thereby keeping prices high and retaining monopolistic profits for himself. The monopolist makes large profits, but the far more serious difficulty is that output does not expand adequately and fails to adjust properly to consumer demand. A broadly pervasive pattern of competition is a second precondition for the effective operation of the market mechanism.

A hundred or more years ago, before giant corporations grew to their present size and influence, we could rely heavily on the free interplay of competitive market forces to bring order out of the seeming chaos of millions of individual economic decisions. There were plenty of economic problems in that earlier uncontrolled economy—financial panics and depressions, low wages and poverty, child labor—to name just a few. But as long as economic power was dispersed, the self-adjusting market economy could be expected to work reasonably well. This was the view, at least, of the laissez-faire liberals who argued for economic freedom from governmental restraints. That view is much less credible today, when, after a century and a half of capital accumulation, much of our economic life is dominated by giant bureaucratic corporations run from the top and influencing the lives of millions of people. A policy of laissez-faire is much less appropriate in a world of giant corporations than it was in a simpler time.

Equity in Income Distribution

The market economy pays incomes to the factors of production in amounts large enough to obtain their services in production. That is, workers, land, and capital are paid only for their usable productive effort. If a man does not work he will not eat, and when he works he will earn an amount equal only to his contribution to total output. His employers have no reason to pay him more, and competition for his services will force them to pay him at least that amount.

There are three important drawbacks to these principles of income distribution as they work in practice. First, not all income is earned; some comes from inherited wealth and favored positions. Second, the uncertainties and luck that prevail in a world in which the future is not revealed can create inequities that have nothing to do with ability or productivity. Third and most important, payments according to productive effort can run counter to the ethical standards of a civilization that values an individual because he is a human being, not solely because he is a producer. Even if there were no unearned income and luck were eliminated, the equity of income distribution in a market economy is a special kind of *economic* equity that does not necessarily coincide with other standards of justice.

For example, suppose that in our whiskey-milk economy, the whiskey industry used large amounts of capital relative to labor per unit of output, while the dairy industry was more labor intensive. As resources shifted from milk to whiskey production, some of the labor used in the economy would become unnecessary at the existing level of wages. The unused supply of labor would tend to bring wages down, while the level of profits in the final equilibrium might rise because more of the economy's scarce capital would be demanded by an expanding capital intensive industry. The new pattern of income distribution would then tend to benefit the owners of capital while the economic position of workers would be worsened. Desirable or not, the market mechanism makes the adjustment, and makes no moral judgments about it. But many people, from social philosophers to revolutionaries, object on grounds of justice and equity.

Disagreements about economic justice have led to some of the most difficult problems of modern society. Socialists have argued for years that profits should go to producers rather than owners and have advocated social rather than private ownership of the means of production. Even when private ownership is accepted as the institutional base of the economy, workers dispute with management over "fair" wages and managerial "prerogatives." Conflicts between wage earner and employer, between worker and owner, have never been fully resolved by the market mechanism. Unless both worker and owner tacitly agree to accept the distribution of rewards created by the self-adjusting market, the system will be continually disrupted. That is a third condition for effective operation of the market mechanism.

Conservation of Resources
The fact that property is privately owned and subject to the profit maximizing decisions of its owner has led to wasteful use of resources. Where forests have been wastefully cut, land exhausted from overuse, and rivers polluted, the reason has usually been that short-run gains can be made by the owner while some of the long-run costs can be shifted to others. It may be quite profitable for a coal-mining company to leave behind exhausted mines from which all the usable coal has been taken, not to mention crippled and silicosis-ridden miners who become wards of the public rather than of the mine companies. At times, it is almost impossible to levy the full cost of resource use, both natural and human, on the producer of the final product. The user of the resource can thus cause waste, with profit for himself but not for society as a whole.

In three areas of concern, society has stepped in to protect itself against potential destructive effects on the resource base through the free market. The first has been in natural resources conservation. Every industrial nation has developed methods to protect land, water, forests, and sometimes other resources from completely free exploitation. But as we all know, much remains to be done. The second concern has been with monetary policy. This sensitive area, in which the value of assets and the supply of money are determined, is controlled in a variety of ways by modern governments in order to avoid the recurrent monetary crises that have plagued the economy in past years and played havoc with the accumulation of the capital. Finally, human resources have been protected from the risks of the marketplace by a variety of social insurance, welfare programs, and protective laws that seek to preserve human values in an uncertain economic environment. Although land, capital, and labor are essential elements of the market economy, no modern nation leaves their disposition solely to market forces.

Individual and Social Goals
The emphasis on individualism that prevails in the market economy can lead to an undue emphasis on expenditures that benefit the individual, and a slighting of those that benefit the total community. Success may come with acquisition of wealth, but status and prestige come only if others are aware of one's success. In the impersonality of modern life the display of wealth through spending has therefore become an important part of the market way of life—*conspicuous consumption*, it was called by the economists John Rae and Thorstein Veblen. This continuing pressure to spend helps to sustain high levels of economic activity, but it also tends to starve public agencies. People don't like to pay taxes, even though the purposes may be highly important for economic growth and well-being. Education, for example, which is largely carried out through public agencies in the United States and is essential

for both individual improvement and economic development, is continually hampered for lack of funds, while the American consumer gratifies his desires for a second automobile, color television, and similar luxuries. This pattern of expenditures may well maximize satisfactions according to the existing pattern of consumer preferences. But the preferences themselves are not independent of the cultural environment of the consumer and the marketing programs of producers. Preferences are in part determined by the social and economic environment within which choices are made. The fact that the market economy tends to maximize benefits does not resolve the problem of whether those benefits are socially desirable.

The Role of Government

Once the implications of a society based on a system of self-adjusting markets are understood, it is easy to understand why government has come to play a substantial role in economic affairs. It is not enough merely to establish the legal framework for the market economy —private property, freedom of contract, inheritance—and to support private economic activity through police protection and enforcement of laws. Those functions, plus national defense, have always been considered essential government activities, even by the most convinced libertarians. Taxes are necessary if those governmental activities are to be supported, and taxes represent one form of interference with private economic activity.

But there is more. The system cannot operate effectively without reasonably full employment, yet it cannot be expected to generate this condition by itself. Competition is necessary for effective operation, yet there are strong incentives for private business firms to reduce or eliminate competition in their own interests. Resources, capital, and people often must be protected against the ravages of the competitive market in order to preserve the

social fabric. Standards of equity must be applied. Some products and services must be produced, yet private interests will not produce them. And there is always the problem of the ultimate goals that individuals and the social system *ought* to seek. All of these considerations have led to a significant intervention of government into economic affairs. In the United States a kind of mixed economy has developed in which a large degree of government influence and direction supplements the system of self-adjusting markets.

It is ironic that the increased role played by government in economic life has created equally difficult problems. The interventionist liberal sought to solve the problems of the economy and curb the power of the giant corporation by enlarging the scope of government activities. Some of the problems have been solved, but in the process another group of great bureaucratic units run from the top has been created. Political power has come to be centralized in the apparatus of the modern national state, and the interventionist liberal is beginning to wonder whether he hasn't created a monster.

Indeed, when the economic power of the large corporation is joined with the political power of the state, as, for example, in the so-called "military-industrial complex," and the entire system gains popular support by providing yearly economic gains and increased affluence for most people, the aims of both the laissez-faire liberal and the interventionist liberal are threatened if not betrayed. This may well be the great economic, political, and philosophical problem of our age: How can we maintain human values in a world in which both economic and political power are highly concentrated and controlled from the top?

Three Types of Economic Choices

The level of production is limited by the amounts of resources, labor, and capital goods available and by knowledge of how to use them. Decisions about production can be divided into three types:

1. If the economy has unused productive capacity and unemployed labor, more of most things can be produced without giving up anything else. This means that there is no economic cost associated with increased output. The unemployed resources can be put to work making more products and services available to everyone. There may be a money cost involved, but "real" costs are zero, because the alternative is to let the unused resources remain idle.

2. If the economy does not have unused productive resources and is operating at its existing capacity, more of one product can be obtained only at the cost of giving up something else. Additional resources can be found to produce more food only by taking resources away from producing other things. In this case there is a "real" cost involved in making choices. We cannot have more of anything without giving up something else.

3. The choices we make between consumption and saving will influence how rapidly the economy's output capacity can be increased. Saving releases resources from the production of consumers' goods and makes them available for investment that will increase output in the future. Higher living standards in the present mean a slower pace of growth, while keeping current standards of living a little lower than they might otherwise be means achieving a higher growth rate, for a period of time, at least.

The Transformation Curve

The three types of choices open to any economy can be illustrated in a little economic model called the *transformation curve.*

- A **transformation curve** is a hypothetical representation of the amounts of two different goods that can be obtained by shifting resources from production of one to production of the other. It is sometimes called a **production possibilities curve** or **production frontier.**

In Figure 1–10 we have taken consumers' goods and investment goods as an example. The table at the right of the figure shows the available production possibilities. If all resources were devoted to investment ($I = 100$), there would be no output of consumers' goods ($C = 0$). That combination is at *A* on the diagram. Alternatively, all resources devoted to consumers' goods would give the combination $C = 100$ and $I = 0$, at point *B*. The intermediate combinations of *C* and *I* are shown by the transformation curve that connects *A* and *B*.

As we increase production of consumers' goods *C*, we have to give up increasing amounts of investment goods *I*. And vice versa. That is the reason for the concave shape of the transformation curve, and is the result of the well-known law of diminishing returns. The first resources shifted away from production of investment goods provide a large increase in output of consumption goods. The next shift brings a smaller increase, and so on. We will have more to say about diminishing returns in Chapter 2, but this illustration helps to introduce the concept. Now let us look at the three types of choices available to an economic system in relation to the transformation curve. In the first case we have unemployed resources and are producing some combination of $C + I$ that lies within the transformation curve (Figure 1–11). Once full employment is reached, consumption can be increased only by giving up some investment, and vice versa (Figure 1–12). Finally, the rate of growth of the economy will depend on the combination of *C* and *I* chosen by the economy when it is fully employed (Figure 1–13).

These propositions are, of course, great simplifications. We choose not only between consumption and investment, but also include public expenditures among our alternatives. This creates a third dimension for our diagram and makes the transformation curve into a transformation surface. Even that is only a beginning, however. Within each of the three

Figure 1–10
The Transformation Curve:
Consumption and Investment

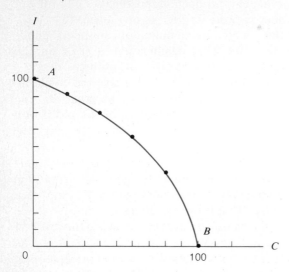

Production Possibilities	
C	I
0	100
20	92
40	81
60	67
80	44
100	0

Figure 1–11
Situation I: Unused Resources

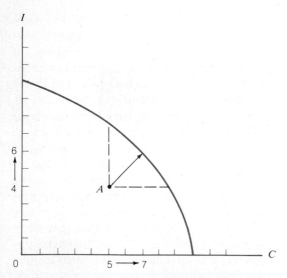

At point *A* the economy produces 5*C* and 4*I*. It could put its unemployed resources to use and increase output to the limits of the transformation curve (say 7*C* and 6*I*) and have more of both.

different categories we can choose between an almost infinite variety of consumers' goods, types of investments, and patterns of public expenditures. The number of alternatives is staggering and cannot possibly be visualized in a geometric model, such as the one shown in this simplified version. The transformation surface develops an almost infinite number of dimensions.

Military Production

Up to this point, the discussion of choice has been purely economic in nature, ignoring considerations of power. In the world as we know it, however, the use of force and compulsion to obtain economic gains is seldom absent, particularly when nations are involved. The resources available to any one nation can be increased by conquest, for example, or favored economic positions may be obtained by use of

Figure 1–12
Situation II: Full Employment

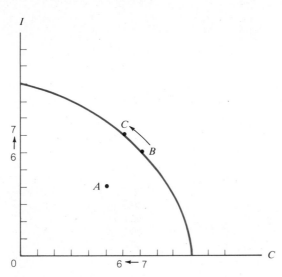

When the economy is operating at its full capacity we can get more *I* only by giving up some *C*. Increasing *I* from 6 to 7 means reducing *C* from 7 to 6 (at that section of the transformation curve).

Figure 1–13
Situation III: Growth

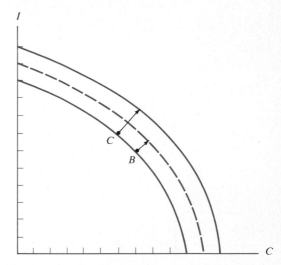

More investment and less consumption pushes the transformation curve outward more rapidly. If we choose *B* the economy will expand more slowly than if we had chosen *C*, where investment is larger.

threats and military-political or economic power. Warfare and the various forms of imperialism are instruments for achieving wealth.

A nation usually must divert resources from both consumption and investment to military equipment in order to gain the power or win wars that bring command over increased resources. Both butter and plowshares are converted into guns, and the lives of young people are sacrificed for future payoffs. The practical choice is not a simple one between consumption goods and investment goods, but a more complex choice among consumption, investment, military goods, and people. Even if we leave people out of the picture, when a nation chooses more military goods it must give up some current consumption.

The political economy of war and imperialism is complex. In Chapter 4 we note that in the modern economy periods of relatively rapid economic growth have been characterized by major wars and arms races. Chapter 30 examines the economics of military spending in peacetime and active warfare. Chapter 37 looks at some aspects of imperialism. At this stage, however, we deal only with the basic proposition that shifting resources from consumption and investment to production of armaments reduces the production potential of the economy. Converting plows and butter to guns forces a nation to have fewer plows and less butter in the future. Figure 1–14 uses the transformation curve to illustrate this proposition.

Figure 1–14
Situation IV: The Cost of Guns

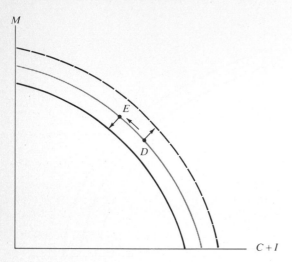

Summary

The United States has a market economy in which the bulk of economic activity is carried on in a system of interrelated markets. Markets both determine the prices at which goods can be exchanged and allocate resources among their alternative uses. Welfare-maximizing consumers and profit-maximizing producers are brought together by the system of self-adjusting markets in such a way that the pattern of production tends to match the pattern of consumer preferences, while resources are drawn into those uses where they receive the highest compensation. A market economy permits individualism to flourish without bringing chaos, and in so doing provides an atmosphere of freedom for individual behavior.

The self-adjusting market economy has limitations, however. There is no guarantee that full employment will prevail. The economy requires a pervasive competition in order to achieve its best results. It may or may not distribute its output according to society's standards of equity. It may not adequately preserve natural resources. It may slight social goals in favor of individual preferences. One result of these limitations of the self-adjusting market economy has been a growing role for government in an effort to add social controls to the system. A system of self-adjusting markets enables people to make choices among alternatives, in which costs are the benefits foregone when only one alternative can be chosen. The logic of choice tells us that rational people will choose those courses of action that are expected to provide the greatest benefits. Choices, moreover, do not involve only the acts of individuals; they also include social decisions that affect both individual action and the alternatives available to people.

Translated into the realm of economics, three types of choices affect all economic activity. They involve:

1. The direction and rate of economic growth.

2. The level of economic activity.

3. The allocation of resources to achieve a desired production pattern and distribution of output.

The simple economic model of the transformation curve was used to illustrate these three types of economic choices.

Key Concepts

markets	law of supply	clearing the market	transformation curve
general equilibrium	demand schedule	change in demand	
law of demand	supply schedule	change in supply	

For Discussion

1. How do the price signals generated in markets lead to a process of economic adjustment? Give some specific examples.

2. How do each of the following conditions prevent a market economy from fully reflecting the desires of consumers?
   a. Pollution from production processes
   b. Monopoly
   c. Poverty
   d. Unemployment
   e. Social goals that have no prices, such as "justice"

3. What actions might government take with respect to the five conditions listed above to cause the market adjustment process to work more effectively?

4. Should some economic decisions be left to the free market and others to government? Which ones should be made by government? Why?

5. "The man who pays the piper calls the tune." Is that true of the free market? Government? Should that be the case?

Chapter 2

Forces of Production

Anthropologists tell us that human beings are tool-using animals. From the earliest known remains of homo sapiens, there is evidence of tools of stone and bone, and the experts presume that wooden tools were also used. These earliest forms of capital goods, or instruments of production, are evidence of the continuing interaction between people and nature to provide subsistence and ease and to increase potential production in order to do so.

Nature does not normally provide material things in exactly the form and place that meet human needs and desires. Human beings have always transformed nature in order to satisfy human wants. In doing so, a variety of instruments of production have been used: the modern cattle feed lot and mechanized slaughterhouse is the direct descendant of the primitive hunter's stone-tipped spear. Natural resources, human effort, and capital goods (such as tools and equipment): these are the basic *forces of production* that have always been used, in a variety of forms, to meet human needs. To these three forces of production a fourth must be added, the knowledge of how to combine the three, which is commonly called technology.

● **Forces of production** are the natural resources, human effort, capital goods, and knowledge used to produce the goods that satisfy human wants and needs.

Accumulation of Capital

The modern economy is, in one sense, a gigantic mechanism for the generation of an *economic surplus* and the *accumulation of capital*. Any economy must reproduce itself by providing sustenance for its producers and replacement of its capital. It must cover its costs of production, producing enough to replace what is used up. But a private enterprise economy does more than that. Enterprises make a profit, which is simply a surplus in excess of the cost of inputs. Indeed, that is their purpose and motivation. Without profit the private enterprise economy would cease to function.

The distinguishing feature of a private enterprise economy, however, is that the surplus is used to increase output. It is transformed into capital goods and knowledge that raise the production potential of the economy. A surplus was generated in other and earlier modes of economic organization, such as those of feudal Europe or the ancient empires, but it was used primarily for luxury living by the aristocracy, to support a large religious establishment, or for maintenance of military power. A relatively small portion was available for economic growth. Rich elites and poor people was the rule. With the rise of capitalism, however, together with the freeing of individuals from feudal constraints and the rise of the national state, the economic surplus was freed from the feudal claims of aristocracy and church to be used to increase the stock of capital.

- The **accumulation of capital** is the process by which an economic surplus is transformed into expanded capacity to produce.
- An **economic surplus** is output above the level required to maintain the existing level of economic activity and reproduce the social order.

Capital consists of two essentially dissimilar elements. One is the actual physical things devised to help in using natural resources, ranging all the way from such simple tools as hoes and hammers to complex ones like petroleum refineries, electrical generating plants, and steel mills. The second form of capital is knowledge stored up in the minds of individuals, or available in written and printed form, that tells people how to build and use capital equipment. Knowledge is by far the most important form of capital: equipment may wear out or be destroyed, but the knowledge of how to make and run it can be used to rebuild, replace, and even improve what has been lost.

A modern industrial economy has three sources of the economic surplus available for capital accumulation. Individuals save, enterprises make profits, and governments collect taxes out of the incomes earned in producing goods and services. This leaves some goods and services unsold and available for use in expanding output and increasing knowledge.

We have two instruments for mobilizing that economic surplus, business firms and governments. A profitable enterprise pays some of the profits to the owners of the enterprise, but large portions are often retained for purposes of investment. In a prosperous economy those profits are large, and retained earnings provide a large fund for expansion. High profits also attract savings from the rest of the economy as owners of those savings seek additional income. The profitable firm taps those sources of capital by borrowing or selling shares in the enterprise. All of this seems ordinary enough, yet we often lose sight of the underlying process. Human effort enters into a production process that generates profit. The profits are plowed back into capital investment and at the same time attract savings from the incomes generated by the production process itself. In this way some of the human effort that enters the production process is transformed first into profits and then into capital.[1]

Taxes can also be used as a means of capital accumulation. Taxes reduce private purchasing power, forcing people to spend less than their earnings. The tax revenues can then be used for several types of public investment. One form of government investment, expenditures on education and health, indirectly increases individual productivity. Governments also provide facilities that reduce business costs and promote business profits, such as waterways, highways, airports, etc. Governments provide direct or indirect subsidies to private enterprises to raise their profits. Finally, governments can invest directly in productive facilities, such as power plants, machinery used by aerospace firms, or even steel mills and oil refineries.

---

[1]The classic analysis of the process by which capitalist enterprises convert labor into capital via profit was developed by Karl Marx in Volume I of *Capital* (1868), where the term "surplus value" is used in place of "profit." Marx considered this process the great contribution of capitalism to human progress, while finding the cause of the downfall of capitalism in its inability to distribute the fruits of progress equitably.

MARX ON CAPITAL ACCUMULATION

Karl Marx gave a unique twist to the analysis of capital accumulation. He pointed out that capital investment increases the economy's capacity to produce without increasing its capacity to consume. Thus, if profits were paid instead to workers and were used to buy consumer goods instead of capital goods, it would be easier to maintain high levels of demand for the final products of the production system. Since that does not happen, the higher the rate of profit the more difficulty the economy would have in maintaining adequate demand for final goods and high levels of output (and profit). Since capital accumulation raises profits, and there is a continuing drive toward capital accumulation in a capitalist economy, Marx saw a growing problem of maintaining prosperity. Periodic crises of increasing severity were built into the private enterprise system because capital accumulation causes expansion of investment at a faster rate than growth of purchasing power.

Marx also showed that it was theoretically possible for the capacity to produce and the ability to consume to increase in a balanced, mutually consistent fashion. He argued, however, that the drive for profit in a private enterprise economy made that result highly unlikely. Marx's discussion of the proposition that rising profits during a period of prosperity create the conditions that bring the prosperity to an end was the starting point for much of the modern analysis of business cycles and economic fluctuations, although most non-Marxist economists don't like to admit it.

Whether the instrument for capital accumulation is public or private, however, the fundamental economic process is similar. Human effort is converted into capital. In one case the instrument is profit and private enterprise, in the other it is taxes and government. Both can be used to accumulate capital.

Business Enterprise and the Profit Motive

The *profit motive* is a crucial element in the process of capital accumulation. The purpose of any business enterprise is to make a profit, to increase the income and wealth of those who own it. Any enterprise that does not make a profit is not long for this world. If expenses consistently exceed revenues the assets of the firm will dwindle to nothing and the firm will disappear from the economic landscape. The successful firm is one that uses its working capital to buy inputs, transforms those inputs into a product, and sells the product for an amount larger than its original capital cost.

$$M \rightarrow C \rightarrow M'$$

where M = original working capital of the firm
C = output of the firm
M' = revenue from sale of C

The profit can then be reinvested in the enterprise to enlarge its operations and make larger profits in the future. Reinvestment of the firm's profits enable it to start the next cycle of production and profit from a larger base and make larger profits in the next time period.

In modern business enterprises, ranging in size from a small mom-and-pop retail store to a giant international conglomerate corporation, this basic relationship is usually stated in the accountant's income statement, which is simply an elaboration of the relationship between M and M': Total revenue from sales minus total cost of producing these sales equals profit. Adding the profit to the original working capital M gives M'.

In a private enterprise economy, profits keep the economy going and provide the resources for capital accumulation and economic expansion. Without profit the motive for continued production disappears. With profit the means for expansion exists, and the desire for still greater wealth assures that a large part of the profit will be reinvested for higher profits later.[2] The economy either expands (because profits are made) or it doesn't function effectively (because profits are inadequate).

Reinvestment of profits to enlarge production is one of two important aspects of the accumulation of capital. The second is technological change, which is financed through profits on the prospect of profits. Transformation of the processes of production enables a firm to increase the rate at which profits are earned. Investing in new techniques can reduce costs and raise the firm's profits per dollar of invested capital. Furthermore, the first enterprise to introduce technical changes gains an advantage over its rivals. Reduced costs give it an advantage in production, and larger profits provide a stronger financial base than more backward firms. It might be argued that in the long run all firms will be on an equal footing as the technical change is adopted by all, but in the meantime there is a clear advantage to the more progressive firms.

Profits generate more profits. They are used to reproduce the firm on an expanded scale, with a larger amount of capital than before, using the same technology. But they also are used to reorganize the production process with a changed technology that enables the firm to increase its rate of profit. Accumulation of capital therefore has both quantitative and qualitative effects.

● The **profit motive** is the driving force of a private enterprise economy. It is the desire for profits which motivates the continuation of production and the accumulation of capital.

Technological Change

An improvement in technology enables more to be produced without increasing the amount of resources, labor, or capital used. More output can be obtained without increasing inputs, by changing the ways in which the inputs are put together. Techniques of production are modified.

The advance of technology can take several forms. New methods of production can reduce production costs. New designs can bring about the production of goods with important new characteristics. Entirely new products can be developed to satisfy human wants more effectively. New techniques of organization, management, or finance may effect important increases in output. All of these forms have the same characteristic, however. They satisfy human wants with less effort or resources. Today's technology sets limits on the amount that can be produced with a given quantity of inputs. Tomorrow's technology can enable the same inputs to produce a larger output.

That basic characteristic of *technological change* has several implications. First, it is possible for output to rise without an increase in the amount of capital. Even if there were no increase in the total amount of capital equipment in use—in a "steady-state" economy, for example—increases in productivity based on technological change can provide for increased standards of living. Normally, of course, in our economy both capital accumulation and technological change take place, and expansion of output occurs for both reasons, but it is possible for improved techniques to be put to use without a net increase in total capital.

Second, a private-enterprise economy has a built-in drive toward continuous technological change. Business enterprises striving for profit find that one way to cut production costs is to introduce new, more efficient methods of production or new improved products. Desire for profit stimulates development and use of ideas that lead to cost reductions and increased output per worker.

A third aspect of technological change is less pleasant. Producing more with the same amount of effort can bring a lighter workload and more leisure for all—or unemployment for

---

[2]Power as well as wealth is a goal. Cartoon in the *Wall Street Journal*: an investment advisor tells his client, "My job is to increase your wealth; turning it into power is your responsibility."

some. Even if enough jobs are available for everyone, technological change can impoverish those whose skills become obsolete. Those who can lay claim to the gains from increased productivity may be enriched while others topple into poverty.

- **Technological change** is the process by which methods of production are altered with the goal of increasing profit and the accumulation of capital.

Resources and Technological Change

Technological change tends to follow the contours of the relative scarcity of the various factors of production. Scarce and expensive inputs will be used sparingly, while relatively abundant and cheap inputs will be used more lavishly. Changes in technology will tend to bring substitution of less expensive inputs for more expensive ones, as efforts are made to minimize production costs. In an economy with relatively abundant natural resources, like the American economy in the nineteenth century, production techniques reflected the relative abundance of natural resources and the relative scarcity of labor.[3] Forests were plentiful, for example, and wood tended to be used widely and wastefully. Wood rather than coal was the favored fuel for heating and cooking. As wood became less abundant it tended to be replaced by coal in both uses. The so-called "balloon" method of light wood frame construction of houses was developed, replacing European methods that required large beams, heavy uprights, and more workers at the building site. Fireplaces accommodated large logs, which wasted fuel but economized on the labor needed to cut or chop the wood. Woodworking

machinery developed in the United States amazed European observers—fast circular saws with thick blades and wide-spaced teeth gobbled up wood, produced much saw-dust, and used power lavishly. These techniques were well adapted to American abundance, but were not widely used in Europe, where wood and power were scarcer. At about the same time, agriculture developed large-scale machinery, like gang plows and reapers, that enabled relatively few people to cultivate great areas of prairie. Such innovations economized on scarce labor power in order to cultivate large tracts of land.

There is another important aspect of technological change. Because technology tends to use relatively abundant resources extensively while using relatively scarce resources intensively, it can contribute to the rapid depletion of exhaustible resources. To some extent that is happening in twentieth-century industrial America. We have in operation a huge amount of fixed capital equipment that was designed to use abundant natural resources efficiently. As those natural resources have become less plentiful, technology has begun to change. Still, a large amount of capital equipment continues to function as it was originally designed to do, and rapidly gobbles up natural resources. It takes time for technological changes to be fully implemented. Meanwhile, relative scarcities of inputs may shift more rapidly than capital equipment can be changed.

The lag can be exaggerated by efforts to shield the old techniques from the impact of economic change. For example, prior to the energy crisis of the 1970s, the prices of energy resources, particularly oil and gas, were regulated in the interests of consumers and industrial users. Artificially low prices encouraged energy use and slowed the development of new technologies that would use the increasingly scarce energy resources more efficiently. By the 1970s much of our technology was outmoded in relation to the relative scarcity of energy resources—witness our gas-guzzling au-

---

[3]Except in the South, where first slavery and later sharecropping with debt-tenure established and preserved a labor-intensive agriculture and held back the development of more technologically advanced methods of industrial production. The economy of the South remained heavily dependent on low-wage labor until well after the second World War.

tomobiles and air-conditioned office buildings with no outside ventilation. When the Arab oil embargo hit in 1973, the economy was unprepared and faced a hectic adjustment in a short period of time. The economy was forced to change quickly to newer patterns of energy use that would ordinarily have come more gradually as energy resources became scarcer.

The lesson to be learned is simple. Technological change tends to respond to the signals given by basic economic relationships. Interfering with those signals can cause serious problems of lagging technological adjustment. Difficulties can arise even without interference, however, because of the large amount of equipment in use that may become outmoded quite rapidly. That problem is compounded when groups with a vested interest in the older technology seek to protect themselves against the changes that shifting relative scarcities require.

Specialization and Large-scale Production

Capital accumulation and technological change open the way to specialization and economies of large-scale production.

Here are some illustrations. An automobile factory is set up as a continuous assembly line operation designed to produce a single basic model in which it specializes. Variations on that model can be produced, but only at a higher cost, as the "extras" added to the base price will indicate, whenever additional features are included. Another basic model will be produced at a different plant, with each plant specializing in a single model in order to produce it most cheaply.

Specialization in automobile production has some limitations, however, for the production plants are usually shut down for several weeks each year to retool for new models. Shifting from one model to another brings reduced output while the changeover is made. Instead of specializing in one model for two, three, or more years, most producers modify their mod-els for marketing purposes, which reduces their production efficiency. If the demand were large enough in a single market area, however, it might be possible for a single plant to produce one uniform model continuously for several years, thereby taking advantage of economies arising from increased specialization.

Specialization, as Adam Smith put it, depends on the size of the market. The larger the demand for a product the greater the possibilities for specialization. As population grows and the economy expands, producers are able to increase their production of single products and thereby reduce costs and increase efficiency. This is why in small towns one finds lawyers and doctors with a general practice, while in large cities a high degree of specialization is common in the legal and medical professions. The specialist, of course, is expected to be more proficient in his particular area than a general practitioner is in that area.

Economies of large-scale production are related to and dependent upon specialization. A single steel mill producing huge quantities of rolled strip steel can be designed for maximum efficiency in production. Specialists can be hired for each job in the process, and because output is so great the individual jobs can be broken down into highly specialized component parts. Management jobs can also be specialized because of the large scale of the operation. There are three constraints, however. One is the size of the market. The scale of production is limited by the amount that can be sold. A second constraint is technology. The scale of output is limited by known techniques and depends inescapably on the current state of the technical arts. The third constraint is management. Somewhere at the top there must be a management specialist who knows how to coordinate all the elements that contribute to large-scale production. Committees and computers can help, and committee or board decisions may be better than one-man management, but at the peak there must be a single decision-making center.

It is quite possible for economies of large-scale production to bring about a situation in which a single unit produces for the entire market. The power plant that supplies an entire region with electricity is one example. The lowest cost production unit generates enough electric power for the whole area, whereas two smaller plants sharing the market would not be able to use the most efficient technology. Growing demand, however, might increase the size of the market enough to support two power plants of the most efficient size. Even growth of the market may not be sufficient to break the monopoly position of the large-scale efficient producer, however: as demand grows there are incentives to improve the techniques of both production and management, increasing the scale of production and reducing costs of production per unit. It is even possible for economies of large-scale production to proceed at a faster pace than the growth of demand, causing the number of producers to fall and competition to diminish. Theoretically, it is possible for technology to advance at a pace fast enough to allow a single monopolist to supply an entire market area and eliminate all competition.

Specialization can also lead to repetitious, dull, and dehumanized work. Assembly line production of automobiles is the classic example. In the early years of this century automobile assembly was carried out by a team of perhaps six workers who assembled the entire automobile from bare chassis to finished product. As demand and output grew, it became possible to place the chassis on a moving trolley while stationing workers along the path to carry out a particular operation or series of operations. Each worker did the same job hour after hour and day after day, and it became possible to increase output by gradually speeding up the line. Efficiency increased, productivity rose, and workers were able to earn higher wages (particularly after unions were organized). But part of the cost was a pattern of work that lacked spontaneity and a sense of

accomplishment. Although the automobile assembly line is an extreme example, it illustrates this less happy face of specialization.

We summarize. Increased output per person can be achieved by *specialization* and *economies of large-scale production*, both of which are made possible by growth of the market and advancing technology, for which accumulation of capital is necessary. But specialization and large-scale production can also lead to unsatisfying work experiences and to monopolistic industries. The ultimate limit to specialization may not be technological in nature, but may well rest in the unwillingness of people to tolerate dehumanized working conditions and the concentration of economic power that accompany large-scale enterprise.

- **Specialization** is the process by which production processes are adapted for a unique or singular purpose.
- **Economies of large-scale production** are reductions in costs of production per unit of output that result from enlarged production facilities.

Labor and Technological Change

Technological change affects labor in a variety of ways. Levels and standards of living can rise as substitution of capital for labor increases the level of output per labor hour. Such advances in affluence depend on two economic relationships, however:

1. The increase in output per worker must rise more rapidly than the number of workers.

2. Workers must share adequately in the distribution of the increase in output created by technological change. If the increase is gobbled up by profits and taxes there would be no increase in general living standards, even if population did not grow.

Substitution of capital for labor may also cause both unemployment and elimination of work skills. Economists have disputed these matters ever since the era of industrialization began, and there is no consensus with respect to the economy as a whole. But the discussions have made it clear that advancing technology makes some skills obsolete, often with disastrous effects on the economic status of workers with those skills. For example, exports of cotton cloth from England to India in the early nineteenth century destroyed the livelihood of millions of Indian handweavers. As they starved it mattered little to them that jobs were created in English factories manufacturing cotton cloth and cloth-making machinery.

The pattern of work skills is also modified by technological change. Introduction of assembly-line mass production into the automobile industry in the early decades of the twentieth century was, in part, motivated by a dearth of skilled labor. However, it also eliminated a large component of skilled labor that was formerly an important part of the production process. Other types of skilled labor in the production of mass-production machinery were created, but in the automobile industry itself there was a general downgrading of workers' skills, as well as fragmentation of work tasks that permitted greater managerial control of the work process.

Two conflicting trends appear to be at work. On the one hand, highly intricate and complex technologies require high levels of skill to design, produce, operate, and maintain the capital equipment used in today's industries. The workers who staff this sector of the economy, although relatively few in number, are highly skilled. The technology they operate is highly capital-intensive. That is, large capital investments and relatively small numbers of workers are employed in producing a large volume of output. A typical example of this type of enterprise is the automated petroleum refinery with a daily throughput of 150,000 barrels of oil and a work force of less than one hundred persons. If this were typical of the economy as a whole, the level of output per person would be tremendously high and the potential level of affluence would be very great.

Unfortunately, there is another side to the situation. The workers who are unable to obtain one of the few jobs available in the capital-intensive enterprises must compete with each other for jobs in the relatively labor-intensive sector of the economy. The historical process of capital accumulation and technical change eliminated jobs in the petroleum refineries, forcing a large portion of the work force into those sectors of the economy with relatively little capital per worker, where wages are relatively low.

In the labor-intensive sector of the economy there is little incentive for firms to substitute capital for labor. The abundance of workers keeps wages relatively low and thereby discourages substitution of capital for labor. This, in turn, preserves the low-wage structure that results from lack of capital and advanced technology.

We find, then, a unique historical development in modern industrial society: a dual pattern of underdevelopment within a developing economy. One sector of the economy moves ahead rapidly to achieve high levels of output per person by utilizing increasingly complex capital equipment in place of people. But the displacement of workers from employment creates conditions in the labor market that keep other sectors of the economy labor-intensive, using an old-fashioned technology. A worker underclass *and* a worker elite are outcomes of the technological change that is an integral part of the process of capital accumulation.

Technological change is a mixed blessing. On the one hand, it makes possible the higher level of output per person that is a chief source of greater affluence and ease. On the other hand, the process of industrialization has substituted capital for labor on a large scale. In doing so it threatens the livelihood of workers and reduces or eliminates their skills while simultaneously creating new jobs and skills for other workers. At a more fundamental level, technological change that originates in the search for markets and profits may well be a major reason for some of the economic and social cleavages that now afflict modern society.

Some Comments

A young economics major might comment that the labor markets in the preceding paragraphs act strangely. Why doesn't the surplus labor displaced by technological change keep wages down in the high-wage, capital-intensive sector, too, thereby eliminating the dual character of the economy? Ah, responds the old economist: labor markets are different from product markets. Labor unions have organized many of the high-technology, high-wage industries to protect their members and to lay claim to as large a share as they can get of the gains from increased productivity. Employers, in addition, can't afford long strikes in highly capital-intensive industries, so they tend to share their gains. Finally, there are often barriers to entry to the high-skill sector of the labor market, such as education, licensing, and discrimination on the basis of race or sex, that serve to strengthen the dual structure of the labor market.

At this point a Marxist student sitting in the back row is likely to observe that the threat of losing their jobs makes workers more docile and amenable to control by the boss, while fractionation of the labor force and the army of the unemployed prevents the working-class unity required for changes in the system. The black woman sitting next to him adds that the whole system is held together by a variety of subsidies to the poor, anyway, and that the financial burden on government will continually increase as the polarization of the economy proceeds. Ultimately, she says, the tax burden will increase to a politically unsupportable level and there will be growing recourse to police power as the situation worsens. All this is nonsense, responds an aspiring business ad-

ministration major: capital investment in new technology is the sure way not only to the profits needed for a viable private enterprise system, but also to a rising standard of living for workers as well.

Barriers to Growth

Even if we set aside the economic, social, and political problems associated with capital accumulation and technological change, there are four barriers to economic growth that must be overcome by any economy interested in greater affluence. They are the population trap, diminishing returns, exhaustion of resources, and failure to use productive resources fully.

The Population Trap

Improved living standards can be achieved only by increasing output faster than the population increases. Man's breeding knows no season. The long run trend in human history has been for the population of the world to grow, despite wars, famines, and other disasters. As a result, the fundamental economic problem becomes one not only of increasing output but of achieving a rate of growth exceeding that of population. Maintaining existing levels of output while population grows means that mankind will fall behind in its efforts to improve its material conditions of life. Raising output only at a rate that matches population growth means stagnation. There are only three possibilities:

1. Where the rate of increase of output is less than the rate of increase of population, the economy moves toward misery.

2. Where the rate of increase of output equals the rate of increase of population, living standards neither rise nor fall.

3. Where the rate of increase of output exceeds the rate of increase of population, the economy can move toward bliss.

Clearly, then, the relationship between output and population growth determines whether or not economic welfare will be increased by capital accumulation and economic growth.

The *population trap* appears when increases in output cause population to grow by providing the means by which death rates can be reduced. An increase in food supplies allows more people to survive, for example. This development affects less developed countries in particular, where birth rates tend to be high and population growth is normally held in check by high death rates. An increase in output may enable living standards to rise temporarily in such a situation, but this in turn may cause a decline in death rates, an increase in population, and a reversion of living standards to their old level.

This sequence of events is at the heart of the Malthusian theory of population, developed by the English economist Thomas R. Malthus (1766–1834) in 1798. Incorporation of this analysis into the body of economic theory of that period led English essayist Thomas Carlyle (1795–1881) to call economics "the dismal science," a verdict that many students concur in, but for somewhat different reasons. Even today, however, the population trap is an important reason why some billions of people in much of the world live at very low subsistence levels. Where the trap has been avoided, it has been done through reductions in the birth rate that parallel the declining death rate. Unless birth and death rates can be brought down together, accumulation of capital and increases in output may have little or no effect on standards of living.

The more advanced nations of the world are more fortunate. For a variety of reasons that are not very well understood, they have arrived at the situation in which both birth rates and death rates are relatively low. Under these conditions an increase in living standards will have little impact on death rates, population will not be induced to rise significantly, and real advances in welfare can more readily be achieved. For much of the rest of the world, however, the population trap is a major problem.

- The **population trap** is the situation in which an increase in output causes or triggers an increase in population.

Diminishing Returns
The second barrier that the processes of economic expansion must overcome is embodied in the *principle of diminishing returns*. Wherever the amount of one factor of production is fixed and cannot be increased, and other factors of production are added to it in the production process, output will be increased as the other factors are added, but after a certain point the increases will gradually decline in size. For example, if one unit of fertilizer is added to unfertilized agricultural land, a relatively large increase in the size of the crop can be expected. Alternatively, two units of fertilizer may increase the crop by more than twice the increase from one unit. At some point, however, the crop increases will stop accelerating and start slowing down, until further increases in fertilizer use will bring little or no increase in output.

- The **principle of diminishing returns** states that as units of a variable factor of production are added to a fixed factor of production, at some point the resulting increases in output will begin to diminish in size.

Experimental studies demonstrating the principle of diminishing returns are most readily found in agriculture, where the acreage of a farm or size of a herd of cattle can be held constant. For example, one study of dairying concerned the effects of varying amounts of feed inputs on the milk output of a large number of cows over a three-year period. The results are shown in Figure 2–1 and Table 2–1.

Diminishing returns are clearly indicated by column 4 in the table. Note also the somewhat erratic nature of the data: they do not fit the

Table 2–1
Feed Input and Milk Output per Cow per Year for 392 Cows Fed at Six Levels

Number of Cows in Each Group	Average Total Digestible Nutrients Consumed (lb per yr)	Average 4% Fat Corrected Milk Produced (lb per yr)	Increase in Milk Output per lb of Increase in Feed Input (lb)
65	5,654	7,626	1.20
60	6,117	8,184	1.62
66	6,575	8,824	1.03
55	7,132	9,400	0.95
52	7,531	9,780	0.50
94	7,899	9,965	

Source: Jensen et al., "Input-Output in Milk Production."

Note: "Total digestible nutrients" includes all types of feed (grain, hay, etc.) expressed as pounds of carbohydrate feed (dry weight) according to feed value. A correction was applied to express all milk production as of a uniform butterfat content.

Figure 2–1
Feed Input and Milk Output Per Cow Per Year

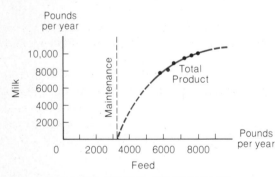

Source: Einar Jensen, John Klein, Emil Rauchenstein, T. E. Woodward, and Ray Smith, "Input-Output Relationships in Milk Production," *U.S. Department of Agriculture Technical Bulletin No. 815,* May 1942.

trend line perfectly, nor is this study a perfect example of the general principle. This is always true of illustrations drawn from actual experience.

The principle of diminishing returns is a basic proposition that applies to any production situation, and it will be met with time and again in this book. Here, however, it is significant in helping to define the basic economic problems faced by any society. It indicates that capital accumulation, by itself, is not enough for sustained economic growth. If the type and amount of natural resources are fixed, and if the work force does not grow, diminishing returns from increased capital accumulation will eventually appear. As returns to capital decline, they will ultimately no longer be large enough to induce consumers to forego present consumption in order to add to the stock of capital.

This proposition of the trend toward a "stationary state" is associated with the name of David Ricardo (1772–1823), a contemporary and friend of Malthus. It became an important building block of the "classical" economics of the nineteenth century, but is given little stress today. The reason for its fall from grace is that the factors of production later proved to be much more flexible and variable than the earlier economists thought, and the presence of a fixed factor, invariable in amount, has not arisen. Population has grown, new areas of the world have been opened for development, increased specialization in production has cut costs, and most important, advances in science and engineering have made possible considerable restructuring of the relationships between factors of production in the production process. All these developments prevented the huge growth of capital that has occurred over the last two hundred years from being limited by diminishing returns. Indeed, there is some evidence that the industrial nations of the world, in spite of their high degree of development, are still in the stage of increasing returns to capital.

Nevertheless, the principle of diminishing returns is important. With a fixed economic base provided by the world's natural resources, capital accumulation alone will not be able continually to generate rates of economic growth large enough to overcome the effects of a rising world population. An additional ingredient is needed: the type of scientific and technological change that raises productivity enough to overcome the long-run tendency toward diminishing returns.

Exhaustible Resources

Many natural resources are not only limited, they are exhaustible. Except for a relatively small supply of hydroelectric power and solar energy, the bulk of the energy resources used today are derived from fossil fuels (coal, petroleum, natural gas) whose supplies are limited by the amounts of organic material preserved in fossilized form within the earth's surface. Other minerals have limitations on their ultimate supply as well, including the iron, copper, and other metals on which modern civilization is largely based.

All *exhaustible resources* have one characteristic in common. Production becomes gradually more costly as the deposits easiest to work and cheapest to draw from are used up. Greater amounts of labor and capital are needed to obtain and transport coal or ores as the mines become deeper, as the richer deposits are exhausted, and as sources further from the market must be utilized. New mines may be opened as old ones peter out, but the very fact that the new ones were not in operation earlier is a good indication that their costs of production are probably higher than those of the old operations.

- **Exhaustible resources** are those whose quantity and/or quality decline when they are used as a means of production.

The fact that exhaustible resources lead to rising costs of production can have significant consequences for economic growth. For example, in the nineteenth century, much of England's predominance in manufacturing rested upon large supplies of rich, easily mined coal. As the mines became deeper and as the richer veins were used up, other coal-producing regions in Germany and France could compete with England more effectively, until by the midtwentieth century English industry had poorer supplies of coal that could be mined only at relatively high costs in comparison with other industrial areas. This exhaustion of cheap coal resources has not been the only reason for England's economic difficulties in the twentieth century, but it is a fundamental one.

The iron ore of the Lake Superior region in the United States may turn out to be a somewhat similar case. Much of the economic strength of the United States has been based on having cheaper iron ore than most other industrial regions of the world. Now that this advantage has been eliminated by exhaustion of the richest Lake Superior mines, the American economy's international position has been reshaping itself, although again there are many other elements in the situation.

The problem is that costs of production rise wherever economic activity is based on an exhaustible resource, unless technological changes can overcome the tendency for costs to increase. New materials, new production techniques, and better organization *can* bring costs down faster than exhaustion of resources pushes them up. On the other hand, they might not, as the case of the British economy in the last fifty years has shown.

Less Than Full Use of Resources

Failure to use productive capacity fully has been one of the chief reasons for the inability of the economy to achieve its full potential for the advancement of human welfare. The causes of that failure will be examined in some detail in Chapters 4 through 14, so here we merely describe three common patterns:

1. Relatively brief *recessions* of perhaps a year or more duration that are characterized primarily by temporary accumulations of goods that cannot be sold at current prices.

2. General *stagnation* in which purchasing power does not rise as rapidly as the economy's capacity to produce. The results are slowly growing unemployment and unused plant capacity, even though the economy may be expanding.

3. *Great depressions* in which basic and fundamental dislocations pervade the entire economy. Massive unemployment, serious financial difficulties, and a major hiatus in capital accumulation and investment characterize the great depressions.

All three of these situations—long and serious depressions, stagnation, and brief recession—are related to the same fundamental cause. Purchasing power either does not keep pace with the potential growth of the economy or it actually declines, creating a gap between the actual level of spending and that required for full use of productive capacity. Seen from the other side of the coin, the capacity of the economy to produce outruns the ability of consumers to buy the output.

Overcoming the Barriers to Growth

These, then, are the barriers to increased wealth:

1. The population trap. Improvement in living standards can literally be eaten up by population increases.

2. The principle of diminishing returns. When one resource, such as land, is fixed in amount, the increased output from added units of other resources tends to fall. Where this is the case, capital must be accumulated at an increasing rate just to keep the economy where it was before. The economy will have to run faster just to stay where it is.

3. Exhaustible resources. Some resources vary in quality even though they may not be completely "fixed" in amount. Where this is the case, costs of production will rise in the long run as the resources are used up, irrespective of the rate at which capital is accumulated.

4. Unemployed resources. The economy can fail to use its full potential, leaving capital and labor unemployed.

None of these problems is insurmountable, however. Four conditions are necessary if the economy is to provide the means for continuing material advances for humanity:

1. The economic system must generate a high rate of capital accumulation. People must be able and willing to devote a substantial portion of their production to building capital rather than to present consumption.

2. A balance between birth and death rates must be established that is largely independent of standards of living so that the population trap may be avoided.

3. The social and economic system must generate a high rate of scientific discovery and technological change in order to avoid the effects of diminishing returns and exhaustible resources.

4. The economy must operate at its potential capacity or very close to it.

Yet these objectives contain fundamental contradictions. A high rate of capital accumulation makes full use of productive capacity difficult when purchasing power fails to keep pace. Technological change tends to eliminate jobs and skills. Economic growth puts pressure on exhaustible resources that increases the tendency toward diminishing returns. The scientific discoveries and technological changes that are a major feature of a modern economy's growth can pollute the environment (as they already have) so that the very continuance of the human race has been cast in doubt. The whole growth process will have to come under greater control if it is not to destroy the ecological system. To these issues we must add problems of poverty and inequality. The affluent society has failed to distribute the benefits of growth to everyone. Progress has not eliminated poverty. The relative incomes of rich and poor have not changed significantly in the last quarter-century, while the tendency for the distribution of wealth to become more unequal has persisted. Meanwhile, the failure of underdeveloped nations to develop their own growth processes, together with rapid population growth, is rapidly dividing the world into nations of haves and have-nots. The political instabilities created by these economic disparities may threaten the viability of the economic system itself.

Spaceship Earth

In the long run, the chief barrier to economic growth is the limited ability of the earth's natural environment to accommodate a growing population and its economic needs. It has become very clear that recent patterns of economic growth and population increase cannot be sustained long into the future unless some rapid changes in technology are achieved. That point was made by Donella and Dennis Meadows and their associates in *The Limits to Growth* (1972). Their computerized projections of recent trends invariably predicted disasters inherent in the limits imposed by one or

more of the earth's exhaustible resources. Disaster may well be avoided, but changes will have to be made as the limits are approached. We are beginning to feel some of those effects already as the era of relatively abundant, low-cost supplies of food and fuel slowly recedes.

Already the expert projections of world population growth are being scaled down. Based solely on demographic factors related to birth and death rates, population experts can project the world's population from the present 3.6 billion to about double that number (6 to 8 billion) by the end of the century and again double (14 to 18 billion) by the year 2100. But when food supply limitations are taken into account the world's population is seen as leveling off at about 5 to 7 billion persons early in the 21st century. And why will it level off? Because of pressure on food supplies in the poorer, less developed nations as a result of famine, disease, and related political and social turmoil. Some experts point to the likelihood that the average calorie intake per person, now about 2200 per day on a worldwide basis, will fall to almost the minimum subsistence level of 1800 daily calories early in the next century. If that happens, billions of people will then be at the margin of subsistence, with the slightest failure of supplies able to trigger massive starvation. The rippling effects of such disasters could have a worldwide impact.

There is an alternate scenario. It is possible that the economy could be organized on a permanently sustainable basis. Renewable resources would be on a perpetual yield basis. Exhaustible resources would be used in ways that would maximize the life of the resource and would enable recycling for reuse. Energy systems would maximize use of renewable fuels (solar energy, for example) and would emphasize the efficient use of fuel while minimizing energy demand. Economic activity would be limited so as not to exceed the environmental regenerative capacities of land, air, and water. In essence, a closed production system would prevail in which a maximum amount of the system's output would be used as inputs, minimizing or eliminating production of wastes. This scenario clearly limits the population to levels consistent with production of food supplies and desired levels of consumption. It also may require considerably greater political ingenuity and technological change than may be forthcoming in time to avoid the first scenario.

Economic growth is still possible in a steady-state or sustainable economy: technological change could continue to increase output per person. Energy use could be based increasingly on use of renewable resources such as geothermal or solar energy and nuclear breeder reactors that produce more fuel than they use. Artificial photosynthesis could produce synthetic foods. With wastes increasingly recycled as production inputs, rising output or increased population would not degrade the environment. As long as technological change led to greater efficiency in energy use, food production, and recycling, capital accumulation could continue. And if population increases were held below those of output, living standards could rise if the gains were well distributed. It is true that ecological and economic factors limit growth, given our present technology, but a different technology, compatible with a sustainable economy, could permit very large gains in living standards for a much enlarged world population.

Few things are produced in nature in the form most useful to people. They must be transformed into the food, clothing, shelter, and other things that are required for human existence, comfort, and ease. This fact is at the root of all economics and much of human history: human beings are engaged in a continuous struggle with a recalcitrant and often niggardly nature to produce the things they need and want.

There are two paradoxes here, however. Humankind is part of nature itself, and its continued existence depends on preservation of the ecological system within which life is maintained. Yet a single-minded effort to extract more from nature can threaten the ecological base. In addition, human beings have social and psychological needs that cannot be satisfied merely by material things. Yet concentration on material things can leave those other needs unsatisfied and human beings far from happy. Economic growth that focuses on material affluence can take the wrong path—and many people today argue that it has—threatening the environment and failing to promote human happiness.

At the root of the problem is a basic contradiction within an individualistic, private enterprise economy. On the one hand, limits are placed on economic expansion and growth by the need to preserve the ecological base of economic activity. On the other hand, individuals see economic activity as a means of increasing their wealth for those with the ability to get as much as they can. Others have done it; why not me? That philosophy, which is a fundamental driving force in the private enterprise economy, is on a collision course with the limits imposed by society's need to preserve its foundations in nature.

We are faced with a challenge. More rather than less is desired by many, particularly those who have less. The gains from affluence can be significant. But economic growth can also be destructive or misguided. Can we so manage our affairs that we will move to a more affluent society that is neither destructive nor inhumane? Much of our future depends on how we answer that question.

What is the path to a sustainable economy? At this stage it can only be dimly perceived. But one point should be obvious. The transition will require a great deal of capital investment in new ways of doing things. The tools of economic progress, capital investment, and technical change will be essentially the same as in the past. But we have come far enough to realize that there is now a further and overriding requirement. We must achieve compatibility with the biosphere that has come to be called Spaceship Earth.

Summary

A modern industrial economy is capable of generating a surplus over and above the goods needed for the continuation and reproduction of the social order. The surplus can be used as capital to expand the economy's capacity to produce. Business firms accumulate capital out of profits, and governments can use the tax system for capital accumulation. In both cases human effort is converted into capital.

Technological change is also a means of increasing the surplus. An improvement in technology enables more to be produced without increasing the amount of resources, labor, or capital used. Technological change tends to respond to the signals given by basic economic relations, using abundant and cheap resources extensively and scarce, expensive resources intensively. Capital accumulation and technological change lead to specialization and economies of large-scale production, which also contribute to production of a surplus and capital accumulation. But they can also contribute to the growth of monopoly and an unsatisfying work environment. Technological change, which substitutes capital for labor, can also bring unemployment and erosion of work skills. In the contemporary economy this trend seems to be leading to a divided society of simultaneous affluence and poverty, of advancing technology and social conflict.

There are four barriers to the economic growth associated with capital accumulation and advancing technology. One is the population trap, in which increased affluence triggers population growth. The advanced nations have been able to avoid it, but many of the less developed countries have not. Second is diminishing returns. Increased amounts of capital applied to limited resources causes growth in output ultimately to decline and level off, unless diminishing returns are overcome by accelerating technical change or economies of large-scale production. The third barrier is exhaustible resources. Costs of production rise when exhaustible resources are gradually used up, unless, once more, that effect is overcome by technical change and economies of large-scale production. Finally, less than full use of resources due to recessions, depressions, and economic stagnation can reduce capital accumulation and slow the application of new techniques—and also reduce output.

The barriers to economic growth can be overcome by rapid accumulation of capital and technological change. The advanced industrial nations have been able to do that over the last two hundred years or more, although interrupted periodically by depressions. But as the industrial economy has spread throughout the world and drawn on all of the world's resources, we stand on the edge of a new era. Both the technology of industrial production and the acquisitive motive that lies behind the process of capital accumulation may be incompatible with the limited resources and ecological foundations of Spaceship Earth.

Key Concepts

forces of production
accumulation of capital
economic surplus
profit motive

technological change
specialization
economies of large-scale production
population trap

principle of diminishing returns
exhaustible resources

For Discussion

1. To what factors would you attribute the decline in capital accumulation and technological innovation in the U.S. in the past decade?

2. Is technological change desirable or undesirable?

3. Has technological change that brought mass production resulted in the "degradation of labor," or has it freed labor from degrading tasks?

4. Is unlimited and continuing economic growth feasible? Desirable?

5. How have the major industrial nations avoided the population trap?

6. Does economic growth lead to greater human happiness? In what ways? If not, why not?

Chapter 3

Social Relations of Production

The forces of production involve interactions between people and things, such as resources and instruments of production. The *social relations of production* involve interactions between people, for example, between employer and employee. In the modern private enterprise economy, which is based on private ownership of resources and intensive use of capital goods, the most important social relations of production are between the owners of capital and the workers. Capital and labor cooperate in carrying on economic activity, yet some of their most important economic interests are in opposition. This chapter examines that fundamental contradiction within the private enterprise economy and its implications for the relationship between capital and labor, the nature of modern business enterprise, the role of government, and the attitudes and ideology of a market economy.

- **Social relations of production** are relationships between people generated by the processes and forces of production. They include direct relationships such as those between buyers and sellers; informal groupings into social classes or economic interest groups; formal organizations such as corporations or government agencies; and economic values, motivations, and ideologies.

Capital and Labor

In a *private enterprise economy* the means of production—resources and capital goods—are largely owned privately. Some capital, such as roads and schools, may be owned socially, but the characteristic pattern is private ownership. Privately owned means of production must be used in conjunction with human labor in order to produce useful and marketable goods. No matter how much the production process is automated, it is created and controlled by some form of human effort. Human beings are the end point of production as well, consuming the output of the production process and enabling the work force to reproduce itself and increase its numbers.

One characteristic feature of a private-enterprise economy is that workers normally do not own the means of production but work for wages and salaries paid by the private individuals or corporations who are owners.

The class struggle as seen by two Captains of Industry from the golden age of the private enterprise economy:

John Pierpont Morgan the elder (1837–1913): "Any employer who pays his labor more than the least he can get them for is cheating his stockholders."

Jay Gould (1836–1892): "I can hire half the working class to kill the other half."

The owners have a continuing interest in increasing the share of profits, while workers have a continuing interest in increasing the share of wages. A fundamental dichotomy, therefore, is at the root of one of the elemental problems of the modern economy: the conflict between the owners of capital and the workers whom they employ.

- In a **private enterprise economy** the means of production are largely privately owned by individuals or business firms owned by individuals.

The conflict is not mitigated by the fact that production requires both capital and labor, or that increased production requires an enlarged capital stock. Both capital and labor benefit from their required cooperation in production and from accumulation of capital. But those factors do not eliminate the conflict between the two.

Nor is the conflict mitigated by the fact that workers accumulate human capital in the form of knowledge and skills. There is a difference between human capital and physical capital such as tools and machinery. An individual can earn an income from his accumulated human capital only if he works, using his human capital along with his labor. Examples are the skilled machine-tool operator, the practicing physician, the teacher, and so on. But ownership of physical capital makes possible income without work for the owner of capital—in the form of rent or profit. In a socialist society, the latter source of income would not exist, and a social class characterized chiefly by income from property would be absent. In a society with private ownership of capital, however, a capitalist class, whose income is derived primarily from ownership of property, is a characteristic feature of the economy.

The market mechanism is, in one sense, an important device for resolving economic conflicts. In the competitive economy, both buyer and seller trade at a price determined by impersonal market forces. Each must accept the market price or not trade at all. There is no room for the individual employer to drive wages down or for the worker to push them up. That conclusion is not true for markets characterized by monopolistic elements, however. Under those conditions there is considerable space for conflict and bargaining.

Even in competitive markets there is conflict lurking beneath the market determination of prices. Market forces of demand and supply are the end product of the actions of large numbers of individuals, each one of whom is trying to maximize personal gains. Underneath the demand for labor by business firms is the continuing effort of employers to pay as little as possible. Behind the supply of labor is the drive of workers to get as much as they can. The market price for labor produced by the interaction of demand and supply is itself the product of the conflict created by an economic system that sets capital and labor at odds. On the surface, the conflict seems to be resolved by the price-making mechanism of the marketplace, but the resolution itself is the outcome of a continuing economic conflict.

There is another element of conflict in a private-enterprise economy. An employer hiring a worker gains command over the worker's labor, and uses that authority to organize the production effort to make a profit. The employer is in a superior position and the employee a subordinate one, establishing a hierarchy of power in which one person dominates another. The working lives of most people are, for the most part, not under their own control, but under the control of others. This situation adds a subtle conflict over authority and power to the conflict over wages and working conditions.

Exploitation

Karl Marx (1818–1883) argued that the conflict between capital and labor originates in the *exploitation* of the working class. His was a sophisticated argument, and in examining it we can learn much about the way a private-enterprise economy functions. Exploitation, as Marx saw it, originates in the production by labor of goods valued at an amount greater than labor's wage. Marx called the difference "surplus value." It includes all income going to owners of the means of production, including what non-Marxist economists call profit, rent, and interest.

Marx argued that all capital is the product of human effort, that it merely embodies the labor of the past, which has become the property of employers. Private ownership of the means of production enables owners to obtain profits, rent, and interest, to transform them into capital by reinvesting them, and to obtain still larger profits. The labor effort that begins as the worker's property ends as capital owned by others.

There is, Marx argued, a constant pressure on business firms to drive down wages, lengthen the working day, and use cheap labor (women and children) in order to make profits and survive in a competitive economy. But Marx recognized that such actions have economic limits imposed by the market. For example, he knew that in a competitive economy wage rates are determined by the market and an employer is unable to get workers if he tries to pay less than the going wage. The more important sources of exploitation, Marx felt, are the larger economic forces that keep wages down and thereby provide for high profits. An army of unemployed is always present in a capitalist economy, he argued, created by lack of purchasing power during depressions and by

substitution of capital for labor in good times. In either case, persistent unemployment keeps wages down for most workers and enables employers to gain a surplus value from the work of their employees.

● **Exploitation**, according to Marx, is the process by which capitalists appropriate a portion of the value of output produced by workers. He called that portion *surplus value*.

Marx's argument is a deep one worth pondering. On the surface, he seems to argue that exploitation is the result of actions taken by business firms to keep costs down and profits high. Beneath the surface exploitation are the impersonal processes of capital accumulation and competitive market forces, which together hold wages down. Ultimately, however, the essential element in exploitation is private ownership of the means of production, which enables the labor effort of workers to be transformed into private capital owned by others.

These outcomes of the capital-labor relationship are often modified, as Marx recognized. Workers can organize unions to bargain with employers, and the unions' enlarged bargaining power can provide a better deal. Social welfare legislation can provide governmental buffers against the worst economic conditions. Living standards can rise from a variety of causes. But according to Marx, underneath the surface there will always lurk the exploitive aspect of capitalism: control of the work process by owners of capital, conscious action by employers to reduce wage costs, unemployment caused by the process of capital accumulation itself, and the transformation of labor effort into privately owned capital by way of business profits.

Alienation

Marx was also one of the first economists to identify *alienation* as an economic problem. In an employer-employee relationship the employer pays a wage or salary in exchange for the labor power of the employees. The product then becomes the property of the employer. The employer sells it for enough money to pay the employees and provide a profit. In the process, the employees exchange the time and effort expended in work, which in reality is a portion of their lives, for a cash payment with which to support themselves and their families.

An intangible element has changed hands also—control over the work process. The workers forfeit command of their own efforts and must work at the direction of the employer. They have no influence over what is produced or how it is made. They do not control the product after it is completed. Their only interest in the process is the pay they earn. The workers work neither to fulfill their own personal goals nor to achieve the goals of the social group to which they belong. Their only concern is their income and what they can buy with it. The work effort is depersonalized; it has become solely a market transaction. In this sense the worker can be said to be estranged or alienated.[1]

One result of the alienation of the worker is psychological. Goals such as self-fulfillment and identification with other people in meaningful relationships give way to economic goals. The economic situation of the worker forces economic goals to the fore by largely eliminating the others. Those most important aspects of daily life connected with making a living come to lack the motivations and relationships necessary to the full development of the human personality. For most people, the satisfactions that make for a humane society are not found in work.

Two ways of compensating for the alienation of the workplace have developed. One is em-

phasis on leisure time and recreation. If work is not satisfying it can be tolerated only with time off and diversions that substitute other satisfactions for those the workplace cannot provide. Another compensation is increased material gains. If only the paycheck is important, incentives can be sustained by increasing the worker's salary or wage. Material gains replace the other motivations that are lacking.

We arrive at an interesting paradox. The psychic effects of the capital-labor relationship require an ever-increasing standard of living to compensate workers for unsatisfying work relationships. Yet the basic psychic needs remain unsatisfied, leading to a further drive for greater material gains. Part of the malaise of the modern industrial society is its inability to satisfy some deep-seated needs of people, in spite of growing affluence.

- **Alienation** is the condition of separation or estrangement of the worker from the product of his or her labor, along with the loss of control over working life. It leads to emphasis on material goals at the expense of more humane values.

Further Considerations

The preceding discussion of the relationship between capital and labor is much simplified—deliberately—in order to get at fundamentals. In reality, there are conflicting interests among owners of capital, for example, between bankers and industrialists or between firms producing raw materials and firms producing finished products. Workers are by no means united, either, but fall into a variety of groups whose interests do not coincide: white collar and blue collar, high wage and low wage, skilled and unskilled, unionized and nonunion, for example. The political leverage of these and other groups will differ from place to place and from year to year.

Socialist economies are not immune from these ills, particularly when organized on authoritarian lines—like the Soviet Union. Capi-

---

[1]Alienation, in the sense used here, is *not* a psychological state, but an objective condition of working life. Wage earners are separated from their product by the employer-employee relationship and the system of wage payments. The fact of separation may have psychic implications, but the psychological condition is the result of a real economic relationship rooted in the economic organization.

tal there is owned by the state rather than by private individuals, but just as in a capitalist economy, workers are separated from their tools and from their product. Problems of conflict, economic justice, and alienation arise there also. The ills of the modern industrial economy are not easily eliminated, and anyone looking for solutions must go beyond merely shifting from private to state ownership of capital.

Technology and Bureaucracy

One of the most striking features of a modern industrial economy is the technology of mass production. It is most fully developed in the basic heavy industry that supplies relatively standard inputs for the light industry that produces a wide variety of finished products for consumers. Goods like steel, petroleum products, copper, aluminum and other nonferrous metals, machinery and electrical equipment, ships and automobiles are manufactured in enormous quantities in huge plants, into which flow large amounts of raw materials and semi-finished products, which employ thousands of workers and produce huge amounts of finished products. Production can be organized on such a large scale because market demand for the final product is also large. Large-scale organizations are also required, and the managerial techniques that control large-scale production are just as important as the engineering technology. These large organizations emphasize economic rationality in decision making, control from the top, and bureaucratic organization. Those characteristics in turn generate a leadership whose goals are wealth and power.

Rationality
The management techniques that make large-scale production possible have three essential features. One is rationality. Every portion of the business operation has to fit into a system in which all the parts interrelate in a smoothly functioning operation. The correct inputs have to be brought together at the proper time and place. A high degree of planning and coordination is necessary for the logistics of production and distribution on a large scale. Furthermore, inputs must be combined in least-cost combinations, more expensive inputs eliminated in favor of cheaper ones, and the revised combinations of inputs introduced without disrupting the production process. Finally, the high cost of capital requires that the entire operation be kept functioning as continuously as possible. All of this adds up to a heavy emphasis on rational decision making based on careful calculations of costs to the enterprise and articulation of actions with goals. A highly rational organization structure is essential to the modern business firm.

Authority
The second notable feature of the modern corporation is control from the top. Decisions about basic policy for the enterprise, about goals and how to implement them, are made by a small circle of top management. The officers of the corporation and the board of directors are, in most cases, the center of authority. Information flows to them from outside the firm and from internal sources. Decisions are made by the managerial group. Directives are passed down through the administrative hierarchy, to be carried out at lower administrative levels. A wide variety of accounting techniques is used to determine how well the organization functions to achieve the goals established at the top, and varied patterns of authority and responsibility may exist. But the fundamental principle is one of central control and central authority combined with information systems and incentives to assure that centrally determined decisions are carried out.

Bureaucracy
The third characteristic of the modern firm is *bureaucracy*. Managerial jobs are just as specialized as production jobs. Each position has a

job description, which specifies the tasks to be performed, responsibilities to higher-ups, and authority over others. A table of organization can be constructed out of job descriptions to show the exact relationships of responsibility and authority among the various jobs, forming a giant pyramid with many at the bottom, few at the top, and a hierarchy of grades in between.

The large corporation, like any bureaucratic organization, must develop patterns of motivations and rewards that bring the career goals of its decision-makers into conformity with the profit-oriented rationality of the firm. This is no easy task, and it is quite possible for the goals of managers to differ from the objectives of the firm. An extreme example is the bank officer who embezzles money from the bank. A more common example is the purchasing agent who gets a kickback from his firm's suppliers rather than insisting on a slightly lower price for his firm. The conflicts between individual and organizational goals develop at all levels of authority in any bureaucratic structure, and are an important reason why large corporations seldom achieve fully their goals of economic rationality. Although the modern business firm outwardly has the twin goals of rationality and efficiency, its bureaucratic form of organization and its hierarchal structure of power prevent it from achieving them.

- **Bureaucracy** is a form of management emphasizing rationality, central authority, a hierarchy of ranks, and specialized jobs.

Corporations also have a problem in determining the most efficient size for a managerial or producing unit. An automobile firm may find that financial management is most effective when handled from a single decision-making center, while production is most efficiently managed when divided into several divisions and only coordinated at the top. A wide variety of organizational patterns have developed within the framework of centralized bureaucratic authority.

This, then, is the modern enterprise: rational, authoritarian, bureaucratic. It seldom operates perfectly, but it is an effective management tool. Its effectiveness is shown by its use wherever modern production technology prevails, whether in a privately owned firm like International Telephone and Telegraph Corporation, or a public enterprise like the Tennessee Valley Authority, or the Ministry for Heavy Industry in the USSR. The Soviet commissar and the U.S. business executive are brothers under the skin.

Wealth, Power, and the Economic Elite

The organizational structure of the modern corporation generates two goals among those who lead it, wealth and power. The person who gets to the top in an authoritarian bureaucracy dedicated to the rational achievement of specified goals must be intelligent and capable, of course. One of the strengths of modern business enterprise is its success in selecting capable and rational leadership. Competency is an essential criterion for success in the large corporation. Many compete for the top positions, but few achieve them.

Those who move to top positions are imbued with a desire for success that drives them to work long and hard at their jobs. Typically, the business executive works a 50- to 60-hour week, often brings work home after closing time, and constantly stresses the drive to succeed. Success is measured in terms of economic gains for the firm and is rewarded not only by promotion within the business hierarchy, but by economic rewards as well. Affluence is one reward for success.

Power is both a means and an end. A person moving up in a bureaucratic organization is sensitive to authority over those below and responsibilities to those above. With others of the same rank competing for a relatively few higher positions, the person who is alert to the acquisition of power and how to use it has an advantage over those who may be equally capable in management but who are a little less astute about organizational politics. The modern large firm, then, selects for leadership a particular type of person. Intelligent, capable, and rational, the rising executive strongly desires success, and success comes in the form of wealth and power. An economic elite emerges that seeks to obtain and hold money and power, and the authoritarian organizations through which they rise provide a means to those ends.

The distinguishing feature of the economic elite of the private enterprise economy is its control over the productive resources (capital) of the economy and over the economic surplus (profits) that enable the stock of capital to grow. It makes the key decisions that control the processes of production and capital accumulation. In the private sector it includes the top management of large corporations, particularly executives of the financial corporations, like banks and insurance companies, through which financial markets function. Finally, the economic elite includes those wealthy individuals and families whose accumulated and often inherited wealth enable them to participate in the important managerial decisions of large firms. Whatever may be said about political democracy in a private enterprise economy, the structure of economic organization and the ownership of property creates an economic oligarchy.

The Role of Government

Government reflects these economic realities. Politics in a private enterprise economy is dominated largely by economic issues, and the functions of government include the maintenance of an effectively functioning economy.

The economy as a whole can be thought of as a going concern, a social enterprise that organizes the processes of production and distribution in such a way that the society continues and prospers. In a private enterprise economy, the organizational structure is based on private property, business enterprise, and the desire for gain. Everyone has an interest in the continuation and effective functioning of the system, for it is through the economy as a whole that workers gain their subsistence and survive and owners and/or managers maintain their wealth and power. Serious difficulties or economic breakdown threaten everyone, whatever their position in the economy.

The most important and fundamental governmental function in a private enterprise economy is the preservation of the economic order. It takes several forms. First, governments maintain the legal basis for the system of private property and the contracts among people and business firms through which economic activity is carried on. Second, governments try to manage conflicts among the many economic interest groups of a complex private enterprise economy. At one level, the daily functioning of legislatures is concerned with the immediate conflict of interests between agricultural, industrial, and financial interests, labor and management, consumers and producers, business enterprise and the general public, and among the many divisions of the business community itself.

At a deeper level, governments help to establish general political and economic arrangements designed to resolve the fundamental economic conflicts between capital and labor in order to prevent those conflicts from tearing the economic order apart. Every major industrial nation has developed such an "accord" between capital and labor in the twentieth century, although in recent years they have tended to become unravelled. In the United States the "accord" involved the following:

1. Collective bargaining between labor unions and management as the chief means for managing the conflict between capital and labor, including government protection of the right of workers to organize and strike, and prohibition of the use of force in labor disputes.

2. Government programs designed to protect workers against the more serious economic threats to their well-being: unemployment insurance, protection against injury on the job, old age insurance and retirement programs, and related legislation.

3. Maintenance of high levels of economic activity and avoidance of serious economic depressions through active use of the government's taxation, spending, and monetary powers.

These programs had the effect of recognizing the need of working people to participate in the gains from growth of economic activity and accumulation of capital. They were, in one sense, an answer to Marx and the socialists who pointed to the economic forces that tended toward exploitation of working people and aggrandizement of the interests of business enterprise. These developments were also favorable to business enterprise. Relative peace between capital and labor enables capital-intensive enterprises to function more effectively and permits capital accumulation to proceed relatively smoothly. Prosperity and rising incomes for workers enable purchasing power to grow and provide the increases in demand necessary for continuing prosperity and growth of wealth and capital. The economic well-being of workers is necessary for the effective functioning of the economic society as a whole, and business interests, particularly big business, have recognized that fact.

A third function of government derives from its role in the compact between capital and labor: opposition to changes in the system of private property and business enterprise. In the United States, for example, the development of collective bargaining, social legislation, and government responsibility for economic growth and prosperity was paralleled by direct repression of radical labor unions during World War I and political and legal harassment of radical movements afterward. U.S. military and foreign policies in recent decades have clearly been dominated by opposition to the spread of socialism and the influence of the Soviet Union, and to the preservation of a world economy open to the activities of U.S. business enterprise. The accord between capital and labor in the U.S. included active government programs to oppose threats to the private enterprise, capitalist mode of economic organization.

Finally, the educational system serves in a variety of ways to strengthen and preserve the economic order. Much of the educational effort, from the earliest elementary school grades through the highest level of graduate training, serves to improve the productivity of labor power at public expense. Part of the benefits accrue to the individuals who receive the education; another part is obtained by the business firms for whom they work. At a more subtle level, the educational system provides an ideology—a system of beliefs—congenial to the preservation of the existing economic and social order. We learn in school that capitalism is good and socialism is bad. In the U.S.S.R. children learn the opposite. This continuing support of government is an essential element in the preservation of the existing system, whatever it may be.

Market Economy and Market Society

A pervasive system of self-adjusting markets draws into itself all the building blocks of the social order. Its inputs are people, natural resources, and the effort of the past—labor, land, and capital in the language of economics—and these inputs are the very things of which the social order is composed. The market economy puts prices on them and allocates them according to economic criteria directed by an acquisitive motive. Everything becomes a commodity, whether it is produced for sale or not.

The functioning of the market economy does not depend on family or community or other social relationships. Allocation of resources is independent of them. In the description of the market system given in Chapter 1 they were not even mentioned. Rather, communities grow and decline according to economic imperatives, people move to where the jobs are, and occupations are selected according to economic advantage. Family, community, and society are not irrelevant to human life, but in a market economy what happens to them is largely the result of economic forces.

When all aspects of society become inputs for a system of self-adjusting markets, the market comes to dominate the social order. People must feed, clothe, and shelter themselves. When they do so in a structure of economic institutions that is largely independent of family, community, or religion, economic activity takes on a life of its own and channels human activity largely along economic lines. Economic goals become the primary goals and economic ends swamp all others. The market economy becomes a *market society*.

- A **market society** is a social system in which economic life is dominated by a market economy and motivated by individual self-interest.

Self-interest and individualism are generated in a market environment. Any individual transaction becomes a contest between buyer and seller to determine which one gains the most. The logic of the market is that each person attempts to get the best deal for himself, and the devil take the hindmost. When market transactions dominate an economy, when the entire social system becomes an extension of the market, that society becomes a group of separate individuals held together by the ties of market transactions and the acquisitive motive. The market system is the glue that holds the social system together and acquisitiveness makes it work.

- **Self-interest** is the desire to maximize individual benefits or satisfactions. It is the chief motivating force of the market economy.

Values in a Market Society

Value judgments are for moralists. The social scientist can only point out that the economic organization and the behavior patterns that drive it reinforce each other. The market cannot decide whether a particular pattern of production is good or bad. It merely adjusts to consumer preferences and to production costs. For example, moral judgments may indicate that a shift from milk to whiskey consumption would be bad for the individual and society. But the market itself can make no judgments of this sort; it only reflects the economic realities that lie behind the demand and supply curves. Nevertheless, a market economy generates a value system consistent with itself and its own motivations. Emphasis on acquisition of material wealth and concern with money is characteristic of a pecuniary society with materialist values. Esteem and approval in a market society go to those who are successful in market activity, those who accumulate wealth and earn large incomes.

This pattern of attitudes and motivations is one of the chief reasons for the growing wealth of our society. It drives people to acquire more; and doing it through the mechanism of the market means that the whole system becomes more productive of material things. The motives that lead individuals to maximize their gains in a market economy push the economy ahead to greater output and to increased wealth.

A price is paid. Where beauty conflicts with profits, profits have a tendency to win out, so billboards line our highways. Where it is cheaper to flush sewage into streams instead of treating it, streams and lakes are polluted. When children finish their educations, their parents may begin to take a dim view of school taxes. A mediocre painting becomes a tourist attraction when bought by a famous art gallery for $5,000,000. The market economy answers the great philosophical question, "What has value?" with the assertion that "if you can sell it, it has value."

Attitudes Toward Work and Wealth

The materialistic value system of the market economy drives individuals on toward producing more in order to acquire more, and no matter how much has been acquired it is always possible to add to the existing pile. The conclusions of David McClelland, an American psychologist, have stressed the *achievement motive,* "*n*-achievement" in his terminology, as the key to economic growth. According to McClelland, people are not born with it, but acquire it in their early training and upbringing when they are taught to do well, to excel, to exceed others, to compete against a standard of excellence. McClelland claims a "society with generally high level of *n*-achievement will produce more energetic entrepreneurs who, in turn, produce more rapid economic development."

- The **achievement motive** is the desire to excel, to achieve goals beyond those presently achieved, or to achieve a given standard of excellence.

A strong motivation to excel, widely dispersed through the social system, may well be part of the attitudinal base of the economy. But why not excel in warfare, or religion, or sports, or the arts? None of these efforts leads to economic activity. It is not a generalized achievement motive that motivates economic life, but achievement motives aimed specifically at material goals such as wealth and possessions. The values of the social system must place acquisition of wealth at a very high level, and those who are wealthy must be given high status because of their wealth, in order that the achievement motive may pay off in economic development. In the modern market economy, attitudes toward both consumption and work are dominated by materialist values and a need to achieve economic success.

Attitudes Toward Consumption

There are two connecting links in our society between wealth, status, and economic motives. One is our attitude toward consumption.

Thorstein Veblen (1857–1929), the American economist, pointed out that the materialistic value system of a market economy puts great stress on the acquisition of wealth and tends to consider those things valuable that have a high market value. The reason is not hard to find. The means of subsistence—food, clothing, and shelter—are obtained by purchase and sale on markets. The worker sells his labor for a wage, and uses the money he obtains to buy what he needs. Without the wage he and his family would starve, or subsist at the very low and degraded level of private charity or public welfare. Success in the marketplace becomes necessary for subsistence, for life itself. It is only to be expected in such a society, argued Veblen, that achievement and success will be measured in monetary terms.

An analogy will make the point clear. In a society based on hunting, the successful hunter has high status because he produces the things necessary for survival. Similarly, in a market economy success in moneymaking brings recognition and approval. The fundamental achievement criteria become pecuniary.[2]

Veblen argued in *The Theory of the Leisure Class* that pecuniary standards of success lead to waste. The wealthy, in order to claim the status their wealth entitles them to, have to prove their affluence by spending conspicuously. Fine houses, many servants, expensive entertainment, or anything that requires large expenditures will do, so long as it is highly visible. This *conspicuous consumption* causes

---

[2]This point should not be pushed too far. An affluent society can afford a multiplicity of values. Recognition of achievement in the arts and sciences does not always bring great monetary gains. But even in those fields the "successful" writer, artist, or scientist earns a good income. If he doesn't, he is not considered successful by more than a group of aficionados. Veblen himself was "unsuccessful." He never rose above the rank of assistant professor and late in life was able to continue lecturing at the New School for Social Research in New York only because former students were willing to help pay his salary. He was one of America's greatest economists, yet he was unable to achieve success in the usually accepted terms of his own time. Late in life he received professional recognition by being elected president of the American Economic Association, but he contemptuously turned down this highest honor that his colleagues could bestow upon him.

pecuniary emulation on the part of others. For example, the jet set lolls on the beaches of Acapulco or the Riviera, so the college sophomore emulates them by going to Fort Lauderdale during spring vacation while his professor rents a villa in Puerto Rico. The result is a pattern of consumption that emphasizes display and expense at all levels in the social system. Veblen called it wasteful, and in terms of biological needs it is. But these patterns of consumption gratify human needs for recognition and status in a market-oriented society with a market-oriented value system. They emphasize spending. There is a built-in drive to increase consumption.

- **Conspicuous consumption** involves expenditures designed to show possession of wealth.

- **Pecuniary emulation** is imitation of the expenditure patterns of the very wealthy by persons of lesser wealth.

Attitudes Toward Work

The second link between wealth, status, and economic motives is the work ethic. Max Weber, a German sociologist, and Richard H. Tawney, an English historian, have argued that the Protestant Reformation in the sixteenth century, together with related changes in Catholic countries, resulted in the rise of an *economic "ethic,"* which greatly stimulated economic growth and promoted the rise of capitalism. During the Middle Ages, they argued, the *approved* motive for economic activity was the preservation of a society within which the individual could prepare for salvation. Acquisition of wealth was frowned upon by the Church because it distracted men from salvation and directed their attention to material things. Wealth itself was not evil, but its pursuit was the wrong path to take.

The Reformation changed all that, according to Weber and Tawney. Martin Luther's concept of the "calling," or the idea that each individual is "called" to the task God wills for him on earth, placed all earthly activities, whether those of businessman or priest, on an equal level. The highest morality lay in fulfilling one's duties in worldly affairs, whatever one's calling. To this was added the Calvinist doctrine of the "elect," the idea that salvation was predestined rather than earned; that individuals had no control over their own fate because God, in his inscrutable ways, had already decided whether they would be damned or saved. This harsh Calvinist doctrine of predestination created serious theological and ethical problems for the individual. Although one's fate was determined, the individual had no way of knowing what it was. How, then, should one behave? Throw all caution to the wind and act in any way one desired, irrespective of the moral laws of the Bible and the Word of God? Or behave according to the religious laws of morality?

The divines had an answer. Anyone destined to be a saint would lead a saint's life on earth. Transgressions of the moral law were a sure sign of damnation. Even doubts about one's salvation might be a sign that one was not destined to live among the angels in the hereafter. The only way to avoid doubt about one's own destiny was to live a pure and moral life, avoiding all temptation. Work hard in one's calling, which after all was the task assigned by God, avoid idleness and luxury, and God's favor would be shown by worldly success. Hard work would leave no time for moral doubts, and wealth obtained by hard work in one's calling would be a sign of divine favor. A *Protestant ethic* emerged, which stressed the virtues of saving and work, traits required for success in a market economy. Material gain was given its ethical letter of credit. The basic point is not that new religious ideas created a new ethic, but that they provided an ethical foundation for behavior characteristic of emerging capitalism.

In the years following the Reformation, according to the Weber-Tawney thesis, the Protestant ethic lost its religious basis and became thoroughly secularized. Hard work, saving, and avoidance of luxury came to be valued because they were useful in accumulating wealth, not because they had religious meaning. Wealth and the respect it brought became ends in themselves. By the mid-eighteenth century the business ethic had become pragmatic and utilitarian, and was the approved pattern of behavior.

The Weber-Tawney thesis has been much criticized. It does not provide an explanation for the rise of capitalism. It does not explain the origins of the acquisitive motive or why Western society puts heavy stress on the need for achievement. It is essentially qualitative rather than quantitative in its analysis and for that reason is somewhat old-fashioned from the modern scientific point of view. But it does help to explain some of the fundamental attitudes toward work and leisure widely found in our society. As we inquire into the attitudes that lead a nation's economy into the path of self-sustaining economic growth, the concept of the Protestant ethic adds to our understanding of why the achievement motive is directed toward material gains.

- The term **economic ethic** refers to the principles of behavior and rules of conduct that prevail in economic activity. The so-called Protestant ethic of modern capitalism stresses hard work and saving as desirable goals.

Consumption, Work, and Economic Growth

At first glance it might appear that Veblen's conspicuous consumption and the Protestant ethic as described by Weber and Tawney are contradictory. One theory emphasizes spending and leisure as central to the motivational pattern of the modern economy. The other stresses hard work, saving, and avoidance of idleness and luxury. They hardly seem consistent with each other. But in the area of ideologies and motivations, consistency need not necessarily be present. The findings of modern dynamic psychology, from Freud onward, have stressed that individual motivations often conflict and are only poorly understood even by the individual. It is quite possible for an individual to work hard and save, to rationally compute each little addition to profit, to hoard capital and use it for maximum advantage *in the role of producer*. That same individual may spend ostentatiously in a display of wealth and status to neighbors and acquaintances *in the role of consumer*. Both patterns of behavior may be quite rational within the scope of modern social and economic institutions.

The important point here is that both behavior patterns contribute to economic activity. Parsimony in a producer expands potential output of an enterprise. Prodigality in a consumer expands demand and keeps pulling the whole economy toward higher levels. Both are needed, one on the supply side of the market and the other on the demand side.

Figure 3–1 diagrams the relationship. On the supply side of the economy, the achievement motive and a materialistic value system lead to a desire for wealth, which stimulates savings, investment, and economic growth. On the demand side of the economy, the same motives and values bring a desire for recognition and status, which leads to the high levels of consumption and aggregate demand necessary to sustain high levels of investment and economic growth. The market economy has generated a value system and motivational pattern that enables the economic system to function effectively.

The Final Contradiction

The motivations of a market economy stress self-interest. Its value system is essentially materialistic, emphasizing acquisition of wealth and the affluent life. These are the motivations and values of an individualistic society, in which each person is responsible only for himself or herself. Maximization of satisfactions of the individual, by the individual, and for the

Figure 3-1
Economic Growth
and the Value System
of the Market Economy

The desire for achievement,
together with a materialistic
value system, creates
conditions on both the supply
side of the market economy
(left column) and the demand
side (right column) that lead
to economic growth.

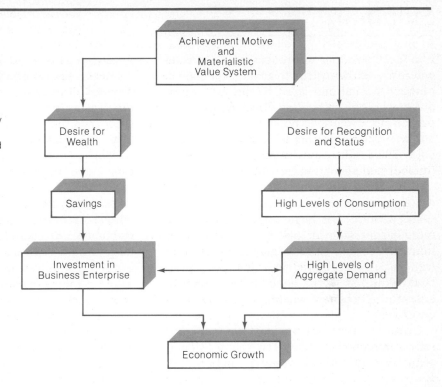

individual is the rule by which such an economy functions.

Yet human beings never exist as socially isolated individuals independent of others and single-mindedly pursuing their own interests. Human life outside some kind of social organization is unknown. The interests of the individual, therefore, must include an interest in the functioning and preservation of the social groups that characterize human life. This inevitably entails a concern for the other people that make up the social order. There is always tension between the goals of the group and the self-realization of the individual. But out of the social relations that have always characterized human life has come the ethical principle that each person has a responsibility for others: "No man is an island. . . ." and "All men are brothers."

The ethics of the market are different. Market exchange operates through conflict. Buyer and seller are opposed to each other, each trying to get the better of the other in the exchange they both desire. Capital and labor are in conflict over the division between wages and profits. A variety of economic interest groups continually seek to change the established rules of the game in an effort to gain economic advantage. Even when the market mechanism establishes the terms on which exchange takes place, it is through conflict within the marketplace that the result is obtained. Conflict pits individual against individual, group against group, class against class. The ultimate contradiction within the market economy is that its social relations of production do not conform to the ethical norms of a humane society.

Summary

The social relations of production in a private enterprise economy lead to an inherent conflict between capital and labor. Gains for owners are maximized by holding down the amounts paid to labor wherever possible, while workers are interested in raising the amounts they are paid. The result of this conflict is exploitation of labor and alienation, according to Marx.

The mass production technology of the modern economy brought a bureaucratic organizational pattern. The large corporation is organized in a hierarchy of jobs, the goal of which is rational decision making and administration with authority centered in a few peak positions. Power is in the hands of an economic elite whose goals are wealth and control over decisions.

Government serves to reinforce and preserve the economic order. The state provides a legal basis for private property and the enforcement of contracts, manages and resolves conflicts, opposes efforts to change the private property foundations of the economy, and provides an educational system that serves to strengthen and preserve the economic order. One vital function of the state was the promotion of an informal accommodation between capital and labor that dampened the inherent conflict between them.

At a deeper level, the social relations of production in the private enterprise economy embody a materialistic value system and attitudes toward work and wealth that enable the market economy to function effectively. Yet this very value system, which stresses individual self-interest and material gain, is at odds with the morality and ethic of human values. The ultimate contradiction within the modern economy lies in the area of ethics and moral values.

Key Concepts

social relations of production

private enterprise economy

exploitation

alienation

bureaucracy

market society

self-interest

achievement motive

conspicuous consumption

pecuniary emulation

economic ethic

For Discussion

1. How does the intrinsic conflict between the capitalist and the working classes manifest itself in the modern economy?

2. Can you identify specific phenomena related to the general condition of alienation? Would they be eliminated if the means of production were controlled by workers themselves?

3. It has been suggested that the pro-labor and welfare legislation of the 1930s in the U.S. was necessary to preserve the private enterprise economy. Do you agree? Why?

4. Would you expect advertising and conspicuous consumption to be prevalent in an economy in which the means of production were owned by workers? Why or why not?

5. What changes do you foresee in the future that would result from the tensions and conflicts present in the U.S. economy today?

6. Is the belief system that stresses democracy and participation compatible with today's economy of big business and big government? Explain.

PART 2

THE LEVEL
OF ECONOMIC
ACTIVITY

The next six chapters deal with the level of economic activity, including output and employment. *Macroeconomics* is the professional term, meaning the economics of the national economy as a whole.

Chapter 4 introduces the topic by describing the chief types of fluctuations in level of economic activity that occur in a private enterprise economy. A brief Chapter 5 provides an overall view of the analysis to come in a presentation of the flow of spending. Chapter 6 explains how the flow of spending is measured, and the appendix to Chapter 6 shows how changes in the general level of prices are measured. Chapters 7 and 8 comprise the heart of the theoretical analysis. Chapter 7 analyzes the tendency of the private sector to achieve a stable level of economic activity, while Chapter 8 analyzes the countertendencies toward instability. Both types of forces are operating at all times. Chapter 9 brings government into the analysis to provide the basis for a discussion of stabilization policy.

Chapter 4

Economic Fluctuations

As this chapter is being written, economists all over the world are involved in a discussion of the probable duration and depth of the recession that began in the spring of 1980 and continued through the winter of 1981. When will the recovery begin? How strong a recovery will it be, and will a new period of economic expansion follow? What are the possibilities of another great depression? Associated with these discussions are problems of government policy. What can governments do to end the recession, increase employment, and establish a firm basis for continuing economic growth? How can these expansionary policies be reconciled with the need to diminish or end the world-wide inflation of recent years? These questions are typical of those that concern many economists in universities, government and business, not only during hard times, but continuously.

The level of output and employment is not the only problem. In recent years high rates of *inflation*—continuing increases in the general level of prices—have complicated the economic situation. Recessions and rising prices are occurring simultaneously. That concurrence is new. Prior to the 1950s, when economic activity fell, the general price level tended to fall as well because of the reduced demand for goods characteristic of a recession. But in recent years the general level of prices has been pushing upward in bad times as well as good, creating a unique problem in economic policy. The medicine for rising prices has traditionally been policies designed to reduce the level of economic activity, but that makes unemployment worse. On the other hand, the prescription for unemployment is policy to stimulate the economy, which makes inflation worse. Policymakers are caught on the horns of a dilemma: whatever they do is wrong.

- **Inflation** is a persistent and widespread increase in the level of prices.

A private enterprise economy is never stable. It is always changing, and one aspect of those changes is continuous flux in the level of economic activity. Four different types of change in the level of economic activity can be observed. The first is economic growth. Increases in the work force, technological innovation, and accumulation of capital—long-run changes that affect the potential level of output —help to determine the rate at which the economy expands. One of the chief features of the world economy in the last two hundred years has been a strong and continuing process of economic growth and expansion.

Rates of economic expansion are not steady and constant over long periods. There are long waves in the level of economic activity forty to sixty years long. These *long waves* comprise two distinct periods. One is a period of relatively rapid economic growth and generally high levels of prosperity. The second is a period of relatively slow growth and hard times. In the history of the modern industrial economy since the late eighteenth century, there have been three full long waves. We appear to be well into the relative stagnation phase of the fourth.

The third type of change in the level of economic activity is the traditional *business cycle*. Its average duration is about four to five years, although it can be as short as two or as long as ten. This business cycle follows four phases: an expansion phase generates an upper turning point, which in turn leads to a recession that ultimately is followed by a recovery. This is the type of fluctuation that economic forecasters are most heavily concerned with and that public policy seems to cope with best. There have been seven of these business cycles in the U.S. economy since the Great Depression of the 1930s.

Great depressions are the fourth type of economic fluctuation endemic to private enterprise economies. There have been four great depressions in the industrial age of the past two hundred years. Three have come in the later stage of a period of relative stagnation in the long waves described above: the 1840s, 1890s, and 1930s. The other, in the 1870s, occurred at the start of a period of stagnation. In each case the great depression began as a phase of a seemingly ordinary business cycle but was transformed into a great depression by a collapse of the financial system. Three of the great depressions of the past were succeeded by the rapid growth phase of the following long wave in economic activity.

This chapter concerns itself chiefly with three types of fluctuation in the level of economic activity: business cycles, long waves, and great depressions. It also introduces the problem of inflation, which is dealt with in great detail later. The three types are closely related to each other. They are also rooted in the forces and relations of production that characterize a profit-oriented private enterprise economy. To put them in perspective, we start with a discussion of the level of economic activity in the U.S. economy in the forty years following the Great Depression of the late 1930s.

U.S. Economic Fluctuations, 1939–1980

Figure 4–1 shows the pattern of economic fluctuations in the U.S. economy from the late 1930s through 1980.

Perhaps the most striking feature of this period is the tremendous economic growth that occurred. Gross National Product (GNP)—the usual measure of annual output—increased from $320 billion in 1939 to $1481 billion in 1980, all measured in constant dollars (1972 prices) to eliminate the effect of rising prices and provide a measure of "real" output. The increase of about 4.6 times was much more rapid than the growth of population from 131 million to 223 million persons, so that output per person rose by about 2.7 times. Much of this period, from 1945 to about 1970, is now seen in retrospect as the "good old days," economically speaking. In the world economy as a whole this was the greatest era of economic growth in human history.

The growth process was uneven, however. The era of rapid growth extended from the recovery from the Great Depression of the 1930s—note the high unemployment rates of 1939 and 1940—to about 1970. GNP increased at a rate of 4.4 percent per year between 1939 and 1969. But during the 1970s the average

Figure 4-1
U.S. Level of Economic Activity, 1939–1980

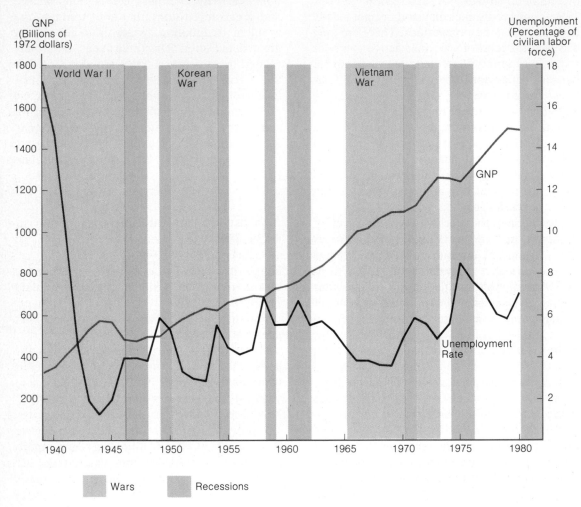

GNP
(Billions of
1972 dollars)

Unemployment
(Percentage of
civilian labor
force)

Wars   Recessions

annual increase in GNP fell to 3.1 percent annually. The U.S. economy reflected the larger pattern of the world economy as it moved into the relative stagnation phase of the fourth long wave of the industrial era during the late 1960s and early 1970s. The U.S. economy also experienced a series of eight business cycles between 1939 and 1980. They were called "recessions" to distinguish them from the Great Depression of the 1930s, which was much deeper and longer than the more common garden variety of business cycle experienced after World War II.

The recessions of the period of rapid growth

were characterized chiefly by pauses in growth or very small declines in output—but with significant increases in unemployment—followed quickly by recovery and resumption of growth. Only the recession of 1946–47 saw a significant decline in GNP, and that was the result, in large part, of conversion from military to civilian production after World War II. At the other extreme, the 1960–61 recession lasted less than a year and the growth process was hardly interrupted. Even the 1970 recession was relatively short and mild.

In the relative stagnation of the 1970s and early 1980s, however, the recessions were more severe. Declines in output were greater, unemployment increased by relatively large amounts, and the poor times lasted longer. Furthermore, unemployment rates remained relatively high even during the recovery between recessions. Greater severity of business cycles is characteristic of periods of relative stagnation.

Causes of Economic Fluctuations

A capitalist economy is driven by the desire for profits. When business firms expect profits to increase there is a strong motive to increase production to take advantage of the good prospects. Workers are hired, investment is increased, funds are borrowed to finance enlarged output, and the entire economic life of the community quickens. On the other hand, when reduced profits are a prospect, business firms reduce their commitments, cut output, and lay off workers. The chief underlying cause of economic fluctuations is to be found here. When prospects for profits improve, business becomes more active. When the outlook for profits darkens, business activity declines.

Expansion of business activity requires increased investment. Even if no increase in the capacity to produce is necessary, enlarged output requires larger inventories of raw materials and finished products to keep the flow of production moving from inputs to final buyer. Furthermore, investment in new plants and equipment is required as production rises to press upon the existing capacity to produce. This process of capital accumulation then generates further increases in economic activity. On the other hand, when prospects for profits weaken, investment in new plant and equipment is reduced. This reduction in spending brings a general decline in economic activity, and cutbacks in production spread. Investment spending is one of the more volatile elements in the economy, and as it rises or falls, so will economic activity as a whole.

Investment and expansion of production can proceed faster than increases in purchasing power. When that happens, the enlarged output cannot be sold at a profit, and expected profits are unrealized. Disappointed business enterprises reduce their output and investment spending. Unless the level of demand for goods rises as fast as the capacity to produce, demand will be insufficient to sustain prosperity. Maintenance of high levels of demand is essential for prosperity.

Profits can also be affected by changes in the relationship between prices of outputs and costs of inputs. When economic activity quickens, selling prices tend to rise more rapidly than costs, and further increases in economic activity are generated as profit margins widen. But if and when costs start rising more rapidly than selling prices, profit margins decline and economic activity is dampened.

These considerations help us understand why a capitalist economy is inherently unstable. Profits are unstable, and expectations of profits in the future are uncertain. The instability of profits is related in turn to two other relationships. One is the changing relationship between the economy's capacity to produce and the purchasing power available to buy its

UNEMPLOYMENT

The unemployment rate shown in Figure 4–1 is more complex than the pure numbers suggest. It is measured by a sample survey in which representatives of the U.S. Department of Labor question several thousand families. The total figure for unemployment and the unemployment rate are then extrapolated from the results obtained from the sample.

A worker is considered unemployed if he or she is out of work and tried unsuccessfully to find work the previous week. Part-time workers are considered employed, even if they would like to be working full time. People not trying to find jobs are not counted at all, on the ground that they are not part of the labor force, even though many might seek jobs if they thought some were available. All of this makes the published figures less than exact. Indeed, the survey methods and definitions have changed so much over the last fifty years that an unemployment rate of 8 percent in 1980 would be roughly the same as 12 percent in 1935. We have cut the unemployment rate by about one-third simply by changing the way it is measured.

Economists distinguish four different types of unemployment. *Frictional unemployment* results from workers moving from one job to another, new workers seeking their first job, and older workers in the process of leaving the labor market. Perhaps 1.5 to 2 percent of measured unemployment is of that sort. *Seasonal unemployment* occurs because of seasonal changes in production in some industries. Retail sales at Christmas season, or harvest work in agriculture, are two examples. The measured employment figures are corrected to eliminate the effect of seasonal unemployment. *Cyclical unemployment* results from the business cycle, or great depressions, and reflects the change in employment that results from changes in the level of economic activity. For example, the increase in the rate of unemployment from 5.8 percent of the labor force in 1979 to 7.1 percent in 1980 would be almost wholly an increase in cyclical unemployment resulting from a recession. Finally, *structural unemployment* results from long-run changes in either the economy or the work force. For example, an increased proportion of young workers in the labor force will tend to increase the unemployment rate, even if there were no change in the level of economic activity, because young workers move more frequently from one job to another. Or a declining industry with a large labor force, such as coal mining in Appalachia in the 1950s and 1960s, may leave other employable workers with few employment opportunities.

How, then, do we define *full employment*? Traditionally, economists have defined it as that level of employment/unemployment at which only the voluntarily unemployed are not working. In terms of measured unemployment, this means only frictional unemployment, so when the measured rate of unemployment is down to, say, 1.5–2.0 percent, full employment prevails. This definition of full employment leaves seasonal unemployment out of account—even though part of it may be involuntary—simply because it is not included in the measured unemployment rate.

In recent years some economists have become disenchanted with this definition. They argue, for example, that getting rid of structural unemployment would require inflationary levels of total spending. Some argue that there is a "natural" rate of unemployment below which prices start rising. These economists would define full employment as that rate of unemployment consistent with a stable general price level, even though much unemployment may be involuntary. These issues will be examined more fully in later chapters.

However we may define full employment or classify an unemployed worker, we should not overlook the nature of the problem. In our society people must have incomes to survive. Those without income-producing property must either work or subsist on the miserable incomes available through various support programs. In addition, the work people do expresses not only their way of life but also their lives as a whole. Work enables people to be somebody, to express themselves, to validate their humanity. Not working destroys the humanity of people as much as it threatens their economic status. Underneath the pure numbers—about 7,785,000 unemployed persons in December 1980—are millions of personal tragedies.

output. The other is the changing relationship between costs of production and selling prices. The interactions of these variables affect profit prospects and generate fluctuations.

Business Cycles

The typical *business cycle* goes through four phases. Economic conditions at the low point of a recession enable profits to rise. A *recovery* begins, which generates a period of *prosperity* in which, ultimately, prospects for profits deteriorate. A *downturn* results that cumulates into a *recession*, which, after a time, brings about a situation in which profit prospects improve and the stage is set for a new recovery. The four phases are shown diagramatically in Figure 4–2.

The business cycle is self-generating. Rising profits cause business activity to quicken, but the very increase in economic activity creates conditions that stop the increase in profits and cause profits to fall. The economy turns from prosperity to recession. The recession itself causes another turn toward higher profits, and a recovery can then begin. The business cycle

feeds on itself, with one stage bringing on the next.

- A **business cycle** is a self-generating fluctuation in economic activity, typically four or five years long, comprising four phases of recovery, prosperity, downturn, and recession.

Recovery and the Cumulation of Prosperity

The succession of business cycles and their stages is continuous, so we can start an analysis of the process at any point. Let's begin with conditions that favor a recovery from a recession. Prices are low relative to those of prosperous times—setting aside here the issue of persistent inflation in order to concentrate on the cycle phenomenon. Costs of doing business have fallen, even though profit margins may be low. Banks have ample reserves on which to base expansion of loans, partly because demand for loans is low in poor times. Business firms reduce their inventories near the end of a decline, which is one reason for low prices. With inventories being liquidated, production falls to levels below current consumption spending. That is, consumer demand is being met partly by goods produced in the past rather than wholly by current production.

Under these conditions a recovery can begin, if only because inventory liquidation ends and production increases to meet current demand by consumers. Consumer spending also increases, as durable and semidurable goods wear out and must be replaced. Sometimes the recovery is aided by a happy event such as a good harvest or retarded by some other influence, such as political uncertainties.

In the early stages of a recovery, selling prices rise more rapidly than the price of inputs. Unemployment tends to keep wages down, and where unions and employers have contracts, the wage is set by the agreement for at least a year. Excess production capacity in the raw materials industries, plus competitive markets in that sector, tend to keep those prices down. Interest rates are low, because

---

Figure 4–2
The Business Cycle

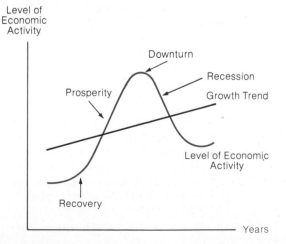

banks have unused lending capacity. Prices of finished products tend to rise, however, as demand increases. With low prices for inputs and rising prices for outputs, profit margins start to increase. The higher profit per unit of output, along with increased output, brings substantial increases in total profits. Managers of business firms become optimistic about the future and implement plans to expand, thereby stimulating investment. The increase in business activity causes employment to rise, and the consumer sector has higher income. The factors combine to bring prosperity.

Prosperity Breeds a Downturn

Prosperity creates conditions that make it increasingly difficult for the upswing to continue. The chief factor is a gradual increase in business costs. Unemployment falls and the resulting tightness in labor markets causes wages to rise as business firms bid for the increasingly scarce labor. Unions negotiate wage increases and additional fringe benefits, which business firms agree to provide in order to avoid strikes and continue making profits. As the raw materials industries approach their output capacity, prices start going up in that sector. In the capital markets, rising demand for credit pushes interest rates up: the lending capacity of banks approaches its limits, and the central bank, fearing inflation, refuses to allow those limits to rise.[1] Rising demand for credit, combined with a limited supply, pushes up the cost of borrowing.

Rising prices of inputs cause profit margins to fall, for it becomes increasingly difficult to raise selling prices in one industry after another. In competitive industries, competition dampens price increases. As full employment approaches, the rate at which consumer incomes rise is also dampened. The consumer goods industries, particularly those producing durable goods, obtained a large boost in demand for their output as the unemployed returned to work at the beginning of the recovery. But with that largely accomplished, those industries now find it much harder to keep selling prices moving up faster than costs. Furthermore, optimistic plans for expansion come to fruition and large supplies of goods come to the market in competition with output from older plants. To put it simply, in the later stages of prosperity, output rises more rapidly than purchasing power. Price increases are harder to institute, and rising costs cause profit margins to decline. In addition, rising inventories of unsold goods further dampen prospects for the future. The economy is ready for a downturn in economic activity.

The Downturn and the Recession

The downturn, like the recovery, can be triggered by the inventory positions of business firms. Inventories rise above the desired level in the later stages of a prosperity as output grows faster than purchasing power. In order to get rid of unwanted inventories, business firms reduce current output. Reduction in output means layoffs of workers, which cause consumption spending to fall. The decline in consumption postpones investment spending, which brings unemployment in the investment goods industries. As business activity declines in this cumulative fashion, inventories cannot be eliminated, and a further round of reduced output ensues.

Selling prices, meanwhile, fall as goods are thrown on the market to realize what can be obtained before prices fall even further. A downturn sometimes brings a "panic" in the goods and money markets. Tumbling prices of goods threaten bankruptcies for both business firms and the banks that have loans outstanding to those firms.[2] Even without such a panic,

---

[1]Chapters 10–13 deal with lending and its limits, and with the role of central banks (the Federal Reserve System in the U.S.) in controlling the money markets.

[2]Nowadays central banks stand ready to act as "lender of last resort" to prevent breakdowns of the financial system like those of 1931–33, but the new international banking system that grew up since 1965 raises questions about whether the devil of financial collapse has been fully exorcised from the body economic. More on that in Chapters 13–14.

the decline in prices and the reduced output bring total profit down, and gloom pervades the business community.

The recession ultimately brings itself to an end, however. Production falls more rapidly than consumer spending, for one thing. The unemployed don't starve: they are sustained by government income support programs and their own savings. Production declines more rapidly, however, as production of investment goods declines to low levels. It is not necessary to buy machinery or build plants when there is plenty of unused capacity, and equipment that wears out doesn't even have to be replaced. The inventory reduction brings output of consumer goods to levels below current consumption.

The decline in production of finished products reduces demand in the markets that supply inputs, and prices decline there as well. Indeed, the fact that production falls more than consumption means that ultimately the prices of things producers buy will fall further than those bought by consumers. As the recession proceeds, the losses that result from liquidation of inventories stop. Ultimately, as prices for inputs fall faster than prices for outputs, profits will appear.

The stage is now set for the next recovery. Profits have reappeared, even though profit margins are low. Inputs are available at low prices. Unwanted inventories have been liquidated and production rises to meet current levels of demand. The increase in production reduces unemployment and starts the next recovery.

Government and the Business Cycle

The description of the business cycle presented here has been deliberately simplified. Emphasis was placed on the private sector, on the self-generating nature of the cycle, and on the cumulative nature of prosperities and recessions. No real-world business cycle will work in exactly that way, and in the modern world governments get involved.

Governments are not neutral where business cycles are concerned. They try to stop recessions and encourage prosperity, primarily by maintaining high levels of aggregate demand. When spending in the private sector lags, governments try to increase government spending to fill the gap between private spending and the full employment level of spending. If prosperity seems likely to push up total spending to levels above the full employment level, thereby causing inflation, governments try to achieve balance through monetary controls and reduced government spending. That is the theory, at least. How well it works is another question, which will be dealt with at length in succeeding chapters.

Long Waves in Economic Activity

Business cycles are closely associated with the business problem of making a profit from current production when faced with changing levels of demand and the day-to-day relationship of costs and prices. The importance of inventories in the business cycle indicates this relationship to relatively short-run changes in output and consumer buying.

Long waves, on the other hand, are more closely associated with the process of economic growth and capital accumulation. Economic growth is not a smooth, even process. Capital accumulation and investment tend to be strong at some times, weak at others. The result is a wave-like pattern around an even longer trend of growth.

- A **long wave** in the level of economic activity is a forty- to sixty-year pattern in which a period of rapid growth is followed by a period of stagnation or slow growth.

A phase of rapid growth and high levels of investment is triggered by the appearance of major innovations in limited sectors of the economy that take the lead in spreading the impetus of rapid growth to other sectors. The phase of rapid growth creates conditions that make it increasingly difficult to sustain rapid growth, however. The leading sectors mature and their growth slows, while growth itself causes prices of resources, labor, and capital to rise and prospects for profits to weaken. These conditions lead to a turn toward slower growth and relative stagnation. During the period of relative stagnation the conditions leading to renewed rapid growth appear: a backlog of innovations and price-cost relationships conducive to investment. In the past, each period of relative stagnation has culminated in a great depression, whose function seems to have been to bring down interest rates, wages, and prices of raw materials relative to prices of finished products, creating profit margins favorable to large-scale investment. Whether the present period of relative stagnation will lead into another great depression remains to be seen.

Long waves have typically lasted forty to sixty years, with each phase—rapid growth and relative stagnation—lasting some twenty to thirty years. Figure 4-3 is a schematic diagram showing what a typical long wave would look like, eliminating other fluctuations from the picture.

The world economy appears to be well into the relative stagnation phase of the fourth long wave of the industrial era. Table 4–1 shows a rough chronology derived from the various scholars who have studied the phenomenon.

The Period of Rapid Growth

Each period of rapid growth was preceded by a great depression, during which the basic forces of production were restructured to set the stage for expansion. Although most prices fall during a depression, prices of raw material fall further and more rapidly than prices of manufactured goods. The chief reason for that disparity is greater competition—and hence price flexibility—in the raw materials industries. A depression also creates downward pressure on wages, because of high rates of unemployment. Unemployment also means that, if there is an economic recovery, wages will not start to rise for some time. Interest rates are low, also because of depressed economic activity, and capital is readily available on good terms. Finally, during a depression the less efficient manufacturing plants are closed and the less efficient machinery is scrapped. Costs of production fall relative to selling prices, setting the stage for a revival of economic activity. Although total output is low and total profits down, the profit margin between costs and selling prices reappears. The economy is lean and hungry, stripped of its fat.

Two or more decades of relative stagnation, ending in a depression, also bring a buildup of innovations and technical change that were not implemented because markets were poor. They provide a potential base for new industries and enlarged investment once basic cost-price relationships are restructured. For example, the first commercial television broadcast was made in 1928 and the first stereo recording was produced in 1930, but these innovations

Figure 4-3
Long Waves in Economic Activity

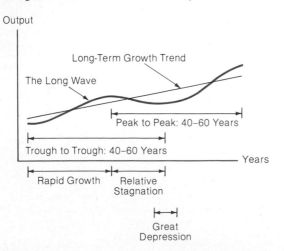

Table 4–1
The Four Long Waves of the Industrial Era

	Trough	Peak	Trough	Great Depression
1	1785–90	1815	1845	1842–49
2	1845	1873	1895	1873–79; 1892–97
3	1895	1914–19	1933	1929–39
4	1933	1968–72	?	?

lay dormant until after World War II, when they were among the new industries that helped to produce the next wave of rapid growth.

With basic economic relationships favorable for investment and economic growth, the profit motive can take over. The entrepreneurial spirit[3] takes advantage of profits to be made from innovations when cost-price relationships are right.[4]

The leading sectors that triggered the rapid growth of 1946 to 1968–72 comprised three groups of industries: durable consumer goods like housing, automobiles and electrical equipment; industries involving new technologies such as electronics, computers and jet propulsion; and service industries such as education and medical care. Many of these industries started small and grew large—TV, or jet propulsion, for example—until they laid claim to a significant share of total spending. Once they matured, however, they grew only as fast as total spending increased and no longer contributed to rapid growth.

The growth pattern of new industries helps to explain both rapid growth and the subsequent slowdown. A new industry, in its initial phase, may expand at a rate of 10–15 percent per year, or even faster. That process cannot go on forever: people have needs other than TV entertainment and travel on jet aircraft. The new industry can grow to claim a larger share of total spending, but sooner or later the share levels off. This process is illustrated in Figure 4–4.

During the early period of rapid growth, the new industry helps to push up the growth rate of output for the economy as a whole, but that

Figure 4–4
Growth Pattern of a New Industry

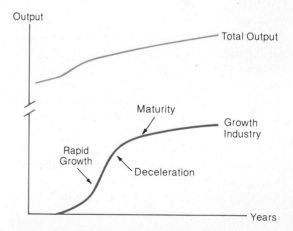

The growth industry matures to ultimately grow only as fast as the rest of the economy. Initially, however, its period of rapid growth imparts an upward tilt to the economy as a whole.

---

[3]Entrepreneur: one who originates and manages an enterprise, particularly a new or untried venture. It is a French word that literally means an intermediary who "stands between" capital and labor as an enterprise organizer.

[4]Example: When ball-point pens were first introduced in 1946 they were marketed at $19.95 each. They cost about $1.25 to produce. The line at Macy's in New York extended out of the store, around the block, and tied up traffic. It was like minting their own money for the early entrepreneurs.

push disappears when the new industry matures and takes its normal position in the consumer's market basket.

The leading sectors contribute to accelerated growth in another fashion. They trigger expansion in industries that complement the leading sector. For example, the interstate highway system in the United States, built largely between 1950 and 1970, required large increases in output of cement and earth-moving equipment. As construction of the interstates gathered momentum, new cement plants and equipment factories were required, adding to the momentum of economic growth. These secondary effects peter out, however. Once the interstate highway system was largely built and construction limited to repair and replacement, new plants to manufacture cement and earth-moving equipment were unnecessary. Supplies were obtained from existing production facilities. The investment required in the 1950s and 1960s to build those new cement and equipment plants was no longer needed, and investment spending triggered by the now mature industry declined significantly.[5]

Military Spending

Spending on armaments is an important source of the dynamism of the rapid growth phases of long waves. This may seem to be a paradox, since military goods do not satisfy human needs and wars are destructive. On the other hand, production of military goods quickens economic activity by providing employment and stimulating investment. Changes in military technology, such as the shift from aircraft, tanks, and battleships to nuclear weapons, missiles, and submarines after World War II,

required the scrapping of old equipment and the factories that produced them and the substitution of new equipment produced in new factories. And, while wars are destructive, they require full mobilization of economic resources and labor to produce at a high level. Countries that mobilize and fight, but do not experience the destruction of actual warfare, like the U.S. in World War II, feel the economic stimulus without bearing the costs.

There is another aspect of the relationship between economic growth and wars. The periods of rapid growth feature new industries in new areas of the world. They change the economic balance of power and in that respect are profoundly unsettling to the locus of political power. The U.S. experienced an example of that shift with the development of the Sunbelt and the relative decline of the industrial Northeast after World War II. Similar shifts occur internationally. When they do, the balance of political power is realigned. If it cannot be done peacefully it is done by warfare. Thus, in the twentieth century the economic expansion of Germany, Japan, and the United States and later the Soviet Union created rivals for the world hegemony that Great Britain was forced to abdicate because of its relative decline in economic strength. The rivalries created by these shifts in economic power helped to generate two World Wars, a number of lesser wars, and two massive arms races, one before World War I and one after World War II. A challenge to the existing balance of political power, resting on a shift in economic power, can bring preparation for war and war itself, which, in turn, provides a stimulus to the economy.[6] In this way the periods of rapid economic growth tend to induce large military spending, which in turn stimulates further economic growth.

---

[5]We shall meet this phenomenon again in Chapter 8 as the "acceleration principle."

[6]See Chapter 31 for a more extended discussion of the economics of war and military spending.

Monetary Expansion

Growth of the money supply and rapid expansion of credit are other characteristics of the rapid growth phase of the long wave. Increased business activity in a private enterprise economy is financed by extension of credit. Business firms borrow to buy raw materials, hire labor, obtain capital, and in general to finance production. Ideally, the loans would be repaid when goods are sold. But in a growing economy the next round of production is enlarged, which requires increased borrowing to finance it. In addition, consumers borrow to buy finished products, and their borrowing increases as their incomes rise. Particularly in the modern economy, in which both production and consumption are financed heavily by extension of credit, debt increases more rapidly than output.

When a period of rapid economic growth begins, the business community has relatively little debt. The ratios of debt to assets and debt to income are low. The same is true for consumers. The reason is simple: the previous period of stagnation and depression has wiped out a significant portion of business and consumer debt through bankruptcies and business failures. In addition, solvent business firms and consumers have reduced their indebtedness to accord with their reduced incomes. So at the start of a period of rapid growth, the financial condition of the economy is good. Improved profit prospects enable business firms to borrow needed funds, and consumers can use rising incomes to increase their borrowing and raise their consumption. The result is that an improvement of economic activity is reinforced by increased borrowing, unhindered by heavy debt burdens.

As rapid growth fueled by expanded credit and growing debt proceeds, the burden of debt rises. A ratio of debt to assets or debt to income that may seem terribly risky to a business firm, or to a bank that lends to the firm, in the early stages of growth seems less risky as economic expansion brings profits that validate decisions to borrow and expand production. Expectations of higher profits are fulfilled in spite of a growing debt relative to assets or income. The financial community calls it "leverage." Where a firm would borrow 75 percent of the capital to finance expansion in the early years of the rapid growth phase, by the end of the phase it may be optimistically borrowing 90 to 95 percent. In the course of a twenty- to thirty-year period of rapid growth, interrupted only briefly by small recessions, the result is a high ratio of debt to income for more and more business firms and for the economy as a whole.

The growth of debt causes new problems. A relatively small decline in a firm's income during the early years of rapid growth will create no difficulty, because the firm has borrowed a relatively small portion of the capital that created the flow of income. But when growth is already starting to slow down in the later stages of growth, debt is typically high relative to income. Even a small decline in the firm's income can create financial difficulties and force a large cutback in its current operations and investment plans. At that stage the financial condition of the economy inhibits further growth, where twenty years earlier it facilitated it.

World Trade and Investment

In the period of rapid growth following World War II, world trade and international investment grew rapidly, aided by reductions in tariffs and trade barriers among nations. The major trading nations negotiated a series of agreements to facilitate trade under the General Agreement on Tariffs and Trade (GATT) of 1946. The trade restrictions that grew up in the phase of relative stagnation from 1920 to 1939 were largely dismantled in the next twenty years. Both international capital investment and trade were greatly supported by stable exchange rates between currencies of major nations in a new postwar financial system negotiated in the Bretton Woods Agreements of 1945. Major programs to provide investment funds for reconstruction of the European economy (Marshall Plan) and development of less developed countries were provided by governments and a variety of United Nations agencies. Expansion of international corporations brought growth of trade, flow of investment funds, and transfer of technology among developed economies as well as between the developed core and the less developed periphery of the world economy. The period from 1945 through the late 1960s was a golden era for international trade and investment, and for profits, as the capitalist economy continued its worldwide development.

After World War II technological innovations such as jet propulsion, computers, and satellite communications greatly improved the ability of business firms to manage operations overseas. The postwar international corporation was born, exporting its highly capital-intensive technology to low-wage areas of the world with large populations. Brazil, Mexico, and other Latin American countries; South Korea, Taiwan, Singapore, and some other Asian nations—all these countries were drawn into the world economy on a large scale because of the possibilities for profit generated by extension of world trade in a rapidly growing economy with a revised technological foundation.

During phases of relative economic stagnation, however, the profit incentive to expand economic activity internationally diminishes. International trade and investment is dampened. Furthermore, weak economic growth or stagnation in the major nations strengthens incentives to protect domestic industries and jobs from international competition. Tariffs and other trade restrictions are imposed to reduce imports, and international trade and investment suffers.

From Rapid Growth to Relative Stagnation

Three changes take place in the later stages of the rapid growth phase of long waves that make it increasingly difficult for the world economy to continue growing rapidly.

1. The sectors that initiated the phase of rapid growth begin to mature. Investment spending in those sectors, which earlier built up a rapidly increasing level of output, is reduced to little more than replacement of existing plant and equipment as it wears out.

2. Prices of basic inputs start to rise as growing demand presses on the capacity to produce in sectors like agriculture and mineral products. Food prices increase. Wages rise as economic growth brings unemployment down to low levels. Interest rates increase. As the cost of inputs rise, either profit margins decline or inflation begins—and either discourages high levels of investment.

3. The high ratios of debt to assets and debt to income built up over several decades discourage further increases in debt. The stimulus to growth afforded by easy borrowing and growing debt is lost.

The maturity of the leading growth sectors, relatively poor prospects for profits, and a weakened financial base turn the dynamism of a decade or two earlier to discouragement, caution, and relative stagnation.

Why don't new growth sectors replace those that matured? The problem is not lack of innovation and entrepreneurship, but a difference in basic economic conditions: high costs of materials, high wage rates, and most importantly, high interest rates. Interest rates are low in the early years of a rapid growth era, say 4–5 percent for established and profitable firms. An innovation that is expected to bring an annual return of 20 percent looks awfully attractive, and even one with a prospective return of 15 percent is very good. In the later stages of the growth era interest rates will be much higher—they would typically reach 15 percent. At those rates of interest, an innovation with an expected return of 20 percent still looks good, but few would be enthusiastic about it because of the risks attached to new ideas. The innovation with an expected return of 15 percent would hardly be given serious consideration.

High interest rates also discourage investment in existing enterprises. Take the steel industry, for example. A new large steel rolling mill can cost about $500 million and will last 50 or more years. With interest rates at 15 to 20 percent it would be foolish to borrow to build one. Long before the plant is worn out, interest rates will be down to half or less of existing rates, if experience is any guide, and a competitive firm will be able to build the same plant at a much lower cost for its capital. The firm that builds will be unable to compete.

The phase of relative stagnation is brought on by the previous twenty to thirty years of economic growth. Fundamental economic relationships in markets for raw materials, labor, and capital discourage innovation, investment, and economic expansion. The heavy burden of debt makes it difficult for firms to borrow heavily, even if they wished to do so. Readjusting those relationships to achieve good prospects for investment and profits takes time— interest rates must fall, prices of raw materials must come down relative to prices of finished products, ample supplies of labor and other inputs must be available, and debt must be reduced even though incomes do not grow. The phase of relative stagnation persists until those readjustments are accomplished.

Some Current Problems

Each phase of relative stagnation differs from the preceding ones. This should be expected,

for fifty or more years bring large changes in the forces and relations of productions. The present phase, which began in the late 1960s or early 1970s, differs in several important respects from earlier ones.

The most important and obvious difference is persistent and increasing inflation. In earlier phases of relative stagnation, prices tended to decline in response to the economy's growing sluggishness. Not this time. Several changes in the economic system contributed to this change:

1. A tremendous increase in economic concentration occurred during the rapid growth period, which gave big enterprise more control over markets and prices.

2. Government programs designed to maintain high levels of employment and income, developed during the 1930s, have further modified the operation of market forces and created upward pressure on prices.

3. Strong labor unions, also a product of the 1930s, have kept wage rates rising in spite of growing unemployment and much slowed increases in productivity.

These fundamental changes combined with the highly inflationary financing of the Vietnam war, the OPEC monopoly of oil production, and rapidly rising food prices to bring an era of inflation amidst stagnation and rising unemployment. A major development in financial markets provided the financing of economic activity at ever increasing prices, in spite of government efforts to prevent it:

4. The new "Eurocredit" banking system, which grew rapidly in the 1960s and 1970s, is able to increase credit and the money supply in unlimited amounts, bypassing the controls of central banks and governments.

These changes in the forces and relations of production created inflationary pressures arising from the conflict between classes and other interest groups. Business firms make lower profits when economic growth slows, and in the big business sector, where firms have some control over prices, efforts have been made to raise prices and thereby sustain profit rates.

Something similar happened in the labor sector. Unions that were successful in obtaining substantial gains in real income for their workers during the period of rapid growth try to continue those gains in the following period of relative stagnation. Their wage demands come in conflict with the profit goals of big business. This conflict is always present in a private enterprise economy, but the problem becomes more acute when the bargains that formerly were satisfactory to both parties can no longer be achieved. But both parties can still seek to increase their money wages and money profits at the old rates, and these excessive demands, which outrun the capacity of the economy to increase output, push up costs and prices.

Government is not immune to these pressures. Tax revenues rise relatively rapidly when economic growth is strong. Government spending programs expand—witness, for example, the rapid growth of spending for highways, education, and medical services, not to mention military spending, by governments at all levels during the 1950s and 1960s. Slowed economic growth means that fewer resources are available to expand those government activities at the same rate, and the drive to continue their growth results in budget deficits, higher tax rates, or both.

Inflation is spurred by the efforts of all three of these claimants to the growth dividend to maintain their gains even though growth has declined. The total of money claims to the national product exceeds the amount available at existing prices, and prices are pushed upward. The process is spurred by the new international banking system, by government budget deficits, and by government policies designed to maintain high levels of aggregate demand. Inflation makes it appear that the gains to which the parties aspire are continuing, even though it is money incomes and not real incomes that are rising. Inflation is a safety valve that defuses, for a time, the struggle between workers, management, and government over a smaller growth dividend.

If inflation is a unique feature of the present relative stagnation phase, the problem of debt burdens is not. In any period of sustained economic expansion like that of 1945–1968/72, managers of business firms tend to lose their fear of indebtedness, and the burden of debt builds up. This occurred in recent decades also. Each $1 increase in value added in the private business sector has been accompanied by an increase in about $1.40 in business indebtedness. The debt/equity ratio for all American corporations reached a historic high in 1977, and by 1980 was only slightly below its peak. Under these conditions a relatively small decline in economic activity can have serious repercussions on firms overburdened with debt.

Something similar has occurred with consumer debt. Installment credit and mortgage debt were major supports for the growth of the consumer durables and housing industries throughout the 1950s and 1960s, but were not overexpanded to dangerous levels until recently. As inflation escalated in the seventies and real purchasing power of consumer incomes declined, families increasingly turned to borrowing to maintain their standard of living. Surging consumer debt helped sustain the recovery from the 1974–75 recession through 1979, but it left consumers with responsibility for payments of interest and principal equal to 23 percent of total consumer incomes, far above the "normal" ratio of about 15 percent. The recession that began in 1980, with its reduced consumer incomes, therefore brought greatly reduced purchases of durable goods as consumers sought to eliminate their excessive debts.

The financial underpinnings of the American

economy are in serious trouble. Both the private business sector and consumers have excessive levels of debt that increase the volatility of the economy. What would have been a relatively mild recession in the 1950s or early 1960s becomes a major recession in the 1980s as a reduced flow of income forces weak business firms and overburdened consumers to reduce their commitments. As the experience of 1974–75 indicates, economic downturns cumulate into significant setbacks. In the 1930s a cumulative debt deflation helped turn what initially looked like an ordinary recession into a major depression. In the relative stagnation of the 1980s the conditions that could bring on a similar episode are present.

Great Depressions

The *Great Depression* of the 1930s began in the United States with a downturn in economic activity in August, 1929, that seemed to be nothing more serious than another recession. The recession came in a very unfavorable economic environment, however. For ten years the world economy had been in a relative stagnation phase that the U.S. economy had avoided, in part. Even in the U.S., however, agriculture had been depressed for a decade, and the automobile industry had reached the end of its first phase of rapid growth some five years earlier. Wage rates were stable while the general price level was creeping upward, causing a slow deterioration of purchasing power. As later events were to make clear, the financial sectors of the U.S. and world economies were in very fragile condition.

- A **great depression** is a severe decline in the level of economic activity, longer and deeper than a business cycle, that usually comes near the end of a period of relative stagnation.

Three events turned the business cycle recession of 1929 into the Great Depression of the

1930s. The first was the stock market crash of October, 1929. Speculation had driven stock prices to artificially high levels that could not be sustained by the reduced flows of business income generated during a period of relative stagnation. The value of capital in financial markets, represented by stock prices, was far above the value of capital as represented by the earnings it produced in the markets for goods and services. The stock market crash realigned those relationships, and stocks lost about 90 percent of their value between 1929 and 1933. By 1933 stocks were a bargain—for those with the cash to buy them and the vision to do so.

The second event was a classic debt deflation, also taking place between 1929 and 1933. The stock market crash made the fragile condition of the economy evident to everyone. Business firms that had built up their debt relative to assets and income during the previous period of speculative euphoria now found it imperative to reduce their commitments. A general rush for liquidity began, involving sale of inventories, cutbacks in production, reduced investment, accumulation of cash, and payment of debt. Tumbling prices, reduced employment, declining incomes, and numerous bankruptcies resulted. The recession cumulated into a general economic collapse.

The *coup de grace* was applied by a collapse of the international financial system in 1931–33 that ended with the closing of the U.S. banks in the spring of 1933. The financial collapse had its roots in the worldwide decline in output and prices, which was particularly strong for agricultural and mineral prices. The largest bank in Austria, the Creditanstalt, had made extensive loans to farmers and mining enterprises in central and eastern Europe during the 1920s, using funds borrowed substantially from German banks. With the large declines in commodity prices of 1930 and 1931, the borrowers could not repay and the Creditanstalt failed. It was well known in financial circles that the Creditanstalt was a large borrower from German banks, so a "run" on the banks began as

Figure 4-5   The Great Depression

A. Gross National Product, 1929–1941

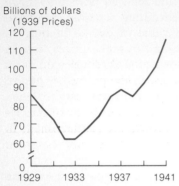

B. Unemployment Rate, 1929–1941

C. Gross Private Domestic Investment, 1929–1941

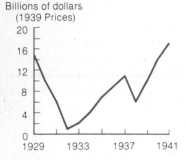

States banks were closed in March, 1933, by government order. What started as a seemingly minor event in central Europe snowballed into the breakdown of the world financial system.

By 1933 the economy reached the bottom of its decline, about 3-1/2 years after the downturn started. The unemployment rate in the U.S. in 1933 was about 25 percent of the labor force, which meant that some 35 to 40 percent of all workers had some spell of unemployment during the year. Business investment was down to a trickle, only about $1 billion. Figure 4–5 shows the long slide from 1929's prosperity to 1933's gloom, the troubled and slow recovery to 1937, a recession in 1938, and the final climb out of the depression at the start of World War II.

During the Great Depression of the 1930s, the basic economic dislocations created by the earlier period of rapid economic growth were finally eliminated. That process had begun in the early 1920s in the rest of the world, which helps to explain why the Depression was less severe in some other countries than in the U.S. By the late 1930s there were large supplies of unemployed labor, interest rates had been more than cut in half, and banks had substantial unused capacity to lend. Cutbacks in agricultural production and in the mining industries provided an ability to expand commodity production, and prices in those sectors of the economy had fallen by a greater percentage than prices of manufactured goods. Business bankruptcies and liquidation of debt by solvent firms provided business enterprises with a newly strengthened financial structure. The weak firms in the financial sector had been weeded out. In manufacturing industries the inefficient plants and equipment had been scrapped, and postponed maintenance provided a potential base for expansion of investment spending. The Depression years, a time of austerity for many families, also created a backlog of potential demand for consumer goods, if only consumer incomes could be

so-called "hot money" was withdrawn to seek a safe haven. The German banks were forced to close and banks in England, France, and the Low Countries were affected. By early 1933 the crisis reached the United States, for American banks had made large loans to German banks during the 1920s to finance German reparations from World War I. The United raised. Ten years of bad times also built up a store of potential new products and production innovations awaiting better economic conditions to trigger their introduction. The Depression had created the conditions necessary for a new phase of rapid economic growth, although few realized it at the time.

The stimulus came with World War II. Spending on armaments in the late 1930s started the process. Huge government spending in the war that began in 1939, with the U.S. entering in 1941, completed the process of triggering the great era of prosperity that followed the war.

Will There Be Another Great Depression?

It is quite possible. The rapid growth of 1945–1968/72 brought large maladjustments in economic relationships: high prices for inputs, deteriorating profit margins, heavy burdens of debt, excessively high prices of common stocks, and high interest rates, to name only the most obvious. The leading growth sectors matured, and while some new ones may be on the horizon, they will remain potentialities until economic conditions become more favorable. Fifteen years of inflation have largely worsened these maladjustments, interfering with the slow process of readjustment that normally occurs during a period of relative stagnation. Two of the chief policy instruments designed to meet the problems of great depressions—government fiscal policy and central bank monetary policy—have been largely neutralized by inflation and the uncontrolled "Eurocredit" banking system.

Only one important readjustment has been even partially accomplished. The excessively high common stock prices of the mid-1960s have already come down by almost two-thirds, in real terms. As of early 1981 the stock price averages were about 5 percent below their 1967 peak, while the general price level was up by over 150 percent. In real terms, common stocks were worth about 35 percent of their value in 1967. The great stock market crash of this era of relative stagnation has already been partially completed, but it took almost fifteen years instead of three and there may still be a long way to go before the slide stops. This is an example of the type of readjustment of prices and values that goes on in a period of relative stagnation and that must be accomplished throughout the economy before conditions favorable for rapid growth are reestablished. In the past it has taken a major depression to complete the job.

Such pessimism may be unwarranted. The policies devised since the 1930s to protect the economy may be effective in preventing a huge drop in incomes, production, and employment. These measures include a "safety net" of income support programs, government spending and tax programs to sustain demand and promote investment, and monetary policies designed to protect the financial system. If inflation can be reduced or ended, these programs could become more effective. It may even be possible for the major nations to overcome their rivalries and bring the new international banking system under control before overexpansion brings a collapse.

The majority of economists are optimistic about the ability of the private enterprise economy, assisted by government, to avoid another great depression. A growing minority, however, is becoming increasingly concerned and some economists, including the author of this text, feel that another great depression is highly probable. Perhaps it will begin at about the time the students reading this book have completed their educations and are entering the job market.

Inflation

Fluctuations in the level of economic activity have been complicated in recent years by continuing increases in the general level of prices —inflation. The period since the mid-1960s is unique: a period of relative economic stagnation and relatively severe recessions accompanied by rising prices. In the past economists took for granted the proposition that economic slack generated falling prices rather than general inflation.

Nevertheless, periods of rising prices have occurred in the past, and a great deal of mythology about inflation has developed. Our first task is demystification. When we look at the record we find:

1. Almost all of the great inflations of the past two hundred years have been short-lived rather than persistent.

2. They have been associated with wars, revolutions, or other political disturbances and their aftermath. Governments, unwilling or unable to finance their expenditures out of tax revenues, turned to printing of money, budget deficits, or both.

3. Increased supplies of money relative to output have accompanied inflation, but that is a surface phenomenon, not to be confused with the underlying causes.

Myths often die hard. Take the explanation of the great inflation of the 16th century. Prices rose persistently throughout the century, up from 100 percent to 300 percent in various parts of Europe. According to the generally accepted theories of historians and economists the cause of the inflation was an influx of gold and silver from the rich mines of the Spanish colonies in the New World, which vastly increased the money supply of Europe when the increased supply of precious metals was coined into money (paper money had not yet been invented). This increase in the money supply forced prices up persistently over a hundred years or more after the discovery of America in 1492.

Right?

Wrong!

Chemists analyzing the presence of trace elements in the European coins of the period and comparing them with ores from the mines have determined that American silver did not go into the coins and was not responsible for the increased monetary use of precious metals (if that occurred at all). Where did the American treasure go? No one knows, but probably into the "plate" and other silver objects of the treasures of kings, nobles, and church, and into payments for imported goods from Asia via the eastern trade routes.

What, then, caused the great inflation of 1500–1600? Probably the best explanation is that it was part of the process in which the economy changed from feudal to capitalist. In the old feudal economy most payments bypassed the market and a great deal of production was for use by peasant and noble households. With the rise of capitalism, however, there was a large and persistent increase in market demand for products. This increasing market demand could not be satisfied at existing prices because a large portion of the output was destined for non-market use and channels of distribution. Prices rose persistently because market demand increased more rapidly than supplies coming into the market, and were not stabilized until the feudal mode of production and distribution had been superseded by the capitalist, market-oriented mode sufficiently to allow increases in aggregate supply to catch up with increases in aggregate demand.

In the process, of course, the money supply increased to accommodate the growing business demand for money and credit. Governments debased the coinage to make the existing supply of precious metals go further. More important, the business community invented new methods of providing credit that involved various paper representations of debt, a process that has been going on in the financial community ever since. The increased supply of money facilitated the working out of the underlying economic forces; it was not the cause of the inflation, but part of the process.

For the American economy, when we look at long-term price behavior over the last 180 years, shown in Figure 4–6, the most striking fact is not the increase in prices, but the wide fluctuations that have occurred. Every large war brought a period of rapid inflation, followed by a period of large price decline when the war ended—except World War II, and we shall have more to say about that shortly. A second fact is that the long-range trend prior to World War II has only a slight upward tilt. From peak to peak—1814 to 1864 to 1919—the average annual increase is negligible and could easily be caused by statistical error. The same is true when the trend is measured from trough to trough—1830 to 1849 to 1897. Even if we try the most unfavorable comparison possible, from the low point of 1897 to the high prices of 1980, the average annual increase is only about 1.5 percent.

Remember that throughout this whole period a continent was being settled and developed, a great industrial and population expansion occurred, and standards of living rose to new heights. Whatever the effect on individu-als may have been, neither rising prices nor falling prices nor wide fluctuations nor relative price stability seem to have had a significant impact on the growth performance of the economy.

In several respects, however, the movement of prices in the last three decades has been different from what we have previously experienced. First, part of the wartime inflation during World War II was postponed until after the war by price controls, rationing, and other measures during the war. Second, the typical postwar deflation, which was usually accompanied by hard times for both business and labor, did not occur. Third, prices were relatively stable from the late 1940s to the late 1960s, moving upward significantly only after escalation of the Vietnam war. The price increases of 1948 to 1968 that caused so much comment in the press and in the political arena are little more than blips when compared with the fluctuations of the past or the increases after 1968. Relatively stable prices were transformed dramatically into escalating inflation in the late 1960s.

Figure 4–6
Wholesale Prices in the United States, 1800–1980

The wholesale price index used for the 1940–1980 period is more comprehensive than the earlier one. This fact probably accounts for its greater stability. A portion of the wide fluctuations in the earlier series is due to the fact that the data are from only five large cities and include a large component of foodstuffs.

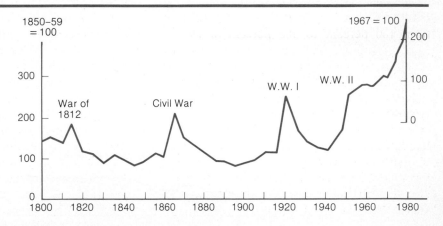

Sources: 1800–1958: *Employment. Growth and Price Levels. Hearings Before the Joint Economic Committee. Congress of the United States* (Washington, D.C., 1959). Part 2, pp. 395–397. 1958–1974: *Economic Report of the President, 1975.*

Prices, 1946–1980

Now some facts about recent trends. Figure 4–7 shows the movement of both consumer and producer prices in the United States from 1946 to 1980. Three periods of relatively rapid increases are shown, separated by periods of relative stability. The first period of inflation was 1946–48, when the suppressed price increases of the World War II years could no longer be held in check. In two years consumer prices rose by 23 percent and wholesale prices by 33 percent. After two years of price stability (producer prices actually fell a little), the Korean War brought a second phase of relatively mild inflation. From 1950 through 1953, consumer prices rose by 11 percent and wholesale prices by 7 percent, a considerably slower pace than in 1946–48.

Then followed a dozen years of relatively stable prices, in which the economy as a whole grew at a slow pace, particularly from 1953 through 1960. In spite of considerable economic slack, however, consumer prices crept steadily upward at a pace of about 1.5 percent annually. Producer prices were considerably more stable, increasing at a rate of only about 1 percent per year, and most of that increase came during or immediately after the Korean War.

The third period of relative rapid increase in price levels came with the escalation of the war in Vietnam, from 1965 onward. Between 1965 and 1973 consumer and producer prices rose by over 40 percent. About half of the increase came in 1971–73, reflecting an escalation in the rate of inflation during those years. Overall, the rise in prices from 1946 through 1973 was between 117 percent (producer prices) and 128 percent (consumer prices). Until 1973 the bulk of the price increase after 1946 was associated with active warfare. During wartime the productive capacity of the economy strains to supply both civilian and military products simultaneously. Purchasing power is increased by wartime government spending, the competition for products and resources intensifies, and prices are driven upward.

Even before 1973 prices of important commodities such as food and petroleum had started to rise persistently. In 1973, however, they began to move upward much more dramatically. The first OPEC increase in the cost of oil in 1973 followed an initial cutoff of oil supplies based on political considerations. A year earlier, in 1972, the U.S.S.R. had a poor harvest,

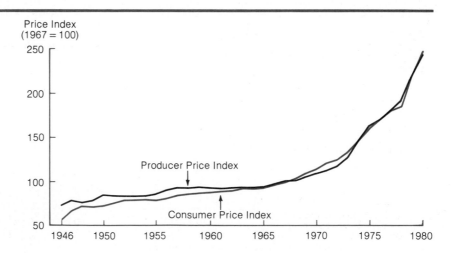

Figure 4-7
Trends in Consumer and Producer Prices, 1946–1980

and grain purchases in the U.S. triggered large increases in the cost of food. These events came at the close of the Vietnam war, and the entire structure of the inflation shifted away from a typical wartime inflation rooted primarily in excessive aggregate demand to a new type of inflation largely caused by increased costs of production. It was this supply-side inflation, accompanied by rising unemployment, that escalated into the ensuing inflationary spiral of the second half of the 1970s.

Runaway Inflation

Some inflations have been known to get out of hand. Several famous examples come instantly to mind: China after World War II, Germany in 1922–23, Russia in 1920–21, France in 1794–97, and this country in 1777–1780. In these inflations prices rose so rapidly and to such heights that the money in use at the particular time lost its value and had to be replaced by a new type.[7]

All of these *runaway inflations* occurred in times of political stress or turmoil. More important, all of the governments involved faced a very uncertain financial situation: demands on government expenditures were rising at a time when it was very difficult to levy and collect taxes. The governments therefore turned to increases in the money supply to obtain the funds they needed. Continuous large injections of purchasing power into the economy through government deficits, financed by newly printed currency, have been the cause of all the principal cases of runaway inflation. Or, put negatively, we know of no case of runaway inflation that was not engendered by a deliberate overexpansion of government spending.

---

[7]The classic joke about runaway inflation: you take your money to market in a bushel basket and bring your purchases home in your pocketbook.

Wartime Inflation

Inflation is characteristic of wars. During wartime income is earned by workers and owners of other resources employed in producing military equipment. Just like any income, much of it is spent on consumption (by consumers) or investment (by business units). But the goods produced for the war are not available for sale: they are shipped overseas and destroyed, for example, in the jungles of Southeast Asia during the Vietnam war. Since income is maintained or increased, but the supply of salable goods is reduced, spending tends to outrun the available supply and prices push upward.

Increasing taxes to pay for military goods is no answer, for as soon as the government pays for the goods the money is back in the hands of consumers and business units. Figure 4–8 illustrates the process quite simply, starting from a peacetime balance between total spending and the supply of goods. War causes a shift in output to the military, reducing supplies available for civilian use. Even if taxes are used to pay for the war, total spending is not reduced, and the goods available for use by civilians must rise in price to absorb the purchasing power created by production of both civilian and military goods. These price increases might be held in check by rationing and price controls, but the basic inflationary conditions will remain as long as part of the product is siphoned out of the nation's markets while full purchasing power is pumped in. Taxes only allow the government to buy the military production without running a budget deficit. They do not eliminate the excessive demand.

Prices and Long Waves

The behavior of prices reflects the underlying economic conditions that prevail in the course of long waves in economic activity. During the phase of rapid growth prices tend to rise as

Figure 4–8
Wartime Inflation:
Imbalance Between
Total Spending and the
Supply of Goods
Available for Sale

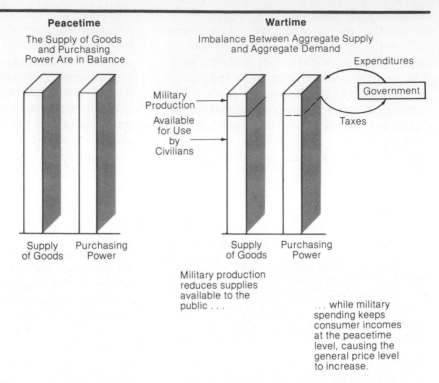

Peacetime
The Supply of Goods
and Purchasing
Power Are in Balance

Supply   Purchasing
of Goods   Power

Wartime
Imbalance Between Aggregate Supply
and Aggregate Demand

Expenditures

Government

Military
Production

Available
for Use
by
Civilians

Taxes

Supply   Purchasing
of Goods   Power

Military production
reduces supplies
available to the
public . . .

. . . while military
spending keeps
consumer incomes
at the peacetime
level, causing the
general price level
to increase.

output rises and demand for goods increases. The later stage of a rapid growth phase is particularly likely to generate price increases, for, as we have seen, production starts to press upon available supplies of raw materials, labor, and capital. The fact that wars and arms races are characteristic of rapid growth phases reinforces the tendency of prices to rise.

The relative stagnation phase is just the opposite. Slowed economic growth creates slack in the economy, and prices tend to fall, particularly in the raw materials industries. Growing rates of unemployment tend to hold wages down. Capital markets ease because of reduced demand for investment funds. These reduced costs of inputs are reflected in generally lower prices. If the relative stagnation phase culminates in a major depression, as has always happened in the past, the general price level can fall quickly and substantially.

The record of U.S. wholesale prices shows these trends. A look back at Table 4–1 indicates that the periods of rapid growth (1845–1873; 1895–1920; 1940–1965) had generally rising prices, even when we ignore the wartime price peaks. The periods of relative stagnation (1820–1845; 1873–1895; 1920–1940) showed generally falling prices.

The present period of relative stagnation is different, however. It has been an era of escalating inflation at a time when unemployment rates are also high and rising. The different experience of the period from the late 1960s to the early 1980s suggests that some new forces are at work in the economy that did not exist in earlier periods. One is the high and rising cost of energy. Another is the changed nature of the economy, in which big business, big labor, and big government are far more significant than in the past. A third is the appearance of new institutions in the money markets that greatly reduce the ability of governments and central banks to control and manage the financial sector of the economy.

Inflation in today's economy is intertwined with problems of relative economic stagnation and slowed economic growth, relatively severe recessions, and high and rising rates of unemployment. It is part of the general problem of the level of economic activity. So at this point we turn to the more general issue, the determinants of the level of economic activity in Chapters 5 through 9. That is followed by discussion of the role of money and the financial system in Chapters 10 through 13 and a more thorough examination of inflation in Chapter 14.

Summary

The level of economic activity in a private enterprise economy is unstable. Economic growth is not steady. Long waves in economic activity, business cycles, and great depressions are characteristic features of the modern economy.

The U.S. economy since the Great Depression of the 1930s illustrates this instability. A period of rapid economic growth lasted until the middle or late 1960s, followed by a period of slowed growth or relative stagnation. Eight business cycles, or recessions, also characterized this period.

The chief cause of economic instability is expectations of profit: business becomes more active when prospects for profits improve, and business activity declines when the outlook for profits darkens. Expansion of economic activity brings investment and increased capacity to produce, which can proceed faster than purchasing power. When that happens the prospects for profit worsen and economic activity turns down. Profits are also affected by the relationship between prices of outputs and costs of inputs. When costs rise relative to prices, profit margins fall and economic activity turns down. Thus, profits reflect underlying economic relationships of output capacity and purchasing power, costs and revenues, and affect the business decisions that determine the level of economic activity.

Business cycles are the result of these forces as they affect levels of output. Four to six years long, business cycles typically pass through four phases: recovery, prosperity, downturn, and recessions. Each phase creates the conditions that lead to the following phase in a self-generating pattern of changing levels of production and employment. The relationship between costs and selling prices is the key to understanding the business cycle.

Long waves of forty to sixty years' duration are related more closely to the process of economic growth and capital accumulation. The period of rapid growth begins with a burst of new investment in several leading industries or sectors of the economy, supplemented by military spending, expansion of world trade, and monetary expansion. Rapid growth ends, however, as the leading sectors mature, prices of materials, labor, and capital rise in response to perhaps a quarter century of rapid growth, and the financial sector of the economy becomes increasingly unstable. The period of relative stagnation that follows performs the function of eliminating the financial problems and restructuring cost-price relationships.

Great depressions have completed that task

in the past. They also have created the conditions out of which the next era of rapid growth could emerge.

The present period of relative stagnation differs from those of the past, however. It is characterized by inflation as well as high levels of unemployment, suggesting that some important changes have taken place in the structure of the economy. At the very least, the concurrence of inflation and unemployment makes the older remedies for each, taken separately, unworkable.

Key Concepts

inflation   long wave
business cycle   great depression

For Discussion

1. Why should business cycles and long waves be an inherent feature of a private enterprise economy?

2. Why are troughs and peaks self-generating in business cycles?

3. Why does a long-wave prosperity phase generate a period of relative stagnation?

4. Major depressions help to set the stage for a succeeding period of relatively rapid growth. Why?

5. What changes might be made in the economy to make it less susceptible to business cycles, depressions, and long waves?

6. Will we have another major depression? Why or why not?

Chapter 5

The Flow of Spending

A prosperous economy requires levels of *aggregate demand* high enough to employ the work force fully.

If business firms do not receive enough from sales of their product to cover costs plus an adequate profit, they will reduce output, lay off workers, and buy fewer inputs. The reduction in output and employment will continue until the flow of payments out of business firms is matched by an inflow large enough to induce them to maintain their level of output. At that level, however, there may be large numbers of unemployed and large amounts of unused capacity. On the other hand, total sales may be so large that business firms seek to expand their output beyond the economy's capacity to produce, bringing inflation. Clearly, the relationship between aggregate demand and the economy's output capacity is crucial to maintenance of economic stability.

- **Aggregate demand** is the level of demand for newly produced products and services in the economy as a whole.

We begin the analysis with the *flow of spending*. The economy's capacity to produce is one limit beyond which production cannot go, but within that limit the level of output depends on the amount of spending. If consumers spend large amounts on products and services, business enterprises will have incentives to produce large amounts. Business firms hire labor, acquire capital, and buy resources, paying out large sums for wages and salaries, rent, interest, and profits. These sums, in turn, become consumer incomes.

Not all income is spent, however. Savings and taxes leak out of the flow of spending and diminish the flow on successive rounds. Unless those leakages are offset by business investment and/or government spending, the flow shrinks, spending declines, and output and employment follow suit. On the other hand, when investment and government spending exceed the leakages created by savings and taxes the flow of spending increases and output grows. In addition, the banking system can create credit and thereby stimulate additional spending by consumers or business enterprise.

- The **flow of spending** is the stream of purchasing power that flows between business firms, governments, banks, and households in the form of income payments, loans, and taxes, and back again through the buying of products and services.

Our explanation of the flow of spending begins with the basic flow between consumers and business firms in the private sector; the second step is to show the crucial role of savings and investment; next, we add money markets and the creation of credit; and finally, we indicate how government participates in the flow of spending.

The Flow of Spending, Consumers, and Business Firms

The flow of spending is such a closely interconnected web of relationships that moving from any starting point will bring the analysis through all of the parts and back again. We can begin with the payment of income from business firms to consumers in exchange for productive services and resources. Owners and employees of business firms supply labor services, land, and capital to productive enterprises in exchange for wages and salaries, rent, interest, and profits. Factors of production are exchanged for incomes. This exchange establishes one part of the flow of spending in the economy.

Business firms transform the resources supplied to them into products and services of other kinds, and, of course, sell them back to consumers. Consumers, in turn, use their incomes to buy products and services from business firms. Income is exchanged for goods. This exchange represents a second part of the flow of spending. These basic exchanges are pictured in Figure 5–1, where the upper loop shows the exchange of products and services between consumers and business and the lower loop the exchange of productive resources and services between business and consumers.

In the process of production some of the capital equipment used by business firms wears out. This is known as *depreciation*. Capital stock has to be replaced if production is to be continued without interruption. A part of the business community's output, therefore, will be used to restock its capital equipment rather than sold to consumers. Productive services and resources are used in producing this part of the nation's output and incomes are paid to consumers for their services and resources, even though the output is retained by business firms for their own use. Since this is a cost of doing business, the prices charged for products and services sold to consumers includes a charge to cover the cost of depreciation. Both the incomes earned by consumers and the costs of the products they buy will reflect the value of the capital used up in production as well as the inputs of new quantities of labor, land, and

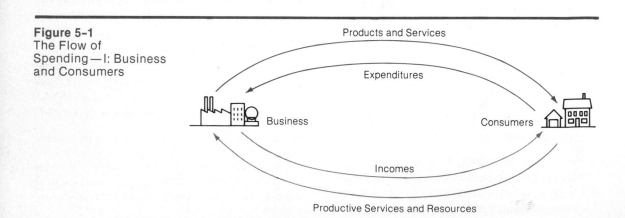

Figure 5–1
The Flow of
Spending—I: Business
and Consumers

Products and Services

Expenditures

Business

Consumers

Incomes

Productive Services and Resources

Figure 5-2
The Flow of
Spending — II:
Depreciation Is
Replaced to Maintain
the Capacity to Produce

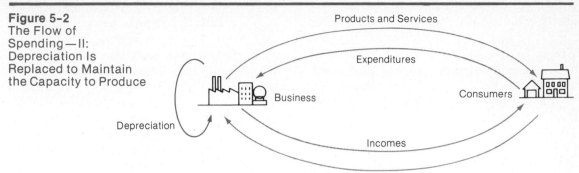

capital. The basic diagram of the flow of spending then appears as illustrated in Figure 5–2.

- **Depreciation** is the loss of capital used up in the production process.

This description of the flow of spending is highly simplified. There are, however, several important aspects that we should note carefully before proceeding further.

1. The flow of money payments is balanced by a flow of real products, services, and resources in the opposite direction. Money payments (the inner ring in the diagram) are the counterpart of resources and products flowing in the opposite direction (outer ring in the diagram).

2. These flows of money payments and real products offer two alternative ways of measuring the flow of spending: by calculating (a) the incomes earned by consumers in the form of wages and salaries, interest, rent, and profits, or (b) the money value of the final products and services sold to consumers or added to the inventories of producers.

3. The flow of spending, as described so far, will neither increase nor decrease in size. Funds flow without interruption between consumers and producers, and between

producers and owners of resources. There are no leakages that might cause instability in the flow of spending or in employment and output.

The reason for the stability just described is worth noting. If consumers spend all their incomes, they will return to producers an amount equal to the sums business firms paid out for the use of productive resources. Since the sums paid out include a normal profit to the owners of enterprises, they should be happy to continue producing.[1] Output will be sustained at existing levels and incomes will continue to be paid to consumers in payment for their labor and productive resources. The level of production and the level of employment will not change. If, however, consumers were to spend less than the incomes they received, they would not buy back from business firms all of the output produced, unsold products would pile up, profits would be inadequate, and business firms would cut back on their employment and output. Conversely, if consumers were to spend *more* than the incomes being currently earned (perhaps by drawing on past savings or

---

[1]The economist defines normal profit in an industry as the level of profit just large enough to keep the existing capital employed in its existing uses, but not so large that any additional capital will be attracted into the industry or so small that some capital will move into other uses.

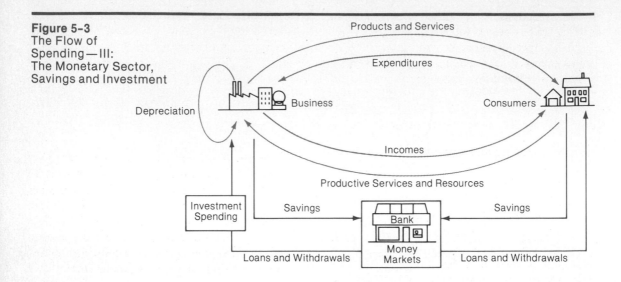

Figure 5-3
The Flow of
Spending—III:
The Monetary Sector,
Savings and Investment

by borrowing), the enlarged purchasing power would encourage expansion of output and increased employment by business firms.[2]

Here is one of the first great principles to be learned from the flow of spending: *the level of employment and output depends on the total amount spent* by the economic units that make up the economy. If total spending, or aggregate demand, according to the economists' lexicon, rises, employment and output will increase and prosperity will bless the land. If aggregate demand falls, employment and output will decline, factories will lie idle, and the economy will be depressed.

Saving and Investment

In the real world, consumers and business firms do not spend all of their incomes; part is saved. Savings from both sources flow into financial institutions such as banks, insurance compa-

nies, savings and loan associations, investment funds, and credit unions, where they represent a pool of liquid assets that can be borrowed by others to finance many purchases. Financial institutions serve as intermediaries in the money markets, gathering the savings of the economy and lending them to borrowers. They also hold funds until their owners withdraw them. They charge for their loans, and the money markets establish the interest rates at which money is made available.

The diagram of the flow of spending can readily be expanded to include the financial sector, as shown in Figure 5–3. This portion of the flow of spending, involving savings and investment, is the part that is responsible both for economic fluctuations (depressions and inflation) and for economic growth. When savings are withdrawn from the flow of spending, the level of aggregate demand is reduced. Some of the income that consumers might spend on products and services is not spent. The incomes of business firms are correspondingly reduced, and they hire less labor and other productive services. This, in turn, reduces the incomes of consumers and their purchasing power still further. The same is true of

---

[2]The alert reader will immediately note the related proposition that changes in total spending can also affect price levels and price relationships within the markets for products and services and for factors of production.

business savings: every dollar set aside in reserves by business firms is a dollar that is not used to hire workers or buy materials for production. It is a *leakage* from the flow of spending and reduces aggregate demand.

- **Leakages** are funds leaving the flow of spending, chiefly through savings and taxes.

Total spending and employment can be sustained at high levels only if the economy's savings are offset by a counterbalancing flow back into the hands of consumers and business firms. The most important *offsets to savings* in the private sector of the economy are:

1. Loans to consumers for the financing of purchases of houses, automobiles, and other durable goods, and for other purposes.
2. Loans to business firms
   a. to finance current operations, and
   b. for investment in new plants, equipment, and inventories.
3. Withdrawal of funds by consumers and business firms (rather than loans) for the purposes listed above.

In any case, unless the leakage of savings is offset by loans and withdrawals from financial institutions, the flow of spending will shrink and the level of output and employment will fall.

- **Offsets to savings** are types of spending that replace savings drawn out of the flow of spending. In the private sector, the chief offsets to savings are business investment and purchases of durable goods by consumers.

The other side of the coin is also important. Borrowing by consumers and business firms can add more purchasing power to the flow of spending than is leaking out in savings. Loans from banks provide the funds. When that happens aggregate demand will also rise. Output

and employment will increase. But prices may also go up, particularly if the economy is at or near its productive capacity. The flow of spending is potentially unstable both upward and downward.

Creation of Credit

Up to this point we have discussed changes in the flow of spending caused by the actions of consumers and business firms. There is another source of change in the flow of spending: the money markets themselves. One of the economy's financial institutions, the commercial bank, can create purchasing power through its loans to consumers and business firms. The way this is done is explained here in simplified form and more fully in Chapter 11. This creation of credit is independent of the incomes earned by consumers or business firms (although they have to be credit-worthy in order to obtain a loan), and can add to the effective demand for products and services. It adds a further source of instability to the flow of spending.

When a shoe retailer borrows from a bank in order to buy his inventories, the bank creates a deposit in the retailer's name that the retailer can then write checks against. The retailer writes a check to a shoe manufacturer to pay for his shoe inventory, the manufacturer presents the check for payment through his bank, and the bank that originally made the loan is obligated to pay. In the meantime, however, the manufacturer gets payments for the shoes he has produced and is able to continue producing more. Purchasing power that did not exist before was created and starts its journey through the flow of spending.

There are limitations on the process. If one bank were to make loans and thereby increase its deposits faster than other banks, it would soon find that checks were coming in for payment very rapidly and that its payments were exceeding its receipts. It would be forced to reduce its loans to keep its incoming deposits and its outgoing payments in balance. But when all banks expand loans together it is easy for a single bank to make new loans because its incoming deposits will be rising also. As a result, during periods of prosperity, when bankers and businesses are optimistic and eager to make higher profits, it is easy for purchasing power to be expanded rapidly by creation of bank credit. In these situations, aggregate demand can rise more rapidly than the economy's capacity to produce and a classic inflationary situation can be created.

Under *easy money* conditions, the creation of credit can readily supplement the earnings of consumers and business firms and add to total purchasing power. On the other hand, hard-to-obtain loans and relatively high rates of interest (*tight money*) dampen down the flow of funds back into the stream of spending and hold back increases in aggregate demand.

• **Easy money** and **tight money** are terms that refer to money market conditions. Money is said to be easy when interest rates are low and loans are easy to get. Money is tight when interest rates are high and it is difficult to borrow.

The potential instability inherent in the banking system has led every advanced industrial nation to devise means by which the creation of credit can be controlled. In the United States, a central bank, the Federal Reserve System, has that responsibility. It has authority to specify the reserve a bank must keep behind its deposits; it controls the total amount of reserves available to the banking system as a whole; and it attempts to influence the availability of credit and rates of interest. In short, it seeks to manage the monetary system in order to promote stability in the flow of spending.[3]

The Role of Government

Consumers, business firms, and financial institutions are not the only actors in the drama of the flow of spending. Governments are also involved. When governments spend money they add to the flow of spending. When they collect taxes they reduce the flow of spending. These flows can be shown diagrammatically much as the flows of savings and investment are shown (see Figure 5–4).

Taxes, like savings, are a leakage out of the main flow of spending. Like savings, they reduce purchasing power and affect the total output of the economy. Government expenditures, like loans and investments, offset the leakage of taxes and raise purchasing power. In the process, governments use their receipts to finance their many and varied programs: public services such as law enforcement and defense, social security and social insurance programs, education, construction of highways and other public facilities, and production of commodities for sale (such as electric power or water supplies in many communities). In some of these programs governments merely transfer purchasing power from one person to another, as from taxpayers to recipients of veterans' pensions. These *transfer payments* do not add to the total output of products and services. In other cases, governments directly employ people who provide services to the public. Or governments may purchase the output of private firms, such as military supplies, or produce goods in their own factories and shipyards. In these instances, government expenditures increase both the total output of the economy and the incomes earned by consumers and business firms. They swell aggregate demand to higher levels by providing productive employment. Government spending, then, can add substantially to aggregate demand.

• **Transfer payments** merely shift income from one economic unit to another. They are not made in return for productive effort.

[3]A fuller analysis of credit creation and money management that gets into the details of the system and the effectiveness of monetary policy is given in Chapters 11 and 12.

Figure 5–4
The Flow of
Spending—IV:
The Government Sector

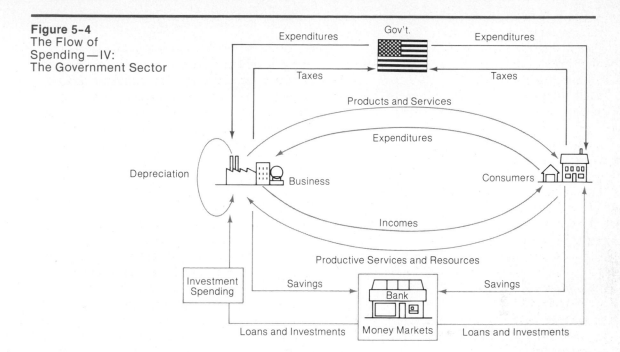

The place of government in the flow of spending goes beyond the fact that government expenditures can add to output and incomes. Control over the flow of taxes and the level of expenditures can be used to stabilize the flow of spending at full-employment levels. If the private sector of the economy does not generate full employment, government expenditures can be increased until full employment is reached. These expenditures can be of several sorts. Transfer payments such as unemployment insurance benefits can be increased, public works projects such as highway construction can be expanded, or purchases from business firms can be increased. In practice, all three types of spending are likely to be expanded simultaneously. Conversely, taxes might be reduced while expenditure levels are maintained. This will sustain the government's contribution to total income and employment while consumers' purchasing power is increased and business taxes are reduced.

In any case, whether government expendi-

tures are increased or taxes are reduced or both policies are followed, the object is to create a deficit in the public finances in which expenditures exceed tax revenues. The deficit will have to be financed by borrowing (sale of government bonds), which will draw funds out of money markets and into the flow of spending. In this way, another offset to savings is created to supplement loans and investments from financial institutions to consumers and business firms. *Government deficits* can also be shown on the diagram of the flow of spending (Figure 5–5).

● **Government deficits** occur when expenditures exceed tax revenues. A **surplus** occurs when tax revenues exceed expenditures.

Conversely, if total spending is too great and inflationary price increases are occurring, government fiscal policy can operate in the opposite direction and *government surpluses* can be created to draw out of the flow of spending more purchasing power than is brought into it,

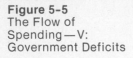

Figure 5-5
The Flow of
Spending—V:
Government Deficits

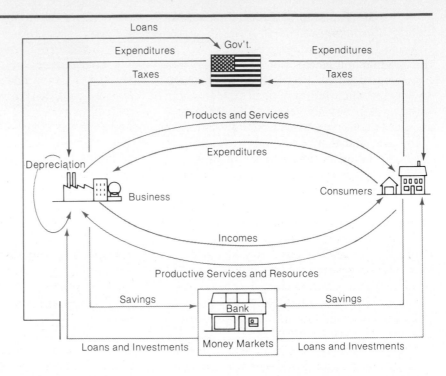

total spending will fall, and the upward pressure on prices will be alleviated.

Government fiscal affairs, then, have three different effects on the flow of spending:

1. Transfer payments shift purchasing power from taxpayers to other persons, presumably in order to achieve social goals not achieved by the pattern of income levels and distribution that would otherwise prevail.

2. Government expenditures provide a variety of products and services through government agencies and add to total incomes, employment, and output.

3. Fiscal surpluses and deficits can be used to promote economic stability. If properly managed, they can reduce—some hope eliminate—the depressions and inflations that would otherwise be generated in the private sector of the economy. This stabi-

lizing function of government expenditure and tax policy is usually coordinated with the policies of the monetary authorities that control the flow of credit. Monetary policy and fiscal policy can be used jointly in an effort to achieve economic stability.

Inflations and Depressions

The flow of spending is continually changing. Although the relationship between income and saving may be a relatively stable one, both the creation of credit and the investment decisions of business firms can vary widely from one year to the next.

When optimism and the expectation of increased business and rising profits are prevalent, the flow of spending can expand readily as investment expenditures and credit creation increase. The resultant increases in aggregate demand can increase optimism still further and induce more expansion. Under these conditions the economy can push forward rapidly and reach levels of full employment. There is nothing that will necessarily stop expansion of aggregate demand beyond full-employment levels. Yet when full employment is reached, output can grow only very slowly. If purchasing power continues to rise rapidly something must give, and that something is the level of prices. Inflation begins, and will continue so long as aggregate demand continues to grow more rapidly than output.

The traditional policy prescription for inflation caused by excessive spending is to tighten the money supply in order to make loans harder to get and to push interest rates up, hold back on government expenditures, and, if possible, run a government budgetary surplus. The policy problem is a difficult one, however, since too vigorous an anti-inflationary policy can start a recession, while too timid a one may not be strong enough to eliminate the excessive demand that is pushing prices up. The economic policymaker's lot is not a happy one.

Inflation is not the only problem. Just the opposite conditions of recession and depression can prevail. Then the problem is one of supplementing the existing flow of spending and of using monetary policies to encourage creation of more credit. Here the problem is simpler, since the unlimited credit of a national government allows it to borrow and spend whatever is necessary to raise aggregate demand to full-employment levels. This may entail an increase in the national debt, but as will be shown in the appendix to Chapter 9, the economic burdens created by such a debt are insignificant when compared with the benefits derived from high levels of output and employment. Indeed we are fortunate, in the mid-twentieth century, to have governments that spend and tax in large amounts: they provide a strong base for high levels of aggregate demand, and relatively small changes in their total budgets can have a large effect on the flow of spending. This was not true of national governments fifty years ago or more, which accounted for a much smaller proportion of total spending.

The fact that aggregate demand in the private sector of the economy is either rising or falling at all times is one of the unpleasant characteristics of the modern economy. This condition in itself creates the changing expectations that in turn spur further changes in the level of aggregate demand and in levels of employment and output. This characteristic of the private sector creates a significant role for government: promotion of greater economic stability. The government sector of the economy can be used to counterbalance the instability of the private sector.

Summary

The level of economic activity is determined by the flow of spending from households to business firms and back. Leakages in the form of savings and taxes are offset by investment and government spending. When they are not fully offset, the flow of spending falls and the level of economic activity declines. The monetary sector is able to supplement the flow of spending by credit created by the banking system, leading to a need for government to manage the money supply. Government budgets can act as a stabilizing element through adjustment of taxes and government expenditures to compensate for the fluctuations inherent in the private sector.

Nevertheless, the flow of spending is inherently unstable and continually changing, and a private enterprise economy always faces the possibility of recession or inflation.

Key Concepts

aggregate demand	leakages	tight money
flow of spending	offsets to savings	transfer payments
depreciation	easy money	government deficits and surpluses

For Discussion

1. Why don't saving and investment automatically balance each other and keep the flow of spending stable?

2. Would you expect investment to be more volatile than savings? Why?

3. If the economy should be at or close to the level of full employment, why should it not stay there indefinitely?

4. If the economy is producing at a level well below full employment, why should it not move rapidly toward full employment?

5. How might the monetary system contribute to economic instability?

6. Explain the basic principles of how government fiscal policies can be used to promote economic stability and full employment.

Chapter 6

Measuring the National Product and Income

Objective evaluation of the performance of an economic system starts with measurements that enable the economist and policy maker to determine the level of economic activity and the direction and speed of its movement. Other quantitative measures can then be used to indicate the way the economy's output is used and how it is distributed. The most important measures of economic performance are national product and income accounts. In this chapter, we define those measures, briefly describe how they are computed, and explain some of their limitations.

The Gross National Product

The most widely used yardstick of economic performance is the nation's *gross national product*, usually abbreviated GNP. It is a statistical invention that sums up, in one neat little figure, the nation's total production in any one year. We can watch it grow over long periods of time. We can observe its fluctuations from one year to the next. Corrected for changes in the price level, it can tell us how the "real" economic conditions have been changing over time. Divided by the nation's population, it can

provide a measure of output per person. Its rate of change can be computed to show the speed of economic growth. Comparisons of the level of GNP with estimates of potential output can tell us if our economic performance is everything it might be.

An increase in GNP tells us that output of products and services has risen and economic activity has grown, provided that we correct the measurement for changes in the general level of prices. Conversely, a fall in GNP indicates reduced output. GNP, then, is a highly useful measure of economic health. But, as we shall see later, it must be used with caution.

- A nation's **gross national product** is the money value of all final products newly produced in a year, in current prices. It measures the value of a year's production purchased by consumers, business firms, and government, plus the difference between exports and imports. All of this adds up to a measure of how much productive effort took place.

GNP as an Estimate

Calculation of the GNP is not exact. It is an estimate based on a wide variety of data gathered by the Department of Commerce from all sectors of the economy. Complete data are never available, and the figures are continually being revised. Sometimes the revisions continue for as much as ten years after the first announcement. Reasonable accuracy, is, of course, maintained. More important, the same calculation techniques are used from one year to the next, so that annual changes are quite accurately measured. If the inexactness of one year parallels that of another, most of the errors of estimation will be washed out by the fact that the methods of estimation were the same.

Why Money Value Is Used

Economists use actual prices prevailing during the year to calculate the gross national product. The many products and services of an economy have to be reduced to some common denominator in order to be added together. That common denominator is their money value, measured by the prices at which they were sold (or if they were not sold but held in inventories, at the value assigned to them by accountants). This provides a value expressed in current prices for all of the component parts of the GNP.

Final Products: Avoiding Double Counting

Only finished products and services that have been bought by their ultimate users are included in the GNP. Products in the intermediate stages of production are *not* included. Take this textbook, for example. It was bought at a bookstore by the consumer now using it, and its value is included in the GNP at its final sale price. A wide variety of intermediate products were used: trees cut and sold to a paper mill; paper, ink, and cloth sold to the printing and manufacturing plant, and so forth. If each intermediate transaction were included, some parts of the book would be included in GNP two, three, or more times. Yet only one book is produced, with a value of only a few dollars. Including the intermediate stages would therefore artificially inflate the total GNP.

The method used by statisticians to eliminate double counting of intermediate products is to calculate the *value added* at each stage of the production process. For example, the value added at the paper-mill stage is calculated by subtracting the cost of pulpwood and other raw materials from the selling price of the paper. The difference will equal the wages and salaries, rent, interest, and profits paid to the factors of production for their productive effort: the value they have added to the value of the raw materials to give the final product its market value. When the value added at each stage is added up, the sum will equal the final selling price of the book. Even inventories and goods in the process of production pose no problem, though they are not yet in the hands of final consumers. The value added by all the productive effort that has gone into them is included in GNP, and their "final" user is considered to be the business firm that owns them as of December 31.

Goods Must Be Newly Produced

In order to be included in the GNP for any year, goods must have been produced in that year. For example, if you bought this book secondhand, the transaction is not part of GNP because nothing new has been produced, no new income has been created or paid out, and no addition has been made to the total stock of goods, except for the services of the clerk and the profits of the bookstore. They are included in GNP because they were useful services newly performed and paid for during the year. But the wholesale cost of the book is excluded because the book was produced in an earlier year and was included in the GNP for that year.

This principle is widely applied. The value of a used house that is sold and bought is not included in GNP, but the agent's commission is. Sales of securities are not included, but brokers' commissions are. The house, the securities, and any existing asset are not newly produced goods, but the commissions are payments for productive services performed during the year.

The Component Parts of GNP

The GNP has three basic component parts: consumption, investment, and government purchases of goods and services. A fourth, smaller one is usually added: "net exports" of goods and services. These four categories are distinguished from each other, in part, by the different economic units that do the buying. More important, they differ because of the factors that influence the level of spending in each category.

Consumption

Personal consumption expenditures are by far the largest component of GNP, amounting to about 63 percent in the United States in recent years. Some of the important types of purchases in this category are:

Durable goods, such as automobiles, furniture, and household equipment.

Nondurable goods, such as food and clothing.

Services, such as housing, transportation, and household operation.

Some idea of the relative size of these expenditures can be obtained from the national product accounts for 1980 (Table 6–1). The figures are in current dollars not corrected for price changes.

Table 6–1
Consumption Expenditures, 1980

	(Billions of Dollars)
Gross national product	2627
Personal consumption	1670
Durable goods	210
Nondurable goods	674
Services	786

Table 6–2
Gross Private Domestic Investment, 1980

	(Billions of Dollars)
Gross national product	2627
Gross private domestic investment	395
New plants and equipment	295
Residential structures	104
Change in business inventories	−4

Investment

Investment, which is called *gross private domestic investment* in the national product accounts, is a particularly crucial part of the GNP because it is the main offset to savings. It also replaces the capital used up in production and increases the economy's capacity to produce. High levels of investment are essential for the maintenance of high levels of output and for the expansion of the economy's capacity to produce. Gross private domestic investment includes several components:

New plants and equipment built or installed by business firms and farmers.

New houses and other residential units.

Changes in business inventories. This component may be positive if business inventories increased during the year, or negative if they declined.

Investment spending in the national product accounts for 1980 is shown in Table 6–2.

● **Investment** consists of goods produced but not sold to consumers, thereby increasing the economy's real capital. More formally, it is real capital formation: plant, equipment, and goods used in production, valued in constant dollars.

Net and Gross Investment

One of the functions of investment is the replacement of capital used in the production process. The share of investment expenditures used for that purpose represents a production cost and does not add to the economy's capacity to produce. It merely replaces what was already there. In that sense it can be thought of as an intermediate product and should not be counted toward the value of newly produced product during the year. This leads to a new concept, the *net national product*, or NNP.

- The **net national product** is the GNP minus depreciation charges:[1]

$$GNP - depreciation = NNP$$

The national product accounts for 1980 showed this calculation, as follows, in billions of dollars:

$$2627 - 288 = 2339 = NNP$$

This tells us that $288 billion of the GNP in 1980 was investment that replaced capital used up during the year, so that the net product was only $2339 billion of goods and services.

Government Expenditures on Goods and Services

Governments at all levels are among the largest spenders in the country. Rather than try to allocate these expenditures to either consumption or investment, the national product accounts lump together all government expenditures on goods and services into a single category. The reason is essentially a practical one: it is the easiest way to do it. Furthermore, as we have already seen, government expenditures can be used as one of the chief instruments for achieving a stable economy. Putting them in a separate category helps economists analyze their influence.

Government budgets are complex documents. Some of the expenditures included in

Table 6–3
Government Purchases of Goods and Services, 1980

	(Billions of Dollars)
Gross national product	2627
Government purchases of goods and services	535
Federal government	199
National defense	132
Other	67
State and local governments	336

them are for direct purchases of goods and services. These enter into the national product accounts because they are payments for newly produced goods and services. Payments of wages and salaries to government employees are included in GNP, on the assumption that government services are useful and productive,[2] and are worth the cost of producing them. But not all expenditures in government budgets are payments for newly produced goods and services. In particular, *transfer payments* are not included in the GNP, even though they make up a substantial portion of most government budgets. A transfer payment merely transfers purchasing power from one person to another without an accompanying production of new goods and services. Typical examples are veterans' pensions, interest payments on the national debt, welfare payments, and social security benefits.

The government component of GNP is large. In 1980, as shown in Table 6–3, state and local governments spent more on goods and services than the federal government, and national defense accounted for the great bulk of federal purchases.

---

[1]In order to confuse noneconomists, depreciation charges are called "capital consumption allowances" in the national product accounts.

[2]That assumption is not made in the Soviet Union, for example, which does not include the wages and salaries of government employees in its calculation of GNP.

Net Exports of Goods and Services

When American business firms sell products and services to foreigners (exports), the production takes place in the United States and income is paid to American workers and business firms. The exports represent newly produced goods and services and should be included in the U.S. GNP even though they may be consumed by foreigners. Conversely, when Americans buy goods and services produced in foreign countries (imports), the production is part of other nations' GNPs. The goods may be sold in the U.S., but they were not produced here and should not be included in our GNP.

The two sets of transactions come close to canceling each other. The difference between the two (exports minus imports) is called "net exports" and is included in the GNP. Thus if exports exceed imports, then our international trade position has brought about a net increase in our output, and a positive contribution is made to GNP. If exports are less than imports, net exports will be negative and GNP will be reduced. The impact on GNP is usually quite small. The relevant data for 1980 are shown in Table 6–4.

Putting the Component Parts Together

We can now put together the component parts of the gross national product:

$$GNP = C + I_g + G + X$$

These symbols stand for the four chief components of gross national product. In 1980, they added up to $2627 billion (Table 6–5).

Table 6–4
Net Exports of Goods and Services, 1980

	(Billions of Dollars)
Gross national product	2627
Net exports (*X*)	27
Total exports (*E*)	341
Total imports (*M*)	314

Table 6–5
Chief Components of GNP, 1980

		(Billions of Dollars)
C	(personal consumption expenditures)	1670
I_g	(gross private domestic investment)	395
G	(government purchases of goods and services)	535
X	(net exports of goods and services)	27
GNP	(gross national product)	2627

Subtracting depreciation, or capital consumption allowances, gives an alternative measure, the net national product NNP. It doesn't matter where the subtraction is made. Depreciation can be subtracted from gross investment I_g to give net investment I_n, and then everything added up to give NNP. Or it can be subtracted from GNP itself.

The National Income

Up to this point we have been discussing the national product and measuring the productive effort of the economy. An alternative approach is to calculate the *national income*, NI, as a measure of how much is *earned* from productive effort.

You will recall from the earlier description of the flow of spending in Chapter 5 that the flow of products in one direction is accompanied by a flow of payments in the other, as shown in Figure 6–1. The national product is derived from the upper loop; it measures final products at the prices at which they were actually bought. The national income is derived from the lower loop. It measures the incomes earned by the factors of production that have been

Figure 6-1
The Flow of
Spending: Money
Payments and
Real Flows

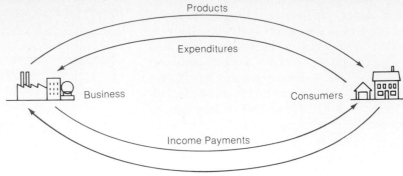

used to turn out the national product of the upper loop.[3]

- **National income** is the sum of payments earned by the factors of production in producing the national product.

NI = wages and salaries + rent + interest + profits

Payments to the factors of production for the use of their labor, land, and capital include:

Wages, salaries, and other payments made to employees (payments for social insurance, health and welfare funds, and other minor items).

Interest paid on loans.

Rental income of individuals.

Business profits, which are usually divided into
—corporate profits and
—income of unincorporated enterprises, professional persons, and farm proprietors.

Do not become confused by the fact that these payments are both incomes to the people

who receive them and costs to the firms that pay them. This dual nature of the payments is inherent in the fact that they are part of the circular flow of spending, and that we are now measuring the national *income* in terms of the earnings of the factors of production.

Not all corporate profits become actual income for individuals. Only part is normally paid out as dividends. A substantial portion is usually retained for spending by the firm itself and another large portion is paid to the government in taxes. Nevertheless, all profits are included as part of the incomes earned in production, just as all wages and salaries are. The reason is simple: profits are considered to be income of the owners of an enterprise whether they are paid out to the owners or not. An idea of what happens to corporate profits can be provided by the figures for 1980 (Table 6–6).

Table 6–6
Corporate Profits, 1980

	(Billions of Dollars)
Corporate profits before taxes	241
Corporate tax liability	80
Corporate profits after taxes	161
Dividends	56
Undistributed profits	105

[3]This explanation has been simplified to get at the essence of the national income; remember that government purchases and business investment must be included, with their products and income payments.

Table 6–7
National Income, 1980

	(Billions of Dollars)
Wages and salaries	1596
Net interest payments	180
Rental income of individuals	32
Business profits (adjusted)	263
Income of unincorporated enterprises	131
Corporate profits (adjusted)	182
National income	2121

There is one additional component of the costs of producing the national product that is not part of the incomes earned by the factors of production. Certain types of business taxes are included in production costs and are embodied in the selling prices of goods and services. These are items such as local property taxes, franchise taxes for public utilities, and similar tax obligations that do not vary with the level of output or earnings of the firm. Accounting procedures normally include these indirect business taxes in the costs of production for the individual firm and they are passed on to the buyer through higher prices. Since the national product is valued at current prices, these indirect business taxes are blanketed into the national product accounts, but should not be

Table 6–8
NI, NNP, and GNP, 1980

	(Billions of Dollars)
National income	2121
Indirect business taxes	212
Minor adjustment items	6
Net national product	2339
Capital consumption allowances (depreciation)	288
Gross national product	2627

included in the national income because they are not earned by any of the factors of production. In 1980 indirect business taxes totaled $212 billion and made up the bulk of the difference between national income and the net national product.

The national income, then, is a measure of the incomes earned in producing the national product, including wages and salaries, interest, rent, and business profits. Table 6–7 shows the component parts of NI for 1980.

The Relationship Between National Income And National Product

The national income and the national product add up to different amounts. The national income does not include indirect business taxes or depreciation charges. The gross national product does, while the net national product includes indirect business taxes but not depreciation charges. All this may seem confusing, but reference to Table 6–8 will help straighten it out.

Remember that there is a reason for having three concepts. Gross national product (GNP) is a measure of total product. Net national product (NNP) is a measure of total product minus the capital used up in production. And national income (NI) measures incomes earned. They tell us different things about the flow of spending and each has its own meaning and use. Figure 6–2 shows the relationship graphically with data for 1980.

Correcting for Changes in the Price Level

All of the measures of national income and product use prices that prevail in the year for which the calculation is made. If comparisons are made between different years, a distortion will appear because of changes in price levels.

Figure 6-2
Relationships Between National Product and National Income Concepts

Figures are for 1980, in billions of dollars.

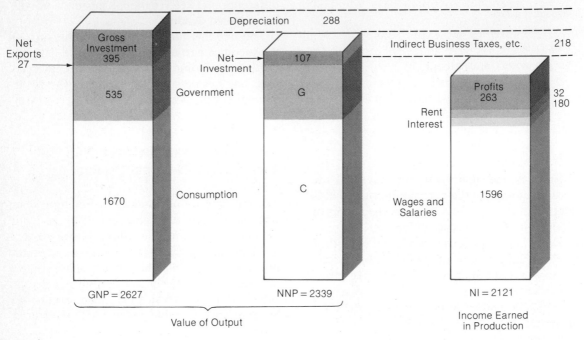

For example, the increase in U.S. national product from $208.5 billion in 1947 to $2627 billion in 1980 reflects both a large increase in output *and* the inflation of prices that took place between those years. An accurate comparison requires elimination of the price increase as a factor in the calculation.

Removal of price trends from national income and product accounts is a time-consuming matter. The first step is the construction of *index numbers* of prices for the various component parts of the national product. This is an intricate process involving the following steps:

1. Selection of a "base period" from which changes are to be calculated. At this time the year 1972 is the base period for calcu-

lation of the national product "deflators," as they are called.

2. Prices in the base period are arbitrarily given an index number value of 100, or 100 percent.

3. Prices in other years are then expressed as percentages of the base year prices.[4] For example, in 1980 consumers' durable goods stood at an index of 156, while services were 178. This means that there was a 56 percent increase in prices of consumers' durable goods between 1972 and 1980 while services rose in price by 78 percent.

---

[4]This is where the calculations become intricate. To learn how these percentages are calculated, see the appendix to this chapter.

The second step in eliminating price trends is to apply the index numbers, or deflators, to the data for national product. There will be no change in the calculations for 1972, since that is the base year and all prices have an index number of 100. But there will be changes in other years. For example, the 1980 calculation of consumers' durable goods will have to be decreased by 56 percent, that for services decreased by 78 percent, and so on for all of the component parts of the national product for each year. When this has been done, the GNP in 1980 will have been calculated on the basis of prices as they existed in 1972 and distortions due to price changes will have been eliminated. Fortunately, all of this work has been done for the hard-working economist by government statisticians, at least for GNP. Data are available for GNP calculated in both current and 1972 prices, as shown in Figure 6–3.

Correcting the GNP for changes in the price level may seem to be a neat, clean little adjustment. But there are pitfalls in using and interpreting the corrected data. The most important arise from the so-called "index number problem." When an index number is constructed for a base year, it is weighted according to the economic importance of the various products and services included. For example, very few television sets were produced in 1946, so they would not be a significant part of the GNP

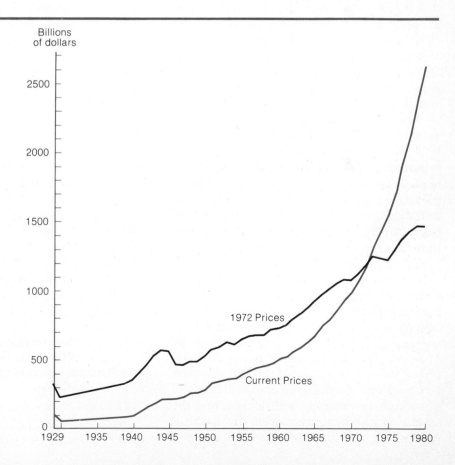

Figure 6–3
U.S. Gross National Product, 1929–1980 in Current Prices and 1972 Prices

computations for that year. If 1946 were the base year for the price index, television sets would be given very low weights in computing the index. By 1972, however, the base year for the national product deflators, television sets were an important part of the market basket of products bought by consumers. They would be weighted heavily in computing the price index. This means that rather different results are obtained, depending on the base year chosen, because of changes in the economy that have occurred. If the GNP is corrected on the basis of 1972 prices and weights, the data for 1946 will be distorted. Conversely, if the GNP in 1972 is corrected using 1946 prices and weights, the data for 1972 will be distorted.

The index number problem is an insoluble one. The greater the economic changes that have taken place over the period for which comparisons are being made, the greater the distortion in the results. Furthermore, comparisons over a time period will be less accurate if the base period of the index number is close to one of the terminal dates of the comparison than if the base period is in the middle, assuming that economic change is relatively steady between the two dates. Deflators based on 1972 prices and weights give a better picture of the economy of 1980 than the economy of 1929. If the two years are to be compared with the least inaccuracies, the national product deflators have to be computed on the basis of prices in 1955 (a midpoint) rather than prices in 1972.

The same problem applies to comparisons between nations. The pattern of consumption in the United States differs from that of the Soviet Union. We consume much beer and little vodka. In the Soviet Union it is just the opposite. We use leather shoes and few made of felt. In the USSR much greater use is made of felt shoes. The GNPs of the two countries will be based on different market baskets of goods and services and will not measure the same things. When comparisons are made, it will be like comparing apples with oranges.

They are both fruits, but there the similarities stop.

The essential point is that the comparisons involve dissimilar things. The use of a common measuring rod inevitably introduces distortions whose extent cannot be accurately estimated. As a result any comparisons of national product or income are only close approximations, whether those comparisons are made between different years in the same country or between different countries in the same year.

What Does the National Product Measure?

It is important to look beyond the definitions of national income and product, as well as how they are calculated, to consider exactly what is being measured. Even a quick look at the concepts indicates several important limitations.

First, some output of new goods and services is not included. Work done at home for consumption by the family is left out, because it does not enter markets and is not bought and sold. This includes, for example, the services of the housewife in cooking, cleaning, and doing other household chores, and also the products of the home workshop operated by her husband. Note the anomaly of this: if the housewife were to take a job outside the home and hire someone to do housework for her, the earnings of *both* would be included in GNP. Unpaid housework done by the wife is not included. Yet an exception is made for farm production consumed on the farm. This is estimated and included in GNP.

○ Question: By how much is the long-term growth of U.S. GNP overstated because of the shift of women into the labor market that has taken place over the last 60 to 70 years?

○ Question: By how much is it understated because of the growth of home workshop production?

○ Answer: No one knows, and the national income accounts won't tell us.

To make the picture more complicated, some items that *do* enter markets and *are* bought and sold are not included in GNP. The most important of these are goods and services illegally traded: the services of the numbers racketeer or gambling-house operator (except where gambling is legal!), bootleg whiskey, narcotics, the services of prostitutes, and so on. Even some income that is legally earned but not reported never gets into the national income accounts at all, such as part of the cash income of some professional people who try to evade income taxes. How important are these items of the "underworld" national income and product? Would you believe 10 percent of GNP? No one knows.

There is a second limitation inherent in the national income and product accounts. The accounts include a wide variety of products and services that merely preserve the existing economy as a functioning entity, or reconstruct parts of it that have been damaged or depleted. We have already seen that one of these items, depreciation of capital, is properly deducted from gross national product to derive a net product available for consumption or investment. But what about expenditures for control of air pollution, garbage removal, sewage treatment, and so forth? Should we include in GNP the services of doctors and hospitals in treating the victims of automobile accidents or cigarette smokers with lung cancer? All of these items, and many more, serve to reconstruct or preserve the economy or the individual as a functioning unit. They make the system whole again rather than adding to the net product. If the national product accounts were to be used as a measure of production available for increasing the national welfare, a large number of additional deductions would have to be made.

These limitations of the national product and income accounts should be borne in mind whenever the accounts are used. The national product measures the value of current output, but not all output is included. The national income measures the incomes earned in producing the national product, but not all income is included. In terms of increased national welfare, too much is included.

But with all their limitations, the national product and income accounts are reasonably useful measures of the level of economic activity and the flow of spending. They are especially useful in showing changes that take place from year to year. They are an essential tool in analyzing how the economy functions and in determining economic policies for the present and the immediate future. Like one's spouse or "significant other," they may not be perfect but they're all you've got.

The Underground Economy

A largely unmeasured or underground economy has grown up alongside the officially measured economic activity captured by the statistics on national income and product. It consists of economic activities that escape measurement because they are not reported to government. These activities may be legal or illegal, market or nonmarket, monetary or barter. They range from illegal transactions in drugs or marketing of pirated popular music recordings to legal transactions like payments in cash to carpenters or doctors who do not report the income in order to avoid taxes.

The growth of the underground economy seems to have been considerably more rapid than the officially measured economy. Early estimates in the mid-1960s placed the underground economy at about 5 percent of gross national product, and this did not include the value of home production (services of housewives, home workshops and gardens, etc.). By 1970 it had grown to 9 percent of GNP and to 15 percent in 1978, according to a study done by the Federal Reserve Bank of Atlanta. A more recent study by Edgar Feige of the University of Wisconsin argues that the unobserved economy grew from about 10 percent of GNP in 1960 to about 27 percent in 1978. The pattern is interesting: from 1960 to 1970 there was little discernible change in the ratio between the two sectors, but an accelerated growth of the underground economy began in 1970 and seems to be continuing at an increasing rate.

Economists are puzzled by the rapid growth of the underground economy. It is easy to understand that unreported illegal economic activity could be as large as 10 percent of GNP—but as much as 25 percent would be hard to believe. Some speculate that high tax rates cause people to move transactions "off the books" in order to avoid taxes. That explanation does not fit the U.S. pattern of rapid growth of the underground economy in the 1970s, however, for tax rates did not rise, although tax payments increased as inflation pushed personal incomes into higher tax brackets. Nor does it fit international comparisons.

In both Italy and Sweden, for example, tax rates are higher than in the U.S., and while tax evasion is a way of life in Italy, it is very limited in Sweden.

Feige has another explanation. He points out that trust in government in the U.S. deteriorated rapidly in the 1970s as a result of the Vietnam War, Watergate, exposure of systematic illegal activity by the Federal Bureau of Investigation, Abscam, and all that. Escalating growth of the underground economy coincided with escalation of distrust of government.

Whatever the causes, be they growth of crime, increased tax burdens, or distrust of government, the underground economy must be taken into account. Economic growth may be more rapid than official figures indicate, employment larger and unemployment rates a bit lower, and the effect of inflation somewhat less. Exactly how much the underground economy affects these measures of economic health and well-being is unknown, for its precise size and rate of growth are not known. But the effect may be considerable.

Summary

The gross national product is the most widely used measure of a nation's economic performance. It measures the money value (at current prices) of all newly produced products and services during a year. Corrected for changes in price levels, it can be used to make comparisons over time. Divided by population, it provides a measure of output per person. Percentage changes from one year to the next can be computed to determine growth rates. It permits rough international comparisons to be made.

The net national product takes into account the fact that some of the nation's stock of capital is replaced each year out of that year's output. The NNP is obtained by deducting depreciation of capital from the GNP.

The national product is a measure of total consumption, investment, government purchases of products and services, and net exports. The national income is the sum of all incomes earned in producing the national product, including wages and salaries (with fringe benefits), rent, interest, and profit. When calculated accurately the two sums are consistent with each other, since each is designed to measure the same flow of spending in different ways.

Measures of the national product and income have serious limitations. The selection of items to be included is somewhat arbitrary. The size of the underground economy is un-

known. And neither GNP nor NI is a good measure of economic well-being.

Key Concepts

gross national product   **net national product**
investment   **national income**

For Discussion

1. Are GNP and NI good measures of the economic performance of a country? Why or why not?

2. What measures of economic performance or economic welfare would be needed, in addition to GNP or NI, to obtain a proper evaluation of a nation's performance?

3. Why are intermediate goods not counted in calculating GNP?

4. Why are transfer payments not included in calculating NI, even though they are part of the income of some people?

5. In what ways can index numbers distort comparisons among different years?

6. Should the unpaid labor of housewives be included in GNP? Discuss.

Measurement of Changes in the General Level of Prices

It is easy enough to measure price changes over a period of time for single goods. It is much more difficult to get a measurement of the overall change in prices. Prices of goods do not change at the same rate, and prices of some goods may be falling even when the general level (average) of prices is rising, or vice versa. Say, for example, that we are interested in comparing the price level of 1974 with that of 1970. If bread were the only commodity produced in the economy, our task would be simple. Knowing the average price for bread in the two years, we could compute the ratio of these prices (called a *price relative*):

$$\frac{\text{Average price of bread in 1974}}{\text{Average price of bread in 1970}} = \frac{\$0.16}{\$0.14} = 1.143,$$
$$\text{or} \quad 114.3\%$$

This tells us that the price of bread in 1974 was 114.3 percent of the price of bread in 1970, or that the price of bread was 14.3 percent greater in 1974 than in 1970.

But one commodity will not do. We are interested in measuring the average price change for a large number of commodities, for example, of consumer retail purchases (as measured by the Consumer Price Index), where prices of different commodities change by different percentage amounts.

To see how such an index is obtained, assume for the sake of simplicity that bread, shirts, and coal are the only commodities that consumers buy, and that the quantities purchased in 1974 are of the same quality and type but differing in amount. (In reality several hundred goods and services are included in the Consumer Price Index.) The data for our example are given in Table 6–9.

If we wanted to keep our efforts simple, we could just add the prices in each year and compare the totals. The total for 1970 is $16.14, while the total for 1974 is $18.66. Prices appear to have risen, but by how much? We might calculate a simple ratio to get the level in 1974 as compared with 1970:

$$\frac{18.66}{16.14} = 1.156 \quad \text{or} \quad 115.6\%$$

We can get an answer that way, but it's not very satisfactory. The method requires adding loaves, shirts, and tons, and this procedure is meaningless.

Let's try again. The price relatives show the increase in individual prices from 1970 to 1974. We could add them together and then get a simple arithmetic mean:

$$\frac{1.143 + 0.875 + 1.250}{3} = 1.089 \quad \text{or} \quad 108.9\%$$

This is a little better; but not much, because it assigns equal importance to each of the three commodities in consumers' budgets.

We are obviously on the wrong track. The trouble is that we have been single-mindedly focusing on prices and ignoring the fact that consumers buy a

Table 6-9
Data for Computing Simple Price Index

	1970		1974		Price Relatives (1974 Price ÷ 1970 Price)
	Price	Quantity	Price	Quantity	
Bread	$ 0.14/loaf	2,000	$ 0.16/loaf	2,200	$1.143
Shirts	$ 4.00/shirt	25	$ 3.50/shirt	30	$0.875
Coal	$12.00/ton	20	$15.00/ton	15	$1.250

market basket of different goods that will have a total cost to them. The average price level is associated with that market basket, and not with just the individual prices.

Let's try that approach. We calculate the cost of the consumers' market basket in 1974, compare it with a similar figure for 1970, and compute the percentage increase:

$$\frac{0.16(2200) + 3.50(30) + 15.00(15)}{0.14(2000) + 4.00(25) + 12.00(20)} = \frac{682.0}{620.0} =$$
$$1.100 \quad \text{or} \quad 110.0\%$$

The trouble with this procedure is that there are two variables, prices *and* quantities. We are interested in measuring the change in only one, prices. The other will have to be held constant so that it does not affect the results.

That's easy to do. We'll pick 1970 as the base, and use the market basket for that year. We can get the value of that market basket in both 1974 and 1970 prices, and calculate the percentage change:

$$\frac{0.16(2000) + 3.50(25) + 15.00(20)}{0.14(2000) + 4.00(25) + 12.00(20)} = \frac{707.5}{620.0} =$$
$$1.141 \quad \text{or} \quad 114.1\%$$

This tells us how much it would cost in 1974 compared with 1970 to buy the same amounts of these goods that were purchased in 1970. The year 1970 is the *base year*, with which the level of prices in 1974 is compared. Therefore 1970 = 100. This is a very simplified version of the method used in computing the Consumer Price Index.

We can now say that since prices in 1974 were, on the average, 114.1 percent of 1970 prices, the value of the dollar in 1974 was 87.5 percent of its value in 1970:

$$\frac{100.0}{114.1} \times 100 = 87.5$$

The "Index Number Problem"

The method we have just worked through is good, but it has some flaws. The index number for any year is expressed as a percentage of the base year. But if the pattern of consumer purchases changes significantly, the comparison will not be very meaningful. That's why a comparison of prices in 1974 as compared with 1874 is only a very rough one. Who buys a buggy today? Or who bought a television set then?

Different market baskets of goods can make a big difference in the results. Suppose, for instance, we were to shift the base year from 1970 to 1974 in the example used above. Between those two years, consumer purchases of bread rose by 10 percent and of shirts by 20 percent, but purchases of coal fell by 25 percent. A rather different pattern of consumer buying has appeared. How much difference will this make in the price index? Here are the calculations, using 1974 quantities as weights:

$$\frac{0.16(2200) + 3.50(30) + 15.00(15)}{0.14(2200) + 4.00(30) + 12.00(15)} = \frac{682.0}{608.0} =$$
$$112.2$$

When 1974 is the base year, then, prices in 1974 were 112.2 percent of 1970 prices. The increase between 1970 and 1974 was 12.2 percent, instead of the 14.1 percent increase calculated from the 1970 base. Which answer is correct? Did prices in our hypothetical economy increase between 1970 and 1974 by 12.2 percent or 14.1 percent? Actually, *both* answers are correct, depending on which base year is chosen!

Statisticians have devised several ways to minimize this "index number problem." But more calculations only take the final result further from reality without entirely solving the problem. The government statisticians who compute our most widely used price indexes have wisely decided to use the simple methods of computation explained here and let those who use the indexes worry about how far their conclusions can be pushed.

One way to minimize the index number problem is continually to update the base period. Most index numbers of prices are used for relatively recent comparisons, for example, in determining how much prices have risen in 1979 as compared with 1978. If the index number has a 1950 base, the comparison of 1979 with 1978 will be less meaningful than if it had a 1978 base. For this reason the common index numbers of prices are usually revised every decade or so, with the base year being moved up ten years each time.

Revising price indexes to keep them up to date creates another set of problems. How does one compare a price index with a 1967 base (like the present consumer price index) to one with a 1957–1959 base, or a 1947–1949 base (like the earlier

Figure 6-4
Consumer Price Index and Major Components, 1967–1979

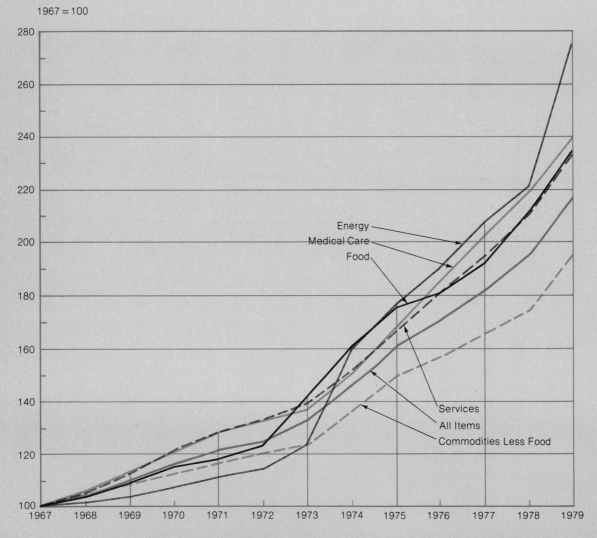

consumer price indexes)? The answer is that one doesn't. The entire index must be recomputed and carried back as far as necessary. Doing that, however, leaves the earlier years of the index so far from the base year that those figures increasingly lose their relevance. That is one reason why the current consumer price index is recomputed only back to 1929.

The Sears Roebuck Catalog, 1897 and 1980

The "index number problem" can be vividly illustrated by comparing the Sears Roebuck mail-order catalog for 1897 (recently republished as a nostalgia item and available in your local library) with a recent catalog from the same firm. Prices were much lower then: men's shirts at 49¢ to $1.50; ladies' dresses at 69¢ to $1.95; kitchen chairs at 34¢ and dining room chairs at $1.10, for example. You'd pay a good deal more for those same items today in an antique shop. Other items aren't available at all today: a surrey with the fringe on top for $48.40, and patent medicines liberally laced with cocaine and other goodies that were touted as cures for almost any ailment, including cancer, heart disease, and impotence. But there weren't any double-knit dresses or bikinis, fashionable ladies' boots, suede jackets, automobile accessories, transistor radios, or stereo albums at any price.

Now, here's the problem: would you rather spend your income on the items in the 1897 catalog at 1897 prices, or on those in the current catalog at today's prices? (Buying and reselling is prohibited in this fantasy.) Which would leave you better off, 1897 goods at low prices or today's goods at high prices? When we compare prices now (about 220) with prices in 1897 (about 22) that is exactly the type of comparison we are making.

Changes Within the Index

Index numbers are a composite made up of many parts. They measure an average of specific elements whose price behavior may differ widely from the group as a whole. Indeed, it would be very surprising if the component parts of a price index moved similarly. The reason we need an index is because they do not. No one price can be used as a proxy for the others, so we have to construct an index that we can use. For example, in Figure 6–4 look at the way some major component parts of the Consumer Price Index have changed in the years since 1967.

Observe the great inflation. All groups of prices rose in the years from 1967 through 1979, as the overall price level rose by 117 percent. But some rose more slowly, particularly commodities other than food (113 percent). But food prices rose by 135 percent, with a particularly large jump in 1973–75, and services also rose by 135 percent. Energy prices rose by 176 percent, particularly after 1973, and the cost of medical care by 140 percent. The movement of the consumer price index as a whole masked some of the more dramatic price increases in the various sectors of the economy.

Chapter 7

Income, Savings, and Investment

The flow of spending is always increasing or decreasing, moving in one direction or the other. But these movements do not continue indefinitely in one direction. There are forces at work that tend to bring them to an equilibrium in which total spending (*aggregate demand*) is just equal to the total cost of production (*aggregate supply*). This equilibrium occurs when withdrawals from the flow of spending (savings and taxes) are just balanced by new funds flowing in (investment and government expenditures). As the flow of spending rises or falls, forces are set in motion that normally tend to bring the outflows into balance with the inflows and stabilize the total.

In this chapter we deal solely with the private sector, leaving government revenues and expenditures to a later chapter, and examine the tendency of the economy to move toward a macroeconomic equilibrium. The following chapter examines the dynamic elements that tend to keep the level of economic activity moving and fluctuating. The supply side is discussed first, then aggregate demand. The latter is broken down into its two component parts, the *propensity to consume* (with its opposite, the *propensity to save*) and the level of *investment*. Aggregate demand and supply are then put together to determine the *equilibrium level of income*. This equilibrium level implies a special relationship between investment and *savings*, which is the final building block of the analysis at this stage. The whole can be summarized in three fundamental propositions:

1. The level of economic activity is determined by the amount of total spending.

2. Total spending will either rise or fall until it reaches a level just equal to the cost of producing the total output (including normal business profits).

3. That equality will be reached when the savings consumers wish to make are just equal in amount to the investment desired by business managers.

The Framework of the Analysis

The principal factors that determine the flow of spending are:

Consumer spending C
Business investment I
Government spending G
Net exports X

Putting all these together, we arrive at a statement of the determinants of aggregate demand Y:

$$Y = C + I + G + X$$

This formulation can be thought of in gross terms, where Y = GNP and I stands for *gross investment* (I_g). Or it can be thought of in net terms, where Y = NNP and I stands for *net investment*, gross investment less depreciation (I_n). Or it can be thought of in terms of national income, where Y is the total net income of the factors of production earned from current production and the other elements in the equation have appropriate deductions made to bring the accounts into balance. But whether conceived in gross, net, or national income terms, aggregate demand is composed of four sources of spending: consumption, investment, government, and net exports. A change in any component of aggregate demand will affect the total.

In examining these relationships in some detail, we shall construct a theory of the process by which the level of aggregate demand is determined. Some simplifying assumptions, which will be dropped later, one by one, are:

1. The economy consists solely of the private sector. There is no government sector; G is thereby eliminated from the basic formulation. This assumption may seem highly unrealistic (and is), but it is made in order to lay out the essential relationships found in the private sector.

2. The economy is closed. There are no imports or exports. This eliminates X from the basic equation. Alternatively, we could assume that the net foreign balance is zero. This would also eliminate the X term.

In some versions of the theory the price level is also assumed to be constant. This is done to emphasize the "real" aspects of the analysis and the close connection between policies to manage the level of GNP and the level of production and employment. The assumption of constant prices can be dropped later, but the theory then takes on the odd look of a machine that has a number of gadgets added to it because the basic model will not work. We know that a change in total spending usually brings about simultaneous changes in both output and prices. So we will use a basic model that allows both prices and production to change as the economy moves toward a new equilibrium level. It will be closer to the approach used by John Maynard Keynes in his *General Theory of Employment, Interest and Money* of 1936 rather than the "reduced" Keynesian theory that assumed constant prices and was popular among American economists from about 1950 to 1970.

The effect of our assumptions is to limit the analysis initially to a closed, private economy with no government contribution to GNP. Our basic formulation, in terms of output, becomes:

$$Y = C + I \qquad (1)$$

That is, the total output of the economy equals the value of output used for consumption and output used for investment.

This basic identity can be stated in terms of income flows as well. The total income of the factors of production either can be used to purchase consumption goods or can be saved:

$$Y = C + S \qquad (2)$$

These two identities are quite similar. The value of total output of the economy (Y in Identity 1) is equal to the incomes paid out in the process of production (Y in Identity 2). Likewise, the value of the consumption goods turned out (C in Identity 1) is equal to the amount spent on consumption (C in Identity 2). Consequently, the value of investment I in Identity 1 must equal the amount of savings S in Identity 2:

$$S = I \qquad (3)$$

This relationship is a fundamental building block of the theory of national income. In the pure private enterprise economy, the amount saved must equal the amount spent for investment. The equality must hold for any level of income and output.

- **Savings** consist of income not spent for consumption.
- **Investment** is goods produced but not sold to consumers.
- **Gross investment** includes replacement of worn-out capital.
- **Net investment** includes only the increase in real capital over and above the amount used up in production.

The Decisions to Save and Invest

Investing and saving are usually done by different people for different reasons. Most capital formation takes place in business firms. An enterprise will attempt to take advantage of possibilities for profit making by building and equipping production plants. Inventories are also needed—raw materials, partly finished products, and final output in the "pipelines" that end in sales to consumers. All of this is part of the real capital required for production. The capital formation undertaken by a business firm can be paid for out of several sources:

1. Earnings retained from current operations or reserves accumulated in the past. These funds are business savings.

2. Borrowing from financial institutions or sale of securities to investors. These sources tap the savings of others and the credit created by bank loans.

Whatever the source of funds, the decision to invest is motivated by a desire for profit and depends on expectations about the future by the decision maker. These expectations can swing widely as events cause business decision makers to become more optimistic or more pessimistic about the future. One important characteristic of business investment is its potential volatility.

By contrast, most saving is done by individuals and families. Saving is not done primarily for profit, although savers usually like to earn as high a return on their savings as they can. Most saving is done to take care of emergencies, to provide for the future, or to make a large expenditure in the future (such as buying a house, sending children to college, etc.). Much saving is regular and contractual in nature, such as payments on many types of insurance policies, mortgage payments on a house and installment payments on a car. Furthermore, savings tend to bear a close relationship to incomes: in the aggregate, the proportion of consumer incomes that goes for savings does not fluctuate widely. Savings, then, are quite different from investment. Saving is done by different people from those who make investment decisions and for different reasons. More important, the relationship between savings and income tends to be relatively stable and the savings people make depend heavily on the income they receive. Investment, however, is much more volatile and depends heavily on the psychological outlook of the business community.

These differences between saving and investment are of crucial importance. Savings must be brought back into the stream of spending if incomes, output, and employment are to be maintained and grow. In a private economy, only business investment can do that job. Yet there is no automatic mechanism to assure that savings generated by full-employment levels of income will just match the amount of investment business managers desire to make.

At this point in the argument we are faced with a paradox: our definitions of savings and investment indicate that at any time they will be equal, yet at that same time the *desired* levels of saving and investment may differ. For example, businesses may have produced $1000 billion of products, of which $100 billion was investment goods they willingly acquired themselves and $900 billion was offered for sale to consumers. But consumers, who received $1000 billion in income, may wish to save only $50 billion and spend $950 billion. In this case business firms will find their inventories falling below the desired level. They are able to invest only $50 billion, not the desired $100 billion. The situation is clearly unstable. Output will be increased as inventories fall and economic activity will expand. Even though savings and investment are equal at $50 billion in the initial situation, the fact that desired savings are less than desired investment causes an increase in the level of economic activity. The paradox, then, involves a distinction between realized levels of savings and investment, and desired levels. As long as the actual and desired levels differ, the level of income and economic activity will change. Only when the actual and desired levels are brought to equality can stability be achieved. We move now to further examination of that process.

- **Desired savings** and **desired investment** are the levels of savings and investment that consumers and business firms *wish* to maintain.
- **Realized savings** and **realized investment** are the levels of savings and investment actually achieved by consumers and business firms.

Aggregate Supply

Business decisions are based on expectations that output can be sold at prices that will recover the costs of production and also allow for at least a normal profit. This means that income payments to the factors of production —wages and salaries, profits, rent, and interest —must come back to business firms in the form of revenue from sales. Unless this amount of income is returned to the stream of spending,

total business revenue will fall below total costs (including a normal profit in total costs), businesses will be unwilling to continue the existing level of production, and output will fall. Conversely, if income from sales is larger than current costs of production, profits will rise above normal and there will be strong incentives to increase output, as well as the enlarged income to do so.

Business firms will produce a given amount of goods and services only if they obtain revenues large enough to cover their costs of production, including a normal profit. This relationship between total costs of production— business expenditures—and revenues enables us to define the *aggregate supply* schedule, which shows the revenues necessary to sustain any given level of production. It is shown in Figure 7–1.[1]

- **Aggregate supply** is the income that business firms require to continue producing a given level of output. It is equal to the amounts expended by business on production costs, including a normal profit.

The aggregate supply schedule pictured in Figure 7–1 has several important characteristics. First, it starts at a minimum level of output Y_m below which output falls to zero. That occurs because there is a level of production below which enterprises obtain sales revenues too small to cover direct (variable) costs of production. Any firm has fixed costs, irrespective of levels of production, such as the cost of capital. Other costs vary with the level of output, such as wages. When revenues are so low that sales do not cover variable costs, a

---

[1] A note on the scales in Figure 7–1. The horizontal axis is in constant prices, enabling us to show the value of output corrected for changes in the price level ("real" output). Thus, if the general level of prices rises, with no change in the amount produced, the locus of Y_F, for example, will not change. The vertical axis is in current prices, however, which enables the analysis to capture "supply side" phenomena such as increased costs of production. If costs of production rise, the expenditures necessary to sustain any given level of real output, such as Y_b, will rise. The entire aggregate supply schedule will shift upward when production costs rise. More on this later in the chapter and in Chapter 14.

Figure 7-1
The Aggregate Supply Schedule

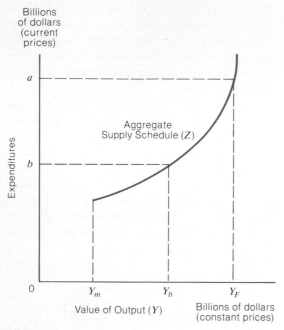

The aggregate supply schedule Z shows the expenditures (measured on the vertical axis) necessary to sustain any level of output (measured on the horizontal axis). For example, at the full employment level of output Y_F business firms would make expenditures equal to $0a$. They would have to receive an equal amount from buyers if they were to maintain that level of output. If the flow of spending provided business firms with proceeds equal only to $0b$, we would expect output to fall to Y_b.

firm will minimize its losses by closing the enterprise entirely. Losses will then be equal only to fixed costs, which will be lower than the total of fixed costs plus the loss on production. Although there has never been a depression serious enough for production to fall to zero, at times the economy has seemed to be heading in that direction, at least to the unemployed worker.

A second characteristic of the aggregate supply schedule is its shape. At relatively low levels of output its slope is less than 1 (less than 45°). This is due to the presence of fixed costs and to relative abundance of low-cost and efficient labor and equipment. When output is small, fixed costs are a relatively large portion of total costs. As output rises, variable costs rise, but—because of the presence of fixed costs—total costs rise more slowly than the increase in output. Furthermore, firms hire the most efficient labor and bring back into production the most efficient machinery as they increase output. This also enables them to raise output more rapidly than their costs rise.

As output increases, however, variable costs per unit of output start to rise. For example, new workers must be trained once the supply of skilled workers among the unemployed is already hired. The slope of the aggregate supply schedule starts rising toward 1 (a slope of 45°), at which output and costs increase at the same rate. Output level Y_b in Figure 7-1 is located in that area of the aggregate supply schedule.

As output approaches the full employment level (Y_F in Figure 7-1) costs of production start to escalate and the slope of the aggregate supply schedule is greater than 1 (above 45°). As the economy approaches capacity production, the markets for labor and other inputs start to tighten. Firms bid more for them, wages rise, and the prices of raw materials go up. In addition, the least efficient labor is hired, and old, inefficient equipment is brought into operation. As costs rise, so do the revenues required to validate the higher levels of production.

These considerations explain why the aggregate supply schedule has the profile of a tilted shallow bowl. It slopes upward because total costs of production rise as output is increased. But at low levels of production output increases more rapidly than costs while costs near full employment rise faster than output.

The level of prices at which output is sold will reflect these movements in production

Figure 7-2
The Aggregate Supply Schedule Shifts
Upward When Costs of Production Increase

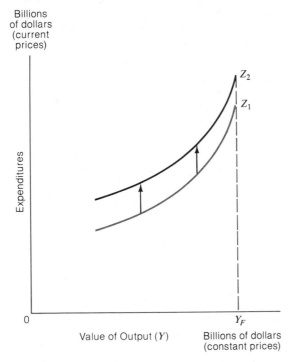

Increased costs of production shift the aggregate supply
schedule upward from Z_1 to Z_2. At each level of output
the revenues necessary for business firms to produce
that output have risen.

costs. When the economy approaches full employment, prices tend to rise because costs of production per unit of output are rising. Interestingly enough, the same is true of low levels of output: in Figure 7–1 costs of production per unit of output are higher at Y_F than they are at Y_b. This means that the general level of prices necessary to validate level of output Y_F will be higher than that needed to validate level of output Y_b.

Shifts in the Aggregate Supply Schedule
The aggregate supply schedule is pushed up-

ward when the cost of production rises. An upward shift means that prices rise to accommodate the increase in costs. Conversely, the aggregate supply schedule shifts downward—prices fall—when production costs fall, assuming, of course, that competition among firms prevails in the economy. Lack of competition may allow monopoloid firms to maintain price levels and raise their profits when prices fall.[2] It is also possible for monopoloid firms to raise prices by more than an increase in costs, using higher costs as an excuse to raise their gains. In a competitive economy, however, prices should quickly follow any movement of costs up or down. Figure 7–2 shows an upward shift in the aggregate supply schedule as the result of an increase in costs of production. At each level of output the revenues necessary to sustain that output are increased. Figure 7–2A shows an upward shift in the aggregate supply schedule as production costs fall.

Production costs can rise for a variety of reasons. The most spectacular instance in recent years was the series of cost increases triggered by the increased price of oil imposed by OPEC in the 1970s. Energy costs rose throughout the world economy, forcing up prices as business firms passed the increases to their customers. Costs of production can be pushed up when the price of any input rises, and when the economy adjusts to the increased costs the prices at which goods are sold will be higher. Some other common causes of higher costs of production and increased prices are:

1. Increased taxes

2. Wage increases that exceed gains in productivity (output per labor hour)

3. Increased interest rates.

---

[2]Monopoloid firms, remember, are those that have some degree of control over the prices they charge, because the markets in which they sell are not perfectly competitive.

Figure 7-2A
The Aggregate
Supply Schedule
Shifts Downward
When Costs of
Production
Decline

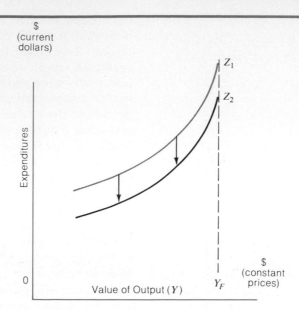

Costs of production can also be reduced, making a lower price level possible, when any of the same variables move in the opposite direction: reduced energy costs, lower taxes, lower interest rates, or increases in productivity that exceed increases in wages. Under those circumstances the aggregate supply schedule shifts downward and competition can bring a lower general level of prices.

Aggregate Demand

The aggregate supply schedule is half of the picture. Aggregate demand makes up the other half. Just as the aggregate supply schedule shows the expected proceeds needed to sustain any single level of output and employment, so an *aggregate demand* schedule will show, for each level of income, how much the various spending units in the economy can be expected to spend.

Those spending units are, of course, consumers and business firms. (We have temporarily excluded from the analysis both government and the net foreign balance.) So we know that the total of aggregate demand comprises expenditures for consumption and business investment, or $Y = C + I$. We turn first to the consumption part of aggregate demand.

● **Aggregate demand** is total spending, the amount businesses actually receive, in the simple income determination model.

The Propensity to Consume
There is a relatively stable relationship between disposable personal income and the level of consumer spending. At very low levels

of income, as in the early 1930s, consumers may temporarily spend more than they earn as they draw on past savings to tide them over the bad times, living off their fat, so to speak, until it is exhausted. At higher levels of income, positive amounts of savings begin to appear, as in the years since World War II, and consump-

tion spending appears as some fraction of disposable personal income.

The relationship between income and consumption is one of the most important building blocks to the theory of income determination. Called the *propensity to consume*, it is shown in Figure 7–3 and in Figure 7–4 with actual data.

Figure 7–3
The Propensity to Consume

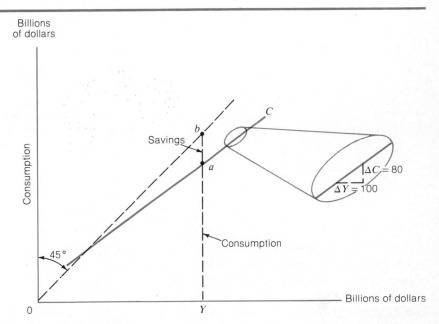

The propensity to consume schedule C shows the amount consumers will want to spend, measured vertically, out of any level of income, measured horizontally. For example, at income Y consumption will equal the height of the propensity to consume schedule at point a.

The dashed line drawn from the origin at an angle of 45° enables us to measure equal distances horizontally and vertically: $OY = Yb$. Since Yb measures total income and Ya is consumption, then ab must equal savings, from our earlier identity, $Y = C + S$.

The enlarged detail shows the slope of the propensity to consume schedule, which has been christened the *marginal propensity to consume* by economists. It measures the propensity to consume out of increases (or decreases) in income, and will be used in the following chapter in discussing dynamic aspects of income determination. The basic rule is that consumer spending rises as consumer incomes rise, but not so rapidly, or

$$\frac{\Delta C}{\Delta Y} < 1^1$$

This relationship is illustrated by assuming that, in the area of the diagram shown, consumers will spend about 80 percent of any increase in income, or

$$\frac{\Delta C}{\Delta Y} = \frac{80}{100} = .8$$

[1]The Greek letter Δ (delta) is used in algebraic notation to mean "change in."

Figure 7–4
The Propensity to Consume, Actual Data, 1939–1980

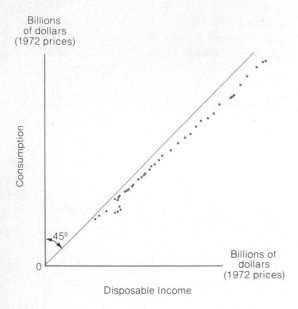

The *propensity to consume schedule* is sometimes called the consumption function in modern economic theory. It has been given that name because there is a systematic relationship between the value of total income and consumption expenditures at any and all levels of output. In algebraic terms,

$$C = f(Y)$$

This formulation summarizes the fact that consumption is systematically related to income. Figure 7–3 merely pictures that relationship for purposes of analysis, and the algebraic statement is a convenient way to conceptualize it.

- The **propensity to consume** is the proportion of income spent for consumption.

- The **propensity to consume schedule**, or **consumption function**, shows the systematic relationship between total income and consumption expenditures at all levels of income.

Underlying these geometric and algebraic formulations is a basic economic truth. The level of consumption spending depends on the amount of income received by consumers, which in turn depends on the level of economic activity through the economy as a whole. The path of cause and effect is primarily

Income → Consumption

That is, changes in the level of consumer spending are the result of changes in the level of income and economic activity. We seldom find changes in the level of income and employment *caused* by changes in consumer spending. It can occur, but when it does, the whole relationship between consumption and income will have shifted. In this case, the propensity to consume schedule in Figure 7–3 will shift its location upward or downward. By stating that $C = f(Y)$ we fix the location of the propensity to consume schedule in Figure 7–3 and postulate a specific direction for cause-and-effect relationships between Y and C.

A moment's reflection will indicate that this implication of the analysis is correct. The two great determinants of consumer spending are tastes and incomes. Although tastes may change, they influence primarily the allocation of spending rather than its amount. Consumers may decide to shift their purchases from whiskey to milk, or from automobiles to Caribbean cruises, for example, but the division between spending and saving tends to be quite stable. When incomes change, however, the level of spending will rise or fall in response. This is particularly true if consumers expect the change in incomes to be permanent or reasonably persistent. Temporary changes in incomes, like windfall gains or losses on securities markets, tend to influence consumer spending much less than changes in the regular flow of income. In other words, movements along the propensity to consume schedule generated by changes in incomes are much more frequent than shifts in the schedule itself caused by changes in the saving habits of consumers.

The Propensity to Save

A *propensity to save schedule* can be readily derived from the propensity to consume. It is the difference between consumption spending and disposable personal income, or, in our simplified analysis, between consumption and the value of output. In Figure 7–3, it is the vertical distance between the propensity to consume schedule *C* and the 45° line.

The *propensity to save* is shown graphically in Figure 7–5. It depicts the relationship between incomes and the amount consumers *do not* spend at each level of income. Net savings are measured vertically, and the value of output *Y* paid to the factors of production is shown on the horizontal axis. The propensity to save schedule is the mirror image of the propensity to consume schedule, with the 45° line as the horizontal axis. Point *b* corresponds exactly to the same point in Figure 7–3.

- The **propensity to save** is the proportion of income not spent for consumption.

- The **propensity to save schedule** shows the systematic relationship between total income and savings at each level of income.

The Level of Investment

Consumer spending is part of aggregate demand. Business investment makes up the rest in the model of a private, closed economy. In the case of business investment, however, there is no functional relationship between investment and total output. Investment spending rises and falls as the expectations of businessmen change. Optimism about increased sales and the structure of costs leads toward substantial business investment. Pessimism can be expected to have the opposite effect. And plans for investment can be modified on a moment's notice if business sentiment should change.

An illustration will make the point clear. Suppose total spending last year was $800 billion, and business investment $80 billion. Will those levels persist this year? Not necessarily. If last year's $800 billion was an increase over the year before of, say, $40 billion, *and the increase is expected to continue this year*, business firms may increase their investment to $100 billion or $110 billion this year. It all depends on how optimistic they are. However, if last year's spending of $800 billion was a decrease from the year before and much unused capacity exists, business firms may cut their investment spending drastically, even though total spending this year is maintained at levels close to $800 billion.

We cannot draw a propensity to invest schedule like that of the propensity to consume. We know, however, that at relatively low levels of total spending investment tends to be small, while at high levels of income it tends to be large. This relationship allows us to draw an investment schedule in which investment rises as the value of output increases. This is shown in Figure 7–6, where an investment schedule is added to the propensity to consume to show the aggregate demand schedule.

The Equilibrium Level of Income

We now have all the equipment needed for an analysis of the *equilibrium level of income*. Briefly stated, the value of output will move to that level at which aggregate demand is equal to aggregate supply. The sum of the amounts

Figure 7–5
The Propensity to Save

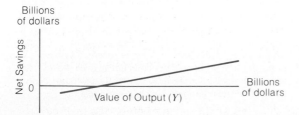

Figure 7-6
The Aggregate Demand Schedule

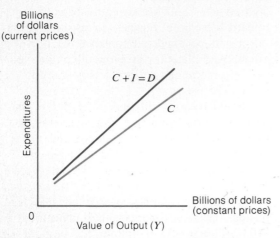

The aggregate demand schedule D is the sum of consumption and investment spending $C + I$ that would occur at each level of output Y, given the existing propensity to consume and the assumed schedule of investment. Note that the distance between C and $C + I$ widens as output increases. That is, I rises at higher levels of output. Investment is not independent of the level of economic activity; higher levels of investment are induced by higher levels of output and expenditure. If investment were autonomous (not affected by the level of output and expenditure), we would draw $C + I$ parallel to C.

consumers are willing to spend and businesses are willing to invest (aggregate demand) must be just equal to the amount required by business to continue the existing level of economic activity (aggregate supply).

If aggregate demand should be above the amount needed by business firms to maintain existing output, the additional demand will encourage business firms to expand production, and the level of economic activity will rise. Should aggregate demand fall below the level required to sustain the existing level of output, business revenues will not cover full costs (including a normal profit), output will be cut back, and economic activity will decline. Only when spending decisions just equal the amount necessary to validate production decisions, in the aggregate, will the level of economic activity remain constant.

- The **equilibrium level of income** is that level of income at which aggregate demand is equal to aggregate supply and desired saving is equal to desired investment.

These relationships are shown graphically in Figure 7–7. The equilibrium level of output in Figure 7–7 is Y_E, assuming the patterns of consumer spending and level of investment embodied in the aggregate demand schedule. At the level of output and expenditure shown in Figure 7–7, the amount consumers are willing to spend and business firms are willing to invest D is just equal to the revenues necessary to sustain that level of output Z. Any other level of output and expenditures will show an

Figure 7-7
The Equilibrium Level of Income

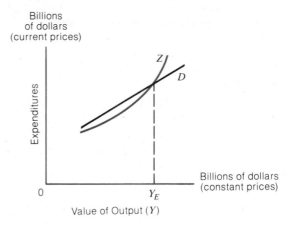

This diagram combines Figures 7-1 (the aggregate supply schedule) and Figure 7-6 (the aggregate demand schedule). The value of output Y on the horizontal axis is also the total income of the factors of production, measured in constant prices. The vertical axis measures total expenditures Y and also the income received by business firms, in current prices. Economic activity will move toward an equilibrium level Y_E at which aggregate demand D and aggregate supply Z are equal.

Figure 7–7A
Adjustment When *Y* Is Less Than Y_E

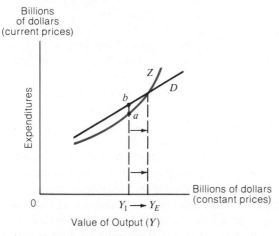

Billions
of dollars
(current prices)

Expenditures

Billions of dollars
(constant prices)

0    $Y_1 \longrightarrow Y_E$

Value of Output (*Y*)

At Y_1 aggregate demand *D* is greater than aggregate
supply *Z*. The excess aggregate demand will push the
level of output and income upward toward Y_E.

Figure 7–7B
Adjustment When *Y* Is Greater Than Y_E

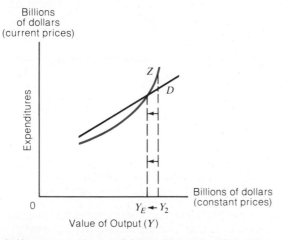

Billions
of dollars
(current prices)

Expenditures

Billions of dollars
(constant prices)

0    $Y_E \longleftarrow Y_2$

Value of Output (*Y*)

At Y_2 aggregate demand *D* is less than aggregate supply
Z, causing the level of output and income to decline
toward Y_E.

inequality between *D* and *Z*, and forces will be
set in motion to move to the equilibrium level.

For example, in Figure 7–7A the level of
output and expenditure, Y_1, is less than Y_E. In
that case aggregate demand is greater than
aggregate supply. Expenditures exceed the
value of current output by an amount equal to
ab. Business firms will find that their inventories are being drawn down below the desired
level—that is, actual investment is less than
desired investment—and they will take steps to
increase their output. The level of output and
expenditures will rise toward Y_E, at which
aggregate demand and aggregate supply are
equal.

In the opposite case, shown in Figure 7–7B,
the level of output and expenditure, Y_2, is
greater than Y_E. Aggregate demand is less than
aggregate supply, that is, firms are unable to
sell all they are willing to produce at Y_2.
Inventories start accumulating above the desired level and output is cut, moving the level
of output and expenditure down toward Y_E.

Only at level Y_E will total expenditures just
equal the value of output, providing no incentive for producers to change the level of production. It is toward this level of economic
activity that the economy gravitates.

The Equilibrium of Savings and Investment
The equilibrium level of income requires an
equilibrium between decisions to save and invest. We already know that savings and investment remain equal as the level of income rises
and falls. But equilibrium requires more than
that. For example, if business overestimates
the level of consumer spending and produces
more than can be sold, it will accumulate
unwanted investment in the form of inventories piling up on shelves. Decisions to reduce
output will follow and the level of economic
activity will fall. Yet throughout the process
savings and investment will equal each other.

A simple numerical example can make this

clear. Suppose that business expects a certain flow of spending to prevail during the coming year (first column), but in fact a different flow actually occurs (second column).

Business Expectations	Actual Results
$Y = 1,000$	$Y = 1,000$
$C = 900$	$C = 880$
$I = S = 100$	$I = S = 120$

In this situation business will find that it has invested $20 billion more than expected or planned. The investment came in the form of unwanted inventories of that amount, since the expectation was to sell $900 billion of consumers goods but in fact only $880 billion was sold. Even though saving and investment remained equal, and the level of investment offset the flow of savings, the situation is not stable. In an effort to eliminate the unwanted inventories, the business managers can be expected to reduce output. Incomes will decline and the level of economic activity will fall.

An equilibrium in the flow of spending requires not only that savings and investment be equal, but also that both savers and investors be satisfied with the amounts of saving and investment they are able to achieve. Two conditions must be satisfied, which in turn imply a third:

1. The savings actually made by consumers must equal the savings they desire to make at existing levels of income:

   Desired savings (S_D) = Realized savings (S_R)

2. The investment actually made by business must equal the investment they wish to make at existing levels of income:

   Desired investment (I_D) = Realized investment (I_R)

3. Since realized savings must always equal realized investment, it follows that an equilibrium level of economic activity requires that

Desired savings (S_D) = Desired investment (I_D)

In other words, economic activity will move toward the level at which desired and realized savings are equal, desired and realized investments are equal, and desired savings equals desired investment. Algebraically:

$$S_D = S_R = I_R = I_D$$

Figure 7–8 illustrates the adjustment process at work. At output level Y_2, the amount of savings withdrawn from the flow of spending is greater than the amount business managers are willing to invest. As long as output continues at that level, unwanted inventories will pile up unsold. This, of course, represents investment businesses do not want to make. Output will be cut back and the level of output will fall toward Y_E. The decline in output will continue as long as savings are greater than desired investment and unwanted inventories are thereby increased. Only at Y_E will this disparity be eliminated and the decline in output halted.

Conversely, at output level Y_1 the economy's savings are below the level of investment desired by business. If the desired level of invest-

Figure 7–8
The Equilibrium of Savings and Investment

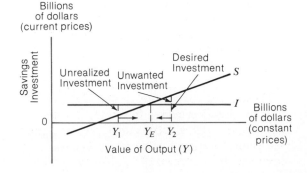

ment in plant and equipment is achieved, then, inventories must shrink below the desired level. If inventories are maintained, there will not be enough resources to sustain the desired expansion of plant and equipment. In either case, output will rise as business firms seek to achieve their investment goals. The level of output will rise toward Y_E and will continue to do so until the disparity between realized and desired investment is eliminated.

The Heart of the Theory

At this point, we can recapitulate the central ideas of the theory of income determination. Using the theoretical framework of a purely private, closed economy, three propositions have emerged:

1. The level of economic activity is determined by the amount of total spending, or aggregate demand:

$$Y = C + I$$

2. The *equilibrium* level of economic activity is the level at which the amount business firms receive from the sale of their output is just equal to the costs of producing it, including a normal profit. This condition prevails when aggregate demand equals aggregate supply:

$$D = Z$$

3. Aggregate demand will equal aggregate supply when the savings consumers wish to make equal the investment expenditures desired by businesses:

$$S_D = I_D$$

These three propositions embody in summary form the elementary theory of income determination. They tell us that four variables determine the level of economic activity and employment: the level of total spending, busi-

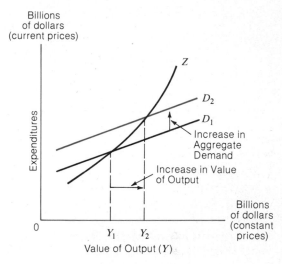

Figure 7–9
Effect of an Increase in Aggregate Demand

As aggregate demand rises from D_1 to D_2 the value of output increases from Y_1 to Y_2.

ness costs of production, the propensity to save and spend, and business investment decisions. Changes in any one of the four will bring changes in the level of economic activity as the economy adjusts to the new conditions. The process of adjustment will continue until a new equilibrium position is reached, at which aggregate demand and aggregate supply are once more equal and desired investment equals desired savings.

We can readily determine the direction of change by postulating a shift in any one of the four schedules involved, assuming no change in the other three. For example, if aggregate demand should increase for any reason, the level of economic activity will rise, as shown in Figure 7–9. Or if investment spending declines, economic activity will fall, as shown in Figure 7–10. Readers can work out other variations by postulating either an increase or a decrease in either of the other two variables that influence economic activity and employment.

Figure 7-10
Effect of a Decline in Investment Spending

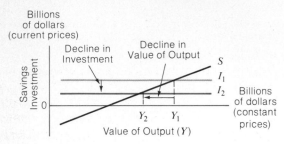

As investment spending falls from I_1 to I_2 the value of output declines from Y_1 to Y_2.

Some Implications of the Theory

The most important single conclusion to be drawn from the simple theory of income determination is that a private economy requires a guiding hand. Will the equilibrium level of income settle at full employment; or at a substantially lower level, bringing unemployment and unused plant capacity; or at levels above full employment, bringing inflation? The answer given by the theory is simple: There is no way to tell. The equilibrium level could fall anywhere and stay there indefinitely, depending on what happens to the four variables that determine it. A level consistent with full employment is only one of many possible levels, and would be achieved in a purely private economy only by chance. Even if full employment were achieved, there is no assurance that it could be maintained. Changes in any one of the four variables could set in motion a chain of events leading to a new equilibrium at either inflationary or depressed levels. Business investment is particularly volatile and cannot be expected to remain at the level required for a full employment equilibrium.

A second conclusion is that the instability of a private economy is inherently difficult to predict. It is hard to tell in advance just what the reaction of consumers, business managers, and borrowers, and lenders is likely to be when changes occur in the economic environment. This lack of predictability makes difficult any kind of policy designed to counter the pattern of instability. Nevertheless, optimism reigns and one of the roles of science in the modern world is to bring intractable natural forces under control. Even if the nature of the economic beast is unpredictable instability, efforts can be made to ameliorate the problems created by its behavior. Those efforts have led in three directions:

1. Development of "automatic stabilizers" designed to reduce the instability of the economy. These measures will be described in Chapter 9 as part of the discussion of government policies and the national income.

2. Use of the government sector of the economy to counterbalance the instability of the private sector. Several instruments of policy are available: taxation and spending (fiscal policy), and management of the monetary sector (monetary policy). These matters will be given considerable attention in the next half-dozen chapters.

3. Forecasting to determine what the economy is likely to do in the near future. Effective forecasting is essential for success in applying economic policies.

There is a still broader and more fundamental implication of the theory of income determination. A private economy will not manage itself, at least with respect to the level of economic activity. The lack of a built-in guidance mechanism that could bring about and sustain economic stability reasonably close to full employment makes government intervention almost inevitable. Whatever may be the merits of a philosophy of laissez-faire, one hard fact remains: a democratic society will hardly tolerate the wastes of an unmanaged economy when its theorists can both explain why the waste occurs and devise ameliorative policies.

Summary

In the simplified theory of income determination, we start with a closed private economy with stable prices, eliminating from consideration the monetary system, the government sector, and the effect of the international economy. In this simple model, savings must equal investment. But since saving and investment are undertaken by different economic units for different reasons, there is no reason to believe that the amount consumers wish to save at full-employment levels of national income will be just matched by the amount of investment business managers wish to make. If desired saving at full employment is greater than desired investment, total spending will fall. The decline in total spending will bring smaller incomes to households and their savings will fall. This process will continue until savings have fallen to the level at which they are equal to desired investment.

Income determination can also be thought of as an equality of aggregate demand with aggregate supply. If total spending is not large enough to compensate business units for the amount they have expended on production, unwanted inventories will accumulate and economic activity will decline. Just the opposite effects will be felt if aggregate demand should push above aggregate supply. Desired investment levels will not be achieved and business firms will expand their production in order to reach them.

Key Concepts

savings	**desired savings**	**aggregate supply**	**propensity to save**
investment	**desired investment**	**aggregate demand**	**propensity to save schedule**
gross investment	**realized savings**	**propensity to consume**	**equilibrium level of income**
net investment	**realized investment**	**propensity to consume schedule**	

For Discussion

1. Explain the role of changes in business inventories in the process by which an equilibrium in the level of income and output is achieved.

2. Explain the paradox that $S = I$ at all times in a private, closed economy, but equilibrium is achieved only when $S_D = I_D$.

3. An increase in the propensity to save can result in a reduction in actual savings. Explain.

4. Show the position of the aggregate demand and aggregate supply curves in a major depression like that of the 1930s. In the absence of government action, what forces, if any, would be likely to move an economy out of that position?

5. Does the modern economy normally tend to produce a full-employment level of national income? Why or why not?

6. Keynes thought that the modern economy normally tended toward a level of economic activity at which there was a substantial amount of unemployment. Do you agree? Explain.

Chapter 8

The Dynamics of Income Determination

Two different kinds of changes can occur in the level of the national product. One is an adjustment toward equilibrium, based on the existing schedules of consumption and investment. The other is a shift in one or both of those schedules. This chapter will analyze the second type of change.

First we show that when the aggregate demand schedule shifts, the level of national product will change by an amount greater than the shift in aggregate demand. This is known as the *multiplier principle*. Second, we show how to calculate the *multiplier*, which relates the size of the change in the national product to the amount of the shift in aggregate demand. Third, we shall discuss the tendency for a change in aggregate demand to set up a cumulative movement in the direction established by the original change, through induced investment. We shall emphasize the case in which a change in demand sets in motion accelerated changes in investment spending (the *acceleration principle*). These three concepts, the multiplier, induced investment, and the acceleration principle, explain why substantial swings in the level of national product are as pervasive as the tendency toward equilibrium.

The Multiplied Effect of Increased Spending

- The **multiplier principle** is the starting point for an analysis of the dynamics of income determination. It can be stated simply: any change in the aggregate demand schedule will result in a change in the value of output greater than the initial shift in aggregate demand.

The principle is illustrated in Figure 8–1. The reason for the larger increase in the value of output is to be found in the operation of the circular flow of spending. An initial increase in aggregate demand, coming perhaps from an increase in investment spending, will bring added incomes to the initial group of business firms that sell the goods. They, in turn, pay out incomes to workers and owners of other factors of production to produce the goods or replace inventories. The consumers who receive this income will then spend a part of it and save some. The amount they spend will become a second round of spending that results in added income for a second group of business firms. This, in turn, leads to a third round of spending, somewhat smaller than the second but

Figure 8-1
The Multiplier

An increase in aggregate demand from D_1 to D_2 (equal to AB on the vertical axis) will move the value of output from Y_1 to Y_2 (equal to AC on the vertical axis). The increase in the value of output is about double the increase in aggregate demand in this illustration of the principle.

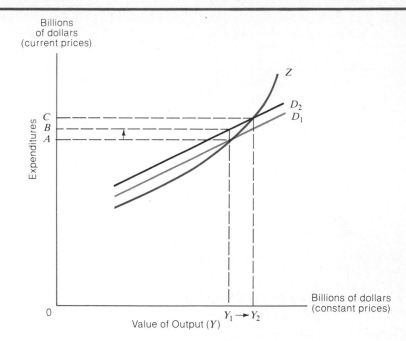

Billions of dollars (current prices)

Expenditures

0

Value of Output (Y)

$Y_1 \rightarrow Y_2$

Billions of dollars (constant prices)

nevertheless a further increase in the total. Additional income and output are generated at each round.

Each round of spending is less than the previous one because some income leaks out into savings each time. Income and output keep rising by smaller amounts each round, until at some point the increase is so small it has no noticeable effect on the total. Technically, the tiny increments of the last rounds of respending will continue until all of the original increase in aggregate demand has shifted into savings and there is no more left to continue around the economy. At that point the increase in output will stop.

A Numerical Example

Assume an increase in new investment, over and above the existing level, of $1 billion. Assume also that consumers will respend half of any increase in income they receive, and that consumer savings are the only "leakage"

out of the flow of spending.[1] Figure 8–2 illustrates what happens.

As the rounds of spending continue, the increase at each round becomes smaller, but continues adding to the total. In this example, the upper limit toward which total spending moves is $2,000,000. At that point the leakage into savings will equal $1,000,000, and the amount of the original increase in spending will have gone into savings, so that there will no longer be any impulse for further expansion. But that is only what the analysis of national income equilibrium in the last chapter would lead us to expect: the value of output will move to a level at which desired savings and desired investment are equal. The important point in

---

[1]In the real world there are other important leakages. Business firms save, too, but we can lump these savings with those of consumers for the sake of convenience. Other leakages flow into governments: taxes, social security, and other deductions, etc. An open economy with foreign trade will have further leakages from the flow of spending. In our example the leakages due to government and foreign trade are excluded, because at this stage we are sticking with our simplified private, closed economy.

Figure 8-2
A Numerical Example of the Multiplier Principle

	New Spending	New Saving
The original increase in investment causes an increase in output and income of . . .	$1,000,000	
The consumers who receive this income spend half . . .	500,000	
. . . and save half.		$500,000
Out of this second round of spending, half is spent by those who receive it . . .	250,000	
. . . and half is saved.		250,000
A fourth round of spending increases output and incomes by half the amount of the third . . .	125,000	
. . . and savings by the same amount.		125,000
At this stage, after four rounds of spending and respending, the total increase in output and incomes is already . . .	$1,875,000	
And the leakage into savings totals . . .		$875,000
The process will continue until these totals are reached . . .	$2,000,000	$1,000,000

this example, however, is that the increase in total output and incomes was a multiple of the original change in the level of investment. In this case the multiple was 2. Of the total increase in aggregate demand ($2,000,000), half was the original increase in investment ($1,000,000) and half was the result of repeated rounds of respending ($1,000,000).

The Multiplier

● The **multiplier** is the factor that relates any change in aggregate demand to the resulting change in the value of output.

In the last example, the multiplier was 2: an increase of $1,000,000 in aggregate demand led ultimately to an increase of $2,000,000 in the value of output. The general relationship can be written as follows:

$$\Delta Y = k(\Delta D)$$

where

Y = value of output
D = aggregate demand
k = the multiplier

If the multiplier were 3, for example, and aggregate demand increased initially by $2 billion, the value of output would rise by $6 billion. The multiplier also works in the other direction: if aggregate demand were to *fall* by $2 billion, and the multiplier were 3, the value of output would fall by $6 billion.

The change in aggregate demand can come from several sources. It may result from a change in investment spending stimulated by a shift in business expectations. It may come from a shift upward or downward in the propensity to consume schedule, resulting from a change in consumer preferences between spending and saving. In the real world, in contrast to our hypothetical example, aggregate demand can be changed by governments. Any change in government spending will change the level of aggregate demand, while changes in tax schedules can shift consumer spending and business investment patterns. But whatever the source, the original change will have a multiplied effect on the economy as a whole.

The Size of the Multiplier

The size of the multiplier depends on the amount of leakages out of the flow of spending. The smaller the leakages, the larger the amount respent and the larger the multiplier. The larger the leakages, the smaller the amount respent and the smaller the multiplier.

The proportion respent out of increases in income is called the *marginal propensity to consume*. For example, suppose consumers receive an increase in income of $3 billion and spend $2 billion of it. The marginal propensity to consume will equal $\frac{2}{3}$. Therefore,

$$MPC = \frac{\Delta C}{\Delta Y}$$

where

MPC = marginal propensity to consume
C = consumption
Y = value of output (total income)

Now go back to our numerical example of the multiplied effect of a change in aggregate demand, in which consumers spent just half of the increase in income they received. What was the marginal propensity to consume in that example?[2]

● The **marginal propensity to consume** is the proportion of an addition to income that is spent on consumption.

In graphic terms, the marginal propensity to consume is the *slope* of the propensity to consume schedule. It tells us how steeply the propensity to consume schedule rises as incomes increase. Figure 8–3 illustrates this relationship.

The marginal propensity to consume determines the size of the multiplier. It determines the amount spent at each round of respending, in an endless but diminishing progression that approaches a limit. The algebra of such infinite geometric progressions gives us the following formula for the multiplier:

$$k = \frac{1}{1 - MPC}$$

Where the marginal propensity to consume is $\frac{1}{2}$, the multiplier will be 2:

$$k = \frac{1}{1 - \frac{1}{2}} = \frac{1}{\frac{1}{2}} = 2$$

Where the marginal propensity to consume is $\frac{2}{3}$, the multiplier will be 3:

$$k = \frac{1}{1 - \frac{2}{3}} = \frac{1}{\frac{1}{3}} = 3$$

The logic of these figures is simple. It rests on the amounts respent at each round of spending. When the $MPC = \frac{1}{2}$ (and $k = 2$), half of all additional income is saved and only half is respent. On the other hand, when the MPC is $\frac{2}{3}$ (and $k = 3$), only one-third of additional income is saved and two-thirds is respent.

---

[2]You're right! 1/2 or 0.5. Figure it out like this:

$$MPC = \frac{\Delta C}{\Delta Y} = \frac{500,000}{1,000,000} = \frac{1}{2}.$$

Figure 8–3
The Marginal
Propensity to Consume

The marginal propensity to
consume is the proportion of
additional income that is
spent on consumption. In this
case the propensity to
consume schedule is drawn
so that consumption rises by
$500,000 for each $1,000,000
increase in income. The
marginal propensity to
consume is ½:

$$MPC = \frac{\Delta C}{\Delta Y} = \frac{500,000}{1,000,000} = \frac{1}{2}$$

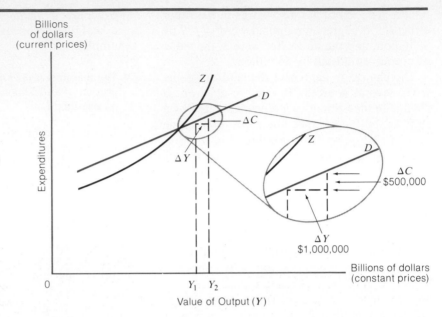

Clearly, in the latter case the multiplied effect on total spending will be larger.

The Multiplier Over Time
Although the size of the multiplier can be readily estimated from the marginal propensity to consume, it is well to remember that the multiplier is part of an economic process that gradually unfolds over a period of time. A change in aggregate demand is felt quickly, but the full effect is spread out over a considerable interval.

Under normal conditions, it takes about three months for an increase in income to be respent. An income generation period, as economists call it, of that length means that there will be four rounds of spending in one year. That number of rounds is enough to include about 80–90 percent of the multiplied effect of an increase in aggregate demand, when the full multiplier lies between 2 and 3. The bulk of the effect is felt within twelve months.

In actual practice the multiplier is usually found within a range of 2 and 2.5 over a year's time. A change in the aggregate demand

schedule will bring about a change in GNP some 2 to 2.5 times as large, in about twelve months. This is a very convenient figure to remember in estimating the probable effects of policies that influence the level of aggregate demand. The chain of respending does not suddenly stop after twelve months, but continues onward in continually decreasing amounts that are usually too small to make much difference when policy decisions are at issue. In this book we shall generally assume a twelve-month multiplier of 2, as an approximation close enough for ordinary use.

If the income generation period should speed up, the multiplied effect of a change in aggregate demand would be felt more quickly. And if the period should lengthen, the multiplier process would work more slowly.

The time pattern of the multiplier is important for another reason. The effect of an initial increase in aggregate demand quickly diminishes, because each round of respending is smaller than the previous one. This will cause the value of output to fall back to its original level unless the original increase in aggregate demand either:

Figure 8–4
The Multiplier: Impact
of a Single Increment
in Aggregate Demand

Assume a single new investment expenditure of
$1,000,000 and an *MPC* of
½. By the end of four income
generation periods the value
of output has fallen back
almost to its original level.

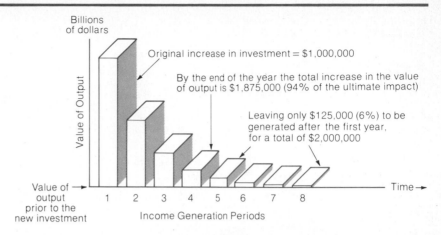

Billions
of dollars

Value of Output

Original increase in investment = $1,000,000

By the end of the year the total increase in the value
of output is $1,875,000 (94% of the ultimate impact)

Leaving only $125,000 (6%) to be
generated after the first year,
for a total of $2,000,000

Value of
output
prior to the
new investment

1   2   3   4   5   6   7   8

Income Generation Periods

Time →

1. Is sustained at the new level.

2. Induces other changes that will provide a comparable increase in aggregate demand.

The diminishing effect of the multiplier is shown in Figure 8–4. It pictures the effect of a single and noncontinuing increase in aggregate demand: A large impact is soon felt, but the value of output quickly falls back to its original level once the effect of the original change wears off.

The value of output will move to a new and higher level, and stay there, only if the change in aggregate demand is continuously sustained through each income generation period. This pattern is shown in Figure 8–5, where the same assumptions are made as in Figure 8–4 except that the new investment spending is repeated in each income generation period. In this case, the value of output rises to approach a limit of $2,000,000 above the starting level.

The Importance of the Multiplier
The multiplier is one of the most important concepts in the theory of the national income. If offers a means of quantifying the impact of changes in aggregate demand and any of its component parts. For example, surveys of business plans may show that next year businesses expect to increase their investment

spending above this year's level by some $5 billion. With a twelve-month multiplier of 2, this change would bring a $10 million rise in the value of output in the coming year. Policy makers in both business and government can use this information to analyze the effects of the change, forecast its impact on other sectors of the economy, and take steps to adapt to the new conditions that will prevail. Both private and public planning will be facilitated.

There is a second way in which the multiplier is important. Since the effect of any change is magnified, it is possible to achieve large results from relatively small beginnings. For example, suppose the economy is currently operating well below its full-employment potential by some $20 billion, and the federal government wants to increase aggregate demand so as to move the GNP upward by that amount. Additional spending will have to be generated by government directly or by stimulating consumer spending or business investment. Whatever the path taken, the amount of new spending required to push the GNP upward by $20 billion is only half that amount when the twelve-month multiplier is 2. The multiplier is a key concept in both economic forecasting and economic policy making, at least for relatively short time horizons. For longer periods its usefulness is limited, because of the uncertainties of induced investments.

Figure 8-5
The Multiplier: Impact of a Continuing Increment in Aggregate Demand

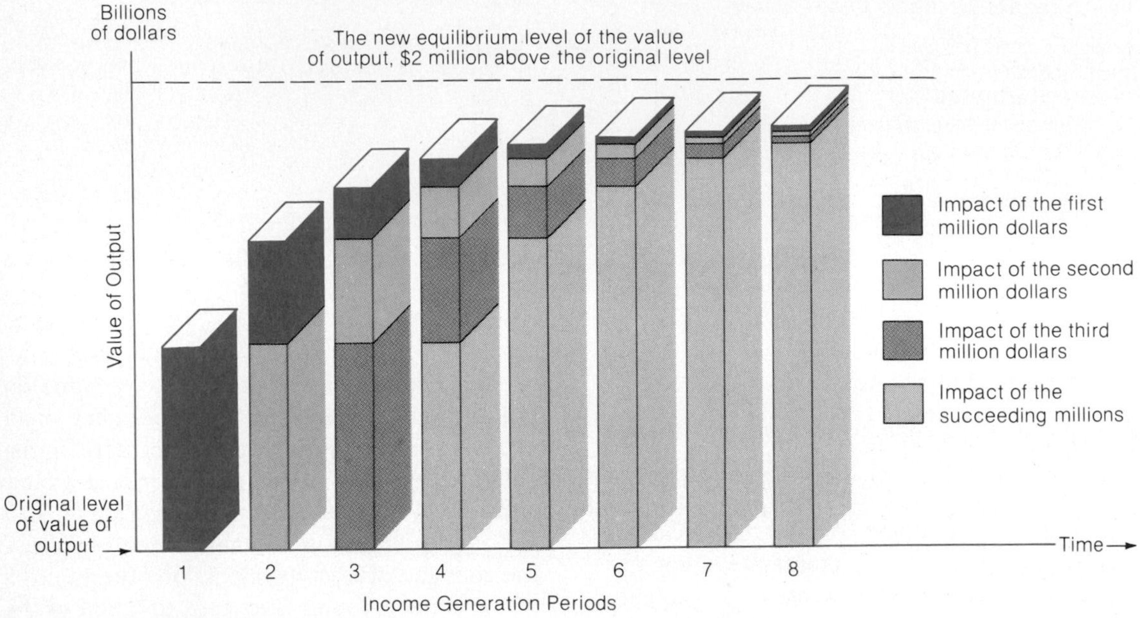

Assume a new investment of $1 million in each income generation period and an *MPC* of ½. In this case the value of output rises to a new level $2 million above the original level and stays there as long as the higher level of investment is maintained.

Induced Investment

Reflect for a moment on the larger meaning of the multiplier: any change in the flow of spending is magnified. In the modern economy, where all the parts are interrelated, this enlarged effect of an original change *must* have an impact on other events, on other parts of the economic system. A change in aggregate demand, therefore, cannot be understood as an isolated event. It is inconceivable that the effects of a single increase in investment, for example, should peter out over a few income generation periods to leave the level of output just as it was before. The very fact that an increase in income has been temporarily generated will induce other changes, for it will have changed the economic environment.

We should expect any change to have cumu-lative effects. A shift upward in the aggregate demand schedule, even a temporary one, will increase incomes and spending. In the process, business firms will be induced to add to their inventories or expand their production capacity. Secondary effects will be felt that will add further to an upward swing in economic activity. This *induced investment* will, in turn, have a multiplied impact on the level of economic activity, continuing still further the process of cumulative change.

- **Induced investment** is new investment stimulated by an initial increase in aggregate demand.

It would be tempting to argue that such a continuing economic expansion, once started, would continue until the economy reached full employment, at which point it would level off.

This, indeed, was the idea behind the "pump-priming" theory of the 1930s. It was hoped that a relatively small increase in government spending would raise incomes and stimulate greater consumer spending, which in turn would induce additional business investment, and so on, until prosperity was restored. And the higher levels of economic activity were expected to generate additional tax revenues.

Unfortunately, the cumulative expansion to full employment prosperity is not always certain. No one knows in advance whether it will or will not occur, since so much depends on business expectations and the climate of opinion in the business community. At some times, such as during most of the years since World War II, the process of cumulative expansion has operated to keep the economy at or close to full-employment prosperity most of the time, although government policies have been very important in providing the proper stimulus. At other times, such as during the Great Depression of the 1930s, a number of advances proved to be abortive, failing to generate the induced investment that would lead to a cumulative expansion toward full employment. Perhaps the pessimism of that era, coupled with the serious economic dislocations of the depression, was so great that a complete change in the economic environment was necessary. Perhaps the stimulus provided by government efforts to prime the pump just was not large enough. Whatever the reason, World War II brought great changes in both of these areas. Government spending increased vastly, and a huge new market for war industries suddenly appeared. There was no question, at that time, about a cumulative movement toward high levels of economic activity. Since business managers knew that huge new amounts of purchasing power were going to be pumped into the economy they increased their own investment spending, and the wartime boom was on. Increased government spending associated with the wars in Korea and Vietnam generated similar effects.

There is, then, a relationship between increases in aggregate demand and the investment component of aggregate demand. An autonomous increase in aggregate demand (that is, independent of the existing flow of spending and level of output) can induce additional investment, to set in motion a cumulative expansion of the economy. Just how much additional investment will be induced and how long the cumulative advance will last is uncertain, however.

All that we have said about cumulative expansion of economic activity is equally true of contractions. An initial decline in aggregate demand will reduce incomes and purchasing power by a multiplied amount. This reduction will not occur in isolation but will spread in an economy of closely interrelated parts. It can easily cause expectations of further decline and stimulate cutbacks in business investment. A self-reinforcing decline in economic activity will have started.

The Acceleration Principle

One aspect of induced investment is particularly important. Called the *acceleration principle*, it embodies two relationships between demand and investment spending.

○ An increase in demand can cause a proportionately much larger, accelerated increase in investment spending. For example, a 10 percent increase in demand may trigger perhaps a 100 percent increase in investment spending as business firms increase their production capacity to meet the increased demand.

○ When an increase in aggregate demand slows its upward pace and begins to level off, a decline in investment spending can occur even if aggregate demand continues to grow.

These two relationships, shown in Figure 8–6, can set in motion a whole series of chain reactions. The accelerated investment induced by an increase in demand will have a multiplied effect on total spending, contributing to a

Figure 8-6
The Acceleration
Principle

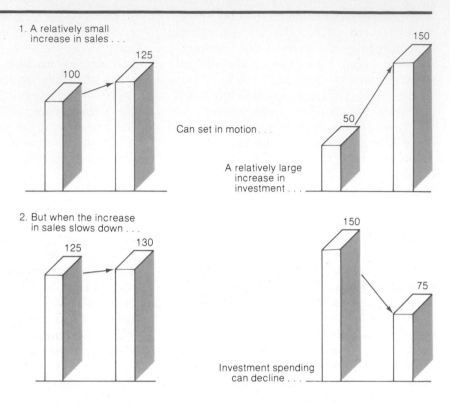

1. A relatively small increase in sales . . .

100 → 125

Can set in motion . . .

A relatively large increase in investment . . .

50 → 150

2. But when the increase in sales slows down . . .

125 → 130

Investment spending can decline . . .

150 → 75

cumulative upswing in economic activity. Yet as economic expansion begins to slow down as the economy begins to reach a peak, the second effect can show up: as aggregate demand starts to level off, even though it is still growing, investment spending can start to decline. The multiplied effect of an investment drop can then start to pull economic activity downward.

A feedback mechanism in the economic system is at work here. A change in aggregate demand induces changes in investment decisions, which in turn have a multiplied effect on aggregate demand. A cumulative upswing can result. As the upswing loses momentum the conditions which end an expansion and create a downturn can appear. Whenever the level of investment spending is tied closely to the level of consumer demand, as in the case of invento-

ries and some other types of investment, these feedbacks can create economic fluctuations.

- The **acceleration principle** states that the amount of certain types of investment is related to the rate of change in demand for the final product.

An Example of the Acceleration Principle

Let us assume, to start with, a business firm that owns ten machines, each of which can turn out 100 units of product each time period. One machine must be replaced each time period, and will last for 10 periods before it must be replaced (see Table 8-1).

1. The firm starts out with sales of 1,000 units in the first time period, requiring full use of its 10 machines and purchase of one new machine to replace one old one.

2. In the second period, there is a 100-unit

Table 8–1
The Acceleration Principle: An Example

Period	Sales	No. of Machines Needed	No. of Machines Purchased		
			Replacement	New	Total
1	1,000	10	1	0	1
2	1,100	11	1	1	2
3	1,300	13	1	2	3
4	1,500	15	1	2	3
5	1,600	16	1	1	2
6	1,500	15	0	0	0

increase in sales, which requires adding another machine to the plant in addition to replacing an old one. This addition increases investment spending by 100 percent to accommodate a 10 percent increase in sales.

3. Now let us postulate an even faster increase in sales, from 100 units to 200 units in the third time period. This will illustrate the proposition that in this situation growth in investment spending requires an increase in the rate of growth in final demand. Two new machines must be added, and total machines purchased rises from two in the previous period to three in this period.

4. Just to clinch the point, suppose sales rise in the fourth period by the same amount as in the third. In this case, there is no increase in investment even though final demand continues to rise.

5. Now what happens when demand for the product continues to rise, but not so fast as before? Let us assume for Period 5 an increase in sales of 100 units. In this case the amount of investment decreases even though output rises.

6. Finally, examine the results of a decline in demand for the final product, when sales fall by 100 units in the next period, back to the level of Period 4. Even though sales are 50 percent above those of the initial period, new investment falls to nothing. This happens because the decline in sales makes it unnecessary even to replace the machine that wears out.

This example of the acceleration principle is shown graphically in Figure 8–7. At their peak, sales were only 60 percent greater than the initial period. Yet the peak in investment was three times the level of the initial period. Furthermore, the investment peak came before sales topped out, and investment had already started downward while sales were still rising.

The Principle Restated
The acceleration principle is based on the relationship between the *level* of investment and the *rate of growth* in final demand. Whenever investment spending is derived directly and closely from the demand for final products:

○ Investment rises when the rate of growth of sales is rising.

○ Investment is constant when the rate of growth of sales is constant.

○ Investment falls when the rate of growth of sales is falling.

To this should be added the concept of acceleration: a change in the level of final sales is reflected in a proportionately much larger change in the level of investment spending.

Some Qualifications
The acceleration principle is easier to illustrate

Figure 8-7
The Acceleration
Principle

Sales kept rising through period 5, but investment spending reached its peak in periods 3 to 4 and was already falling in period 5. By period 6 investment spending was down to zero even though sales were 50 percent more than in period 1.

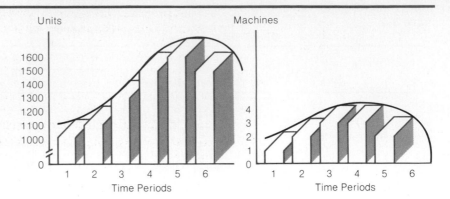

in a hypothetical example than in the real world. Few business firms maintain a fixed relationship between sales and investment spending. Long-range planning of capital expenditures in most large firms is seldom based on short run swings in sales. Nevertheless, some types of investment depend to a substantial degree on sales, including much inventory accumulation and a significant amount of investment by railroads and public utilities.

A more important qualification is that the principle does not apply when there is a significant amount of excess capacity. In those circumstances, a large increase in sales may have little impact on investment as old equipment is brought back into use before new investment is made.

The principle must also be modified by the way in which expectations influence decisions. Business executives don't wait until they have reached capacity operations before they start adding to their production capabilities. They anticipate needs and plan for them in advance whenever they can.

As a result of these three factors, the swings in investment spending that might be expected to result from the operation of the acceleration principle tend to be smoothed out.

Significance of the Acceleration Principle
In spite of these qualifications, the acceleration

principle is important. It doesn't apply to all investment spending, but where it does apply, it creates significant economic problems.

1. Investment spending will fluctuate more widely than demand for final products.

2. Investment spending can start to decline while sales are still rising.

These two phenomena help to explain why a private-enterprise economy is inherently unstable. When an industry is at or near capacity levels of production, a continued rise in aggregate demand will bring about an accelerated increase in investment spending. Even before capacity output levels are reached, the anticipation of that condition can set the principle in motion. The enlarged investment spending then feeds back to the economy a further increase in aggregate demand.

Once a rise in aggregate demand begins to slacken off, however, the operation of the acceleration principle can cause investment spending to decline. The feedback effect of this decline in investment will slow the growth of aggregate demand still further and can set the stage for a general downturn in business activity. Timing of these effects, however, is uncertain. When expectations enter the picture, the downturn in investment spending can come even sooner. If time is required to make investment decisions effective, or to change them, the decline in investment spending may lag behind the original changes in aggregate demand.[3] But whatever the case, an unstable economy is the result.

The Acceleration Principle and Economic Growth

The acceleration principle is also important in the process of economic growth. Almost any important industry illustrates the principle at work. Take railroads as an example. The American railway system was built, for the most part, between 1850 and 1914. Investment in rail lines, bridges and stations, and rolling stock was considerably greater in the 50 years before 1914 than in the 50 years after. In the earlier years investment was for expansion as well as replacement, while in the later years there was little expansion. Investment in railroads after 1914 was limited primarily to replacement (and to new types of equipment resulting from technological change). As a result, before 1914 the expansion of railroads and the investment spending that went along with it was a major stimulant to American economic growth. After 1914, economic growth came from other sources.

The automobile industry showed a similar pattern, but with two important differences. Once the productive capacity of the industry had been built up by the late 1920s, investment in expanded facilities was sharply curtailed, until demand for cars started moving up once more in the years after World War II. Investment by automobile companies for purposes of expansion slowed considerably after the late twenties. But investment of another sort appeared, in jigs, dies, and tools needed for the annual model changes. The built-in obso-lescence of annual models helped to sustain investment spending. So did technological change, which brought larger and faster cars. The roads built in the 1920s and 1930s had to be replaced by the expressways of the 1950s and 1960s. A burst of public investment spending was required because of improved automobiles, which would have been necessary even if total sales of cars and trucks had not risen.

The long run relationship between investment and aggregate demand may well be the most important aspect of the acceleration principle. Roughly speaking, *stability of investment spending requires continual expansion in the rest of the economy*. If expansion slows down in the rest of the economy, a decline can be expected in investment spending. Such a decline will, in turn, serve to reduce expansion in the rest of the economy and contribute to a general economic stagnation.

This relationship is, of course, not exact and precise. Technological change can promote investment. So can changes in consumer tastes. And business expectations will influence the level of investment spending. In addition, a growing economy will require larger replacement of capital equipment from year to year. These factors may offset or modify the long run effects of the acceleration principle. Underneath it all, however, stands the fundamental relationship embodied in the feedback mechanisms of the acceleration principle: a sustained level of investment spending requires a sustained rate of growth in the economy as a whole.

Expectations

Some of the economic mechanisms that relate changes in investment spending to the level of aggregate demand and vice versa are now apparent. The multiplier shows how an increase in investment spending (or any other type of spending) will push total spending up by more than the original increase. Induced

---

[3]Most empirical studies of the acceleration principle show that it is felt with a time lag, usually three to six months, rather than instantaneously.

investment introduces a feedback mechanism through which an increase in total spending promotes further increases in investment, and the acceleration principle shows how the induced investment can ultimately lead to a downturn. Expectations and anticipations are important throughout these relationships. For example, no one can tell *how much* new investment will be induced by a specific increase in total spending, even though we know that under such circumstances there would be a *tendency* for investment spending to increase.

Expectations and Investment

Forward planning in business reduces expectations to actual quantities of projected sales and revenues, and from them derives production, personnel, and financial plans. In the process, investment decisions emerge from the comparison of expected rates of return on capital investment with the rate of interest that the company would have to pay on borrowed capital.

A hypothetical example will show how these factors influence a firm's decision. An electronics manufacturing firm contemplating construction of a new plant to manufacture transistor radios must decide on the size of the plant it wishes to build. The management can borrow the capital at an interest rate of 6 percent, and has no control over this cost of capital.[4] Putting its analysts to work, it develops the projections listed in Table 8–2. Pretend that you are a member of the board of directors responsible for making the investment decision and that profit maximization is the major criterion applicable in this case. You would also like the firm to obtain as large a share of the market as it can get without compromising the profit

maximization goal. How much should the firm invest in its new plant?

The investment decision emerges almost intuitively. Profits will be maximized with an investment of either $6,000,000 or $7,000,000. An operation of the larger size is slightly preferable, however, since it will provide for higher output and a larger share of the market. This solution has a very special characteristic: the increase in expected returns due to raising the capital investment from $6,000,000 to $7,000,000 is $60,000 (see Column 4), which is exactly equal to the cost of borrowing the additional $1,000,000. A general rule is involved here:

○ A profit-maximizing firm will increase its investment up to the point at which the expected rate of return on additional new investment is just equal to the rate of interest.

The principle is illustrated in Figure 8–8. Only one of these two factors is an objective, measurable one. The rate of interest is determined in the money markets and any firm can determine its investment costs quite accurately. The expected rate of return on new investment, however, is the result of the planning process itself. It is an expectation, and may or may not materialize. Like all expectations, it is intangible and ephemeral. It may be based on projections of recent costs and sales, and on highly sophisticated forecasts of the future. But recent trends need not necessarily continue and forecasts are often wrong. As new information is received, the forecasts will be revised and the expectations based on them will change. As a result, the decision to invest may be changed or scaled downward or upward, or its timing changed.

In other words, the schedule of the expected rate of return on additional new investment (called the marginal efficiency of investment) can shift upward or downward, leading to changes in the level of investment. That, in turn, will bring multiplied changes in the level

---

[4]Even if the firm made the investment out of retained earnings and paid no interest charge on the capital, the cost would be the same. Presumably, the firm would be able to lend the money to someone else at the market rate of interest and earn the interest charge on the loan. The cost of using the capital in its own business is the amount the firm would have to give up by not lending the money to someone else.

Table 8-2
Electronics Manufacturing Co. Proposed Transistor Radio Division

(1) Additional Capital Investment (Millions of Dollars)	(2) Cost of Capital (6%)	(3) Expected Average Annual Return on Operations	(4) Expected Increase in Return Due to Additional Investment	(5) Expected Profits Column (3) Minus Column (2)
1	$ 60,000	$ 90,000		$ 30,000
2	120,000	175,000	$85,000	55,000
3	180,000	255,000	80,000	75,000
4	240,000	330,000	75,000	90,000
5	300,000	400,000	70,000	100,000
6	360,000	465,000	65,000	105,000
7	420,000	525,000	60,000	105,000
8	480,000	580,000	55,000	100,000
9	540,000	630,000	50,000	90,000
10	600,000	675,000	45,000	75,000

[4]Even if the firm made the investment out of retained earnings and paid no interest charge on the capital, the cost would be the same. Presumably, the firm would be able to lend the money to someone else at the market rate of interest and earn the interest charge on the loan. The cost of using the capital in its own business is the amount the firm would have to give up by not lending the money to someone else.

of aggregate demand, which may induce still further changes in investment spending, including some of the type illustrated by the acceleration principle and others that result from further changes in expectations. Clearly, the schedule of investment spending, which looks so stable when we draw it in our diagrams, can move rather substantially if economic conditions are right.

Expectations and Consumer Spending
The schedule of the propensity to consume can also shift in response to consumers' expectations. There is a tendency among economists to assume that it remains stable, that with a given level of GNP we can predict the level of consumer spending rather closely. Much of the time that is true: the propensity to consume does not fluctuate widely in response to economic conditions but is tied closely to income. Once in a while, however, it does shift, creating repercussions that are very difficult to anticipate.

One recent instance occurred in 1968. A 10 percent income tax surcharge was passed by

Figure 8-8
The Level of Investment Spending

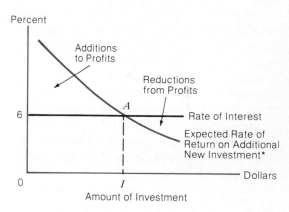

As investment is increased toward *I*, each additional amount of new investment adds to profit. Profits are maximized at *I*, and any further amounts of new investment start bringing total profits down. To the right of *I* the cost of the new investment is greater than the revenues it adds, while up to *I* the added revenues are greater than the cost.

*John Maynard Keynes christened this concept "the marginal efficiency of capital." The standard terminology used by contemporary economists is "the marginal efficiency of investment."

Congress early in the year;[5] it was designed to reduce consumer spending and diminish the inflationary pressures created by high levels of military spending for the Vietnam war. Most economists expected the surtax to have that effect. After-tax income would be reduced by about 10 percent and a multiplied decline in GNP was expected to occur, reducing the pressure on prices to rise. But consumers were too smart for the economists. They also knew that military spending was pushing prices up, and that their money would buy less the longer they held it. They reacted by maintaining their levels of spending, in spite of higher taxes. Savings fell from about 7.5 percent of disposable income to about 6.25 percent. This upward shift in the propensity to consume was financed in part by borrowing, in part by reduced savings, and in part by higher wages and salaries brought by inflation. The effects of the tax surcharge were cancelled by the effects of a change in consumer expectations and a shift upward in the propensity to consume.

Consumer behavior is becoming less stable over the years, largely because of the increased amounts of discretionary income in consumer hands. Many consumers are becoming wealthier and better educated; they have accumulated substantial savings and have huge credit facilities at their service. Years ago they may have purchased to fill their needs, but now they buy to satisfy their tastes as well. Consumers can borrow or use savings to buy now, or they can postpone their purchases until later. Spending depends not only on ability to buy, but on willingness as well. In addition, consumer spending has become a much more important factor in the economy as incomes have risen. All of these developments have contributed to an increase in the importance of consumer anticipations and expectations.

The Moving Economy

We can now summarize the results of our analysis of income determination. The economy is continually moving toward an equilibrium level of income and output. The movement toward that equilibrium can set in motion changes in both the investment and consumption schedules. These changes mean that the equilibrium position is itself changing, even though the tendency to move toward it remains. We are brought to the realization that the level of economic activity is continually moving, never settling down at a single point. A dynamic pattern is always found.

In addition, there is the problem of growth. Since any economy moves along a growth path, another dimension must be added to the dynamics of income determination. The factors crucial to growth, such as accumulation of capital, changes in technology, education and science, and the process of innovation, interact with the determinants of the level of aggregate demand to produce a continually changing economy. Actual achievement of the equilibrium described in Chapter 7 is well-nigh impossible in a private enterprise economy.

---

[5]A 10 percent tax surcharge, or *surtax*, means an increase of 10 percent in the consumer's tax payment. For example, a tax of $100 would be increased to $110. It does not mean that an additional 10 percent of total income would be paid in taxes.

Summary

The movement of the level of income to an equilibrium depends on the existing schedules of consumption and investment. If one of these schedules changes, there will be a move to a new level of income. In the simple theory of income determination, we usually assume that the propensity to consume does not change, and that changes in the investment schedule are the dynamic element.

A change in investment spending has a multiplied effect because of the respending that takes place in the circular flow of spending. The size of the multiplied effect depends on the leakage of savings out of the circular flow. Hence, the size of the multiplier depends upon the marginal propensity to consume:

$$k = \frac{1}{1 - MPC}$$

A multiplied change in aggregate demand can change business expectations, inducing further changes in the level of investment.

A particularly important form of induced investment is that affected by the acceleration principle. Where investment expenditures are directly tied to the level of sales, a relatively small change in sales can bring a relatively large change in investment. The key to the acceleration principle is that the amount of investment depends on the rate of change in final sales.

These three relationships, together with changes in expectations, impart a dynamism to the level of economic activity that continually keeps it in flux in spite of the forces at work that tend to create an equilibrium. At the same time, the forces of equilibrium keep the system from expanding or contracting without limit. A change in one direction tends to generate more change, yet the equilibrium forces tend to bring the system to rest. The result is continuing flux rather than stability.

Key Concepts

multiplier principle	**induced investment**	**marginal propensity to consume**
multiplier	**acceleration principle**	

For Discussion

1. Explain the relationship between the multiplier and the marginal propensity to consume.

2. How does induced investment contribute to the upward cumulation of prosperity during a business cycle?

3. One implication of the acceleration principle is that a business cycle upswing cannot continue indefinitely. Why?

4. How do the acceleration principle and induced investment help us understand the phenomenon of the growth period in long waves?

5. Would you expect the marginal efficiency of investment to be relatively stable or volatile? Explain.

6. Would you expect the level of investment to fluctuate widely or remain relatively stable? Why?

Chapter 9

Government and the National Income

Our analysis of national income determination has concentrated up to this point on the private sector of the economy. Chapter 6 looked at the tendency for an equilibrium level of national income to emerge from the interaction of consumption, savings, and investment. Chapter 7 examined some of the simple dynamics of the system—the multiplier, induced investment, the acceleration principle, and the effect of expectations and uncertainty. The picture that emerges is one of a fluctuating economy in which economic stability seems impossible to achieve.

This conclusion is of the utmost importance. It means that a policy of laissez-faire has to be paid for with unemployment, business failures, insecurity, lost production, or inflation. The personal costs to individuals and the economic loss to society can be high. The problem lies in relationships between large, impersonal economic variables over which individuals have little control. No matter how hard an individual works or how good a business manager may be, the instability of a private-enterprise economy can wipe out the savings of a lifetime or a business enterprise in a few short months. In a success-oriented society, the most poignant

fact of all is that luck rather than effort can determine one's economic destiny.

Modern nations have turned to governments to promote greater economic stability as the only significant alternative, short of socialism, to the instability of a private-enterprise economy. In the absence of mechanisms in the private sector that might keep an economy stable at full-employment levels of activity, governments have stepped in to do the job.

Achievement of a stable, full-employment economy is not easy. The economy is not static, for its capacity to produce increases continually. The policies that bring full employment this year may be inadequate next year. Furthermore, the goal of full employment may not be fully consistent with the goal of stability in prices. Difficult compromises may have to be made between unemployment levels and price changes in an effort to hold back inflation.

One way that government can intervene in economic affairs to promote full employment and economic stability is through its powers to tax and spend, which compose what is commonly called *fiscal policy*. The government budget can be manipulated so as to increase or decrease aggregate demand and thereby influence the level of employment and output as well as the incomes received by producers. The basic concepts underlying fiscal policy have already been outlined in Chapter 5, and need only be restated here in summary form:

○ Taxes reduce aggregate demand by taking purchasing power away from economic units that would otherwise spend a large portion of it.

○ Government expenditures on products and services add to aggregate demand by channeling purchasing power back into the flow of spending.

It follows from these two principles that economic activity can be slowed down by raising taxes and/or reducing government expenditures. These actions reduce the flow of spending. They are appropriate when the economy is becoming "over-heated," to use the jargon of the financial community, and price increases are the chief threat to stability. Conversely, economic activity can be increased by tax reductions and/or larger government expenditures, which have the effect of increasing the flow of spending and enlarging aggregate demand. These measures are appropriate when unemployment threatens to increase and the economy needs a boost.

● **Fiscal policy** refers to taxation and spending on the part of the government. It is developed in the budget, whose size and balance or imbalance indicates how the government is trying to move the level of aggregate demand. Fiscal policy should be clearly distinguished from **monetary policy**, which deals with government control of the monetary system.

These basic propositions are only the beginning, however. They must be integrated into the general analysis of national income determination, which has been outlined in two previous chapters. In addition, there are several important qualifications and additions that to-day's sophisticated knowledge of fiscal policy requires. Finally, the general strategy of fiscal policy needs further elaboration.

Government and the Determination of the National Income and Product

When government spending is added to our hypothetical economy, which heretofore has been purely private, a new factor is added to the determinants of aggregate demand. Government purchases of goods and services, in addition to consumption and investment spending, now determine the level of national product and income. The basic equation becomes:

$$Y = C + I + G$$

where G = government purchases of goods and services.

Correspondingly, the uses to which income is put must be expanded. People not only spend and save, they also pay taxes. The equation for the uses of the national income becomes:

$$Y = C + S + T$$

where T = taxes paid to government.

The identity between savings and investment that prevailed in the private economy is also changed when government enters the picture. Withdrawals from the flow of spending still equal additions to the flow, but now there are two items on each side. The total of savings plus tax payments must equal the total of business investment plus government purchases of goods and services; or

$$S + T = I + G$$

This does *not* mean that considered separately, savings equal investment and taxes equal government purchases. Those equalities may prevail, but not necessarily so. The essential identity is between withdrawals from and additions to the flow of spending, no matter how the two sides of the equation are constituted.

Finally, the conditions for national income equilibrium are changed. Expectations and plans are still important, but more factors have entered the picture. The national income will move toward that level at which desired savings plus taxes equal desired investment plus government spending. That is,

$$S_D + T = I_D + G$$

This last point is very important. It tells us that desired savings do not have to equal desired investment in order for a given level of national income to be sustained. Government spending and taxes are just as important as the plans and expectations of the private sector. The national income can be maintained at a level at which desired savings substantially exceed desired investment, as long as government spending is larger than tax revenues by an equal amount.

For example, suppose we have a situation in which desired savings equal $75 billion, but desired investment equals only $60 billion. We would normally expect aggregate demand to fall until the two were brought into equality. But the decline need not necessarily occur: if government expenditures equal $100 billion and tax revenues only $85 billion the gap would be filled and a sustained level of national income achieved. In terms of the equation that defines the national income equilibrium,

$$S_D + T = I_D + G$$
$$75 + 85 = 60 + 100$$
$$160 = 160$$

Since withdrawals from the flow of spending (the left side of the equation) are equal to increments to the flow of spending (the right side of the equation), *and the desires of both savers and investors are realized*, a sustainable level of national income is achieved. It is achieved, however, only with a government *budget deficit* of $15 billion, which is equal to the difference between desired savings and desired investment. If the imbalance were in the opposite direction it could be countered by a *budget surplus*.

Remember that this is only a hypothetical example, and that achieving these relationships in the world outside of textbooks is quite complicated; but it does illustrate the basic point: government fiscal policy can be used to achieve and sustain a level of national income consistent with full employment.

- A **budget deficit** occurs when government spending exceeds revenues. A **budget surplus** occurs when government revenues exceed expenditures. The balance between government revenues and expenditures is the chief fiscal instrument for influencing the level of aggregate demand.

Government Expenditures and Aggregate Demand

Although aggregate demand is increased by government spending and reduced by tax revenues, the effects are not symmetrical. Common sense might tell us that if government purchases of goods and services are increased by, say, $10 billion, and taxes are raised simultaneously by an equal amount, there will be no net change in the national income and product. In this case, however, common sense is wrong, and knowing the reason helps us to understand the economic effects of fiscal policy more fully. Expenditures made by the government affect aggregate demand directly, while taxes do not. A government purchase of military equipment, for example, enables a business firm to produce and to employ resources in the production process. Output and incomes are directly increased by the amount of the government purchases, and that amount then has the usual multiplied effect on aggregate demand.[1] Taxa-

---

[1]Not all government expenditures add to output and employment. Some merely transfer incomes to consumers from taxpayers. These *transfer payments* include such items as social security payments, veterans' benefits, unemployment insurance benefits, and similar payments, which are not made in payment for products or services. In this chapter we will use the term government expenditures to mean only government purchases of products and services.

tion, however, exerts a direct influence on the propensity to consume rather than on aggregate demand as a whole. As a result, the multiplied effects on aggregate demand are of a different magnitude.

Let's look first at the direct effects of government expenditures on aggregate demand. With government in our model of the economy, the national product comprises three components:

Y = consumption expenditure
   + private investment
   + government purchases

  = $C + I + G$

This can be shown on the standard diagram of income determination by adding to the schedule of the propensity to consume C, both private investment I and government purchases of goods and services G. This gives us a schedule for aggregate demand, and the level of national product is determined by the intersection of that schedule with the aggregate supply schedule. In Figure 9–1 that intersection is shown at E.

Figure 9–1 shows that the effect of government expenditures on aggregate demand is quite similar to that of private investment. The multiplied effect is felt, and its size is determined by the marginal propensity to consume. To check on your knowledge of these matters, assume a $15 billion increase in government expenditures, no change in taxes, and a marginal propensity to consume of $\frac{2}{3}$. By how much would the national product be increased?

The answer: $45 billion. An MPC of $\frac{2}{3}$ means a multiplier of 3, and 15 billion times 3 equals $45 billion.[2]

The process also works in the other direction. A cut of $15 billion in government expenditures, with no change in taxes and a

---

[2]To review:

$$k = \frac{1}{1 - MPC} = \frac{1}{1 - \frac{2}{3}} = \frac{1}{\frac{1}{3}} = 3$$

Figure 9–1
The Effect of Government Expenditures on the National Product and Income

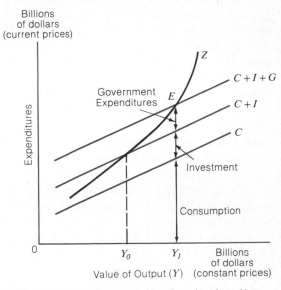

Adding G to $C + I$ brings the national product from Y_0 to Y_1. Notice how the multiplied effect of G is similar to that of I, both depending on the slope of C (which is, as we know, the marginal propensity to consume).

multiplier of 3, would bring a decline in aggregate demand of $45 billion.

Taxation and the Propensity to Consume Schedule

Taxes, on the other hand, do not directly affect aggregate demand and the level of economic activity. Their initial effect is on disposable (after-tax) income. Part of that income is saved, and these savings reduce the effect of a change in taxes, as compared to a change in government expenditures. An illustration should make the point clear. Assume that consumption expenditures are $400 billion annually, savings equal $100 billion, and the marginal propensity to consume is $\frac{2}{3}$, giving us a multiplier of 3. In this situation, the federal government reduces taxes by $15 billion. How much will the national product rise?

If your answer was $45 billion ($15 billion ×
3), you're wrong. The correct answer is $30
billion. Why?

First, a tax reduction of $15 billion adds that
amount to disposable income, but an *MPC* of $\frac{2}{3}$
means that only $10 billion will be spent and $5
billion will be saved. Second, applying a multiplier of 3 to an increase in spending of $10
billion gives us a total increase in aggregate
demand of $30 billion. This $30 billion increase
in aggregate demand, coming from a $15 bil-
lion decrease in taxes, compares with the $45
billion increase that would result from increased government spending of $15 billion.
The indirect impact of tax changes means that
they have a smaller quantitative effect on aggregate demand than government expenditures.[3] The shift in the propensity to consume
schedule set in motion by a tax increase is
shown graphically in Figure 9–2.

The Balanced-Budget Multiplier

We can now return to the paradox stated
earlier in this section: an increase in government spending, when accompanied by an equal
increase in tax revenues, is not neutralized. It
serves to increase aggregate demand by an
amount equal to the increase in government
spending. Just the opposite is true of a
balanced-budget decrease in government
spending (expenditures and tax revenues cut
by an equal amount). Aggregate demand will

Figure 9–2
Effect of Taxes on the Propensity to Consume

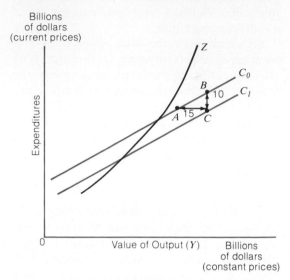

A tax increase of $15 billion (*AC*) moves the propensity to
consume schedule downward from C_0 to C_1. The decline
in consumption spending is $10 billion (*BC*), and is
determined by the slope of the consumption schedule.

fall by an amount equal to the cut in government spending.

This relationship is known as the *balanced-
budget multiplier*, and is equal to 1. As an
example, we can use the assumptions and
calculations made in the two preceding sections
of this chapter. Assuming an *MPC* of $\frac{2}{3}$ ($k = 3$),
we showed that an increase in government
spending of $15 billion would raise the national
product by $45 billion. A simultaneous in-
crease in tax revenues of $15 billion would
bring a decline of only $30 billion in the
national product by $45 billion. The net in-
crease of $15 billion is just equal to the original
increase in government expenditures.[4] The results are shown graphically in Figure 9–3.

- The **balanced-budget multiplier**, which is equal to 1, means that a change in the size of a balanced budget affects aggregate demand in an equal amount.

Perhaps the easiest way to understand the balanced-budget multiplier is to think of it in terms of the flow of spending. Taxes take money from the private sector and expenditures put it back in equal amounts. The net result is no change in the money flows that originate in the private sector. But in the meantime government has used the funds to purchase products and services, causing output, employment, and incomes to increase by an amount equal to the government purchases.

As a result, the total flow of spending is just that much larger. The flow of spending originating in the combined private and public sectors is increased.

Compensatory Fiscal Policy

An active fiscal policy helps to compensate for the ups and downs inherent in the private sector. When the private sector loses its dynamism and sinks below the full-employment growth path, government fiscal policy can be used to bring aggregate demand closer to the full-employment level. Taxes can be reduced, expenditures increased, and total spending

Figure 9-3
The Balanced-Budget Multiplier at Work

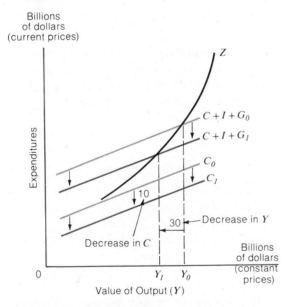

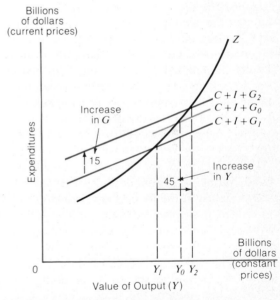

I. The Impact of Increased Taxes An increase in taxes of $15 billion brings C down by $10 billion (when $MPC = \frac{2}{3}$). Y_0 is reduced to Y_1, a decline of $30 billion ($k = 3$).

II. The Impact of Increased Spending When the government spends the $15 billion it raised from increased taxes, G increases by $15 billion, setting in motion a $45 billion increase from Y_1 to Y_2.

The balanced-budget multiplier works through two simultaneous but distinct steps. Taxes decrease consumption by an amount less than the tax. Spending increases aggregate demand by an amount equal to the spending. When changes in taxes and spending are equal the result is change in national product equal to and in the same direction as the change in G.

Figure 9-4
Compensatory Fiscal
Policy

Compensatory fiscal policies add to aggregate demand in recessions ▦ and reduce aggregate demand during inflations ▦ to keep the economy on a relatively stable growth path ▬

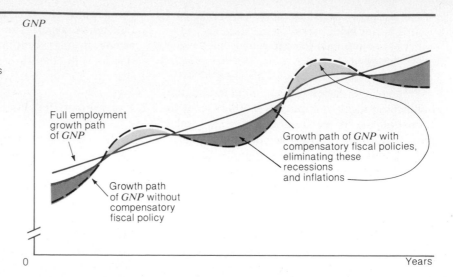

thereby enlarged. When the private sector becomes overly dynamic and inflation threatens, just the opposite policies can be used to dampen the economy. Taxes can be raised and expenditures cut, and some of the excessive aggregate demand that is causing the trouble thereby eliminated. It is too much to expect that recessions or price increases can be eliminated altogether, but a proper *compensatory fiscal policy* can keep the economy close to its full-employment growth path, as shown in Figure 9–4.

The easiest way to increase aggregate demand during recession periods is to incur a budget deficit at the federal government level, or reduce a surplus from an earlier period. With a multiplier of 2, the deficit will add to purchasing power an amount equal to twice the deficit. The deficit can be achieved by reducing tax rates, increasing spending, or both. If a deficit is not wanted, the same effects can be obtained by increasing both spending and tax revenues. In this case the added spending will have to be about twice the amount required if a deficit were achieved, since the balanced budget multiplier is approximately 1 instead of 2.

A budget surplus is the easiest way to reduce inflationary pressures, although again the same effect can be obtained through a balanced budget decrease in spending that is twice as large.

Automatic Stabilizers
The federal budget has several components that automatically produce a stabilizing effect on aggregate demand. The most important are the progressive personal income tax, unemployment compensation, and social security payments. The progressive personal income tax is the most important of these *automatic stabilizers*.

• **Automatic stabilizers** are aspects of the flow of spending that tend to counterbalance increases or decreases in aggregate demand, without any policy actions being taken.

As GNP rises, personal incomes rise and some taxpayers move into higher tax brackets. They then pay a larger proportion of their incomes in taxes. Since this happens to many taxpayers across the country, the revenues of the federal government rise faster than GNP. Disposable personal income rises more slowly than GNP, thereby slowing down the pace of economic expansion.

Just the opposite effect occurs as the economy heads toward a recession. The proportion of income paid in taxes declines as incomes fall and families move into lower tax brackets. Disposable personal income falls more slowly than GNP, consumption spending tends to hold firm, and the decline in GNP is slowed.

Unemployment compensation programs have a dual effect. Unemployment falls when the economy is on an upswing, reducing government payments to the unemployed. At the same time, payroll deductions for payments into the unemployment insurance trust fund go up, because more workers are employed. Receipts rise, payments fall, and the net effect is to reduce the flow of spending. During a recession the flow is reversed. As unemployment rises, payments into the trust fund decline because fewer people are employed. For the same reason, unemployment compensation payments rise. The net effect is to increase consumer incomes and bolster the flow of spending.

Social security payments act somewhat differently. In good times or bad they remain the same, thereby providing a certain amount of stable income for one group of consumers, even though other incomes may fluctuate. Contributions to social security fall during recessions, however, because fewer workers are employed. These changes take place automatically unless the payments are changed by law. Figure 9–5 shows the three chief automatic stabilizers.

Some quantitative estimates will provide insight into how the automatic stabilizers function. At the start of the 1980 recession a $60 billion decline in GNP was associated with a 1 percent decline in employment (roughly one million working people). A fall of that amount in GNP and employment would bring a decrease of roughly $20 billion in federal tax revenues and an increase of about $4 billion in expenditures for unemployment compensation. In other words, the federal budget deficit would increase by about $24 billion. Applying

Figure 9–5
The Automatic Stabilizers

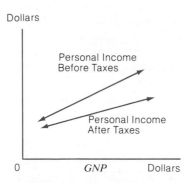

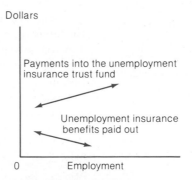

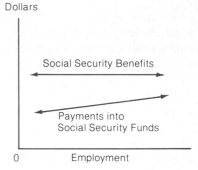

A. The Personal Income Tax After-tax incomes rise more slowly than pretax income, as the proportion of income paid in taxes goes up. Just the opposite effects occur when incomes fall.

B. Unemployment Insurance As employment grows withdrawals from the flow of spending rise and injections into the flow of spending decrease. The opposite effects occur when employment declines and unemployment rises.

C. Social Security Benefits Social security benefits tend to be stable regardless of the level of GNP, while payments into social security funds rise automatically as employment increases.

a multiplier of about 2 gives a total stimulus to the economy of about $48 billion. About 80 percent of the original decline of $60 billion would be automatically offset. There is a time lag, of course. Although the process starts at once the full effect is not felt until about a year has elapsed.

The automatic stabilizers help keep the economy on a relatively even keel. They can't do the whole job, however. Their most important function is to slow down the swings in the economy, thereby giving policy makers a little more time to assess the situation and determine the best course of action.

The National Economic Budget

The *national economic budget* is a device for analyzing the balance in the national economy between potential output and potential aggregate demand. On one side, it provides an estimate of how large the gross national product is likely to be, based on estimates of consumer spending, investment, and government purchases. On the other side, it provides an estimate of how large the GNP could be if it were to follow the economy's full-employment growth path. In other words, the national economic budget provides an estimate of the economy's potential growth in the coming year, a forecast of potential aggregate demand, and an estimate of any gap between the two. Economic policies to bridge the gap can then be devised. An example will clarify the concept. Assume the following situation in the current year:

$$Y = C + I + G$$

where

Y = $800 billion
C = $600 billion
S = I = $75 billion
G = $125 billion (with a balanced budget)

Let's also assume that there are 4 million

persons unemployed, and that an increase in GNP of $25 billion would provide employment for just 1 million of the unemployed.

The first step in creating a national economic budget is to estimate the potential growth of the economy. Such an estimate requires forecasts of the growth of the work force and the increase in productivity. We can use the following estimates.

1. Increase in the work force (corrected for changes in the length of the work year and other factors) = 1.5 percent.

2. Increase in output per laborhour = 3.5 percent.

Together, these factors provide an estimate of about 5 percent growth in GNP, from $800 billion to $840 billion.

We could add, however, enough spending to reduce significantly the total number of unemployed. Cutting it in half, from 4 to 2 million, would bring the total down to just about the frictional unemployment level (approximately full employment). This would require an additional increase of $50 billion in GNP, making a total of $890 billion. Such an increase would be very large, over 10 percent, and could cause difficulty if it triggered a growth so rapid that it could not be slowed down sufficiently in the following year. It would perhaps be wiser to aim for only half that reduction in unemployment, from 4 to 3 million, requiring only $25 billion more in total output.

We are now able to make an estimate, on the supply side, of the potential output of the economy for the coming year:

GNP in the initial year	$800 billion
Potential growth at 5% per year	40 billion
Additional output obtained by reducing unemployment by 1 million persons	25 billion
Goal for coming year	$865 billion
Required increase over previous year	$ 65 billion

The next step is to make an estimate of the expected aggregate demand during the coming year. Two methods have been widely used in recent years. One is the use of surveys in which a sample of consumers and business managers are asked what they expect to spend during the coming year on such items as automobiles and housing (in the case of consumers) and on plant and equipment (in the case of business). While there may be a gap between intentions and their realization, several of these surveys are widely available and remarkably accurate. They provide estimates of C and I.

Government spending is particularly easy to estimate, since planned budgets are prepared and published well in advance, and actual spending usually differs little from budgets. Information on government spending plans can be used to supplement surveys of consumer and business plans to provide insight into spending levels in the immediate future.

A second method for estimating aggregate demand that is increasingly coming into use is the computerized econometric model. The factors that influence aggregate demand are highly complex, but refined statistical estimating techniques are able to provide close estimates. Since all types of spending are related to each other systematically, by way of the circular flow of spending, the multiplier, and the acceleration principle, it is possible to bring all of them together in a system of simultaneous equations. The entire system, or model, can then be solved with the aid of high-speed computers. Several of these models are now available for research and forecasting purposes. They are all based on the fundamental Keynesian equation we are familiar with.

$$Y = C + I + G + X$$

All of the models break down C and I into their component parts: durable and nondurable consumer goods (for C); and housing, plant and equipment, and inventories (for I); and so on, each with a separate equation. Each model also has equations for estimating price changes, employment, and other variables. The basic concept is the same for each: several equations are used to estimate the component parts of C, several for I, estimates of G are taken from budgets, and the model puts them all together to provide an estimate for Y, or gross national product.

Surveys, econometric models, and perhaps other techniques are used to provide estimates of expected spending for the forthcoming year. Continuing the example started above, suppose the forecast shows an expected increase in GNP from $800 billion to $820 billion, as follows:

$$C = \$610 \text{ billion}$$
$$I = \$\ 80 \text{ billion}$$
$$G = \$130 \text{ billion}$$
$$GNP = \$820 \text{ billion}$$

Note the interrelationships in this estimate. Investment is expected to increase by $5 billion from the initial year's $75 billion, and government spending by $5 billion. A multiplier of 2 (which is close to the one that prevails in the economy) will mean a GNP increase of $20 billion, implying a $10 billion increase in consumption.

Now we have problems. The expected increase in GNP is only half of that needed to provide jobs for a growing and more productive work force. If the estimate turns out to be accurate, unemployment will increase rather than decrease. Instead of falling by 1 million, unemployment will rise by about 800,000 persons. The national economic budget at this stage does not show a balance between the capacity to produce and the capacity to consume, but instead a growing deficit in aggregate demand that will continue to grow unless appropriate measures are taken to stimulate spending.

One way to fill the gap may be through increased government spending, without an increase in taxes, designed to bring GNP up to $865 billion from the expected $820 billion.

With a multiplier of 2, that would mean, at first glance, a federal budget deficit of $22.5 billion:

Required GNP	$865 billion
Expected GNP	$820 billion
Gap	$ 45 billion
Additional spending needed ($k = 2$)	$22.5 billion

All of the additional spending need not be from the federal budget, however. A higher GNP may well induce higher levels of business investment than business managers were planning. Going back to our econometric models or surveys may tell us that a GNP of $865 billion will bring investment spending of $85 billion instead of the planned $80 billion. The additional I will enable the government deficit spending program to be reduced by $5 billion.

A second revision will also have to be made. Taxes will rise as GNP goes up. In order to get a deficit of the necessary $17.5 billion ($22.5 billion minus $5 billion for induced investment), it will be necessary to reduce tax rates so as not to increase total taxes. Let's say that our econometric models predict that with existing tax rates and a GNP of $865 billion, tax revenues will rise by $7 billion, acting as a drag on the growth of aggregate demand. Tax rates will have to be reduced to eliminate that drag.

We can now restate the goals and policies of the national economic budget for the coming year. The goal is an increase in GNP large enough to provide for growth of 5 percent plus a reduction in unemployment of 1 million persons. A GNP of $865 billion will be needed. Achieving that growth would require the following spending:

$$C = \$632.5 \text{ billion}$$
$$I = 85 \text{ billion}$$
$$G = 147.5 \text{ billion}$$
$$\text{GNP} = \$865 \text{ billion}$$

The investment total comprises the $80 billion planned by business firms on the basis of their existing anticipations, plus $5 billion induced by the larger-than-expected growth in GNP. Government spending comprises $130 billion already planned for, plus a deficit of $17.5 billion. Tax revenues remain the same as expected (130 billion) because of the planned reduction in tax rates to compensate for the growth in taxable income. The government deficit and induced investment provide the increase in spending of $22.5 billion needed to raise GNP by $45 billion ($k = 2$) above the expected level.

This is only one combination of policies that might be adopted. Tax rates could be reduced still further, providing a larger disposable personal income and higher C. Taxes on business firms could be adjusted to stimulate more I. Monetary policy could be eased to promote greater I. All of these policies would enable the increase in G (and the deficit) to be reduced. The policy mix that is finally selected may be extremely complex, and many alternatives are available. The example used here was highly simplified but it shows the way in which the national economic budget can be used.[5]

The Dynamics of Fiscal Policy: Fiscal Drag

We have already noted some of the effects of changes in aggregate demand on tax receipts and the adjustments in fiscal policy that they might require. These dynamic aspects of fiscal policy are especially important in a growing economy, where the level of GNP changes from year to year. Government must adjust itself to these changes and the impact they have on its fiscal position.

A change in GNP, either upward or downward, changes the amount of income received by consumers in the form of salaries, wages, and other payments. Since much of the revenue of the federal government is obtained from income taxes, a change in the level of incomes will be reflected in a change in tax revenues. A change in government revenues, in turn, af-

---

[5]The term "national economic budget" is a dirty word in Washington: it smacks too much of economic planning, which it is. Conservative members of Congress will have nothing of it. Nevertheless, the process we have explained above describes what the President's Council of Economic Advisors does and embodies in its annual report, but in a more complex fashion.

fects the budget position of the federal government: higher tax receipts can produce a budget surplus, or move a deficit budget into balance, or increase an already existing budget surplus. And we already know that shifts of these sorts in the federal budget affect the level of GNP and the pace of economic growth. Any government that uses its financial operations to seek full employment and satisfactory rates of economic growth must take these feedback effects into consideration when it establishes its budget and determines its economic policies.

These dynamic relationships became matters of general public interest in the United States in the mid-1960s. The situation was this: recovery toward full-employment levels of GNP from the recession of 1960–61 and the relatively stagnant economy of the 1950s was proceeding well. But as GNP rose, the tax receipts of the federal government rose even more rapidly. This was caused by the fact that the federal income tax is progressive; as people moved into higher income brackets their income tax rates rose and they paid a higher proportion of their income to the federal government. As a result, federal budget deficits were smaller and the spur given to continued economic expansion was diminished. Estimates made by government economists showed that the federal budget would come into balance well before full-employment levels of GNP were achieved, if expenditures did not increase and the growth of revenues continued. Under those conditions there would be a substantial budget surplus if the economy were able to reach full employment.

There is nothing wrong with a budget surplus, taken by itself. But the policy dilemma was that the surplus would start appearing well before full-employment levels of GNP were reached. Its multiplied effect on aggregate demand would act as a brake on further increases and make it more difficult for the economy to reach full employment. Instead of stimulating the economy, the federal budget would act as a drag, slowing down the desired expansion (see Figure 9–6).

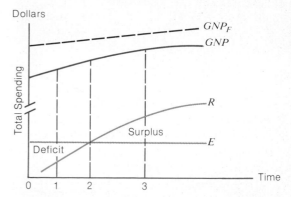

Figure 9–6
The Problem of Fiscal Drag

GNP_F is the full-employment level of GNP, and E is the level of budget expenditures. At 1, revenues R are less than expenditures E; the budget deficit pushes up GNP relatively rapidly. At 2, the rise in R eliminates the deficit, and a balanced budget has a neutral effect on GNP. At 3, however, rising revenues R create a budget surplus, which acts as a drag on increases in GNP and prevents achievement of the full-employment level of GNP.

In order to avoid this *fiscal drag*, three alternative policies were available. First, government expenditures could be raised from year to year to match the increases in revenue and retain the budget deficit that was providing much of the stimulus for expansion. Second, tax rates could be reduced to slow down the increase in revenues. Finally, tax reductions and expenditure increases could be used together to achieve the same results. Indeed, if the proper tax rate structure and expenditure level were selected, it would be possible for the budget deficits to continue, but to diminish each year, until the budget was balanced at full-employment levels of GNP. Some economists thought that this would be the ideal situation; diminishing deficits would bring the economy to full employment, followed by growing surpluses if GNP moved into an inflationary situation (see Figure 9–7).

• **Fiscal drag** is the tendency of tax receipts to rise more rapidly than aggregate demand, thereby holding back further increases in GNP.

Figure 9-7
Solving the Problem
of Fiscal Drag

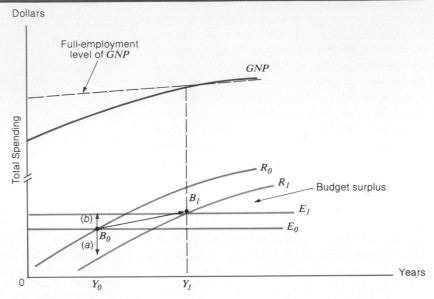

One way to solve the problem of fiscal drag: In year Y_0 reduce taxes (a) from R_0 to R_1 and raise expenditures (b) from E_0 to E_1. This action increases the budget deficit in year Y_0, but it stimulates a stronger growth of GNP by moving the balanced-budget position from B_0 to B_1. By year Y_1, the economy has been moved to full employment with a balanced budget. Beyond Y_1 the budget surplus dampens down further increases in GNP.

A qualification: If you want to reach full employment before year Y_1, larger tax reductions and spending increases will be necessary, but they will have to be partially rescinded as the economy approaches full employment in order to eliminate inflationary pressures originating in fiscal policy.

The policy actually selected in 1964–65 was a combination of a substantial tax reduction together with a small increase in expenditures. The result was continuation of the drive to higher levels of GNP, which brought with it an increase in tax receipts even though the tax rates were reduced. The budget deficit turned to a surplus. Many people, including a number of prominent congressmen and senators, didn't believe it would actually happen. After all, they asked, how could reduced tax rates and increased spending cause a surplus to appear? It all seemed quite paradoxical to those who were unfamiliar with the dynamics of fiscal policy. They did not realize that both tax reductions and increased spending would push GNP to higher levels, which would then generate greater tax revenues.

That is exactly what happened. Tax rates were reduced in 1964, primarily on personal incomes, by amounts that would have resulted in a revenue loss of about $13 billion if the GNP had remained at the same levels as before. Instead, GNP jumped by over $51 billion, and tax revenues rose by $5 billion.

The policies of 1964–65 were revived in somewhat different form in 1980–81 as part of the policies of the Reagan administration. The Kemp-Roth proposal, named after its congressional sponsors, proposed to cut personal income taxes 30 percent over a three-year period (later scaled down to 25 percent over 27 months). The tax cut was designed to increase consumer spending and, favoring upper income groups, to promote private savings and increase the funds available for investment. The goal was to stimulate aggregate demand and reduce unemployment. The tax cut was also expected to reduce the federal budget deficit, for budget revenues would increase more rapidly than the level or aggregate demand. Whether it would eliminate the deficit entirely after three to five years, as its advocates believe, is problematic, but the general economic logic behind the plan was certainly valid. Assuming no change in government expenditures, an increase in aggregate demand would increase tax revenues to close and ultimately eliminate the gap between revenues and expenditures. Critics called it "voodoo economics," but it was nothing more than a variation of the policies pioneered in the early 1960s, modified by proposals designed to specifically stimulate investment spending.

The chief difficulty with this strategy in 1980–81 was the presence of high interest rates that hindered economic expansion. Without increased incomes and output, the tax reductions could be expected to bring larger instead of smaller budget deficits. One part of the strategy (high interest rates) negated the other (economic stimulus).

The Full-Employment Budget

The concept of the *full-employment budget* emerged from the experience of the mid-1960s. It is a variant of the national economic budget, in which the economy is presumed to be at full employment. An estimate is made of budget revenues at the full-employment level of GNP, based on existing tax rates. Current government expenditures are then planned at that level, to provide a balanced budget at full-employment. The current level of GNP however, may be below the full-employment level, and revenues correspondingly low. Expenditures based on full-employment revenues would mean a current budget deficit, which would push the economy toward full employment. On the other hand an overfull-employment GNP would generate revenues greater than expenditures based on full employment, and the resulting surplus would tend to bring GNP down and reduce inflationary pressures. Table 9–1 shows these relationships.

Table 9–1
The Full-Employment Budget

	A	B	C
	(Billions of Dollars)		
GNP	1900	2100	2300
Tax revenues	400	470	500
Expenditures	430	470	470
Deficit (−) or Surplus (+)	−30	0	+30

Table 9–1 uses approximate data on GNP and federal budget revenues for 1978–80, just to show what the approximate magnitudes are. *B* is the full-employment budget, with expenditures planned at a level equal to full-employment revenues. If *A* were the actual situation the resultant deficit would push GNP toward the level of *B*. If *C* were the current situation the surplus would push GNP down in the direction of *B*.

- The **full-employment budget** is an estimate of the national economic budget at full employment, designed to establish the level of federal expenditures that would equal revenues obtained at full employment with the existing tax system.

The full-employment budget provides a rule of thumb that helps to keep fiscal policy from either overly stimulating or restraining the economy. But there may be times when greater stimulus or restraint may be warranted. No mechanical rule will fit all situations. On the other hand, the concept calls attention to an important issue. If the government budget is in deficit at full employment the resultant borrowing implies an expansion of the monetary system that could itself add to inflationary pressures.

An Active Fiscal Policy

We can now summarize some of the basic principles of fiscal policy. Perhaps the most

FISCAL POLICY IN A RECESSION

The recession of 1974–75, which accompanied the OPEC oil boycott and price increase, was the most severe recession experienced by the American economy up to that time since the end of World War II. The figures below capture some of the process of decline and recovery:

Year	GNP	C	I_g	G
		(billions of 1972 dollars)		
1973	1,235	768	207	253
1974	1,218	761	184	258
1975	1,202	775	143	263
1976	1,273	821	173	263

The decline in GNP between 1973 and 1975 was about $33 billion (2.7 percent), even though consumer spending, after an initial decline, increased by 7 billion in 1973–75 and government purchases of goods and services rose by $10 billion. The chief decline came in business investment, which fell by $64 billion (30.8 percent). The episode provides a good example of the volatility of business investment, and its multiplied effect on the entire economy.

The chief reason for the rapid recovery is to be found in the federal budget. Look at the figures for the deficit in the federal accounts:

Year	Federal Budget Deficit (billions of current dollars)
1973	14.8
1974	4.7
1975	45.2
1976	66.4

During the initial year of the recession the federal government actually contributed to the severity of the decline by allowing the budget deficit to fall. But policy was quickly turned around (1976 was a presidential election year, and you know what that means) with a tax cut, extension of unemployment insurance benefits, and increased spending in almost all categories of the budget. The federal deficit increased by over $40 billion in 1975, with an additional increase of more than $20 billion in 1976.

The 1976 budget deficit of over $66 billion came at a time when the economy was already starting to come out of its slump, and its large size undoubtedly contributed to the upsurge of inflation that followed recovery from the recession. On the other hand, perhaps the 1976 budget deficit was too small: the incumbent president was narrowly defeated.

important point is that it is impossible for government fiscal action to be neutral with respect to the level of economic activity. As long as a government performs services or buys products, it affects aggregate demand. The only truly neutral government is a nonexistent one.

Since government fiscal activity cannot be neutral, a fiscal policy must be developed. Even a policy of not directing taxation and spending toward achievement of macroeconomic goals implies a policy judgment that

those goals are secondary to others. For example, the tax system might be thought of solely as a source of revenue for essential government programs, and the effects on employment and growth ignored. In this case, the policy judgment is that fiscal policy ought not to be used to achieve macroeconomic policy goals.

Contemporary opinion takes the other tack. Fiscal policy is seen as an instrument to aid in the achievement of greater economic stability. It can help develop an environment within which individuals and business firms can function more effectively. Fiscal policy enables society to choose, within limits, the level of aggregate demand it wants. There are no easy solutions, however. Fiscal policy must be used carefully. It must be active, continually revised in the light of economic events, the direction in which the economy is moving, the level of employment and prices, and all of the other available indicators of the state of the economy's health.

Summary

We know that government action is necessary to maintain full employment and stable growth. The primary tools for that purpose are taxation and government purchases of products and services. When they are added to the analytical model, the level of aggregate demand becomes

$$Y = C + I + G$$

The conditions for equilibrium become

$$S_D + T = I_D + G$$

Taxation and government spending do not have a symmetrical effect on the level of aggregate demand. Taxes change the propensity to consume schedule, which means that a portion of any tax reduction will go into savings and not affect aggregate demand. Conversely, a tax increase will reduce both spending and savings. Government expenditures affect aggregate demand directly, however. The result is a balanced budget multiplier equal to 1. That is, a change in government spending accompanied by an equal change in tax receipts to keep the budget balanced will change aggregate demand by the amount of the change in government expenditures.

A compensatory fiscal policy can use government spending and taxes to reduce the fluctuations characteristic of the private sector, aided by the "automatic stabilizers." Budget surpluses dampen inflationary pressures and budget deficits counter recessions, and the national economic budget can be used to analyze the existing situation and to organize the strategy of economic policy.

Key Concepts

fiscal policy	**budget surplus**	**fiscal drag**
monetary policy	**balanced-budget multiplier**	**full-employment budget**
budget deficit	**automatic stabilizers**	

For Discussion

1. Should the federal government always strive for a balanced budget? Why or why not?

2. How does an increase in government spending combined with an equal increase in tax revenues lead to a net increase in national income?

3. What are the major automatic stabilizers, and how do they work?

4. Explain the connection between fiscal drag and a progressive income tax.

5. How can a tax reduction, with no change in government spending, bring about a reduced budget deficit?

6. Has the use of fiscal policy had a stabilizing or a destabilizing effect on the American economy in recent years?

Appendix *9A*

The Economics of the National Debt

A macroeconomic policy whose goal is economic stability may bring increases in the national debt. Deficits in periods of economic slack may be larger than surpluses during inflationary periods, leading to an increase in the federal debt. An increase in debt need not be harmful to the economy, however, and it may be beneficial.

Most people think that the national debt will have to be "repaid" at some time or other. It won't. Most people believe that the national debt is a burden on future generations. It isn't. Even if we tried we would find it almost impossible to shift the burden of the national debt to our children. Most people believe that the national debt can become so large as to bankrupt the federal government. Impossible! Most people think that a large national debt is a burden on the economy. It need not be, if it is managed properly.

There is no economic limit to the size of the national debt, and a rising debt can bring important benefits. Any burdens that may arise appear only if the national debt is managed improperly or if it is increased or decreased at the wrong time for the wrong reasons.

The federal government, unlike you or me or General Motors Corporation or the State of Arkansas, has an unlimited line of credit. It can always borrow more, if it wishes, at existing rates of interest. Indeed, the federal government is the only economic unit in the national economy for which

that is true. All other economic units can borrow only finite amounts, based on their income, wealth, and credit history. The reason is simple: the federal government controls the money supply and can use the money supply to create its own line of credit.

World War II provides an example. When the Treasury wished to borrow, say, $5 billion to pay for another batch of tanks, guns, ships, and aircraft, and the banking system was loaned up so that it could not absorb any more government securities, the Federal Reserve System (our central bank) would step in and buy $1 billion of the new issue of Treasury bonds. Like any open market purchase, this created $1 billion of new reserves for the banking system. The banks were then able to buy the remaining $4 billion of Treasury bonds through the process of multiple expansion of bank credit. It almost seems too simple, yet that is exactly how most of the expenditures of World War II were financed. The process is known as monetizing the national debt, since it results in an increase in the money supply almost as great as the increase in debt.

There is one drawback to financing a war, or any other government expenditure, in this fashion. It adds to total spending without adding to output. If this is done when the economy is close to full employment, it can cause rising prices. If done at the wrong time, an increase in the national debt is inflationary. But if done at the right time—that is, when there are unemployed workers and unused plant capacity—the increase in debt can add to total output and to economic welfare. The increase in GNP is a net gain, because the resources and laborpower would otherwise lie unused.

An important truth emerges: a rising national debt can benefit the economy if it occurs when there is economic slack. It can hurt the economy if it occurs when there is little or no economic slack.[1]

Whether the debt is a burden or not also depends on what the money is used for. If the debt is increased to pay for weapons of destruction that are shot up on the battlefield, the resources used are gone and have not contributed either to economic growth or economic welfare. On the other hand, if the debt is increased to provide jobs for the unemployed or assist the needy or build highways, it will increase welfare and promote growth. A second truth emerges: a rising national debt can hurt the economy if the funds are used wastefully. It can benefit the economy if the funds are used wisely.[2]

But what if the debt continues to grow and becomes very large—will it not then be a burden on the economy? A large debt can be a burden if it results in a redistribution of income. If interest payments on the debt are paid out of tax revenues, there will be a shift of income from those who pay taxes to those who own government securities. If the taxpayers are poor and the bondholders rich, the economy will be worse off.[3] Fortunately this is not a significant problem in the United States. Although government securities are largely owned by people with more than the average holding of wealth, the progressive federal income tax takes a larger than average share of tax revenue from them. While there may be a small income redistribution effect from paying interest on the national debt out of tax revenues, economists who have tried to measure it have been unable to find any significant shift. We conclude, therefore, that if a nation's tax system is based on ability to pay, there will be no problem of income redistribution arising from paying interest on the national debt.

Interest payments might be a burden for another reason, even if, as suggested above, they come out of one pocket and go right back into the other. Taxes to finance interest payments may have incentive effects on taxpayers. The folklore is that taxes reduce incentives, but they can also increase them. An increase in taxes will lower after-tax incomes, which may cause people in a success-oriented economy like ours to work harder in order to maintain their incomes and living standards. Economists who have studied the effects of taxes on incentives have been unable to decide which effect is stronger. We know that taxes can change the direction of economic activity, but there is no evidence to show that the present level and pattern of U.S. taxes affects the total amount of economic activity either favorably or unfavorably. Since interest payments on the national debt are so small relative to total federal tax revenues (about 10 percent) the incentive effects must be exceptionally small. Remember, too, that it is always possible to borrow to pay interest on the national debt, since there is no economic limit to the debt's size. That can be done if payment of interest out of taxes is ever felt to be a burden.

For the same reason, the national debt need never be repaid. Old debt matures, but it can always be replaced by new debt. If the banks are loaned up and can't take any more, the debt can always be "monetized" by Federal Reserve action. This happens almost every month, in fact. Old issues of federal securities mature, the Treasury sells new securities to replace them if it wishes, and the Fed sees to it that the money markets can absorb the new issue. No one in either the Treasury or the Fed expects anything else. The national debt is like a forest, in which each tree must eventually die but the forest goes on indefinitely.

If all of this applies to us, it also applies to our children. Future generations will be no more burdened by the national debt than we are. Even if they wished to repay the debt—and they don't ever have to do that—they will be repaying it to themselves. They will probably just replace old debt with new, just as we do. With proper attention to the tax system, there need be no significant incentive or income distribution effects, even if the debt is a great deal larger than it is now. And if changes in the size of the debt are managed with proper regard to timing and purpose, it can bring beneficial rather than harmful results.

---

[1] The alert reader will note that it is not the debt itself that benefits or hurts the economy, but the deficit it finances.

[2] Here again, the debt is not the culprit or the hero, but the expenditures it finances may be either wise or foolish.

[3] See Chapter 28 for an explanation of why total welfare can be reduced by shifting income from the poor to the rich.

Two qualifications are in order. First, if economic growth is slowed down, today's debt can burden future generations. For example, if we increase the national debt during a period of full employment, the deficit adds to inflationary pressures, and if the price increases draw resources away from investment and economic growth, future generations will have less. A better example is a wartime deficit, financed by increased debt, which draws resources into destruction rather than progress. But note this: most of the losses from these misuses of the national debt are borne by the generation living at the time. Only a small portion of the burden can be shifted to future generations by way of investment and the rate of economic growth.

The second qualification concerns the effect of government borrowing on the money markets. A deficit requires that the Treasury borrow from the private sector of the economy, increasing the demand for funds. When there is substantial slack in the economy this increase in demand in the money markets has little impact, for banks and other lenders will have funds available for purchase of government securities that would otherwise not be used. The increased sale of treasury securities will not push interest rates up.

During times when money markets are already tight, however, increased Treasury borrowing will cause interest rates to rise. This will *crowd out* some of the private borrowing in the money markets as well, and higher interest rates will dampen spending and investment in the private sector.

- **Crowding out** is the phrase used to describe the reduction in private borrowing when increased government borrowing causes higher interest rates and absorbs a portion of the funds available to borrowers.

During a period of inflation, like that of the late 1960s and after, lenders tend to keep all of their funds in loans, money markets are generally tight, and interest rates are high. Under those conditions, an increase in the government budget deficit, which brings a rise in the demand for loanable funds, will push interest rates up and crowd out some private borrowers. On the other hand, a reduction in the budget deficit will reduce demand for loanable funds, ease the money markets, and tend to bring interest rates down in a period of strong inflationary pressures. A budget surplus in such times would be even better. As the government debt is reduced, funds that formerly were lent to the government would be freed for loans in the private sector, where the increase in the supply of loanable funds would ease money markets and lower interest rates.

The basic rule is that an increase in the government debt tends to create tightness in the money markets, while a decrease in the government debt tends to bring monetary ease. These effects are negligible when a considerable degree of slack exists in the money markets, reflecting slack in the economy as a whole. But they can be important when the economy is at or near full employment or when inflation is significant. Once again, we conclude that the debt itself is less significant than changes in its size and that the timing of the changes is the more important factor.

All that we have said about the national debt applies only to an internally owned debt. A national debt owned largely by foreigners, as the U.S. debt was up to the Civil War, can be a real burden. The payments of interest and principal, while made in U.S. dollars, are turned into foreign currencies by the recipients, who want to spend the money at home rather than here. For that to be done, U.S. goods must be sold abroad to make the foreign currencies available. There will be less of our GNP left at home to meet domestic needs. Some of it will be exported and used by foreigners as we pay back what we borrowed from them. U.S. citizens will be that much poorer.

The national debt should be thought of as an instrument of national economic policy, to be used along with other policy instruments to achieve and sustain a full-employment economy. The deficits that are financed by the national debt can bring important real benefits in high levels of employment, output, and economic growth. Deficits should not be avoided with the thought that they result in a growth of debt, for the debt itself is no problem if it is properly managed. Proper management means, however, that deficits at times of full employment should be avoided. On the other hand, if the private sector grows slowly, government spending is needed to keep the economy on the full-employment path. When that happens the rise in the national debt should not be viewed as unfortunate, but as the inevitable accompaniment of the proper economic policies.

PART 3

THE MONETARY SYSTEM

An understanding of the monetary system is essential for a full grasp of the instability inherent in a private enterprise economy. Chapter 10 introduces the role of money in the economy, with an appendix on the monetary functions of gold. Chapter 11 shows how the modern banking system creates most of the money supply, while Chapter 12 shows how the Federal Reserve System tries to control the money supply and stabilize the money markets. A brief appendix to Chapter 12 describes recent legislation relating to the money markets. Chapter 13 returns to the main line of the theory developed in chapters 4–9, and deals with the interrelationships between money and the level of economic activity. Finally, Chapter 14 treats inflation, the great macroeconomic problem of our time.

Money does not directly relieve the necessities of life, but is an instrument artificially invented for the easier exchange of natural riches.

Nicholas Oresme, *De Moneta* (ca 1360)

The Use of Banks has been the best Method yet practis'd for the Increase of Money. . . . So far as they lend they add to the Money, which brings a Profit to the Country, by imploying more People, and extending Trade.

John Law, *Money and Trade Considered* (1720)

The importance of money essentially flows from its being a link between the present and the future.

John Maynard Keynes, *The General Theory of Employment, Interest and Money* (1936)

Chapter 10

Money

There are three different ways of thinking about the role of money in the modern private enterprise economy—the neoclassical, monetarist, and post-Keynesian. The neoclassical approach treats money markets as if they were exactly the same as the market for anything else, with a supply and a demand that generate a price, which in this case is a rate of interest. This view leads to treating money in the framework of a general equilibrium of all markets in which relative prices are determined. With the rise of Keynesian economics this approach was modified to include the national income and product equilibrium in the general model. Money, however, is seen essentially as a means by which the exchange of commodities is facilitated rather than as a major determinant of the equilibrium, although it is recognized that the rate of interest and the quantity of money, as part of the general equilibrium, influence and are influenced by adjustment of the system.

The monetarist approach takes up a problem that neoclassical theory has a great deal of difficulty with, the general level of prices. Monetarists argue that the quantity of money determines the level of prices, whatever may be the system of relative prices established in the general equilibrium of markets. Although many economists agree with that conclusion when applied to long-run tendencies, the attempt to apply it to immediate or short-run movements of the general price level is highly controversial.

The post-Keynesian view of money differs from both the neoclassical and the monetarist positions. Post-Keynesians analyze money as an integral part of processes of production and distribution that take place over time in a world of a known past and an unknown future. Money is not simply another commodity among many others but is created as part of the process of producing goods, and the money market functions differently from those of other commodities. Money and money markets respond to the needs of the economy at large for financing, and at the same time add to the instability of the system as a whole.

In many respects there is truth in all three of the approaches to understanding money and the monetary system. In this chapter we select from each the elements that seem to fit best the reality of the modern economy. From the neoclassical analysis we take the concept of money as a means of exchange and the functions it performs in a market system. Next come a definition of money, the forms that money takes in the modern economy, and how much of it there is. That inquiry leads naturally into a discussion of the quantity theory of money and the monetarist position on the general level of prices in the long run. We then turn to the role of money and debt in the process of production and distribution as developed in post-Keynesian theory.

Money as a Medium of Exchange

The use of money as a medium of exchange is often illustrated by a parable. Imagine a Robinson Crusoe economy made up of only one individual. He has no one else with whom he can exchange things, so he has no need for money. Even a small group of people, living in isolation, could exchange goods and services by barter. But a highly complex economy based on voluntary buying and selling in a system of interrelated markets would find a barter system cumbersome and inconvenient. It may be difficult for an individual who has a commodity to exchange for other things to find someone else who has what he wants and wants what he has. Finding him would take time and effort that could be used more productively doing other things. The use of money avoids this drawback of a barter system. With money in use, the goods could be sold for money to anyone, and purchases made from anyone else. As far as the individual is concerned, the person who wants what he has can be different from the person who has what he wants. Any economy based on market exchange would invent money if it did not already have it.

○ Four chief functions are performed by money in an exchange economy. Money acts as (1) a means of payment, (2) a unit of value, (3) a standard of deferred payments, and (4) a store of value.

Money as a Means of Payment
The process of exchange creates an obligation on the part of the buyer to make a payment to the seller. Money paid to the seller discharges that obligation. The buyer can, of course, pay something else, as when a professional baseball team trades a pitcher for an outfielder and a shortstop. But in most transactions a payment in the form of something generally acceptable in making payments is preferred.

The general acceptability of money is vital, for it maximizes the freedom of choice of the person who receives payment. For example, the baseball team may strengthen its playing ability by a trade, but it must have cash to operate its stadium or pay its traveling expenses. Selling the pitcher's contract to another team instead of trading him would enable the team to do that. Money enables people to buy what they want, when they want it, in the quantities desired.

In the modern economy people and business firms must continually buy things and make payments. Money is always being paid out: "Like water, away it flows." Yet income is irregular. Some people get paid weekly, others twice a month, others once a month. The income stream for any single economic unit usually does not exactly coincide with the payment stream. As a result, most people and business firms maintain some holdings of cash to meet their day-to-day needs and carry on the normal transactions of the economy. Economists call this the *transactions demand* for money.

Money as a Unit of Value
The monetary unit acts as a measuring rod that measures the value of any kind of commodity or service. An automobile is worth, say, $3,000, or a certain house $25,000. These values are expressed in dollars, which is the monetary unit, as the most convenient way of stating the value. This function of money results from its general acceptability as a means of payment. Since transactions are completed by making money payments, the automobile or house is valued at the number of dollars for which it can be exchanged. Common stocks,

for example, are normally valued at the price paid for them in the last transaction.

The usefulness of money as a unit of value cannot be overestimated. Accountants know only too well that the condition of a business firm depends on the value attributed to widely different assets, such as cash, accounts receivable, real estate, machinery, and "good will." Assets can't be added up and a net worth determined for the firm until all are expressed in a common unit. The monetary unit serves that purpose.

For money to perform its function as a unit of measurement, its value (or purchasing power) should remain relatively stable. A yardstick that grows or shrinks is of limited usefulness. Yet the value of money depends on what it will buy, that is, on the general level of prices, and does rise and fall as price levels change. One reason for concern about inflation is the difficulty it creates when business firms must make decisions in the face of a changing unit of value.

Although fluctuations in the value of money are inevitable, money has the advantage of relative stability of value. The value of any single commodity, such as wheat or corn, fluctuates more widely than prices in general. Relative to other prices (in markets where prices are not controlled) the purchasing power of money shows a high degree of stability under normal conditions. Nevertheless, the existence of a unit of value that itself fluctuates in value creates problems for the economy.

Money as a Standard of Deferred Payments
Any measure of value and means of payment will become the unit in which future payments are expressed. The modern economy has a huge amount of contracts for payment at some time in the future, or debts; in the United States in 1979, for example, debts amounted to some $4248 billion. In addition, there are such things as long-term salary contracts, leases on property, and contracts for sale of mineral products for long periods of time.

Deferred payments require stability in the value of the monetary unit. Rising prices hurt people who receive future income and benefit those who make future payments. If you borrow today and repay the money after ten years, and prices have gone up in the meantime, you will be repaying money that has less purchasing power than the money you borrowed. The lender, on the other hand, will have lost on the transaction. This is the chief reason why so many bankers (who lend money for a living) insist on maintaining "sound" money that does not decline in value over the years. Just the opposite situation prevails if prices fall over a period of years and the value of the monetary unit rises. Borrowers lose and lenders gain.

These effects of a changing value of money assume greater importance as the economy grows. More people become borrowers and lenders, or acquire ownership interests in financial institutions. Deferred payments assume greater importance in the everyday lives of more and more people. As this trend develops, the issues of equity and economic self-interest associated with changes in the purchasing power of money become more important, stimulate political interest, and lead to a growing concern on the part of government with prices, price levels, and management of the monetary system.

Money as a Store of Value
Since money can be used to make purchases at any time, it is the most convenient form in which to hold assets. Its instant convertibility into other things makes it a highly desirable way to hold wealth. Money, however, is sterile. It does not earn an income. Coins and paper money in your pocket are valuable enough. They give you power to buy things as you need them, to meet emergencies, and even to take advantage of good buys if they should come along. But they do not earn anything for you as long as you hold them.

Money, however, can be transformed into other assets simply by buying them. And those assets can pay an income to the holder. For example, you can deposit cash in a savings account. The bank will make interest payments to you to encourage you to leave your money there while the bank lends it to a borrower at a somewhat higher interest rate. Or, alternatively, you can buy government securities, which will earn a little more income and involve slightly more risk (their price may fall while you hold them). In each case you have given up a highly liquid asset (cash) in order to obtain a somewhat less liquid asset that earns some income. The income you earn is a payment for giving up *liquidity* and for assuming some risk.

In this sense, money is just like any other asset. It combines liquidity, risk, and earning power. In the case of money, the liquidity is almost perfect while the risk and earning power are nil. Other assets will have less liquidity but more earning power and more risk.

- **Liquidity** is a difficult concept to define. It refers to that quality of an asset that enables it to be used in exchange. Money, for example, can always be used to make a purchase or pay a debt. Other things can be used to make payments only after they have been converted into money. The time, cost, and effort required to make that conversion determines the liquidity of an asset. The greater the time and effort, the less the liquidity. For example, a checking account is a more liquid asset than a savings account. You can write a check for a payment at any time of day or night. But money from a savings account can be obtained only during banking hours and only by making a visit to the bank office (except when withdrawals are made by mail, which may take two or more days).

  The flexibility achieved through liquidity is maintained at the cost of earning power and (sometimes) safety. The more highly liquid checking account earns little income, but the less liquid savings account earns more. Cash, which is more liquid than a checking account, earns nothing, and is less safe—it is a prime target for a thief. Thieves like liquidity, too, in their victims.

Owners of assets always have the option of holding their wealth in a variety of forms. Most investors hold some money at all times, and distribute their other wealth among a wide variety of other assets with differing combinations of liquidity, safety, and earning power: savings accounts, government bonds, corporate or municipal bonds, common stocks, real estate, precious metals, or jewelry, and many other forms. The various proportions of each in an investor's "portfolio" depend on the investor's expectations about the future. If investors expect prices of certain assets to rise, they invest some of their cash in those they expect to rise the most. Expectations of increased value from holding other assets reduce their desire to hold cash. On the other hand, if investors expect prices of assets to fall they will sell some of their assets and shift to greater liquidity all down the line. But they probably won't liquidate entirely and hold all their wealth in cash, since their expectations might be wrong.

In this fashion, investors, speculators, and managers of assets, following their own self-interest, influence not only the money markets but the markets for financial assets of all kinds. As their expectations change, their desire for liquidity versus income will shift, and there will be repercussions on the level of output and income as well as on the money and securities markets. Money is an asset, and, like any asset, the demand for it can change as the expectations of consumers, business people, and speculators change. This *demand for money as an asset* will shift with changing business conditions and the expectations of businesses, and in doing so will have an impact on the level of employment and output.

"Near Money"

Some assets can be so readily converted into money with so little risk of loss that many people look upon them as almost the same as money. For example, a college student at the University of Michigan typically uses a savings rather than a checking account for temporarily holding funds. Even though banks allow only three withdrawals per month without charge, students manage to avoid the service charges applied to small checking accounts. They deposit their cash monthly and carry the amounts needed in between their thrice-monthly withdrawals. They tend to hold larger amounts of cash this way, but in other respects there is no appreciable influence on their spending behavior.

People or business firms with larger amounts of cash at their disposal will use short-term government securities or large-denomination certificates of deposit in a similar way. For example, a corporation may have cash totaling several hundred thousand dollars that is not needed right away. The money can be invested in 30-day or 90-day Treasury "bills" (short-term promissory notes of the federal government) to earn a little income until the money is needed and the bills are sold.

These types of assets are sometimes called *near money*. They are almost as liquid as money itself and, used in this way, earn very little. For some purposes it can be useful to treat them as money, particularly if "total liquid assets" are the subjects of analysis. But in this book they will be treated as nonmonetary assets, albeit the ones next to money itself on the liquidity-of-assets continuum.

- **Near money** refers to highly liquid assets that can readily be exchanged for money.

In recent years several new types of near moneys have appeared. Banks can now automatically transfer funds from a customer's savings account to his or her checking account. This practice in effect transforms the savings account into a checking account. Savings and loan associations allow depositors to write drafts payable on demand against their accounts. Mutual funds that invest in short-term money market securities allow their customers to write checks against their accounts. These practices greatly widen the assets that can be used to make payments, and have blurred the formerly clear distinctions between checking accounts, savings accounts and investments.

A Definition of Money

- **Money** is an asset that is generally acceptable in making payments, in the uses to which it is ordinarily put.

This definition is both broad and narrow at the same time. It includes coin and paper money because they are customarily used for a wide variety of small retail transactions. But even those forms of money are not acceptable for some payments. Try paying a New York taxi-cab driver with a $100 bill, for example. This definition also includes checking accounts in banks, because checks are used in making payments in a wide variety of purchases. But not in all. You can't buy a newspaper with a check, where a coin will do; and there are many types of retail transactions in which checks are not accepted.

The inclusion of *demand deposits* (checking accounts) in the money supply is important. By far the largest volume of transactions is carried out by using checks to make payment. Upwards of 95 percent of all transactions, measured in dollars, in the United States are carried out with checks. Furthermore, most checking accounts are created out of the economic activity of business firms, and the amount of checking accounts in existence at any time is closely related to the level of economic activity. This form of money is not created by government but by the private sector of the economy: as we shall see in the following chapter, checking accounts are created by banks in their efforts to make a profit for their stockholders. Governments impose constraints on this private creation of a portion of the money supply, but checking accounts remain a private obligation and not a public one.

Table 10–1
Money Supply of the United States
(billions of dollars, as of February 1980)

Currency in circulation	106.9
Demand deposits	261.2
M–1A	368.1
Other checkable deposits	16.5
M–1B	384.6

Table 10–2
Near Moneys in the United States
(billions of dollars, as of February 1980)

Savings accounts and small time deposits	1074.7
Large time deposits	228.3
Money market mutual funds	56.7
Other near moneys	59.7
	1419.4

At this point the definition of money becomes a bit murky. Traditionally, the money supply has been defined to comprise currency in circulation and demand deposits in commercial banks. But with the appearance of other types of deposits subject to check it would seem logical to include them as well. And what about the near moneys that can quickly be transformed into checking accounts? Because of these confusions the money supply is measured in several ways. We start with currency in circulation and demand deposits in commercial banks for the narrowest measure of the money supply (M–1A) and then add other checkable deposits for a somewhat broader measure (M–1B). This is the measure of the money supply that will be used in this book (see Table 10–1).

Some economists would include in the money supply various types of savings accounts, time deposits, and mutual funds against which checks can be drawn, so we include another table that shows these near moneys.

The Value of Money
One of the most widespread of economic fallacies is the belief that money derives its value from some kind of "backing" or "security" that guarantees its value. Gold is the asset usually nominated as the source of the *value of money* by the makers of this myth. The belief dies hard, but like the unicorn, it is pure mythology.

It is true that coins are made from metal, which has a market value as pure metal. But their market value is usually considerably less than the face value of the coin. If it were not, the coin would be melted down for the value of the metal; which is why silver dollars don't circulate anymore.

Paper money in the United States is not even issued by the national government, but by the Federal Reserve system. Although the governors of the Fed are appointed by the President, with approval by the U.S. Senate, its operating units are owned by the banks that are members of the system. Nor is this paper money a promise to pay. It is identified on its face as a:

Federal Reserve Note
The United States of America
One Dollar

and there is no statement that anyone is obliged to pay anyone else when the slip of paper changes hand. Take a $20 Federal Reserve Note to a Federal Reserve Bank, demand payment, and you will get another $20 bill.

But surely, you might respond, our paper money is "backed" or "secured" by something. Indeed it is. The Federal Reserve Banks must hold a "reserve" of either government securities or promissory notes from private business firms equal to the value of Federal Reserve notes in circulation. Most of the reserve is government bonds. But hold on a moment—a government bond is just a promise to pay a certain amount of money at some future time. And the money in which it is paid is nothing but our friend the Federal Reserve note. We have come full circle. Your $20 bill is a government promise to pay, which is secured by another promise to pay, which in turn is payable in the first promise to pay.

If money does not derive its value from any intrinsic qualities or from its backing or security, where does its value come from? One clue can be obtained from the functions of money described earlier in this chapter. Money is generally acceptable in making payments. It derives this acceptability in part because the government will take it in payment of taxes. More fundamentally, it is limited in quantity. Money doesn't grow on trees. It cannot be obtained for the asking. It cannot be plucked out of the air. In order to obtain money, something else must be exchanged for it. People work for it, thereby exchanging services for money. Other people sell things in order to get money.

○ Money is worth what it will bring in exchange, just like any other asset. The value of money is determined by the value of the commodities it will buy. If prices rise the value of the dollar falls, because it will buy less. The *purchasing power* of the monetary unit determines its value.

The Quantity Theory of Money

In the relatively simple economy of preindustrial Europe, in which the creation of money was independent of the level of production, a simple relationship between the quantity of money and the level of prices could be observed. If a government increased the quantity of coins or paper money faster than production grew, prices tended to rise. The reason was simple. The amount of goods available for sale was being bid for by an increased purchasing power, and the market adjustment process brought higher prices. Or if the quantity of money remained the same while output fell, perhaps because of war or crop failure, a similar imbalance occurred and prices rose. Or if coins were exported to buy foreign goods, prices tended to rise.

These observed relationships led to the famous *quantity theory of money,* which holds that changes in the quantity of money cause changes in the level of prices, that the level of economic activity itself is influenced by the quantity of money, and that in the long run the value of money depends on the quantity in circulation. The quantity theory was formalized by the American economist Irving Fisher (1867–1947) in the equation of exchange. This proposition is a statement of the truism that the total amount spent in an economy equals the value of all goods purchased. Fisher stated it in the following form:

$$MV = PT$$

where

M = the quantity of money
V = the velocity of circulation of money
P = the general level of prices
T = the number of monetary transactions.

Solving for P yields

$$P = \frac{MV}{T}$$

or, in words, the general level of prices is determined by the quantity of money, the velocity of its circulation, and the level of economic activity. If the latter two factors remain constant or if changes in one offset changes in the other, then changes in the quantity of money will cause changes in the level of prices.

Fisher assumed that the economy in the long run would operate at full-employment levels, and he argued that the quantity theory applied only to that "normal" condition. He also believed that in the long run the *velocity of circulation of money* (the number of times during the year that the money supply was spent) tends to remain stable, and his empirical studies showed that it tends to change only

MEASURING MONEY

The rapid development of "near moneys" in recent years—assets with a high degree of liquidity—made the definition of money quite murky. The Board of Governors of the Federal Reserve System, therefore, adopted some new definitions to try to bring some order into measurement of the supply of money.

M–1A Currency plus demand deposits at commercial banks (except deposits by other banks, foreign banks and official institutions, and the U.S. government). As of November 1979, $372 Billion.

M–1B M–1A plus other checkable deposits. This is the most widely used measure of the money supply, $388 billion as of November 1979.

M–2 M–1B plus savings deposits, small time deposits (under $100,000), money market mutual fund shares, and two types of "overnight" assets (redeemable the next day): "repurchase" agreements of U.S. commercial banks and "Eurodollar" deposits by U.S. residents in Caribbean branches of member banks. $1510 billion in November 1979. Eur-odollars are dollar deposits in banks outside the U.S.; repurchase agreements are a form of loan from one bank to another.

M–3 M–2 plus large denomination time deposits and longer term repurchase agreements. $1759 billion in November 1979.

L. M–3 plus other liquid assets, such as short-term obligations of the U.S. Treasury, U.S. savings bonds, bankers acceptances, and commercial paper (short-term IOU's of business firms), and other Eurodollar deposits held by U.S. citizens. $2,124 billion in November 1979.

So, there you are—four measures of the money supply ranging from $372 billion to $1,759 billion and one measure of liquidity of $2,124 billion (as of November 1979). Everyone is still confused, but no one wants to admit it. The definitions are arbitrary, of course. Holdings of gold and silver, for example, are not included, simply because no one knows how large they are. Nor are other forms of wealth included, even though they also have the quality of liquidity. As one wag commented, "Soon we'll have M–20: M–19 plus old master paintings."

very slowly. Under these assumptions the equation of exchange tells us that if the supply of money M increases at about the same rate as economic activity T, the price level will remain stable. Prices will fall, however, if M increases more slowly than T; and prices will rise if M rises more rapidly than T.

The quantity theory of money was also developed into an explanation for business cycles and depressions as well as inflations. During the nineteenth century banks rather than governments became the most important source of money and credit, and checking accounts in banks became the chief form taken by money. (The next chapter explains how banks create credit and add to the money supply by making loans.) Many economists argued that overexpansion of the money supply by banks could bring excessive expansion of production and rising prices, leading to a financial crisis when expansion of bank loans reached its limits. During the ensuing recession, excessive contraction of the money supply would make things worse and add to the forces of depression. The solution to the problem seemed clear: manage and control the lending activities of banks so as to stabilize the supply of money and credit at the level necessary for a full-employment level of economic activity. The Federal Reserve System was born in the United States, and central banks were established in other countries, to manage the monetary systems of the nations of the world and thereby achieve economic stability.

This monetary theory of depressions was heavily discredited during the Great Depression of the 1930s, and the quantity theory of money went into a long eclipse. The depression itself was attributed by most economists to fundamental problems in the economy as a whole and not only to difficulties in the monetary system. Insufficient aggregate demand was the chief problem, and the Keynesian analysis focused on that issue. Monetary explanations for the depression seemed irrelevant. Furthermore, recovery in output and employment was the immediate policy goal, the problem of price levels was secondary, and the long run orientation of an approach like Fisher's equation of exchange could not come to grips with the short run objectives of economic recovery. The quantity theory of money fell into disrepute.

Revival and Revision of the Quantity Theory

The quarter-century after World War II saw a great revival of the quantity theory of money. These were years largely of full employment, interrupted it is true by periodic recessions, but characterized principally by vigorous growth and relatively high levels of employment. These were close to the conditions postulated by Fisher's analysis of the long run relation between prices and the money supply. Those years were also characterized by persistent increases in price levels. The bulk of the price increases were attributed by Keynesians to excessive aggregate demand during times of war: the aftermath of World War II, the Korean War, the Vietnam war. But a persistent creeping inflation seemed also to be at work, even during recessions, that could nor be explained adequately by the Keynesian theory of national income. Led by Milton Friedman of the University of Chicago, many economists began to turn back to the quantity theory of money.

The basic propositions of the quantity theory were modified in order to fit the new national income concepts. Fisher's equation of exchange was altered, replacing transactions T with total output Q (an analog of GNP, or total output of final products). The altered equation became:

$$MV = PQ$$

where

M = the quantity of money
V = the velocity of circulation of money (relative to GNP)
P = the general level of prices
Q = total output (GNP)

Solving for P yields

$$P = \frac{MV}{Q}$$

which is essentially the same as the older formulation, except that the Keynesian GNP is the measure of economic activity used.

A Modernized Quantity Theory of Money

Contemporary "monetarists"—those economists who support the modernized quantity theory of money—analyze the level of income and output, and price levels, in terms of the demand for and supply of money. The key proposition is that there is a normal relationship between the demand for money and the level of GNP. For example, suppose that when GNP is $1000 billion consumers will be willing to hold cash of $250 billion in currency and checking accounts. The ratio in this case is 4 to 1. In monetarist terms, $V = 4$: if the supply of money is spent four times during the year it will be just sufficient to buy the GNP of $1000 billion. This relationship defines the equilibrium that relates the money supply to the level of output at the existing level of prices.

Now let's see what happens if the equilibrium is disturbed. Let the supply of money *M* be increased to $275 billion, with no initial change in GNP. Economic units will now have an additional $25 billion they do not wish to hold as part of their assets. They will spend it instead. Spending it will add to aggregate demand and GNP will rise. GNP will continue to rise until the 4:1 ratio between GNP and *M* is once more established. With *M* = $275 billion the equilibrium GNP will be $1100 billion. If the former level of $1000 billion was at the production capacity limit of the economy the increase in GNP will bring a 10 percent rise in the general price level.

In terms of the revised equation of exchange, $MV = PQ$, the old and new equilibria look like this:

1. Original equilibrium
$$(250)(4) = (1)(1000)$$

2. New equilibrium, with unchanged prices, enlarged output
$$(275)(4) = (1)(1100)$$

3. New equilibrium, with higher prices, unchanged output
$$(275)(4) = (1.1)(1000)$$

In the real world these relationships would only be approximated, because other factors would probably not remain constant. But the basic tendency would be there.

To check your understanding of these relationships, work out what would happen if the original equilibrium (*M* = $250 billion; GNP = $1000 billion) were disturbed by a decrease in *M* to $200 billion? Would *P* decline by 20 percent to 0.8? Would *Q* fall by 20 percent to $800 billion? Or would both decline, each by somewhat less than 20 percent, until a new *PQ* equilibrium is reached at a level of 80 percent of the old? The last is the general rule, with the first two the limiting cases: the economy would be deflated to 80 percent of its former level:

$$MV = PQ$$
$$(200)(4) = (800)$$

- The **quantity theory of money** is the theory that price levels and economic activity are directly related to the quantity of money. Sometimes the theory is stated in the form of the equation of exchange $MV = PQ$, which relates the quantity of money *M* and its velocity of circulation *V* to the level of economic activity *PQ*, where *Q* stands for the economy's GNP.

- The **velocity of circulation of money**, in the modernized quantity theory, is the ratio of GNP to the money supply (Q/M).

The Monetary Rule

Economists who support the modernized quantity theory of money generally do not advocate an active policy of manipulating the money supply to compensate for the short run ups and downs of the economy. The predominant view among them is that such a policy would add to the instability of the economy.

Rather, they argue that the money supply should increase at about the same pace as output. A growing economy needs additional supplies of money. If *M* does not rise as fast as *Q*, *P* will fall (assuming *V* remains the same). Falling prices will then have a retarding effect on additional investment and growth of the economy will slow down. On the other hand, if *M* rises faster than *Q*, *P* will rise. The ensuing inflation will either bring on a downturn, or cause savings to fall and the rate of growth to drop, or both. The monetary rule then becomes:

○ In order to sustain stable economic growth, that is, full employment and price stability in a growing economy, the supply of money should increase at approximately the same rate as the real growth rate of output.

Why do we use the word "approximately" in the rule? Because the velocity of circulation of money seems to show a tendency to increase over the long run. The chief reason for a rising *V* seems to be the growing efficiency of banks and business firms in using and transferring funds and the development of new economic institutions, such as credit cards, that enable existing supplies of money to be used more effectively in handling transactions. But whatever the reason, there seems to be a long run pattern of a slowly rising *V*, which means that *M* should increase at a rate slightly below the growth rate of *Q* in order to compensate for increases in *V*.

One final caveat: all this is very much simplified. This explanation of the modernized quantity theory of money was designed to get at the underlying concepts, stripped of their complications. No economist, monetarist or otherwise, would argue that the real world is as simple as this explanation. But the basic point stands out: there is a long-run relationship between the demand for money, on the one hand, and the level of output and prices, on the other. The relationship may be highly complex, but the monetarist would argue that it prevails in the long run.

Money and Inflation

The monetarist view of the economy attributed the high rates of inflation of recent years very largely to increases in the money supply that outstripped the growth of output. Here, for example, is a quotation from an editorial in *The Wall Street Journal*:

> Inflation results when the Fed expands the supply of money faster than the economy expands the supply of goods. Factors such as spurts in the price of oil or food have some short-run effect, but over any meaningful period of time are only excuses. To understand why we have had increasingly serious inflation, look at the history of monetary growth: an average yearly rate of 7.4% to mid '74 from '72, 6% to '72 from late '66, 3.8% to '66 from mid '62, and 1.8% to '62 from '52.[1]

This view was echoed in the *Review* of the Federal Reserve Bank of St. Louis, which has been an important spokesman for the monetarist position for many years:

The basic underlying cause of the inflation currently being experienced in the United States is simply that the growth trend of money has been accelerating over the last ten years, approaching a 7 percent rate on average over the last three years. This has resulted in a growth of demand for goods and services that is much greater than the long-term average growth of real output.[2]

All economists will agree that the money supply is important, but the extent of its significance and how it affects other aspects of the economy is open to debate. We shall see later that the causes of inflation are far more complex than those quoted here, for instance.

Money and Debt

In a capitalist economy money consists of two distinct elements related to the processes of production and distribution. The simplest element is currency (coins and paper money) used by consumers to make daily purchases. The second part is the credit created by lenders to finance the continuing operation of economic units. The bulk of that credit is extended by commercial banks in the form of loans to consumers and business firms and is measured, roughly, by the amount of demand deposits in the banking system. This credit may take the form of an installment loan to a consumer, loans for purchase of inventories by retail or wholesale sellers, or a line of credit for use as general working capital by a manufacturing enterprise, to give some common examples. In each case the extension of credit provides funds that will have to be repaid in the future: a *debt* is created. Repayment depends on the ability of the borrower to generate a stream of income in the future, out of which there will be a large enough surplus to repay the loan.

---

[1]*The Wall Street Journal*, October 11, 1974.

[2]Federal Reserve Bank of St Louis *Review* 56, 9 (September 1974): 22.

● A **debt** is a deferred payment, created when a borrower arranges to repay an agreed upon sum to a lender.

For example, when a bank establishes a line of credit for a manufacturing firm, with the funds to be used for general operating expenses, both the lender and the borrower expect that the sale of goods produced by the firm will provide a flow of revenues large enough to pay the costs of production and distribution, plus principal and interest on the loan, plus a normal profit to the firm. The manufacturing firm is then in a position to enter contracts with suppliers to obtain raw materials and semifinished goods for use in the production process. The suppliers, in turn, can now obtain credit from other banks to finance their operations. Meanwhile, the original manufacturing firm is able to hire labor with a promise to pay workers by the day, week or month. The employees will then be able to borrow to buy automobiles or other goods on the basis of the income they expect to receive in wages and salaries.

A capitalist economic system functions, then, through an interlocking web of debts based on an ongoing process of production and distribution. Each debt results in the creation of purchasing power for some economic unit. In the process money is created. It increases in amount as economic activity grows. When economic activity declines, so does the amount of money and debt. Seen in this light, money is not merely a means of exchange, nor is its quantity independent of the production process affecting only the general level of prices. Money is created as part of the process of production and distribution. The amount of money increases as economic activity grows and decreases when economic activity declines.

Debt and Economic Activity

Any transaction will result in debt. Even when you buy a newspaper at the corner newsstand, a debt is created, although in that case it is extinguished almost immediately by payment in cash. In most cases, however, debt is not immediately paid, and the transaction results in a deferred payment (debt) of some kind. The important point to remember is that economic activity gives rise to deferred payments. The presence of these debts is an indication of economic activity. The less the economic activity, the fewer will be the number of transactions and the lower will be the level of debt. Just the opposite is also true: the more the economic activity the greater the total amount of debt.

There is a clear relationship between debt and economic activity:

○ If the level of debt is reduced, the flow of spending will decline and employment and production will fall.

○ If the level of debt is increased, purchasing power will rise and employment and production will grow until the economy reaches full employment, at which point prices will start to rise.

In sustaining or increasing purchasing power, it makes little difference where the borrowed funds come from or who does the borrowing. Public debt will stimulate the growth of purchasing power just as well as private debt. Private borrowers spend the money they borrow, and so do governments. In both cases the money enters the stream of spending and adds to aggregate demand.

As we saw in Chapter 4, during a period of economic expansion debt grows more rapidly than output and incomes. Business debt is incurred because firms expect the funds they borrow to generate a flow of income sufficient to pay off the debt and interest on the loan, and earn a profit as well. Consumers expect their future incomes to be large enough to pay interest and principal on the loan. Lenders have the same expectations, which is why they are willing to risk making a loan. Figure 10–1

Figure 10-1
Debt and Economic Activity, 1946–1979

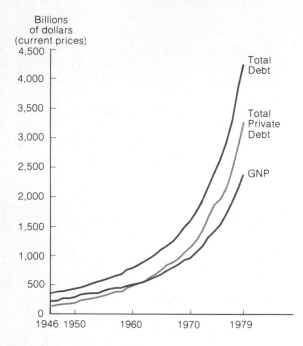

shows this process at work from 1946 to 1979. Between 1946 and 1979, GNP rose by 1025 percent and total debt increased by 1100 percent, but private debt increased by 2862 percent. During the same period, public debt rose by only 297 percent, from $243 billion to $964 billion.

Monetary Instability

Commitments to pay debts must be met if the system of production and distribution is to continue. If business firms are unable to pay their debts, the viability of the financial institutions that made the loans is weakened, and their ability to continue lending is reduced. Firms unable to repay their debts will also find that they are unable to obtain additional financing and will have to reduce output and employment. The reduced flow of spending will spread the financial problem to other parts of the economy. If the firms and banks in difficulty are large and prominent, a general loss of confidence in the financial system and the network of debt can cause a general rush on the part of firms, banks, and individuals to obtain cash. The economic system is vulnerable to *financial crises* from time to time unless it is protected from them.

- A **financial crisis** is a situation in which the ability of many debtors to meet their commitments is doubtful, threatening the stability of the financial system.

The economy itself creates the conditions that generate financial problems. When economic conditions are good, the economy stable, and the flow of funds uninterrupted and growing, business firms take on added debts in order to expand operations and increase their profits. The growth of economic activity causes spending to grow, which validates the decisions to expand production. Banks, of course, are happy to lend and increase their profits, too. Under these conditions, both borrowers and lenders become less cautious. Riskier activities are financed, debts grow more rapidly than the assets of borrowers, and payments of principal and interest rise relative to the incomes of both business firms and consumers. Firms begin to anticipate a rising flow of income, and when their debt is refinanced, it is increased relative to their assets and income. If the increase in income does not occur they will be in trouble, unable to repay the commitments they have incurred. At that point a slowdown in economic activity can start the debt cycle spiraling downward.

The instability of a private enterprise monetary system is not merely theoretical. Financial crises followed by "debt deflation" have occurred periodically, and a rising ratio of debt to incomes and assets is characteristic of any period of sustained prosperity. In the years after World War II in the U.S. economy the period up to the mid-1960s of sustained growth and minor recessions was free of serious financial strain, but a continuing increase in debt led to a weakened financial structure. The result was a succession of "credit crunches," as they have come to be called, in 1966, 1970–71, 1974–75, and 1980. Serious difficulties were avoided only by the Federal Reserve System's prompt action to support financial markets.

Accommodation and Protection

The financial system requires two contradictory types of assistance. On the one hand, it must meet the financial needs of business enterprise —creation of debt to finance production and distribution. The banking system will normally perform that function well, generating the money supply needed by consumers and business firms to carry on normal economic activity. But that *accommodation* function requires that banks hold adequate reserves to provide the loans needed. Central banks—the Federal Reserve System in the U.S.—were invented to see to it that the banking system is able to provide the credit required by the economy. How that is done and how the central bank attempts to manage the money supply is explained in Chapter 12.

But accommodation also means that funds are provided for financing the growing debt burden characteristic of prosperous periods that leads to unstable financial conditions. The possibility of financial crises due to rising debt burdens requires that protection be provided to prevent collapse of the financial system. That protection function is also performed by central banks, which must be ready to provide funds in an emergency to either the financial system as a whole or to individual financial enterprises. The central bank is the system's *lender of last resort*, as it is called, and we will have more to say about that in Chapter 12.

- **Accommodation** is the process of providing adequate funds to business and consumers to finance production and distribution.
- The **lender of last resort** is the central bank, which must be ready to provide funds in situations that threaten a financial collapse.

A paradox arises because the central bank's performance of its accommodation function creates the conditions that require it to protect the system and act as a lender of last resort. The central bank cannot prevent financial instability, it can only attempt to prevent financial difficulties from becoming a financial breakdown. In recent years the Federal Reserve System has succeeded in performing its protection function effectively when financial crises threatened. In 1933 it was not successful.

Summary

Money acts as a medium of exchange in a market economy. It functions as a means of payment, a unit of value, a standard for deferred payments, and a store of value. As an asset, it has a high degree of liquidity and can be used to acquire other assets. All assets have varying degrees of liquidity, and those that can most readily be transformed into the means of payment are called near monies. The simplest definition of money is that it is an asset that is generally acceptable in making payments, in the uses to which it is ordinarily put.

The money supply of the United States is dominated by demand deposits (checking accounts), which are supplemented by paper money and coins. Only the coins are issued by the federal government. Paper money is issued by the Federal Reserve System, and checking accounts are created by privately owned banks.

The value of money is determined by its purchasing power and not by any intrinsic value or backing. According to the quantity theory of money, prices are directly related to the quantity of money, and an increase in the money supply at a rate approximately equal to the real growth of output is necessary for stability in the general level of prices.

Money is an essential element in the financial system of a private enterprise economy. Money and debt are created when economic activity rises or falls. The process of financing production, distribution, and investment leads to financial instability, however, and a central bank is necessary both to assure the creation of an adequate supply of money and credit and to protect the financial system from its own instability.

Key Concepts

liquidity	quantity theory of money	financial crisis
near money	velocity of circulation of money	accommodation
money	debt	lender of last resort

For Discussion

1. What characteristics does money possess that make it desirable as a medium of exchange?
2. What are the key assumptions required to make the quantity theory of money?
3. Why do people hold money when it does not earn any income for them?
4. According to the post-Keynesian analysis, what role does the supply of money play in determining the level of economic activity?
5. What are the implications for government policy of the three perspectives on the role of money?
6. Which of the three theories of the role of money—neoclassical, monetarist, and post-Keynesian—is most nearly correct, either alone or in combination?

Appendix 10 A

The Monetary Functions of Gold

Gold and silver have been monetary metals since ancient times. Coins minted from those metals circulated widely. Gold and silver were for years the basis for defining the monetary units of the major commercial nations of the world, and until World War I most paper currencies were normally redeemable in gold or silver coins.

In the twentieth century, however, those two precious metals gradually relinquished their central positions in the monetary systems of the world. The amount of money and credit within an individual nation is no longer tied to reserves of monetary gold. Gold is still used in the international monetary system, but even here its importance has been greatly reduced by changes that occurred over the last fifty years.

The "Gold Standard"

Contrary to general belief, the so-called "gold standard" is no older than the nineteenth century. Its heyday was the period between the Napoleonic wars and World War I, an era of economic growth, industrialization, relatively stable international political conditions, and British hegemony in the world economy. The era of the gold standard may be said to have begun with passage of the Coinage Act of 1816 by the English Parliament. Its demise came with World War I and the suspension of gold payments by the Bank of England in 1914, although

that measure was thought to be only a temporary wartime expedient. Efforts were made after the war to put Humpty Dumpty back together, but he was never the same again.

The gold standard of 1816–1914 embodied several key provisions in a nation's monetary system:

1. The monetary unit was defined in gold. For example, the Gold Standard Act of 1900 in the United States defined the gold dollar as equal to 25.8 grains of gold nine-tenths fine (fineness is a measure of purity). This tied the "value" of the monetary unit to the price of gold.

2. The government undertook to coin gold at the offical standard, subtracting something (seignorage) to cover the costs of the mint. That is, anyone could take gold bars to the Treasury and exchange them for the equivalent amount of gold coins. This provision tied the amount of gold coins in circulation to the amount of gold available.

3. Paper money was redeemable in gold. Any legal tender, whether issued by the government itself or by private banks, could be exchanged for gold coins. In this country that meant currency circulated by national banks as well as by the federal government. This provision tied the amount of paper money to the nation's gold reserve. A government might issue more paper money than its gold reserve, but not much

more: it always had to face the possibility that people would try to redeem paper money and get gold. Any government wishing to maintain monetary stability would be careful to avoid the risk of a "run" on its paper money by limiting the amount issued to a sum close to its gold reserve. In practice most countries issued paper money only up to the limit of the gold reserve.

Many countries made exceptions to these rules. For example, the United States Treasury issued silver certificates redeemable in coined silver dollars, but they were a minor part of the money supply. Other exceptions prevailed in other countries, but the basic concept was the same everywhere: gold was the ultimate reserve for a nation's monetary system.

The gold standard had two important effects. First, it placed a limit on the amount of money available. This was done in two ways. Gold coin and paper money were directly limited by the requirements of the gold standard. Bank credit was indirectly limited. We shall subsequently see that creation of credit by the banking system is limited by the amount of currency in circulation (in the absence of any legal limits). Since the amount of currency under the gold standard was limited by the gold reserve, a limit was also placed on the amount of credit that banks could extend.

Second, the gold standard created fixed relationships between the moneys of the various nations of the world. Each monetary unit—dollar, pound, franc, mark, yen, and other—was defined in specific amounts of gold. These fixed relationships created monetary equivalents for every currency in terms of every other currency, and efforts were made to maintain those ratios in the money markets. Table 10–3 shows the value in dollars of some of the world's leading currencies, based on their definition in gold in 1968, before devaluation of the dollar finally brought the system to an end. That is, the par value of the Italian lira was 0.2 cent, the German mark 25 cents, the English pound $2.40, and so on.

At the present time the values of the various currencies of the world rise and fall in response to supply and demand in the world's money markets. There is no effective "par value" for the dollar or any other currency. Currency prices "float" in response to market forces. Gold is still held by na-

Table 10–3
Value of Important Currencies in Dollars, 1968

Country	Currency	Par Value in Dollars
England	Pound	$2.40
France	Franc	.203
Germany	Mark	.250
Italy	Lira	.002
Japan	Yen	.003

tions, however, as a means of settling balances in international payments, but even that use for gold is highly restricted. The "gold standard" as it existed before World War I is dead.

Gold in the U.S. Monetary System

The experience of the United States with the gold standard is both interesting and instructive. Our first effort to establish a sound monetary system used a bimetallic standard based on both gold and silver. The Coinage Act of 1792 defined the dollar in terms of gold (24.75 grains) and silver (371.25 grains). This was a ratio of 15 to 1, that is, $24.75 \times 15 = 371.25$. The ratio was very close to the relationship between the prices of gold and silver in commercial markets and seemed reasonable at the time. But the price of silver soon fell (relative to gold) until the market ratio was close to $15\frac{1}{2}$ to 1. As a result, gold disappeared from circulation and the country was, in fact, on a silver standard.

The reason for the disappearance of gold was that silver could be brought to the mint and exchanged for gold at the ratio of one ounce of gold for 15 ounces of silver. The gold could then be exchanged on world markets for $15\frac{1}{2}$ ounces of silver. A profit of one-half ounce of silver could be made on each set of transactions. As long as this differential was greater than the costs of the transactions plus shipping costs, silver would be imported into the United States, exchanged for gold at the Treasury and the gold exported for sale abroad. The result was that the country's gold reserve disappeared and was replaced by silver. It was an illustration of Gresham's law that the cheaper metal circulates and the more expensive one disappears, or "bad money drives out good."[1]

The disappearance of gold from circulation did not make much difference to the nation's economy and caused no problems for anyone until gold was discovered in North Carolina and Georgia. Then it became politically expedient to "keep the gold at home." The result was passage of the Coinage Acts of 1834 and 1837, which revised the ratio of gold to silver to almost 16 to 1. The dollar was revalued to 23.22 grains of gold, but left at 371.25 grains of silver, for a ratio of 15.988 to 1. Since the market ratio was only about 15.73 to 1 at the time, gold was worth more at the mint than in the open market and the flow of metals was reversed. Gold was imported into the United States and exchanged at the Treasury for silver until all the silver was gone and the country's monetary reserve consisted of gold. Gold coins circulated instead of silver, except for subsidiary coinage in which the silver content was so far below the face value of the coins it was not worth while to melt them down.

The United States was now, in effect, on the gold standard while paying lip service to bimetallism. The Coinage Act of 1853 reduced the use of silver to subsidiary coinage (less than $1 face value). After the Civil War, a sop was thrown to silver mining interests by requiring the Treasury to coin silver dollars as "backing" for silver certificates, which circulated as paper money. Then, after the bitter political campaign of 1896 in which the monetary system was the chief issue, the victors passed the Gold Standard Act of 1900 to put the nation firmly on a gold-based standard of value. Except for the Civil War years and their aftermath (1861–79), when gold payments were suspended, the United States was on a gold standard from 1834 to 1934.

In those years, the nation's monetary system changed radically. Prior to the Civil War a wide variety of paper money appeared and circulated. Most of the nation's monetary gold came to rest in the vaults of the Treasury rather than circulating as gold coin. The development of fractional reserve banking made possible a large expansion of bank loans based on relatively limited reserves, to parallel the vast economic growth of the nation. This made possible a large expansion of the money supply based on relatively small reserves of gold.

In theory, the gold standard should have brought stability to the monetary system. Reserves of gold would permit issuance of a limited amount of paper money, which in turn would permit creation of a limited amount of bank credit. As long as banks lent for legitimate business purposes such as financing investment or harvesting crops, the loans would be sound and excessive expansion of credit could be avoided. The money supply would adjust itself to the needs of the economy. This was the theory behind the National Banking System, which prevailed from 1864 to 1914. National banks, which did the bulk of the banking business, were required to keep their reserves in cash—gold coins, gold certificates, or silver certificates. This meant that once the gold standard was restored in 1879, bank reserves were ultimately redeemable in gold and the amount of bank credit was limited by the size of the nation's monetary gold supply.

But this system did not bring stability. For example, when the Treasury bought gold—and this was an erratic rather than a steady flow—it issued new gold certificates to pay for the purchase. This expanded the money supply. When the new currency was deposited in banks, the reserves of the banking system were increased, to act as a base for further expansion of bank credit. This expansion took place because of Treasury gold purchases, whether the economy needed a larger money supply or not.

Instability could also occur because of the public's desire to hold currency. When cash was needed at Christmas, Easter, or harvest time, it would be withdrawn from banks, reserves would dwindle, bank loans would be cut, and shortages of credit would appear just when the economy needed expansion. Far from bringing stability, the gold standard promoted wide swings in economic activity through large fluctuations in the credit structure.

Nor was inflation prevented by convertibility of paper money into gold. The United States in 1897–1914 experienced a severe and prolonged peacetime inflation. Prices rose by almost 50 percent in a little over 15 years. Gold discoveries in Alaska, Colorado, and Australia, plus improved methods of

---

[1]Gresham's law was named after Thomas Gresham (1519–79), one of Queen Elizabeth I's advisors on monetary affairs, who neither originated nor ever stated the idea. He was famous for other aspects of monetary policy. The rule that the least valuable money would circulate instead of the most valuable is found in early writings on the precious metals that date from the fifth century B.C. It was probably known but not written down long before then.

obtaining gold from ores, increased gold production substantially. Most of the new gold moved into monetary reserves. The fractional reserve banking system multiplied the effect of the new gold on the monetary system. "Easy money" pushed the expansion of purchasing power upward faster than output expanded and prices rose persistently, not only in the United States but in other nations as well.

An important change in the system came in 1913, with passage of the Federal Reserve Act, and the present era of managed money began. Under the new system the supply of money was to be adjusted to promote the stability the old system could not achieve. The amount of money came to be limited by men rather than by the gold reserve. Nevertheless, the fiction of a gold base for the monetary system was retained, largely for psychological reasons. Some people feared that the new system might lead to an unlimited inflationary expansion of the money supply and demanded provisions that put a lid on the potential expansion of credit. Consequently, the act required the Federal Reserve banks to keep a gold reserve against their liabilities: 40 percent against Federal Reserve notes and 35 percent against deposits. But in order to prevent interference with the real purposes of the act, the Board of Governors was empowered to set aside the gold reserve requirement if the need arose.

The Fed, as the Federal Reserve Board is commonly called, never allowed its management of the monetary system to be influenced by the gold reserve requirement. The money supply was managed solely with respect to the need for money and credit, and reserves of member banks have been increased or decreased by the Fed in response to general business conditions rather than the stock of monetary gold. Whenever monetary expansion caught up with the gold supply, the gold reserve requirement was reduced by act of Congress. The first occasion came during World War II, when monetary expansion was required to help finance the nation's military effort. In 1945, Congress reduced the gold reserve requirement for both Federal Reserve notes and deposits to 25 percent. The second occasion was in 1965, during the period of serious imbalance in the U.S. balance of payments, when the gold reserve behind deposits in the Federal Reserve banks was eliminated completely. The requirement of a 25 percent gold reserve against Federal Reserve notes was all that remained, and that was removed in 1968. These actions merely formalized what had already become a fact: the supply of money was completely freed from any relationship to gold.

In the meantime, most of the other requirements of the gold standard had been eliminated in 1934. The Great Depression brought both financial collapse and much greater intervention into economic affairs by the federal government. One of the major reforms was in the monetary system, and the gold standard was one of the first things to be changed. Convertibility of paper money into gold was ended. Gold was available from the Treasury only for settlement of international accounts through central banks. American citizens were allowed to own gold only for manufacturing purposes and in jewelry or decorative objects after 1934. Gold, for all practical purposes, was no longer a monetary metal in the United States after 1934.

Gold and the International Economy

Even after the United States formally abandoned the gold standard with regard to domestic monetary affairs, it continued to define the dollar in terms of gold in order to maintain orderly international monetary relationships. Most other countries did the same. The gold standard as it had existed prior to 1914 virtually ceased to exist. What remained was the so-called "gold exchange standard," in which the world's currencies were defined in gold, and gold could be used to settle balances between central banks.

The dollar was part of this system at $13\frac{5}{7}$ grains of gold, a figure established in 1934 in a reduction from the level of 23.22 grains that had lasted for almost exactly one hundred years. This was the "devaluation" of the dollar, which fixed the price at which the Treasury would buy gold at $35 per ounce. The devaluation had little effect on the domestic economy, but the new U.S. price for gold soon became one of the important cornerstones of the international monetary system.

New international financial relationships were established after World War II a conference at Bretton Woods, N.H. in 1945. The U.S. Treasury agreed to buy any gold offered to it at $35 per ounce to provide a stable anchor for the relative values of the world's major currencies. Other nations agreed to maintain the value of their currencies at a fixed level relative to the dollar. The purpose of the arrangement was to provide a stable financial base for world trade and investment.

These arrangements lasted for almost a quarter of a century, but broke down under the impact of large-scale U.S. private investments abroad and U.S. government expenditures overseas during the Vietnam War. Huge deficits in the U.S. balance of international payments were absorbed by foreign central banks in order to maintain the value of foreign currencies relative to the dollar, as required by the Bretton Woods agreements. The result was increased inflation abroad, and, generally, a shift of foreign assets into American hands. These assets increased the speed with which U.S. corporations were able to increase their investments abroad and helped finance U.S. military expenditures in Vietnam. In essence, the Bretton Woods system enabled the U.S. government to promote the interests of U.S. international corporations and shift part of the real burden of the Vietnam war to foreigners. Power and greed cause governments as well as individuals to do terrible things. When other governments refused in 1971 to cooperate any longer, the system broke down.

In 1971, with abandonment of the Bretton Woods agreements, the U.S. Treasury stopped buying gold and the value of the dollar was allowed to "float" on the international money markets. Governments and central banks still own a large part of the world's gold supply, and the high price of gold has vastly increased the value of those assets. But gold is not even used any more to settle international payments among governments or central banks. It is hoarded as an ultimate reserve in case of a financial crisis.

Gold and Inflation

Worldwide inflation from the mid-1960s through the 1970s and into the 1980s has given gold a new importance and significance. As prices rose and the value of the dollar and other currencies fell, money began to lose its function as a store of value. That always happens during rapid and continuing inflation. Why hold assets in the form of money when it will buy less and less as time goes on? Owners of wealth turn to assets that hold their value in spite of generally rising prices, real estate, diamonds, old master paintings, and precious metals like gold, silver and platinum. All of these goods share a special quality: their supply is either fixed or grows very slowly. Annual production of gold is relatively small compared to the total stock in existence, and demand for gold in jewelry or industrial production uses up a large portion of new output. The available supply is relatively fixed, and most of that is held by the world's central banks. This fixed supply, however, is one of the factors that gives gold its charm. Since the supply of money rises rapidly during an inflation, goods with a relatively fixed supply will become increasingly scarce relative to the growing amount of money, and their value measured in money will rise. Precious metals have another quality: they occupy small space and can be transported easily from place to place and hidden from greedy governments in case the inflation should generate serious political instability. These factors combine to create a growing demand for gold and other precious metals during an inflation. Gold becomes an important store of value, which means that it starts taking on some of the functions of money that the usual forms of money lose during an inflation.

Gold also rises in value during a depression and for essentially the same reason: holders of wealth lose confidence in the monetary system and seek to hold their wealth in forms other than money. During a depression, the flow of income falls, and business firms face increasing difficulty in meeting their commitments to their creditors, the banks. A serious depression threatens a financial crisis in which deposits in banks are insecure. This insecurity causes holders of wealth to seek a safer haven, and gold becomes a better store of value. The basic principle is that during periods of serious economic instability like inflations and depressions money starts to lose some of its functions while gold increasingly takes on those functions.

Chapter 11

The Banking System and the Creation of Credit

Banks perform a crucial function in a modern, private-enterprise economy. They lend money to consumers and business firms, a procedure that creates both debt and purchasing power. At the same time, bank loans create the checking accounts, or demand deposits, that constitute the most important part of a nation's money supply. The lending power of banks has built-in constraints, however, that limit the ability to create credit. This chapter will discuss the lending functions of banks, the mechanisms through which the banking system creates checking accounts, and the constraints that limit creation of credit. It also discusses the emergence since the mid-1960s of a new international banking system and some of the problems it has brought.

Banks and the Money Supply

Loans from banks are essential to a modern economy. They enable business firms to finance production and distribution, and they enable consumers to finance many kinds of important purchases.

Consider the simple purchase of an automobile by a consumer. Relatively few buyers pay cash. Most people use their old car as part or all of the down payment and borrow the rest. They might borrow directly from a bank, or they might borrow through the dealer's finance company. It makes little difference, however, because the finance company gets its funds from a bank loan anyway. Let's follow one of these loan-financed transactions and see what happens (see Figure 11-1).

Note carefully just exactly what happened: the borrower's bank has acquired an asset (the promissory note) and created a liability (the demand deposit against which the borrower can write checks which the bank must honor). As for the borrower, he got a new asset (the checking account, which he exchanged for a car) and a new liability (the promissory note). The seller merely exchanged one asset (a car) for another (an increase in his bank account). The total of assets and liabilities increased, and some new purchasing power for the borrower was created that did not exist before. All this was done by a series of paper transactions that created both a loan and a new demand deposit.

Figure 11-1 An Automobile Loan

The buyer of the automobile goes to his bank to borrow enough money to buy the car. He signs a promissory note, which specifies the amount borrowed and the terms of repayment, and pledges the car as security in case he can't repay in cash. In return, the bank creates a checking account in the name of the borrower equal to the amount borrowed.

In order to complete the transaction, a check equal to the amount borrowed is made out to the automobile dealer and signed by the borrower, who gets delivery of the car in exchange for the check.

The automobile dealer deposits the check in his bank. His account is credited, and he can now write more checks against it to carry on his business activities.

The dealer's bank then sends the check to the borrower's bank for collection, and the funds are transferred from the borrower's bank to the dealer's bank at a clearinghouse.

Ultimately, the check gets back to the borrower's bank and the amount of the check is deducted from the borrower's bank account. At this point all of the settlements have been made and the funds have been transferred to the account of the automobile dealer.

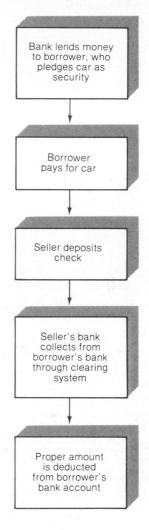

The ultimate security for the loan and the "backing" for the newly created money is the automobile pledged as security for the loan. More important from the point of view of the economy, however, is the fact that an important transaction was financed and the sale of an automobile occurred. Everyone gained. The buyer got his car, the dealer made a sale, and the buyer's bank acquired an income-earning asset. It was all made possible by an addition to the economy's stock of money and to the total of debt.

The lending powers of the banking system are of critical importance in the system of money, debt, and credit. Bank loans create both debt and purchasing power. Let's turn now to the conditions that limit their ability to make loans, starting with clearing of checks and then moving on to the process by which loans are increased.

Clearing of Checks

When a check is deposited in the same bank on which it is drawn, the process of keeping the accounts is very simple: the bank merely credits one account and debits the other. When more than one bank is involved, the process is a little more complicated, since funds must be shifted between banks as well as between accounts. To simplify the process and avoid shipment of cash from one bank to another, the banking system makes use of the *clearinghouse*, where all the banks in a city or larger area have accounts. Any one bank will send checks drawn on other banks to the clearinghouse, instead of directly to the other banks, and will receive payment by having its account at the clearinghouse credited. At the same time, checks drawn against it are sent to the clearinghouse by other banks, and its account there is debited. At the end of a business day the bank will have a net change in its account entered on the books. In this way checks are "cleared" without any cash changing hands.

Here is a highly simplified example of how the process works, using three banks and a single clearinghouse:

Bank *A* sends in checks totaling $100,000 drawn against Bank *B* and $60,000 drawn against Bank C

Bank *B* sends in checks totaling $120,000 drawn against Bank *A* and $90,000 drawn against Bank *C*

Bank *C* sends in checks totaling $70,000 drawn against Bank *A* and $110,000 drawn against Bank *B*

Table 11–1
Balances of Banks A, B, and C at the Clearinghouse

Bank	Credits	Debits	Difference
A	$160,000	$190,000	−$30,000
B	210,000	210,000	0
C	180,000	150,000	+ 30,000
Totals	550,000	550,000	0

The balance of the various banks at the clearinghouse are shown in Table 11–2. In this case, Bank *A*'s account would be reduced by $30,000 while *C*'s would be increased by $30,000. No change would occur in *B*'s account.

One or two days like this at the clearinghouse would make little difference to any of the banks involved. But if the situation were repeated day after day, *A*'s clearinghouse account would have to be replenished by either a cash deposit or a loan from the clearinghouse. Long before that, however, Bank *A* would take action to eliminate its negative clearinghouse balances by reducing its loans to its customers so that they would not write so many checks.

Bank *C* is in just the opposite situation. Its account at the clearinghouse is increasing. If this situation continues indefinitely, Bank *C* will have a substantial amount of idle assets on which it could be earning some income. It will have strong incentives to increase the volume of loans it makes to its customers. As it does so, its positive clearinghouse balances will gradually be reduced until its account is no longer increasing.

Bank *B*, unlike the other two, has achieved perhaps the ideal situation from the banker's point of view. It has not increased its loans so much that its clearinghouse balance is declining, yet it has lent enough to keep all its assets at work earning an income.

An important principle is at work here. Bank *A* has expanded its loans more rapidly than the system as a whole, and Bank *C* more slowly. This has caused a drain on *A*'s assets while *C* has accumulated unused assets. Both will ultimately act to bring their loan policies into conformity with those of the entire banking system.

- The **clearing of checks** is the process by which checks are debited and credited to the bank on which they are written. Balances at the clearinghouse result in increases or decreases in the reserves of individual banks and thereby influence bank lending policies.

A single bank cannot indiscriminately increase its loans and thereby increase the amount of demand deposits in the economy. If it does, it will get into trouble at the clearinghouse and have to reduce its excessively expansionist policy. But if all banks act together the banking system as a whole can increase loans, and the money supply, without much hindrance. For then any one bank's credits at the clearinghouse will increase as fast as its debits. Negative balances will not develop so long as the bank does not expand its loans faster than the other banks.

Bank Reserves and Expansion of Credit

Any bank must hold *reserves* of cash to meet the needs of depositors who wish to withdraw funds. Reserves are also needed to cover temporary debit balances at the clearinghouse. If debits and credits balance at the clearinghouse, however, and customers deposit as much as they withdraw, those reserves might never be used. They could be reduced to very low levels relative to total demand deposits, large enough to cover only bad loans. This is exactly what a modern private enterprise banking system does. It expands demand deposits to a large multiple of its reserves. As long as all banks expand their loans simultaneously so that none has an adverse clearinghouse balance, it is

theoretically possible for total demand deposits to grow continuously and without limit.

- **Bank reserves** are funds held by banks to meet withdrawals by depositors and cover adverse balances at the clearinghouse.
- The **multiple expansion of bank credit** is the process by which demand deposits in the banking system as a whole are increased to a multiple of the systems reserves.
- A banking system that operates in this fashion is called a **fractional reserve** banking system.

The only economic limit to credit creation by banks is the fact that the use of currency in hand-to-hand circulation rises as bank deposits and economic activity increase. Experience has shown that these ordinary needs for cash amount to about 2 percent of the total demand deposits in the economy. This sets a limit to the expansion of bank credit even if there were no legal or other restraints on bank lending. The limit is the amount of cash available: the banking system must have cash reserves of perhaps 2 percent of any increase in demand deposits to satisfy the demand of the general public for pocket cash.

Prudence may call for larger reserves, however. A bank may not be able to collect on all of its loans as they come due, but it must honor all the checks drawn against it if it wants to stay in business. Consequently, a reserve must be held against potential bad jugment on the part of the bank's lending officers and against the uncertainties of a changing economy. But these are not large items, and in normal good times a reserve of perhaps 5 to 10 percent is usually enough to take care of them. Even this reserve need not be held in cash. It can be invested in readily salable short-term government bonds, called Treasury "bills," that mature in 90 days or less.

In summary, then, no single bank can indiscriminately lend to its customers without limit. It must keep a sharp eye on its clearinghouse balances to make sure that its loan policies are not creating a continuous drain of cash. It must make sure it has enough cash on hand to meet its customers' needs for hand-to-hand currency. It must be careful to make safe loans that the borrowers can reasonably be expected to repay, and it must keep some highly liquid reserves to compensate for mistakes.

But although each and every individual bank must follow a policy of caution and safety, the banking system as a whole can expand loans, and the money supply, to a point at which demand deposits are ten to twenty times the amount of reserves held by the banking system. Furthermore, if each bank seeks to maximize its profits, there will be a strong tendency for the system as a whole to expand demand deposits to the maximum level permitted by reserves and the rules of safety. Indeed, if there were no legal requirement that banks hold reserves, and no money was needed for hand-to-hand circulation, and all bank loans were perfectly safe, the banking system could expand loans and demand deposits *without limit*.

The Function of Bank Reserves

Bank reserves do not make the banking system safe. Their function is to limit the amount of money created.

First, the problem of safety. Multiple expansion of credit rests on public confidence in a bank's ability to honor checks drawn against it. In the absence of any arrangements to protect the system, unwise extension of credit by a single bank can result in failure to meet its obligations, and public confidence in the whole system might deteriorate. A "run" on all banks can start, bringing the whole system down. Similarly, economic events entirely outside the banking system, such as a stock market crash, might cause a similar "run". Since the system as a whole has cash reserves equal to only a fraction of total demand deposits, any concerted effort on the part of depositors to get cash instead of holding bank deposits can cause the system to fail.

As long as demand deposits exceed the cash assets of the banks, the system is vulnerable. Reserves could prevent a breakdown only if they were equal in amount to the total of demand deposits. Short of that requirement two devices have been used to preserve the system. One is the guarantee of bank deposits, up to $100,000, to assure the depositor that his money is safe. The second is the existence of a "lender of last resort," the Federal Reserve System, which stands ready to lend funds to any bank that has assets that can be used as security. Together, these arrangements keep depositors from panicking and can provide funds if a bank should have a temporary need. The only reasons for bank failures nowadays are bad management, thievery, or both, on the part of bank officers.

The problem of limiting the creation of credit is far more important. The flow of spending can be affected quite significantly by extension of credit. Yet a profit-oriented banking system has every reason to expand credit, whether or not expansion may be desirable at the time. Some mechanism to restrain the system is needed, and it is provided by the reserves banks are required to hold.

We turn now to the multiple expansion of bank credit, the mechanism by which it takes place, and how it is limited by a required reserve.

Multiple Expansion of Bank Credit

In the United States, the reserves a bank must hold are set by the Board of Governors of the Federal Reserve System, within limits fixed by law. The reserves themselves are on deposit in the Federal Reserve banks,[1] which also operate the regional clearinghouses for clearing of checks. This means that as checks are cleared

---

[1] "Till money" (cash on hand) held by banks is also part of bank reserves, but amounts to only a small part of the total.

through the banking system the reserves of individual banks rise or fall.

At the present time the Fed requires a *reserve ratio* averaging out at about 1 to 5. That is, banks must hold $1 in reserves for every $5 in demand deposit. The required reserve varies with the amount of demand deposits in the individual banks, but the average for the system as a whole is about 20 percent, or 1 to 5. As a result, the banking system is able to create and maintain demand deposits about five times as large as its reserves.

- The **reserve ratio** is the proportion of reserves to demand deposits. It is now about 1:5 or $1 of reserves for each $5 of demand deposits.

For example, in November 1979, the reserves of all banks that were members of the Federal Reserve System totaled $43.1 billion. Those reserves supported a total of $192.4 billion in demand deposits. The ratio of reserves to demand deposits was just a little more than 22 percent. The banking system as a whole was "loaned up" at the time; that is, all of the reserves were required to back up the existing level of demand deposits. There were no excess reserves, and banks had borrowed about $1.9 billion from the Fed to meet their reserve requirements.

The process by which this five-to-one expansion takes place is not complicated. But banks can't just write loans equal to five times their reserves. If they did, they would quickly have adverse balances at the clearinghouse and would have to cut back. But even though one bank can make loans equal only to the *free reserves* it has, the banking system as a whole will end up with loans and demand deposits equal to five times its reserves. Here is how it works.

- **Free reserves** are those not needed as a reserve against the existing amount of demand deposits. That is, they are funds available for lending. Free reserves and **excess reserves** are the same thing.

The Starting Situation

We can begin our example with a reserve ratio of 20 percent. That is, all banks are required to keep a reserve of $1 for every $5 of demand deposits. We propose to increase the amount of reserves available to the banking system and then show (1) the process by which multiple expansion takes place; and (2) the limit imposed by the reserve ratio.

All the banks in the system are assumed to be loaned up. That is, existing demand deposits are exactly five times the available reserves and there are no free reserves in excess of those required. The banks are eager to lend and are unwilling to hold excess reserves, so that any new funds they receive will be used for new loans to eager customers.

Step 1: The Creation of New Reserves

We now provide our banking system with $100,000 in new reserves. This is easily done. The usual method is for the federal reserve banks to buy government bonds. This purchase will automatically increase the reserves of the system. It happens like this:

The treasurer of a Federal Reserve bank writes a check for $100,000 to pay for the bonds. The check goes to a dealer in government securities, who deposits the check in his bank. His bank then sends the check through the clearing system. At the clearinghouse, located at the regional Federal Reserve Bank, the bank's account will be credited. That account at the clearinghouse is the bank's reserve, however, and is now $100,000 larger. The easiest way to understand how bank reserves are influenced by Federal Reserve purchases of government securities is to visualize the path taken by the check used to pay for the bonds (Figure 11–2). The crucial step is the third one, in which a commercial bank sends the Fed's original check back to the Fed for collection, and is paid by having its reserve account increased by the amount of the check.

What has happened as a result of the transaction? First, the person who formerly owned

Figure 11-2
Purchase of Securities
by a Federal Reserve
Bank Increases
Member Bank Reserves

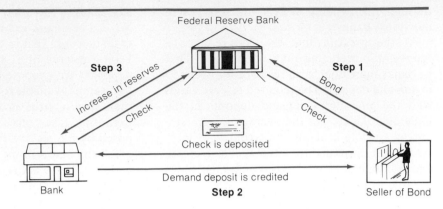

$100,000 of government bonds now has $100,000 more in his checking account. His total assets have not changed, but they are now held in a demand deposit instead of government securities. The bank has a new obligation, or liability, in the form of $100,000 in demand deposits, but it has additional assets in the form of $100,000 in reserves. Its balance sheet for the transaction will show the following:

Assets		Liabilities	
Reserves	$100,000	Demand deposits	$100,000

The Federal Reserve bank has also had an increase in both its assets and its liabilities, with its balance sheet showing the following changes:

Assets		Liabilities	
Government securities	$100,000	Member bank reserves	$100,000

The net result for the banking system when the Federal Reserve bank buys a new asset is a corresponding increase in demand deposits and reserves of the member banks.[2]

Step 2:
The First Stage of Multiple Expansion
No bank likes to hold unused reserves that could be put to work earning income for its stockholders. In this case the bank that got the original increase in reserves will now find that its reserves are $80,000 greater than those required by a reserve ratio of 20 percent. These are "free" reserves, which the bank can use in any way it wishes. Its officers will want to lend that money to a customer, and when they do its balance sheet will change:

Assets		Liabilities	
Reserves		Demand deposits	$100,000
Required	$ 20,000		
Excess	80,000		
	$100,000		

---

[2]Just the opposite occurs when the Federal Reserve System sells government securities. By reducing its assets it reduces the reserves of the banking system. Work out the exact process for yourself by following the transaction through from beginning to end.

The customer who gets the loan will quickly put his money to use, writing checks that will be deposited in other banks. As those checks pass through the clearing system, funds will be shifted from Bank I to a second group of banks. Both demand deposits and reserves will move as the transactions are cleared. This is what will happen:

Assets		Liabilities	
Reserves	$100,000	Demand deposits	$100,000
Loans	80,000		80,000
	$180,000		$180,000

By the time the funds have been cleared to the second group of banks, Bank I will have arrived simultaneously at its final position.

Assets		Liabilities	
Reserves	$100,000	Demand deposits	$180,000
less	80,000	less	80,000
	20,000		$100,000
Loans	80,000		
	$100,000		

This balance sheet of Bank I's final position contains in microcosm the multiple expansion of demand deposits. Compared with Bank I's initial position, the bank has succeeded in reducing its reserves to the minimum level required to cover its demand deposits. It did so by making loans to its customers. This action increased the demand deposits and reserves of other banks, which then were in a position to repeat the process.

This analysis also tells us why Bank I cannot lend five times the amount of its excess reserves. If it were to lend $400,000 to its customers ($80,000 × 5) it would lose $400,000 of reserves to other banks through the clearing system. This would bring its total reserve position $300,000 below where it started, while its demand deposits would be up by $100,000. Since it started out all loaned up, it would now be $320,000 short in its required reserves. It is for this reason that no single bank can lend more than the free reserves it has.

Yet in our example so far, total demand deposits have risen by $180,000, even though new reserves in the system remain at $100,000 —and the process of expansion has not yet ended.

Step 3: The Second Group of Banks Expands Its Loans

The second group of banks is now in a position of holding excess reserves. They need only $16,000 as a reserve against the new demand deposits of $80,000 they have acquired. $64,000 is available in free reserves and can be lent to their customers, who will in turn write checks against their new deposits. After those checks have cleared, the balance sheet of the second group of banks will look like this:

Assets		Liabilities	
Reserves	$ 16,000	Demand deposits	$ 80,000
Loans	64,000		
Total	$ 80,000		

Step 4: Effects on Other Banks

A third group of banks will receive new demand deposits and reserves of $64,000 when the checks from the second group of banks clear through the system. They in turn, will find themselves with excess reserves, will lend to their customers, and arrive at a new loaned-up balance sheet. Just to test your understanding of the process, see if you can fill out the blanks in the following balance sheets for the initial and final positions of the third group of banks.

Initial position

Assets		Liabilities	
Reserves	–	Demand deposits	–
Loans	–		
Total	–		

Final position

Assets		Liabilities	
Reserves	–	Demand deposits	–
Loans	–		
Total	–		

You should have been able to work it out correctly. Answers are given below.[3]

Ultimately, the banking system as a whole will expand loans up to the point where all free reserves have disappeared. All of the new reserves will be required at the higher level of demand deposits. Table 11–2 shows the expansion pattern.

The expansion has now come to an end. All the new reserves are being used as backing for the expanded level of demand deposits. The banking system has created an additional $400,000 of new money to supplement the original increase of $100,000, and a 5-to-1 expansion of the money supply has taken place.[4]

---

[3]*Initial position*

Reserves	$64,000	Demand deposits	$64,000
Loans	0		
Total	$64,000		

Final position

Reserves	$12,800	Demand deposits	$64,000
Loans	51,200		
Total	$64,000		

[4]The algebraic formulation for the multiple expansion of demand deposits is similar to the formula for the national income multiplier:

$$dD = \Delta R \left(\frac{1}{r}\right)$$

where D = demand deposits, R = reserves, and r = reserve ratio. In the example used here the solution is

$$\Delta D = \$100,000 \left(\frac{1}{0.2}\right) = \$100,000 \times 5 = \$500,000$$

Some Qualifications

The process we have just described was broken down into its component parts in order to explain it systematically. In actual practice, all of the banks expand their loans together rather than in the strict sequence described here. An increase in reserves quickly spreads throughout the system and most banks start out with excess reserves. They all try to reduce their reserves to the required level by increasing their loans, and as they all expand, the system as a whole succeeds in reaching its upper limit of expansion.

A bank need not make loans for the multiple expansion to occur. It may buy securities or other investment assets, and this will have the same effect as a new loan. The bank will buy the assets by check and the check will be deposited in the seller's checking account. The result will be an increase in the system's demand deposits just as if a loan were made.

Leakages

There are two factors that might prevent the full expansion to five times the new reserves (in our example). One is the leakage of cash into hand-to-hand circulation. Some of those who acquire larger demand deposits will want some of their assets in cash, and will withdraw some from the banking system. This leakage will have to come from the reserves of the banking system. The result will be a slightly smaller expansion.

Suppose, for example, that 2 percent of the new reserves were drawn out in cash as the system expanded. The new reserves available to the system would be only $98,000 and the new level of demand deposits would be

$$\$98,000 \times 5 = \$490,000$$

or 2 percent less than if there had been no leakage.

Table 11–2
Multiple Expansion of
Demand Deposits

	Demand Deposits	New Loans	Required Reserves
Bank I	$100,000	$ 80,000	$ 20,000
Second group of banks	80,000	64,000	16,000
Third group of banks	64,000	51,200	12,800
Fourth group of banks	51,200	40,960	10,240
Total for first 4 groups of banks	295,200	236,160	59,040
Total for remaining groups of banks	204,800	163,840	40,960
Final result	$500,000	$400,000	$100,000

Excess Reserves

The second factor that could keep expansion below the theoretical limits is the holding of excess reserves by the banking system. Suppose, for example, that each bank in the system decided to hold not just 20 percent reserves but an additional 5 percent of any new reserves it received. Bank officials may do this for a variety of reasons, say in preparation for large seasonal demands for loans a little later, perhaps at Christmas or Easter; in expectation of higher interest rates; or perhaps because of pessimism or prudence. Whatever the reason, they will be, in effect, imposing a greater reserve requirement upon themselves than is necessary, and the expansion of credit will be less than the maximum possible:

$$\$100,000 \times 4 = \$400,000$$

Excess reserves can be very important. If businesses are not eager to borrow and banks are not eager to lend, as during recessions or depressions, large amounts of excess reserves can pile up. This happened during the depression years of the 1930s, when the banking system at times had as much as $5 billion in excess reserves. This experience illustrates an important point:

○ **Expansion of the money supply is not automatic.** Although an upper limit is defined by the amount of reserves and the reserve ratio, the expansion of the system depends on the economic climate as seen by both business firm and bankers. Bankers must be willing to lend, and business firms and consumers must be willing to borrow.

The International Banking System

Until the late 1960s the world's monetary system consisted primarily of separate systems of banks in each country, each of which operated on the basis of fractional reserves and expanded credit to some multiple of total reserves. Each major nation also had a central bank whose chief functions were to manage the nation's money and credit, protect the system from financial crises, and help manage financial relationships with other countries. There were, to be sure, financial relationships between the economies of the various countries, and they were quite important. However, they were largely private transfers of funds from one nation to another, particularly for purposes of investment and for making payments in international trade.

In the late 1960s a new *international banking*

system began to appear. It receives deposits, transfers funds, and makes loans in currencies other than those of the countries in which the bank is located. For example, a bank in Switzerland lends U.S. dollars to a large international corporation instead of lending Swiss francs. The system has come to be called the Eurobank system, because most of the banks involved in the early days were in Europe, including the European branches and subsidiaries of U.S. banks. It has spread, however, to other financial centers such as Tokyo, Hong Kong and Singapore, and to places like the Bahamas and the Cayman Islands, where the wealthy find tax havens and bank regulation is largely nonexistent. The units that make up the new international banking system include the external or foreign departments of banks in those places, including the foreign branches or subsidiaries of U.S. banks.

The Eurobank system had an interesting origin. It began in the early 1950s during the cold war between the U.S. and the Soviet Union. The state trading agencies of the Soviet Union, fearing that the U.S. government might block or seize their deposits in U.S. banks, transferred those deposits of U.S. dollars to banks in England that agreed to hold and transfer them on demand. The English banks, of course, could use the U.S. dollars for short-term loans to international borrowers and make a nice profit on the deal. Expansion of Eurocredit loans followed, the chief borrowers being international corporations, governments, and other large banks—high finance. The U.S. dollar was the favored currency, partly because the dollar was widely used in international trade and finance (the U.S. is the world's largest importer, exporter, and supplier of funds for international investment). In addition, the price of oil is denominated in dollars and most international purchases and sales of oil are made in dollars. About 75–80 percent of all Eurocurrency deposits are dollar deposits.

The chief reason for the development of the Eurobank system (Eurocredit, Eurodollar—there are a variety of names) was the desire of bankers to increase their profits. Central banks limit the expansion of fractional reserve banking systems in order to achieve a more stable economy. Reserve requirements in the United States limit the amount of profit-making loans the banks can make. In most European countries, loans are limited to some percent of a bank's assets, but the effect is the same: loans and profits are limited. Loans made in foreign currencies are not subject to these limits, however. Thus, a large U.S. international corporation may find that it is unable to increase its borrowings from U.S. banks because the system is loaned up, but that it can borrow dollars from the foreign branches or subsidiaries of U.S. banks. The loans made by those foreign branches are limited only by prudent banking practice and not by the reserve ratio and limited reserves.

The international banking system is, then, a free, private-enterprise banking system that makes loans and in so doing creates money for the use of borrowers. The loans are made in foreign currencies, however, and mostly in U.S. dollars. It provides a huge potential for expansion of the world's money supply, without the limits that are now imposed by central banks on the money and credit systems of individual countries.

- The **international banking system**, sometimes called the *Eurobank*, *Eurocurrency*, or Eurodollar system, consists of banks that hold deposits, transfer funds, and make loans in currencies other than those of the country in which the bank is located. About 75–80 percent of its loans and deposits are denominated in U.S. dollars.

Growth of International Lending
Expansion of the international banking system has been rapid. Total deposits in the system were only about $50 billion as late as 1968, but by the end of 1980 the total was about $1500

billion. No one is sure of the exact amount because the banks in the system don't have to report to any central authority. Of that total, some $1100–1200 billion was denominated in dollars. Note, in passing, that the domestic supply of dollars in the U.S. monetary system was about one third the total of international dollars and that the entire domestic money supply of the various nations of the world outside of the socialist bloc was approximately equal, in 1980, to the money supply created by the international banking system. About half of the world's money supply is now supplied by the international banks.

Inflation and International Banking

The international banking system has been and continues to be an important source of worldwide inflation. In the years since 1968 international lending increased the world's money supply at a rate of about 10 percent annually, while total output in the world economy rose at an average annual rate of about 3 percent. If the monetarist theory of the relationship between the growth of the money supply and increased output is correct, this overexpansion of credit was responsible for a worldwide rate of inflation of 7 percent.

The financing of oil imports has been particularly inflationary. In 1979 the net "oil deficit" of nations importing oil was about $75 billion. That is, oil importing nations had to borrow that amount from the international banking system to obtain the dollars needed to pay for oil imports. The loans were not for the purpose of increasing output, but merely to keep normal economic activity going. So the result was to raise the world's money supply by $75 billion, which had the usual multiplied effect on the world's flow of spending, without significantly raising world output of goods for sale. Result: more inflation.

Dangers Inherent in the System

The continuing expansion and growth of the international banking system is undermining the system itself. The basic problem is that money is being created, mostly in the form of dollars, more rapidly than output can increase. The resulting inflation reduces the value of the money being created, and ultimately the willingness of people to accept it. As confidence in the value of money deteriorates, large holders of money seek to hold their assets in the form of other things. Money starts to lose its functions in the economy, and gold, silver, old master paintings, and real estate are sought as ways to hold wealth. In the present situation we can therefore expect a long-run decline in the value of the dollar, which is the chief type of money created by the international banking system, interrupted by short periods of recovery or stability, and a continuing rise in the value of other things, unless the rapid expansion of international bank lending of dollars is greatly reduced or halted.

A second danger is present. Loans create debt, and the burden of debt grows when it increases faster than output and income. As the ratio of debt to income rises, the financial system becomes increasingly fragile. A significant downturn in economic activity can prevent borrowers from meeting their debt commitments. Under those conditions a general financial crisis can occur. Remember 1931–33, when exactly such a sequence of events brought the breakdown of the banking systems of one nation after another.

There is a third danger. About one-third of all deposits in the Eurobank system represent interbank deposits—funds of one bank deposited with another. This means that if (when) the system starts to collapse, all the banks in the system will be affected and the financial crisis will quickly spread to the banking systems of all major nations.

The new international banking system is subject to all the ills of an unregulated and uncontrolled fractional reserve banking system: potentially unlimited expansion, growth of debt faster than income, and the potential for financial crisis. It lacks a central authority to limit and manage the expansion of credit, to protect the system from its own excesses, and to act as a lender of last resort in time of crisis. Interestingly enough, many of the bankers that operate in the system understand its fragility and have made several proposals to create protections and introduce limits. Each plan has been wrecked by conflicting interests among the major nations and the desire to maintain an obviously profitable business. So far, greed has prevailed over reason.

The Need for Control

Money and credit are the lifeblood of a private-enterprise economy. Both the existing level of economic activity and economic growth require an appropriate level and expansion of the money supply. Yet money and credit are provided by profit-making business enterprises, the commercial banks, whose primary obligation is to their owners, not to the economy as a whole. An individual bank will maximize its profits when it has expanded its loans to the highest level consistent with safety. When all banks do this, a very large expansion can occur, which may or may not be consistent with the welfare of the economy as a whole. A stable economy may require constraint.

At other times the banking system may be loaned up, and unable to provide adequate amounts of credit. At these times the banks need additional reserves in order to expand loans.

It is for these reasons that all modern nations regulate the monetary system. In the United States loans are made by individual banks, who thereby ration the available credit among potential borrowers. But determination of the total amount of credit has been taken out of their hands. The next chapter explains how.

Summary

Banks provide credit to business units and consumers, an operation vitally important to a modern economy. By making loans, banks create purchasing power in the form of demand deposits. If there were no legal limits placed on the process, this creation of money would be limited only by the need to keep a small reserve on the part of banks. This multiple expansion of credit is characteristic of modern banking. Indeed, if all banks expanded loans at the same rate and at the same time, there would be no limit to expansion.

Reserves do not provide safety. They limit the expansion of credit.

The process of multiple expansion of credit occurs because profit-seeking banks try to lend to their customers any funds not required for reserves. They reduce their reserves to the minimum level by loans that bring them a profit. The system as a whole ends up with a total of demand deposits larger than its reserves, even though no one bank has lent out any money it did not have.

Since this process obviously affects aggregate demand and the level of economic activity, all modern nations try to manage their monetary systems.

In recent years a new international banking system has emerged. It comprises the foreign departments of banks located outside the U.S. and the foreign branches and subsidiaries of U.S. banks. These banks hold deposits, transfer funds, and make loans in currencies other than the currency of the country in which they are located, but largely in U.S. dollars. About half of the world money supply outside the socialist countries is now in the form of deposits in banks of the international monetary system. Although it performs important banking functions, this new type of banking has created serious problems of inflation and financial instability, largely because it is not controlled by, or protected by, any central bank or similar organization.

Key Concepts

clearing of checks
bank reserves
multiple expansion of bank credit
fractional reserve

reserve ratio
free reserves
international banking system

For Discussion

1. Assume a 20 percent reserve ratio and no excess reserves or cash leakages. Work through the process by which the banking system expands the money supply beyond an initial increase in reserves of $1000.

2. How do cash leakages and excess reserves affect the process of credit expansion?

3. What would be the advantages and disadvantages of a 100 percent reserve ratio for demand deposits?

4. Why is a central bank necessary for the stable operation of the U.S. banking system?

5. How might excessive expansion of credit in the Eurocredit market be controlled?

6. Can a central bank control the supply of money without affecting the level of economic activity? Explain.

Chapter 12

The Federal Reserve System and Monetary Policy

Money and credit do not manage themselves. They respond to the needs of the economy and the desires of millions of borrowers. The efforts of banks to make a profit influences the money supply and the flow of credit. The need of business firms for credit to finance production and distribution influences the demand for funds. The form in which financial institutions and consumers wish to hold their assets—money, securities of various kinds, other things—affects the money markets. All of the millions of economic units make decisions about money and credit, and the decisions may or may not add up to a consensus that contributes to economic well-being. A guiding hand is needed to assure that the monetary system contributes to the general economic health of the community. The central bank performs this function.

Functions of a Central Bank

A central bank seeks to provide the stability that an unguided monetary system lacks. It has four chief functions:

1. Accommodation. The central bank provides the reserves necessary for the banking system to perform its normal function of lending to business and consumers to finance the processes of production and distribution. It also operates the central clearinghouses for the settlement of accounts between banks, including the clearing system for checks.

2. Lender of last resort. The central bank has responsibility for maintaining the viability of the banking system, the network of credit, and the system of financial institutions. To this end it must stand ready to prevent the sort of financial panic and bankruptcies that, in the absence of a central bank, would characterize a private enterprise economy. This function of the central bank is not part of its daily operations but must be done periodically. Between the mid-1960s and 1980, the Federal Reserve System intervened in the money markets four times in order to avert a potential financial crisis.

3. Fiscal agent for the government. The treasury has its chief bank account at the central bank, out of which it makes payments and into which tax collections flow.[1] More

---

[1]A qualification. In most countries, including the United States, the Treasury holds a portion of its bank balances in commercial banks.

important, the central bank usually maintains a market for government securities and can provide an unlimited line of credit to the national government. This function of the central bank is of special importance today. As long as the central bank cooperates, there is no limit to the size of the national debt.

4. Managing the monetary system. The most important job of the central bank, the one it must perform at the highest policy levels, is to manage money and credit:

A. The daily and weekly changes that take place in the money markets must be smoothed out, so that they do not interfere with the normal processes of production and distribution. Temporary shortages or surpluses of funds in the money markets can affect business activity, and should be counteracted.

B. When the economy begins to falter, unemployment increases and output falls; the job of the central bank is to *ease* conditions in the money markets. This is done by increasing the amount of loanable funds and pushing interest rates down.

C. When the economy becomes overheated, with high levels of employment and output and prices starting to rise, the task is just the opposite. The central bank tries to *tighten* the money markets by decreasing the availability of credit and pushing interest rates up.

D. All this is done within the framework of an expanding economy. Economic growth requires increased debt and an increase of currency in circulation. As the central bank "leans against the wind" of recession or inflation, it must keep in mind the long-term need for expansion of both credit and money in order to facilitiate economic growth.

5. International monetary management. Any one nation's monetary system is connected with those of other nations and the international economy. The balance of international trade and payments, the value of a nation's currency in international money markets, prices and interest rates all affect and are affected by what happens in domestic money markets. Those who make decisions for the central bank must keep these relationships in mind: domestic and international monetary stability are interrelated.

These are the great principles of central banking. Yet central banks do not order the commercial banks to lend more or lend less. They cannot specify interest rates. They cannot force banks to lend or businesses to borrow. But they can encourage and cajole. They can create situations in the money markets that cause others to act in desirable ways. In essence, the job of the central banks is so to structure the money markets and credit system that bankers and businesses voluntarily act in ways that further the general public interest.[2]

The Federal Reserve System

The United States set up its central bank in 1914, after passage of the Federal Reserve Act in 1913. We were one of the last industrial nations to do so; Italy and Russia preceded us, and some countries, like Sweden and England, preceded us by more than 200 years. The American central bank is part of the *Federal Reserve System*. The entire system comprises three principal units:

1. The member banks

2. Twelve regional Federal Reserve Banks

3. A Board of Governors

The Board of Governors and the twelve regional banks carry out the functions of the central bank.

---

[2]It's easy enough to say that a central bank manages the money supply "in the public interest" or "with the goal of economic stability" in mind. But how are these phrases to be defined and who is to define them? Policy conflicts can easily arise.

- The **Federal Reserve System** is the U.S. central bank, which is made up of a Board of Governors and 12 regional banks that do the bulk of the commercial banking business.

There are almost 15,000 commercial banks in the United States. Of these, about 5,400 are members of the Federal Reserve System. There are a number of qualifications and requirements for membership, which are changed occasionally by Congress, but the membership comprises almost all of the banks of significant size. Although member banks include only 45 percent of all commercial banks, they hold 85 percent of all demand deposits. Member banks are required by law to keep their reserves on deposit in the Federal Reserve Bank for their region.[3] This automatically makes them part of the Fed's clearing system for checks, and insures that any changes in the money markets will affect the banks' reserve position.[4]

The twelve regional Federal Reserve Banks, with their twenty-four branches are *not* owned by the federal government, but by the member banks in each region. Each member bank is requried to buy stock in the regional Federal Reserve Bank equal to 3 percent of the member bank's capital plus surplus. The member banks earn a dividend of 6 percent on this stock, with all profits above that going to the U.S. Treasury.

The officers and policies of the Federal Reserve Banks are not controlled by the member banks, however. Their top policy-making and operating officers are appointed by the Board of Governors of the Federal Reserve System.

Each Federal Reserve Bank has nine directors, only six of whom are elected by the member banks. Three are appointed by the Board of Governors, including the Chair and Vice Chair. In addition, the appointments of the president and vice president of the regional banks must be approved by the Board of Governors. These top officers can be removed by the Board of Governors, and this power gives the Governors ultimate control over policy. There have been disagreements over policy matters between the Board of Governors and presidents of the regional Federal Reserve Banks from time to time. But in each case the regional president has played the game, and has not tried to sabotage the Board's policy.

The guiding force of the system is the Board of Governors, located in Washington. Its seven members are appointed for staggered 14-year terms by the President, whose appointments must be confirmed by the Senate. The Board of Governors has certain administrative responsibilities and supervisory powers over the twelve regional banks and their branches, but its most important function is management of the monetary system. The Board controls the instruments of monetary management and determines the goals of monetary policy.[5] The system is privately owned, but controlled by public appointees whose chief responsibilities are the guidance of the money markets toward paths consistent with the general welfare.

The Board of Governors is not independent of other federal agencies that deal with economic policy. It is expected to coordinate its money market management with the policies of

---

[3]In addition, currency held in their vaults by member banks counts as part of their reserves.

[4]Banks that are not members of the Federal Reserve System keep their reserves with member banks. Some participate in the clearing of checks directly, by maintaining accounts at the regional Federal Reserve banks, and others indirectly through their reserve accounts with member banks. In recent years several proposals to bring all commercial banks into the system have been made.

---

[5]A Federal Advisory Council of 12 members representing the Federal Reserve Banks advises the Board of Governors but has no direct powers. The Federal Open Market Committee (12 members, 7 are are the Board of Governors and 5 named by the Federal Reserve Banks) determines policies for the entire system with respect to purchase and sale of government securities. These are the only two instruments the 12 regional banks can use to influence the policies of the Board of Governors, except for informal channels.

the President and the executive branch of the government, including the Treasury, the Office of Management and Budget (OMB), and the President's Council of Economic Advisors. These agencies, together with the Board of Governors, make up the group responsible for development and implementation of national economic policy, within the framework of presidential and congressional responsibility.

There has been considerable debate over how independent the Board of Governors is or ought to be. The Board's position is that it was established by act of Congress and is responsible to Congress for carrying out the purposes of the act and other congressional legislation. In practice, however, national economic policy is a seamless web, and those responsible for one sector cannot ride off in directions different from those taken by others. This means that the Fed must cooperate with other agencies if its legal responsibilities are to be fulfilled. On the other hand, the President cannot order the Fed to take action and, although he appoints the members of the Board of Governors, he cannot remove them. This forces the executive branch (Treasury, OMB, Council of Economic Advisors) to reach agreement with the Fed on most major issues of economic policy. There have been disagreements in recent years, but by and large the two groups have cooperated effectively. Nevertheless, some economists and members of Congress feel that the Fed should not be independent and that all economic policy agencies should be directly coordinated by a single agency within the executive branch of the government.[6]

---

[6]The chief deterrent to independent action by the Fed is the fact that Congress can always change the law. Independent action by the Fed may lead the President to ask Congress to subordinate the Board of Governors to the executive branch. A popular President with a significant majority in Congress could probably get such legislation through. So the Fed can maintain its independence only by not exercising it, except on relatively unimportant matters. It's a good example of the proverb that power disappears if it is used.

Managing the Monetary System: Techniques

We have seen that the creation of demand deposits is limited by:

1. The amount of reserves held by commercial banks, and
2. The reserve ratio, that is, the proportion that must be maintained between reserves and demand deposits.

For example, with a reserve ratio of 20 percent and reserves of $1,000,000, a bank could maintain demand deposits totaling $5,000,000. The chief instruments of monetary policy are designed to act on these two limiting factors. The money managers of the central bank can change either the amount of reserves or the reserve ratio. The resulting change in the reserve position of the banks will be felt in the money markets by changes in the availability of loans and the interest rates borrowers pay.

Other actions can be taken, but they are much less important. The central bank can change the rate of interest it charges on loans to commercial banks. Or it can try to influence the money markets by exhortation, advice, and public statements. Some direct regulation of interest rates or terms of loans in special areas of the money markets may be available. Any good central bank will use any or all of these instruments of money management if appropriate, but in the end the reserve position of the commercial banks is the key to effective action.

Open Market Operations
The Federal Reserve System can change the amount of reserves held by commercial banks by buying or selling government securities. The term *open market operations*, comes from the fact that the transactions are carried out in the New York market for government securities, a market open to anyone, rather than directly

with the federal government. Just as you or I would do, the New York Federal Reserve bank will telephone a broker to make a purchase or sale and will pay by check,[7] an action that can create new reserves.

● **Open market operations** are the purchase and sale of government securities by Federal Reserve banks.

This process is important enough to merit careful review in greater detail, and is basically very simple.

○ Whenever the Fed acquires an asset the reserves of the member banks are increased.

The reverse is also true.

○ Whenever the Fed sells an asset the reserves of the member banks are decreased.

When the Open Market Account buys government securities it pays for them by a check written on a Federal Reserve Bank. The seller of the securities deposits the check in his bank, which sends the check through the clearing system. At the clearinghouse, which is the regional Federal Reserve Bank, the reserve account of the seller's bank is credited and the new reserves are now available.

It is very useful to see what happens to the balance sheets of the participants. First, the seller of the government securities has exchanged one form of asset for another, for

Before		After	
Assets	*Liabilities*	*Assets*	*Liabilities*
Bonds $100,000		Demand deposits $100,000	

[7]The purchase or sale is made by the manager of the Fed's Open Market Account, under instructions from the Federal Open Market Committee, which operates out of the Federal Reserve Bank of New York. Purchases are made at the lowest available prices and sales at the highest, at the time of the transaction.

example, $100,000 of government securities for $100,000 in demand deposits.

Meanwhile, the buyer of the securities, one of the Federal Reserve banks, has acquired both an asset and a liability:

Assets		*Liabilities*	
Government securities	+$100,000	Member bank reserves	+$100,000

And the commercial bank has also increased both its assets and its liabilities:

Assets		*Liabilities*	
Reserves	+$100,000	Demand deposits	+$100,000

The member bank can then set in motion the chain of multiple expansion of credit by making loans and investments that reduce its new reserves to one-fifth of its new demand deposits, its excess reserves will move to other banks, and the process can go on until the system is once more loaned up.

The process works equally well in reverse. Sale of government securities will decrease the reserves of the banking system. When the Fed sells an asset, it is paid by a check from the buyer. The Fed collects by deducting the amount of the check from the reserve account of the member bank. By the time the transaction has been completed, the buyer's demand deposit has been reduced by the amount of his purchase of government securities. Instead of a demand deposit, he has government bonds. The commercial bank has lost reserves, but its demand deposits have been reduced by the same amount. The Federal Reserve Bank has reduced its assets by sale of the bond and this has led to a reduction in its liabilities, the reserves of the member banks.

Open market operations are controlled solely by the Board of Governors and its Federal Open Market Committee. The member banks have no option whatsoever. Whenever the Board wants to do so, it can raise the banking system's reserves by buying government securities, or lower the reserves by selling. There is no limit to the amounts that can be bought: the system is kept solvent by the fact that increased reserve account liabilities are balanced by increased assets. There is a limit to the amount of government securities the Fed can sell, since it owns a finite quantity, but even that limit is flexible. The Fed can always "sell short" if it has to. That is, it can sell securities it does not have, borrowing them from a broker, and buying them later for delivery. But this is a theoretical rather than a practical limit to open market sales. In March 1980, for example, the Fed owned some $116.8 billion of U.S. government securities, more than enough for any foreseeable need.

Furthermore, open market operations of any size can be carried out, and on very short notice. A small increase or decrease in reserves can be made very quickly, a large change very slowly, or vice versa. Open market operations are a flexible means by which the reserve position of the banking system as a whole can be changed, to almost any extent that the Board of Governors feels is advisable.

Reserve Requirements

The ability of the banking system to expand credit can also be affected by changing the *required reserve ratio*. This method of controlling the money supply is not used very often, however, because it has a large impact on the money markets. The Fed has found that a soft touch is usually better than a bludgeon.

- The **required reserve ratio** is the proportion of reserves to demand deposits required of member banks.

The Board of Governors is empowered to set reserve requirements for all financial institutions that hold "transactions" accounts, savings accounts, and time deposits. The system is in a transition period of eight years duration, however, under legislation passed in 1980. See the appendix to this chapter for further details.

First, transactions accounts. These accounts include demand deposits, NOW (negotiable order of withdrawal) accounts in savings and loan associations, and ATS (automatic transfer system) accounts—checking plus savings—in commercial banks. The required reserve against the first $25 million of transaction accounts is 3 percent. The required reserve for amounts above $25 million will be between 8 and 14 percent when the 1980 law is fully operational in 1988, but it was fixed at 12 percent initially.

To illustrate: a bank has deposits in transaction accounts of $100 million. Its required reserve against those accounts is $9,750,000, computed as follows:

3 percent of $25 million	$750,000
12 percent of $75 million	$9,000,000
Total	$9,750,000

Second, savings accounts and time deposits. There is no required reserve against those accounts held by individuals. But "nonpersonal" savings accounts and time deposits—held by business firms, for example—have a required reserve of 3 percent, with a possible range of 0–9 percent by 1988.

Finally, the Fed has complete flexibility in times of crisis. It can establish any level of reserve requirement for up to 180 days in an emergency. These reserve requirements are complex and are summarized in Table 12–1.

Changes in reserve requirements have a large effect on the reserve positions of member banks. A one-half of one percent decrease in required reserves, if made early in 1980 would mean an increase in free reserves of some $1,340 million. At a 1 to 5 ratio of reserves to

Table 12–1
Reserve Requirements for Financial Institutions*

Type of Account	Reserve Requirement (percent)	
	Initial	Range
Transaction		
$0–25 million	3	3
over $25 million	12	8–14
Savings and time		
personal	0	0
non-personal	3	0–9

*Note: The initial reserve requirements are specified in 1980 legislation; the range is to be phased in between 1980 and 1988.

demand deposits, that amount of reserves could be the basis for $6.7 billion of demand deposits. That is a significant amount of new purchasing power.

Changes in reserve requirements are seldom used to force banks to reduce their loans. This may seem paradoxical, because it is such a good weapon to use for that purpose. The problem is that a forced reduction in lending can be very hard on business firms that just happen to be caught with a need to renew their old loans, and would discriminate against businesses that are short of working capital. This is the condition of small business most of the time, while big firms often have substantial reserves. The impact of changes in reserve requirements is not felt evenly throughout the business community. Instead, an increase in the reserve ratio is used most often to sop up the excess reserves of the system and make it more sensitive to open market purchases and sales, rather than to change the amount of loans outstanding.

The Federal Reserve Discount Rate
When a member bank borrows from its regional Federal Reserve Bank, it must pay interest on the loan, just as you or I or General Motors Corporation must pay interest when we borrow. The rate of interest charged by the Feder-

al Reserve when member banks borrow is called the Federal Reserve *discount rate,* or sometimes the *rediscount rate.*[8]

Borrowing from the Fed affects the reserve position of the borrowing bank. For example, if a bank suddenly finds itself without adequate reserves, it can borrow the required amount, using government securities as collateral for the loan. The regional Federal Reserve Bank then credits the member bank's reserve account by the amount of the loan. Exactly the opposite occurs when the member bank pays off the loan. The regional Federal Reserve bank takes payment by reducing the member bank's reserve account.

Banks don't like to borrow from the Fed. Moreover, a bank that is continually in debt to the Fed will sometimes receive an inquiry about why it is always in trouble, and perhaps a reprimand. So most banks borrow only on a temporary basis and only when they must bolster their reserve positions. The Fed encourages this attitude on the part of the member banks. It keeps the banks from borrowing more than they absolutely need, and thereby makes it easier for other instruments of credit control to operate more effectively. In fact, until recently the Fed assumed that no bank would borrow unless its reserve position made the loan absolutely necessary, and almost never turned down a bank's request for a loan.[9]

---

[8]When a member bank borrows at the Fed it usually uses government securities as *collateral*, or security for the loan. When the loan is repaid, the bank pays back the amount of the loan plus interest, say 4 1/2 percent, for the time it held the money. This is called *discounting* and the interest rate is the *discount rate*. In England it's called the *Bank rate*, meaning the Bank of England.

A second procedure is available. The member bank may sell to the Fed some of its commercial paper (promissory notes from business firms to whom the bank has made loans). The sale will be at a discount of 4 1/2 percent. This is called rediscounting (because the bank has already charged interest on, or discounted, the original loan) and the interest rate is the rediscount rate. The Federal Reserve discount rate and rediscount rate are always identical. The rates will vary with the length of maturity of the loan and may differ from one Federal Reserve district to another.

[9]Late in 1966, the presidents of the twelve Federal Reserve banks announced that the Fed's loan policies would be based on the general economic conditions of the country. Up to that time, loans to member banks had been based solely upon the bank's "credit worthiness" and upon the value of the collateral for the loan.

The Federal Reserve discount rate is not a very effective way of influencing credit conditions and the money markets. In the first place, the initiative for a loan must come from the member banks. The Fed takes a passive role, waiting for the member bank to ask. Lowering the rate will not do much to encourage banks to borrow, however, because of the reluctance of member banks to be in debt to the Fed. Raising the rate won't have much impact either, because when banks have inadequate reserves they have little alternative but to borrow.[10]

Secondly, the Federal Reserve discount rate must remain close to the rate of interest on short-term government securities. There is an interesting relationship here. If the Federal Reserve discount rate for a 90-day loan is 10 percent while the rate of return on a 90-day Treasury bill is 12 percent, a smart banker will borrow from the Fed rather than sell his Treasury bills in order to adjust his reserve position. Doing so will increase the system's reserves at a time when the Fed may not want greater ease in the money markets.

On the other hand, if the discount rate is well above the interest rate on Treasury bills, banks will sell their government securities before they come to the Fed to borrow. This puts the Fed out of touch with the money market climate and makes it more difficult to decide how to use the instruments of credit control. As a result, the Federal Reserve sets its discount rate to follow very closely the fluctuations that occur in the yield on Treasury bills. Yet that interest rate is the result of supply and demand conditions in the money market, which in turn have been influenced by other instruments of credit control.

In spite of all this, the discount rate does have some uses as an instrument of credit control. It is watched by bankers and speculators as a confirmation of the trends they have already observed in other market rates of interest. When the Fed raises the discount rate, the action is understood as confirming the fact that interest rates have risen and that money markets have become tighter. The psychological effect is to cause a little more tightening. When the Fed lowers its discount rate just the opposite occurs. Bankers and others in the money markets know that an easing of money market conditions has occurred, and there is a tendency to a little more ease in lending as a result. Thus we have an intriguing paradox: one of the least effective of the instruments of monetary management is one of the most closely watched indicators of money market conditions.

Moral Suasion

It is sometimes possible for the Fed to influence credit conditions by public statements, by private discussions with bankers, and by developing "voluntary controls." For example, in 1966, when there was great concern over the nation's balance of international payments, the federal government, in cooperation with the Fed, developed a program to limit foreign loans by banks. There were no compulsory controls, just a set of guidelines that banks were asked to abide by. There was a very high degree of compliance. The circumstances were good: domestic money markets could absorb all the loans the banks could make and interest rates were rising so banks went along with the voluntary limitations on their foreign loans that the Fed asked for. Besides, there was always the threat of compulsion if the voluntary system didn't work. The episode indicated that "jawbone controls" could work under the proper conditions.

Sometimes, however, they do not work. Late in 1979 the Fed asked large banks not to make loans that were primarily for speculative purposes. The object was to reduce demands

---

[10]A bank can always pay the penalty for inadequate reserves, which is 1 percent more than the discount rate on the amount of the inadequacy. It is cheaper to borrow from the Fed than to pay the penalty rate, however.

for credit that were pushing interest rates to extremely high levels. Nevertheless, a number of leading banks continued to make large loans to a group of speculators in the silver market and to their brokers. These loans contributed to the financial crisis of the spring of 1980. The bank officials who made the loans explained that they were unaware of the fact that the funds were for speculative manipulation of the silver market—which means that the bankers were either lying or incompetent, take your pick. The incident was an excellent example of the failure of moral suasion to act as an effective means of credit control.

Most of the time moral suasion is used only to set the stage for later action. A speech by a member of the Board of Governors may be a prelude to significant open market operations or use of some other credit control instruments, and may be part of a combined operation designed to achieve just the proper state of tension or ease in the money markets. Standing alone, it may have little effect. But as part of a pattern that includes use of open market operations and changes in the discount rate, it could have a significant psychological effect on the money markets.

Special Credit Controls
The philosophy of the Federal Reserve System is to apply general tightness or ease in the money markets as a whole. It seeks to leave decisions about the use of the available funds to the forces of the money markets themselves. In the Fed's view, competition among lenders and borrowers should determine how the funds will be allocated among their alternative uses. This traditional policy is quite consistent with the development of modern economic theory: the level of economic activity must be managed in order to achieve economic health, but the allocation of resources can be left to market forces (if monopoly can be avoided) in order to achieve economic efficiency.

But from time to time even the Fed accepts some modification of this basic principle and uses special credit controls that affect only one segment of the money markets. One area of special concern is speculation on the stock market. If speculators borrow a large portion of the money they need to buy stocks, there will be considerably more speculation than if such borrowing were limited. For a variety of reasons—chiefly the stock market crash of 1929—Congress has given the Fed power to limit that type of borrowing by setting *margin requirements*. The proportion of the selling price of securities that the buyer is required to put up in cash is called the "margin." Thus, when margin requirements are set at 70, this means that 70 percent of the purchase price has to be cash and only 30 percent can be borrowed. The Fed can set margin requirements at any level. In recent decades they have been fixed between 50 and 90, depending on how the Fed has assessed the speculative pressures existing in the securities market.

The Fed also has power to fix the ceilings on interest rates on time deposits. These are the maximum rates that member banks can pay to depositors on savings accounts and other time deposits, including time certificates of deposit. These ceilings are used to limit the amount of savings deposits that member banks can attract from outside the Federal Revenue System. By raising interest rates on savings deposits, member banks can cause the general public as well as large investors to shift their time deposits from savings and loan associations and savings banks to the member banks. During periods of tight money, there is strong incentive for the member banks to get funds in this way. But the whole point of tight money is to prevent further expansion of credit. Imposing limits on the interest rates that member banks can offer on time deposits closes this loophole and makes the other means of credit control more effective. Controls over maximum interest rates will be phased out by 1986, however, under the new 1980 legislation.

The Fed has authority to do a variety of other things to manage the markets for money

THE FEDERAL RESERVE SYSTEM AT A GLANCE

Structure
Board of Governors: 7 members with 14-year
  terms.
12 regional Federal Reserve banks.
about 5,425 member banks (1980).

Monetary Policy
Decided by the Federal Open Market Committee,
whose voting members are the 7 members of the
Board of Governors, the president of the Federal
Reserve Bank of New York, and the presidents of
four other regional banks, who rotate in one-year
terms. Presidents of the other Federal Reserve
banks attend meetings of the committee but do
not vote.

Process
The "trading desk" of the Federal Reserve Bank
of New York buys and sells government securities

for the system as a whole, dealing with about 35
firms that buy and sell government securities.

When the Fed buys securities it pays the seller
by check. The seller deposits the check in a
commercial bank, which increases demand deposits. When the commercial bank deposits the
check in a Federal Reserve Bank, its reserves
are increased.

When the Federal Reserve Bank of New York
sells securities it receives a check from the
buyer. It collects from the commercial bank
against which the check was written by reducing
the reserves of the commercial bank by the
amount of the check. When the commercial bank
deducts the amount of the check from the buyer's
bank balance, demand deposits are reduced.

and credit. It can impose a variety of direct or indirect controls on consumer credit and the corporations that lend to consumers via loans or credit cards. It can impose reserve requirements on mutual funds that invest in the money markets. It can impose a variety of special charges and reserve requirements on financial institutions to deal with special rather than general problems in the money markets. In normal times the Fed shies away from these actions, following its policy of applying a general stimulus or constraint and allowing the effects to be allocated among various portions of the money markets by the markets themselves. But the need for special credit controls has increased in recent years, partly because in recent decades new practices and institutions developed in the money markets that the more general credit controls could not effectively reach, and partly because the effectiveness of general credit controls has been significantly reduced by the growing internationalization of

the money markets, about which more will be said later in this chapter.

The Federal Reserve System as Lender of Last Resort

A lender of last resort has responsibility to prevent the sort of financial instability that could lead to a large scale bankruptcy of financial institutions. The problem is inherent in any fractional reserve banking system in which the obligations of banks are much greater than their reserves. During a serious downturn in economic activity business firms may not be able to repay their loans from banks. If, at the same time, large depositors seek to withdraw funds from the banks, the banks may not be able to pay. Such a "run" on the banking system can cause the entire financial system to break down as depositors rush to withdraw their funds in a "panic." At such times the central bank is expected to make funds available to the commercial banks so they can meet the demands for withdrawal of funds, restore confidence in the system, and stop the run.

In the spring of 1933 such a panic occurred in the United States, leading to a breakdown of the entire banking system and the "bank holiday" in March of that year. The Fed was unable to halt the panic, and some argue that it did not try very hard. There is some question, however, as to whether stronger action would have been effective. As we noted in Chapter 4, in 1931 the Creditanstalt, the largest bank in Austria, failed. It had made large loans in eastern Europe to farmers and mining enterprises. Those debtors were unable to repay because of large declines in commodity prices in 1930 and 1931. Failure of the Creditanstalt was quickly followed by a run on the other Austrian banks. It was known that the Austrian banks had borrowed large sums from German banks, which they were now unable to pay. Smart investors then began to withdraw their funds from German banks, and the run on those banks soon caused them to fail. By this time the uneasiness spread to England and France and their banks were in trouble. In addition, it was known that a number of important U.S. banks had made large loans to German banks to assist in financing payment of World War I reparations by Germany. The run thus shifted to U.S. banks by late 1932 and early 1933 and huge sums were withdrawn for transfer abroad, forcing the federal government to close the nation's banks. The dominoes were toppling. From small beginnings in a peripheral part of the world economy a financial storm arose that largely destroyed the world financial system, including that of the United States.

Note that the heart of the problem was not a horde of small depositors lining up at the banks to withdraw their savings, although there was some of that at the end. The basic cause of the debacle was withdrawal of large amounts of so-called "hot money" by big depositors seeking a safer haven in another country.

Much has been done since 1933 to reduce the possibility of a similar financial panic. The Federal Deposit Insurance Corporation was established to guarantee small deposits (the upper limit is now $100,000). Similar organizations guarantee deposits in savings and loan institutions and savings banks.

More important, the Federal Reserve System now acts much more effectively as a lender of last resort to bolster the financial system when it is in trouble. There have not been situations as serious as 1933, but the Fed has had to act as a lender of last resort four times in recent years. In 1966 it prevented the collapse of the savings and loan industry. In 1970 it protected the market for commercial paper (short term business loans). In 1974–75 it prevented the collapse of the Franklin National Bank from spreading to other major banks, and in 1980 it helped prevent the failure of the First Pennsylvania Bank, averted a major financial collapse that could have resulted from speculation in the silver market, and again came to the rescue of the savings and loan industry. In each case the Fed's intervention brought large amounts of new reserves into the banking system.

Provision of additional reserves for the banking system is the key to rescue operations by the central bank. The system is in trouble either because banks or other financial institutions are unable to meet the demands of their depositors or there is the possibility of severe loss of confidence in their ability to do so. Some agency must provide funds to prevent collapse. That agency is the central bank, which can either buy in the open market to provide reserves to the system as a whole or rediscount (buy at a discount) some of the assets of a particular bank to provide reserves directly to it.

The 1980 rescue of the First Pennsylvania Bank, the largest bank in Philadelphia, is one example of the process. The bank's management had made a series of serious errors of judgment speculating in government securities. As knowledge of the bank's condition spread, the monetary authorities feared a run would force it to close. All of this was happening at a time of great tension in the money markets associated with speculation in silver and other commodities and problems for the savings and loan associations. The stage was set for a major financial collapse if nothing was done to prevent the failure of one of the country's largest banks. So the monetary authorities stepped in to provide assistance: a loan of over $200 million from the Federal Deposit Insurance Corporation to the First Pennsylvania Bank, and a reported loan of $800 million from a syndicate of other large banks. In addition, the regional Federal Reserve banks apparently agreed to rediscount several hundred millions of dollars of the financial assets of the First Pennsylvania Bank and to provide the other large banks participating in the rescue with the reserves necessary to make their loans to First Pennsylvania without interfering with their other operations. All of this meant a potential increase in new reserves for the banking system of at least $1 billion. The exact amount of the new reserves created for the purpose will never be known. In the long-standing tradition of central bank secrecy, these operations are carried out with as little information announced to the public as possible on the theory that a financial panic might develop if the public knew the system was in trouble.

The First Pennsylvania rescue was almost simultaneous with another rescue operation, the details of which are even more obscure, to prevent the speculative collapse in the market for silver from spreading to other commodities markets and to securities markets. This operation apparently required an even larger injection of new reserves into the banking system than the First Pennsylvania operation. Again, only the insiders know the amount of new reserves created for this purpose.

When the central bank acts as a lender of last resort the other goals of monetary policy must be set aside. Massive injection of new reserves into the banking system is required whenever the central bank prevents the collapse of some sector of the financial system. Yet the flooding of the financial system with increased liquidity may come at a time when inflation is strong, and a sudden easing of the money markets may create further inflationary pressures. The central bank's function as lender of last resort can seriously interfere with its ability to manage and stabilize the monetary system.

This is exactly what happened in the period since 1965. The strong inflationary pressures created by the war in Vietnam, very large increases in the cost of energy, and rapid growth of international banking helped create the financial environment and practices out of which came the monetary problems of 1966, 1970–71, 1974–75, and 1980. At a time when inflationary pressures called for monetary restraint to dampen the increase in prices—when the Fed should have been consistently leaning against the inflationary winds—it was forced periodically to do exactly the opposite, and on a large scale.

There is a second serious side effect of lender of last resort operations: they often validate unsound financial practices. For example, in 1974, as part of its rescue of the Franklin National Bank, the Fed extended the guarantee of domestic bank accounts to deposits in the foreign branches of Franklin National. The purpose was to prevent a run on the foreign branches that might move to other banks and start a general financial collapse. But the effect was implicitly to guarantee all deposits in branches of all U.S. banks overseas. Protecting them in this fashion greatly reduces the risk attached to those deposits and encourages further expansion of the bank loans that create international accounts. And, as we saw in Chapter 11, the rapid growth of those deposits is a classic example of unsound expansion of credit in an unsupervised banking system.

There is an interesting paradox inherent in the central bank's function as lender of last resort. On the one hand, it is absolutely essential that a private banking system organized around the profit motive have a lender that can stand above the hurly burly of the money markets to provide stability for the financial system. All economic activity must be financed, and the money market provides the financing. If financial institutions fail and are unable to perform their functions effectively, the economic system as a whole will be crippled. The lender of last resort has a responsibility to prevent such a collapse.

On the other hand, the financial practices that lead to trouble are part of the system itself. Thus, when the First Pennsylvania Bank began speculating in government securities, it was only trying to enlarge its profits. The speculation, however, came to interfere with the bank's function as financier of production and distribution. By rescuing the bank the Fed implied that banks would not have to pay the full price of unsound financial practices. Rescuing the system as a whole creates an environment in which destabilizing financial behavior is implicitly condoned.

The Limitations of Monetary Policy

Experience with monetary policy in the last quarter-century has brought to the fore a whole series of limitations on its use. Banks have developed a good deal of flexibility in their loan policies by juggling their asset portfolios. Substantial time lags between action by the Fed and effects in the money markets have become evident. Forecasting of economic conditions and the effects of monetary policy is often difficult. The effects of action by the Fed are not always evenly spread through the economy. And in recent years the growth of the international banking system has seriously interfered with the effectiveness of monetary management within national boundaries.

These limitations mean that monetary policy can be only one arm of national economic policy, and not the principal one. It must be strongly supplemented by other action if economic policy goals are to be achieved.

Secondary Reserves

Banks have developed a good deal of flexibility, making it difficult for the Fed to maintain the close control over money markets it would like to have. The chief source of flexibility is the so-called *secondary reserves* of the member banks. These are highly liquid assets, mostly federal government securities, owned by banks. These holdings can be used to foil the actions of the Fed, at least for a short period of time.

Suppose the Fed wishes to tighten the money markets. There is no need for quick action: the Fed manages its open market operations so that free reserves gradually fall as the GNP rises and bank loans increase. As more and more banks become loaned up, they face the unhappy task of telling their customers that funds are not available. Rather than send them away to borrow elsewhere from a competitor, a bank will probably decide to sell some government securities out of its portfolio. This will provide the cash for loans to customers. The bank, in other words, shifts the composition of its earning assets from government securities to loans. It will do so for two reasons: it can earn more on the loans than on the securities, and it will keep its customers satisfied.

As a result of this action, however, the supply of funds for business loans keeps rising even though bank reserves have not been increased. The money markets have not been significantly tightened and the Fed's objectives have not been achieved.

When the banks sell government securities someone has to buy them. Since the Fed is not the buyer, it has to be someone in the private, nonbank sector of the money markets, probably an insurance company, investment fund, or some other large investor. When investors buy the securities their bank accounts, which were being held as an asset, are reduced. But the banks that sell the securities immediately lend the money to someone who wants to spend it. Bank deposits that were idle are thus activated; money that was held as an asset is then spent.

Eventually the money markets will begin to tighten up, however. As sales of government securities mount, their prices will fall. This will happen partly because the supply offered in the market is increased, and partly because the holders of idle bank deposits must be given some incentive to shift the form in which they hold their assets. As the price of government securities falls, their yield will increase, which is equivalent to an increase in the rate of interest. As the price falls, the banks will have to take increasing losses as they sell their government securities, and this is discouraging.[11] For a time they can raise interest rates to compensate, but eventually this will start discouraging their customers. Sooner or later, the process of liquidating "secondary" reserves will start slowing down and come to an end. But it may take months, and in the meantime, funds for bank loans to their customers have not been significantly affected.

That isn't true of interest rates, however. The yield on Treasury bills will start rising quite soon after the banks start selling them. This will bring the Federal Reserve discount rate up, as the Fed keeps it in accord with the yield on Treasury bills. Other interest rates will also start moving upward, as investors and lenders start shifting their portfolios into higher-yielding Treasury bills. Tightness in the money markets will begin to show up in rising interest rates before bank lending starts to slow down.

- **Secondary reserves** are highly liquid assets, mostly government securities, owned by banks that can be sold to provide cash for loans to customers.

Time Lags in Monetary Policy

The level of production and employment is not affected immediately by the Fed's efforts to tighten the money markets. Just how long the lags may be is not clearly known. And, of course, they will differ as circumstances change in the money markets and in the economy as a whole. Just to give you an idea of the range of opinion among economists on this matter, some believe that about half of the effect of open market operations will be felt within about six months and the bulk of the effect within a year. At the other end of the scale are those who argue that significant effects are not felt for perhaps nine months to a year, while the full effects require two to three years before appearing. Many economists just throw up their hands and refuse to guess.

But there is agreement on one point: there are serious time lags between action by the Fed and effects on the money markets, and even longer lags in effects on GNP. These lags make it imperative that the Fed move carefully. It is quite possible that actions by the Fed, taken many months ago in the direction of tight money, will start to catch hold right in the middle of an economic downturn. In the intervening time the economy may have moved from overheating to slack, requiring easy money instead of tight. So the perverse effects of monetary policies may be contributing to the downturn instead of leaning against it.

Just the opposite may also be true. The Fed may try to stimulate recovery from a recession by easing the money markets, only to discover

---

[11]Note the connection between interest rates and bond prices. Suppose a $1,000 bond carries an interest payment of 5 percent per year. The payment will be $50. Now let the price of the bond fall to $900. The $50 payment provides a yield (on the purchase price) of 5.55 percent:

$$\frac{\$50}{\$900} = 5.55 \text{ percent}$$

If this is a government bond, and the Treasury wants to sell more bonds after the price has fallen, it will have to offer a payment of $55.55 on a $1,000 bond. The interest rate will have risen.

Alternatively, the Treasury could still market bonds with a face value of $1,000 and an annual "coupon" of $50, but it would get only $900 for them. The effective interest rate will still be the new and higher level established by the market.

that when the ease occurs the economy is pushing on the full-employment ceiling, and the money markets need tightening.

Information and Forecasting Problems

Time lags in the effects of monetary policy put a great premium on economic forecasting and adequacy of information. In order to know what to do today, the Fed must have a good notion of what the condition of the economy is likely to be in six months or a year, when the effects of today's actions or inactions will be strongly felt. Yet the Board of Governors does not even know what is going on currently. All it has is information on the recent past, and the more recent its information the less accurate it is likely to be. Incomplete and inaccurate facts are the raw materials for decisions.

The problems of economic forecasting are severe. But the Fed is faced with an additional problem. The Board of Governors must coordinate its forecast of the time lag built into its monetary policies with its forecast for the economy as a whole. Both can be in error. When that happens serious mistakes in monetary policy can be made.

The Board of Governors cannot avoid the problem by doing nothing. That also is a policy, for it implies that the economy is operating on an even keel and nothing needs to be done. There are three policy alternatives. The Board can lean toward tighter money to slow down economic expansion and reduce present or potential inflationary pressures. It can lean toward easier money to encourage an increase in economic activity or keep an expansion going. Or it can take a neutral position, which implies that the economy doesn't need a nudge in either direction. But in all three cases accurate information and good forecasts are necessary for good results.

Portfolio Adjustments and Monetary Policy

Banks are not the only economic units to make *portfolio adjustments* (changes in asset holdings) when money market conditions change. People who make their living in the money

markets adjust more quickly, perhaps, and to a greater extent than others, but changes in the availability of money and credit affect everyone. And just like the adjustments made by banks, this general accommodation made by the public may have results unforeseen by the monetary authorities.

- **Portfolio adjustments** are shifts in the holding of liquid assets throughout the private sector in response to changes in the money markets.

Suppose, for example, that the public has become accustomed to a gradually expanding supply of money and near money, that is, currency, demand deposits, and time deposits, to meet its need for liquid assets, and feels comfortable about the amount it holds in relation to its other assets. As the economic theorist would explain the situation, portfolios are in equilibrium and there is no tendency to sell assets and acquire money, or vice versa.

If, then, the money supply declines or fails to grow as fast as it had been growing, people will find themselves squeezed. They will try to bring their holdings of money back into equilibrium with their other assets. To do so they will sell some of their other financial assets, such as securities. Business people caught in a financial squeeze of this sort will try to reduce their inventories in order to rebuild their cash positions. They will reduce their output and lay off workers or slow down their investment in new plants and equipment.

These efforts to return to a new liquidity equilibrium will, in a chain effect, influence the incomes and assets of others. They, in turn, will try to reach a new adjustment in which they feel comfortable again with their holdings of cash and other assets. The ultimate result is extremely difficult to forecast, or even to measure. Attitudes toward portfolios and liquidity are essentially psychological, depending upon optimism or pessimism about events. The situation is always new, and even though, objectively, it may be similar to past situations, people can react differently than they did in the past. Although the general direction of the effect of monetary policies on portfolio decisions can be estimated with some confidence— tight money will normally cause people to shift toward greater liquidity, for example—the extent and timing of the reaction is extremely difficult to assess. Policy makers, therefore, find it difficult to determine the proper extent and timing of monetary policy. They tend to be careful and cautious, moving slowly and in relatively small steps.

The Uneven Impact of Monetary Policy

Adjustments in the money markets often affect some sectors of the economy more heavily than others. This is particularly true as the markets tighten up. There is some evidence, for example, that large borrowers are among the last to feel the effects of tight money, and small borrowers the first. For example, residential construction is done by relatively small firms; and home purchases by individuals are relatively small transactions. In both construction loans and mortgage loans the availability of credit seems to be very quickly affected by tighter monetary conditions. Similarly, sales of consumer durable goods are quickly affected.

The main differences in impact arise from differences in the extent to which companies rely on loans for their operations. Most large corporations obtain a large portion of their capital for investment and operations from their earnings. These firms will be little affected by tight money because they borrow relatively little. Most small firms, however, operate to a substantial extent on borrowed funds, and traditionally finance much of their expansion with loans; these firms will be influenced significantly by tight money. They will find that, relative to the larger firms, their operations are restricted by the rationing of credit by banks and their costs are higher because interest rates have risen. Even though banks may make an effort to avoid favoring large borrowers, these differences of operation between

large and small firms tend to work toward de facto discrimination against small business firms.

Monetary Policy and the International Monetary System

The monetary system of the United States is closely tied to that of the rest of the world. That relationship became even closer after the development of the so-called Eurobank or Eurocredit system since the mid-1960s. There is now a highly developed and well articulated international monetary system, and its "key currency" is the United States dollar. This monetary system enables funds to be transferred quickly from the banking system of one country to another in response to changes in interest rates, risks, economic conditions, and political events.

For example, an increase in interest rates in United States money markets will tend to draw funds from abroad into the United States. One result will be to dampen the rise in U.S. interest rates by increasing the supply of funds available to borrowers. One might suppose that interest rates would rise abroad, but that would occur only if the world money supply were limited, and that is not the case. The Eurobank system can create the supply that the market calls for at existing interest rates. The result of these relationships is to greatly reduce the effectiveness of the monetary policy instruments available to the Fed.

Suppose the Fed wishes to tighten the United States money markets to dampen inflationary pressures. A large open market sale of Treasury bills by the Fed would normally draw reserves from the banking system, reduce bank lending and cause interest rates to rise. But with a flexible international banking system this effect is greatly reduced. Overseas financial institutions, including branches of U.S. banks, shift funds into the U.S. economy, and U.S. multinational corporations borrow dollars overseas. The result is that a large-scale open market sale by the Fed has only a relatively small effect on U.S. money markets.

Open market purchases designed to ease U.S. money markets suffer the same fate. The goal of open market purchases is to increase the supply of available funds and bring interest rates down. Instead, much of the new reserves may be siphoned off by large banks to their international branches, where the funds can earn larger profits because the international branches have no reserve requirements. Money markets within the U.S. are not strongly affected.

These examples illustrate one of the hardest facts of monetary policy. The development of international banking on a large scale in recent years has greatly undermined the ability of central banks, including the Federal Reserve System, to manage effectively their national monetary systems. It is going too far, perhaps, to say that the U.S. monetary system is out of reach of the controls exercised by the Federal Reserve System—but such a conclusion is closer to reality than many would like to admit.

The Uses of Monetary Policy

Monetary management is a highly complex job. It entails much more than simple manipulation of the instruments of monetary control to keep the economy on the right track. Secondary reserves give the member banks a good deal of flexibility in responding to changes in money market conditions. Serious time lags appear between Federal Reserve actions and effects in the money markets. These problems are compounded by difficulties in forecasting, by unexpected portfolio changes, and by the sensitivity of domestic money markets to international monetary influences.

The policy implications of these limitations are important. Monetary policy alone cannot be relied upon to achieve the stability needed by a modern economy. The best that it can do is to "lean against the wind." On the one hand, if the economy is operating at levels below full employment, the Fed can promote ease in the money markets. But monetary ease cannot assure that banks will lend and businesses will borrow in just the amounts necessary to bring the economy to full employment. Indeed, too much ease in the money markets could lead to a speculative expansion of economic activity that could not be sustained, leading to later difficulties in both the money markets and in output and employment.

On the other hand, if the economy is overheating and a policy of tighter money markets is adopted and carried out, excessive tightness can bring about a downturn in economic activity. Yet if the money markets are not tightened enough in such a situation, an inflationary expansion could get out of hand and also lead to a downturn later on. There is a fine line monetary policy must follow, a golden mean of neither too much nor too little, yet the line is very difficult to find and adhere to.

Complicating the problem is the possibility that significant shifts in monetary policy may induce the very swings in economic activity that the policy seeks to avoid. Turning the flow of credit up and down shifts the economic environment within which decisions are made, first to expansion and then to contraction. Unless used very gingerly, monetary policy might itself provoke a pattern of boom and bust. Anything more than "leaning against the wind" could be dangerous.

Monetary policy can't do the whole job of controlling short run fluctuations in economic activity. Monetary policy and fiscal policy must supplement each other. When monetary policy leans toward ease, the tax and expenditure policies of the federal government should be expansionary. The two policies will complement and assist each other in achieving the necessary increase in GNP. In contrast, when monetary policy leans toward tightness, federal fiscal policy should be moving toward reductions in total spending, either through tax increases or spending reductions or both. Monetary policy is an essential instrument of economic policy, but it can be used only for limited purposes, has limited effects, and must be coordinated with appropriate fiscal policies if it is to be effective.

The Fundamental Dilemma of Monetary Policy

Coordination of monetary and fiscal policy is difficult. Fiscal policy tends to have an expansionary bias. When significant economic slack prevails, it is relatively easy for the federal government to reduce taxes and increase spending. Those measures are popular with voters. But when the time comes for economic restraint, it is difficult to cut spending and raise taxes. Congressmen and senators who vote that way don't get reelected.

Furthermore, if spending programs are desirable, if there is a net gain to society from them, the programs are worthwhile in good times as well as bad. If we need missiles and H-bombs, or if we need medical research programs and the myriad other things government spends money on, we should have them irrespective of whether the economy is doing well or badly. Conversely, if the programs are not desirable, why should they be placed in operation just to increase employment and output? A countercyclical fiscal policy that involves increases and decreases in public spending to stabilize aggregate demand will involve an inefficient allocation of resources. When times are bad there could be too much spending on programs that are not needed, while in good times there may be inadequate spending on desirable programs. Efficient allocation of resources to social uses and stabilization of the economy can be incompatible goals.

These considerations combine to cause policymakers to put responsibility for economic constraint very heavily on monetary policy. An expansionary bias in fiscal policy forces a bias toward monetary constraint onto policymakers at the Fed. The result is a tendency toward tight money and high interest rates. Yet these are the conditions that hold back investment and expansion of the economy's capacity to produce—and it is exactly these sorts of supply-side constraints that exacerbate inflationary pressures. The effort to use monetary policy to compensate for some of the political and economic limitations of fiscal policy helped to bring on the economic difficulties of the early 1980s.

Summary

The basic rationale for management of the monetary system by a central bank is that the private operations of individuals and banks can bring instability that is not in the best interests of the economy as a whole. The central bank seeks to ease the money markets when slack appears in the economy and to tighten them when expansion becomes too rapid or threatens inflation, while at the same time facilitating economic growth. It also acts as a lender of last resort to preserve the viability of the financial system.

The Federal Reserve System is the central bank of the United States. It comprises some 5,700 privately owned member banks, 12 Federal Reserve Banks and a Board of Governors. The central banking functions are carried out by the Board of Governors and the Federal Reserve Banks.

The instruments of credit control available to "the Fed" are open market operations, changes in member bank reserve requirements, changes in the Federal Reserve discount rate, "moral suasion," and some special credit controls. The lending power of the member banks is determined by their reserve position, which in turn is controlled by the Fed primarily through the amount of reserves made available, largely through open market operations.

Monetary policy has important drawbacks that limit its usefulness, including the fact that banks usually hold secondary reserves; time lags that exist between actions by the Fed and their actual impact; difficulties of forecasting; portfolio adjustments in the business world; the uneven impact of tight money on different sectors of the economy; and the impact of the international monetary system. As a result of these difficulties monetary policy alone cannot be expected to stabilize the economy. It must be used together with fiscal policy.

Key Concepts

Federal Reserve System
open market operations
required reserve ratio

secondary reserves
portfolio adjustments

For Discussion

1. Should the policies of the Fed be brought under the control of the President, or should the Fed remain independent? Explain.
2. In what ways do the functions of a central bank conflict?
3. What is meant by the "accommodation" function of a central bank?
4. Why is the "lender of last resort" function of the Fed necessary?
5. Does the rise of the Eurocredit banking system indicate that there should be a shift in monetary authority from the national to the supranational level? Why?
6. What are the chief limitations on the use of monetary policy?

Appendix 12A

1980 Changes in Monetary Controls: The Depository Institutions Deregulation and Monetary Control Act

The national policy of monetary management ushered in by the Federal Reserve Act of 1913 was strengthened during 1933–35 by a wide variety of legislation that increased the powers of the Federal Reserve System, guaranteed bank deposits, regulated securities exchanges, and restructured the capital markets for agriculture, housing, and business investment. The bulk of this legislation was designed to stabilize money markets and the flow of credit into needed uses and to diminish speculation. One effect of this restructuring was to reduce competition by defining more precisely the areas within which commercial banks, savings and loan associations and firms in the securities market could function.

Large changes in the money markets occurred in the years after World War II. In particular, commercial banks devised a variety of ways to avoid Federal Reserve regulations and to enter sectors of the money markets formerly dominated by savings and loan institutions and securities firms. Securities firms invented money market mutual funds, which enabled them to encroach on territories dominated by commercial banks and savings and loans. Commercial banks moved into the international money markets, which enabled them to get back into investment banking, a sector of the money markets from which they had been barred after 1935. One result was that money management by the Federal Reserve System began to lose its effectiveness, and the money markets were plagued by growing instability and widening fluctuations in interest rates. Competition was eroding both monetary regulation and the protected position of the great vested interests of the money markets.

The credit crunch of 1966 brought demands for action. Both the commercial paper market and the savings and loans had to be rescued from collapse by a massive easing of credit by the Fed, which seriously interfered with anti-inflation policy at just the time that escalation of the Vietnam War was increasing inflationary pressures. After much discussion, numerous studies, and passage of preliminary legislation, the Depository Institutions Deregulation and Monetary Control Act of 1980 was passed. It gave everyone something. The Federal Reserve was provided with broader authority to regulate reserves of all deposit institutions, instead of only commercial banks, and increased authority to require reporting of data needed for money management. New reserve requirements for nonmember banks and thrift institutions are to be phased in over a period of eight years. The Fed lost power to control interest-rate ceilings on deposits, which delighted the commercial banks and savings and loans, but the Fed was glad to give up this authority, which was an albatross around its neck in the newer environment of money market competition. Elimination of interest-rate ceilings will take place over a six-year period. State interest-rate ceilings on most types of loans were overridden, which pleased all lenders. Nationwise authorization of NOW (Negotiable Order of Withdrawal) accounts enabled savings and loan associations to compete for checking accounts with commercial banks, which were authorized to establish immediate electronic transfers between checking and savings accounts, to enable them to compete with the savings and loans. Savings and loan associations and savings banks were given broader authority to extend their investments in the money markets.

One little-noticed but potentially very important provision allows the Board of Governors to impose reserve requirements on overseas deposits in U.S. banks and their international branches or subsidiaries. This provision has not been implemented, because it would reduce the ability of U.S. banks to compete with foreign rivals. Restriction of credit creation in the so-called Eurocredit or Eurocurrency banking system is badly needed, and this provision of the 1980 act would enable the Board to implement an international agreement to do so, if one should be worked out in the future.

The new legislation affects the money markets in several ways. Federal Reserve authority is extended by bringing all institutions holding deposit accounts within the scope of the Fed's reserve requirements. Competition among those deposit institutions—commercial banks, savings and loan associations, savings banks, and money market mutual funds—is increased. The flow of funds into mortgage markets

will be stabilized by enabling savings and loan associations to compete for funds, unrestricted by interest rate limits. Rapid shifting of large amounts of money among savings and loans, banks, and money market mutual funds should be reduced by the ability of all three to compete more closely with each other. Stabilization of the money markets is the objective.

A cynic might argue, however, that the 1980 legislation will enable the Fed to create a general economic disaster as it pursues its policy of driving interest rates up and keeping them high in its attempt to diminish inflationary pressures through the money markets. In the past, efforts to pursue that policy were short-circuited. High interest rates created a succession of credit crunches in particular sectors of the economy that forced the Fed to help the money markets. Now that all sectors of the money market can compete with each other for funds, no one sector is threatened, but all may be vulnerable to a general credit crunch. The revised money management framework increases competition and gives the Fed greater authority, but it also requires greater wisdom on the part of the Board of Governors, and that cannot be legislated.

---

*Further Reading: The Federal Reserve Bank of Chicago has published an excellent little article on "The Depository Institutions Deregulation and Monetary Control Act of 1980" in *Economic Perspectives*, Vol. IV, Issue 5 (Sept./Oct. 1980). Send for it at P.O. Box 834, Chicago, IL 60690; it's free.

Chapter *13*

Money and the Level of Economic Activity

The relationship between the monetary system and the level of economic activity is one of the more controversial topics in the macroeconomic analysis of the modern economy. The previous chapters of this book stressed two propositions:

1. All economic activity must be financed, and the basic task of the monetary system is to provide that financing.

2. Management of the supply of credit by a central bank is needed to minimize the instability inherent in a private enterprise financial system.

We also know that there is a tendency toward equilibrium in the level of income and output at which desired savings and desired investment are realized, as well as a strong tendency toward fluctuations in the level of income and output. It is also clear that the money markets affect the level of economic activity. There is obviously a pattern of interaction between the level of economic activity and the monetary system. This chapter, and its appendix, explores these relationships: the determinants of the rate of interest, the effect of the rate of interest on levels of investment and economic activity, and the relationship of the national income and output to the monetary system.

The Rate of Interest

When anyone borrows money he pays a price for it. That price is the rate of interest.[1] From the lender's point of view, money, which is a highly liquid asset, is given up in exchange for a less liquid asset, such as a promissory note, a government bond, or some other promise to pay. The payment received by the lender in exchange for the use of his money is, in effect, a payment for giving up liquidity.

Liquidity Preference, Money, and Interest Rates

The stock of money (currency plus demand deposits) in the economy at any time must be held by someone, either in their pockets or in their checking accounts. There is no other

---

[1]There are many rates of interest in the economy, depending on the type of loan, the borrower, the length of time of the loan, uncertainty, risk, and other factors. They are, however, systematically related to each other in a continuum. To simplify matters, the term "rate of interest" will be used as a proxy for the range of rates of interest that actually prevails.

Figure 13-1
The Liquidity Preference Schedule

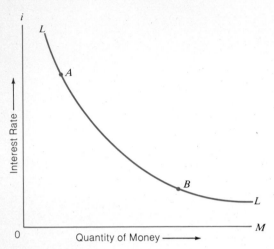

At high rates of interest (and high rates of return on security investments) economic units will be willing to hold only small amounts of cash, point A. When interest rates are lower a larger amount of cash will be held, point B. Note how the liquidity preference schedule, LL, becomes parallel to the axes at its extremities, at the upper level because of the need for some cash to carry on normal economic activities, and at the lower level because yields on securities are too low to cause holders of cash to shift their holdings.

place for it. For example, if there is more money available than people desire to hold in their cash balances, those who have it will buy other assets. They will accumulate more of such near moneys as government bonds and other securities. Doing so will cause the prices of those securities to rise. As their prices go up their yield, or rate of return, will go down.

Take as an example a government bond with a face value of $1,000 and an annual interest payment of $80 (8 percent of face value). Let the price rise to $1,100. The payment of $80 now represents a yield of only 7.27+ percent. Just the opposite happens if the price of the security should fall. The yield would rise above 8 percent. For example, if the price of the bond fell to $900 an $80 payment represents a yield of 8.9 percent.

When the yield from existing securities falls,

new securities can be sold only at interest rates equivalent to the yield on old securities of a similar type. Any attempt to sell them for more will find no takers. For example, if our bond with a face value of $1,000 and an annual payment of $80 sells in the securities markets for $1,050 (yielding a return of 7.6+ percent), any newly issued $1,000 bond could be sold for about $1,000 if it carried an annual payment of $76. This is an interest rate of 7.6 percent, which is the same as the yield that could be obtained by buying an old bond on the open market. The basic idea is a simple one: the desire for liquidity (given the existing supply of money) determines the prices of securities *and* the rates of interest at which new loans can be made.

The desire for liquidity is given a special name by economists: *liquidity preference*. It can be defined as the cash that economic units will be willing to hold at various rates of interest. If interest rates are high, investors will be willing to hold only relatively small amounts of money in cash. On the other hand, if interest rates are low they will have less desire to lend or buy securities and will hold more of their

Figure 13-2
Liquidity Preference Increases

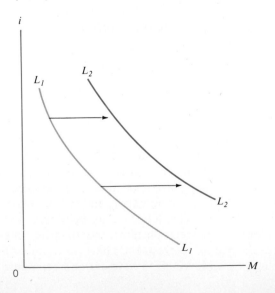

assets in cash. Shown on a diagram, the liquidity preference schedule will look like Figure 13–1.

- **Liquidity preference** is the desire for liquidity. More formally, the amount of cash economic units will be willing to hold at various rates of interest. In this context, the rate of interest is the payment necessary to induce a lender to give up the liquidity embodied in cash.

The liquidity preference schedule is like a demand curve for money. The vertical axis shows the price of money and the horizontal axis shows the amount of money. The schedule itself shows how much money will be held at the various prices, just as a demand curve shows how much of a commodity consumers will be willing to buy at various prices. Just as a demand curve will shift its position as consumer tastes change, so the liquidity preference schedule will shift as the desire for liquidity changes. An increase in the willingness to hold cash shifts the schedule to the right (Figure 13–2), a decrease shifts it to the left (Figure 13–3).

Figure 13–3
Liquidity Preference Decreases

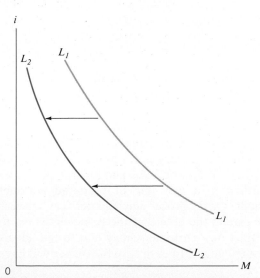

Figure 13–4
Simple Monetary Equilibrium

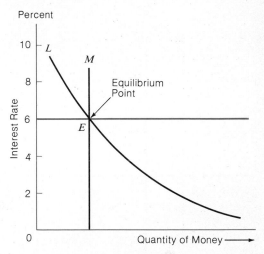

E is the point at which the amount of money people wish to hold equals the amount available to be held. This equality determines the rate of interest. If the rate of interest were higher, *M* would exceed *L*, people would buy securities, their prices would rise, and yields would fall, bringing interest rates down toward *i*. Just the opposite would occur if interest rates were below the *i* shown in the diagram. *L* would exceed *M*, securities would be sold, their prices would fall, their yields would rise, and interest rates would go up. *M* is drawn as a vertical line on the assumption that the quantity of money is unchanged.

The Monetary Equilibrium
The liquidity preferences of economic units interact with the supply of money available to determine the rate of interest. This occurs in much the same way that demand and supply interact to determine the price of a commodity. With a given liquidity preference schedule and a given supply of money, there is a unique rate of interest at which economic units will be willing to hold the existing amount of money. This condition defines the simple monetary equilibrium toward which the money markets will tend to gravitate. It is shown in Figure 13–4.

Figure 13–5 shows what would happen if the quantity of money were to increase while the

Figure 13–5
Money Supply Rises

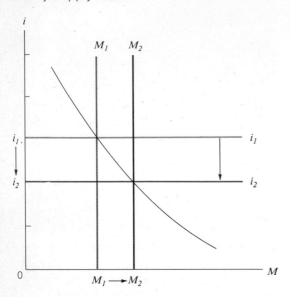

With a given liquidity preference schedule, an increase in M from M_1 to M_2 will bring interest rates down from i_1 to i_2.

Figure 13–6
Money Supply Falls

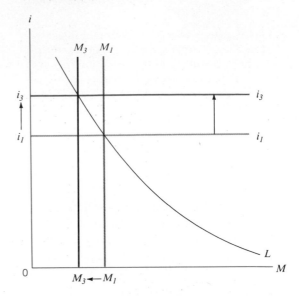

If the quantity of money declines from M_1 to M_3, and L remains unchanged, interest rates will rise from i_1 to i_3.

desire for liquidity remained the same. Interest rates would fall. On the other hand, interest rates would rise if the supply of money fell while liquidity preferences remained the same. That is shown in Figure 13–6.

We can also show what would happen if the desire for liquidity were to change while the quantity of money remained the same. Figure 13–7 shows the effect of an increase in the desire for liquidity. Figure 13–8 shows what happens when the desire for liquidity decreases.

The rate of interest equates the demand for liquidity (liquidity preference) with the supply of liquidity (the quantity of money). In that sense it is no different from any other price. The money markets are like any other markets in that they tend toward an equilibrium in which the rate of interest serves to balance the quantity of money and the liquidity preferences of people who hold money and other assets.

This monetary equilibrium does not stand alone, however. The rate of interest affects the level of investment and thereby the level of output and income. We turn now to that relationship.

Investment Decisions and the Rate of Interest

People in business are continually faced with a wide variety of investment opportunities. The owner of a grocery store, for example, may be able to expand business and enlarge profits by putting in a new line of prepared gourmet foods. Or the grocer may add delivery services to extend the area that the store serves or, to attract new customers, may add to the advertising budget. In each case the owner will have

Figure 13-7
Liquidity Preference Rises

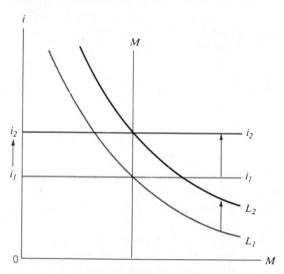

As the desire for liquidity rises from L_1 to L_2, with no change in the quantity of money M, assets are sold. The fall in their price brings yields and interest rates up from i_1 to i_2. At the new interest rates the owners of assets would just as soon hold on to them as sell them, and a new monetary equilibrium has been established.

Figure 13-8
Liquidity Preference Falls

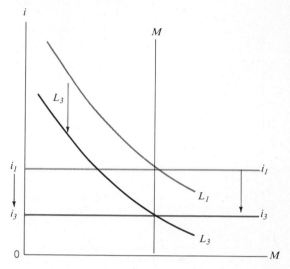

As the desire for liquidity falls from L_1 to L_3, with no change in the quantity of money M, interest rates fall from i_1 to i_3.

to invest additional capital, which will cost a price. And in each case the expansion will be expected to add to revenues.

A rational owner will make no investment unless the expected rate of return is greater than the *cost of capital* (which is the interest rate on money borrowed). Only if that is the case can the owner expect to add to profits. Furthermore, as long as there is any investment for which the expected rate of return is greater than the cost of capital, a business manager will try to borrow the money for it. If the rate of interest exceeds the expected rate of return on new investment, however, it would be foolish to expand further.

● The **cost of capital** is the cost to the borrower of funds obtained for investment. In the context of this chapter, it is taken as equal to the rate of interest.

The Marginal Efficiency of Investment
Economists give the name *marginal efficiency of investment* to the expected rate of return on new investment.[2] It is shown in Figure 13–9. The schedule of the marginal efficiency of investment slopes downward and to the right, like a demand curve. The reason is that rational business firms will first make the most profitable (expected) investments, saving the less profitable ones for later. As the total amount invested is increased, each succeeding investment has a slightly lower expected rate of return than the one before. The rate of return on the last dollar invested declines as the total rises.

---

[2]In this terminology "marginal" refers to the fact that we are dealing with increases to or decreases in the total, while "efficiency" refers to the expected rate of return. We could use the term "expected marginal rate of return on investment," but that phrase is just too big a mind-breaker.

Figure 13-9
The Marginal Efficiency of Investment

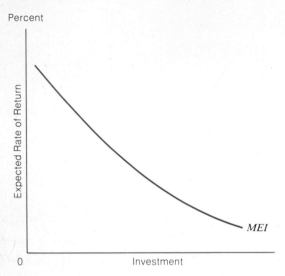

Percent

Expected Rate of Return

0   Investment

MEI

● **Marginal efficiency of investment** is the expected rate of return on new investment.

The *MEI* schedule shows *expected* rates of return on new investment. It is not a phenomenon that can be measured in the marketplace, like the quantity of money or the rate of interest. It is a psychological phenomenon that depends on the state of mind of business managers. It can fluctuate widely from time to time, depending on how they view future prospects. The estimation of the course of future events is crucial in determining investment decisions.

The Rate of Interest and the Level of Investment

We are now able to connect the rate of interest with the level of investment. Business firms can be expected to push the level of investment up to the amount at which the rate of interest is equal to the marginal efficiency of investment. Figure 13-10 shows the analysis.

Figure 13-10A shows how the level of interest rates is determined by the liquidity preference schedule and the quantity of money. Figure 13-10B shows how that rate of interest, together with the marginal efficiency of investment schedule, determines the amount of investment. As long as the *MEI* is greater than the rate of interest, an additional amount of investment is expected to add more to revenues than the money would cost. Investment will be increased up to the level at which $i = MEI$. Beyond that point at which $i = MEI$, the *cost of capital* will be greater than the returns that can be expected. This investment will not be made.

In this link between the monetary sector and the level of national income, the equilibrium in the money markets in which $M = L$, determining the rate of interest, is supplemented by another equilibrium in which $i = MEI$, determining the level of investment.

We can manipulate Figure 13-10B to become more familiar with the relationship it involves. For example, what happens if business executives become more optimistic than they were earlier, that is, if their expectations about the future improve? The *MEI* curve would shift to the right; and we should expect them to increase their investment expenditures, as in Figure 13-11.

If such a change were to occur when the economy was already at full employment, the resultant multiplied increase in aggregate demand would set in motion inflationary price increases. The monetary authorities could then be expected to take action to raise interest rates. The effect would be to reduce the level of investment as shown in Figure 13-12. Similar shifts would occur, but in the opposite direction, if business managers became more pessimistic or if the monetary authorities brought interest rates down. You can work out these diagrams yourself.

Figure 13–10
Investment and the Rate of Interest

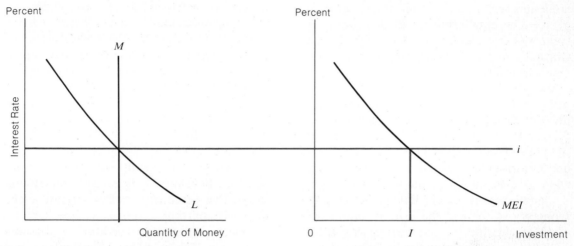

A. The interest rate is determined by the quantity of money *M* and liquidity preference *l*.

B. Investment is determined by the rate of interest *i* and the marginal efficiency of investment *MEI*.

Figure 13–11

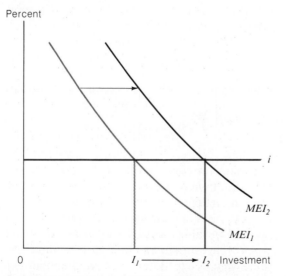

Optimism about the future shifts the *MEI* curve to the right. With no change in the rate of interest, investment will rise from I_1 to I_2.

Figure 13–12

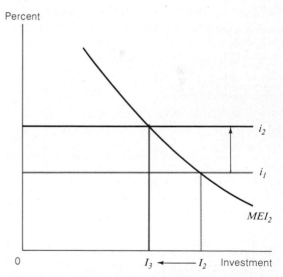

An increase in interest rates from i_1 to i_2 causes the level of investment to fall from I_2 to I_3, assuming no further shift in the *MEI* schedule.

Money and Aggregate Demand

We can now take the final step in linking the monetary sector to the level of aggregate demand. The equilibrium level of national income was shown in Chapter 6 to be the level at which desired savings equals desired investment, as in Figure 13–13.

We have just finished showing how the level of investment is determined, given the schedule of the marginal efficiency of investment, by the level of the rate of interest. Since the rate of interest is determined in the money markets, and in turn influences the level of investment, while investment affects the level of aggregate demand, there is a clear linkage between the monetary sector and the level of output and employment. Indeed, the vertical axis of Figure 13–13 is the same as the horizontal axis of Figure 13–10B. This enables us to show the linkage visually in Figure 13–14.

The rate of interest is determined by the intersection of the liquidity preference schedule and the quantity of money schedule in Figure 13–14A. The level of investment is determined by the intersection of the rate of interest with the marginal efficiency of investment schedule in Figure 13–14B. Finally, the investment schedule intersects with the propensity to save schedule to determine the level of national income in Figure 13–14C. We have

linked the *monetary equilibrium* $(L = M)$ to the *real equilibrium* $(S_D = I_D)$.

- **Monetary equilibrium** is a condition in the money markets in which the existing money supply is willingly held by economic units.
- **Real equilibrium** prevails at the level of economic activity at which desired savings and desired investment are realized.

Some Qualifications

The synthesis of monetary and national income equilibria developed here has some limitations. In the first place, the rate of interest affects several important elements of the national income equilibrium in addition to business investment. The most important are consumer purchases of durable goods and housing construction. Expenditures for those purposes influence aggregate demand and the national income, just as business investment does. They might be included in the analysis at the same intermediate stage as business investment, perhaps in the following fashion:

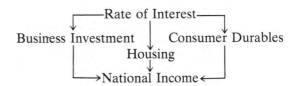

Spending on consumer durables and housing has a multiplied effect on national income in a fashion analogous to the relationship between interest rates, investment, and NNP. We can think of durables and housing as merely other types of investment and treat them in much the same way. They differ, however, in that the motives for those types of spending differ from the motives for business investment, and other factors than interest rates and expected rates of return affect them.

Figure 13–13
Equilibrium of Saving and Investment

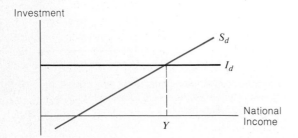

Figure 13–14
The Monetary Sector and the National Income Equilibrium

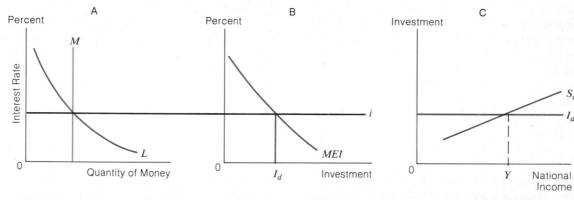

In A the rate of interest is determined by liquidity preference L and the money supply M.

B shows that the level of desired investment is determined by the rate of interest i and the marginal efficiency of investment MEI.

Finally, in C the level of national income is determined by desired investment I_d and desired savings S_d.

These practical difficulties are accompanied by some analytical problems. Two of the key variables are psychological in nature, liquidity preference and the marginal efficiency of investment. The desire to hold cash can change drastically and quickly in response to both economic and political events. So can the expected rate of return on investment. A recent example: election of a socialist president in France in May, 1981 triggered a sharp drop in prices on the French stock exchange as the present value of shares in French companies fell sharply in the minds of investors. Expectations of future earnings were revised downward and investors shifted from stocks to cash.

Economic events also affect expectations about the future. A rise in economic activity can itself create optimism. In that case, the liquidity preference schedule will shift down and the schedule of the marginal efficiency of capital will shift upward. Interest rates may not change, if the increase in economic activity is accompanied by an appropriate increase in the quantity of money, but expectations of rising profits can bring greater investment and a further growth of economic activity. In this sequence of events any change in the level of economic activity becomes cumulative, and the analysis reinforces the description of the business cycle of Chapter 4.

The fact that the psychological variables can shift drastically and quickly gives the monetary and real "equilibrium" a special quality. It does not mean that either the monetary system or the level of economic activity remain stable. What it does mean is that within the pattern of change in the level of economic activity there are two variables that are potentially highly unstable. The policy implication is that the other variables, the quantity of money and the rate of interest, must be managed by the monetary authorities in a way that tends to counterbalance the uncontrollable psychological variables.

Summary

Changes in the monetary sector are reflected in changes in the level of economic activity. The rate of interest is determined by the interaction of liquidity preference and the quantity of money. Interest rates, together with the marginal efficiency of investment, determine the amount of investment. Investment, together with the propensity to save, determines the level of economic activity.

A monetary equilibrium is achieved in which the existing supply of money is willingly held at the existing rate of interest. While this equilibrium is being achieved, the level of output and income is also moving to a new real equilibrium in which desired investment is equal to desired savings. The mutual adjustment of the two equilibrium processes brings a general equilibrium that involves both the monetary and real sectors.

The adjustment process can also start in the real sector. For example, the expected rate of return on new investment can change in response to changing business attitudes about future events. Changes in the prices of investment assets will occur and their yields will change. This development will, in turn, affect attitudes toward the holding of cash assets, and the adjustment will be spread into the monetary sector. Wherever it starts, the movement toward a new equilibrium will involve both the level of economic activity and the monetary system. The "equilibrium" in this analysis does not mean stability, however, for the psychological variables, liquidity preference, and the marginal efficiency of investment can change quickly and substantially. The analysis identifies the variables that must be managed—the money supply and interest rates—in order to overcome the instability inherent in expectations about the future.

Key Concepts

liquidity preference
marginal efficiency of investment
cost of capital

monetary equilibrium
real equilibrium

For Discussion

1. How has the rise of the Eurocredit system affected the exercise of monetary policy within the U.S. economy?
2. What determines the rate of interest in the short run? The long run?
3. Explain how monetary policy affects the level of economic activity.
4. What monetary policies are appropriate when the economy is close to full employment and prices are rising?
5. What monetary policies are appropriate when there is significant unemployment and stable prices?
6. What monetary policies are appropriate when unemployment is high and prices are rising?

Chapter *14*

Inflation

During the 1970s inflation became the chief macroeconomic problem of not only the United States, but the world economy as well. It was not a traditional inflation, however, because it was accompanied by rising unemployment. This combination of rising prices and growing unemployment was difficult to explain within the framework of accepted economic principles, for it had been generally assumed that prices would not rise significantly when output could be increased to meet a growing ability to buy. If inflation was caused by "too much money (or buying power) chasing too few goods," why did prices rise when goods production could be increased? The inability to answer that question satisfactorily left a policy gap as well. Remedies are directed at causes, and if causes cannot be identified, the remedies cannot be developed. This chapter investigates the problem of inflation, seeks to identify causes, and then suggests some relevant policies.

We first identify two different types: inflation caused by excessive aggregate demand and its wartime variant, and supply-side inflation caused by increased costs of production. Each can lead to an upward inflationary spiral of prices as increased demand and rising costs generate further price increases. There are self-limiting aspects of an inflationary spiral, but they can be swamped by expectations of further inflation that keep the upward spiral going.

Furthermore, the modern economy is inflation prone, because of the government's high-employment policy, labor markets in which inflationary pressures can be generated, and the administered prices of big business. Contrary to the arguments of the monetarists, autonomous increases in the money supply are not a significant cause of inflation. Money is not dropped from heaven like Biblical manna, but is created by banks to accommodate the needs of business. An increased money supply accompanies inflation, but the causes of inflation lie deeper. Among the causes in recent years has been accelerated conflict among capital, labor, and government for the reduced economic surplus resulting from slowed economic growth.

Policy to control inflation is as complex as the causes. Simple remedies and quick fixes do not work. At one extreme is the strategy of making the poor pay the costs of inflation by generating a depression strong enough to liquidate the accumulated inflationary pressures.

At the other extreme is a strategy of controls and economic planning to spread the sacrifices across the board. The Reagan administration is trying the first alternative, and the planning/ equal sacrifice solution does not seem feasible. The immediate prospect is for either continued inflation or a major depression.

Aggregate Demand and Inflation

Increases in the general level of prices can occur when aggregate demand grows more rapidly than aggregate supply, pressing on the economy's capacity to produce. This is *aggregate demand inflation*. We can show the relationship by use of the analysis and diagrams developed in Chapters 7 and 8, illustrated in Figure 14-1.

We start from a situation in which aggregate demand D_1 is below the full employment level Y_F. There is substantial unemployment and idle capacity. Prices do not increase as long as costs of production do not rise, and the aggregate supply schedule Z remains fixed.

Now postulate a shift upward in aggregate demand to D_2, which is just below the full employment level. Costs of production per unit of output rise, as indicated by the steeper slope of the aggregate supply schedule. The rise in costs is caused by the need to hire less-productive labor, use less-efficient machinery, and pay higher prices for raw materials. At this stage, inflation is moderate, perhaps 2 to 5 percent annually, and the rate of unemployment is relatively low—perhaps 3 to 5 percent of the labor force as a whole, although the unemployment rate will vary among different segments of the labor force. As aggregate demand increases from D_1 to D_2, prices creep upward as production costs rise.

A second stage of inflation could be reached if aggregate demand increased further, to D_3. In this case aggregate demand is greater than the level necessary to reach full employment

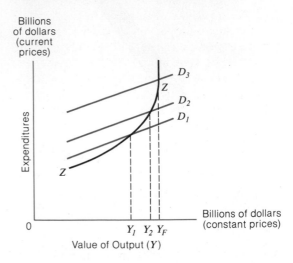

Figure 14–1
Aggregate Demand and Inflation

Billions of dollars (current prices)

Expenditures

Value of Output (Y)

Billions of dollars (constant prices)

With a given aggregate supply schedule Z and aggregate demand D_1, prices do not rise because the level of output Y_1 is well below full capacity output Y_F. At aggregate demand D_2, however, the level of output and income Y_2 is high enough to cause costs and prices to rise, as indicated by the relatively steep slope of the aggregate supply schedule Z. When aggregate demand is at D_3 an inflationary spiral can begin because D_3 is well above the intersection of Z and Y_F.

and full production capacity. Markets are tight, shortages appear, and prices move upward rapidly.

- **Aggregate demand** or **demand-pull inflation** is caused by excessive aggregate demand or demand pull, when production is at or near capacity.

When the cost increases occur within the domestic economy, the results are somewhat different. In that case an upward shift in the aggregate supply schedule is accompanied by an upward shift in the aggregate demand schedule. The increase in aggregate demand occurs because higher costs to producers mean higher incomes for other economic units. For example, an increase in the price of domestic oil will raise costs of production for all firms that use it as an input, but it will also raise the incomes of those who sell the oil. The increase in aggregate demand will be less than the upward shift in the aggregate supply schedule, however, since part of the increase in income will be saved.

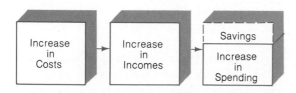

Thus, aggregate demand will rise as a result of an increase in production costs. But because of savings the increase in spending will not fully counterbalance the increase in costs of production. The result will be an increase in unemployment along with an increase in prices—stagflation once more—but the loss in employment will be less severe than in the case of higher costs for imported raw materials.

Figure 14–2 shows this more general case. It adds to Figure 14–1 an increase in aggregate demand somewhat smaller than the increase in aggregate supply and indicates the decline in output that results.

✳ Aggregate Supply and Stagflation

An increase in costs of production will also cause an increase in the general price level. Known as *aggregate supply inflation*, it operates on the supply side of the economy, however, through the aggregate supply schedule. In this case, however, the increase in prices is accompanied by a decline in employment. This combination of price increases plus rising un-

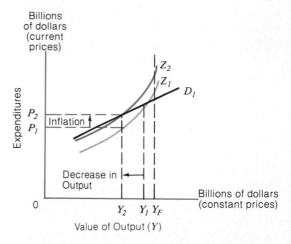

Figure 14-23
Aggregate Supply and Stagflation-I

With a given level of aggregate demand D_1 an upward shift in the aggregate supply schedule from Z_1 to Z_2, because of increased costs of production, causes a decline in output from Y_1 to Y_2. The increase in prices is indicated by the vertical distance between Z_1 and Z_2, shown on the vertical axis by the increase from P_1 to P_2.

employment has been dubbed *stagflation* by economists.

When costs of production rise any given level of output can be sustained only at a higher price level that allows producers to earn a normal profit. The amount of revenue necessary to sustain the given level of output rises by the total increase in costs. The aggregate supply schedule shifts upward. When that happens, if there is no change in the aggregate demand schedule, the level of output and employment will fall, as shown in Figure 14–3.

The outcome shown in Figure 14–3 is characteristic of cost increases on imported goods, such as, for example, imports of oil. The higher cost of oil is imposed on the domestic economy and prices rise, but the revenues and incomes from the higher costs go abroad and are spent there, so there are no changes in aggregate

Figure 14-3 2
Aggregate Supply and Stagflation-II

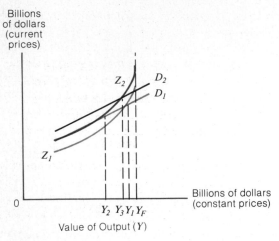

Billions
of dollars
(current
prices)

Z_2 D_2
       D_1

Z_1

Billions of dollars
(constant prices)

0

Y_2 Y_3 Y_1 Y_F

Value of Output (Y)

An upward shift in the aggregate supply schedule from Z_1 to Z_2 if not compensated by an increase in aggregate demand, would bring output down from Y_1 to Y_2. But aggregate demand rises from D_1 to D_2, due to higher incomes, so the fall in output is only from Y_1 to Y_3. The increase in D is less than the increase in Z because of savings.

demand in the domestic economy. The result is a relatively large decline in output and employment, as shown.[1]

● **Aggregate supply** or **cost-push inflation,** or **stagflation**, is caused by increases in the costs of production. It is accompanied by rising unemployment.

The Inflationary Spiral

When inflation starts, prices and costs, wages and profits can spiral upward. Increased aggregate demand can drive costs up, wages move up (wages are prices, too), and increased sales revenues usually mean higher profits. The money supply rises as banks meet the needs of their customers for the increased credit required at a higher price level. An upward spiral of prices, costs, wages, profits and money supply results.

It is easy to confuse the process of the *inflationary spiral* with the causes of inflation. To distinguish the cause from the process, we can examine what happens in the economy when aggregate demand continues to rise after the economy has approached its capacity to produce.

As markets begin to tighten, producers and sellers observe that shortages of both raw materials and finished products are starting to appear. Sellers realize that they can raise their prices without suffering a loss in sales. They do so, and profits start to rise. With profits rising, producers begin to bid for the factors of production so that they may take advantage of greater profit possibilities. Prices of raw materials move upward. Interest rates go up as suppliers of capital take advantage of tighter money markets. Competition among employers for increasingly scarce labor causes wage rates to rise.

During an aggregate demand inflation, most prices will rise, some more and some less, depending on the specific sectors of the economy into which the excessive demand flows most readily. This includes the prices of the factors of production—wages, profits, and interest rates—which are also pulled upward by the general tightness to be found in markets throughout the economy. Some of these prices, particularly wages and interest rates as well as prices of raw materials, are major components of the production cost of other products. When these costs rise they exert pressure on business firms to raise the prices of finished products and services if they can. This imparts the so-called "spiral" effect to an inflation.

The inflationary spiral can begin with excessive aggregate demand, as shown in Figure

[1]Economists love to pick nits: some of the increased income for foreigners is bound to find its way back into the domestic economy, and there will be some increase in aggregate demand as a result. We ignore that effect for clarity in exposition and because the effect is small.

14–3. Without output already at the full employment level, the excessive aggregate demand causes prices to rise. Some of those prices are the prices of inputs into the production process, so costs rise, and the aggregate supply schedule shifts upward. An inflationary spiral can then be set in motion. An increase in aggregate supply brings an increase in aggregate demand of a somewhat smaller amount: costs to business firms represent incomes for consumers, who save a portion of the increase. Aggregate demand rises in another round of inflation, there is another upward shift in aggregate supply, and the price spiral continues. Eventually the inflationary spiral should slow down and stop, with equality between D_3 and Z at a considerably higher level of prices. That eventual equilibrium at full employment, with stable prices, may be a long way off, however, if the inflationary spiral creates expectations of further inflation.

A similar spiral can occur as a result of an upward shift in the aggregate supply schedule. In this case prices rise and output falls, as shown in Figure 14–2. Rising prices trigger demands for higher wages and salaries as workers seek to protect their standard of living. Lenders demand higher interest rates to maintain the value of their funds; firms raise prices to protect their profits and asset values; and banks accommodate by generating the increased funds necessary to support the economy at the higher price level. Another round of increases in costs pushes the aggregate supply schedule upward, with a corresponding but smaller increase in the aggregate demand schedule and a further drift downward of output and employment. Employment falls as prices rise—the classic symptoms of stagflation.

The inflationary spiral, then, has two variations. Each has its origins in a different source of inflation. When inflation originates in the demand side of the economy with aggregate demand rising faster than aggregate supply, output and employment are at the level of full utilization of output capacity and the labor force, and excessive aggregate demand pushes up prices. When inflation originates on the supply side of the economy, however, the result is stagflation. Increased costs push up prices, but the upward price spiral is accompanied by gradually rising unemployment. In both cases the inflationary spiral is characterized by both the upward pull of rising aggregate demand and the upward push of increased costs of production.

● An **inflationary spiral** is a continuing and self-reinforcing rise in the general price level that combines demand-pull and cost-push elements.

Factors Limiting an Inflationary Spiral

Even when an inflationary spiral is at work, the economy generates a number of anti-inflationary conditions that tend to slow down an inflation and bring it to a halt. Here are some of the most important:

1. *Tight money.* Bank credit expands as the GNP increases and prices rise. But sooner or later the banks will become loaned up, interest rates will rise, and the expansion of bank credit will stop—unless, of course, the central bank feeds new reserves into the system.

2. *Taxes.* A progressive income tax will take a larger and larger bite out of rising incomes as people move into higher tax brackets. Taxes become a larger proportion of income, and a larger withdrawl from the flow of spending.

3. *Government transfer payments.* As incomes rise, some transfer payments decline, such as unemployment compensation. Others, like veterans' benefits and social security payments, remain the same and become a smaller proportion of the growing flow of spending.

4. *Holdings of cash and other liquid assets.* As prices rise, consumers need more

money for daily use. Withdrawal of money from bank reserves helps further to tighten the money markets. A related phenomenon is the need for larger cash balances by both business firms and consumers: as prices rise the purchasing power of liquid assets declines, and the value of those assets must be increased in order to maintain the same conditions of liquidity, so bank balances are increased. This effort to maintain liquidity is another reason why the money markets become tighter.

However, during an accelerating inflation, attitudes toward liquidity change as everyone tries to turn money assets into real assets. When that happens, the prevailing attitudes toward liquidity promote speculation and further inflation.

5. *Imports and exports.* As domestic prices rise relative to prices abroad, imported goods become better buys, and some of the increased aggregate demand is funneled out of the domestic flow of spending. Exports decline at the same time, because their prices rise and foreigners buy less. This decline reduces the domestic flow of spending.

6. *Stable incomes.* Some groups in the economy have fixed or relatively stable incomes, such as people on pensions. Their real purchasing power declines, and further price rises are thereby discouraged.

7. *Increases in output.* The output capacity of an economy rises even when prices are going up, thereby reducing inflationary pressures.

8. *Increases in production costs.* During an inflation costs of production increase as wages and salaries, interest rates, and prices of raw materials increase. Unless aggregate demand continues to rise, cost increases cannot be passed on to consumers, profit margins decline, and firms cut back production and employment.

9. *Declining real incomes.* An accelerating inflation, like that of 1967–1980, causes prices to rise faster than incomes for an increasingly large number of consumers. When that happens consumers are able to buy less and output can start to fall. This situation, together with rising production costs, helps turn an inflation into a recession or a depression.

These last two points indicate the real dangers of an inflationary spiral. Price increases bring rising costs of production, but although incomes also rise, they eventually start falling behind the increase in prices. The result is a recession or depression, as output is cut back and a downturn in economic activity begins.

At this juncture, government policy is important. There are essentially only two policy choices. Government can stimulate the economy to avoid a recession, but that will keep the inflationary spiral going. This seems to be the traditional choice in the early stages of an inflationary spiral, when the increases in prices are relatively modest. The other alternative is to allow the decline in economic activity to occur and even to encourage it with tight money policies, in order to stop the inflationary spiral. This policy is characteristic of the later stages of an inflationary spiral, when government policy strategists conclude that the political unrest arising from continuing inflation is a greater danger to their continuance in office than the political unrest that would be generated by a recession. The chief factor limiting an inflationary spiral is public opinion.

Expectations and Inflation
Expectations of continuing inflation can counteract the factors that normally tend to limit an inflationary spiral. If business firms expect prices to continue rising they can be expected to buy materials and equipment now rather than later. Doing so will tighten markets further and promote further price increases. Consumers will also tend to buy now in order to get

ahead of expected price increases. Pressure from higher demand will then push prices up.

Expectations of rising prices can have an important impact on interest rates. Lenders, expecting higher prices and a lower value of money in the future, will demand higher interest rates. For example, let the rate of interest with stable prices be 6 percent, reflecting the "real" earnings of capital. Now start prices rising, so that lenders expect a 4 percent rate of inflation in the future. If they lend money today at 6 percent its real purchasing power will only rise by 2 percent when the loan is repaid. In order to protect themselves they will try to raise the interest rate to 10 percent.

Business firms will be willing to pay the higher interest rates if they also expect higher prices or expect that they will be able to raise their prices without significantly reduced sales. Higher prices will enable producers to meet the increased costs imposed by higher interest rates. Higher prices will also enable them to maintain the value of their capital investment.[2]

Higher prices charged by business firms create demands by workers for higher wages and salaries as they seek to maintain their standard of living in the face of increased prices. Unions, expecting prices to rise in the future, will seek wage increases that allow their members to keep up with inflation. Employers will pass on similar wage increases to their nonunion workers to avoid losing them and to prevent the discontent that could reduce efficiency and productivity.

Meanwhile, the banking system accommodates its customers with the increased loans made necessary by the higher prices, wages, salaries and interest rates. The money supply rises as the economy finances the increased commitments made necessary by higher prices. Lenders, of course, expect the increased commitments, even at higher interest rates, to be validated by the increased flow of incomes expected to follow higher prices, wages and salaries.

Expectations of higher prices and continuing inflation can keep an inflationary spiral going, whether the inflation results from increasing aggregate demand or from rising costs and an increase in the aggregate supply schedule. The deflationary forces that tend to slow and halt the inflation can be swamped by expectations of continuing inflation.

Runaway Inflation

Some inflations have been known to get out of hand, in spite of the self-limiting changes in the economy that an inflation generates. Several famous examples come instantly to mind: China after World War II, Germany in 1922–23, Russia in 1920–21, France in 1794–97, and, further, this country in 1777–80. In these inflations prices rose so rapidly and to such heights that the money in use at the particular time lost its value and had to be replaced by a new type.[3]

All of these *runaway inflations* occurred in times of political stress or turmoil. More important, all of the governments involved faced a very uncertain financial situation: demands on government expenditures were rising at a time when it was very difficult to levy and collect taxes. The governments therefore turned to increases in money supply to obtain the funds they needed. Continuous large injections of purchasing power into the economy through government deficits, financed by newly printed currency, have been the cause of all the principal cases of runaway inflation. Or, put negatively, we know of no case of runaway

---

[2]The value of capital falls when interest rates rise, unless the stream of income generated by the capital also rises because of increased prices. Example: with stable prices let a $100 capital investment earn a profit of $10 annually (10 percent), which is also equal to the rate of interest. Let interest rates in the money market rise to 20 percent, and the value of the capital investment will fall to $50. Why? Because $50 lent in the money markets will earn $10 annually, the same as the capital investment. Now let the producer raise his prices to increase his annual profit to $20. The value of his capital will rise to $100 because it earns just as much as $100 lent in the money markets.

---

[3]The classic joke about runaway inflation: you take your money to market in a bushel basket and bring your purchases home in your pocketbook.

inflation that was not engendered by a deliberate overexpansion of the money supply, carried out as a conscious policy by the government.

● **Runaway inflation** continues indefinitely until money loses its value. Past runaway inflations have always been caused by government fiscal or monetary policy, since an ordinary inflation tends to be self-limiting.

Money and Inflation

According to the quantity theory of money, the general price level will rise if the money supply grows more rapidly than the economy's total output. In the equation of exchange $MV = PQ$, if the money supply M rises while its velocity of circulation V and the level of business activity Q remain unchanged, the price level P must rise. This simple relationship is deceptive, however. The supply of money is not an autonomous variable, with money being dropped from a helicopter into an unsuspecting economy. The money supply is created by banks as they meet the demands for credit of business firms, consumers and governments. When aggregate demand rises or costs of production increase, the demand for credit increases to finance enlarged commitments to pay in the future. Banks accommodate their customers, and the central bank creates reserves to enable them to do so. The increased money supply is generated by growing economic activity.

It is correct, then, to argue that inflation is accompanied by an increase in the money supply. But the underlying cause of the inflation is either excessive aggregate demand or rising production costs, or both, and not simply the rise in the money supply.

The monetary aspects of inflation are nevertheless important. If total spending were to rise by 10 percent, for example, while output increased by 5 percent, the extra 5 percent would have to come from the monetary sector. The quantity of money M and/or its velocity of circulation V would have to rise in order to make possible the extra growth of spending. The extra spending, in turn, would push up prices. Thus, an inflationary increase in aggregate demand is accompanied by an increase in the money supply. The process works in the other direction as well. An increase in the money supply means that either money in circulation or demand deposits have increased, and in either case spending is greater. A rise in demand deposits occurs because consumers and business firms borrow to increase their spending, and money in circulation increases because economic units are spending more and need more pocket money or cash in the till. Normally, then, an increase in aggregate demand is accompanied by an increase in M or V, and an increase in M or V is a sign of greater economic activity. When those events occur while the economy is pressing upon its output capacity, either generally or in key basic industries, the general price level rises.

An increased money supply also accompanies inflation triggered by cost increases and an upward shift in the aggregate supply schedule. Increased costs mean that the commitments of business firms to buy materials, hire workers, buy inventories, and so on are increased. These commitments must be financed by increased extension of credit by banks and other financial institutions, which means an increase in the supply of money. The banking system accommodates its customers at its loan windows, and the central bank accommodates the needs of banks for increased reserves. Failure to do so would bring on reduced output and higher unemployment rates, or, as in recent years, increased borrowing in the international money market.

Beware, then, of the *monetarist fallacy*. Inflation is not caused by printing of money by governments, and a sophisticated monetarist would not argue that it is. Inflation can be caused by excessive aggregate demand brought about by government deficit spending at a time of full employment. The deficit must be financed, however, either by printing money (the old-fashioned way) or by borrowing (the modern method). In either case, the money supply is increased, but it is the increase in total spending that creates both the inflationary pressure as well as the increase in the money supply.

- The **monetarist fallacy** is the belief that excessive increases in the money supply cause inflation.

The basis of the monetarist fallacy is the idea that the money supply is independent of the level of economic activity, that M can be increased or decreased independently of PQ, in the equation of exchange. If that were the case, the cause-effect relationship would be $M \rightarrow PQ$, and when PQ presses upon the capacity to produce, then P rises. In the modern economy, however, the supply of money rises or falls in response to the need to finance economic activity. That is, $PQ \rightarrow M$, and when PQ presses upon the capacity to produce or costs of production increase, then P rises.

So when you hear someone say, for example, "assume an increase in the supply of money . . .," or "If the government prints more money . . .," or "Let the money supply increase by 50 percent . . .," you know you are about to be treated to another example of the monetarist fallacy.

The Inflationary Environment

We noted earlier in Chapter 4 that up to the late 1960s the bulk of the inflation since World War II in the United States was associated with wartime excess demand. Between the wars prices were relatively stable. But even the periods of price stability were marked by an upward creep that persisted from year to year with little pause. When a larger than usual slack appeared in the economy, the upward creep slowed and even temporarily halted. But

when the GNP started rising and unemployment rates fell, the upward creep began once more and seemed to move faster as the unemployment rate dropped.

The behavior of the general price level was quite different in the hundred years prior to World War II. In that era it was characterized by large swings upward and downward, with the peaks and troughs of the long waves showing no consistent direction over the long run. Prices in the 1960s, for example, seem to have been at about the same level as they were just after the Civil War, in 1865. No persistent upward creep of prices is found in the earlier period.

The difference between the two eras suggests that important changes have occurred in the economy that have made it more vulnerable to inflation. In particular, three structural elements seem to have made the economy vulnerable to an upward creep of prices:

1. Government's commitment to high levels of employment and output

2. Relationships between changes in productivity and changes in wage rates

3. Administered prices

4. Changes in the labor market

High-Employment Policy

Government commitment to a policy of economic growth and high levels of employment provides a guarantee that markets will be relatively tight. Both fiscal and monetary policies are used to move aggregate demand upward at a rate approximately equal to the annual expansion of aggregate supply. Relatively low unemployment rates are the goal.

These two conditions, growing aggregate demand and relatively tight labor markets, provide the basic conditions for an upward creep in prices. In effect, government policies assure workers of jobs at prevailing wage rates and assure employers that their output will be sold at prevailing prices. If, for other reasons, wages and prices should be raised, the national government stands ready to provide the levels of aggregate demand needed to prevent unemployment or falling sales. This policy removes one of the chief deterrents to an upward creep in prices. It provides both labor and management with assurances that the agreements they reach about wages and prices will not serve to reduce either employment or sales.

Productivity, Prices, and Labor Unions

Strong unions and big business go together. Industries like steel, automobiles, chemicals, coal mining, and machinery manufacturing are characterized by large firms that deal with well-organized unions. There are some exceptions: textile manufacturing (where firms are generally not large) is mostly nonunion, and some strong unions operate in industries where small business predominates (trucking and clothing manufacture). The general rule, however, is that strong unions bargain with strong employers.

The result is usually a standoff, with neither side able to make significant gains at the expense of the other. This is an important point: collective bargaining between partners of roughly equal strength usually limits the gains unions can obtain for their workers. Under those conditions opportunities for wage increases are created by two factors: (1) increases in output per laborhour; and (2) the ability of the employer to raise prices. Any wage increases that go beyond productivity gains will reduce the employer's profits, unless the higher costs can be passed on to consumers by way of higher prices. If prices can't be raised for fear of lost sales, the union will find strong management resistance to wage increases that exceed increases in productivity.

On the other hand, even an employer in a strong bargaining position finds it hard to hold wage increases below productivity gains, especially at times when aggregate demand is rising

and unemployment rates are low. At those times the bargaining position of the union is strong, the employer is prosperous, and both parties expect wage increases to be forthcoming.

Usually, then, strong unions are able to obtain wage increases that match increases in output per laborhour, but they usually can't get wage increases that exceed the growth of output per laborhour. There are exceptions, and when they occur they raise production costs, but the general rule is that productivity and wages rise at approximately the same rate.

For example, U.S. Department of Labor data show that for the years from 1947 through 1972 the average annual increase in output per laborhour was 3.0 percent, which was almost exactly equal to the average annual increase in real compensation per hour of 2.9 percent. These trends are not always the same in the short run, but they tend to even out. Thus from 1960 to 1965, real hourly compensation[4] fell behind advances in productivity, and labor's share of the economy's total product fell from 63 percent in 1960 to 61 percent in 1965. But by 1969, rather large increases in hourly compensation brought labor's share back to the 1960 level. In the long run these disparities have tended to correct themselves, and compensation and productivity have moved up together.

It might appear on the surface that if hourly compensation (wages) does not exceed productivity gains, there is no need for employers to raise prices. Unfortunately, that is not the case. Unions, for the most part, represent production workers rather than white-collar workers and are mostly found in the capital intensive industries, where productivity tends to rise more rapidly than in other sectors of the economy. However, wage increases to production workers spread to white-collar workers in

---

[4]Real compensation per laborhour includes wages plus the estimated value of fringe benefits for *production* workers. It is corrected for changes in the price level to make it comparable with productivity measures, which are calculated on a real basis.

the same industry, and to workers in other industries, where productivity gains don't match those of the unionized production workers. When this *wage spread* occurs, costs of production rise and exert an upward pressure on prices.

- A **wage spread** is the spread of wage increases from sectors of the economy with large productivity gains to sectors with low productivity gains. The result: rising production costs in the latter.

For example, when the United Automobile Workers union negotiates increases in wages and fringe benefits for production employees, the auto firms will raise the wages and salaries of clerks, typists, and other white-collar workers, and even management personnel. The companies want to keep those workers happy (and not give them a reason to organize). The spreading effect does not stop there. When production workers at the Willow Run auto assembly plants get wage increases, the price of haircuts goes up in nearby Ann Arbor; the owners of barbershops raise the salaries of their barbers to keep them from quitting and taking jobs in the auto industry, and the increased costs (there has been no increase in productivity in barbering since electrical clippers were introduced fifty years ago) are passed on to consumers in higher prices. The effect of the wage increase has spread to other sectors of the economy. In those other sectors the wage increase exceeds productivity gains.

The phenomenon of wage spread is one of the chief reasons for rising production costs during periods of high prosperity. There are others as well: less efficient workers are hired as unemployment decreases, interest rates rise as money markets tighten, less efficient machinery is reactivated, and so on. Costs per unit of output do rise, on the average, for the economy as a whole. Labor costs are an important part of that upward push of costs, even when labor unions get no more for their mem-

bers than productivity gains make possible. The wage spread sees to that.

These relationships in labor markets help to explain why labor costs tended to creep upward during the periods of relatively stable prices between 1945 and 1965. Wage rates in unionized industries rose at about the same pace as productivity. But, in the nonunion sector they tended to rise more rapidly than productivity.

The relationship changed when an inflationary spiral began in the late 1960s and picked up speed in the 1970s. Unions sought wage increases that would maintain their members' real incomes. This meant wage increases more rapid than gains in productivity. Business firms were able to provide those large wage increases because inflation enabled them to raise prices enough to protect their profits. Prices could be raised because rising wage rates pushed up aggregate demand, which was bolstered further by government spending designed to reduce the unemployment engendered by rising costs. Wage rates kept pace with rising prices, even though they increased more rapidly than productivity.

There was a fundamental difference, however, from the earlier experience. Before 1965 an upward creep in labor costs was a cause of mild inflationary pressures, particularly in the nonunion sectors of the economy. After 1965 the inflationary spiral facilitated and validated increased labor costs. The increase in labor costs was not an independent cause of inflation, but was only one component part of an ongoing inflationary spiral.

Administered Prices

The presence of big business and *administered prices* adds another dimension to the inflationary environment. The term administered prices refers to prices that are controlled to some degree by business firms, rather than solely by competitive market forces. We shall examine this phenomenon at some length later in this book. At this stage, however, we need only note that administered prices are common in many manufacturing industries, particularly those dominated by a single large firm or by a few firms. These are the same industries in which organized labor is strong and wage rates are determined through collective bargaining.

- **Administered prices** are prices whose level is wholly or partially controlled by large firms.

Where administered prices prevail, the price leader or leaders have some influence over prices. They are able to raise prices when costs rise. Their freedom to do so may be relatively great, or it may be limited, depending on the circumstances of the industry. But one thing is sure: the weakness of the forces of competition means that prices are not readily reduced. Occasionally problems will develop that force administered prices down. Excess capacity and foreign competition brought price reduction in steel in 1968, for example. In addition, list or announced prices are temporarily reduced with some frequency in a number of administered price industries. But the general rule is that administered prices can move up much more easily than they can move down.

The upward bias of administered prices creates an upward bias in the price system as a whole. It is one of the chief reasons for the failure of price levels to fall during recessions and for the ease with which they rise when the country is prosperous.

There is more than an upward bias, however. When aggregate demand is strong and markets are tight, it is relatively easy for price leaders in administered price industries to raise prices without suffering a loss in sales. This ability to raise prices can make them less vigorous in resisting union demands for higher wages at the collective bargaining sessions. They have an added option open to them. They can agree to wage increases equal to productivity gains, and then add some more to be recaptured by price increases. Union leaders are as well aware of this possibility as business leaders, so the result, in administered-price industries, can be wage increases that exceed productivity gains. When that happens, the wage spread will be even greater and the increase in production costs still larger.

Structural Change in the Economy

During the 1950s a significant shift in military technology occurred, away from wheeled vehicles and aircraft and toward missiles and electronic equipment. The economy felt the impact of that shift through increased demand for electronic equipment and higher prices in that sector of the economy. Demand fell in the automobile and aircraft industries, but prices of their products did not decline. Output and employment were reduced but prices were maintained. Prices in the automobile industry, and in steel, its chief raw material, are administered prices, and they tend to resist downward pressure from the market even when substantial excess capacity appears. Electronics, by contrast, was a rapidly expanding industry in which demand was growing. The added military buying pushed prices up. The net result for the economy as a whole was an upward swing of prices: prices did not fall in the sector in which demand fell, but prices rose in the sector in which demand rose.

Those events illustrate one reason why the economy's inflationary environment helps produce an upward creep in prices. Changes in production costs, development of new products, and shifts in consumer demand may make it possible for prices to fall, and if prices were flexible downward they would do so. But the built-in rigidity of administered prices prevents that outcome, particularly when aggregate demand is kept high by government economic policies and the wage spread phenomenon is at work.

The Changing Labor Market

At one time it was very unfashionable for economists to argue that the structure of the labor market was related to the persistence of unemployment while prices were rising. This was in the 1950s and 1960s, when macroeconomic theory featured demand management as the almost exclusive method for promoting conditions of stable full employment. The idea was that macroeconomic stability could be achieved through fiscal and monetary policies that adjusted aggregate demand, leaving decisions about allocation of resources to the free operation of the market. In this view, the functioning of the labor market was no problem and should be left alone. If there was unemployment, an increase in aggregate demand through a tax cut or increase in government spending would take care of the problem. There was little need for special training or relocation programs for workers who lost their jobs because of automation and technological change, for example.

Even then, however, a minority of economists argued that labor markets were segmented and did not function in the same way as product markets. One segment of the labor market was the labor force normally employed in the big business, advanced-technology, unionized, high-wage, "primary" sector. The other was the work force employed in the competitive, labor-intensive, nonunionized, low-wage, "secondary" sector. When aggregate demand increased, it was argued, the primary labor force became fully employed and prices began to rise before the far more volatile secondary labor force reached full employment. Furthermore, as aggregate demand rose, marginal workers would be drawn back into the secondary labor market to keep the measured unemployment rate high. All of this was complicated by a growing number of young people and women entering the work force for the first time, many of them seeking jobs in the secondary sector.

Now fashions have changed, and the majority of economists recognize that the structure of the labor market makes a difference. When unemployment of "prime" workers—white, male, 25–45 years of age—falls to 1.5–2 percent, prices can be expected to start rising, even though unemployment rates for other groups may be very high, say 40–50 percent for black, female, 16–19 year-olds.[5]

The dual labor market described here came to maturity in the years after World War II. It was generated out of a wide range of disparate and seemingly unconnected events: large scale migration of blacks from the South to northern cities and of Puerto Ricans to the mainland U.S., increased numbers of women in the labor force, an upsurge of young workers because of the baby boom after World War II, segregation and discrimination in the labor market and crowding of women and minorities into low-wage occupations, automation and technological change in the primary sector of the labor market, and the movement of manufacturing industry to overseas locations. By the 1970s it was apparent that a significant amount of unemployment was due to these accumulating structural changes in the labor market. Increased aggregate demand, even when it led to inflation as it did during the Vietnam War, had little impact on this "structural" unemployment. There was, indeed, a significant drop in unemployment of the structural type during that war, but it came primarily because young people were drafted into the armed forces or stayed in school to avoid the draft.

These changes in the labor market help to explain why unemployment accompanied rising prices. Full employment would be achieved in the primary sector of the labor force while unemployment rates were high in the secondary labor market. Government efforts to reduce the overall unemployment rate still further then created inflationary pressures in those sectors of the economy employing primary workers. By the 1970s it was not unusual to find that, at the peak of a business cycle, the

[5]The definition of "prime" worker is, of course, sexist and racist, but it reflects labor market behavior. In a market economy the word "prime" is applied descriptively to workers in the factory and beef going to the slaughterhouse.

unemployment rate for the economy as a whole was 6 percent, for primary workers 2 percent, for secondary workers 14 percent, with an inflation rate of 10 percent.

Inflation and Economic Conflict

The behavior of prices in the period after the second World War is also related to some other fundamental changes taking place in the modern capitalist economy. Labor unions came of age, and their programs, policies, and actions significantly affected economic affairs. They wanted secure employment and a rising standard of living for their members, and an important influence on public policy of all kinds. Business enterprise came increasingly to be dominated by large firms with growing control over the economic environment in which they functioned. Retained earnings gave large corporations increased control over the process of capital accumulation; acquisitions, mergers and advertising brought influence over markets and prices; and great size brought political influence. Governments also increased the scope of their activities, their regulatory powers, and their tax revenues.

The period of rapid economic growth from the end of World War II to about 1968–1972 enabled the two chief private economic-political interests to achieve their goals. Workers in the United States and other industrial nations gained greater economic security than ever before. Wages and standards of living rose, and prospects for the younger generation appeared to be favorable. Business profits were high; corporations grew; and opportunities for wealth and power for business leaders increased. Economic growth provided an annual economic surplus that enabled both labor and capital to make impressive gains. It also allowed government to provide the services both groups desired: full employment policy, housing and transportation subsidies, large national defense expenditures, expansion of health and education programs, and other social services. Prosperity and economic growth fueled a stable political accord among the claimants to economic gains. And in spite of the Cold War and the independence movement in the Third World, U.S. economic and military power provided a relatively stable economic environment that brought expanded world trade and investment.

Four developments brought serious problems, however. First, economic growth slowed, and the annual economic surplus was cut in half. In the United States, the average annual rate of economic growth fell from almost 4.5 percent in the 1946–1968 period to just over 2 percent in 1969–1979. The gains that labor and capital had become accustomed to over a quarter century were no longer available.

Second, development of the international economy freed business firms from much of their earlier dependence on unions and government. Shifting production overseas could take advantage of low-wage labor. Capital was available from the international banking system, and the less developed nations often provided attractive tax concessions and other inducements. Many European firms took advantage of emigrant labor from southern and eastern Europe and North Africa. U.S. firms used labor from Mexico and the Caribbean. In this environment the political accord between labor, capital, and government became increasingly fragile.

Third, demands on government increased. During the period of rapid growth, 1946–1968, a substantial group of people remained poor and their prospects for betterment became dimmer. These were the minorities and other groups that were largely bypassed in the growing affluence of the period. These problems increased in the 1970s when economic conditions shifted to relative stagnation. Problems of pollution and environmental protection also escalated as economic activity increased.

Finally, U.S. world hegemony was threatened by war in Vietnam between the Soviet-backed Communist regime in the North and the American-supported government in the South. A strategic decision was made by the U.S. government to hold the line at that point. It was this war that turned the limited inflation of the period before 1965 into accelerating inflation after 1967.

Heightened inflationary pressures were one outcome of these events. The U.S. government tried to finance the war in Vietnam without significantly raising taxes, which would have reduced the growth of affluence among taxpayers. The resulting budget deficits were an important cause of rising prices after 1967. More generally, slower economic growth and an increased need for government expenditures placed a growing strain on the budgets of federal, state, and local governments as expenses rose faster than tax revenues. Government claims on the economic surplus continued to rise at a time when the surplus contracted.

Workers, meanwhile, attempted to maintain the growth in their living standards at the level to which they had become accustomed. They pushed for increased wages and salaries and added to their debt in order to do so. Business firms, aiming to sustain the profits of the more prosperous times had a double reason for raising prices in the face of demands for higher wages and salaries: costs were rising and expansion of markets had slowed.

In the institutional environment of the late 1960s and 1970s—big government, big business, big labor—these excessive claims on the reduced economic surplus led to inflation. Higher wages and salaries stimulated price increases as business firms sought to maintain their profit margins. The banks, together with the new international banking system, provided the necessary financing of these larger commitments, along with increased consumer credit and mortgage debt. Increased incomes brought higher tax revenues for government through the progressive income tax, sales taxes and property taxes. Yet the gains to workers,

business and government were illusory. Higher money wages, for example, were negated by higher prices. As each group sought to maintain its gains by another round of increases in wages or profits or tax revenues, the inflationary spiral worsened.

The huge increases in oil prices that occurred after 1973 shifted income and wealth from the oil importing nations to the oil exporting countries. Each economic interest group within an oil importing country like the U.S. could then try to protect itself by shifting the burden to other groups. But doing so only worsened the inflationary pressures created by the higher cost of energy.

The potential conflicts inherent in a private enterprise economy can always be eased by economic growth in which the bulk of the population shares. But, when growth slows down, the conflicts are heightened. Inflation is one way in which the increased conflicts manifested themselves in recent years. Why not in the past? Because the environment of big business, big unions, and big government had not yet matured.

The Policy Problem

Inflation has many faces. One is the demand-pull aspect that originates in excessive aggregate demand. The other is the cost-push of increased costs of production and an upward shift in the aggregate supply schedule. The two are united in an inflationary spiral in which increases in aggregate demand bring increased costs that push total spending up—and so on for more rounds of the spiral. Nor should we forget the increased money supply that accompanies and facilitates an inflationary spiral, or the expectations of continued inflation that keep it going.

Another aspect of the problem is the creeping inflation associated with the modern economic structure of big business, big labor, and big government. In the institutional environment of modern capitalism, with administered prices, wage rates determined by collective bargaining, and government commitment to high levels of economic activity, a persistent cost-push can add further to the upward push of prices. Finally, a slowed rate of economic growth brought efforts by big business, big labor, and big government to sustain their earlier gains in ways that brought higher prices and increased costs.

A comprehensive anti-inflation policy will have to take all of these aspects of inflation into account. It is obvious that the solutions are not simple. Indeed, if inflationary pressures are inherent in the modern structure of the private enterprise economy, it may not be possible to eliminate inflation entirely without some significant changes in the economic system.

Deflation as a Remedy for Inflation

The classic remedy for inflation is deflation. That is because the significant inflations of the past originated in excessive aggregate demand. The clear remedy is to eliminate the cause. In the modern world this would mean a restrictive fiscal and monetary policy:

1. A balanced government budget or even a surplus of tax receipts over expenditures. Government spending could also be reduced. A budget deficit is to be avoided.

2. Restrictive monetary policies designed to prevent the banking system from increasing the amount of money and credit made available to the private sector. The resultant tightness in money markets would raise interest rates and discourage private borrowing, and reduce economic activity.

The basic strategy is to reduce spending by governments, consumers, and business firms. Reduction of aggregate demand will then ease the pressure on prices in the markets for goods, labor, and capital. As prices slow their rise, expectations of further price increases change, and the economy moves to a "soft landing"

with little or no increase in unemployment but with the inflationary excess of aggregate demand eliminated.

This textbook scenario applies, however, only to aggregate demand inflation and has serious limits when attempts are made to apply it to the new type of aggregate supply inflation, as the U.S. government found out in 1979–1980. The basic danger is that the deflation scenario will generate a serious depression.

Indeed, in the era before demand management was an accepted government policy strategy, aggregate demand inflations had a nasty habit of curing themselves by creating a depression. The inflationary spiral typically began to push prices up faster than incomes. For a time expansion of credit kept purchasing power rising fast enough to keep up with rising prices. As the banking system became loaned up that support came to an end, however; buying fell, and a downturn in economic activity resulted. The typical aggregate demand inflation brought on its own deflation as economic activity and prices spiraled downward.

The deflation remedy was tried in 1979–1980, at least partially, when the Fed used its relatively limited monetary policy instruments to cut off the massive increase in credit that had kept the inflationary boom of 1976–79 going for several years after incomes had begun to lag behind prices. To everyone's dismay, instead of a soft landing, the policy generated an old-fashioned steep recession.

At the root of the problem was an effort to apply the remedies appropriate for an aggregate demand inflation to an aggregate supply inflation. With costs rising, an increase in credit and loans was necessary just to maintain the existing level of economic activity. Failure to make that increased credit available brought a reduction in economic activity while rising costs went untouched.

Price Controls

A second common remedy for inflation is direct control of prices, wages and profits. The strategic idea is to short-circuit the inflationary spiral by stopping the higher prices that lead to higher wages and profits and bring about another round of increases in aggregate demand. Price controls, however, do not attack the causes of inflation, whether the cause is rising purchasing power or increasing costs of production. Their purpose is to keep the inflation under control while other policies are used to bring the increases in aggregate demand or production costs under control.

By themselves, price, wage and profit controls are difficult to apply. Goods find their way into illegal markets where controls are evaded and prices move up to what buyers are willing to pay. Producers devise means to avoid controls. Items with low profit margins are dropped, and buyers have to buy higher priced goods instead. Manufacturers require "tie in" sales that make buyers take a second item in order to get the one they really want. Products are "redesigned" to be new and exempt from controls or salable at a higher price. Quality of products is reduced, and free services or discounts are eliminated. Inferior products are shipped on a "take it or leave it" basis. Goods are exported rather than sold on the domestic market where controls are in effect. The ultimate effect is disappearance of goods from normal market channels. This is what critics of price controls mean when they say that controls don't work.

Price controls work during wartime, however, and not because patriotism replaces greed as an economic motive. They work because they are part of a larger scheme of wartime planning, allocations, and labor market controls. For example, during World War II, if a firm raised its prices beyond the allowable limit, it lost its allocated supplies of raw materials. A union that demanded wage increases above the limits found that its members lost their exemption from the military draft. Price controls work when they are part of a system of planning that has teeth in it. Even then, their usefulness is limited. They do not solve the

problem, but merely buy time in which to apply more fundamental remedies.

Incomes Policy

An *incomes policy* seeks to restrain increases in the incomes of all the factors of production. The policy includes restraints or controls on wages, profits and all other types of income. An incomes policy is designed to prevent an inflationary spiral by keeping incomes from rising, but it does not prevent increases in aggregate demand triggered by government deficits, or wartime spending, or increases in business investment or consumer spending financed by extensions of credit. Nor can an incomes policy prevent inflation from the supply side that is brought on by cost increases such as higher prices for oil.

• An **incomes policy** limits prices, wages, profits, and other incomes in order to diminish inflationary pressures.

Since it involves sacrifices an incomes policy must be seen by all major interest groups as both fair and necessary, either for their own benefit or for the good of the nation as a whole. One group cannot be expected to accept restrictions on their incomes while other incomes are unrestricted. Thus, an incomes policy that restricts wage increases but leaves profits uncontrolled will quickly lose the support of workers and unions.

Several interesting proposals for an incomes policy have surfaced in recent years. One was the *wage and price guideposts* of the 1960s. First developed in 1961 and 1962, they emphasized controls over wages as a means of slowing down the cost-push aspects of rising prices. The major proposition was that wages in any industry should be allowed to rise by no more than the average increase in output per laborhour for the economy as a whole. Price policies would reflect these wage increases. If output per laborhour were to rise by, say, 3 percent, no wage contracts could provide for a more rapid wage increase. Prices should be reduced in those industries whose increases in productivity exceeded the national average, for in those industries costs of production would be falling. On the other hand, industries in which productivity gains were less than the national average would have rising costs of production, and they should be allowed to raise their prices. Exceptions could be made for special cases. The idea was that price declines would offset price increases and the average level of prices would remain stable.

- **Wage-price guideposts** are standards for wage and price changes designed to hold inflationary pressures in check.

The guideposts did not have a happy history. For a time they seemed to hold back some wage and price increases, but this was in 1963–65, when there was still considerable slack in the economy and price increases were small. As the economy moved closer to capacity and unemployment rates fell below 4 percent, inflationary pressures grew and the guideposts gradually gave way. In 1965, wage settlements in the steel and shipping industries were kept within the guideposts after some struggle, but early in 1966 a much publicized breach was made in the construction trades in New Jersey. Later in 1966 the guidepost principle was completely defeated in settling a strike of airline machinists, and from 1967 onward less and less was heard of them.

What was the trouble?

The chief source of difficulty was the process of inflation itself. By 1967 the economy had reached levels so close to full employment that further tightening of markets began to pull prices up. All of the inflationary pressures were beginning to appear and the inflationary spiral was beginning. Exhortations and political appeals could not keep them in check as aggregate demand continued to rise. While wage and price guideposts might help to retard the upward creep of prices growing out of the relationships between big business and big labor, they were no match for the strong pressures of an inflationary spiral fed by excessive aggregate demand. Guideposts were the wrong medicine for the disease.

A second difficulty was the failure of the guideposts to do anything about profits. Unions looked upon the guideposts as a limit placed on the gains available to workers. They were hardly enthusiastic to begin with and became positively antagonistic when they saw profits rising substantially. For example, between 1963 and 1968 average weekly earnings in nonagricultural industries rose from $88.46 to $107.73, or 10.5 percent. During the same five-year period corporate profits after taxes rose from $33.1 billion to $51.0 billion, or 54.1 percent. Although comparisons of this sort are not very meaningful, the relatively large gains for business made workers feel that they were bearing the chief burdens imposed by the guideposts.

An important principle is involved. Government can ask economic interest groups to make sacrifices for achievement of national goals, price stability in this case, but unless the groups themselves perceive the sacrifices as being approximately equal they will eventually become disenchanted. This happened to the wage and price guideposts as soon as it became clear that they were helping hold back wage increases while profits were rising rapidly.

Failure of the guideposts led to proposals for a broader incomes policy for the United States. First, it is necessary to have a set of guidelines against which any proposed increases in wages and prices can be judged. Even though our experience with the wage-price guideposts has not been favorable, something like them would have to be used to provide indicators of what might be allowable and what prohibited.

Second, a *public review board* independent of other economic policy-making agencies (along the lines of the Federal Reserve's Board of Governors) could be established to enforce the guidelines. Several proposals along this line have been made, some as long ago as the mid-1950s. These proposals envisage that all wage agreements in a wide range of industries would be submitted to the board for its approval or disapproval, within the framework of noninflationary guidelines. Price increases in administered-price industries would also be submitted to the review board prior to being instituted. Some proposals would have the public review board hold hearings and publicize its findings that a proposed wage settlement or price increase is or is not consistent with the guidelines for price stability. If not, the increase could still go into effect, either immediately or after a waiting period. The overall objective would be to alert and mobilize public opinion as the chief deterrent to inflationary pressures. Advocates of this proposal argue that large and well-known corporations may not wish to antagonize public opinion by going ahead with price increases disapproved by the public review board.

Third, proposals have been put forth for a variety of enforcement procedures either to delay or to prohibit the institution of a wage settlement or price increase deemed to be inflationary. The most imaginative *tax-based incomes policy (TIP)* would use a corporate income tax surcharge as the chief deterrent. If wages or prices or dividends or salaries of corporate officers were increased beyond the guidelines, the corporation would be subject to an increased corporate income tax, say 50 percent rather than the normal 46 percent. The surcharge could even be progressive, with the rate increasing the more the wage or price or dividend or salary increase exceeded the guidelines.

An intriguing concept lies behind this suggestion. It puts pressure where it belongs, on the decision makers in administered-price industries. If business executives know that reduced profits after taxes will be the inevitable result of wage settlements that increase their costs, unions will find getting such settlements increasingly difficult. Keeping profits down if prices are raised can help keep wage increases within limits consistent with stable prices.

In another TIP proposal, tax incentives would be given to employers who kept wage increases below a specified rate, while workers who get wage increases below the target would get tax credits. The carrot instead of the stick.

- A **tax-based incomes policy (TIP)** would use tax penalties or tax benefits to enforce or motivate an incomes policy.

Controlling Costs of Production

An incomes policy would affect wage claims and other sources of income, but it would leave other costs of production unaffected. Costs of energy, food, and raw materials can rise to push up costs of production. These costs are not controllable in the long run, and their increase causes economic burdens. At best, an incomes policy would allow the burdens to be shared equitably and prevent them from generating an inflationary spiral.

Energy costs are another matter, for they can be raised unilaterally by the OPEC cartel. Repeated increases in the price of oil in the 1970s were a significant cause of stagflation in that decade as the aggregate supply schedule of the industrial nations shifted upward. This aspect of inflation is generated by human action—efforts to shift wealth from energy users to energy producers, using the monopolistic powers of market control and price fixing. It can be countered by actions designed to stabilize the cost of energy. We will examine this problem in a later chapter, but we note here that any comprehensive anti-inflation program will have to deal with the cost of energy.

Controlling Inflation

A workable anti-inflation program is beginning to fall into place. It would consist of policies designed to control both aggregate demand and aggregate supply.

The first objective is stabilization of the

THE CONSERVATIVE PROGRAM

In the absence of a coherent incomes policy at the national level, a business-oriented policy emerged in the early 1980s that would allow business claims to the economic surplus to dominate. It consists of the following:

1. Restrict the claims of government by limiting or reducing government expenditures. Military spending should be increased, however, to contain the influence of the U.S.S.R. The reductions would come in services to the public and assistance for the poor.

2. Reduce or eliminate government regulations that increase business costs, particularly in the areas of environmental protection and occupational health and safety.

3. Reduce taxes on business and provide tax incentives for business investment.

4. Provide a general tax reduction to increase incentives to work and save—and to gain political support for candidates advocating the conservative program.

5. Create a policy of fiscal restraint and tight money to combat the immediate problem of inflation, even at the cost of significant increases in unemployment.

The underlying strategy of this program is that the unemployment created by the anti-inflation component will be offset by the employment created by reduced costs and increased investment. In the long run it would enable business enterprise to obtain a larger share of the economic surplus. It is, implicitly, an incomes policy oriented toward business goals. The first five points embody the economic strategy of the Reagan administration when it achieved power in 1981. The goal of a balanced federal budget was at least postponed, or perhaps abandoned, in order to achieve a large increase in military spending, however.

Simultaneously, and off the national political stage, a sixth element in the conservative program has developed:

6. Weaken the bargaining power of labor unions by exploiting loopholes in the labor laws, retaining and strengthening state laws that make organizing difficult, and shift production to nonunionized areas where possible. This anti-union campaign is carried on largely outside the political arena and with little publicity.

aggregate supply schedule. A three-point program applies here:

1. An incomes policy with guidelines for wages, profits, and other incomes that are perceived by all major interest groups as both fair and workable, together with effective incentives and/or penalties.

2. An energy program designed to stabilize energy costs. This issue will be discussed later, and several alternatives will be proposed, including deregulation of energy prices, price controls, or both.

3. Strict price, wage, and profits controls with effective enforcement powers to hold the line while the long-term program is developed and until the incomes policy is worked out.

The second objective, once the aggregate supply schedule is stabilized, is to stabilize aggregate demand at or near the full-employment level. A three-pronged policy applies here as well:

1. Use of fiscal and monetary policies designed to bring unemployment rates for the prime labor force down to the level of frictional unemployment only—about 2 percent for white males twenty-five to forty-five years of age.

2. Economic development programs to reduce unemployment in the secondary labor force. These might include tax incentives for business firms to hire secondary workers or locate new plants in inner city areas, training programs, and relocation programs.

3. Monetary policies that refrain from driving interest rates up and hindering the investment necessary for adequate economic growth and increases in productivity.

Finally, there are international aspects of the inflation problem. Some form of cooperation with other major nations to control credit creation in the international banking system and the oil import problems of other countries is needed. This cooperation may not be either politically or economically feasible. But a major cause of the international inflation is inflation in the U.S., which causes OPEC to raise the price of oil in dollars, requiring oil deficit nations to borrow more dollars in the international banking system, which adds to worldwide inflation. An effective anti-inflation program in the U.S. would go a long way toward easing international inflation problems. Even within the United States, however, there would be a great deal of difficulty in obtaining political support for a proper anti-inflation program. The economics of it is much simpler than the politics.

Summary

Inflations can have two sources, excessive spending (aggregate demand inflation) and increased costs of production (aggregate supply inflation). Aggregate supply inflation is accompanied by rising unemployment (stagflation). Both basic types can lead to an inflationary spiral, particularly when expectations of rising prices swamp the effect of other factors that normally tend to dampen inflationary price increases. Although many people think an increased supply of money is the cause of inflation, it is not. An increase in the money supply accompanies an inflationary spiral, but the underlying causes are to be found on either the demand or supply side.

In the modern economy prices tend to rise because of the institutional structure of the economy. Government-supported full-employment policies, administered prices in the big business sector of the economy, and strong unions in one part of the labor market tend to keep aggregate demand, price levels, and wage rates from falling. In that environment, technological change and changes in the structure of final demand tend to create an upward creep of prices, while a growing duality in labor markets tends to raise the unemployment rate. Conflict between big business, big labor and big government over a diminished economic surplus also created inflationary pressures in the 1970s.

Anti-inflation policy must address a complex network of causes. The policy suggested here seeks to stabilize both aggregate supply and aggregate demand. Aggregate supply would be stabilized by an incomes policy and an energy policy designed to hold cost increases in check, and by a short-run program of wage, price, and profit controls. Aggregate demand would be stabilized by the usual fiscal policies, supplemented by special programs to increase employment in the secondary labor force, and by monetary policies designed to keep interest rates down to levels consistent with strong economic growth. International cooperation on monetary controls and oil import problems would also be desirable. The political difficulties associated with such far-reaching solutions suggest, however, that the problem will remain unresolved in the immediate future.

Key Concepts

aggregate demand inflation	runaway inflation	incomes policy
aggregate supply inflation	monetarist fallacy	wage-price guideposts
stagflation	wage spread	tax-based incomes policy (TIP)
inflationary spiral	administered prices	

For Discussion

1. Discuss: Inflation is essentially a monetary phenomenon.
2. Explain why shifts in either aggregate demand or aggregate supply can lead to inflation.
3. What institutional changes on the national and international level have made the economy more prone to inflation? Explain.
4. Explain how conflicting claims on a shrinking economic surplus have provided a powerful cause for ongoing inflation.
5. What causes an inflationary spiral to continue? To end?
6. What should be done to prevent inflation?

Appendix 14 A

Inflation and Government Policy

The Inflation-Unemployment Tradeoff

During the 1960s there seemed to be a tradeoff between unemployment and inflation. When unemployment was relatively high in the first half of the 1960s, prices were relatively stable. For example, in 1962, when the unemployment rate averaged 5.5 percent the consumer price index rose by only 1.1 percent. But as unemployment fell prices tended to rise more rapidly. In 1965 an unemployment rate of 4.5 percent was accompanied by a 1.5 percent increase in prices; and in 1969, when the unemployment rate had fallen to 3.5 percent prices rose by 5.4 percent. The figures in table 14–1 show the relationship.

Table 14–1

Year	Price Changes	Unemployment
	(Percent)	
1960	1.6	5.5
1961	1.0	6.7
1962	1.1	5.5
1963	1.2	5.7
1964	1.3	5.2
1965	1.5	4.5
1966	2.9	3.8
1967	2.8	3.8
1968	4.2	3.6
1969	5.4	3.5

There seemed to be a relationship between the two variables. As unemployment rates fell below 4–5 percent the rate of increase in prices escalated, and the more unemployment was reduced the faster prices seemed to rise.

A ready explanation seemed at hand. The English economist A. W. Phillips published a study in 1958 on the relationship between unemployment and wage rates in England between 1861 and 1957. He showed that wage rates tended to rise when unemployment rates were low, and vice versa, providing empirical verification of an old hypothesis about labor markets—that labor unions are able to obtain good wage increases when labor markets are tight but make relatively few gains when labor markets are easy. American economists seized upon this study to explain price behavior during the inflation of the 1960s, under the name "the Phillips curve." Wages are the most important component of production costs, they argued, and Phillips' relationship between wages and unemployment is readily translated into a relationship between prices and unemployment: price increases accelerate as unemployment rates fall. The argument was particularly appealing during the 1960s, when statistics seemed to verify the hypothesis. Furthermore, the theory provided an alibi for those economists who had trouble explaining why the expansionary economic policies of the 1960s were bringing price increases before full employment was reached. *Wage-price guideposts* were needed, they argued, to hold prices in check while continued expansionary policies brought unemployment rates down. Business sentiment also favored the idea that unions were largely responsible for rising prices and that wage increases should be held in check.

Figure 14–4 shows the Phillips Curve hypothesis as it developed in the 1960s and 1970s, with the solid color line indicating the relationship between the unemployment rate and the rate of change in prices. The dashed and dash-dot lines show the presumed upward shift in the Phillips Curve that occurred in the 1970s.

The theory of the Phillips Curve began to disintegrate in the early 1970s. The clear relationship between unemployment rates and prices disappeared. For example, in both 1972 and 1974 the unemployment rate was 5.6 percent. According to the theory, the rate of price increase should have been the same in both years. It wasn't: in 1972 prices rose by 3.3 percent, in 1974 by 11 percent. Another

example: the unemployment rate fell between 1971 and 1972, from 5.9 to 5.6 percent. The theory said that price increases should accelerate, but instead the rate of price increase fell from 4.3 to 3.3 percent. Some theory! Table 14–2 shows the unemployment-price relationship for the 1970s.

In order to rescue the theory, some economists began to argue that the Phillips Curve had shifted upward in the early 1970s—the dashed color line in Figure 14–4—and upward again after 1973—the dash-dot black line. The reason, some argued, could be traced to changes in the structure of the labor force. There were more hardcore unemployed in the labor market, young men and women without adequate training and skills and without much work experience. As the proportion of these workers increased in the work force as a whole, it was argued, the unemployment rate at any given level of prices would rise. If employers were to hire these workers, prices would have to rise to compensate employers for higher training costs, lower worker

Figure 14-4
The Phillips Curve,
1960–69 and 1970–79

Between 1961 and 1969 there seemed to be a clear tradeoff between changes in prices and changes in the unemployment rate (solid color line). Then came 1970–73, which didn't fit the pattern. Some economists argued that the curve shifted outward (dashed color line), with a second outward shift after 1973 (dash-dot line).

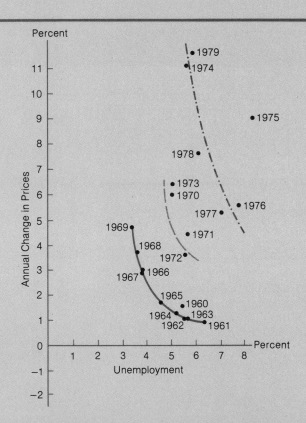

Table 14–2

Year	Price Changes	Unemployment
	(percent)	
1970	5.9	4.9
1971	4.3	5.9
1972	3.3	5.6
1973	6.2	4.9
1974	11.0	5.6
1975	9.1	8.5
1976	5.8	7.7
1977	6.5	7.0
1978	7.7	6.0
1979	11.3	5.8

Figure 14–5
Natural Rate of Unemployment and the Short-Run Phillips Curve

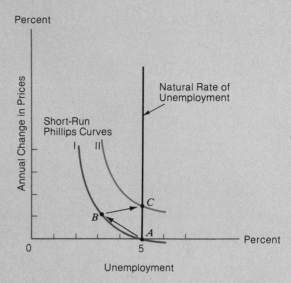

Starting from A, government policies increase aggregate demand to reduce unemployment to 3 percent. Prices start rising, however, bringing the economy to B, where the unemployment rate is 3 percent and the inflation rate is 1 percent. Increased costs and other adjustments, however, move the economy to C, where unemployment is once more at 5 percent, the natural rate, while the inflation rate is 1.5 percent.

productivity, and increased labor turnover. This line of argument led to proposals for large-scale training programs to increase the employability of "marginal" workers.

A second group of economists wanted to "zap labor." They argued that the presumed upward shifts in the Phillips Curve were the result of increased bargaining power by labor unions, which enabled them to obtain large wage increases that exceeded productivity gains, forcing business firms to raise prices, while the government saw to it that aggregate demand rose to prevent any increase in unemployment. This explanation led to the conclusion that the wage increases presumed to be at the source of the problem should be limited.

Finally, another group of economists used the concept of the Phillips Curve to argue in opposition to the use of fiscal policy as a stabilization device. They argued that there was a natural rate of unemployment, say 5 percent, at which the general level of prices was stable. If government tried to reduce unemployment below that level, it could succeed temporarily, but prices would rise. This would create a "short-run Phillips Curve" in which reduced unemployment is associated with higher prices. But the higher prices would entail higher production costs, adjustments in people's expectations and in the money markets, and unemployment would start rising again toward the natural level. That is, the Phillips Curve would shift upward. This theory is shown in Figure 14–5.

The disputes engendered by the Phillips Curve

hypothesis are instructive. They show that a great deal of presumably scientific economics is heavily burdened by ideological baggage. Three different interpretations are associated with three different political positions. One favors continued use of policies designed to manage aggregate demand plus training programs for the unemployed, which could be labelled the liberal Keynesian position. A second also accepts aggregate demand management but would supplement it with wage controls, the conservative Keynesian position. The third rejects demand management and blames it for inflation, a conservative anti-Keynesian position that many monetarists adopt. It is the sort of academic debate that will be decided at the ballot box, and not at the level of rational analysis.

PART 4

COMPETITIVE MARKETS

Up to this point we have dealt with the macroeconomic processes at work in a private enterprise economy, showing why and how the contrary tendencies toward equilibrium and disturbance result in a continually fluctuating level of economic activity. We now turn to the microeconomics of the system of interrelated markets that was described in simple terms at the very beginning of the book. We start with the relatively simple case of competitive markets (Part 4) before moving on to the more complex and realistic patterns of monopoloid markets (Part 5).

Chapter 15 provides an overview of the underlying forces behind the functioning of markets: a review of how prices are determined by the interaction of demand and supply; the concepts of adjustment at the margin, rational action, and costs, as they are used in the analysis; and the nature of a market equilibrium. A most important fundamental principle emerges: both parties involved in an exchange benefit when the exchange is truly free and uncoerced.

Chapter 16 looks at the demand side of the market, analyzing the principle that lies behind the downward sloping demand curve: utility diminishes at the margin as quantity consumed is increased, and how that principle is applied to decisions to work, save or spend, and buy commodities. An appendix presents an alternative analysis of consumer preferences that is preferred by many economists.

Chapter 17 introduces an important and useful concept, elasticity of demand. It helps us understand and measure the relationship between a change in price and a change in quantity demanded, thereby filling out our understanding of the slope of the demand curve.

Chapter 18 looks behind the supply curve at costs of production. Its purpose is to show why and how the supply curve slopes upward in the market in the short run, and how costs of production behave in the long run.

Chapter 19 sums up the adjustment process in competitive markets. It is one of the most important in this book. The analysis takes the adjustment through three conceptually different time periods: market, short run, and long run. In reality they overlap, but are separated here for analytic purposes. The conclusion is one of the oldest and most fundamental truths about competitive markets: in the long run, prices tend to equal costs of production.

Chapter **15**

The Basic Economics
of Market Systems

Chapter 1 portrayed the functioning of a system of interrelated markets and showed in simple terms how a competitive market economy tends to adjust the pattern of production to the wants of consumers. This chapter goes behind the allocative mechanics of freely adjusting markets to show why such a market system tends to maximize benefits to individuals, assuming that individuals are rational and markets free to respond to their decisions. Our purpose here is to set forth the essential elements of the market system as a whole prior to examining its component parts. The analysis assumes that the economy is made up of a very large number of independent units and that there are no constraints on the market adjustment process.

Freedom, Constraints, and Market Forces

The allocative mechanism of a market system involves many millions of independent decisions made by many individual consumers and producers. Advocates of the market economy as a way of organizing economic life emphasize the individual freedom implicit in a freely operating market economy and the individual benefits derived from it. But it must be remembered that freedom always operates within constraints. In the case of the free market, those constraints are market forces, all-pervasive, impersonal, and not amenable to control by individuals (except where monopolistic conditions exist). Those market forces determine prices for everything bought and sold in the market system. Values in exchange are determined within a market framework.

Relationships between prices provide individuals with the alternatives on which decisions are based. Decisions about what to buy, what to produce and sell, which resources to use for which purposes, and what to pay for resources depend on prevailing prices. These prices are the constraints within which the individual functions. The market system itself constrains individual behavior.

The constraints of the market are more rigid and intractable than those of any government. For example, if you have a product you would like to produce and sell for support of yourself and your family but can't find enough buyers or anyone to provide you with capital—well, that's tough. You had better try something else, even if it requires a style of life less attractive to you. Millions of farm families found this out the hard way in recent decades. By contrast, if government prohibits certain types of economic activity, such as traffic in narcotics, the prohibition can be overcome by engaging in them outside the law, or by bribery, or both. Thousands of members of the underworld have exploited these opportunities in recent decades, to their great joy and profit.

Economic planners know about the limits imposed by the market. When a government edict, or a government allocation of resources, or an attempt to fix prices, collides with market forces, the market usually wins. Illegal markets during periods of rationing are an example. For example, the simple supply-demand-price diagrams explained in Chapter 1 can be used to show how illegal markets for gasoline could develop out of gasoline shortages when rationing attempts to keep prices down.

In normal markets, shown in Figure 15–1, the interactions of demand and supply determine the price P_1 and the amount sold Q_1.

A reduction in supplies coming into the market, like that of 1972–73 during the Arab oil boycott, causes the market supply schedule to shift from S_1 to S_2 in Figure 15–2, leading to a higher price P_2 if no controls are imposed. The supply curve is shown becoming a vertical line because of artificial limits imposed by the political authorities.

Now let us imagine that government steps in to prevent the price rise and fixes the price of gasoline at the original level (Figure 15–3). At the controlled price P_1, the quantity demanded exceeds the available supply by amount AB. This excess demand will still push the price upwards toward the market equilibrium P_2. The only way to prevent it is by rationing and by police action against illegal markets. If the

Figure 15–1
Step 1: The Market for Gasoline in Normal Times

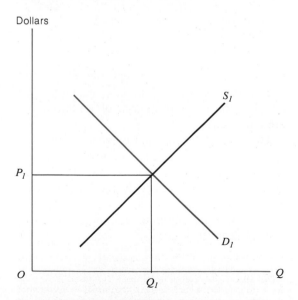

Demand (D_1) and supply (S_1) interact to determine the market price (P_1) and the quantity sold (Q_1).

Figure 15–2
Step 2: Limited Supplies of Gasoline Normally Cause Its Price to Go Up

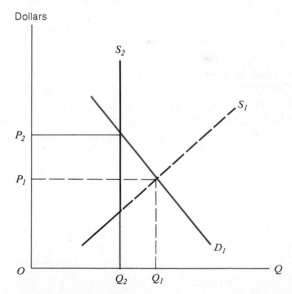

Restrictions on supply by OPEC move the market supply from S_1 to S_2, to push the market price to P_2. At the higher price, less is sold (Q_2).

Figure 15-3
Step 3: Government Imposes Price Controls Designed to Keep the Price of Gasoline at the Pre-Shortage Level

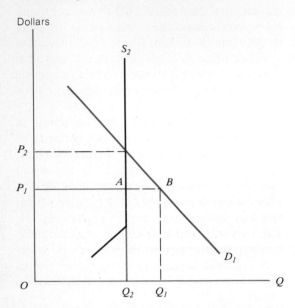

In order to prevent price from rising to P_2, price controls establish a legal price at P_1, with quantity sold remaining at Q_2.

Figure 15-4
Step 4: The Legal Price and Illegal Market Price

At price P_1 there is considerable unmet demand $(Q_1 - Q_2)$, which pushes the price upward toward P_2, resulting in an illegal market price whose level depends on the effectiveness with which the fixed price is enforced.

police action is weak and ineffective, the price will move up toward P_2; gasoline will be sold on the illegal market at the higher price; and supplies will tend to disappear from the legal channels of distribution. The illegal market will take over (Figure 15–4). The illegal market price will fluctuate between P_1 and P_2, depending on the amount of police power applied and the force of psychological appeals, always tending upward toward P_2.

The only ways open to governments to prevent illegal markets are patriotic appeals and force. Both can be effective, depending on how strong the psychological appeals are and how much force is applied. The result of their interaction with the market forces that push prices upward is indeterminate. That is, the

prevailing price in the illegal market will fall somewhere between P_1 and P_2, depending on how vigorously the price controls and rationing are enforced.

The market mechanism is indeed powerful. Its effects can be modified somewhat, but the extent of that modification is limited and temporary for the most part. In the long run, the market forces that allocate resources and determine incomes tend to dominate efforts to control them.[1]

---

[1]Why should a government ration commodities? Why not let the market allocate them, even in wartime? The answer is that the market would allocate goods to those who can pay the higher price caused by restricted supply. Gasoline would go to the rich for their pleasure boats, for example, instead of to workers who need gas to drive to work. Rationing and price controls are used to achieve goals that would not be achieved through the market mechanism.

Marginal Analysis

Market forces normally operate through small increases and decreases. This is particularly true of competitive markets composed of many buyers and sellers. It is less true of markets dominated by a few large sellers or buyers, but even there the decisions involve changes from one position to another.

Here is an example. You are the operator of an automobile service station, and have to determine how long you want to remain open. Should you close at 10:00 P.M., 11:00 P.M., or midnight, or should you stay open still longer? As a business manager, you want to make as much money as you can, and you don't care to operate when your costs exceed your revenues.

One part of the problem can be set aside immediately. No matter what your hours of operation, you have certain *fixed costs* that must be paid, such as rent, your own salary as owner or manager, accounting and other business services, and similar items. Since these bills must be met anyway, they have no relevance to a decision about whether to stay open an additional hour or to close an hour earlier.

Other costs will increase or decrease with the hours of operation. These *variable costs* include the wages of the attendant, the cost of gasoline and other items sold, the cost of utilities for the added hours, and some other items. However, longer hours will bring in additional revenue. As long as the additional revenues exceed the costs incurred from longer operation, total profit from the enterprise will rise. That relationship is the key:

○ When additional revenue exceeds additional costs, total profit rises.

Examining the changes in revenues and costs will show the direction in which total profit is moving.

Now suppose that in experimenting with different closing times, you have accumulated the information in Table 15-1. This information

tells you that between 10:00 P.M. and 11:00 P.M. your additional receipts average $122 and your additional expenses are $86, with a net addition to profits of $36, and so on to 2:00 A.M. Up to midnight your profits rise, but decline thereafter. If you are interested in maximizing profits, you will keep the station open at least until midnight, but will certainly close before 1:00 A.M. Further experimentation may indicate a 12:30 A.M. closing time, if you wish to refine your decision still further. But at some time between midnight and 1:00 A.M. the additional costs will start to exceed the additional revenues, and you will be losing money unnecessarily.[2]

This way of thinking about decisions is called *marginal analysis*. Although applied here to a business decision, the method is applicable to any maximization problem. It is particularly relevant in the market economy because market prices can be used as measures of benefits and costs, at least as a first approximation.[3]

● **Marginal analysis** is the theoretical method that analyzes market forces in terms of marginal units, marginal benefits, and marginal costs. The **marginal unit** is the last unit bought or sold. Economists call increases or decreases around

---

[2]The figures used here are real ones, somewhat simplified, taken from the operation of a service station run by a nonprofit enterprise, with which the author was associated, that employed the hardcore unemployed. We wanted to close at midnight, but the oil company that leased the station to us wanted it open all night. It was located at an expressway exit and they wanted to sell gas, whether we made money or not. So the lease was written to require 24-hour operation. It is of such material that the relationships between big enterprise and small are built.

[3]Economists have to be very careful here. Prices do not always measure full benefits and full costs. We have met this problem before and will keep coming back to it from time to time. For example, the cost of education is greater than the direct costs of the buildings, faculty, and other resources used in educating students. It also includes the value of the things students could be producing, but are not, because their time is spent in school. Likewise, the benefits are broader than those that accrue to the individual student and for which he might be expected to pay. They include the benefits others derive because educated people contribute more to society as a whole. As a result, the price charged for education (tuition) is less than the full cost to society, and also less than the full benefits. Subsidies are provided to educational institutions (even private ones), and indirectly to students, because of these disparities.

Table 15.1

Hours of Operation	Additional Receipts (Hourly)	Additional Variable Costs (Hourly)	Change in Profits (Additional Receipts Minus Additional Variable Costs)
10 P.M.-11 P.M.	$122	$86	+$36
11 P.M.-12 P.M.	84	72	+ 12
12 P.M.-1 A.M.	32	48	− 16
1 A.M.-2 A.M.	26	44	− 18

that unit *the margin*. Benefits derived from satisfactions obtained from consumption of the last unit are called **marginal utility** or *marginal satisfactions*. The benefits and costs associated with the last unit are **marginal benefits** and **costs**.

Rational Decisions

Marginal analysis is the key to rational decision making in economic affairs. Indeed, it is a key to rational decisions in many fields. Take military strategy, for example. A commanding general has the goal of subduing an enemy. He has at his disposal a limited amount of resources in the form of men, guns, ammunition, ships, airplanes, and other materiel. A good general will seek the strategy and tactics that will achieve his goal with the minimum expenditure of resources, so that he will have the maximum amount left to take care of the next enemy. At each step in his campaign he must weigh the potential gains against the potential losses. Only if the gains are greater than the losses will he be better off and the step be worth taking.[4]

This formal type of economic analysis is characteristic of decision making in economic affairs. Business firms in competitive markets seek out that path of action which they believe maximizes their profits. Some may seek immediate profit and go for a quick killing. Others may develop a strategy to maximize profits in the long run. But one thing is clear: the business firm that does not try to make the largest profits will operate at a disadvantage when competing with those that do. It will generate less capital out of profits, and will have greater difficulty in obtaining capital from the capital markets. Investors certainly seek the greatest gains (taking risk and uncertainty into account), and their behavior gives the advantage to profit-maximizing firms. In a growing, competitive economy, the prosperous firms will be those that maximize profits, while those that do not will fall by the wayside.

With consumers the situation is less clear. An argument can be made, on logical grounds, that consumers seek to maximize the satisfactions they obtain from the use of their resources. They wouldn't be "rational" if they didn't. But that proposition is impossible to prove. Any pattern of behavior, no matter how odd or perverse it may appear to be, will fit the proposition that the person involved gets pleasure out of it. Masochists like to be whipped, and sadists like to whip them, for example.

Consumer behavior is influenced by the social system. People are educated in patterns of action that fit the standards and values of their family, community, work group, church, and

[4]This type of analysis has its limits. This example from military strategy does not take into consideration the use of atomic weapons. Since both the U.S. and the USSR have such a large "overkill" ability, one cannot overcome the power of the other without being destroyed itself. While this situation doesn't make the two nations any friendlier, it does avert open warfare and channels their rivalry into other areas. As long as the leaders remain rational the world won't be destroyed.

other groups that affect their lives. Their choices are not "free," but are constrained by the social institutions in which they function. For example, a college professor does not act like a Mohawk war chief, even though he may give vent to some fierce emotions when watching a football game or grading examinations.

Social patterns, social environments, social attitudes, and habit, then, all influence consumer behavior. The social environment may make available a relatively large area of decision making for individual choice. Or it can restrict those choices to a relatively narrow area. In either case, however, the economic analysis of markets is based on the assumption that there will be opportunity for rational consumers to compare positions at the margin and to make welfare-maximizing decisions.

Reflect for a moment on the last time you ordered a dinner in a restaurant. How did you decide on steak, rather than lobster, or roast beef, or anything else on the menu. Consciously or unconsciously, there was a comparison of benefits to be derived from the alternatives, compared with the prices at which they were available. You made the selection you "liked" the most, given your tastes, the money you had at the time, and all of the other constraints that you may have felt. An economist would argue that within that framework, a welfare-maximizing decision was made.

All of these examples of rational action involve a comparison of benefits and costs at the margin, with the objective of maximizing net benefits. In all cases there is a choice among alternatives, and there are constraints imposed on the choice. That is the meaning of rational behavior as it is analyzed in economics.

The Nature of Costs

You win a free trip to Bermuda, with all expenses paid. Would you refuse to go? Some people would, strange as that may seem. Why?

Because they may feel that it would be better for them to spend the time doing other things. Example: the college professor who knows he is dying from an incurable cancer may want to finish the book he is writing that will finally get down on paper the unpublished results of his latest researches. He just can't afford the time a trip to Bermuda would take.

Another example: the business manager with a big deal on the fire, who stands to gain much more than the cost of a Bermuda vacation. If the deal goes through successfully, the gains might finance ten vacations. In this case the vacation in Bermuda is very expensive.

These two examples have one thing in common. The alternatives are worth more to the people involved than the free vacation. The costs of taking the vacation are greater than the benefits. Even though there are no direct monetary costs, there are other costs involved in the choices. Those costs are the benefits given up because an alternative course of action is taken. Everyone has a variety of ways to use time and resources. Some ways provide greater benefits than others. A rational choice selects the use that provides the maximum benefit. The cost of that choice is the benefit that could be obtained from the next most favorable use of time and resources.

All choices involve *opportunity costs* of this type. Keep this principle in mind. It is one of the fundamental concepts of the logic of rational action in any sphere of life. No matter what choices we make, we must give up something in order to get what we want. Nothing in this world is free.

● **Opportunity costs** are the benefits or satisfactions that could have been obtained by choosing something else.

The Market Equilibrium

The concept of equilibrium is fundamental to an understanding of how a market economy works. It is a simple proposition: any system reaches equilibrium when the forces that operate within it are in balance. One force neutralizes another, leading to a stable relationship in which the existing pattern remains unchanged.

The solar system is a classic example of physical equilibrium; in it, the gravitational forces and motions of sun, planets, and satellites have established a relationship that holds the system unchanged. There is motion within the system, and the system as a whole is moving, but the units within the system are so related to each other that their movements are repeated endlessly. Even Halley's comet returns periodically, following its odd but predictable track.

Two forces within the economy lead to *market equilibrium*: benefits and costs. Benefits are the force that causes people to take action. Costs provide the limits to that action. When an action is contemplated, rational individuals balance the marginal benefits they expect to obtain against the marginal costs. When the marginal benefits exceed the marginal costs, they take the contemplated action. When they don't, they stay where they are.

The general principle can be stated in another fashion. If at the existing price charged for a commodity, the marginal benefits to consumers of increased output are greater than the marginal costs to producers, strong economic forces are set in motion to increase the output. Only when the marginal benefits from additional output fall to equality with the marginal costs (or marginal costs rise to equal marginal benefits) will there be no advantage to increased output. We should think of it in this way: as long as any consumer can increase benefits by an amount more than the increased costs to any producer, the self-adjusting market is not at its equilibrium position.

Here is a hypothetical example. The price of milk is 35¢ per quart. But Joey Schlemiel is willing to buy an additional quart of milk at that price. That is, he judges that the benefits to himself that could be derived from another quart of milk are worth more than 35¢ worth of anything else, including savings. On the other hand, Billy Schlimazel would be willing to produce and sell one more quart of milk if he were paid 35¢ for it. His costs would be less than that amount. In a competitive market with a reasonably free system of information, Schlemiel and Schlimazel are brought together and make their transaction. Indeed, that is exactly the function performed by competitive markets. Both will gain. Schlemiel will have acquired milk, which he values at more than 35¢, while Schlimazel will have acquired 35¢, which is worth more to him than the milk. The two will continue to trade until Schlemiel is no longer willing to pay more than 35¢ for a quart of milk, or until Schlimazel finds that producing and selling another quart costs him more than 35¢.

But why would Schlemiel stop buying milk at a price of 35¢ per quart? The fact that he does stop indicates that he would rather spend the next 35¢ on something else. At some point, Schlemiel decides that other opportunities for consumption (or saving) are equally attractive to him. At that point the market price becomes a measure of both benefits and costs associated with the last quart purchased.[5]

Marginal benefits to buyer = Market price
= Marginal costs to buyer

Now let's look at the seller. Suppose Schlemiel has all the milk he wants at a price of 35¢, but Schlimazel's cost of producing and selling another quart is only 33¢. It would clearly be to Schlimazel's advantage to lower the price, thereby inducing Schlemiel to buy more. And if he didn't lower his price, in a competitive market someone else would. So Schlimazel reduces his price as long as the price exceeds his additional costs. He will continue to do so until the price is just equal to the cost of producing and selling the last quart of milk, including whatever return will be large enough

---

[5]The concept of cost used here is opportunity costs, discussed a few pages back.

to make it worthwhile for Schlimazel to continue his operations.

Schlimazel, then, continues to produce additional milk until the revenues he obtains from selling one more quart are no greater than the cost of producing that quart. At that point he can no longer add to his profits, and the market price will measure both his revenues and his costs:

Marginal revenues to seller = Market price
= Marginal costs to seller

The essential element in reaching and preserving the market equilibrium is equality of marginal benefits and costs. As far as Schlemiel is concerned, the benefits from the last quart of milk he purchased are worth *to him* just what he paid for it, say 33.5¢, and neither more nor less. As for Schlimazel, the price of 33.5¢ provides gains just large enough to compensate him for the costs and effort of producing that last quart. Benefits and costs for both buyer and seller have been equalized at the margin.

Marginal benefits to buyers
= Marginal cost to buyers = Market price
= Marginal cost to sellers
= Marginal benefits to sellers

When that situation has been reached, neither buyer nor seller can improve his position, the price does not change, and the pattern of production and sales continues without change. The market is in equilibrium.

- **Market equilibrium** is a stable relationship among market forces that leaves existing patterns unchanged. It occurs when all economic units have equated costs and benefits at the margin.

Maximization of Benefits

The market equilibrium that emerges from profit-maximizing behavior by sellers and welfare-maximizing behavior by buyers has one extremely important characteristic: the total of

benefits to both buyers and sellers is maximized.

The buyer, Schlemiel in our example, added to his total benefits with each quart of milk he purchased. But he finally stopped buying. If he were acting rationally, he must have decided that the added benefits were not equal to the added costs. For the last quart of milk he bought, however, Schlemiel must have decided that the additional benefits were at least equal to the additional costs. If he adds benefits every time he buys an additional quart, it must follow that when he stops buying he has maximized the total benefits he obtains. If he could add more net benefits, he wouldn't stop buying.

As for Schlimazel, the seller, his task was easier. He could calculate his revenues and his costs in dollars and cents. He could see that additional sales added to his net gains up to the last unit sold. But he stopped expanding his sales because another unit sold would add more to his costs than to his revenues. He also had arrived at a position that maximized his net gains.

The principle can be generalized for the economy as a whole. If each Schlemiel is at his best position, and each Schlimazel is too, it is not possible for the group as a whole to move to anything better, at least for this set of transactions. Benefits to the group are maximized when each individual in the group maximizes his own benefits.[6]

Some Conditions

Maximization of benefits through the market mechanism, while a pervasive and continuing tendency wherever buyers and sellers exchange

---

[6]The group as a whole can get together and decide that it is mutually beneficial to reduce individual benefits for each person in order to provide things that will be used jointly, such as parks or schools or nuclear weapons. This does not change the basic principle: the resources left in the hands of the group members will be allocated to achieve maximum benefits when each member of the group has achieved a position of maximum benefits.

with each other, requires a number of conditions. Without them the maximization of benefits can only be approximated. The chief conditions are these:

1. Free markets. If markets are free of controls by both public and private sources of power, consumers and sellers are better able to select those paths of action that maximize their benefits. This is the most powerful argument against both private monopoly and public regulation. Constraints against freedom of action in the market limit the maximizing behavior of individuals.

2. Information. Both buyers and sellers must know about all the alternatives open to them. If they don't, they will not be able to maximize their benefits. For example, informative advertising helps, while deceptive advertising hinders the achievement of maximum benefits.

3. Full substitutability of the factors of production. Just as buyers and sellers must have full knowledge of all alternatives and access to them, so producers must be free to use resources for all purposes. Capital must be freely substitutable for labor, for example, in order that producers may be able to minimize costs of production and produce what consumers want. If the technological relationships in production processes are rigid, the flexibility of adjustment of the entire economy is reduced, and the alternatives open to producers are limited.

In essence, a flexible economy with the greatest freedom of choice and the largest amount of information widely available to all is the one in which maximization of benefits can proceed the farthest. Anything that reduces flexibility of adjustment, knowledge, or freedom to choose will compromise the achievement of maximum benefits.

This proposition is the heart of the ideology of capitalism. The social philosophy that advocates laissez-faire as a policy rests on the economic analysis that connects individual decisions with maximum benefits by way of free markets. It is this philosophy, with its accompanying economic analysis, that Adam Smith systematically developed in the eighteenth century and that became the starting point for modern economic analysis.

Ideology is one thing; theoretical analysis is something else. In the process of working out the economics of self-adjusting markets, we learn a great deal about the world in which we live. However imperfect it may be, much of our economic activity takes place in the framework of a system of interrelated markets. Many markets are not free of private and public controls, knowledge is less than perfect, and resources are often immobile. Nevertheless, by starting with a model of competitive markets, we can learn the essential elements of how market forces operate and develop a norm against which less competitive market situations can be judged. We can then move to consideration of monopoloid markets with various limitations on alternative choices and look at how markets might function in a socialist economy. In doing so, we shall obtain a richer understanding of the larger alternatives facing the contemporary world.

One final point: rational allocation of resources is also a goal of socialist economies. It can be accomplished without the compulsions required by central planning if market principles are followed for allocating resources, as we show in Chapter 36. Indeed, market socialism may be even more effective than market capitalism in fitting the pattern of production to the pattern of human needs.

We embark, then, on an analysis of the theory of markets in greater detail.

Summary

The interaction of supply and demand in self-adjusting markets indicates that market forces move powerfully toward their own equilibrium. They provide strong constraints within which economic activity is carried on and within which economic policy must function.

The market adjustment process involves small increases or decreases in moving from one position toward another. Although this process of adjustment is always going on and never comes to a halt, it can be analyzed as if it were moving from one equilibrium position to another through a series of small changes. This theoretical method is called the marginal analysis.

The market system is pushed toward equilibrium by the efforts of consumers and producers to maximize their individual net benefits. Individual comparisons are made of benefits and costs at the margin, and the costs of any choice are essentially the benefits from other choices that have to be foregone. The result of individual choices is a general equilibrium in which market prices play a key role. For any one good, marginal benefits to buyers = marginal cost to buyers = market prices = marginal cost to sellers = marginal benefits to sellers. This pattern of market equilibrium represents a welfare-maximizing position for both buyers and sellers.

This solution is subject to important conditions, all involving the flexibility of the market and complete freedom of choice by both buyers and sellers: markets must be free of public and private constraints, alternatives must be fully known, and factors of production must be fully substitutable for each other. Although these conditions are never fully present except in a theoretical analysis, the self-adjusting market can be expected to move toward a welfare-maximizing equilibrium to the extent that it does have freedom and flexibility to adjust.

Key Concepts

marginal analysis   marginal utility   marginal costs   market equilibrium
marginal unit   marginal benefits   opportunity cost

For Discussion

1. Economists argue that *rational action* involves comparison of marginal costs with marginal benefits. Do you agree?

2. Would you expect more than one price for a single good to be present in a competitive market? Why?

3. What would you expect to happen if the government tried to fix the price of a commodity above the market equilibrium price?

4. The pursuit of self-interest by both buyers and sellers in a competitive market leads to an equilibrium in which both are satisfied with the result. Explain.

5. Explain and give a concrete example of opportunity costs.

6. Benefits to buyers and costs to sellers are different, like apples and oranges. How can they be equal at the margin?

Chapter 16

The Rational Consumer and the Law of Demand

This chapter examines the behavior of consumers and the "law of demand": consumers tend to buy less at higher prices and more at lower prices. The analysis is based on the assumption that decisions are directed toward maximizing net benefits. The concept of utility and the principle of diminishing marginal utility are used to analyze the consumer's decision-making process. These concepts are then applied to consumer decisions about work and leisure, spending and saving, and the allocation of expenditures on different goods, resulting in a market demand curve. The discussion then shifts to the law of demand in its simple and more general formulations, and goes on to discuss the shape of the demand curve.

The Rational Consumer and the Concept of Utility

Behind the demand for a good lie the decisions made by individual consumers. People decide whether to work more or less, to save and to spend, and what to buy. Consumers generally know what they want: food and shelter, a certain amount of ease and comfort, a little

variety of experiences, the self-satisfaction that comes from doing something well, security against the uncertainties of the world, some approval from their fellows, and leisure. They also have a pretty good idea of how they value any one of these goals when compared with the others. Most consumers also know how much any one good will contribute to the achievement of these goals. And the market economy provides them with a set of prices at which any good can be purchased.

Consumers can use this information to maximize their satisfactions. Some may wish to maximize their wealth, measured by its money value. Others may have different goals: to be an outstanding creative writer or artist, to develop religious piety, to contribute to world peace, to gain power over other people. Whatever the goals, a rational person will use his resources so as to maximize the benefits he gets from the resources at his disposal.

Utility is the term most commonly applied by economists to the benefits or satisfactions obtained from a good or from a particular course of action. An individual will save because the utility he obtains from saving a dollar is greater than the utility he could get from spending it.

He works because the utility derived from his earnings is greater than the utility obtained from leisure. He buys an automobile because its utility is greater to him than the utility obtained from spending on other things. In each case, the crucial factor is the relationship between the individual and the good, and not the good itself. This is an important point: each individual values things differently from every other individual. A rare stamp may be valued highly by a stamp collector, but not by someone who collects old books. Utility is not an inherent quality of the good, like its weight or color, but, like beauty, exists in the eyes of the beholder.

We should be more specific: people make choices. If they do so after considering alternatives, there must be a basis for comparison. The alternatives must have something in common; this common characteristic is the relative utility they provide to the individual.

- The term **utility** refers to the benefits derived by individuals from goods or from a particular action. Utility is not inherent in something, but is derived from the relationship between an object and a person.

Utility and Freedom of Choice
Since individuals differ in their evaluation of things, it behooves us to recognize the differences. If, for example, we require all students to learn a foreign language as a condition of granting a college degree we may hit the preferences of some right on the nose. But not of others. Many probably would prefer taking other courses that would be more useful to them than the language courses. If we want to maximize utility, then, freedom of choice is necessary. This principle applies to the economy with particular force. Free choice among alternatives makes it possible for consumers to maximize the utility they obtain, and in so doing to maximize their welfare as they interpret it. If consumers are rational, they will proceed to do exactly that.

Diminishing Marginal Utility

The more we have of a good, the less we desire more of it. This widely observed characteristic of human behavior is fundamental to an understanding of the market economy. Economists have developed it into the principle of *diminishing marginal utility*. Here is an illustration:

Mr. *X*, who enjoys drinking beer, would derive considerable utility from having a bottle with dinner each night. If he could increase his consumption so that he could have beer after dinner, too, he would increase his total utility, but probably not by the same amount as that obtained from just one bottle. A third bottle would bring still more utility, but a little less than the second bottle did. This process could go on, with additional beer consumption bringing him more utility at a diminishing rate, until one more bottle would add nothing at all to his utility.

We might even set up a hypothetical utility schedule for Mr. *X*, as in Table 16–1, showing his consumption of beer, the total utility obtained from it, and the *marginal* (additional) *utility* derived from additional bottles of beer.

Table 16–1
Mr. *X*'s Utility Schedule for Beer

Bottles per Day	Total Utility	Marginal Utility
0	0	9
1	9	8
2	17	7
3	24	6
4	30	5
5	35	4
6	39	3
7	42	2
8	44	1
9	45	0
10	45	−1
11	44	−2
12	42	

Table 16–1 shows us that Mr. *X*'s utility from beer consumption increases as he consumes more, up to 9 bottles per day. After 10 bottles, total utility begins to decline: maybe he starts to feel bad after that much drinking.[1] The right-hand column shows the marginal utility derived from each additional bottle of beer, falling slowly until it reaches zero with the tenth bottle and continuing into the negative range if consumption were to continue beyond that point.

The information in Table 16–1 is shown graphically in Figure 16–1. Total utility increases by an amount equal to the marginal utility derived from each additional unit, reaching its peak at 9–10 units and declining thereafter. Marginal utility shows its typical declining path.

Figure 16–1 has a steplike appearance because we are dealing with moderately large units of consumption. If beer could be stored and consumed in very small amounts the rectangles would become very narrow and the steps would become continuous lines, as shown by the curves in Figure 16–1.

One property of the marginal utility curve in Figure 16–1B should be noted. The area under it at any level of consumption is equal to the height of the total utility curve (Figure 16–1A) at that level of consumption. This means that total utility can be measured in two ways. It will often be convenient to use the area under the marginal utility curve to measure total utility.

- **Diminishing marginal utility** refers to the decrease in marginal utility as the quantity of a good increases within a given period.

The Decision to Work

Most consumer incomes come from work. The decision about whether to work or not must be made by everyone. Once made, there is another decision about how much to work. A housewife may decide not to work outside the home at all. Her husband may take a job for 35 hours a week, instead of one for 40 hours. And he has the opportunity for "moonlighting" at a second job to increase his income.

Rational consumers will balance the gains and costs at the margin. On the one hand, money earned from work provides goods with utility. On the other hand, leisure has its uses too: it provides the time needed to enjoy income, for one thing. More leisure means less income from work, while more work means less time to enjoy the income.

We show in Figure 16–2 how our rational man, Mr. *X*, would make a decision on this matter. The figure is constructed as a box diagram based on a working day of 18 hours (allowing six hours for sleep),[2] which Mr. *X* has to allocate between work and leisure. Marginal utility is measured vertically, hours of work per day from left to right on the bottom of the diagram, and hours of leisure per day from right to left at the top. The curve for the *MU* of work declines as hours of work increase, and so does the curve of the *MU* of leisure, but starting from the other side of the diagram. The curves cross at 8.5 hours of work and 9.5 hours of leisure. At this point Mr. *X* has reached an optimal situation. If he adds more work time, he must reduce his leisure. In that case, the marginal utility of the work is less than the marginal utility of the leisure. He will be worse off if he trades leisure for work

---

[1]One of Red Skelton's famous skits when he was just starting his career as a comic in the mid-1930s was a how-to-dunk-a-doughnut routine, which he did on the three-a-day vaudeville circuit. I was in the audience once when he stopped in the middle of the skit, threw away the half-eaten doughnut, and exclaimed, "I can't eat another one of these awful things. Three a day for six days a week is more than a man can stand." His marginal utility from doughnuts was negative.

[2]We have simplified the problem by giving Mr. *X* six hours for sleep. He could restructure his problem by reducing that time and reallocating the nonsleeping time between work and leisure. There is a story about a wandering Talmudic scholar, back in the old country, who had 24 pupils. He spent an hour a day with each one. So when he acquired a 25th pupil, he decided to get up an hour earlier.

Figure 16–1
Total and Marginal Utility

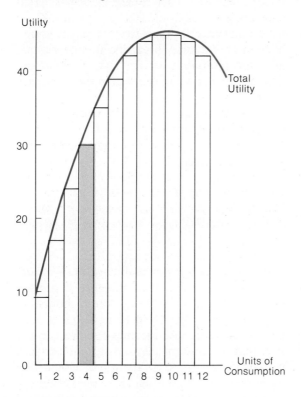

A. Total Utility Each rectangle shows the utility obtained from consuming the indicated units of the good.

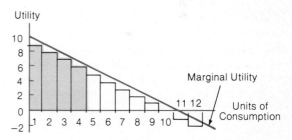

B. Diminishing Marginal Utility Each rectangle shows the amount of utility added to the total by an additional unit of consumption.

The shaded area in diagram A equals the shaded area in diagram B. The total utility from four units of consumption equals the sum of the marginal utilities derived from the first four units. In diagram B, the area under the marginal utility curve is equal to the total utility for that number of units, while utility derived from the marginal unit is equal to the height of the marginal utility curve:

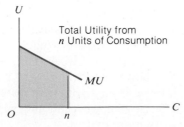

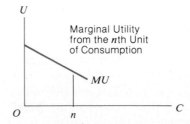

Figure 16-2
The Decision to Work

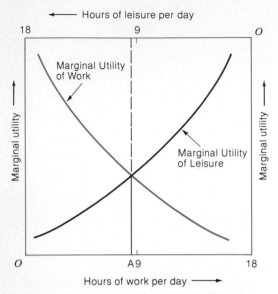

The individual will increase his hours of work up to *OA*, for every hour of work up to that point brings him more utility than that hour spent not working. Just the opposite is true for work time in excess of *OA*: the extra leisure is more desirable than the added work.

beyond 8.5 hours. He will also be worse off if he trades work for leisure. The last hour of work brought him more utility than one more hour of leisure would have provided. If he doesn't work that hour he will be giving up more than he gets. Mr. *X*, then, will maximize his total utility when

$$MU \text{ of work} = MU \text{ of leisure}$$

Substitution and Income Effects

The decision to work changes as the rewards for work shift. For example, what would happen to the decision regarding work versus leisure if wage rates were to rise, say from $4 to $5 per hour, in a particular occupation? Workers would be attracted to that occupation from others for which wages had not risen, of course. But how would the workers already in that occupation react to higher wages? Two conflicting forces would start to operate. First, we would expect workers to work longer hours, assuming, of course, no artificial barriers such as union limitations or employer regulations. One reason is that an increase in the wage rate makes an hour of leisure more costly. It means $5 foregone instead of $4. Some workers would decide that it's better to substitute some work for some leisure. This reaction is called the *substitution effect*.

● The **substitution effect** is the substitution by consumers of relatively low-priced goods for relatively high-priced goods caused by a change in price.

An *income effect* would also be felt. Workers would discover that their incomes had risen even without their working longer hours. A wage increase from $4 to $5 per hour is a 20 percent increase. As incomes rise we can expect that demand for all products and services will also rise. Workers, therefore, would buy more food, more housing, more of everything. Leisure is one of the benefits they could afford more of, with their higher incomes. Some workers might decide to work a little less and have more leisure time.

● The **income effect** is the change in demand for a good when consumers' real income changes.

In the case of any one worker the substitution and income effects would be at work simultaneously. The higher cost of leisure would push him toward longer hours, while increased income would push him toward shorter hours of work. For any one individual the new equilibrium would depend on the relative strength of the substitution and income effects, and we can't tell whether he would work more or less.

OPPORTUNITY COST REVISITED

The decision between work and leisure is a good example of the principle of opportunity cost. The cost of an hour's earnings is the utility derived from an hour's leisure. And vice versa. The rational individual recognizes this fact. The cost of going to college includes the income the student could have earned as a producer, for example. And once in college the cost of studying for an economics examination is the benefit that could have been obtained from doing something else. Every choice we make involves these comparisons; and maximization of benefits (happiness?) requires that we equalize utilities at the margin.

The Relationship Between Hours of Work and Income

If theory won't give an answer, what can we determine by looking at the facts? Chiefly, we learn that the income effect dominates in this case: people tend to work less as their incomes rise. The most convincing support for that conclusion comes from historical data that show reduced hours of work accompanying rising earnings. Here are data for workers in the private, nonagricultural sector of the economy, for example:

> Average weekly earnings *rose* from $68.13 in 1947 to $108.36 in 1972 (measured in 1967 dollars to correct for changes in the price level). Meanwhile, average hours worked per week *fell* from 40.3 to 37.2. A 60 percent increase in earnings was accompanied by an 8 percent decrease in hours worked.

Additional evidence comes from studies of hours and wages in different industries. Here the evidence is less conclusive, because of a wide variety of other factors at work, such as differences in technology, composition of the work force, structure of industries, and so on. But these studies also tend to show that high wage rates are associated with shorter hours.

This conclusion is quite significant. It tells us that one of the benefits of economic growth (rising real incomes) is increased leisure. Economic growth makes it possible for people to work less and do other things with their time. Our conclusion also suggests that higher taxes are likely to get people to work more rather than less. We often hear the argument that high income taxes on large incomes reduce work incentives. Yet if the income effect of lower earnings after taxes dominates the substitution effect of reduced rewards for work, which is what the data tell us, people will work harder if taxes take a larger proportion of their income.

The Decision to Save

The decision to save or spend is much like the decision to work. Some people are eager to consume and do not want to postpone the gratification of their desires. They will save relatively little. Others are more concerned about the future and are willing to postpone some consumption until a later time. They will save more. In either case, the utility from future consumption must be balanced against the utility of present consumption.

There is another factor in saving, however. Money saved now can be lent to others who want to spend it now, enabling the saver to earn additional income. That income also has utility for its recipient. Saving, then, has two different sources of utility for an individual. One is the utility of future consumption from the savings. The other is the utility of present consumption from the return earned by savings. Together they make up the utility derived from saving.

The rational consumer will make his decision about saving and spending so as to equate the marginal utilities involved. With a given amount of income, he will increase his spending, dollar by dollar, and reduce his savings

Figure 16-3
The Decision to Spend or Save

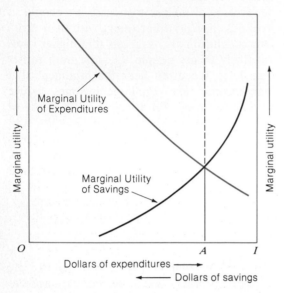

The consumer will spend *OA* and save *AI*. Up to that amount of spending, a dollar spent will bring more utility than if that dollar were not spent. Expenditures greater than *OA*, however, will bring less utility than savings would bring.

correspondingly, until the utility derived from the last dollar spent just equals the utility obtained from the last dollar saved. Figure 16–3 illustrates the process.

Figure 16–3 is much like Figure 16–2, except that it deals with a finite amount of income instead of a finite amount of time. Marginal utility is shown on the vertical scale, dollars of expenditures on the bottom horizontal scale, and dollars of savings on the top. The appropriate marginal utility scales for Mr. *X* are drawn. You will observe that in his scale of values spending brings greater utility than saving, for the marginal utility curve for expenditures lies higher on the diagram than the marginal utility curve for savings. As a result, he spends most of his income and saves relatively little, even after equating utilities at the margin. Another individual, with a different standard of values, will decide differently.

Rational Mr. *X* will increase his expenditures up to point *OA*, where the vertical line on the diagram is drawn. Up to that point each dollar spent brings him more utility than if he had saved that dollar. The portion of his income greater than *OA* (the *AI* segment of his total income) will be saved, for in that area of the chart a dollar saved provides greater utility than a dollar spent. At *OA* the marginal utilities are equal.

The rule for maximizing total utility from spending and saving is similar to the rule for other decisions:

$$MU \text{ of expenditures} = MU \text{ of savings}$$

Allocating Expenditures

Rational decision making when there are only two alternatives is simple enough. The concept of opportunity costs tells us that the benefits from one must be compared with the benefits from the other. The concept of marginal utility leads to the maxim that the utilities derived from the last units of each must be equated if benefits are to be maximized.

The same maxim can be applied to decision making when there are many different alternatives. This type of problem arises when the income among the many hundreds of products and services available to it in the market. It is a universal problem, and every household must solve it. The solution is to equate the marginal utilities derived from the last dollar spent on each alternative.

We start with Mr. *X*'s household, whose members have already decided what the trade-off between work and leisure will be. That decision determines their income. They have also made a decision about how much to save, which determines the income available for purchase of products and services. Now they must decide what and how much to buy. In making that decision the participants have a pretty good idea of their preferences (marginal utility schedules), and the prices they will have to pay.

Following the rule that marginal utilities must be equated, the rational consumer household will equalize the utility derived from the last dollar spent on each item bought. This rule can be written as:

$$\frac{MU_a}{P_a} = \frac{MU_b}{P_b} = \frac{MU_c}{P_c} = \cdots = \frac{MU_n}{P_n}$$

where

MU = marginal utility
P = price
a, b, c, n = products and services (goods)

You may wonder why we put the market price in this equation. That is done because units of different commodities are not comparable: one apple and one automobile mean different things. But dollars are comparable. A dollar spent on apples can be measured against a dollar spent on automobile transportation. So we use marginal utility per dollar (MU/P) as the unit for comparisons between goods. This rule for maximization of utility is subject to one condition: the household must use up all of the income that is allocated for spending. If

not, it could increase its consumption of all goods, keeping their marginal utility per dollar equal, and add to total utility. This condition can also be expressed as

$$E = Q_a \cdot P_a + Q_b \cdot P_b + Q_c \cdot P_c + \cdots + Q_n \cdot P_n$$

where

E = total expenditures
Q = quantities purchased
P = prices of the various goods
a, b, c, n = goods

This tells us that the sum of the amounts spent on all goods must equal total expenditures.

Figure 16–4 provides a diagrammatic illustration of the rule for rational expenditure allocation. The vertical axes show marginal utility per dollar for each good. The horizontal axes measure quantities of each good. The horizontal line I cutting across the four diagrams shows the income level that will use up the X family's income when allocated so that MU/P for each good is equal. (A larger income would show I lower down, with more of everything being bought, while a smaller income would have I higher up and less being bought.)

Figure 16–4
Rational Allocation of Expenditures by a Consuming Unit

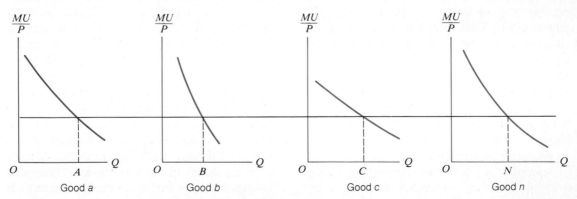

The rational consumer will allocate expenditures so that the marginal utility per dollar spent on each good is equal, subject to the condition that the entire income allocated for spending is used up.

In Figure 16–4, *MU/P* is equal for all goods, but a different quantity of each good is purchased.

The General Equilibrium of the Household

We can now summarize the conditions under which a rational household will maximize its utility. First, it will equalize the marginal utility of work and the marginal utility of leisure:

$$MU_W = MU_L \qquad (1)$$

Second, it will equalize the marginal utility of expenditures and the marginal utility of savings:

$$MU_E = MU_S \qquad (2)$$

Third, it will equalize the marginal utility per dollar spent on goods:

$$\frac{MU_a}{P_a} = \frac{MU_b}{P_b} = \frac{MU_c}{P_c} = \cdots = \frac{MU_n}{P_n} \qquad (3)$$

Finally, it will use up all of the income allocated to purchases of goods:

$$E = Q_a \cdot P_a + Q_b \cdot P_b + Q_c \cdot P_c + \cdots + Q_n \cdot P_n \qquad (4)$$

All of these decisions will influence each other. They are not made seriatim, but simultaneously. Indeed, many economists eliminate the first two conditions by lumping them into condition (3). That can be done if leisure and savings are included in the definition of goods. They have been kept separate here to indicate that decisions on those matters are of a different order from decisions about purchases of goods and services.

These four conditions define the results of utility maximization by the rational household or rational consumer. We can presume that consumers will behave in this fashion in any situation involving choices. At the very least, lack of coercion will provide the opportunity for choices to be made in this fashion. Any consumer will be able to maximize his satisfac-

tions and welfare, as he defines them, if he wishes to do so.

However desirable this pattern of free choice may be, the world is never perfect. Two considerations may effectively prevent the exercise of rational choices: consumers may not be rational, and social institutions may interfere with freedom of choice. In either case, welfare maximization will be short-circuited and a less-than-best solution emerge. These considerations create difficult problems of theory and policy that will be discussed later in this chapter and at various points throughout the book.

From Individual Demand to Market Demand

Having examined decision making by the rational consumer, we return to his demand for a single good, and use that as the basis for deriving a market demand curve for that good. First, we make the assumption that, for purposes of the analysis, everything is kept constant except the price and quantity of the good under consideration. Incomes, tastes, prices of all other goods, decisions to invest, along with anything else that might affect the outcome, are not allowed to vary. This assumption enables us to isolate what happens in the market for a single good.

Second, we start with the individual consumer and his marginal utility schedule for the good, which is shown in Figure 16–5. We ought to emphasize that the utility scale on the vertical axis is known only to the consumer himself. It is the basis for his comparisons of this good with all the other goods he could buy. But no one else knows what that scale looks like.

However, we do know something about one point on the scale and one point on the marginal utility curve. After the consumer allocates his expenditures, he buys, at the market price, a certain quantity of good *a*, shown in Figure 16–6 as *OA* on the horizontal axis. Since the consumer has purchased the marginal unit at

Figure 16-5
The Consumer's Marginal Utility Schedule for
Good *a*

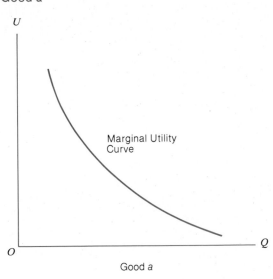

Figure 16-6
The Consumer Buys at Price *P₁*

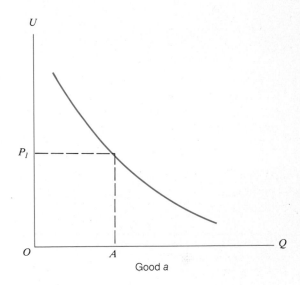

price P_1, we conclude that the utility derived from that purchase was just worth it to him, and that therefore the price is a proxy for the marginal utility.

Third, we can vary the price, hypothetically at least, and derive other points on the marginal utility curve, as shown in Figure 16–7. In this way we can create a different vertical scale on the diagram by converting utility to price, just as the consumer himself would do it when faced with alternative prices in the actual market. We end up with the consumer's demand curve for good *a*, shown in Figure 16–8. This demand curve shows, like any demand curve for an individual, the quantities of the good that the consumer would buy at varying prices, within the range of price changes consistent with the *ceteris paribus* assumption that no other variables change.

Substitution and Income Effects Once More
In the case of the consumer's demand curve for a good, substitution and income effects nor-

mally point in the same direction. (You should recall that in the case of the work-leisure decision a few pages back they tended to offset each other.)

Take the substitution effect. A reduced price will encourage the consumer to substitute good *a* for other goods. Doing so will increase satisfactions, for by substituting a now cheaper product for relatively higher priced ones the consumer can gain the same amount of utility as before and still buy more. Clearly utility will be increased and the substitution will be made.

Or the income effect. A lower price for good *a* means that the consumer's real income has risen. Even without any substitution the consumer can buy exactly what he or she bought before the price of *a* fell and have some income left over. The surplus can then be used to buy more of everything, including good *a*. Both the substitution effect and the income effect lead to increased purchases of good *a* when its price falls. The conclusion is that the consumer's demand curve slopes downward to the right.

Figure 16–7
The Consumer Buys at Several Prices

Figure 16–8
The Consumer's Demand Curve for Good *a*

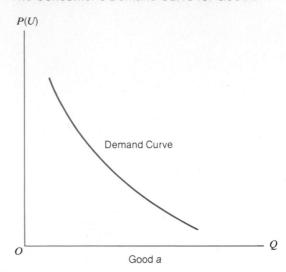

The Market Demand Curve

Having derived the individual consumer's demand curve for good *a*, we can take the last step toward obtaining the market demand curve by adding up the demand curves (or schedules) for all consumers. At each possible market price for good *a*, each consumer will buy a given amount. Adding up these amounts for all consumers gives us one point on the market demand curve. Doing the same thing for each price will lead us to the entire market demand curve, as Figure 16–9 illustrates.

The market demand curve for any good reflects the countless decisions made by millions of consumers. Those decisions, in turn, reflect the choices made by consumers on the basis of their individual preferences, which are rooted ultimately in their values and goals. This is the first step in the argument that in a market economy free choice among alternatives by rational consumers offers the opportunity, at least, for society to maximize the welfare of those who participate in it.

The Simple Law of Demand

Most of us, living as we do in the midst of a market-oriented society, are intuitively aware of the relationship between the price of a good and the amount buyers are willing to buy: the higher the price, the less bought in a given period of time. Conversely, if the price is lower, more will be bought. This is the *simple law of demand*, a general relationship between the price of a commodity and the amount demanded that can be expressed in a variety of ways:

1. Algebraically: $D_a = f(P_a)$. This is the general proposition that the demand for good *a* is systematically related to its price.
2. Geometrically: The demand curve, which pictures the relationship between price and the quantity demanded for good *a*, as in Figure 16–10.
3. Arithmetically: The demand schedule, as shown in Table 16–2, which gives the actual data used in constructing the demand curve for good *a*.

Figure 16–9
Adding up Individual Demand Curves to Obtain a Market Demand Curve

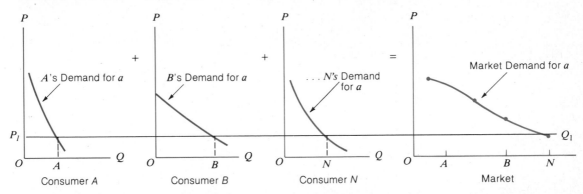

At price P_1, consumers A, B, and N will buy quantities OA, OB, and ON, respectively, which are shown on the right-hand diagram as segments OA, AB, and BN, respectively, designating point Q_1 on the market demand curve. Other points on the market demand curve can be similarly located and the entire curve will appear as shown.

Both the figure and the table show the classic functional relationship: consumers normally buy more at a lower price than they do at a higher price.

- The **simple law of demand** states that $D_a = f(P_a)$.

The normal relationship expressed by the simple law of demand can be readily illustrated. Figure 16–11 shows consumption and prices of apples in the United States between 1949 and 1960. For each year, the amount consumed and the average price per bushel is plotted as a single point, with price measured horizontally and consumption measured vertically. A demand curve for apples has been drawn as a straight line that approximates the relationship between consumption and price shown by the scattered data for each year. The points on the chart fall in a rather narrow band around the

Table 16–2
Demand Schedule for Good a

P_a	Q_a (Units)
$10	10,000
11	9,000
12	8,000
13	7,000

Figure 16–10
Demand Curve for Good a

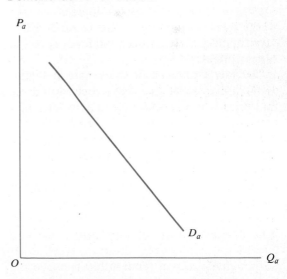

The demand curve shows that at higher prices less will be purchased, while at lower prices more will be bought.

Prices and
Consumption of
Apples, 1949–1960

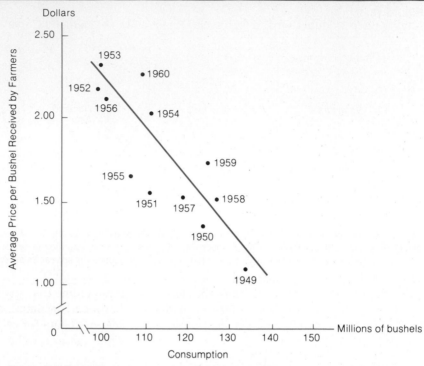

Source: U.S. Dept. of Agriculture, Agricultural Statistics: 1963 (Washington: U.S. Government Printing Office, 1963).

demand curve, although none fall exactly on it. The demand curve for apples slopes downward to the right. This indicates that consumers buy more apples at lower prices and fewer apples at higher prices.

The fact that most of the points in Figure 16–11 are close to the demand curve tells us that price is an important element in determining consumer behavior in the market for apples. The fact that all the points lie off the demand curve itself and are scattered around it in a random pattern indicates that other factors also influence consumer purchases of apples.

The General Law of Demand

Although there is a relationship between the price of a good and the quantity demanded, the large variation in the data suggests that other forces also influence the quantity of a good that consumers are willing to buy. Indeed, there are so many things other than price that affect consumer decisions to buy that a whole profession of market analysts has sprung up to advise business firms about them. The more important additional forces are:

1. Prices of other goods. Purchases of one good will vary with the prices of other goods. If the price of chickens falls, some consumers will buy less beef and more chicken, substituting chicken for beef in their diet. If the price of shoes falls, and consumers buy more shoes, demand for shoelaces will probably increase. If rents rise substantially, creating a squeeze on consumer incomes, purchases of movie

tickets, magazines, and more expensive cuts of meat may be reduced. The general rules are these:

A. Where commodities are good substitutes for each other (chicken-beef), the effect of changes in the price of one on the sales of the other may be large.
B. Where products complement each other (shoes-shoelaces), a change in the price of one will affect its demand *and* the demand for the other.
C. In some cases, where purchases of a good take up a substantial portion of consumer incomes (housing), a change in its price (rent) can affect the demand for everything else.

2. Income. The level of family income is an important determinant of the amount of a good that is purchased. Generally speaking, the higher the family income, the greater the demand for goods of all kinds. For most goods, if family incomes rise while the price of the good does not change, total purchases will rise. Demand for the good is said to increase, and the entire demand curve shifts upward and to the right (Figure 16–12). In some cases an increase in income may lead to a fall in demand for a good. For example, higher incomes may cause families to consume less bread and more meat. In this case bread would be called an inferior good: demand for it falls as incomes rise.

3. Distribution of income. Patterns of expenditure change as incomes rise. The very poor spend a very large proportion of their incomes on housing and food, save very little, and do not spend a great deal on books, travel, entertainment, education, and the like. The very rich, on the other hand, spend smaller proportions of their income on housing and food, and

larger proportions go for savings, entertainment, travel, and so on. Since dollars represent votes in the marketplace, and turn up as demand for goods, a shift in the pattern of income distribution will shift the pattern of market demand.

4. Population and its characteristics. A large population means a potentially high demand for goods, and increases in population mean increases in demand for most goods. The characteristics of the population are also important. Better educated people tend to buy more medical care and education. A population of small families will need more housing units than a population of large families, and the type of housing unit will differ as well. A young population consumes more food than an older population of equal numbers: food intake rises to a maximum during the teen-age years and then declines as people grow older.

5. Tastes and preferences. Many of our tastes and preferences are determined by the so-

Figure 16–12
Effect of Increase in Family Income on Demand for a Good (Usual Case)

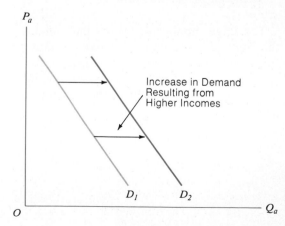

cial institutions in which we carry on our lives and by the ways we are brought up. Catholics will eat substantial amounts of fish; and many Jews eat little pork. Corn-meal and grits are popular in the South, bagels and lox in the New York area, scrod in Boston, and pralines in New Orleans. Not very many North Americans eat breadfruit, which is popular in the South Pacific, but we do import large volumes of bananas and pineapple.

Within any society individual tastes will vary, and that, of course, makes for diversity and wide availability of choices. Perhaps more important, tastes can change rapidly for many people simultaneously, creating the fashions and fads that are especially prevalent in affluent economies with large amounts of discretionary income over and above the amounts required for necessaries.

6. Stocks of durable goods. An affluent society will also have built up substantial stocks of durable goods in use, such as houses, household furniture and appliances, electrical equipment, automobiles, and the like. Demand for new units will be heavily influenced by the age and condition of the existing stock. Once acquired, they need only be replaced as they wear out or become obsolete.

The large number of factors that influence the demand for a commodity requires that we state the law of demand in more general form, to emphasize the fact that the price of a good is not the only determinant of the amount purchased.

- A **general law of demand** states that

$$D_a = f[P_a, P_b, \ldots, P_n, I, (S), t]$$

where

D_a = demand for good a
P_a = price of good a
$P_b \ldots P_n$ = prices of other goods

I = income
S = stocks, in parentheses because it affects only durables or storable items
t = time, a proxy for those factors that change relatively slowly, such as tastes, income distribution, and population

This formulation tells us that demand for a good depends on its price, the prices of other goods, consumer incomes, stocks on hand (if the good is durable or storable), and a variety of other factors that change slowly over time. It is a much more general statement than the simple law of demand, $D_a = f(P_a)$, which relates demand directly to price alone.

A Problem in Methodology and Its Solution

The general law of demand, while far closer to reality than the simple law of demand, is much less useful in analyzing the operation of a market economy. For a wide variety of analytical problems we should like to be able to take an established price as given, and then proceed to analyze how business managers adjust their decisions to it. Yet many of the ways in which producers adjust to market prices affect incomes and their distribution, prices of other goods and, indeed, all of the components of the general law of demand. This creates difficulties in the analysis, because then the demand curve starts jumping around instead of standing still. This, in turn, affects business decisions, which affect the factors that influence demand, which . . . well, to facilitate the analysis, something has to be done to anchor the demand curve so that the rest of the market adjustment process can be carefully worked out.

The solution is to assume constancy of all but one factor in the general law of demand. We can *assume* that prices of other goods do not change, that incomes, stocks, income distribution, tastes and preferences, population and its characteristics, and all other influences except the price of the good itself, remain constant for

Figure 16-13
Change in Quantity Demanded

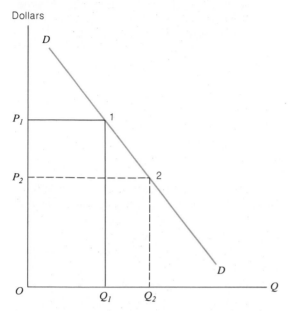

Dollars

Given the demand curve *DD*, points 1 and 2 show different combinations of price and quantity. If the price were P_1, the quantity demanded would be less than if the price were P_2. A change in price brings a change in the quantity demanded.

Figure 16-14
Decrease in Demand

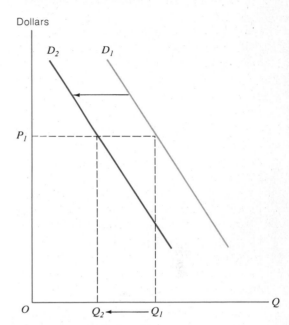

Dollars

A decrease in demand occurs when, without a change in price P_1, the quantity demanded falls, $Q_1 \rightarrow Q_2$. The demand curve D_1 has shifted to the left D_2.

purposes of the analysis. This is the famous *ceteris paribus* (other things remaining the same) assumption that is a feature of much economic analysis. Making this assumption reduces the law of demand to its simple form:

$$D_a = f(P_a)$$

and keeps the demand curve firmly anchored in one place on the page.

Change in the Quantity Demanded
Our formulation of the simple law of demand implies that it exists only at one moment in time. Each point on the demand curve is an alternative to any other point on the curve at that moment in time. In Figure 16–13, if the price were P_1, the *quantity demanded* would be Q_1. Alternatively, if the price were P_2, the

quantity demanded would be Q_2. These are alternative positions on the same demand curve and in the same demand schedule. A change in the quantity demanded means a shift from one point to another on the same demand curve *in response to a change in price*.

- **Quantity demanded** refers to the amount of a good that would be sold at a given price.

Change in Demand
Both the demand schedule and the demand curve shift with a *change in demand*. A change in demand means that consumer tastes have changed, or one of the other factors in the general law of demand has changed, so that the whole curve shifts, as shown by Figures 16–14 and 16–15. A change in demand means that a different quantity will be bought *at the same price*.

Figure 16–15
Increase in Demand

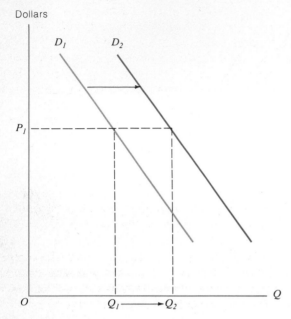

An increase in demand occurs when, without a change in price P_1, the quantity demanded increases, $Q_1 \rightarrow Q_2$. The demand curve D_1 has shifted to the right D_2.

Distinguishing Between Change in Quantity Demanded and Change in Demand

Students of economics must always keep in mind the difference between a shift along the demand curve (change in quantity demanded) and a shift of the demand curve itself (change in demand). They each result from a different cause. A shift along the demand curve results from a change in price, with no change in the conditions that determine the demand schedule. A shift of the demand curve itself implies that the factors that determine the demand schedule have changed. This distinction may seem inconsequential, but failure to grasp it can result in some ludicrous errors. For example, reasoning like the following has even crept into the *Congressional Record*, not to mention

hundreds of examination papers written by college students:

> A tax on automobiles will cause their price to rise. The increase in price, however, will cause consumers to buy fewer cars. This decrease in demand will bring the price back down to its former level.

You should be able to explain the fallacy in this line of argument. If you can't, reread the material on change in quantity demanded and change in demand and try again.

The Demand Curve at a Moment in Time
One other technical point about the demand curve must be emphasized. The demand curve as it emerges from the simple law of demand exists only at a single moment in time. That moment must be long enough to encompass changes in price and consequent shifts along the demand curve. But the moment in time must be short enough so that consumer tastes and incomes, the prices of other goods, stocks of durable goods, and other longer range factors can't change enough to cause the demand curve to shift.

How long is this theoretical moment in time? Some economic theorists consider it to be instantaneous. Others call it a "day," and still others simply say that the theory has no time dimension. Whatever the period of time, it is long enough to enable price to change but too short for any other changes to occur. The demand curve that exists during that moment in time is usually called the *market demand curve* and the time itself is usually called the *market period*.

The Demand for Apples Reconsidered
Earlier in this chapter the demand for apples was used as an example of the relationship between price and quantity demanded. We used data from a twelve-year period, however, and then had the audacity to draw in a demand curve for apples for the entire time. Isn't that moment in time a little long? Won't incomes,

tastes, and other factors have changed over such a long period of time? Of course, the answer is yes. The data shown in Figure 16–11 are subject to the influence of all the factors that are included in the general law of demand, which is why the individual points are scattered around the trend line. But the fact that a demand curve based on price and quantity alone emerges easily from inspection of the data shows that, in this case, the relationship between price and quantity overwhelms the effects of all other factors. It also tells us that in spite of the restrictions and qualifications necessary to state the law of demand correctly for purposes of economic analysis, there is a strong basis in reality for the proposition that for any commodity during a given period of time, the higher the price the smaller the quantity demanded, other things remaining the same.

Summary

The rational consumer determines his choices in a fashion designed to maximize his total utility. He does that by equating utilities at the margin. The decision to work equates the marginal utility of work with the marginal utility of leisure:

$$MU_W = MU_L$$

That decision determines his income, which he allocates between spending and saving by equating the marginal utility of expenditures with the marginal utility of savings:

$$MU_E = MU_S$$

Expenditures are then allocated to maximize satisfactions by equating the marginal utility of a dollar spent on one good with the marginal utility of a dollar spent on any and all other goods:

$$\frac{MU_a}{P_a} = \frac{MU_b}{P_b} = \frac{MU_c}{P_c} = \cdots = \frac{MU_n}{P_n}$$

assuming that the total income is spent:

$$E = Q_a \cdot P_a + Q_b \cdot P_b + Q_c \cdot P_c + \cdots + Q_n \cdot P_n$$

We are then able to derive the demand for any one commodity on the part of a single consumer, add them all up for all consumers, and arrive at the market demand for the commodity.

The simple proposition that more of a commodity is sold at a lower price than at a higher price embodies a complex series of problems of economic analysis. The simple law of demand,

$$D_a = f(P_a)$$

is a variant of the general law of demand,

$$D_a = f[P_a, P_b, \cdots, P_n, I, (S), t]$$

which is more accurate but less convenient for analyzing the functioning of markets. The simple law of demand is derived from the general law by assuming that all variables except P_a remain constant. This assumption fixes the locus of the demand curve, but at the cost of reduced generality.

The law of demand applies only to a single moment in time. Demand may shift from one moment in time to another, but this phenomenon must be carefully distinguished from alternative positions on the demand curve at a single moment in time.

Key Concepts

utility

diminishing marginal utility

substitution effect

income effect

simple law of demand

general law of demand

quantity demanded

For Discussion

1. Are consumers rational?

2. Mrs. Jones buys two commodities A and B such that

$$\frac{MU_A}{P_A} > \frac{MU_B}{P_B}.$$

How can she improve her total utility without increasing her total expenditure?

3. Expenditure on advertising tends to push the price of a good up. And at a higher price, consumers buy less of the good. If this is true, why do firms advertise?

4. The simple law of demand says that a demand curve is sloped downward to the right. Is it consistent with the law of diminishing marginal utility? Explain.

5. An empirical approach to construction of the market demand for a good is shown in Figure 16–11. What are the possible problems with this approach?

6. If personal income taxes were reduced, would you expect people to work more or less? Explain.

Are Consumers Rational?

Some economists prefer an alternative approach to the theory of demand that is more closely associated with theories of general equilibrium. It starts from the idea that prices and quantities demanded of all commodities are related to each other in two ways. A decline in the price of one good will cause consumers to both increase expenditures on that good, because it is cheaper relative to other goods, and buy less of other goods, because they are relatively more expensive. Cheaper goods are substituted for more expensive goods, which is the substitution effect.

A decline in the price of the one good also increases the real income of consumers. Money income may stay the same, but it will buy more. This income effect enables consumers to buy more of all goods, not merely the one whose price fell.

The basic idea is that the simple law of demand, $D_a = f(P_a)$, does not tell the whole story. Rather, a change in the price of one good will affect the demand for *all* goods by way of substitution and income effects. The consumer will adjust all of his or her purchases of all goods when a change occurs anywhere in the system of prices. This Appendix works out some of the implications of that idea.

The Indifference Curve

We start by simplifying the problem. Contemplate a single consumer with a given income, all of which is spent on two commodities only, at prices deter-mined in the market. Let the commodities be designated as *A* and *B*. The consumer buys both commodities, but will be indifferent between different combinations. That is, he would be equally willing to have, for example, combination $6A + 1B$, $3A + 2B$, $2A + 3B$, $1A + 6B$, etc. To put it another way, each combination would give equal satisfaction, or utility, to the consumer, who would not care which combination he had. The consumer is indifferent among them. This situation can be shown graphically in the form of an *indifference curve*.

The indifference curve is drawn with a convex curvature when viewed from the origin, with the slope becoming flatter as we move down the curve. This shape means that as the quantity of one good is increased and the quantity of a second is decreased, the consumer is increasingly reluctant to give up the second. The scarcer a commodity, the greater is its value to the consumer, at the margin, and more of the first good is required to get the consumer to give up an additional unit of the second. Thus, in Figure 16A–1 and the numerical example above, if the consumer has $3A + 2B$ he or she would be willing to give up $1A$ to get $1B$ to reach the combination of $2A + 3B$. But giving up another unit of *A* would require an additional 3 units of *B* to compensate for the lost utility of the second unit of *A*. The scarcer a good, the greater is its utility at the margin.

As we move along an indifference curve, the rate at which the consumer substitutes one good for another changes as his consumption of one increases relative to another. Economists call that rate the *marginal rate of substitution* of one good for another, and it is important in determining the point at which the consumer maximizes satisfactions.

The Indifference Map

Figure 16A–1 is only one of the many indifference curves. We could have started with a higher level of utility, $6A + 2B$ instead of $6A + 1B$, for example, and derived a second indifference curve, each point on which would indicate a higher level of utility than any point on the first indifference curve. In this way we can show an *indifference map* of many curves, with a higher level of utility as one moves further out from the origin, as shown in Figure 16A–2.

The indifference map is like a topographical map, but with contours that show levels of utility instead of altitude. Each indifference curve is an *equal utility contour*. As the consumer moves out from the origin, from one indifference curve to another, he or she will move to higher levels of utility. Movement along an indifference curve, however, will bring no change in utility, but it will bring a different combination of goods.

The Budget Line

Choices are constrained by the consumer's income. Only so much can be purchased with a given income. In our example we can endow our consumer with enough income to buy $6A$, if the whole amount is spent on A; or $4B$ if the total income is spent on B. These two points enable us to define the consumer's *budget line*, which shows all the possible combinations of $A + B$ that the consumer can buy with the available income. The budget line is shown in Figure 16A–3.

The slope of the budget line is determined by the

Figure 16A-1
A Consumer's Indifference Curve

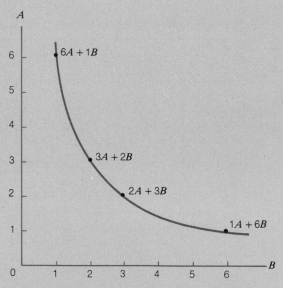

The combinations of $A + B$ that provide equal utility can be shown as an indifference curve. All combinations are equally desirable to the consumer.

Figure 16A-2
A Consumer's Indifference Map

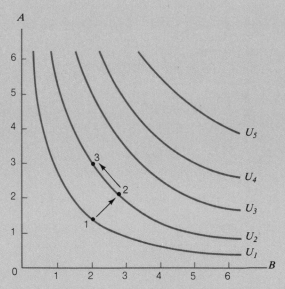

An indifference map is made up of many indifference curves, U_1, U_2, U_3, U_4, U_5, . . . U_n. Satisfaction (utility) increases as the consumer moves up from one indifference curve to another, as in 1 → 2, but movement along a curve, such as 2 → 3, neither increases nor decreases the consumer's satisfaction (utility).

Figure 16A-3
The Consumer's Budget Line

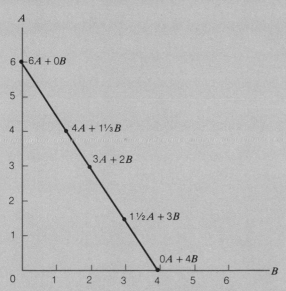

The budget line shows the combinations of $A + B$ that the consumer can buy, from one extreme of $6A + 0B$ to $0A + 4B$, with such intermediate combinations as $4A + 1\frac{1}{3}B$, $3A + 2B$, and $1\frac{1}{2}A + 3B$.

Figure 16A-4
The Consumer Maximizes Utility

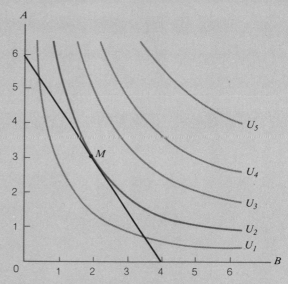

Constrained by the budget line, the consumer maximizes utility by moving to the highest possible indifference curve, or utility contour (U_2), which is reached at point M. At that point the budget line is tangent with U_2. The consumption bundle at that point ($3A + 2B$ in this case) maximizes the consumer's utility, given his or her income.

relative prices of A and B. That is, $6A$ are equal in value to $4B$. If the market price of A is $10, the price of B would be $15. The slope of the budget curve in Figure 16A–3 is, therefore, 3/2 (ignoring its sign, which would be negative to show a downward slope).

The Consumer Maximizes Utility

We can now put together the consumer's indifference map with the budget line to determine which combination of $A + B$ will maximize the consumer's utility. The consumer is free to choose any combination of $A + B$ that can be bought, given constraints imposed by income. That is, he or she can move along the budget line, substituting one good for another, until the highest possible level of utility is reached. The highest level will be found on the indifference curve furthest from the origin. This point, where the budget line is tangent to that curve, is shown in Figure 16A–4 at M.

The highest utility contour is reached when the consumer, moving along the budget line, cannot cross a utility contour to arrive at a higher one. That situation occurs when the budget line just touches, but does not cross, a utility contour. In Figure 16A–4 point M allows the consumer to reach contour U_2, at a combination of $3A + 2B$.

At point M, the point of tangency, the slope of the budget line is exactly equal to the slope of utility contour U_2. Both have a slope of 3/2 at that point, as indicated by the ratio of $3A/2B$ on the utility contour at that point, which is the same as the slope of the budget line. At this point the marginal rate of substitution (the slope of the utility contour) is equal to the slope of the budget line. The basic rule is that utility is maximized when the marginal rate of substitution is equal to the slope of the budget line.

This rule from preference theory is equivalent to

the rule derived from utility theory, that the consumer maximizes utility when the marginal utility per dollar is equalized for all commodities:

$$\frac{MU_A}{P_A} = \frac{MU_B}{P_B} = \cdots \frac{MU_N}{P_N}$$

The same result is obtained in preference theory. At point M in Figure 16A–4 the slope of the utility contour is the same as the slope of the budget line, and both equal 3/2. The slope of the utility contour represents the marginal rate at which the two goods are substituted for each other at that point, which can be written as:

$$\frac{MU_B}{MU_A}$$

We already know that the ratio of prices of the two commodities is:

$$\frac{P_B}{P_A} = \frac{3}{2}$$

Since at point M the marginal rate of substitution (slope) of utility contour U_2 is equal to 3/2, we can now write:

$$\frac{MU_B}{MU_A} = \frac{P_B}{P_A}$$

A simple algebraic transformation[1] shows that this formulation is exactly the same as:

$$\frac{MU_A}{P_A} = \frac{MU_B}{P_B}$$

Voila! At point M the marginal utility of the last dollar spent on each good is equalized, and the consumer has maximized the utility derived from spending his or her income on the two goods.

---

[1]Here is the algebra, for those who may have forgotten. First cross-multiply the fractions.

$$\frac{MU_B}{MU_A} = \frac{P_B}{P_A} \text{ becomes}$$

$MU_A \times P_B = MU_B \times P_A$. Now divide both sides by P_B, cancelling where appropriate. The equation becomes

$$MU_A = \frac{MU_B P_A}{P_B}.$$

Finally, divide both sides by P_A, cancelling again, to reach

$$\frac{MU_A}{P_A} = \frac{MU_B}{P_B}.$$

Changes in Income

So far, the analysis has focused chiefly on defining the point at which utility is maximized. We can now turn to how that point is affected by changes in income and changes in price. Income is first.

A change in our consumer's income can be shown by a shift in the locus of the budget line. An increase in income enables the consumer to buy more of both goods. The budget line shifts outward, enabling a higher utility contour to be reached, with greater satisfactions or utility. A decrease in income is shown by an inward shift of the budget line, and the consumer moves to a lower level of satisfaction. In Figure 16A–5 we show an increase in income and the shift to a new utility maximization.

Figure 16A-5
Increased Income Shifts the Budget Line Outward

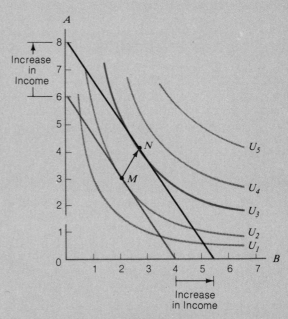

An increase in income shifts the budget line outward, enabling the consumer to increase total utility as he or she moves from UC_2 to UC_3. The utility-maximizing point moves from M to N. In this case we increased the consumer's income by \$20, equal in value to $2A$ or $1\frac{1}{3}B$ at the prices used in our example.

Changes in Price

Price changes can be shown somewhat differently. Return to the consumer's original budget, where we showed a price ratio of

$$\frac{P_B}{P_A} = \frac{3}{2}.$$

Next, double the price of B, so that the ratio is now

$$\frac{P_B}{P_A} = \frac{3}{1}.$$

It now takes three units of A to get one unit of B, where formerly 1-1/2 units of A could be exchanged for one unit of B. Since the consumer's income remains where it was at the beginning, it will still buy $6A$. But it will now buy only $2B$. The budget line has rotated. Figure 16A–6 shows the rotation and the new point (L) at which utility is maximized.

The price increase for B caused the budget line to rotate from the origin at $6A$, while at the other end it

---

Figure 16A-6
Change in Price Causes the Budget Line to Rotate

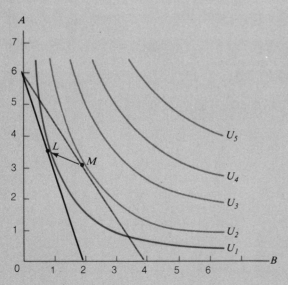

Doubling the price of B causes the budget line to rotate from a ratio of 6/4 to 6/2. The consumer moves from the M to L, maximizing utility by consuming a larger amount of A and less B.

moved from $4B$ to $2B$. The new point of tangency with an indifference curve is at L. The consumer has moved down from utility contour U_2 to U_1, with a lower level of utility and a new combination of $A + B$ that maximizes utility under the new conditions that prevail.[2]

Income and Substitution Effects

We can now separate the effect of substitution of cheaper for more expensive goods from the effect of changes in real income. The increase in the price of B just described resulted in a decline in purchases of B and increased buying of A. Part of that change resulted from the fact that consumers substitute relatively cheaper goods for relatively more expensive goods as prices shift. But part of the change also resulted from the fact that, with higher prices for B, the consumer's income will buy less. The consumer's real income has fallen. These two effects, the substitution effect and the income effect, can be distinguished from each other on the preference map. Figure 16A–7 shows how that is done.

In Figure 16A–7 the price of B doubled, moving the consumer to a lower level of satisfaction on utility contour U_1 at point L. The lower level of utility represents a decline in real income, the extent of which can be measured as if it were simply a decline in money income. That is shown by a new budget line, the dashed line in Figure 16A–7, drawn parallel to the first, but tangent to U_1 at point K. Point K and point L show the same real income because they are on the same utility contour, U_1. If nothing but a decline in real income had occurred, the new utility maximizing combination of $A + B$ would be at point K.

The consumer ends up at L, however, not K, because with the higher price for B there will be substitution of A for B, moving along utility contour U_1 to L. The move from K to L entails no change in satisfaction, because both points are on the same utility contour. But it does embody the substitution of the cheaper good A for the more expensive good B.

---

[2]To clinch your understanding of price changes, postulate a doubling of the price of A instead of B. What happens then? In that case the budget line rotates from the horizontal axis at point $4B$, with the other end resting at $3A$.

Figure 16A-7
Income and Substitution Effects

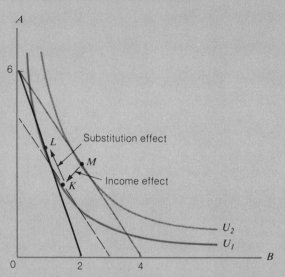

The increase in the price of B moved the consumer down from utility contour U_2 to U_1. This reduction in real income is equivalent to a reduction in money income shown by the dashed line, which is tangent to utility contour U_1 at point K. The shift from M to K shows what would have happened if only the consumer's income had changed. The new equilibrium is at L, however, as shown by the new price line. The difference between K and L results from substituting A, the less expensive good, for B, the more expensive good, at the same level of real income.

The income effect in Figure 16A-7 is the shift from M to K. The substitution effect is the move from K to L. In practice only a single movement would be observed, from M to L, but it is composed of two separate elements.

The Demand Curve and the Indifference Map

The analysis of consumer preferences does not lead directly to a demand curve that relates prices to quantities demanded for a single good. A demand curve can be derived from the indifference map, however. To do so, we will vary the price of one commodity while leaving the prices of all other commodities unchanged. That is equivalent, on the indifference map, to using one axis for the commodity whose price will be changed (B), and the other axis for all other commodities (A). We endow the consumer with a given income, say $100, which allows us to calculate a price for B: four units of B absorb the entire income, so the price of B is $25. At that price, according to Figure 16A-6, our consumer will buy 2 units of B. When the price of B is doubled, however, the same figure tells us that purchases will fall to .85 units of B. We now have two points on a demand schedule:

Price of B (dollars)	Quantity Demanded (units)
25	2
50	0.85

In similar fashion, other points on the consumer's demand schedule can be obtained and a demand curve constructed. Figure 16A-8 provides a graphic illustration of the technique.

In Figure 16A-8 a third price is added to the two shown in 16A-6. In the third instance the price is reduced to $16.67 ($6B = 100), at which price the consumer will buy 4 units. An entire demand curve for the product can be built in this way for the individual consumer. And the individual demand curves can be summed to produce a market demand curve for the product.

Summing Up

The chief advantage of preference theory is its greater generality. It shows that any change in price for any good has repercussions throughout the economy. This is a more general proposition than the simple law of demand, which relates a price change to the quantity demanded only for the good whose price has changed. In addition, preference theory enables income and substitution effects to be separated from each other, which is useful for some more advanced analyses of price and quantity relationships. Finally, by relating the results of economic changes directly to utility contours a wide variety of direct welfare considerations may be opened for analysis.

Figure 16A-8
Deriving the Consumer's Demand Curve from the Indifference Map

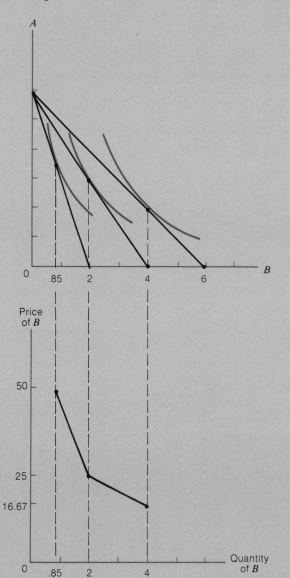

Demand Schedule of *B*	
Price of *B*	Quantity Demanded
$50.00	0.85
25.00	2
16.67	4

Changing the price of commodity *B* relative to the prices of all other commodities, assuming no change in the preference map or income of the consumer, shown in the upper part of the diagram, generates a demand curve, three points of which are shown in the lower diagram. The key step connecting the two is to establish an initial dollar price for *B* at one point by assuming a given dollar income for the consumer.

For the purposes of this book, however, these points are simply elaborations on the basic point that needs to be made about consumer demand. The desires of consumers generate a market demand for goods, which can be expressed in demand schedules and demand curves. Indeed, for that purpose the utility analysis of demand is better: derivation of demand curves from indifference maps is a relatively complex process.[3]

The two analyses are fundamentally similar. Both are based on the concept of utility and define rational behavior as an effort to maximize satisfactions. Both utilize the general and simple laws of demand, although preference theory starts from the general and moves to the simple while utility theory reverses the process. And both provide the starting point for an analysis of the behavior of markets that runs from the desires of consumers through the market adjustment process to a pattern of production.

---

[3]Preference theory has some important limitations. The most important is that "rational" consumer behavior must be defined in a highly restrictive way to fit well-behaved indifference maps, in which indifference curves do not cross or touch, have no discontinuities, and no bumps. The result is a metaphysical consumer who does not act like anyone, and who exists only in an ideal world. Utility theory accords with reality more closely, taking people as they are, with all of their imperfections. Preference theorists have tried to adapt the theory to the real world by arguing that preferences are "revealed" by what consumers actually do. This theory of revealed preference doesn't solve the problem, however, because it retains the assumption of well-behaved indifference maps and its implications for consumer behavior. Economists sometimes argue about the silliest things.

The Theory of
Consumer Preferences

There are three possible explanations for consumer behavior. Decisions can be thought of as purely haphazard or random, such as the "impulse buying" storekeepers try to encourage. Decisions can also be thought of as conforming to habit and custom, following accepted or learned modes of behavior. Or they can be thought of as acts of deliberate choice among alternatives. We have emphasized the last interpretation for a variety of reasons:

1. There is more consistency in consumer behavior than is implied by the "random" explanation.

2. There is more variety than the "habit" explanation would suggest.

3. Surveys of consumer behavior patterns indicate a high degree of thoughtful consideration of alternatives, especially for large purchases.

This is not to say that impulse and habit are unimportant determinants of consumer behavior. They undoubtedly are significant. But even impulse buying may satisfy some important psychological needs of the buyer, and habit is often only the ingrained rationality that comes from experience. The presence of impulse buying and habitual patterns of consumption may be evidence of rationality rather than irrationality!

Furthermore, all consumers don't have to be rational all of the time, in the sense described in this chapter, for the market adjustment process to work effectively. Only some need be rational at any time in order for the results to be desirable. If a business firm wants to maximize profits, it must attract the largest possible number of customers to the product and to the establishment itself. The offering of the firm must be an attractive alternative to the marginal buyer. The decisions made by the marginal buyer, based on a careful evaluation of alternatives, will determine the decisions of producers at the margin, and the market will adjust accordingly. If other consumers buy on impulse or in habitual ways, their behavior will also influence the market, but their decisions won't matter for those consumers who are trying to maximize their welfare. So we can accept the proposition that some buyers make many random decisions and some are creatures primarily of habit. As long as some make rational decisions and the market responds to them, the market adjustment process will move toward welfare maximization for those who care about it.

The Rational Consumer: Ideology and Policy
The theory of demand sketched in this chapter can be thought of in two ways. In a narrow sense, it tells us what to expect on the demand side of the market when we analyze the processes of price formation in a market economy. Normally, the amount of a good that consumers are willing to buy will be larger the lower the price. And vice versa: at higher prices, less will be bought. This general rule must be qualified, however, for changes in incomes, tastes, and prices of other goods can overwhelm the relationship

between price and quantity in a single market for a single good.

More broadly, the theory of demand has important ideological and policy implications. It shows that in a market-oriented economy there is a tendency toward maximization of welfare that is deeply rooted in individual behavior. To the extent that consumers are rational and freedom of choice prevails, a market economy at least has the opportunity to achieve maximization of individual welfare. If the processes of production respond effectively to patterns of consumer demand, the whole economy can be directed toward that goal by the market adjustment process.

Four qualifications must be entered at this point, all of which must have occurred to the reader. The first qualification is that the ability of the market mechanism to respond to consumer choices is limited by restrictions placed upon it. Some of the most important of those restrictions are imposed by the structure of business enterprise itself, in the monopoloid character of many of our important industries. These problems are examined in Chapters 20–23.

The second is that the pattern of consumer choices in the economy as a whole is strongly affected by the distribution of income and wealth. We can analyze the implications of consumer choice, given the existing pattern of income distribution, and argue that the market leads to an efficient outcome that tends to maximize consumer welfare subject to the constraint provided by the existing pattern of income distribution. That conclusion immediately raises the issue of what pattern of distribution of income and wealth is most likely to bring the highest degree of consumer welfare. We devote Chapters 24–28 to that question.

The third qualification is that some choices are social choices rather than individual ones. They are made largely through government, and involve use of resources for such things as military purposes, public parks, sewage disposal and water supplies, and a whole range of other *public goods*, as they are called. Some very difficult issues of resource allocation and welfare maximization are involved here, and we devote Chapters 29–33 to them.

The fourth qualification concerns advertising, which may shift consumer preferences toward goals desired by sellers rather than buyers. We examine that issue next, albeit briefly. These qualifications should not obscure the thrust of the theory of consumer choice, however. Without minimizing the problems of income distribution, social choice, and market restrictions, the basic conclusion remains: subject to those constraints, the market mechanism provides a powerful means for making welfare-maximizing decisions.

Advertising and Consumer Behavior

The economic effects of advertising are strongly disputed. Part of the reason is that the advertising industry advertises itself, and usually uses its normal technique of playing upon emotions rather than providing information. Part of the reason is that hard facts are difficult to obtain. Because advertising is only one part of a complex pattern of business strategy its specific effects are hard to isolate. Out of the welter of argument and counterargument several important propositions emerge, however.

On the positive side, to the extent that advertising provides information to consumers it helps them make better decisions. Increased knowledge of alternatives and the qualities of products can enable buyers to select those goods that best meet their needs. There is a considerable amount of informative advertising: classified advertisements in newspapers, trade advertising in technical or professional journals, and some mail advertising, for example. But advertising of that sort is only a small part of the total.

The bulk of advertising expenditure—about 75 to 85 percent, depending on whose estimate one uses of the some $40 billion spent on advertising each year—is spent on competitive advertising of a relatively few products, such as detergents, personal products like deodorants and shaving cream, and durable goods like automobiles. The goods themselves are essentially similar in their qualities, so firms try to differentiate them using emotion-based appeals, and the advertising image becomes part of the total product bought by the consumer. This type of advertising may be absolutely necessary for the individual business firm's effort to maintain or enlarge its share of the market in competition with other firms that advertise, but it raises the cost of the product to the consumer. Benefits to the individual firms cancel each other out, while the costs are a net loss to the economy as a whole. Whatever benefits consumers obtain in the form of relatively small amounts of information are swamped by the excessively large advertising expenditures of producers. The inherent irrationality of advertising is to be found in this paradox: actions that are eminently rational from the point of view of the individual business firm are irrational from the social point of view.

But what of the argument that advertising can enlarge the market for a product, making possible economies of large-scale production and bringing lower prices to the consumer? This is a favorite contention of the advertising industry. Unfortunately, there are no known cases in which that has occurred. It may be possible for advertising to sustain or increase the sales of one firm's output (Ford cars, Salem cigarettes, for example), but all of the research devoted to the effects of advertising cannot document a single case in which the market for a product (automobiles, cigarettes) has been enlarged, except very temporarily. *Moral:* Don't believe the wolves when they tell you how pleasant it is to be devoured. We shall return briefly to this point when we deal with the economics of monopoloid markets in a later chapter.

One reason for the inability of advertising to have a significant effect on consumer purchases (of products, not brands) is that consumers do not believe the claims made in advertisements. One of the few strong conclusions that emerges from the many studies of the impact of advertising is that the average buyer believes most advertising claims are deceptive. That is the reason why much advertising nowadays makes no claims about the quality of the product, but is designed primarily to keep the brand name in the public's mind.[1]

Finally, we come to an argument made by critics, that advertising fosters the growth and preservation of materialistic attitudes, of overemphasis on spending for goods people don't need. There is little evidence for this argument, either. Indeed, most of the evidence from surveys of consumer attitudes indicates a high degree of rational behavior and consideration of real benefits when consumers decide to spend, although this evidence concerns purchases chiefly of durable goods. Furthermore, if consumers are largely sceptical of advertising it is not likely that advertising will change their attitudes. Far more likely is the proposition that acquisition of

material things is deeply engrained in many people and that advertising tries to take advantage of that attitude in order to sell particular products and brands. We should be very sceptical of the argument that advertising causes spending to rise and savings to fall.

What can we conclude about the effect of advertising on consumer behavior? A relatively small amount of advertising provides information to consumers, but the bulk of advertising expenditure seems to be wasteful. Advertising may induce consumers to shift their buying from one brand to another, but seems to have little or no effect on their decision to buy one product or another, or to increase their buying relative to saving. Consumers seem to retain their essentially rational approach to spending in spite of the barrage of conflicting claims and emotional appeals. Nevertheless, a significant amount of resources and effort are devoted to advertising that apparently provides no benefit to the economy as a whole or to individual consumers, however beneficial and necessary it may be to individual business firms.

Widening the Area of Choice

To achieve a pattern of welfare maximization, consumers must have freedom of choice and must approach their decisions in a rational manner. Public policy designed to achieve these goals would address itself to promoting an adequate flow of information to consumers about qualities and quantities of the goods they buy, about the potential harmfulness of products, and about the terms on which purchases can be financed. In an economy such as ours, with a highly advanced technology affording many highly complex products, there is a need to protect consumers against the effects of inadequate information.

Policies designed to promote greater freedom of choice among products are also important. In our economy they entail primarily the encouragement of competition among producers. For if producers compete with each other for the consumer's dollar, they will produce the things consumers want, and their profits will depend on how well they do so. The quest for profits will continually force producers to try out new products and to change old products in an effort to gain a greater share of the total market. This pervasive tendency in competitive markets

[1] A cynical joke that surfaces periodically among people who work in advertising: "But if it's not deceptive, how can it be advertising?"

provides a long-run, endless drive toward greater variety and extended choices. In contrast, one of the shortcomings of monopolistic practices and protected market positions among producers is the long-run tendency for consumer choices to be restricted. Probably the most pervasive barrier to the development of greater freedom of choice between products is the existence of monopolistic market control practices among producers.

Another vital area in which freedom of choice is restricted is in choice of occupation. Such a statement may seem strange in a country that prides itself on its openness and freedom of opportunity. But reflect for a moment on just a few of the things which restrict occupational choice in our society:

Tuition charges in institutions of higher learning, coupled with wholly inadequate scholarship and other aid programs.

Poor (sometimes abysmal) school systems in many central city and rural areas.

Discrimination in employment, which has effectively barred blacks, Spanish-speaking Americans, Indians, other minority groups, and women from many job opportunities.

Wide disparity in income and wealth, which tends to open opportunities for children of the wealthy and narrow them for children of the poor.

These and other restrictions on choice of occupation influence the choice between work and leisure and the income that can be earned by many individuals and families. If we wish to take advantage of the potential of a market economy for maximization of welfare, public policy will have to address itself to these problems.

When we move into the area of commodities and services, we find large opportunities for choice, but even here there are some formal restrictions. Narcotics, LSD, and marijuana are all banned. So is prostitution and, in many places, gambling. Sale of pornography is sometimes limited. All of these restrictions are imposed by a society that, rightly or wrongly, wishes to preserve certain standards of morality and to eliminate a variety of behavior patterns considered to be antisocial and harmful.

Informal restrictions on choice can be far more significant than legal restrictions. Blacks know what this means. Patterns of housing segregation, and resulting segregation in schools and other aspects of life, are still a long way from being ended. Until very recently, housing segregation was supported by "restrictive covenants" in deeds to houses, which were enforceable in the courts. They no longer are, but the patterns persist and, for a variety of reasons, may even be increasing. Other informal restrictions on blacks developed in hotels, restaurants, public parks, and other public accommodations, and some of them are still to be found in spite of legislation and court orders. Nor are blacks the only group subject to these constraints. Indians and Mexican-Americans have felt similar discrimination, especially in the western and southwestern states.

Perhaps the most important restrictions are those related to the distribution of income. The poor have far fewer choices than the wealthy simply because they have fewer resources at their disposal. Choice between work or leisure is limited by the need for income. The needs of the family limit savings. There is little discretionary income above that needed for necessities. As incomes rise, choices in all of these areas expand, until the very wealthy have few restrictions. Many of the restrictions on choice we have noted here are eased as incomes rise.

We find, then, that choices *are* restricted and that the restrictions do not apply equally. Some serious minority-group problems seem to persist interminably. Yet within the framework of restrictions, consumers have much freedom to make choices that will maximize their satisfactions. After all the qualifications, there is a substantial degree of rationality in consumer behavior. Most people seek to do the best they can for themselves in this sometimes trying, sometimes frustrating, sometimes idiotic world. One way to make it a little less trying, frustrating, and idiotic is to widen choices and opportunities.

This analysis assumes rational behavior on the part of the consumer, which is not an unreasonable assumption. The analysis is also subject to some important qualifications: consumer choices are restricted by the pattern of income distribution, only individual choices are included, not social choices, and the institutional framework is assumed to be one of freely adjusting markets. Advertising, however, does not seem to seriously diminish consumer rationality, whatever its other effects may be.

Nevertheless, the fundamental thrust of the theory is tremendously important: subject to the constraints just summarized, the market mechanism could be a powerful instrument for achieving maximum welfare for individual people.

Chapter 17

Elasticity of Demand

We have explained why there is a functional relationship between quantity demanded and the price of a good. We did not attempt to discuss the quantitative relationship between Q and P, however. For example, if the price of automobiles is raised by 10 percent we would expect the quantity sold to decline, other things remaining the same, but will sales fall by more than 10 percent or less? Or, if the marketed wheat crop increases by 5 percent, prices should fall—but by more or less than 5 percent? These quantitative relationships between changes in P and changes in Q involve the elasticity of demand.

An Example: California Grapes

When the United Farm Workers Union organized the grape workers in California's San Joaquin Valley in the 1960s, the growers fought the union vigorously. Even after the wineries recognized the union and reached agreements on wages, the growers of table grapes (grapes sold as fresh fruit) refused to recognize the union and refused to bargain over wages, hours, conditions of work, or anything else. A strike of the grape pickers escalated into a national boycott of table grapes—California produces over 90 percent of the supply—and *la huelga* ("the strike") became *la causa* ("the cause") and something of a national issue. Why were the growers of table grapes so adamant in their resistance to the union, when the growers of wine grapes were not?

One reason for the intransigence of the growers of the table grapes is the relationship that prevails between the price of table grapes and the quantity sold, which is illustrated in the table.

	1964	1965	Percentage Change
Production (1000 tons)	3,145	3,975	+26.4
Average price per ton	$55.80	$41.00	−26.6

Between 1964 and 1965, production rose by a little over 26 percent, and prices fell by almost exactly the same proportion. As a result, total revenues to the producers were almost the same in the two years:

1964 production (1000 tons)	3,145
Average price per ton	$55.80
Total revenue	$175,491,000

1965 production (1000 tons)	3,975
Average price per ton	$41.00
Total revenue	$162,975,000

Even though the price of grapes in 1964 was $14.80 per ton more than in 1965, total revenues exceeded those of 1965 by only $12.5 million.

Under these circumstances, significant wage increases to the grape pickers would reduce the profits of the producers. Price increases would be associated with an equally proportionate decline in sales, leaving total revenue unchanged. Here is the sequence of events:

1. Wage increases lead to higher costs of production, which cause employers to . . .

2. Raise their prices, but . . .

3. Increased prices are accompanied by an approximately equal percent decline in sales, which means that . . .

4. Total revenues do not change significantly. Therefore . . .

5. Profits must decline, since costs of production have risen.

The dilemma is laid bare: what one party gains, the other loses.

This was not true of grapes used in the manufacture of wine. For a variety of reasons, the quantity of wine sold is little affected by changes in price. The wineries, then, could pass on to their customers any increases in production costs. Total revenues would rise, enabling the wine producers to recapture the bulk of any increase in wages paid to field labor used in picking the grapes. Wage increases could be passed on to the retail customer, and would not come out of the producers' pockets. It was this characteristic of the market that enabled the Farm Workers Union to obtain wage increases and union recognition from the wineries with relatively little difficulty. With table grapes, however, total revenues remain roughly stable even when prices rise or fall. Producers may charge higher prices if their costs rise, and total revenues will remain about the same. But total costs will have risen, leaving the producers with lower profits.

The difference is a difference in elasticity of demand. Wine grapes have an *inelastic demand*: price changes have little impact on the quantity demanded. Table grapes have *unit elasticity*: price and quantity demanded change in the same proportion. Some other products may have an *elastic demand*: a small change in price is accompanied by a large change in the quantity demanded.

- Demand is **inelastic** when the relative (percent) change in the quantity demanded of a good is less than the relative (percent) change in the price of the good.

- Demand is **elastic** when the relative change in the quantity demanded of a good is greater than the relative change in the price.

- **Unit elasticity** prevails when the relative (percent) change in the quantity demanded is equal to the relative change in the price of the good.

The Concept of Elasticity

Elasticity is a term economists have borrowed from mathematicians. It is a measure of the relative changes in two related variables. For example, in the simple law of demand, a fall in price is associated with an increase in the quantity demanded. This relationship is more than merely an association, however. The cause-and-effect relationships involved enable us to conclude that, other things remaining the same, a fall in price causes an increase in the quantity demanded. In this instance, the increase in quantity demanded is a *dependent variable* (its change is caused by a change in another variable), while the fall in price is the *independent variable* (the cause of the change in the dependent variable).

We can now define *elasticity*, as it is used in

economics. Elasticity is the ratio between the relative change in a dependent variable and the relative change in an independent variable. The word *relative* in this definition is important. Changes in quantity demanded are measured in tons or bushels or gallons or some other unit. Changes in price are measured in dollars. The units are not comparable. To make them comparable, the changes can be transformed into percentages, that is into relative changes or ratios. Thus, an increase in the quantity of grapes sold of 100,000 tons, due to a fall in the price of grapes of five cents, is not very meaningful. But it is meaningful to say that a 2 percent decline in price brought about a 1 percent increase in the quantity sold.

- **Elasticity** is the relative change in a dependent variable associated with a relative change in an independent variable.

Price Elasticity of Demand

We can now define *price elasticity of demand*, in which price is the independent variable and quantity demanded is the dependent variable.

- The **price elasticity of demand** is the relative (percent) change in quantity demanded of a good associated with the relative (percent) change in the price of the good

or

$$E_d = \frac{\text{percent change in quantity demanded}}{\text{percent change in price}}$$

Elasticity of Demand and Total Revenue

One simple way to think of elasticity of demand is to relate it to total revenue. For example, suppose a relatively small decline in price is associated with a relatively large increase in the quantity demanded. The total revenue from sales rises, and demand is said to be elastic. This relationship is shown in Figure 17–1.

Figure 17-1
Elasticity of Demand and Total Revenue

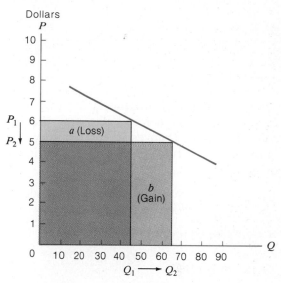

At a price of $6 per unit, 45 units are sold, for a total revenue of $270. In the diagram, total revenue is equal to the area of the quadrangle bounded by $6 on the vertical axis and 45 units on the horizontal axis.

When prices are reduced from $6 to $5 (16⅔ percent), the amount purchased goes up to 65 units (almost 45 percent), and total revenue goes up to $325. The new total revenue is equal to the area bounded by $5 on the vertical axis and 65 units on the horizontal axis.

The increase in total revenue is shown by inspection: rectangle *b* is larger than rectangle *a*, which means that the entire rectangle bounded by P_2Q_2 is larger than the rectangle P_1Q_1.

Now suppose a relatively large decline in price were associated with a relatively small increase in quantity demanded. In this case total revenue would decline.

Price	Quantity Demanded	Total Revenue
$6	45	$270
5	50	250

That relationship is characteristic of inelastic demand.

When total revenue does not change with a change in price, unit elasticity prevails.

Price	Quantity Demanded	Total Revenue
$6	45	$270
5	54	270

Measuring Elasticity of Demand

Price elasticity of demand measures the responsiveness of changes in the quantity demanded of a particular good to change in its price:

$$E_d = \frac{\text{relative change in quantity demanded}}{\text{relative change in price}}$$

It would be computed as follows:

$$E_d = - \frac{dQ}{Q} \div \frac{dP}{P}$$

where

Q = quantity demanded
dQ = change in quantity demanded
P = price
dP = change in price

Note: The formula for elasticity of demand has a minus sign because the demand curve slopes downward. The relative change in quantity demanded would then be negative, so a minus sign is introduced to make the answer a positive number.

Here is a relatively simple example, using data from Figure 17–1.[1] In this instance, the change in quantity demanded is greater than the change in price and E_d is greater than 1. This is characteristic of elastic demand.

$$E_d = - \frac{dQ}{Q} \div \frac{dP}{P}$$

$$= - \frac{20}{45} \div \frac{-1}{6}$$

$$= \frac{0.444}{0.167}$$

$$= 2.65[2]$$

Demand can be elastic, inelastic, or have unit elasticity, depending on the responsiveness of changes in the amount demanded to changes in price:

○ *Unit elasticity (E = 1)*—A change in price causes an equally proportionate change in the amount demanded. When this happens there is no change in the total amount spent on the good (Figure 17–2).

○ *Inelastic demand(E <1)*—A change in price causes a less-than-proportionate change in the amount purchased. In this case total revenue will rise if prices go up and fall if prices are reduced (Figure 17–3).

The limiting case for inelastic demand is E = 0. In that case the quantity purchased remains the same, irrespective of price, and the demand curve is vertical (Figure 17–4).

○ *Elastic demand(E > 1)*—A change in price causes a more-than-proportionate change in the amount purchased. In this case total revenue will fall if prices go up and will rise if prices go down (Figure 17–5).

---

[1]These calculations assume that prices change while all other variables remain the same. They don't in the real world. For example, we used the case of California grapes, and it all seemed very simple and straightforward. It isn't. Between 1964 and 1965, consumer incomes and other prices changed, along with P and Q for California grapes. Those other factors also affected Q. Statistical estimating techniques can be used to eliminate much of the influence of those other factors—you will learn how to do this if you study *econometrics*—but the raw data we used earlier still retain their influence. When all extraneous factors are eliminated, the price elasticity of demand for grapes turns out to be about 0.9, which is slightly inelastic. Since consumer incomes rise from year to year, however, the effect of rising incomes combined with consumer reactions to price brings the observed relationship in the marketplace to just about unit elasticity.

[2]This answer is only an approximation that gives the rough dimensions of the answer. Why? Because the elasticity of a curve applies only to a single point, while in this case we are measuring it over an arc between two points. The calculation used here is based on a single point only, that comprising the $6 price and 45 units of sales. A closer approximation (but still an approximation only) could be obtained by computing an average elasticity over the whole arc. You will learn how to do that in your advanced courses in economic theory.

Figure 17–2
Approximate Unit Elasticity

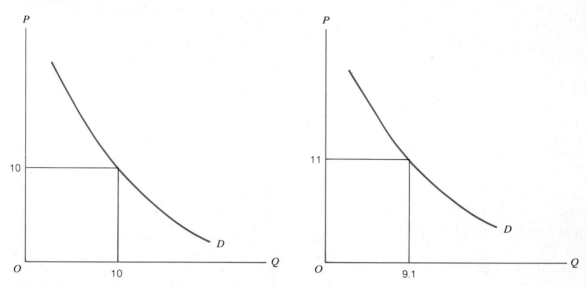

The price rises from $10 to $11, causing sales to fall from 10 to 9.1 Total revenue remains the same at approximately 100. The *PQ* rectangles in the two diagrams are about the same size.

Figure 17–3
Inelastic Demand

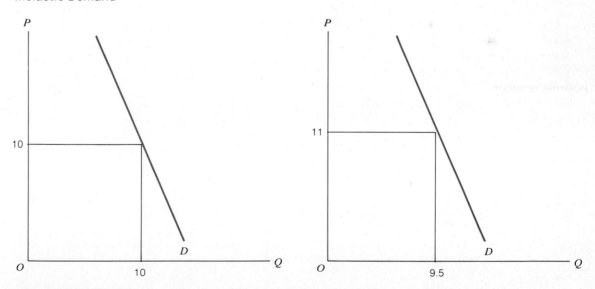

A price increase from $10 to $11 is accompanied by a decline in purchases from 10 to 9.5. Total revenues from sale of the good have risen from $100 to $104.5. The second *PQ* rectangle is larger than the first. The elasticity of demand in this case is less than unity: it computes to −0.45.

Figure 17–4
Perfectly Inelastic Demand

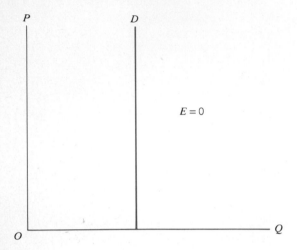

The limiting case for elastic demand is one in which a price increase reduces sales (and revenues) to zero, while a price decline raises sales (and revenues) to infinity. Where demand is perfectly elastic the demand curve is horizontal (Figure 17–6). Real-world examples of infinitely elastic or infinitely inelastic demand curves do not exist, but the limiting cases are helpful in clarifying the concepts.

Elasticity and the Demand Curve

Although we usually assume that a steeply sloping demand curve is relatively inelastic, while a demand curve with a shallow slope is relatively elastic, appearance can be deceiving. The slope depends on the scales used in drawing the demand curve. For example, in Figure 17–7, the elasticity of demand is the same in both cases, even though the line on the right slopes more steeply than the one on the left. The reason is that the horizontal scales are different. It is quite possible for a highly inelas-

Figure 17–5
Elastic Demand

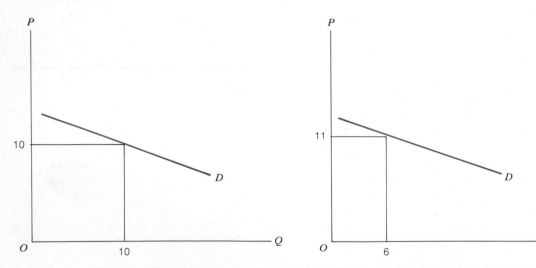

A price increase from $10 to $11 has brought total sales down from 10 to 6, and total revenues from $100 to $66. The computed elasticity of demand is 4.

tic demand curve to show a very shallow slope in a diagram if the intervals on the horizontal scale are widened. Conversely, an elastic demand curve can be given a steep slope by narrowing the intervals on the horizontal scale.

A second difficulty arises because the elasticity of a line or curve will normally change at different points on the line or curve. The special curve drawn with unit elasticity at all points is an exception. The usual case is one in which elasticity changes from one point to another. The phenomenon of changing elasticity can be illustrated by the example of a straight line, shown in Figure 17–8.

When the price of a commodity is low, its demand may be highly inelastic, while at a higher price its demand may be elastic. Thus, when the price of gasoline was low there was little competition from substitutes, and demand was highly inelastic. At a higher price (relative to substitutes) demand for gasoline becomes less inelastic as consumers substitute other goods for gasoline.

Figure 17–6
Perfectly Elastic Demand

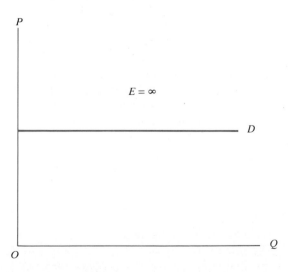

Interpreting Measures of Demand Elasticity

Recent studies of automobile demand show a demand elasticity of 1.2 to 1.5. That is, a 1 percent increase in the price of automobiles will be accompanied by a decrease in sales of 1.2 to 1.5 percent. Conversely, if prices were cut by 1 percent (it happened in 1975!) sales could be expected to rise by 1.2 to 1.5 percent. In this case the demand is elastic: the percent change in sales is greater than the percent change in price.

Sometimes our knowledge of elasticities of demand can be deceiving. Large reductions in price for products with relatively inelastic demand can open up large new markets that did not exist before the price reductions. Automobiles provide the classic example. Prior to 1910 automobiles were a high-priced product with a relatively inelastic demand. Manufacturers in the industry knew that price reductions had a relatively small impact on the industry's sales. Then along came Henry Ford's Model T, a new product (the first low-priced car) for a new market (the average family), with new methods of financing consumer purchases (installment buying) to tap the new market. Sales zoomed upward at the new low price, and the entire industry was transformed. It is not fair to say that only the price changed, for the Model T was a new product for an untapped sector of the market, but the automobile was now manufactured for a market with relatively elastic demand, in place of the old market with a relatively inelastic demand.

Another Example: Gasoline

How do consumers react to changes in the retail price of gasoline? The answer to that question is vital to the oil companies, to governments (which raise revenues for highways from the gasoline tax), and to all those citizens who are concerned about highway congestion and conservation of resources. A 1973 study showed an elasticity of demand for gasoline in the short run of 0.4 and in the long run of 0.7. These figures mean that a moderate price

Figure 17-7
Slope and Elasticity

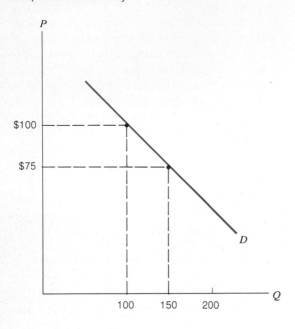

Figure 17-8
Elasticity of a Line

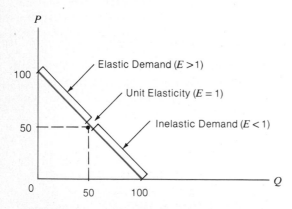

increase of, for example, 2.5 percent would be quickly accompanied by a 1 percent drop in sales. In the long run, as consumers adapted to the higher cost of transportation by shifting to other methods or by traveling less, consumption of gasoline would ultimately drop by about

1.75 percent if the price remained 2.5 percent above the original level. The demand for gasoline is relatively inelastic, but it is more inelastic in the short run than in the long run.

There is an important lesson to be learned from this example. One way to conserve resources is to raise their prices. If energy resources are scarce their prices will rise and that, in turn, will lower their use. Just how much their use will be lowered depends on the elasticity of demand for the product. The price increase will also stimulate greater output, thereby contributing to the elimination of the shortage from the supply side of the market as well, a principle explained earlier.

**Factors That Influence
Price Elasticity of Demand**
The price elasticity of demand is influenced by the characteristics of the product or service. When there are lots of close substitutes for a

good, price elasticity of demand is high. For example, a Ford is a close substitute for a Chevrolet. If the price of Chevrolets goes up while the price of Fords is unchanged, the number of Chevrolets bought by customers should decline substantially. Customers will shift to Fords. The demand for Chevrolets, then, is elastic.

When the amount spent on a good represents a large percentage of the average consumer's income, a relatively small change in its price should have a relatively large impact on the quantity demanded. For example, a 20 percent increase in the price of a candy bar will raise its price by only 3–4¢ (or reduce its size correspondingly) and should have little effect on the quantity bought. But a 20 percent increase in automobile prices would mean about $1200 more. This is a substantial bite out of the average income, and could mean a significant reduction in automobile purchases. We should expect that the demand for candy bars would be more inelastic than the demand for automobiles.

When the good is a necessity without close substitutes, such as bread, a rise in price will usually have little effect on sales. But if it is a luxury, like truffles, then the demand will be more elastic under normal circumstances. The reason is that the necessity will have to be purchased even if the price is higher, while the luxury, by definition, need not be bought if the price rises.

Other factors influence the price elasticity of demand for any commodity, but those mentioned here are probably the most important. Table 17–1 summarizes them.

Apply these characteristics to the market for grapes. The demand for wine grapes is relatively inelastic because the demand for wine is inelastic. Wine takes only a small share of consumer incomes and, when entertaining or otherwise using wine, there are few good substitutes for it. While a luxury, wine is customarily used as an adjunct to various patterns of dining and entertainment, which largely deter-

SOME PRICE ELASTICITIES OF DEMAND

Estimates of demand elasticities require elaborate statistical techniques to eliminate all of the influences on the quantity demanded of a good other than its price. It's easy to wave the magic wand of *ceteris paribus* in the theory, to reduce the general law of demand to the special. It is a good deal more difficult to do so when working with real data. Nevertheless, economists try, and we list below some of the better estimates of demand elasticities culled from the economics literature.

Inelastic Demand

Newspapers and magazines	0.1
Coffee	0.25
Potatoes	0.3
Cigarettes	0.3–0.4
Shoes	0.4
Gasoline	0.4–0.7
Legal services	0.5
Doctor's services	0.6
Housing	0.9

Unit Elasticity

Police protection	1.0

Elastic Demand

TV sets	1.2
Refrigerators	1.2–1.6
Automobiles	1.2–1.5
Sports equipment	1.3
Airline travel	2.4
Canned tomatoes	2.5
Fresh peas	2.8
Foreign travel	4.0
Fresh tomatoes	4.6

Source: H.H. Houthaker and Lester D. Taylor, *Consumer Demand in the United States* (2nd ed., Cambridge, Mass.: Harvard University Press, 1970); Donald S. Watson, *Price Theory in Action* (2nd ed., New York: Houghton Mifflin and Co., 1969).

Table 17–1
Characteristics of Goods That Affect
Elasticity of Demand

Elastic Demand	Inelastic Demand
Good substitutes	Few good substitutes
Large share of consumer incomes	Small share of consumer incomes
Luxuries	Necessities

mine how much is used, and price has little impact on how much is bought.

Table grapes, on the other hand, have numerous good substitutes (other fruit) and are a luxury food. Demand for them would be elastic except that they take up such a small share of consumer incomes, and, after all, nothing else tastes quite like a fresh grape. The resulting situation is very close to unit elasticity of demand.

Summary

Price elasticity of demand links relative changes in the quantity demanded of a good to relative changes in other variables, such as the price of the good (price elasticity of demand), the price of another good (cross elasticity of demand) or incomes (income elasticity of demand). An elastic demand is characterized by relatively large changes in quantity demanded associated with relatively small changes in the other variable. An inelastic demand is just the opposite. Unit elasticity occurs when the relative changes in the two variables are the same.

More specifically:

Elastic Demand: A one percent change in price is associated with a change in quantity demanded greater than one percent. $E > 1$

Inelastic Demand: A one percent change in price is associated with a change in quantity demanded less than one percent. $E < 1$

Unit Elasticity: A one percent change in price is associated with a change in quantity demanded equal to one percent. $E = 1$.

Key Concepts

inelastic demand   **elasticity**
elastic demand   **price elasticity of demand**
unit elasticity

For Discussion

1. Whenever a public transportation system has a deficit, the first thing that may be proposed is a fare increase. Under what conditions would an increase in fares reduce the deficit? Increase the deficit? Explain.

2. The tobacco industry is not strongly opposed to taxes on cigarettes. Why not?

3. A relatively inelastic demand for the product enables labor unions to gain wage increases from employers relatively easily. Why?

4. The demand for cigarettes is known to be highly inelastic. Would this also be true for a particular brand of cigarette?

5. Collusion among sellers to control the price of a commodity is more likely in cases in which demand for the product is inelastic than in cases of elastic demand. Why?

Appendix *17A*

Other Measures of Demand Elasticity

The sensitivity of quantity demanded to price is only one relationship that can be measured. The quantity of a good that consumers will buy is also influenced by incomes and by the prices of other goods. The concept of elasticity applies to these relationships and they will be introduced briefly.

Cross Elasticity of Demand
When commodities are good substitutes for each other, or if they complement each other, a change in the price of one will bring changes in the quantity purchased of the other. This relationship is called *cross elasticity of demand*. It is computed in a manner similar to the measurement of ordinary price elasticity:

$$E_{dx,y} = \frac{\text{relative change in quantity of } x}{\text{relative change in price of } y}$$

or

$$E_{dx,y} = \frac{dD_x}{D_x} \div \frac{dP_y}{P_y}$$

where

$$D_x = \text{quantity demanded of } x$$
$$dD_x = \text{change in quantity demanded of } x$$
$$P_y = \text{price of } y$$
$$dP_y = \text{change in price of } y$$

And cross elasticities can be unitary, elastic, or inelastic.

Cross elasticities of demand can indicate whether goods are good substitutes for each other. For example, if the price of Chevrolets goes up, the number of Fords sold will rise. This will happen because some who would buy Chevrolets at a lower price switch to Fords when the price of Chevrolets goes up. The cross elasticity of demand between the two is positive, showing that they are good substitutes for each other in the eyes of buyers.

Complementary goods show just the opposite effects. If the price of bagels goes up the amount purchased will fall, and so will purchases of goods eaten with bagels, such as lox (and perhaps cream cheese). In this case, the cross elasticity of demand is negative, indicating a complementary relationship between the two products.

- **Cross elasticity of demand** is the relative change in the quantity demanded of a good associated with the relative change in the price of another good.

Income Elasticity of Demand
Changes in income also affect the demand for goods. This relationship is called the *income elasticity of demand*.

$$E_i = \frac{\text{relative change in quantity}}{\text{relative change in income}}$$

or

$$E_i = \frac{dQ}{Q} \div \frac{dI}{I}$$

where

Q = quantity purchased
dQ = change in quantity purchased
I = income
dI = change in income

Like other measures of elasticity, it can be unitary, elastic, or inelastic.

- **Income elasticity of demand** is the relative change in the quantity demanded of a good associated with the relative change in consumer incomes.

The income elasticity of demand can be significant. Recall the price elasticity of demand for automobiles, which is 1.2 to 1.5. Well, the income elasticity of demand for automobiles has been variously estimated at 2.5 to 4.2. That is, a 1 percent increase in consumer incomes will be accompanied by a 2.5 to 4.2 increase in sales of automobiles; a decrease in incomes has the opposite effect. It is for this reason that a slight recession in the national economy can cause a significant depression in Michigan, where the automobile industry is centered. And, of course, a nationwide economic recovery makes Michigan quite prosperous. Particularly in the Detroit area, "When the national economy sneezes Detroit has pneumonia."

So if you want to go into a more stable business, pick one with a relatively inelastic income elasticity of demand, like coffee, with an income elasticity of demand that has been estimated at 0.2 to 0.5. Sales don't change much even if consumer incomes do. Incidentally, the demand for coffee is also price inelastic, the coefficient being about 0.25. Which means that the amount of coffee people drink doesn't respond much to changes in either incomes or price.

Key Concepts

cross elasticity of demand   **income elasticity of demand**

Chapter *18*

Behind the Supply Curve

Let us review for a moment. Chapter 1 showed that a system of freely operating markets tends to generate a pattern of production that matches the pattern of consumer wants. Building on that concept, Chapter 15 showed that such a system tends to maximize satisfactions by equating benefits to consumers at the margin with costs to producers at the margin. Chapter 15 began a more detailed analysis of the system. Going back to the demand-supply-price analysis of markets sketched in Chapter 1, it focused on the demand side of the market and the factors that determine the locus and shape of the demand curve. Chapter 16 then went behind the demand curve to the concept of marginal utility as the basis of consumer wants.

Now the focus of the analysis shifts to examine how the producer responds to consumer demand. The analysis occupies two chapters. This chapter deals with two aspects of the decision-making process for individual producers: the principle of profit maximization and the principle of least-cost combination of inputs. Chapter 19 then examines the producers' decisions regarding output, plant capacity, and production processes in competitive industries,

as they respond to the price for their product established by the interplay of market forces.

The analysis developed in these chapters will be used as a basis for examining the economics of big business, with its monopoloid markets, that prevails in the contemporary American economy (Chapters 20–23) and socialism (Chapters 33–35). It is not merely an academic exercise. The theory of competitive markets develops an understanding of how markets operate that will be useful both in analyzing some of our economy's important problems and in judging how well it functions.

Business Decisions and Analytical Time Periods

Although business firms make a wide variety of decisions, we are most directly concerned with how they respond to the consumer's demand for their products. The decisions involve:

1. How much to produce with the existing plant and equipment.

2. What size of new plant to build.

3. What production processes to use.

4. How to respond to changing relative scarcities among the factors of production.

These decisions can be analyzed in terms of two different time periods, *the short run* and *the long run*. The key difference is that in the short run some inputs are fixed, while in the long run all inputs can be varied. Short-run decisions about the level of output from existing plant and equipment can take effect almost immediately. Additional workers can be hired or some of the present work force laid off. Some inputs, however, cannot be varied. The company's plant and equipment must either be used or lie idle (unless it can be sold, rented, or leased to someone else). At least part of the management must be retained, whatever the level of output. In other words, in the short run some inputs are fixed. The firm, in basing its decisions on the cost of its inputs and the price of its outputs, has the additional constraint of its existing plant.

When the firm decides on the size of plant and selects from among a variety of available production processes, the implication is that all the factors of production can be varied within the existing state of the production arts. The firm has enough time to select the process it feels is best and to build the size of plant appropriate to that technology. For example, a steel firm can use several different technologies. It can use natural ore as a raw material, or beneficiated ore that has some of the impurities removed, or iron pellets that have a very high iron content, or steel scrap. Whatever the decision, a different type or style of reduction furnace and supporting facilities are required for each type of ore. Each source of iron requires different proportions of coal, limestone, and other inputs. Finally, whatever production process it chooses, the firm will have to select a preferred scale of operations. It can build a large or small plant for processing the ore and transforming it into steel. In terms of our time periods, this is the long run. All of the inputs can be varied, within the alternatives provided by existing technology and knowledge of production processes. The firm adjusts to the cost of its inputs and the price it can get for its product, but without the constraint imposed by an existing plant.

Ultimately, even the techniques of production can be considered as a variable. As new methods of production are devised the firm is freed from the constraints imposed by the existing technology. Furthermore, as the economy grows, the relative abundance of labor, land, and capital can shift; their relative prices can change; and the firm will have to adapt to those changes. Ultimately, firms are free to respond to the relative scarcity (and prices) of their inputs without constraints imposed by plant size, existing production processes, or existing knowledge.

These time periods, the short run and the long run, are theoretical constructs that help us analyze the decisions facing the business firm. They correspond to reality in that firms make those decisions in fact. They differ from reality in that the decisions often overlap each other, as do the actual time periods required in the business world to carry out the decisions. Nevertheless, for the purpose of analyzing the response of firms to demand conditions, it is convenient to separate the two different time periods:

- The **short run**: with a fixed plant, a given process of production, and existing prices of inputs, the firm decides how much the plant will produce and what price will be charged for its output. In competitive markets, where price is determined by market forces, only the level of output is at issue.

- The **long run**: with existing technologies given, the firm decides what size and type of plant will be built. All inputs are variable and substitutable for each other.

Profit Maximization: Basic Principles

Do you remember the example of the filling station operator who was trying to decide on his closing hours? It contains in microcosm the central elements of business decisions about using existing facilities to maximize profits. You will recall that the rule for profit-maximization was that output should be increased as long as additional revenues (marginal revenue, *MR*) exceed additional costs (marginal cost, *MC*). Profits will be maximized at that level of output at which marginal revenue and marginal cost are equal, $MR = MC$.

That is half of the profit maximization problem. It concerns how the firm adjusts output to the price it can get. The second part of the problem is internal to the firm, and conerns how it organizes the production process to minimize the cost of production per unit of output. The internal problem is resolved by a process analogous to the way the rational consumer allocates his income, that is, by applying the equimarginal principle to the firm's inputs. Lower-cost factors are substituted for higher-cost ones at the margin, until costs at the margin are equalized.

Both of the criteria for profit maximization involve production costs, and the next step in the analysis is to look at the cost structure of the firm. A preliminary issue needs to be dealt with, however. Why should we assume that business firms maximize their profits? Aren't other goals important, too, such as growth, market power, survival? Indeed they are, but one cardinal point stands out. When business firms compete strongly with each other, they are forced to stress profits as a primary goal: the firm that succeeds in maximizing profits not only makes money for its owners but also has better chances for survival than a firm that does not maximize profits. When competition is reduced or eliminated, however, there is less pressure on the individual firm to maximize profits. A variety of other goals or motivations for business behavior may develop. But in a competitive economy the profit-maximizing firm survives and flourishes, so we start our analysis with the simplifying assumption that the firm seeks to maximize its profits.

Normal Profits Are Part of a Firm's Costs

The production cost incurred by a business firm is the amount it must pay for all of the inputs required to keep operating. Labor must be hired, materials purchased, management paid. Funds must be obtained to buy or lease productive equipment. All of these payments to owners of the factors of production are part of the firm's production costs.

A *normal profit* must be included in the costs of production. If a firm does not earn profits at least as large as those that could be earned by producing something else, the owners of the capital will take it out of the industry and put it to work elsewhere. This is the principle of opportunity costs at work, and it applies to business firms as well as to consumers. Just as a firm must pay wages as high as those its workers could earn elsewhere, so it must pay a return to capital just as high as the amount the capital could earn by being used to produce something else.

- **Normal profit**, then, is the return to capital just large enough to keep it employed in its current uses. It is as much a part of the costs of production as any other payment to a factor of production.

In our analysis of the business firm, normal profits will always be included in the costs of production. All of the cost schedules developed and subsequently used in our analysis of markets have a normal profit included in them.

Total, Fixed, and Variable Costs

Every business manager knows that to make a profit, total revenues must be larger than total costs. If they are not, he will be dipping into his working capital and ultimately will be unable to pay his bills. One portion of total costs is the operating costs directly associated with output, such as wages and salaries, materials, rent and utilities. They must be covered by revenues or the firm will be quickly forced to close down as its operating capital is used up. These operating costs vary with the level of output and are called *variable costs*.

In the short run, some costs are *fixed costs*. They are incurred no matter what the level of operations may be. Primary among them are those associated with the firm's plant and equipment: the cost of the capital that went into it and the administrative costs necessary to keep it running. They are present essentially because the plant and equipment are fixed elements in the firm's operations: they cannot be eliminated; their cost is fixed.

- **Variable costs** are those that vary with the level of output.
- **Fixed costs** are those incurred regardless of the level of output.

In the long run, however, the size and nature of the firm's production plant are variable and the fixed costs become variable costs. In terms of the cost structure of the firm, this is the important distinction between the short-run and long-run periods and the decisions pertinent to each.

Total costs include both variable and fixed costs. A firm cannot survive in the long run if its total costs exceed its total revenues. In the short run, however, in determining the level of output that maximizes profits or minimizes losses, only variable costs need be considered. Fixed costs can be ignored for that decision. Why? The reason is that no matter what the level of output, fixed costs remain fixed. In a comparison of one level of output with another to determine which is more desirable, the only difference is the variable cost. The fixed costs in the two comparisons cancel each other. We can see this relationship clearly in the hypo-

Figure 18–1
Total, Fixed, and Variable Costs

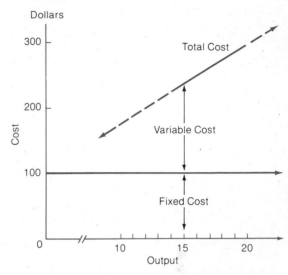

Adding the rising variable costs to given fixed costs gives the rising total cost line.

thetical example given in Table 18–1 and shown in Figure 18–1.

- **Total costs** consist of variable costs plus fixed costs.

Marginal and Average Costs

Two other cost concepts are important for an understanding of profit maximization: marginal cost and average cost. *Marginal cost* is the change in total cost that is associated with a change in output of one unit. Since total cost and variable cost rise by equal increments, marginal cost can be computed from either one. *Average cost* is the cost per unit of output. Like any average, it is obtained by dividing the total by the number of units. In any analysis of the market adjustment process, two different average costs are useful, average total cost and average variable cost:

Table 18-1
Total, Fixed, and Variable Costs

Quantity of Output	Total Cost TC	Fixed Cost FC	Variable Cost VC	Change in TC = Change in VC
14	$213	$100	$113	
15	226	100	126	$13
16	240	100	140	14
17	255	100	155	15
18	271	100	171	16
19	288	100	188	17
20	306	100	206	18

Total cost is the expense associated with production at each quantity of output, rising with the increase in output.
Fixed cost is the expense incurred irrespective of the quantity of output. It would be the same if output were zero or 100 units.
Variable cost includes all expenses not included in fixed costs, so that $TC = FC + VC$. It also increases as output increases, and the amount of the change is the same as the amount of the change in total costs. When put on a chart, as in Figure 18-1, the total cost curve rises, the fixed cost curve is horizontal, and variable costs are the difference between fixed and total costs.

Table 18-2
Marginal and Average Costs

Quantity of Output	Total Cost TC	Marginal Cost MC	Average Total Cost ATC	Average Variable Cost AVC
14	$213		$15.21	$ 8.07
15	226	$13	15.07	8.40
16	240	14	15.00	8.75
17	255	15	15.00	9.12
18	271	16	15.06	9.50
19	288	17	15.12	9.89
20	306	18	15.30	10.30

$$\text{Average total cost} = \frac{\text{Total cost}}{\text{Output}}$$

$$\text{Average variable cost} = \frac{\text{Variable cost}}{\text{Output}}$$

These cost concepts can be illustrated by taking the example given in Table 18-1 and extending it, as in Table 18-2.

- **Marginal cost** is the change in total cost associated with a change in output of one unit.

- **Average cost** is the cost per unit of output, either for total cost (average total cost) or for variable cost (average variable cost).

The Shape of the Average Total Cost Curve

Table 18-2 shows the typical pattern followed by average total costs. They fall, reach a low point, and then start rising. Why? The reason is that the firm has fixed factors of production (hence fixed costs) to which other inputs are added in order to increase output. The law of diminishing returns comes into play. Initially, the output attributable to a one-unit increase in the variable factors of production rises, then levels off, and falls. If the input is considered a cost, this is equivalent to saying that costs per unit of output fall, reach a minimum, and then

Figure 18–2
Typical Average Cost Curve

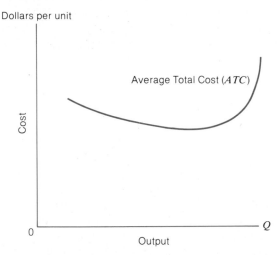

Dollars per unit

The word "typical" is important. Average cost curves can show wide variations in their shape, within the "bowl" or "U" shape derived from the principle of diminishing returns. As drawn here, the *AC* curve is influenced very strongly at the right-hand side of the diagram by engineering capacity limits, and probably is close to the usual situation. In some cases, particularly in retailing, the bottoming out seems to be a horizontal section rather than only a point. Whatever the variations, however, the simple bowl shape is the typical case that we shall use in the analysis.

relationships can be illustrated by data from Table 18–2.

Quantity of Output	Total Cost	Average Total Cost	Marginal Cost
1. When *ATC* is falling, *MC* < *ATC*.			
14	$213	$15.20	
15	226	15.10	$13
16	240	15.00	14
2. When *ATC* is constant, *MC* = *ATC*.			
16	$240	$15.00	
17	255	15.00	$15
3. When *ATC* is rising, *MC* > *ATC*.			
17	$255	$15.00	
18	271	15.10	$16
19	288	15.20	17

A similar relationship exists between marginal costs and average variable costs. Here is an example in which the data shown in Table 18–2 are extended to lower levels of output.

Quantity of Output	Total Cost*	Average Variable Cost	Marginal Cost
7	$150	$7.14	
8	156	7.00	$6
9	163	7.00	7
10	171	7.10	8

Fixed cost = 100.

This example shows that when *AVC* is falling, *MC* < *AVC*; when *AVC* is constant, *MC* = *AVC*; and when *AVC* is rising, *MC* > *AVC*.

The Cost Structure of the Firm in the Short Run
The short-run cost structure of a typical firm can now be completed. The bowl-shaped average cost curve is associated with a marginal cost curve that cuts it from the bottom, crossing at the lowest point on the average cost curve, and lying above the average curve be-

start rising. The typical shape of the *ATC* curve is shown in Figure 18–2.

The Relationship Between Average and Marginal Costs
Table 18–2 also shows the typical relationship between marginal costs and average total costs. Indeed, it illustrates the relationship between any average and marginal quantities. When average total costs are falling, marginal costs are below *ATC*. When average total costs are at their lowest point, marginal costs equal *ATC*. When average total costs are rising, marginal costs are higher than *ATC*. These

Figure 18-3
Average and Marginal Costs
in the Typical Firm

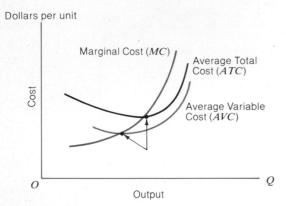

Dollars per unit

As *MC* rises, both *AVC* and *ATC* bottom out; *MC* crosses *AVC* and *ATC* at their lowest points; and the continuing rise of *MC* causes *AVC* and *ATC* to start rising also.

yond that point. This cost structure is shown in Figure 18–3.

Profit Maximization for the Firm

A firm will maximize its gains, or minimize its losses, at the level of output at which its marginal costs are equal to its marginal revenues, or where *MC* equals *MR*. This principle is so important for the analysis that follows in later chapters that it must be clearly understood at this stage of the argument.

The concepts of marginal cost and marginal revenue should be reviewed:

MC = additions to total cost resulting from one additional unit of output

MR = additions to total revenue resulting from the sale of one additional unit

The principle can be best understood for those cases in which the firm is a *price taker*. That is, the firm takes as given the price at which it sells each unit of output, set by the market in a competitive economy; by a planning agency in a socialist regime; or by a price control board in a wartime economy. Whenever the firm is a price taker, the price at which it sells its output becomes its marginal revenue as well. No matter how much it sells, one more unit of output can be sold at the existing price; and if one less unit is sold, total revenues are reduced by an amount equal to the existing price. The price is equal to marginal revenue, $P = MR$. In this case profits will be maximized where $P(MR) = MC$. This proposition can be readily understood from Figure 18–4, which shows a firm's marginal cost curve, *MC,* and the price at which its products are sold. To simplify matters, we assume that the firm can sell all it wants at the market price, so that the price represents both its average revenue per unit sold and its marginal revenue, *MR*.

Suppose this firm were to produce and sell one more unit than q. In this case the added cost would exceed the added revenue and net profits would decline, as shown in Figure 18–5.

On the other hand, suppose the firm were to produce and sell one unit less than q. In this case the revenues it lost would be greater than

Figure 18-4

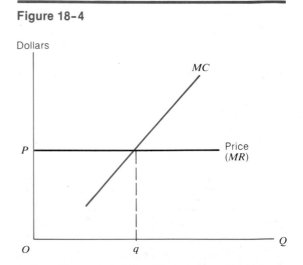

Dollars

Profits will be maximized at output q, where $MC = MR$.

Figure 18-5

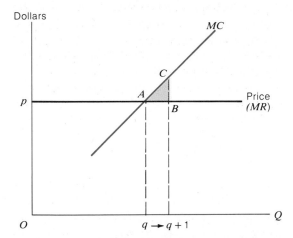

Raising output and sales from q to $q + 1$ causes costs to go up by more than revenues, reducing profits by the area of triangle *ABC*.

Figure 18-6

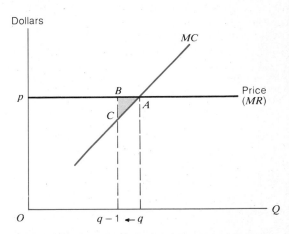

Reducing output and sales from q to $q - 1$ causes revenues to fall more than costs, reducing profits by the area of triangle *ABC*.

its reduction in cost, and it would forego net gains it could earn, as shown in Figure 18–6.

The logic of this situation is clear. As long as the firm increases its output and sales up to the level of q it will be adding to its gains. In that range of output and sales, $MR > MC$. But increases in output beyond q will reduce its total profit, for at those levels of operation $MR < MC$. Profits can be maximized only at output and sales equal to q, where $MR = MC$.

The Supply Schedule of the Firm

Its marginal cost curve becomes the supply schedule for a price-taking, profit-maximizing firm. It will produce and sell that quantity of output at which $MC = MR$, which represents a single point on its marginal cost curve. If the price were to change, profits would be maximized at a changed level of output, and again MC would be equal to MR but at a different point on the MC curve. This proposition is illustrated in Figure 18–7. Whatever the price, the output at which profits are maximized is determined by the MC curve.

The Shutdown Point

Each firm has some level of output below which it will not find operating worthwhile. That *shutdown point* is defined by the intersection of the firm's MC curve with its average variable cost, $MC = AVC$. It is shown in Figure 18–8. Here is the logic behind that conclusion. When price is at p_1, the firm will minimize its losses with output q_1. It will be losing money, because revenue per unit is below total cost per unit, for $P < ATC$. At a price above p_1, something above average variable cost will be earned, and a contribution will be made to paying some of the fixed costs and/or to normal profit. Below price p_1, however, $MR < AVC$. This means that the firm is not only failing to earn a normal profit and its fixed costs, but also failing even to earn its operating or variable costs. By closing down its operations, it can reduce its losses to only its fixed costs and normal profit. The firm will not operate in the output range between O and q_1. Output q_1, with price p_1 is its shutdown point (see Figure 18–8).

Figure 18-7
The Supply Schedule of the Firm

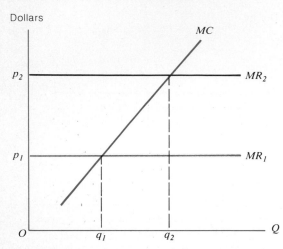

When the price is at P_1 the profit maximizing firm will produce and sell output q_1. If price were to rise to P_2, the firm would increase its output to q_2.

Figure 18-8
The Firm's Shutdown Point

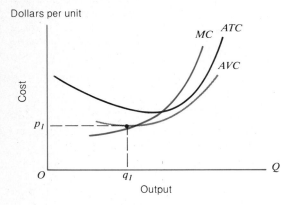

Output

The supply schedule of the price-taking firm, then, is its marginal cost curve for that range of output above the level at which $MC = AVC$.

- The **shutdown point** is the level of output below which a firm will not operate because it is not even earning its variable costs. At this point $MC = AVC$.

The Supply Curve for the Industry

The industry's supply schedule can now be determined. It is obtained by adding up the amounts each firm would be willing to supply at various prices. Those amounts are derived from the marginal cost schedules of the individual firms. Very simply, the supply schedule for the industry is the sum of the supply schedules, or marginal cost curves, of the individual firms. This relationship is shown in Figure 18–9.

Minimizing Costs

At the same time that our firm is maximizing its profits, given its cost structure and the selling price for its product, it seeks to minimize its production costs. Minimum costs per unit of output are as important for profit maximization as selection of the level of output at which $MR = MC$. There are strong incentives to move the entire cost structure of the firm downward, and we can expect that any firm competing strongly with others will continually seek ways to shift its internal operations toward lower production costs. Competition is a great spur toward efficiency.

The key to reduced production costs is substitution of lower-cost inputs for higher-cost ones at the margin. If the cost of labor falls, relative to the cost of other inputs, business firms can be expected to substitute labor for other factors of production. This basic principle applies throughout the production process.

In the short run, when the existing plant and production processes are fixed, the firm has some opportunities to substitute factors of production for each other, but the opportunities are relatively limited. Production relationships have already been determined largely by prior decisions about which production processes to use and what size plant to build. Even then there is some flexibility in replacing untrained for trained personnel, in substituting a machine for workers (or workers for a ma-

Figure 18–9
Adding Marginal Cost Curves of Individual Firms to Obtain Supply Curve for Industry

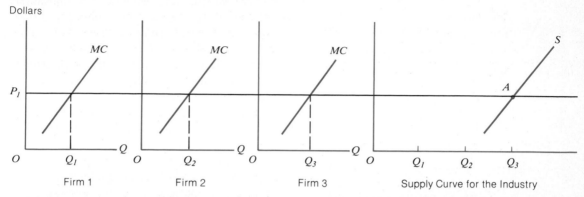

At Price P_1, the three firms will produce and sell quantities Q_1, Q_2, and Q_3, which are summed at point A on the industry's supply curve. Other points on the industry's supply curve are obtained in the same way.

chine, which doesn't seem to happen much these days), and in reorganizing little bits and pieces of the production process to reduce production costs.

In the long run, however, processes and plant size become flexible, and the possibilities increase for substituting one input for another. The firm does not have much freedom to push its average and marginal cost curves downward very much in the short run, but in the long run it can push them down as far as the existing knowledge of technology and science will permit.

Marginal Costs and Economic Welfare

Behind the supply curve for any commodity lie the costs incurred by producers. In this chapter we have treated those costs in monetary terms, because that is how they are seen by the firm and that is how they influence the firm's decisions. But we should never forget that behind those monetary costs to the firm are real costs to the economy as a whole. Units of labor and physical plant and equipment are used that

could have other uses producing other things. The monetary costs to the firm are the way the market system expresses the opportunity cost to the economy as a whole. So when we say that costs at the margin determine the amounts that profit-maximizing producers are willing to supply to their customers, there is more to the matter than merely the principle of profit maximization.

Chapter 16 explained that the demand curve for a commodity is based on utility to the buyer at the margin. This chapter has added that the supply curve reflects costs to the producer at the margin. Since we know that demand and supply are equal at the market price, it follows that the market adjustment process creates an equilibrium at which marginal utility to the buyer equals marginal costs to the seller:

$$MU = MC$$

Figure 18–10 illustrates this proposition, using a supply-demand-price diagram.

The equality of marginal costs and marginal utility at the market price indicates that the net benefits are maximized. For example, referring to Figure 18–10, if output were one unit greater

Figure 18-10
Market Equilibrium Revisited

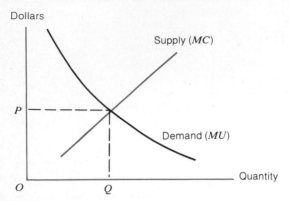

At the market price P, buyers will take quantity OQ, which is the same amount that producers are willing to supply. The money value to consumers of the last unit purchased, that is, the height of the demand curve Q, is exactly equal to the additional costs incurred in producing that unit. Benefits at the margin are equal to costs at the margin. $MU = MC$.

than Q, the additional costs to producers (MC) would be greater than the additional benefits to consumers (MU). There would be a net loss of welfare. On the other hand, if output were one unit less than Q, consumers would be giving up marginal benefits greater than the cost savings to producers. Clearly, benefits to the society as a whole will be maximized at Q. We should remember, too, that these are real benefits and costs, with the monetary values merely reflecting the satisfactions obtained by consumers and the effort expended by producers.

A market equilibrium, then, tends to maximize net real benefits to the economy as a whole. The drive of consumers to maximize their satisfactions together with the efforts of producers to maximize their gains, worked out in the environment of a freely adjusting market system, moves the society toward a welfare-maximizing result.

This conclusion is subject to a series of important, already familiar qualifications. The existing distribution of income and wealth is taken for granted. Prices have to reflect all of the costs of production, social as well as private. There can be no restrictions on freedom of action in the market, either by private monopolists or government bureaucrats. "Public goods," or those that would not be provided by private enterprises motivated by profit, are excluded from the analysis. These are important limitations. Nevertheless, the basic concept is one of the most important ideas in the modern social sciences, for it suggests that properly structured markets can work effectively to promote human welfare. They don't solve all of our problems, but for some they may work quite well.

Summary

Producers' efforts to maximize profits lie behind the supply of goods brought to market. Those efforts respond to two objectives: the desire to maximize net revenues in the market, and the desire to minimize production costs within the firm.

Maximization of net revenues in the market occurs when marginal revenues equal marginal costs. When the firm is a price taker, its MC curve above the shutdown point becomes its supply curve. Individual firms' supply curves can then be added to arrive at a market supply curve for the industry as a whole.

As for minimization of costs within the firm, that is brought about by substituting lower-cost factors of production for higher-cost ones at the margin until the point where MR/P is equal for all inputs.

When the market supply curve for a good is based on marginal costs, as it is for price takers, it also reflects real or opportunity costs to the economy as a whole. This enables the market-adjustment process to equate marginal benefits to buyers with marginal costs to producers and thereby maximize net benefits for the system as a whole.

Key Concepts

the short run	variable costs	marginal cost
the long run	fixed costs	average cost
normal profit	total costs	shutdown point

For Discussion

1. Why does profit maximization require that marginal cost be equated with marginal revenue?

2. Average variable cost is assumed to increase beyond a certain level of output. Why?

3. In the short run, operating at a loss may be better than shutting down. Why? When is it better to shut down operations entirely?

4. Explain why in the short run the competitive firm's supply is its marginal cost curve.

5. If the typical firm in a competitive industry makes extranormal profits, what would you expect to happen to the industry's supply? Why?

6. When additional firms enter a competitive industry, what would you expect to happen to the typical firm's profits?

Chapter 19

Market Adjustment Under Competitive Conditions

Our discussion of the general theory of markets up to this point has covered basic principles, the theory of demand, and the costs that lie behind the supply curve. We are now ready to go beyond the simple supply-demand-price relationships and examine the way in which producers adjust their output to the market prices for the goods they sell. Since we are now interested only in the reactions of producers, we do not consider any changes that may occur on the demand side of the market. We analyze producers' decisions: how much to produce, whether to enter or leave the industry, what size plant to build, and what production processes to use.

The simplest place to start is with competitive industries in which neither sellers nor buyers can influence prices in the market. That is, we assume that the number of sellers and buyers is so large, and each is so small relative to the size of the market as a whole, that all accept the market price as a factor in their environment over which they have no influence. These conditions are characteristic of *pure competition*, which will be described in the following section.

Pure Competition

A purely competitive industry requires a number of sellers so large that the action of any one firm has no appreciable effect on the fortunes of the other firms. Each firm can seek to maximize its profits without fear of retaliation from other firms. There are no "enemy" firms or rivals that have to be watched: the only factors that influence the firm's decisions are its internal cost structure and its external market conditions. In other words, the output of any one firm is so small when compared with the output of the industry as a whole that its actions are not significant enough to influence market prices.

There are not many markets in which these conditions exist. The market for wheat or other basic farm products is one. Others come close. However, our purpose here is not to describe any single market accurately, but to get at the basic market adjustment mechanism that works to a greater or lesser extent in many different markets.

Some additional assumptions will also help to simplify the analysis:

1. All firms in the industry produce a single homogeneous product. That is, as far as the buyers are concerned, the product of each firm is identical to the product of any other firm in the industry.

2. There is full freedom of entry into the industry and exit from it for all potential sellers. Patent restrictions, long-term contracts, exclusive supplying agreements, and other restrictions on entry do not exist. Firms are also free to leave the industry if profits are too low.

- These assumptions define **pure competition** as economists generally use it: many firms; single, homogeneous products; free entry and exit.

Perfect Competition

Mobility of resources is closely allied to freedom of entry and exit. The factors of production must be free to move from place to place, from industry to industry, and from entrepreneur to entrepreneur. Of course, time must elapse while the factors are moving and being rearranged, and this has led to the distinction between the long run and the short run in economics. But whatever the time period, factors of production must be free to move anywhere in the economy in order that the market adjustment process may freely respond to the desires of consumers and the desires of producers.

To complete the picture, each producer must have full knowledge of the market and the opportunities available there. It is obvious that this condition cannot be achieved, but it isn't too far wrong, either. Wrong decisions in the market lead to economic extinction if firms persist in them. We can assume that business managers tend to make correct decisions, as if they had perfect knowledge, simply because those who make poor decisions are forced out

of the market by their more successful competitors.

A perfectly competitive industry cannot be found. *Perfect competition* requires full mobility of resources and full knowledge, in addition to a large number of firms, a homogeneous product, and free entry. Nevertheless, we make all these assumptions in order to simplify the analysis of the market adjustment process, knowing full well that the analysis will not describe reality. But it will help us understand the essential elements of the market adjustment process.[1]

- **Perfect competition** is a situation with all the characteristics of pure competition, plus full knowledge of all alternatives on the part of the buyers and sellers, and unrestricted mobility of all resources.

Demand for a Firm's Product

Our assumptions tell us that in a perfectly competitive industry the individual firm can sell any amount of its product at the existing market price. This conclusion follows from the requirement that the firm's output is so small, relative to the size of the market as a whole, that its actions will not affect price. As a result, the demand curve for the single firm is a horizontal line at the market price. This situation is shown in Figure 19–1.

In a competitive industry the individual firm must take the price of its product as a given element. If it is constrained in this way, it is freed in another: it can sell any quantity at that price. If the firm tried to charge a higher price, it would sell nothing; customers would go to

---

[1]A general principle of scientific method is involved here. A methodology is selected with a definite purpose in mind, and may be quite inappropriate to another purpose. Here our purpose is analytical knowledge that will later be put to use in understanding reality. But we do not confuse the analytical model with reality any more than the engineer confuses the algebraic formulation of the stress factors in a steel bridge with the bridge itself.

Figure 19–1
Demand Curve for a Single Firm

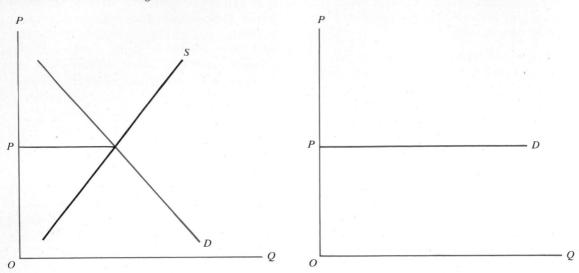

Interaction between demand and supply determines the market price . . . which then defines the single firm.

other sellers of the identical product. Yet there is no incentive to sell at less than the going market price, since the firm can sell any amount it wishes at that price. Its demand curve is infinitely elastic at the existing price. Since the demand curve is horizontal, average revenue is constant. We already know that when average revenue is a constant, it equals marginal revenue, or $AR = MR$. The market price is therefore equal to the firm's average revenue and to its marginal revenue:

$$P = AR = MR$$

The chief immediate problem facing the firm then becomes one of deciding which level of output will maximize its profits. This is the first step in the process of market adjustment.

Price Takers and Price Makers
In the purely competitive model, the firm is a *price taker*. That is, it accepts the price determined in the market and adjusts its operations to the market price. This condition distin-

guishes the purely competitive firm from those in monopoloid markets, where the individual firm has a greater or lesser degree of choice with regard to the price of its product. Firms in that situation can be termed *price makers,* although the degree of influence they have over the price of the product may vary widely.

The Firm in the Short Run: Choosing the Level of Output

We shall assume that the firm has plant and equipment already at hand. Its cost structure is like that described in the last chapter. That is, its average cost per unit of output falls for a time, and then starts to rise. The appropriate marginal cost curve follows from the shape of the average cost curve. The firm's demand curve, of course, is fixed at the market price, so that price equals marginal revenue and average revenue.

Putting these elements together enables the

Figure 19-2
The Competitive Firm Determines Level of
Output at Which Profits Are Maximized

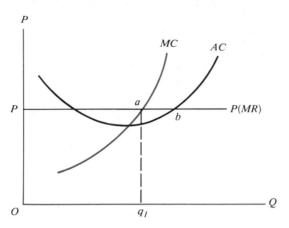

With the given cost structure and market price, output
level q_1 will maximize profits. Up to that point additional
revenues MR exceed additional costs MC as output
increases. This adds to profits. Beyond that point
additional costs MC exceed additional revenues MR as
output goes up. Profits fall beyond q_1. Point a designates
the profit maximizing output. Question: Why are profits
not maximized at b?

Figure 19-3
Extranormal Profits

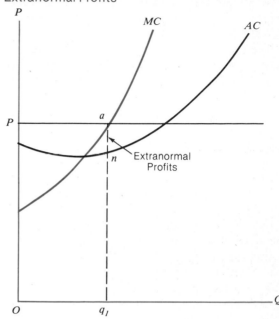

This segment of Figure 19-2 shows extranormal profits
per unit equal to *an*, the difference between average
costs per unit and the market price.

firm to determine the level of output at which
profits are maximized. Remember that $MR = MC$ is the profit-maximizing condition. The
firm will select the level of output at which that
condition prevails. An example is given in
Figure 19-2.

Figure 19-2 was drawn in a special way. It
was deliberately structured so that the firm
would make *extranormal profits*. Normal profits (just large enough to keep the firm operating) are included in average costs. But at
output level q_1, the selling price is greater than
average costs. The difference is extranormal
profits, shown in Figure 19-3.

The firm making extranormal profits shown
in Figure 19-2 is maximizing its profits with the
existing plant and equipment at the going
prices for inputs. But the industry as a whole
has not reached an equilibrium because the

extranormal profits should induce other firms
to enter the industry. We turn to the process
that brings the industry into equilibrium.

● **Extranormal profits** are those above the normal
profits that are included in the firm's costs.

The Industry in the Short Run:
Entry and Exit of Firms

When the typical firm is making profits greater
than those necessary to sustain it, additional
producers will be attracted into the industry.
They will move in from industries in which
price-cost relationships do not enable firms to
make extranormal profits.

The entry of new firms will add to the supply

of the product available on the market. The additional supplies will bring prices down. As prices fall, the extranormal profits of individual firms will diminish and ultimately disappear. When that happens, there will no longer be any incentive for new firms to enter the industry, supplies available for sale will no longer rise, the market price will stop falling, and the industry will have achieved an equilibrium. Figure 19–4 shows the equilibrium position of the individual firm when that result occurs.

Just as extranormal profits encourage firms to enter an industry, profits lower than normal will cause firms to leave. This will have exactly the opposite effects from those just explained. Supplies in the market will fall and prices will rise. This adjustment will continue until the market price equals average costs of production for the typical firm. At that point producers will be earning normal profits and the incentive to leave the industry will be gone. We can summarize the adjustment process as a whole, then, by looking at the position of the individual firm.

○ *When the typical producer is making more than normal profits,* the market adjustment process causes prices to fall (Figure 19–5).

○ *When the typical producer is making less than normal profits,* the market adjustment process causes prices to rise (Figure 19–6).

○ *When the typical producer is making normal profits,* and no more, the market adjustment process stops. Both firm and industry have reached equilibrium (Figure 19–7).

Equilibrium in the Industry as a Whole

The process by which the industry as a whole reaches equilibrium involves two distinct steps. First, each firm selects the level of output that maximizes its own profits, given the market price for its product. This decision does not affect prices in the market, for the firm is a price taker in a competitive industry. Second, the number of producers is determined by the pattern of entry into and exit from the indus-

Figure 19–4
Equilibrium of the Firm in a Competitive Industry After Extranormal Profits Have Been Eliminated

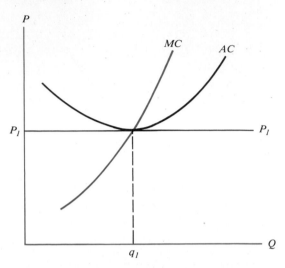

The extranormal profits of Figure 19–2 have disappeared after entry of new firms into the industry brought the market price down to P_1. This firm recovers all costs and earns a normal profit at output q_1.

Figure 19–5

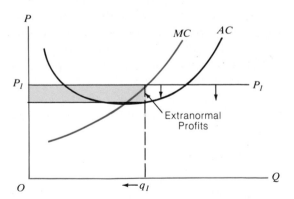

Extranormal profits cause new producers to enter the industry; supply increases and the market price falls.

Figure 19–6

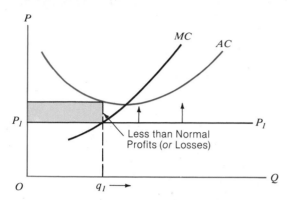

Profits below normal (or losses) cause some existing producers to leave the industry; supply decreases and the market price rises.

Figure 19–7

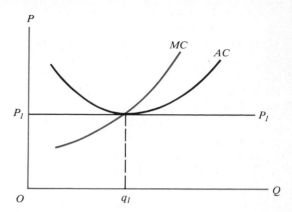

When profits are at the normal level, producers have no incentive to either enter or leave the industry. Equilibrium prevails.

try. Decisions of many firms to enter or not enter affect the total supply in the market and, consequently, the market price. When the market price reaches that level at which the number of producers is stabilized, the industry will be in equilibrium. Each firm remaining in the industry will have reached a profit-maximizing level of output as a result of its own internal decisions, and the number of firms will be established by the process of entry and exit. There will then be no tendency for the market price or quantity sold to change. The *market equilibrium* of supply-demand-price is achieved simultaneously with the *short-run equilibirum* of the firm and the industry, as illustrated in Figure 19–8.

- **Market equilibrium** is a condition in which supply and demand in the market are equal at the prevailing price, which therefore tends to remain where it is.

- **Short-run equilibrium** is a condition in which the individual firm is operating at the level of output that maximizes profit. Short-run equilibrium of the industry pevails when the quantity produced by the typical firm is such that $P = MC = AC$.

A Methodological Problem: Is There a "Typical" Firm?

Our analysis of the market adjustment process under competitive conditions used the device of the "typical" firm. The concept simplified the analysis, but in doing so it enabled us to sweep under the rug several troubling analytical problems.

All producers are not alike. Some are more efficient than others. Some are more alert to the need for change and adjustment. Some have better management. As a result of these differences, the cost curves of individual firms will differ. Production costs will be higher for some, lower for others. A market price that enables one firm to make normal profits will leave another with losses, while yet another may make profits substantially above the normal level. Under these circumstances, are we justified in resting the analysis of market adjustment on the actions of a "typical" firm?

Economic theorists have attempted to solve this problem in a variety of ways. One is to assume that all firms have exactly the same production costs, and that the differences that actually occur are "rents" paid to the factors of

Figure 19-8
Achievement of Equilibrium in a Competitive Industry

Stage I

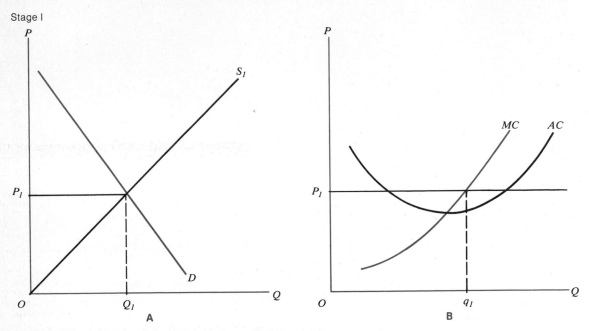

The initial position of the market equilibrium produces price P_1 and output (sales) Q_1 (diagram A). This position does not produce equilibrium in the industry because the typical firm makes extranormal profits (diagram B), attracting additional producers into the industry and leading to Stage II (diagrams C and D).

production. For example, suppose a retail store has a particularly favorable location, such as Broadway at 34th Street in New York. It would have to pay a high rent for that location, and the landowner, if he were a good bargainer, could extract rent payments that entirely eliminated the more than normal profits of the retailer. Even if the store owned the land itself, a proper economic accounting of costs would charge off a portion of the "profits" to implicit rent. In this way, any special advantage that a firm might have over its competitors—location, patent rights, astute management, and so forth —could be allocated to rent or royalties. Likewise, any significant disadvantages of location or cost can be attributed to negative rents or royalties. The result is to bring costs of production of all firms to equality and make all of their cost curves identical.

A second way out is to assume that most firms are like the typical firm. This recognizes the possibility of differences in costs between firms. The luckier or more efficient ones will expand and grow. The less efficient will contract and tend to die off. The great majority will continue in business, adjusting as best they can to the competitive market environment. As for firms entering an industry for the first time, we can expect them to be in the middle range; they would not come in if they did not feel reasonably sure that they could meet the competition, but they would not have the experience to match the best.

Both these ways of solving the problem of difference in cost curves end at about the same place. The first is closer to an analytically rigorous and "correct" analysis. But it gives up a good deal of reality. The second is more

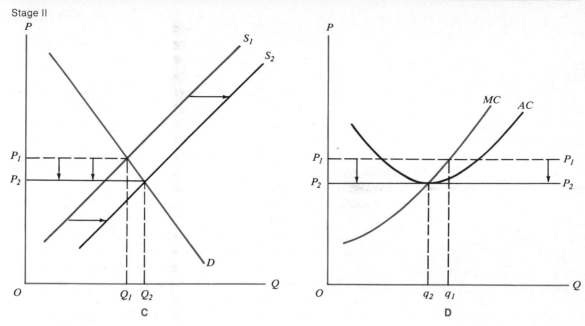

Stage II

C

D

Entry of new firms increases supply in the market from S_1 toward S_2, causing the price to fall from P_1 to P_2 and the amount produced (sold) to increase from Q_1 toward Q_2 (diagram C). The decline in market price causes the typical firm to reduce its output (sales) from q_1 to q_2 (diagram D), with a downward movement along its marginal cost curve. When the market price falls to P_2, the extranormal profits of the firm are gone, entry into the industry stops, supply in the market stabilizes at S_2 (diagram C), and the industry has reached its equilibrium.

realistic and better fits our intuitive understanding of the situation. However, it lacks the analytical rigor of the first approach. The important point is that both are consistent with the analysis of the market adjustment process as we have described it.

The Long Run: Size of Plant and Long-Run Costs

As we moved in our analysis from the equilibrium of the firm to the equilibrium of the industry, new firms could enter the industry and build new plants. Existing firms would also be able to build new plants, selecting a larger or smaller size or even adopting a different technology. What was fixed in the short run becomes variable in the long run, and the fixed

costs of plant and equipment become variable costs. An illustration will help clarify the distinction between long and short run. When a steel producer operates a blast furnace, the output of pig iron from the furnace can be varied with different types of inputs, but only within limits. Iron ore with a 50 percent iron content may allow an annual output of 200,000 tons. Using an enriched ore containing 65 percent iron may raise the annual output to 250,000 tons, partly because the input is richer and partly because it takes less time to burn out the impurities. The firm must then decide whether a shift to higher grades of ore, which also cost more, will bring greater profits or not. To the economist this is a short-run decision: the fixed costs of the blast furnace have been incurred, and the only issue is the variable costs of the inputs.

A long-run decision concerns whether or not to build a blast furnace at all and, if so, the size at which it should be engineered. When these fixed costs can be varied, the firm can choose between blast furnaces or electric furnaces, or direct reduction in oxygen furnaces, and all at a variety of capacity levels that in turn will vary with the quality of the inputs. The firm is in the position of having to choose the most efficient combination of all factors of production, and all of them can be varied in amount. There are, of course, technological limitations on the proportions in which the factors of production can be combined. But there are no fixed amounts of any one factor to limit the choices, as in the short-run case of existing plant and equipment.

In the long run, each one of the variety of plants among which the firm can choose will have a different cost structure. A small plant may have relatively high costs, while costs in a larger plant may be lower. A still larger plant may run into higher costs because of technological problems, management difficulties, or other organizational problems. The possible choices can be compared with each other, as in Figure 19–9. Three alternative plants with different output capacity are shown. Plant 1 is a small, relatively high-cost plant. Plant 3 is a large and also a relatively high-cost plant. Plant 2 is the one with the lowest cost structure. It is, of course, the one a competitive firm will seek to build. The long-run average cost curve, *LRAC*, represents the choices the firm has. It is drawn in a dish-shaped form to indicate that cost structures change with plants of different size, and it becomes a smoother curve the larger the number of alternatives. The long-run marginal cost curve, *LRMC*, shows the

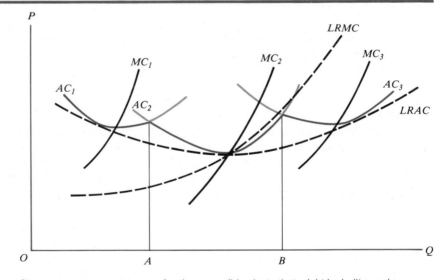

Figure 19–9
Long-Run Costs for the
Firm in a Competitive
Industry

Short run average cost curves for three possible plants that might be built are shown (AC_1, AC_2 and AC_3). The heavy line shows the long run average cost curve (*LRAC*) that a firm will plan on as its sales increase. It will shift from Plant 1 to Plant 2 when sales increase beyond *OA* and from Plant 2 to Plant 3 when sales are greater than *OB*. If the firm had an infinite number of plants to choose from, the *LRAC* curve (or "planning curve") would take on the shape of the dashed line. Any firm that wanted to survive in a competitive industry would have to build Plant 2, which has the lowest cost structure. The lowest point on its *AC* curve coincides with the lowest point on the *LRAC* curve. Note the *LRMC* curve that is associated with the *LRAC* curve.

Figure 19–10

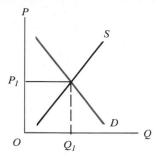

A. Market Equilibrium

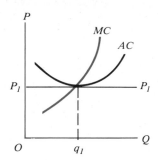

B. Short-Run Equilibrium

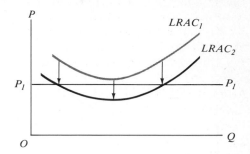

C. Long-Run Equilibrium

marginal costs associated with the *LRAC* curve.

We have just noted that the competitive firm will select the plant that, in the long run, has the lowest cost of production.[2] The logic behind that selection is that if it doesn't, other firms will, and it will be ultimately driven out of business by more efficient producers. The result is that all surviving firms will have selected plants close enough to the best size to enable them to compete with the most efficient firms in the industry.

This lowest-cost plant is the only one that can maximize profits in both the short run and the long run. Of all possible plant sizes, it is the only one in which marginal costs equal average costs in both time periods. This is shown in Figure 19–9: $MC_2 = AC_2$ at the same level of output at which $LRMC = LRAC$. By contrast, $MC_1 = AC_1$ at a different level of output from that at which $LRMC = LRAC$.

We can use the *LRAC* curve to show what happens in the long-run adjustment process when technology changes or the prices of inputs change:

1. Supply and demand interact to determine prices in the market, and existing firms adapt to that price by selecting their profit-maximizing level of output. But let us now assume that they all have old-fashioned plants: a new technological discovery makes it possible to build plants with lower cost structures. This situation is shown in Figure 19–10. The short-run equilibrium of the industry (Figure 19–10B) has been shattered by technological changes, which move long-run average costs downward from $LRAC_1$ to $LRAC_2$ (Figure 19–10C).

2. Firms both within and outside the industry discover that new plants will make extra-normal profits by selling at the existing market price, P_1. Figure 19–11 shows the comparison.

3. As more plants come into production, old ones are scrapped. Competition starts to pull the market price down as larger supplies come on the market. Ultimately a new short- and *long-run equilibrium* is established. The newer and lower long-run cost structure (Figure 19–12C) causes selection of the plant shown in Figure 19–12B. The lower costs enable the industry as a whole to reduce price and increase output (Figure 19–12A) until the price comes down to a level at which ex-

---

[2]The alert student will point out that this conclusion is obvious, and that we did not have to draw the long-run average cost curve to prove it. Correct! The *LRAC* curve was introduced at this point because it can move upward or downward as costs of inputs rise and fall or as technology changes, and firms have to adjust to those changes too, as we have seen.

Figure 19–11

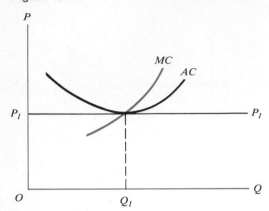

A. Short-Run Equilibrium, Old-fashioned Plant

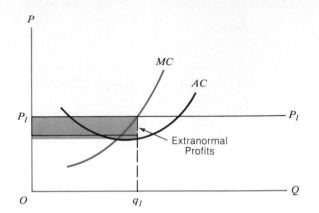

B. New, More Efficient Plant

Figure 19–12

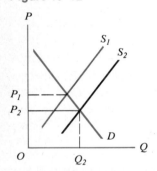

A. Market Equilibrium

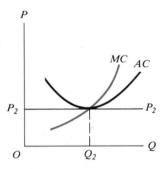

B. Short-Run Equilibrium

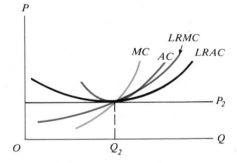

C. Long-Run Equilibrium

tranormal profits have been eliminated (Figure 19–12B). This is the new equilibrium of the industry. Supply and demand are equated in the market, and price equals marginal costs and average costs for the individual firm in both the short run and the long run.

● **Long-run equilibrium** is a condition in which individual firms have built the lowest-cost plants, and entry or exit of firms has brought profits equal to normal profits to the typical firm.

Economies of Large-Scale Production

One special attribute of the long-run cost curve was the starting point for the modern theory of monopoly and monopoloid markets. Suppose demand in the market is not large enough to support a large number of independent producers, each with a lowest cost plant (Plant 2 in Figure 19–9). What if only two or three such plants could be supported by the existing demand for the product? In that case, the number of sellers would be too few for competition to prevail, for the decisions made by any one seller would affect the other sellers.

In some cases only one seller might be able to supply the entire market and monopoly would prevail. This situation would occur if a single plant (such as Plant 1 in Figure 19–9) could supply the whole market. Even if demand were to increase, a somewhat larger, lower-cost plant could be built to supply the whole market at a somewhat lower price than before (if the monopolist could be induced or forced to lower his price). Economies in production can be achieved by increasing the scale of output in the declining sector of the long-run average cost curve, still with only a single producer in the industry. Economies of large-scale production may make it impossible for competitive conditions to prevail. This topic is discussed in greater detail in the following chapter as part of an inquiry into the economics of monopolistic industries.

Constant, Increasing, and Decreasing Long-Run Costs

The analysis up to this point has assumed that market demand does not change: the demand curve stands still, and the profit-maximizing firm in a competitive industry adjusts to market demand on the basis of its cost structure. The result is the long-run triple equilibrium of the industry in the market, the short run, and the long run.

But what happens if demand changes, if the demand curve shifts its position? In one sense, nothing happens to change the essential elements of the adjustment process. The firm and the industry merely adapt to the new environment and arrive at a new triple equilibrium based on the changed conditions of demand. That conclusion, while correct, ignores some of the things that can happen to the location of the long-run cost curve. We should analyze that problem in order to complete the picture of how the adjustment process takes place.

In a growing economy, the increases in

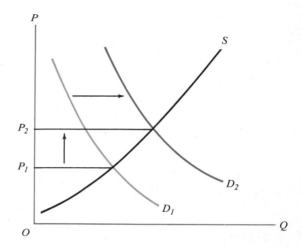

Figure 19–13
Increases in Wealth and Income Create Increases in Demand for Goods

wealth and income that accompany growth bring increases in the demand for a variety of goods. For example, more leisure time promotes the expansion of recreation industries, tourism, reading of books and magazines, and entertainment of all kinds. The market for a large range of products and services expands. In terms of our analysis, demand for those goods increases and the demand curve shifts upward and to the right in the usual supply-demand-price diagram, that is, from D_1 to D_2 in Figure 19–13. The increase in demand brings prices up from P_1 to P_2. We know from our earlier analysis that this price increase will raise profits for the typical firm above the normal level, drawing new producers into the industry. The resultant increase in supplies coming into the market will start bringing prices down until the extranormal profits are gone.

At this point the structure of *costs in the long run* comes into the picture. If cost conditions do not change, the new plants will have the same short-run costs as those of the old producers, and extranormal profits will not be

Figure 19-14
Long-Run Adjustment: Constant Costs

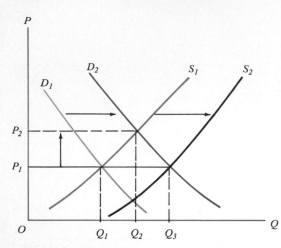

A. Market Equilibrium

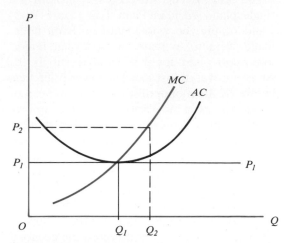

B. Short-Run Equilibrium

In diagram A, the increase in demand from D_1 to D_2 causes price to rise from P_1 to P_2 and output to increase from Q_1 to Q_2. The higher price attracts new firms and supply increases from S_1 to S_2, which then brings P back down to its old level because cost structures have not changed. As for the typical firm (diagram B), the original increase in D that shifted prices upward from P_1 to P_2 caused it to increase its output from Q_1 to Q_2. As new producers came into the industry and prices fell back to P_1, output was reduced back to Q_1. In the industry as a whole, however, the increase in supply to S_2 caused total output to rise to Q_3 (diagram A). The net result is enlarged output for the industry, no change in prices or costs, and reestablishment of the original equilibrium of the typical firm.

eliminated until prices have come down to the old level (see Figure 19–14).

The situation shown in Figure 19–14 may be called constant costs in the long run. As growth of demand for the industry's product stimulates increased output, the cost of inputs, or materials, labor, capital, and so on, does not change. The long-run adjustment of the industry can be made without higher costs of production or higher prices.

Another industry may have increasing costs in the long run. In that case, the cost of one or more inputs rises as the industry expands in response to increases in demand. It is often an input from land or natural resources that figures in the cost increases. Firms in an industry using iron ore as an input, for example, will discover that their raw material costs go up as the richest and most readily available deposits

of iron ore are used up, and as growth requires the opening up of new, higher-cost mines. We can analyze the process in Figure 19–15.

In this instance, the supply curve for the industry rises in the long run (S_L in Figure 19–15A). That is, as demand increases with growth of the economy, the industry produces a growing output, but at steadily rising prices. In the long run more can be produced, but only along a path in which the triple equilibrium of the industry is achieved at rising prices.

The final case is the industry with decreasing costs in the long run. This is just the opposite of the increasing-cost industry: prices of some inputs fall when the industry expands in response to rising demand. There can be several reasons for declining costs of inputs. As an industry grows, some of the services it needs can be provided by outside firms. Maintenance services may have to be done by each firm, but if several firms are located near each other, an independent, specialized, and more efficient supplier of maintenance services may be organized to provide those services more cheaply than they can be carried out by the firms themselves. Another example: growth of an industry may develop specialized labor skills in the labor market that may be hard to find if the industry is small and demand for the skills is correspondingly small. Again: suppliers of materials may be able to reduce their costs (and prices) as the industry's demand for the materials is going up. In each of these instances the reduced costs of inputs are due to growth of the industry as a whole and not to the actions of any single firm. They are therefore called external economies, that is, savings external to the firm and not due to its internal decisions.

External economies are the chief source of decreasing costs in the long run. As demand for the industry's product goes up and the industry expands, external economies bring long-run average costs down, and the industry's supply curve takes on a downward slope (see Figure 19–16).

Cost conditions, then, come in three variations in the very long run, depending on what happens to the costs of inputs:

○ **Constant costs:** Prices of inputs stay the same.

○ **Increasing costs:** Prices of inputs rise.

○ **Decreasing costs:** Prices of inputs fall.

All of these trends in the long run are consistent with the equilibrium of a competitive industry. They show that this equilibrium can move up or down, or stay where it is, as far as costs are concerned, within the framework of a growing and changing economy.

Figure 19–15
Long-Run Adjustment: Increasing Costs

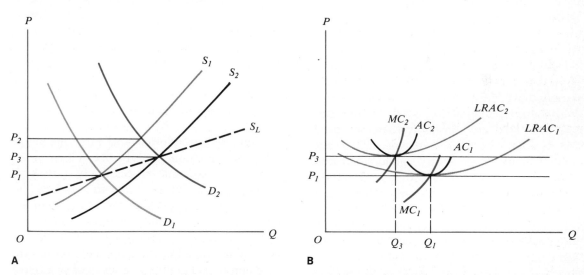

A

B

Demand increases from D_1 to D_2, pushing prices up immediately to P_2. The large extranormal profits bring in new producers and supply starts to increase from S_1 toward S_2. But the increased demand for inputs causes long run costs to rise from $LRAC_1$ toward $LRAC_2$. Declining prices from increased supply and rising long run costs meet at price P_3, at which point a new triple equilibrium has been established. The new price P_3 is higher than the old P_1.

Figure 19–16
Long-Run Adjustment: Decreasing Costs

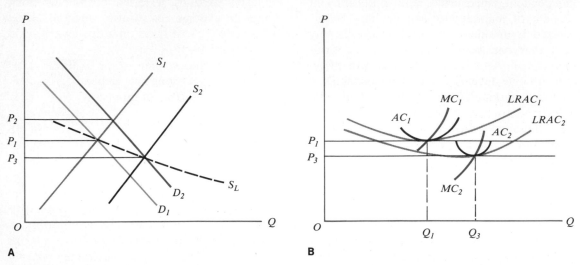

A

B

The increase in demand from D_1 to D_2 pushes prices up to P_2, drawing new firms into the industry. Expansion reduces long run costs from $LRAC_1$ to $LRAC_2$, due to external economies, while at the same time supply rises from S_1 to S_2. The decreased long run costs bring a new equilibrium at price P_3, which is lower than the original price. The supply curve (S_L) slopes downward in the long run.

Review: Three Analytically Different Time Periods

Analysis of the market adjustment process is usually divided into three analytically distinct phases, outlined in Figure 19–17. These time periods have been separated for purposes of analysis only. In practice, market prices and quantities sold are constantly changing, firms are deciding on their levels of output and capital expansion programs, and long-run cost relationships are shifting and causing adjustments in capital outlay programs of individual firms. All of the decisions and trends are related to and influence each other, and all are simultaneously adjusting to conditions of price and cost.

The Market Adjustment Process in Perspective

The ideas developed in this chapter are some of the most important in all of economics. They

are a distillation of the essential elements of Adam Smith's *Wealth of Nations* (1776), David Ricardo's *Principles of Political Economy* (1817), and Alfred Marshall's *Principles of Economics* (1890) as amended and developed by a host of other economists up to the present day. In one form or another they comprise a central portion of the tool kit of all economists today.

Why are they so important? First, the method is a classic example of the use of logic in the analysis of economic processes. It starts with assumptions about behavior that reduce the problem to manageable proportions. Then the problem is divided into segments, "time periods" in this case, which allow one variable at a time to be studied while the other variables are held constant. Finally, by a series of successive approximations, the whole process under study is put together in such a way that any or all variables can change, yet the investigator has a sure understanding of what is happening to the system as a whole.

Second, the market adjustment process tells us how markets function, in general and in their essential elements. There are no perfectly competitive markets. Yet whatever the imperfections and constraints, any market will adjust itself to the changes that are continually taking place in our world. The process of adjustment will have much in common with the competitive model, once the specific characteristics of the market system in the real world are taken into account. One of our tasks later will be to analyze the market adjustment process as it exists under a variety of other conditions, including monopoly, a variety of monopoloid situations, and a planned economy. In each case, the analysis of the specific situation will hark back to the fundamentals of market adjustment in the perfectly competitive market.

The theory of the competitive market system is important for a third reason. The role of the profit motive in a private economy becomes very clear. This motive is the driving force behind the adjustment process. The business manager, in an effort to maximize profits, makes decisions about output levels, size of plant, technology, and whether to enter or leave the market, which bring the industry into equilibrium in the short run. Decisions on profit maximization also determine the long-run equilibrium. Even though only a few people earn the profits, it is profits that motivate the decisions.

Finally, and most important, the market adjustment process has important implications for welfare and efficiency. Earlier we concluded that rational consumers allocate their incomes to maximize utility, an action we equated with maximization of welfare. We also showed that in the market equilibrium, where supply and demand are equal at market price and the market is cleared, welfare is maximized because marginal utility to the buyer and marginal cost to the seller are equal. We were able to show that, as producers adjust their actions to consumer demand, they do so at the minimum possible real cost. The price that prevails in the long run in a competitive econo-

Figure 19-17
Three Analytically Different Time Periods of Market Adjustment

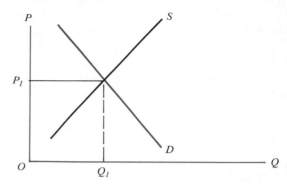

A. The Market Period   Demand and supply are already determined. Their interaction in the market determines the price and the amount sold.

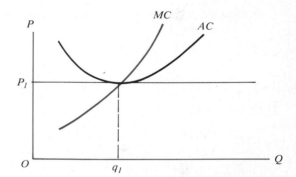

B. The Short Run   The individual firm has its plant and equipment (capital is a fixed cost), but other inputs are variable. The firm determines its level of output.

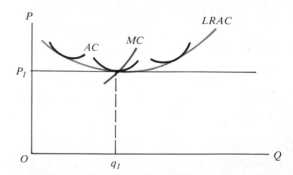

C. The Long Run   All costs are variable. The firm selects the size of plant and amount of capital investment it wishes.

my cannot be any lower for the existing level of output. The equilibrium of the firm and industry cannot produce prices any lower. In other words, producers bring resources together in the least-cost combinations, to produce at the lowest unit costs just that combination of goods that brings maximum welfare to consumers. When we understand this point, we realize why the idea of a self-adjusting market economy has had such a hold on the minds of so many people. And, as we shall see in a later chapter, the analysis can be applied just as well to a socialist economy as to a capitalist economy. Nevertheless, we must remember that this is a theoretical model only. Achievement of the welfare-maximizing results depends on the existence of four conditions, and they are not always found in a real life economy:

1. Consumers must be free to choose among the goods available in the market. This means the absence of rationing, either in wartime or in a planned economy, and the absence of legal restrictions imposed by government (such as prohibition of liquor or marijuana).

2. Markets must be free of controls over prices or quantity of sales, by either public authorities or private monopolies. It is in this respect, the existence of private monopolistic controls, that our economy shows its most serious deviation from the competitive model. Some types of planned economies are also subject to strong controls over producing units by government agencies, but, as we shall subsequently

see, this deficiency is not necessarily present in all types of planned economies.

3. The entire price system must be organized in such a way that prices reflect real production costs. If that does not happen the resulting triple equilibrium will not have much meaning so far as maximization of welfare is concerned. Monopolistic practices in our economy can prevent this condition from prevailing, and poor planning can have the same result in a planned economy. Failure to include such items as the social costs of pollution in the prices of goods will also cause market prices to differ from real costs.

4. All outputs (and inputs) must have prices attached to them. This condition is satisfied for goods produced privately, but goods supplied by governments are not always priced and sold. Public goods do not fit neatly into this process.

5. The outcome of the market adjustment process reflects the distribution of wealth and income as well as consumer wants. As we shall see in Chapter 28, there is reason to believe that a more equalitarian distribution of wealth and income will probably generate greater net welfare than a less equal distribution.

The world is different from the theory, but the theory enables us to make judgments about the world. We will use the theory for that purpose later, particularly in discussions of economic planning and monopolistic practices.

Summary

In a purely competitive industry, the profit-maximizing firm adjusts its output to the level at which marginal cost equals marginal revenue. If the typical firm makes extranormal

profits at that level of output, new firms will enter the industry. If less than normal profits are made, some firms will leave the industry. Those shifts will cause the market supply to shift, which will cause the market price to change. At the same time all firms are building the size and type of plant at which production costs are minimized. These adjustments tend toward a triple equilibrium of market, firm, and industry in which demand and supply are equal at the market price, the typical firm is maximizing profits at a level of output that also minimizes average costs of production, and no firm makes either more or less than a normal profit. As production techniques and relative scarcities of the factors of production change, the entire system will adjust as it continually seeks to reach a condition of simultaneous equilibria in market, firm, and industry. The result is that prices tend toward the level that just covers cost of production, including normal profit as part of the cost.

Key Concepts

pure competition

perfect competition

extranormal profits

market equilibrium

short-run equilibrium

long-run equilibrium

For Discussion

1. Explain why in a competitive industry the individual firm's demand curve is a horizontal line, while the industry's demand curve slopes downward as sales rise.

2. Explain the triple equilibrium of a competitive industry.

3. How can a competitive market economy simultaneously result in maximum welfare of consumers and maximum profit for producers?

4. How does technological change affect the market adjustment process in a competitive industry?

5. Profit is the driving force of the market adjustment process in a competitive industry. Explain.

6. Can competition survive if costs of production in the long run are continually declining because of economies of large-scale production? Explain.

PART 5

MONOPOLOID MARKETS

Few markets are competitive in the sense in which that term is used in Part 4. The modern economy is dominated by big business, and its dominant role seems to be increasing rather than diminishing. Chapter 20 documents the position of big business in the economy and how it has been changing. It defines the difference between competitive and monopoloid markets: competitive markets produce a horizontal demand curve for the product of the individual firm, while firms in monopoloid markets have a downward sloping demand curve for their product. Chapter 20 also introduces the three chief analytic types of monopoloid markets: pure monopoly, which is as rare as pure competition; monopolistic competition, which is common in retail trade; and oligopoly, which is characteristic of much industrial production.

Chapter 21 focuses on the basic theory of monopoloid markets. It shows that the beneficent results of competitive markets cannot be achieved. Monopoloid markets generally result in profits for sellers and prices to consumers above the competitive norm. Even when entry of new firms occurs or is threatened, causing extranormal profits to disappear, other economic inefficiencies of monopoloid markets prevail.

Chapter 22 analyzes oligopoly, focusing on the price and market strategies of firms in sectors of the economy dominated by a limited number of giant enterprises. Emphasis is placed on practices of price leadership and markup pricing, and on the various techniques used to maintain market control.

Chapter 23 examines government policy toward big business. We find a curious dichotomy. Antitrust laws seek to prevent monopoloid economic practices, but have done little to prevent the growth of oligopoly that uses those practices. Regulation has been largely ineffective in protecting the public and has instead protected the position of big business in the regulated industries; some of this old style regulation is being dismantled. The new regulation of recent years has far broader purposes and is, of course, under attack from business interests. Other aspects of government action have given support to private efforts to control markets. There is a clear conflict between the felt need of the public for protection against the behavior of big business, but business and financial interests have become too powerful for much to be accomplished.

Chapter 20

Big Business in the American Economy

The competitive model helps us to understand how markets function, but we should be careful not to apply it uncritically to the contemporary American economy. Few markets have the characteristics of pure competition, and many are far from it. Much of the American economy is dominated by large firms with a considerable degree of market power, which enables them, within limits, to influence prices, exclude competitors, influence public policy, and affect the flow of capital.

On the other hand, pure *monopoly* is also rare. The case of a single firm as the only seller of a product, with no competition, is largely of theoretic interest. Nevertheless, some aspects of the pure monopoly case are important in understanding the effect of market constraints in general, just as the theory of purely competitive markets adds to an understanding of the general nature of the competitive aspects of real-world markets.

- **Monopoly** literally means *a single seller*. It refers to an industry in which one firm supplies the entire output of a commodity.

In between the extremes of perfect competition and pure monopoly lie the many different types of market structures that make up the modern private enterprise economy. Two are particularly important: *monopolistic competition* and *oligopoly*. Monopolistic competition is characterized by a relatively large number of sellers, but market imperfections of various sorts introduce some of the characteristics of monopoly into the functioning of the market. Oligopoly is a situation in which there are relatively few sellers, each one of which is able to influence the market price and quantity sold, and thereby to affect the situation of the other sellers in the market. Most markets in the modern economy fall into these two categories, and exhibit characteristics similar to some of the essential elements of the analysis of pure monopoly. For this reason we label them *monopoloid*, to emphasize the fact that they comprise a common class of economic phenomena: pure monopoly, monopolistic competition, and oligopoly have some important characteristics in common that distinguish them sharply from perfectly competitive markets.

The key distinction between competitive and monopoloid markets is control over price by the individual firm. In competitive markets the firm is a "price taker." That is, the price is set in a competitive market, and the individual firm has no influence on the market price. It takes the price as a given datum, and then tries to maximize profits within that constraint. In a monopoloid market, whether it is a case of pure monopoly, oligopoly, or monopolistic competition, the decisions of the individual firm affect the market price: the firm is a "price maker." The ability of the firm to influence or control the market price depends on the nature and structure of the market, and is almost never complete or absolute. Monopoly, oligopoly, and monopolistic competition differ from each other in the extent of market control that individual firms can exercise, for example. But their common characteristic is that, in a greater or lesser degree, individual firms can influence the market price.

- **Monopolistic competition** is characteristic of markets with a relatively large number of sellers. Individual firms can influence the market price and quantities of goods sold.
- **Oligopoly** means literally *few sellers*. It is applied to an industry dominated by a small number of firms.

The distinction is important. Competitive markets tend to bring highly desirable results: goods desired by people at prices that just cover the necessary costs of production. Monopoloid markets do not achieve those goals, and they have a further undesirable tendency to shift income and wealth into the hands of the monopoloid firms and those who own or control them. One of the fundamental propositions that emerges from the analysis of monopoloid markets is that they tend to concentrate economic benefits, wealth, and power in the hands of the few, in contrast to the tendency of competitive conditions to disperse benefits, wealth, and power very widely among the many.

Big Business Defined

The terms *big business* and *large enterprise* are often used in two different ways. The more common usage denotes the relatively few giant enterprises in the economy as a whole, such as, for example, the 500 industrial firms and the 50 financial institutions with the largest assets. *Fortune* magazine publishes an annual census of those corporations that has become almost a part of our folklore. From time to time various governmental or private studies use a larger

Table 20–1
Types of Market Structure Compared

Market Structure	Number of Producers	Product Differentiation	Degree of Control Over Price	The Firm's Demand Curve	Examples
Perfect competition	Many	Identical products	None	Horizontal	Some farm products
Monopolistic competition	Many	Varies from much to little product differentiation	Varies from much to little control over price	Downward sloping sloping	Retail trade
Oligopoly	Few		Price leadership is common	Uncertainty can create a "kink"	Steel, autos, machinery
Monopoly	One	Unique product without close substitutes	Very great	Identical with demand curve for the product	Some public utilities

number—1000, 1500, or perhaps 2500. Whatever the specific number, these corporations are the largest of the millions of business enterprises in the country. They are the firms whose actions can affect the entire country or an important segment of the economy.

Big business also denotes a firm that is large relative to the other firms in its industry, but that may be small in comparison with corporations in the "Fortune 500." Furthermore, a moderate sized firm in the steel industry or some other highly capital intensive industry may be larger (measured in terms of sales or assets) than a "giant" in another industry such as food services or dry cleaning. A firm may be "big" in its own sector of the economy, but quite insignificant in the economy as a whole.

In this book the terms *big business* and *large enterprise* are used in the first sense, defining big business as those firms that are the largest in the economy. Their very size means that their actions affect large numbers of employees, customers, and the general public, and they are therefore objects of social concern. Large firms of that size often are able to influence the markets in which they operate—a topic central to the inquiries of this and succeeding chapters. The results of those inquiries can often be applied to the other type of "large enterprise" as well, those firms large in their own sector of the economy but small relative to the economy as a whole.

Size, then, can be thought of in both an absolute and relative sense. We use the term big business largely in an absolute sense, but recognize that some of the conclusions about the giant-size firms in our economy can be applied to firms that are large only in relation to their own markets.

Some Key Facts

The American economy is dominated by large corporations. Although there are some 11.5 million business enterprises in operation, the key sectors of the economy on which modern high standards of living are based, including manufacturing, transportation, communication, utilities, and finance, are the natural habitat of big business. Even in sectors dominated by small firms, such as services, wholesale and retail trade, and construction, some giants are to be found. And some supercorporations straddle several sectors of the economy as diversified "conglomerates."

The place of big business is expanding, although the trends are sometimes difficult to discern because of the constant flux and change going on in a modern economy. One way of getting a rough measure is to look at the share of GNP originating in those sectors of the economy dominated by oligopoly and large firms, as compared with sectors dominated by small firms. Taking the private domestic economy alone (eliminating the government sector and foreign trade), those sectors dominated by large firms originated about 60 percent of GNP in the mid-1970s as against 55 percent in 1950. The share originating in sectors of the economy dominated by small enterprise fell correspondingly from 45 to 40 percent. The predominance of big business is due more to mergers than to internal growth of firms. Compare, for example, the 200 largest manufacturing firms in 1947 and in 1968. Their share of all manufacturing assets rose from 42.4 percent to 60.9 percent. The total increase between the two dates was 18.5 percent. The increase due to mergers and acquisitions was 15.6 percent, while the effect of industry growth was only 5.2 percent. This means that, without mergers and without growth of the industry, the share of manufacturing assets controlled by the 200 largest industrials would actually have fallen to about 40 percent, but because of internal growth and because of mergers their share rose dramatically.

Stages in the Growth of Big Business

Three great periods of mergers and acquisitions transformed the basic structure of the American economy into its present state. The first came around the turn of the century (1897–98 to 1902–3), and marked the culmination of the transition to a truly national economy and the development of capital markets capable of taking large securities offerings. Great combinations were organized in many basic industries, as well as in mining, railroads, and utilities. Where formerly some industries had many small and medium sized firms, typically one giant corporation appeared that was either close to a monopoly or had gained such a large share of the market that it clearly dominated the others and managed prices and other market conditions with considerable freedom.

The classic example was the formation of the United States Steel Corporation in 1901 as a merger of corporations that produced about two-thirds of the nation's steel. The new company reached back to control its sources of iron ore, coal, and other raw materials, and forward to plants fabricating steel products. Railroads and shipping companies bound the integrated operations together. Close ties were maintained with banks, investment banking firms, and insurance companies by providing them with representation on the board of directors of U.S. Steel. These financial ties enabled the corporation to raise large amounts of capital in the midst of the depression of 1907 to gobble up Tennessee Coal and Iron Corporation, which had inconveniently developed a low-cost process for producing high-grade railroad rails that threatened to take a large and profitable market away from U.S. Steel. The dominant market position of U.S. Steel enabled it to fix the basic price of steel products with little fear that any of the lesser companies would do anything but follow the leader, enabling the corporation to make nice profits in spite of the excessive capital structure imposed on the firm by the bankers who financed it.

The basic contours of the twentieth century industrial economy in the U.S. began to take form in this first period of mergers. Large firms with a dominant share of the market were formed in basic manufacturing industries. Groupings of railroads dominated transporta-

tion: Union Pacific-Southern Pacific-Illinois Central and Great Northern-Northern Pacific-Burlington in the West; the Pennsylvania and New York Central groups in the Northeast; the Southern and Atlantic Coast Line-Louisville and Nashville systems in the Southeast; the Missouri Pacific system in the Southwest. American Telephone and Telegraph Corporation and Western Union dominated communications. Investment banking centered in J.P. Morgan and Co. and Kuhn, Loeb and Co. In manufacturing industries such as flour milling, meat packing, and others, large firms oriented to national markets drove out of business or acquired smaller firms producing for local or regional markets. Standard Oil dominated the oil industry. As the big business sector grew, the more competitive small business sector retreated.

The first merger movement subsided after the securities market slump of 1903–4, which was followed by a period of slower economic growth to the time of World War I. This intermediate period saw the first significant enforcement of the antitrust laws against big business, additional railroad legislation, and the passage of further antitrust legislation in 1914.

With the return of rapid economic growth and buoyant securities markets after World War I, a second merger movement began (1924–25 to 1930–31). There was a difference this time: lesser firms merged to challenge the industry leaders. In steel, for example, where in 1920 U.S. Steel was a goliath among pygmies, by the early 1930s Bethlehem, Republic, and several other companies had been put together by merger and acquisition to create the present oligopolistic structure of the industry. This pattern was repeated in most of the manufacturing sector. Where single-firm monopoly or dominance had appeared in the first merger movement, dominance by groups of firms (oligopoly) evolved during the second.

There were exceptions to this pattern. The automobile industry in the 1920s began the process of attrition of small firms, which left the industry with progressively fewer producers as time passed. In public utilities, the second merger movement left the entire nation dominated by three giant firms, which were broken up during the Great Depression of the 1930s, partly by the collapse of their rickety financial structures, and partly by federal legislation and regulation.

The third merger movement began in 1944–45, and continued to the early 1970s. The number of mergers tended to grow from year to year through the postwar years, culminating in a great spurt in the late 1960s. Merger activity did not begin to fall until the extremely tight money and the queasy securities market of 1969–1970 appeared. The industries most heavily affected were food and beverages, chemicals, metals, electrical and nonelectrical machinery, textiles and clothing, petroleum, aerospace, and transportation equipment. Other active fields included railroads, airlines, banks and insurance companies, hotels, and food retailing. The pace of merger activity in this period seems to have been little affected by new antitrust legislation in 1950 that was intended to discourage mergers as a means of corporate expansion.

The quarter-century of sustained merger activity after World War II was dominated by the largest companies—those with the most internal capital accumulation, the best access to capital markets, and the greatest public visibility. Large firms not only dominate their industries, they also dominate merger activity. For example, 1072 large manufacturing firms were merged into other companies; the 200 largest manufacturing companies gained 57 percent of their assets by participating in those mergers.

The merger movement of the quarter-century after World War II featured the growth of conglomerates and the international spread of big business. A conglomerate is a firm with major operations in a variety of different industries. For example, one unit may be a steel company with operations that range all the way from coal and iron ore mines through steel mills to fabricating plants. A second unit may be a group of insurance companies; a third unit may be a real estate development firm; a fourth unit may be a chemicals and plastics manufacturing firm; and so on, as the firm uses its retained earnings to acquire firms already established in new lines of activity.

There are several motives for conglomeration. Profits from the financing of acquisitions and mergers are important. So is the desire to avoid risks by diversifying: if one industrial sector is in the doldrums, another may be prosperous. The antitrust laws may make continued growth in a single industry undesirable. Large retained earnings not paid to stockholders as dividends may be available for investment, and the best profit prospects may be found in developing sectors of the economy quite different from the firm's customary lines of business. So we find that a typical conglomerate will have divisions or subsidiaries in a variety of manufacturing industries, finance, service industries, transportation, wholesale and retail trade, and so on.

The same factors lay behind the international expansion of big business. In the 1945–1970 period of rapid expansion overseas, U.S. business investment abroad increased by about $3.5 billion annually. It was particularly strong in petroleum, electronics and other "high-technology" industries. The growth of world trade, jet aircraft, and speedy communications pulled American corporations increasingly into world markets. Manufacturing companies opened branch plants or subsidiaries abroad, or acquired foreign firms. To give some idea of the extent of U.S. penetration, about one in 14 workers in Scotland is employed by subsidiaries of U.S. firms and over 20 percent of British exports are intrafirm transactions of U.S. subsidiaries with their parent firms. In 1970, the overseas portion of International Business Machines Corporation contributed more profit to the company than its domestic operations did. Large U.S. banks followed manufacturers with branches and acquisitions. Some European and Japanese firms took the same path, and a group of truly international supercorporations is beginning to appear. This development is still in its early stages, but the internationalization of world capitalism is now firmly established with a network of international corporations in manufacturing, finance, communications, transportation, and trade.

The natural history of big business shows a three-stage development, marked off by three periods of numerous and large-scale mergers and acquisitions. Around the turn of the century there was a period in which giant firms were formed to dominate particular industries. In the 1920s oligopoly—dominance of markets by several large firms—became the rule. Finally, in the 1960s and 1970s oligopolistic firms spread out into new sectors of the economy to become diversified conglomerates on an international level.

Can Competition Survive?

The urge to merge rests upon some important forces within the modern economy. The technological imperative is strong. Much industrial technology requires the use of highly expensive equipment that can be used only for a single purpose or for very limited purposes. A steel rolling mill can cost up to $500 million, together with its supporting and auxiliary equipment, and it can be used only to produce steel strips and sheets. Its high cost requires either full and continuous use, or else prices high enough to cover interest on the capital investment and payment of the standby crew during the mill's downtime. A number of industries have similar problems, including chemicals, petroleum refining, railroads, automobile production, much machinery manufacturing, and more. In these and similar industries price competition could drive prices down, in the short run, to levels that cover only variable costs, leaving all firms

with losses, unable to cover their high fixed costs and unable to convert their plants to any other use.

It is understandable that in an industry with those characteristics existing firms would try to keep out newcomers (many of whom are already barred by high capital requirements), protect their markets from competitors, and maintain price levels. Division of markets and price fixing should be expected. Where those actions are legal, as in most European countries, formal market-sharing and price-fixing agreements are common, and the groups involved are called *cartels*. In this country such collusion is illegal, so American industry has turned to merging instead. At least up to 1950 there was little legal hindrance to mergers that brought significant market power, as long as it was not used in a predatory or "unreasonable" manner against other firms. As a result, American industry is characterized by a few large multiplant firms and oligopolies which, as we shall see, tend to follow policies that stabilize market shares and bring price structures that are flexible upward but are hard to move downward.

A second factor in the urge to merge is the financial profit that can be obtained. This element in mergers has always been strong. If manipulated properly, a merger can provide large savings on taxes for the firm itself, resulting in larger aftertax profits per share and a higher price for the company's stock. Our tax system provides a variety of so-called "tax losses" that can be used by an acquiring firm. This benefits both management and stockholders, while the higher profits and stock price can be used to finance another merger. This has, indeed, been the path followed by a number of conglomerates in recent years—until investors discovered that these financial manipulations really didn't affect the long-term profitability of the business operations themselves. In addition, there are profits to be made by financial institutions and law firms that manage the mergers. In some cases of large mergers, the fees for their services have ranged upwards to tens of millions of dollars.

Finally, we come to profits themselves. Large mergers of firms in the same industry can bring the market power that eliminates or dampens competition and brings extranormal, monopolistic profits. This temptation is always present, for one characteristic of monopoly positions is higher-than-normal profits.

Beyond these immediate causes of the merger movements, there is another and perhaps even more significant underlying cause: the need for economic planning. A modern industrial product is a highly complex item, whether it is an automobile, a jet aircraft, a computer, or a radio. Its complexity requires that a very large number of raw materials and semifinished products be brought together at exactly the right point in time and space to assemble the finished product. The automobile assembly line, for example, has a series of other assembly lines feeding into it such items as engines, transmissions, steering assemblies, wheels, and so on, all the way back to the fabrication of steel sheets and castings in steel mills and foundries. The market system is a wonderful mechanism for coordinating the flow of all the inputs, for it enables the firm to buy what it needs at the going price to assure the availability of all the necessary components. But the market has its flaws. Delivery schedules may be missed and gaps may develop in the pipelines. If that happens, the huge assembly plant may have to close down (as it does nowadays if there is a strike in a small supplying plant), at considerable cost to the enterprise and its employees. These uncertainties could be overcome by holding substantial inventories of all the inputs, but the capital tied up there is also expensive. With proper coordination and a continuing, planned flow of inputs controlled by the enterprise itself, these higher costs of downtime and large inventories can be cut or eliminated. The enterprise moves back to control its supplying plants and forward to control its distributors, creating a system of continuous

flow from raw materials to retail sale under its own management. Planning replaces the market as the coordinating mechanism.

Note the importance of large capital investment in this relationship. Costly assembly facilities, like the automobile assembly plant, make downtime expensive. Where that is not the case, as in home building, delays due to imperfect coordination are much less expensive and integration of operations much less necessary.

Once a firm is integrated back to its suppliers and forward to its distributors to keep a complex, expensive plant operating efficiently, it becomes strongly concerned about the stability of its markets and prices. The integrated system requires assured outlets for the product at prices stable enough to form the basis for production planning that may take years from product design to market. Add to that the large capital investment required, and all of the elements for a push to achieve market power are present. The economic risks associated with the use of a complex, expensive technology in a market system introduce the true technological imperative: an attempt to achieve coordination through planning rather than the market, which leads in turn to large size of firms and a drive to achieve control over markets and prices. This trend is not present to an equal extent in all sectors of the economy. It is found most strongly in the technologically advanced sectors, however, which helps to explain why they are the habitat of big enterprise.[1]

Well, can competition survive? Probably not, at least in the form implied by the economic theory of competitive markets. The economic costs of competition when expensive, single-purpose equipment is used; the profits to

---

[1]The contribution to production planning made by economic stability helps us understand why big business needs big government—notwithstanding some vocal protests. Government policies designed to promote full employment and economic growth produce the lush natural environment in which the large modern corporation can flourish. Other types of firms can flourish, too, but the big enterprise requires it.

be made from mergers; the attraction of extra-normal profits; the need for long-range planning—all of these factors point to a natural evolution of giant enterprise with significant market power. The history of the past hundred years confirms that analysis, and the analysis helps to explain the history. Nor does the growth of big enterprise seem to be coming to a halt. There is probably more to come.

Oligopoly in American Industry

Manufacturing is the most important sector of the U.S. economy. It originates about 30 percent of GNP. The growing dominance of large firms in that sector is illustrated by data reported in a special study of corporate mergers prepared for the Federal Trade Commission.

In 1968 the 200 largest industrial corporations controlled over 60 percent of the total assets held by all manufacturing corporations.

The 100 largest manufacturing corporations in 1968 held a larger share of manufacturing assets than the 200 largest in 1950.

The 200 largest in 1968 controlled a share of manufacturing assets equal to that held by the 1,000 largest in 1941.

A very large proportion of U.S. manufacturing industries are dominated by a relatively few large sellers. A *concentration ratio* is the proportion of value added (roughly, selling price less cost of raw materials) by the largest domestic firms in an industry, usually calculated for the four largest firms. These ratios can be adjusted to reflect the fact that some markets are local rather than national, such as the markets for bricks, concrete, newspapers, milk, and bread. In the automobile industry about 95 percent of value added is accounted for by four firms, in steel about 55 percent, in drugs about 75 percent, and so on. When

adjusted to account for local and regional market patterns, about one-third of all value added in manufacturing is produced in industries with concentration ratios over 70 percent. Almost 80 percent of value added is from industries with concentration ratios over 40 percent. The average degree of concentration in American industry is about 60 percent. Only 12 percent of value added in U.S. manufacturing is from industries in which the top four firms hold less than 30 percent of the market.[2]

- A **concentration ratio** is the proportion of value added by the largest firms in an industry. Four-firm concentration ratios are the ones most commonly used.

Although the pattern varies widely, most oligopolies in American industry are dominated by a single giant firm, with several other large ones trailing behind. This pattern of *unbalanced oligopoly* usually features strong price leadership by the dominant firm. Often, the industry leader is as large as the next two largest firms together; the second largest firm is as large as the third and fourth firms together, and so on down the line. *Balanced oligopoly* is not common, although it exists in a few industries. It is characterized by several firms of about the same size, strength, and market power. Industrial chemicals is one industry that might qualify as a balanced oligopoly, although each of the principal firms tends to dominate in particular product markets within the industry. Some typical examples are shown in Figure 20–1.

- In a **balanced oligopoly** the leading firms are approximately the same size. An **unbalanced oligopoly** has a single firm that is considerably larger than the other leading firms.

[2]These figures have been calculated from government data by William G. Shepherd and reported in *Market Power and Economic Welfare* (New York: Random House, 1970), pp. 104–108.

Table 20–2
Oligopoly in Some Important American Industries.

Market and Leading Firms	Approximate Market Share (Percent)
Motor vehicles (3 firms) General Motors, Ford, Chrysler	70–75
Petroleum refining (4 firms) Standard Oil (N.J.) (now Exxon), Texaco, Gulf, Mobile	40–50
Iron and steel (4 firms) U.S. Steel, Bethlehem, Armco, Republic	50–60
Industrial chemicals (4 firms) Du Pont, Union Carbide, Dow, Monsanto	60–70
Aluminum (3 firms) Alcoa, Kaiser, Reynolds	80–90
Copper (3 firms) Anaconda, Kennecott, Phelps-Dodge	60–70
Metal containers (2 firms) American Can, Continental Can	80–90
Aircraft (3 firms) Boeing, McDonnell-Douglas, General Dynamics	80–90
Aircraft engines (2 firms) General Electric, United Aircraft (now United Technologies)	90–100
Drugs (4 firms) American Home Products, Merck, Pfizer, Lilly	70–80
Soaps and related products (3 firms) Proctor and Gamble, Colgate, Lever	60–70
Dairy products (3 firms) Borden, National Dairy, Carnation	60–70
Automobile tires and tubes (3 firms) Goodyear, Firestone, Uniroyal	70–80
Television broadcasting (3 firms) CBS, NBC, ABC	80–90

Profits and Big Business

There is a clear relationship between a firm's share of the market and its rate of profit. The larger the share of the market the higher the rate of profit. This is not a universal rule, but there is a clear tendency or trend in that direction.

The tendency for high profits and large market shares to go together can be modified by particular conditions in individual industries:

1. Where barriers to entry are high profits tend to be higher than where barriers to entry are low.

2. When oligopolistic firms cooperate to form a "shared monopoly" profits are higher than when oligopolists fight each other.

Figure 20–2 shows these relationships.

The higher profits made by large firms—and by those able to limit competitors or cooperate with rivals—gives those firms a further advan-

Figure 20-1
Two Types of
Oligopoly

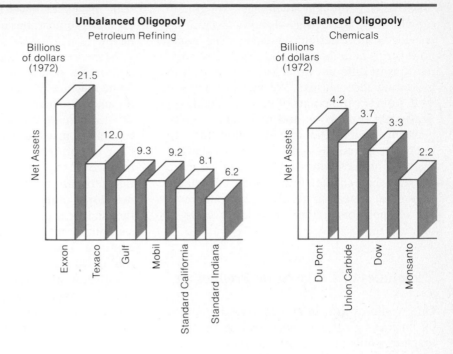

Unbalanced Oligopoly
Petroleum Refining

Billions
of dollars
(1972)

Net Assets

21.5 Exxon
12.0 Texaco
9.3 Gulf
9.2 Mobil
8.1 Standard California
6.2 Standard Indiana

Balanced Oligopoly
Chemicals

Billions
of dollars
(1972)

Net Assets

4.2 Du Pont
3.7 Union Carbide
3.3 Dow
2.2 Monsanto

Figure 20-2
Relationship Between Market Share
and Rate of Profit

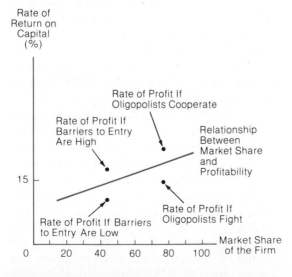

Rate of
Return on
Capital
(%)

Rate of Profit If
Oligopolists Cooperate

Rate of Profit If
Barriers to Entry
Are High

Relationship
Between
Market Share
and
Profitability

15

Rate of Profit If
Oligopolists Fight

Rate of Profit If Barriers
to Entry Are Low

Market Share
of the Firm

0   20   40   60   80   100

Adapted from William G. Shepard, *The Economics of Industrial Organization* (Englewood Cliffs, N.J.: Prentice-Hall, Inc., 1979), p. 63.

tage. Relatively high profits mean that substantial funds are available for expansion out of retained earnings. In addition, relatively high profits mean ready access to borrowed funds from the capital markets. Firms with lower rates of profit operate at a double disadvantage: lower profits provide less capital available from retained earnings and poorer access to the capital markets. The result is a long-term, pervasive tendency for the large firms to get bigger and the smaller firms to fall behind. We should not be surprised to find a growing tendency for large firms to become increasingly dominant in the private enterprise economy.

Is Big Business More Efficient?

Dominance of the U.S. economy by large enterprises must naturally raise the issue of whether their large size is the result of greater efficiency. If big business produces at lower average costs of production than smaller enterprises, such economic advantages would help explain why such firms develop as well as provide a justification for them. The issue, however, is complicated, and simple cost comparisons of different firms are both difficult to make and inconclusive. We will examine the issue from several points of view: economies of large-scale production and their limits, multiplant firms, and the role of innovation. To anticipate the conclusions a bit, we shall argue that big business does not seem to be more efficient than smaller firms. What advantages they have appear to result from monopoloid market positions rather than lower costs of production.

Economies of Large-Scale Production

One would expect, in an economy dominated by business giants, a chorus whose theme is that the giants are big because they are more efficient than smaller firms. They produce and distribute goods at lower cost. Love those friendly giants. Particularly in the years since World War II, in an era in which the dominance of large firms grew, there was strong interest in studies of the relationship between the size of firms and economic costs.

There are a number of reasons why larger production units can provide lower average costs of production than smaller units. Workers learn by doing, and become more efficient as they gain experience. Costs of production tend to be lower when people work continuously, producing a single product instead of shifting from one operation to another. This principle applies to relatively simple products like clothing and shoes, as well as to complex items such as computers and aircraft. A similar principle applies to machinery: once a machine is set up to process a particular item, it can continue indefinitely, but changing the setup to do another job uses time when the machine is not producing, as well as requiring labor to change the setup. A standardized output on a large scale makes for lower average costs. Consumers may grumble, but production managers are happy.

At the level of the plant itself there are other economies obtainable from larger outputs. Some machinery, such as boilers, steel furnaces, and oil refinery vessels, can be expanded in size to increase output more rapidly than the cost of the machinery rises. For example, doubling of output may result from an increase in the size of the machinery by only two-thirds. Furthermore, repairing specialized equipment may force other machinery to be idle, unless the plant is large enough to have several of the specialized machines so that production can continue. Thus, a steel rolling mill may have to shut down when the steel furnace that supplies it with raw steel has to be relined, unless the plant is large enough to have several steel furnaces to continue supplying the rolling mill.

Larger plants can develop other economies. It may be feasible to hire a cost accountant to continually study ways of reducing costs: a single person can guard the entrance to a large plant as effectively as a small plant; a single first aid station can service many workers as well as a few. Any plant requires a manager, and in a large plant the manager's salary can be spread over a larger output, thereby reducing average costs of production.

These economies of increased scale of production have limits, however. In almost all instances they are subject to diminishing returns. Somewhere in the enterprise there is a factor of production that is limited or fixed in amount, so that continuing increases of another factor or factors ultimately fail to pay off. Machinery may become unwieldy or subject to increasing stresses as it becomes larger. The most efficient size for one part of a complicated production process may not fit the most efficient size for other parts of the process. Workers can become dissatisfied and work less efficiently if specialization and repetition are pressed too far. If the labor market on which the plant draws is small, an enlarged work force may require higher wages. Managerial control and supervision can become less effective as the size of the operation expands. To these technical and organizational issues should be added the problem of risk. A large plant can be disabled by a fire, flood, or strike. So can a smaller plant, but the risk of large-scale disruption is reduced if output is decentralized in several small plants. Transportation costs can also limit economies of scale. The larger the production from a single plant or complex of plants, the more must be sold and the larger must be the market area. Costs of transportation will increase more rapidly than output and average costs will rise.

Finally, there are dynamic problems in a changing economy. A large plant with a large and highly specialized output can have trouble coping with economic changes that require a major shift in the product or the production process. The U.S. automobile industry in the 1970s is a good example of the difficulties that large production units can have. The firms had to adjust to higher energy costs and consumer demands for more energy-efficient cars. New production facilities were needed, but heavy investment in existing plants made management reluctant to build new ones. Even if mass production creates economies, large size can retard changes required to keep production up to date.

We can close this discussion of costs and the scale of production with a simple conclusion: there is, in most industries, an optimal or best size of production plant. Economies of large-scale production define that optimum size. But those economies ultimately disappear, further expansion can take place only with higher costs, and still larger plants can produce only at higher costs per unit of output. In terms of our earlier discussion of costs of production, the long-run cost curve does not continue declining indefinitely as quantity of output rises. This means that, except for some possible exceptional cases like local or regional utilities, the present high levels of economic concentration cannot be attributed to greater efficiency of large production units.

Multiplant Firms

The limits to economies of large-scale production are one reason for the appearance of multiplant firms. Retained earnings, plowed back into the enterprise, provide for corporate growth and expansion. For a time, economies of scale lead to expansion of a single plant. But as the potential for reduced costs at one operation diminishes and disappear, operation of a second plant, often at another location in an entirely different market area to save on transportation costs, becomes the more profitable use of retained earnings.

Among economists who have studied multiplant firms there seems to be general agreement that these firms have few advantages with respect to production costs. That is, a single firm with six plants, for example, each of the most efficient size, will not have lower costs of production than six separate firms, each with the optimal size plant. The multiplant firm may have some advantages in specialized management services, in producing a wider range of products, and in reduced risk of disruption of output, but these advantages, if present, are small.

Multiplant firms have other advantages, however, and most of them are associated with the monopoloid position of large multiplant enterprises. First, they are able to advertise and promote their products more readily than smaller firms. The cost of large advertising campaigns, spread over a large output, will not raise average costs significantly, while the resultant increase in customers may enable the firm to raise its selling price. The small firm, on the other hand, often does not have the resources to mount large promotion campaigns. The large firm has the advantage because it is large, not because it is more efficient.

Second, large multiplant firms have advantages in capital markets that are not available to smaller firms. Some of these advantages provide real economies, although they are small. It is cheaper for a bank to process one large loan than six smaller loans, for example, and the risk of disruption is less for a multiplant firm. But the chief advantage of large firms is the close relationship they develop with large financial institutions. This relationship provides good access to large amounts of capital when it is needed. Furthermore, when a bank or insurance company has millions of dollars in loans and investments committed to a large firm, there are strong incentives to keep the firm operating and provide the capital to see it through difficult times. The large multiplant firm is, therefore, better able to withstand severe business recessions, to survive competitive battles, and to buy out rivals. Bigness provides the financial alliances that promote bigness.

Third, large multiplant firms can develop the market power to dominate the pricing policies of an industry. This price leadership enables dominant firms to establish prices that give them higher profits than other firms. The price leader must set prices that are acceptable to the other large firms in the industry, or those firms won't follow the leader, but that constraint leaves considerable leeway for the leader to select a price that is best for itself.

Multiplant firms tend to earn higher profits than single-plant firms, but those favorable results depend primarily on their monopoloid characteristics: large size, market dominance, and financial connections. Multiplant operations are able to provide some economies that can lower average costs per unit of output, but they are relatively small. On the other hand, diseconomies associated with managing and coordinating large, complex, and dispersed operations are also present, and they can be substantial. So is big business more efficient than smaller enterprises, as its propagandists and sycophants claim? The bulk of the evidence points to a negative answer.

Big Business and Innovation

It is sometimes argued that big business is more innovative than small enterprise, that the economy must tolerate monopoloid market positions because they provide the high profits that are used for research and development of new products and processes. Not so. Here again, the evidence is against bigness. The record shows that the highest levels of innovation and investment occur in what might best be termed medium-sized firms. Innovation is strongest among firms with sales of up to about $250–400 million. Above that level there is little or no increase in innovation. The moderate-sized firm seems to be most favorable for innovation.

These findings are understandable. In competitive industries with numerous small firms, each enterprise is too busy surviving to devote much effort to research and innovation, and capital for these purposes just isn't available. The economist's model of perfect competition is not fertile ground for innovation.

Strong monopoloid positions are not conducive to innovation, either. There are several reasons: the number of sources for innovation are restricted; there is little incentive to gain a strong market position through research and development; and barriers to entry keep out innovating firms. There is a great deal of research and development done by large firms, but most is designed to protect existing market positions, for example, concentration on patents that protect existing patents by covering surrounding areas or by making small advances over existing technology. Indeed, much of this type of research has the effect of slowing down innovation through control of discoveries that could threaten existing products or processes.

The best results seem to come from firms that are large enough to generate enough resources to mount substantial research and development programs but that are not so large that they have a strong market position to protect. The other important source of innovation is, of course, the individual entrepreneur working alone or with a small group to develop something really new—but that person is very likely to sell out to a large firm that has access to the capital necessary for full development of the innovation. Large firms have a favored position in the race to gain control over innovations, even though they are not particularly good innovators themselves. A case in point is the new science of genetic engineering, which was developed largely in university laboratories supported by funds from the federal government. Small research-oriented firms were spun off from that base. At that point large conglomerate firms got into the act, not by setting up their own research laboratories, but by investing in gene-splicing companies doing research they might be able to develop further.

Innovation is, however, an important means by which the entrenched positions of large firms can be challenged. New products, materials, and technologies that promise reduced costs or expanded markets represent an attack on the economic status quo. And when established firms seek to gain control over the innovation process they become part of it themselves, using new products and processes continually to stake out growth positions. Examples are found, for example, in the chemical and pharmaceutical industries, where *some* of the leading firms have been important innovators.

On the other hand, it is quite possible that the process of innovation itself may be administered for purposes of stability while new firms are kept out by various barriers to entry. The automobile industry is a good example. Since the late 1920s, when the industry took on its present tight oligopoly form, every significant technological advance was introduced first on foreign cars, whether developed initially by a U.S. company or not. The bulk of U.S. research and development spending is related to the military and is financed by the federal government, and the most innovative firms tend to be medium-sized rather than either the giants or the small ones. While the general

proposition that some degree of business size and oligopolistic structure may be most conducive to technological advance and its diffusion, it is difficult to justify the dominance of major industries by one or a few giants on the ground of innovation.

Financial Advantages of Large Firms

The chief advantage of large firms is financial. Their large size provides not only large amounts of retained earnings from profits, but also relatively high rates of profit derived from their strong market positions. High rates of profit are then able to attract capital from the capital markets. Finally, business alliances with large banks and insurance companies assure financial support when needed.

The combination of large retained earnings, attractiveness to outside investors, and financial alliances gives large firms a favored position in the process of capital accumulation. They are able to mobilize large amounts of capital to take advantage of new, profit-making opportunities on a scale not open to firms with smaller economic resources. For example, in the new field of microwave communications, four firms are moving toward dominance. Only one, M.C.I. Telecommunications, is a relative newcomer. The others built their positions using capital retained from earnings in other sectors of the economy: telephone communications (American Telephone and Telegraph Corporation), manufacturing and communications (International Telephone and Telegraph Corporation), and railroad transportation (Southern Pacific Corporation). This new industry, already dominated by four firms, will probably be joined by the U.S. Post Office if it succeeds in its effort to develop microwave delivery of mail. All but one of the smaller companies that attempted to enter the field have already fallen out, unable to compete with the huge capital resources available to the giants.

There are many other cases. For example, Warner-Lambert, a pharmaceuticals and consumer products conglomerate, entered the bread-making business in 1978 by absorbing a highly successful bakery in the New York metropolitan area and expanding it to a nationwide operation, using large retained earnings from other operations. "Lack of capital" led the local bakery to look for a buyer, according to the *Wall Street Journal*, even though it was a highly profitable operation, and its successful expansion was due in large part to its "well-heeled parent." In another recent merger Westinghouse, the electrical equipment manufacturer, acquired Teleprompter, the nation's largest cable television firm, using its strong alliances with important financial institutions, plus its large internal cash flow to raise the purchase money. Westinghouse and its financial allies could also supply large amounts of capital to Teleprompter for the rapid expansion of cable television expected in the 1980s.

In both of these instances each of the coupling firms benefited. The large conglomerate gained entry to a potentially highly profitable field, while the smaller firm gained easy access to capital for expansion. But with respect to the changing structure of wealth and power, these mergers are examples of the big getting bigger by taking over the pioneering and innovative advances made by others. Warner-Lambert gained access to an innovative and successful marketing technique, while Westinghouse acquired the fruits of successful entrepreneurship in a new sector of the communications and entertainment field. Neither giant took the initial risks; they let others do that. But once the innovation proved successful they were able to gain control.

The Financial Sector

A high degree of concentration also prevails in the financial sector of the U.S. economy. In addition, large financial institutions exercise a substantial degree of control over large firms in other sectors of the economy, creating an even greater degree of economic concentration than that brought about by the recent move toward conglomeration of monopoloid firms into giant units.

Commercial banking shows approximately the same oligopolistic structure as industry. Although there are over 14,000 commercial banks in the United States, the 50 largest hold about half of all deposits and the 10 largest about 30 percent. Concentration on a national scale has increased rapidly in recent years: the 50 largest have a substantially larger proportion of all bank assets than the 100 largest fifteen years ago.

Most cities have a high concentration ratio in banking. The average four-bank concentration ratio for the 15 largest metropolitan areas had been climbing slowly to about 70 percent by the late 1970s. Smaller cities had even greater concentration ratios, with two-bank concentration ratios averaging over 70 percent for the smallest metropolitan areas.

Significant changes are taking place in banking concentration. By 1980 a clear trend toward national banking operations by the large commercial banks in New York, Chicago, and California was evident. As the large banks spread their operations, banks in smaller centers seek to protect themselves by mergers, acquisitions, and expansion to strengthen their share of statewide or regional business. Commercial banking is in a transition toward a much smaller number of units and a higher degree of concentration.

Banks are in a particularly strategic position with respect to large business firms. The chief business done by banks involves loans to business firms, and in the case of large banks, to large enterprises. These relationships are intimate and stable, like marriages used to be. The firm relies on a continuing "line of credit" from the bank, and the bank comes to know a great deal about the firm. Banks must know about their risks, and they maintain close relationships with the officers of the firms they serve. Bank officials are often members of boards of directors of large customers, but these ties merely formalize the informal relationships that exist between large and regular borrowers and their lenders. Furthermore, banks seldom compete for steady customers of other banks, knowing that a live-and-let-live policy protects their good customers from raids by other banks. Commercial banking contributes to the monopoloid structure of the American economy in two ways. First, most financial markets are dominated by a small number of relatively large banks, and a relatively few large banks service the giant corporations. Second, the close ties between big banks and big corporations bind big industry and big finance together, creating an even larger community of interest.

Insurance companies make up a second major segment of the financial markets, with total assets in 1973 of $252.4 billion. There are over 1500 life insurance companies in the United States, but the 10 largest hold about 55 percent of all life insurance company assets, the 20 largest about 65 percent, and the 50 largest about 80 percent. Insurance companies occupy a strategic position in the capital markets. Most life insurance policies provide for payment of premiums that build up a "cash value" over and above the funds necessary to pay claims. This cash value represents savings made by the policy holder that are invested by the insurance company. These investments are channeled primarily into mortgages on both residential and business real estate, corporate bonds, and, to a lesser extent, into common stocks. Thus, in the 1950s and 1960s about half of all new issues of bonds of nonfinancial corporations were acquired by insurance companies—and this represented about 45 percent of all external financing of those corporations. Sorry, but more recent data are just not available.

In the years since World War II, two other financial institutions have moved to positions of importance in financial markets. These are mutual funds and pension funds. A mutual fund is an investment fund in which an individual buys shares. The money is then invested in securities or other assets, and dividends or other income of the fund are either reinvested or paid out to the owners. The mutual fund is usually managed by a separate, privately owned company that is paid a fee for its managerial services based on the amount of assets in the fund. Mutual funds and other investment companies have grown rapidly. Their ownership of securities reached $70 billion in 1975, rising from a little over $1 billion in 1949 and about $10 billion in 1959. The 10 largest mutual fund groups held about 60 percent of the total.

Pension funds invest the assets of private retirement programs. Most of them are managed by the trust departments of commercial banks, thereby adding further to the economic clout of those institutions. In 1969, private pension funds in the U.S. owned some $106 billion of assets, including $40 billion of common stock. Their holdings are rising at a rate of about $5 billion annually. The growth of pension funds is expected to accelerate sharply in the near future. They are expected to have total assets of about $200 billion by the early 1980s and will be generating an annual flow of $10 billion of new funds each year. These are only the private funds: public pension funds of federal, state, and local governments are equally large.

Although the concentration of control of these huge assets is difficult to measure exactly, these institutions make up a relatively cohesive financial community with many informal and sometimes formal ties binding them together. There is a high degree of concentration in each sector of the financial community. Commercial banks run the bank trust funds and manage most of the private pension funds. Many insurance companies are moving into the business of managing and selling mutual funds. Many banks, through their trust departments and the pension funds they manage, control large blocks of their own stock. Finally, there are many instances of interlocking directorates between large financial firms and between financial firms and other large business enterprises.

Corporate Interest Groups

The only comprehensive study of informal *corporate interest groups* in the U.S. economy was done for the year 1935. It was limited to the 250 largest corporations of that era, and showed that at least eight "more or less clearly defined interest groups," including 106 of the 250 with nearly two-thirds of the combined assets, could be identified through interlocking directorates alone.

Two clustered around large New York banking interests. By far the largest involved the greatest investment bank of that era, J. P. Morgan and Co., and the First National Bank of New York, together with 39 of the 250 largest corporations. The second largest was built around another investment bank, Kuhn, Loeb, and included 15 major corporations.

Three interest groups were constructed from the firms dominated by family interests, the Rockefellers (mainly in oil), the Mellons (companies headquartered primarily in Pittsburgh), and the Du Ponts (chemicals, GM, and related firms). The other three were loose groupings of companies related to each other through important banks in Boston, Cleveland, and Chicago.

Although the economy has changed quite sharply since the years of the Great Depression —firms have grown, changed, and merged, and whole new industries have appeared—the pattern of corporate interest groups continues. The membership and structure of any one group may shift, however. For example, when Richard K. Mellon died in 1970 his obituaries noted that the Mellon family still owned dominating interests in six major corporations, listed here with their assets.

Gulf Oil Corp.	$8.1 billion
Aluminum Corp. of America	$1.5 billion
Mellon National Bank	$4.9 billion
Koppers Co.	$0.5 billion
Carborundum Co.	$0.3 billion
General Reinsurance Co.	$0.3 billion

The family also held, in addition to their interests in these firms with total assets of $15.6 billion, a substantial interest in the First Boston Corporation, an important investment bank associated with a number of large firms headquartered in New England, and Richard Mellon himself owned a $20 million investment in the stock of General Motors Corporation.

The interest groups centering around banking interests also remain. A 1968 investigation by a subcommittee of the House Committee on Banking and Currency showed that the Morgan banking group, much changed and transformed, was still strong. It was based on the Morgan Guaranty Trust Co. of New York, whose commercial bank deposits of $7.3 billion made it one of the large New York banks, but by no means the largest. Its trust department, however, managed assets of some $17 billion. In these trust accounts it held 5 percent or more of the common stock of 72 corporations. Its officers are on the boards of directors of more than 100 companies. Together these companies in which Morgan Guaranty has an important investment or managerial position had total assets of almost $30 billion.

Another study of the 200 largest U.S. nonfinancial corporations in the late 1960s indicated that 56 could be placed in just six corporate interest groups. Three centered in New York financial institutions: Chase Manhattan Bank, the Morgan group of banks, and two closely related investment banks, Lehman Brothers and Goldman, Sachs and Co. Another was the Mellon group. Two others were based on the largest banks in Cleveland and Chicago. There is a network of relationships that makes cousins of entire broods of economic giants.

- **Corporate interest groups** are formed when several corporations ally with each other via stock ownership, interlocking directorates, or financial ties.

Interlocking Directorates

One of the most important ways in which large corporations are related to each other is through a common, or interlocking, body of directors. It is illegal for a member of the board of directors of one large firm to also sit as a board member of a competing firm. But it is not illegal for board members of two competing firms to be members of the board of a third noncompeting firm. Thus, it would be illegal if Mr. *A* were on the board of both General Electric Co. and Westinghouse Electric Corp. But it would not be illegal for Mr. *A* and Mr. *B* each to be on the board of the Bankamerica Corp., with Mr. *A* also on the General Electric board and Mr. *B* on the Westinghouse board. These indirect *interlocking directorates* are quite common, providing meeting places for corporate executives who are supposed to manage competing interests.

- **Interlocking directorates** are formed when an individual is on the board of directors of several different firms. Interlocks can be *direct* (one person on the board of more than one firm) or *indirect* (directors of two different firms on the board of a third firm).

It is difficult to estimate, or underestimate, the significance of these informal relationships. For example, in the electrical equipment industry a complicated system of interlocks tied the four chief firms together—General Electric, Westinghouse, Western Electric, RCA—through other industrial firms and financial institutions, and tied the large companies to smaller firms in the industry and to potential customers, suppliers, and competitors. This was the industry that, after a long history of incidents of price fixing, developed the greatest illegal price-fixing and market-sharing conspiracy in our history during the 1950s and early 1960s. The legal informal ties and illegal conspiracies may have had no connection whatsoever, and interlocking directorates do not necessarily lead to violation of the law, but one is not surprised when the two occur in the same industry.

The Federal Trade Commission has documented the wide prevalence of interlocking directorates throughout American industry and the ties they create between industrial and financial firms.[3] Hardly any large-scale manufacturing industry is free of them, and almost all of the large firms are involved. According to the FTC, interlocking dictorates

Tend to limit or eliminate competition.
May forestall the development of competition.
May give rise to communities of interest and create a united front against any who threaten habitual relationships or established preeminence.
Evoke preferential treatment in the distribution of materials in short supply.
May . . . create preferential access to market outlets.
May establish a vertical relation that assures adequate credit to favored companies and a withholding of credit and capital from their competitors.

Interlocking directorates are one of the main ways in which intimate ties between nominally independent firms are created and sustained. They help to formalize other ties, based on customer-supply relationships, credit and other financial connections, and stock ownership, maintaining a subtle web of relationships among the group of large firms that dominate much of the American economy.

---

[3]*Report of the Federal Trade Commission on Interlocking Directorates* (Washington, D.C.: U.S. Government Printing Office, 1951).

Trade Associations

When firms are few, it is relatively easy to achieve cooperative behavior and community of interest. When they are numerous the task is more difficult. Some type of formal organization is necessary. In the American economy that need has been met by formation of the *trade association*.

A trade association is an organization through which firms in an industry or trade combine to further their common interests. The antitrust laws prohibit them from engaging in practices that restrict competition and most of them have never been charged with illegal activities. However, many of them do things that tend to create common patterns of behavior among their members. Among these activities are promotion of common cost-accounting methods (which tend to create a common cost basis for pricing); reporting of prices (which tends to identify and isolate price cutters); and reporting of sales and inventories (which can promote market sharing and restriction of output). The danger is that these relatively harmless activities will pass by imperceptible stages into illegal conspiracies. Over 200 legal actions have been brought against various associations that have been accused of price fixing, division of markets, allocation of customers, and restriction of output.

The most important function of trade associations is their political activities. They are among the most important lobbyists with government administrators and legislatures at all levels of government. When firms in an industry wish to promote or hinder legislation, appropriations, and administrative rulings, the contacts with government are usually carried out by the industry's trade association.

- A **trade association** is an organization of firms in the same line of business whose objective is to further the common interests of its members.

Stockholder, Manager, and Financier

The stockholders of most large corporations have become little more than risk takers, delegating their functions as managers to corporation boards of directors. Although they remain the legal owners of the enterprise, they no longer control the making of policy. This *separation of ownership and control*, first pointed out by Thorstein Veblen in his *Theory of Business Enterprise* (1902) and documented by Adolf Berle and Gardner Means in *The Modern Corporation and Private Property* (1932), rests upon very wide dispersal of stock ownership. A typical giant corporation has hundreds of millions of shares of common stock outstanding, held by millions of shareholders. Most shareholdings are under 1,000 shares. If a shareholder disagrees with the management's policies, he or she can protest or even vote a handful of shares against the management at the annual shareholder's meeting. But the only effective action is to sell the shares. The shareholder has a financial role to play but has no avenue to policy decisions. Risk taking, yes. Control, no. The effect of wide dispersal of ownership, the difficulties in making one's voice heard, plus the ease with which securities can be bought and sold, usually leaves management in command.

Management's independence is further strengthened by its ability to use profits and other internal flows of cash for investment purposes. Expansion can, and does, come largely from profits and depreciation allowances for large firms; some three-fourths of all investment spending by the 500 largest nonfinancial corporations comes from that source. This pattern may well benefit the stockholders in the long run if it raises the value of their shares enough to compensate them for reduced dividends. But whether they like it or not, the stockholders have little to say about the matter of having smaller dividends in return for the potential of higher stock value.

● **Separation of ownership and control** is the situation in many corporations, in which management is largely independent of stockholder control, largely because of wide dispersal of stock ownership.

Some large firms are controlled by wealthy individuals or families who own enough common stock to dominate. In a large corporation in which most stockholdings are small and widely dispersed, ownership of 5 percent of the stock may be enough for control and over 10 percent is certainly enough. One study for the year 1963, using 10 percent ownership as the dividing line between owner and management control, found that owner control prevailed for 33 of the 200 largest U.S. nonfinancial corporations. A 1967 study, using the same dividing line, found that 11 of the top 100 corporations were controlled through stock ownership by a single individual or family.[4] Wealthy capitalists have definitely not disappeared from the economic scene.

Control by financial institutions is also important. The trust departments of commercial banks are in a particularly strategic position with respect to control of business enterprises. These units hold and manage the assets of wealthy individuals and families, the endowment funds of many colleges and other nonprofit institutions, and the pension and benefit funds of many labor unions. In carrying out their functions as financial managers, bank trust departments usually have authority to vote the shares of common stocks in their care. These holdings are also highly concentrated. By the mid-1970s the ten largest bank trust departments held about one-third of all assets held by bank trust departments, including about half of all employee pension and benefit fund assets.

A significant amount of control of giant corporations by financial institutions has developed. One study of corporate control showed that in 1967–69, 67 of the 200 largest nonfinancial corporations in the United States were controlled by financial institutions through either ownership of common stock or voting rights over managed assets. Another 11 of the 200 largest firms were partly controlled by financial institutions and partly by large individual or family stock ownership. Thirty of the 200 firms were controlled by individual or family ownership, and two others were partially so controlled. There was no identifiable center of control for 85 others, which means that control lay with the firm's management rather than with stockholders or financial institutions. Five firms fitted into none of the three chief categories. Of the 200 largest nonfinancial institutions, a little over one-third were controlled by financial institutions, perhaps one-fifth by very wealthy individuals or families, and over 40 percent by management insiders.[5]

The influence of large financial institutions was further documented in a 1978 report by a U.S. Senate subcommittee. The subcommittee staff examined control of common stock in 122 of the largest U.S. corporations whose common stock comprised 41 percent of the market value of all outstanding common stock in the United States—which is itself an indication of corporate concentration. It found that 21 large investment institutions, including 11 banks, 4 insurance companies and 6 investment company groups held "significant voting strength" in the 122 corporations. Part of the stock controlled by the 21 financial firms was owned directly, and part was controlled through trust, pension, and investment funds managed by the financial institutions. The study did not charge that the financial firms controlled the 122 giant

---

[4]Robert J. Larner, "Ownership and Control of the 200 Largest Nonfinancial Corporations," *American Economic Review*, Vol. LVI, No. 4, Part 1 (September 1966) pp. 777–87. Robert Sheehan, "Proprietors in the World of Big Business," *Fortune*, Vol. LXXV, No. 7, (June 15, 1967), pp. 178–83.

[5]For further details see David M. Koltz, *Bank Control of Large Corporations in the United States* (Berkeley, CA: University of California Press, 1978).

corporations, but it did show that the financial firms controlled more than 5–10 percent of their voting stock, which is the figure that many economists believe will normally bring control of a large corporation whose stock ownership is widely dispersed. Even this study probably underestimated the extent of financial control of large corporations, however, for it did not include stock owned by individuals but held by brokerage houses, which can exercise voting rights if the individual owner does not.

The Business Elite

The business leaders of the rather small number of large firms that dominate the American economy (200, 250, 500, 750?) necessarily compose a small group. At the most it comprises a cadre of perhaps five to ten thousand persons: top executives and directors, partners in big law and accounting firms, chief executives of important financial institutions. It is a tiny fraction of the total adult population.

As a group, the business elite comes predominantly from an urban, white, Protestant, upper or upper-middle income background. Recent studies of the social and economic characteristics of post-World War II business leaders by W. Lloyd Warner and James C. Abegglen, C. Wright Mills, and J. William Domhoff, building on studies of earlier periods by Frank Taussig and C. S. Joslyn, and William Miller, show very few immigrants or sons of immigrants, small numbers from farm worker or lower white-collar backgrounds, relatively few Catholics and Jews, and no blacks. About 10 percent of them inherited their top positions by moving into family dominated companies. About 5 percent were entrepreneurs who built their own companies. Some 10–15 percent were professional men, mostly lawyers, who moved into top business positions after professional success. The majority of business leaders, however, some 70 percent, moved to top positions by working up through the business hierarchy. This is a much greater proportion than in the past. Seventy-five years ago the entrepreneurs and family connected managers were far more important (68 percent), the career executive much less important (18 percent), and the proportion of lawyers and other professionals was about the same as now.

These data suggest that the business elite is a relatively open one. It brings in recruits from outside the already existing elite group, and this tendency appears to be increasing. The chief source of recruits is the system of higher education. The business elite has always had more than average education, and today that is truer than ever. The educational system is an important screening mechanism and the cost of education helps to explain why so many of the business elite are from upper and upper-middle income groups. They tend to be drawn heavily out of the Ivy League colleges (from which most of the managers from "old wealth" families graduate) and out of the large state universities (where most of the career executives get their educations).

This first level of screening at the college level is supplemented by executive training programs and on-the-job training. There the aspiring top manager is indoctrinated with the business point of view and the ideology of management, there he or she learns to "fit in" with those already at the top, and there he or she develops the "good judgment" that top management requires. Since advancement depends on the judgment of those already at the top, a premium is placed on development of viewpoints and life styles that already prevail. As Mills put it, "In personal manner and political view, in social ways and business style, he must be like those who are already in, and upon whose judgments his own success rests." The business elite is a self-perpetuating and self-selecting group that develops a common set of values, an accepted mode of behavior, and an unspoken but recognizable set of goals.

Its value system, in particular, stresses the desirability of wealth, both for the individual and the nation, and accepts as generally beneficent the institutions of private property and the national state. Indeed, strengthening and preservation of those institutions seems to be a fundamental point of agreement among the business elite, irrespective of individual political persuasion.

Summary

The American economy is dominated by giant corporations, particularly in those sectors we look to for the sources of high and rising standards of living and technological progress. If there is any trend, it is toward increased concentration, primarily through mergers rather than internal growth of firms. The dominant pattern in industry is not monopoly, but oligopoly, with many important industries being characterized by a leading group of large firms in which a single firm is significantly larger than the other big ones. These positions of dominance are sustained by barriers to new firms, chiefly product differentiation with large selling costs, and large-scale production with large capital requirements. Other barriers can include patent control and control over raw materials. The financial sector also shows a significant degree of concentration in banking, insurance, and control over trust and pension funds.

Large multiplant firms tend to be more profitable than smaller firms. Higher profitability does not necessarily mean greater efficiency, however. There are limits to economies of large-scale production that seem to be reached well before the size of giant firms is attained, and the advantages of multiplant firms appear to be derived largely from their ability to influence markets and gain favored access to financial resources. Nor do large firms lead in innovations. Market control plus financial strength are the chief reasons for the higher profitability of the economic giants.

The big business community is bound together in several ways, chiefly through corporate interest groups, interlocking directorates, and trade associations, in addition to the financial ties that function through the relatively highly concentrated financial sector. Stockholders have relatively little control over the policies of large corporations. Rather, control rests very heavily with business management itself, financial interests, and a few wealthy families. The business elite is a relatively open one, but it is a self-selecting and self-perpetuating group that passes on a business ideology from one generation to the next.

This structure is a far cry from that envisaged by the pure theory of competitive markets. We should not expect it to function in the same fashion as the economy of the theoretical firm in a theoretically competitive environment. Nor does it, in fact. In succeeding chapters we analyze the performance of the monopoloid sector, first by examining the general cases of monopoly and imperfect competition and then by taking a closer look at oligopolistic markets. Then we examine the relationships between government and business that have developed in an economy dominated by oligopolies. We shall be dealing throughout with the problem of economic power—its uses, its effects, and how it might be brought under control.

Key Concepts

monopoly
monopolistic competition
oligopoly
concentration ratio

balanced oligopoly
unbalanced oligopoly
corporate interest groups
interlocking directorates

trade association
separation of ownership and control

For Discussion

1. In view of the spread and growth of oligopoly in the U.S. economy, do you think competition will die out?

2. Discuss: Profits of U.S. corporations should grow for the good of the economy and the nation as a whole.

3. Give some examples of both economies of large-scale production and diseconomies of large-scale production.

4. Should the federal government break up oligopolistic big businesses to restore competition and protect consumers?

5. Is the growth of big business the result of malfunctions in the market mechanism or of natural economic forces in a market economy?

6. Discuss: The centralized structure of big business and big government is desirable because both are necessary to maintain U.S. power in the world.

Chapter 21

Monopoloid Markets: The Fundamentals

When the average person buys or sells common stock listed on the New York Stock Exchange, he trades at the market price prevailing at the time of his transaction. He has no control over the price. Rather, he decides only whether he will buy or sell and, if so, how much. This condition is characteristic of market competition.

The New York Stock Exchange is *not* an example of perfect competition, however. If a large mutual fund wishes to buy or sell stock in large quantities, say 400,000 shares of stock in which normal trading is about 25,000 shares daily, that single transaction can have a decided impact on the prevailing price. A large purchase will pull the price up, while a large sale would push it down. This condition is characteristic of imperfect markets: the seller or buyer can influence the market price.

In terms of economic analysis, the monopoloid market differs from the competitive case in that the individual firm can increase its sales only by reducing its price. This chapter examines the economic consequences of that difference. It starts with an analysis of pure monopoly to show that the optimal results of pure competition are not achieved. Monopoly brings a higher price and different level of output than the competitive case, making it impossible for the economy to produce efficiently or to maximize consumer welfare. We then move to the case of monopolistic competition, in which a number of firms, each with a downward sloping demand curve, compete with each other. In spite of competition that eliminates monopoly profits, price is still high and output restricted when compared to the competitive case.

- **Monopoloid markets** are those in which the demand curve faced by the firm slopes downward to the right. More can be sold only if price is reduced.

These findings are of the utmost significance. They show that even without the deliberate manipulation of markets by monopolies—even if "competition" prevails—common forms of market structure in our economy bring a less than optimal outcome.

The Demand Curve Faced by the Firm

For purposes of economic analysis, the demand conditions faced by the individual firm define the fundamental difference between perfectly

Figure 21-1
Demand for Its Product as Seen by Firm in
Perfectly Competitive Industry

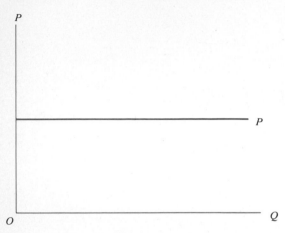

More can be sold at the existing price.

Figure 21-2
Demand for Its Product as Seen by Firm in
Imperfectly Competitive Industry

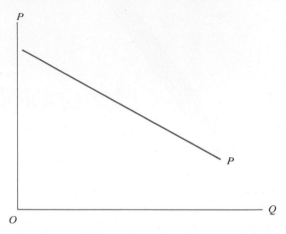

More can be sold only if price is reduced.

and imperfectly competitive markets. In one case the seller can sell all he wishes to sell at the market price. In the other, the seller is able to sell more only if he reduces his price. If he wants a higher price he will have to accept a smaller quantity of sales. The difference can be shown graphically by drawing typical demand curves as they are faced by sellers in the two circumstances, shown in Figures 21–1 and 21–2.

**Average and Marginal Revenue
Under Imperfect Competition**
When the demand curve for a firm's product slopes downward to the right, as in Figure 21–2, marginal revenues no longer coincide with average revenues. Since more can be sold only if price is reduced, and the price must apply to all units sold, the additions to revenue (marginal revenue) must be less than the price (average revenue). This condition is illustrated in Table 21–1 with a hypothetical example in which the selling price falls as the quantity sold is increased. When the firm sells 10 units the price per unit (average revenue) is $25. Total

sales revenue is $250. But for the firm to sell 11 units instead of 10, the price would have to be reduced to $24 per unit for each of the 11 units sold. Total sales revenue would rise to $264, an increase (marginal revenue) of $14. Increasing the quantity sold to 12 would require a further price reduction to $23 per unit, generating total sales revenue of $276 and a marginal revenue of $12.

This example is only another illustration of the basic arithmetic relationship, explained in Chapter 18, that when an average quantity is falling, the corresponding marginal quantity lies below it. It is particularly applicable to the analysis of imperfect markets, however, for they are characterized by the phenomenon of falling average revenues for the individual firm as output rises. That characteristic relationship is a feature of all the analytical models of imperfect markets.

The implications of a downward sloping demand curve for the firm are important. It means that the results found in the purely competitive market cannot be achieved in an imperfectly competitive one. Why that is true

Table 21–1
Price and Marginal Revenue Under Imperfect Competition

Quantity Sold	Price (Average Revenue)	Total Revenue	Marginal Revenue
10	$25	$250	
11	24	264	$14
12	23	276	12
13	22	286	10
14	21	294	8
15	20	300	6

will become evident when we examine two limiting cases: monopoly (a single seller of a product) and monopolistic competition (many sellers, but all facing a downward sloping demand curve). For the present, it is sufficient to say that the downward sloping demand curve makes it impossible to achieve the triple equilibrium of market, firm, and industry characterized by pure competition.

Monopoly

The simplest case of imperfect markets is that of a single seller. The demand curve he faces will be the same as the market demand curve for the product, and it will slope downward to the right (Figure 21–3). The monopolist is the industry, and the market demand curve is the firm's demand curve.

● **Monopoly** exists in a market with a single seller (or single firm).

The monopolist will, of course, have cost conditions similar to those of any firm, except that he may not feel the same pressure toward highly efficient operations that are felt by the competitive firm. In the short run, with his existing plant and equipment, average costs for the monopolist will fall, reach a low point, and then rise. Marginal costs will rise to cross the average cost curve at its lowest point, as in

Figure 21–3
Demand Conditions Faced by a Monopolist

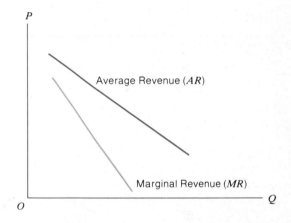

Figure 21–4. What level of output and price will the monopolist choose? We can start with the assumption that he seeks to maximize his profits. He isn't worried about potential competitors because he controls all necessary patents, or owns some essential raw materials, or has colluded with potential competitors to exclude them from the market. These arrangements free him to concentrate single-mindedly on maximizing his gains.

Profit maximization requires that marginal cost MC equal marginal revenue MR. This is true for the monopolist, with his downward sloping demand curve, just as it is true for the competitive firm with its horizontal demand

Figure 21–4
Cost Conditions Faced by a Monopolist

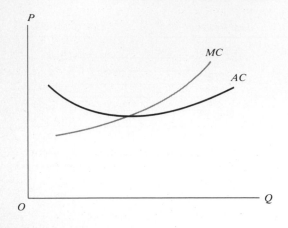

MC. When the profit maximizing monopolist compares his cost and revenue conditions, he will be able to determine the unique level of output and price at which $MC = MR$ and at which profit is greatest. That situation is illustrated in Figure 21–5. $MC = MR$ at output Q_1 with price P_1 (remember that the demand curve AR tells the monopolist the price he can get for any level of output).

Pause for a moment to check your understanding of this analysis. Why does the monopolist select the output at which $MC = MR$? Why not where $AR = AC$, or where $AR = MC$? When he has selected output Q_1, why does he market it at a price equal to AR? Why not a lower price equal to AC? The answers are to be found in the explantions above, so be sure you know them before going on.

Monopoly Profits

The price and level of output fixed by the profit-maximizing monopolist in this example enables him to earn higher than normal profits. Earlier we defined normal profits as those necessary to provide incentive for producers to continue producing. They are included in the average costs pictured in the diagrams. Whenever the price of a good exceeds its average costs of production, extranormal profits are being made. This situation exists in the case of the profit-maximizing monopolist, and is shown by the shaded rectangle in Figure 21–5. At output Q_1 and price P_1, cost per unit is Q_1A, which includes a normal profit. Revenue per unit is Q_1B. The difference AB is extranormal profit per unit. Since the number of units sold is equal to OQ_1, the total extranormal profit is $AB \times OQ_1$.

In a competitive industry the lure of extranormal profits would draw new firms into the industry, bringing prices down and reducing profits. The monopolist considered here does not have to face this trauma, however. We have endowed him with the means of keeping competitors out, and where he has that power he is free to maximize his profits without

Figure 21–5
Output and Price Set by a Profit-Maximizing Monopolist

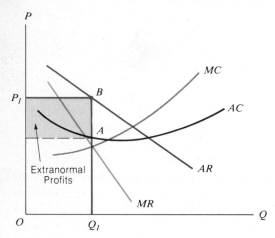

$MC = MR$ at output Q_1, which can be sold for a price equal to P_1.

curve. If marginal revenue MR is greater than marginal costs MC, then as output and sales increase, profits will rise. As soon as MC moves above MR, total profits will begin to fall. Hence, profits will be greatest when $MR =$

Figure 21-6
Monopoly

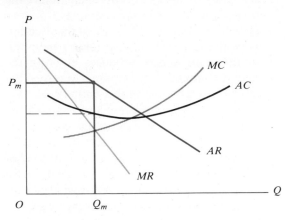

Figure 21-7
Competition

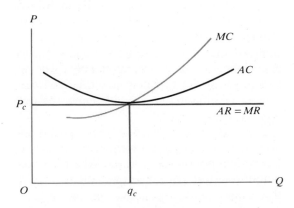

interference. We shall shortly examine the situation in which the monopolist does have to worry about potential competition (or enforcement of antitrust laws) and show how he is likely to adapt to these horrors.

Monopoly and Competition Compared
If we compare the results of monopoly with those of competition, the evils of monopoly stand out quite clearly. Compare the equilibri-

um of the profit-maximizing monopolist (Figure 21–6) and a competitive industry made up of individual firms in equilibrium (Figure 21–7). To make the comparison we assume that the lowest point on each average cost curve is at the same level. This is purely an "as if" comparison designed to show the differences that would prevail if production costs were similar in the two cases. That is, we are trying to separate the effects of monopoly from those of technology. Under these assumptions, the firm in the monopolized market charges a higher price than the price in the competitive market ($P_m > P_c$). Its cost of production per unit of output is higher: in Figure 21–6, AC at output Q_m is higher than AC at output q_c in Figure 21–7. And the monopolist makes extranormal profits while the competitive firm does not.

This comparison assumes that monopoly and competition are real alternatives for each other, that the nature of technology and markets is such that a multiplant firm has a monopoly in an industry that otherwise could be competitive. That condition is clearly unrealistic, and was established merely for convenience in pointing up the nature of monopoly. What of the real world, in which market imperfections prevail? Technology and the structure of markets may make it impossible to achieve the conditions necessary for competition and may leave a market with only one seller. In that case we can still sustain the basic conclusions that when the monopolist maximizes his profits the price he charges is above the price that would equal minimum average costs; he makes extranormal profits; and the production plant is not operating at peak efficiency.

Furthermore, since price is above minimum average costs it is also above marginal costs, and one of the basic conditions for economic efficiency and maximization of consumer welfare ($P = MC$) is not achieved. It is impossible for benefits to consumers at the margin to equal costs to producers at the margin in the case of the profit-maximizing monopolist.

Figure 21-8
Monopoly Pricing Designed to Forestall
Potential Competition

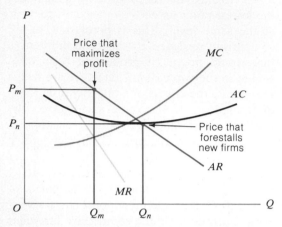

Output Q_n is sold at a price just equal to average cost P_n, in order to prevent entry of new firms. At this price the firm is taking a loss on its marginal units ($MC > P$) and would probably do so only under the greatest pressure. The price that maximizes profit P_m is higher than the price that forestalls competition, as shown by the greater height of the vertical line at Q_m as compared with Q_n.

The Monopolist and Potential Competition

Few monopolists are ever in a position that enables them to forget completely about potential competition. Even the owner of an exclusive patent must fear the development of a new technology that achieves the same results as his. The firm that controls its sources of raw materials has to consider the possibility of newly discovered resources.

These considerations can lead a monopolist to depart from a simple profit-maximizing strategy and move to one designed to limit potential competition. He will increase output and reduce price in an effort to meet a larger portion of the market demand while accepting lower profits. It is even possible that, at one limit, he will reduce his price and increase his sales so as to earn no more than a normal profit. To the extent that a monopolist is willing

to accept lower profits, he will reduce the threat of potential competition. He can also reduce the possibility of prosecution under the antitrust laws with the same strategy.

How far will he go? The logic of the situation tells us that, *in extremis* and under the imminent threat of a new producer entering the industry, a monopolist may move to prices that eliminate extranormal profits entirely. He will reduce his price and increase his sales until the selling price just equals average cost at the enlarged output. In that case his position would be that shown in Figure 21-8. Instead of producing output Q_m, at which the selling price maximizes profit, the monopolist will sell output Q_n at a price that equals average cost.

Monopoly Prices: The Limits

We can now review the limits within which we can expect monopoly prices and output to be established. At one extreme is the high price and low output of the monopolist who single-mindedly pursues the goal of profit maximization. At the other extreme is the lower price and higher output of the monopolist who insures against the threat of potential competition by eliminating any profits above the normal level.

In practice, both considerations—profits and potential competition—are in the minds of most monopolists. As a result, the price and output selected will fall between the two limits, the exact locus depending on the relative strength of the two motives in influencing the monopolist's actions. The economic analysis cannot provide a specific answer, but only a range within which the solution will fall.

Nevertheless, one conclusion is evident. The monopoly price will be above the competitive price, and the level of output will be different.[1]

---

[1]There is one possible case in which the monopoly solution and the competitive solution coincide: if the monopolist seeks to forestall all potential competition by eliminating extranormal profits, *and* his AR curve crosses his AC curve at its lowest point. This concurrence would be accidental, however.

This means that the optimal welfare results of the competitive case cannot be achieved. The extent of the departure from the norm is not accurately determinable, however, because the monopoly solution is indefinite within upper and lower limits.

We should note, too, that even potential competition can discipline a monopolist to sell more at lower prices than he would if he were fully free to maximize profits. He probably would not go all the way to the price and output at which $AR = AC$, but he can be expected to move partially in that direction from the higher price and lower output at which profits are maximized. The moral is interesting: the threat of competition can have some influence even when competition itself is absent.

Monopolistic Competition

Competition between sellers does not necessarily bring about the conditions needed for perfect competition. Far more common is the case of monopolistic competition, in which there is a substantial number of sellers with each one facing a downward sloping demand curve. It combines some of the features of the competitive model with some of the monopoly model.

• **Monopolistic competition** exists in a market with many sellers, each one of which can sell more only at a lower price.

The distinguishing feature of monopolistic competition is that each seller would do less business at a higher price, but would not lose all his customers to sellers charging lower prices. Conversely, at a lower price he could increase his sales, but would not take away all the trade from competitors charging more.

Here are some examples of monopolistic competition:

1. Retail gasoline sales. There is considerable competition among retailers, but buyer loyalty to brand names and other intangibles retain customers against lower prices charged by some dealers.

2. Ladies ready-to-wear clothing. Sales competition with large advertising expenditures creates partially protected markets for individual sellers.

3. Retail drugstores. Customary price markups maintain relatively high prices, but entry of new stores pulls profits down to the normal level and maintains considerable excess capacity. Lower prices would mean larger sales per store, and fewer stores.

These three examples taken from many possible ones indicate some of the chief features of monopolistic competition. It can be found almost anywhere, but is especially prevalent in retail trade. One of its characteristics is sales competition through advertising and use of brand names designed to obtain consumer loyalty to the product of a specific firm, even though the product may be the same as the product of another firm or insignificantly different. Finally, much monopolistic competition is characterized by *markup pricing*, in which a fixed percentage is added to direct costs in order to determine the final selling price to the customer. One effect of markup pricing is to shift competitive practices away from the use of lower prices and toward advertising and other types of sales competition.

All of these examples of monopolistic competition have one characteristic in common: the firm faces a downward sloping demand curve. If it wished to sell more, prices would have to be reduced. In order to avoid this type of competition, alternatives are sought that will maintain sales in the face of higher prices (brand names, advertising) or that will mute price competition in the whole trade (markup pricing).

Monopolistic competition is a complex phenomenon. In analyzing it we will first take the simple case of a few firms in a trade from which new firms are excluded. Next, we will show what happens when entry into the industry or trade is unrestricted.

Monopolistic Competition with Restricted Entry

We start by examining the case of competition between numerous firms in an industry from which additional firms can be excluded. But the firms are not so numerous that the demand curve for the individual firm is horizontal. The firm's demand curve is downward sloping, but not to the same extent as the monopolist's.

When there is a single seller of a product, the firm's demand curve is the same as the market demand curve. If several additional firms are in the market, each will get a share. Total demand will be divided among them. Furthermore, the demand curve facing any one of the sellers will be more elastic than that in the market as a whole. This is true because a higher price will lose customers to other sellers in the same market as well as to other products entirely. And a lower price will draw trade from other sellers as well as money that otherwise would be spent on other products. If we picture additional firms entering a monopolized market the firm's demand curve will shift in two ways. First, it will move to the left as its sales fall. Second, the slope will diminish. Figure 21–9 shows what happens.

In the case of monopolistic competition, if we assume that each firm seeks maximum profits, the results are analogous to those of the profit-maximizing monopolist, with the exception that the firm's demand curve is almost sure to lie in a position that entails excess production capacity.[2]

---

[2]A special definition of plant capacity is involved here. The *economic capacity* of a plant is the output level at which *AC* is at its lowest point. The physical or technological capacity is greater than that output level. Excess capacity exists when the output level is below the one at which *AC* is minimized. In the discussion that follows, we shall use the word *capacity* to mean economic capacity as defined here.

Figure 21–9
The Firm's Demand Curve as New Firms Enter a Formerly Monopolized Market

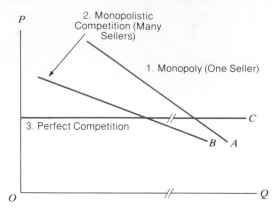

The monopolist's demand curve is shown at *A*. With additional sellers in the market, the demand curve for any one will be the intermediate area *B*. If there are enough firms the industry will be perfectly competitive, with each firm having a horizontal demand curve *C*.

Figure 21–10 shows the result. The firm maximizes profits at output Q_1, where $MR = MC$. It charges price P_1 and makes extranormal profits equal to the shaded area. Output is below optimal capacity, since Q_1 is a smaller output than the level at which $MC = AC$. All of the numerous firms in the industry will operate that way.

Monopolistic Competition with Free Entry

The extranormal profits earned by the firm in the restricted entry case will continue to attract additional firms into the industry or trade. If that should happen, the individual firm's demand curve will continue to shift downward and become flatter, approaching more closely the horizontal demand curve of the perfectly competitive industry. The individual firms may differentiate their products by using brand names, advertising, and creating customer loyalty. As more firms enter, however, the shifting locus of the firm's demand curve will ultimately eliminate extranormal profits. This

Figure 21-10
Monopolistic Competition with Restricted Entry

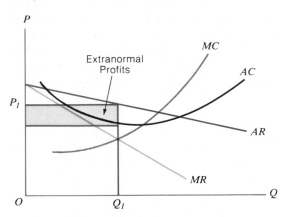

The firm's demand curve has shifted downward and become flatter than the monopolist's demand curve. But there are still extranormal profits; prices are higher than the perfectly competitive level and output is below the firm's capacity (defined as the output at which $MC = AC$).

Figure 21-11
Monopolistic Competition with Free Entry

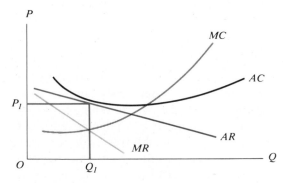

Extranormal profits are gone ($AR = AC$), profits are maximized ($MR = MC$), but because $MC < AC$ the firm has excess capacity and the price is higher than it would be if the industry were perfectly competitive.

Note: Why does $MC = MR$ at the same sales level at which $AR = AC$? The answer is derived from the mathematics involved. The AR curve is tangent to the AC curve at quantity Q_1. The mathematics of marginal, total, and average quantities is such that at the point of tangency of two average curves, the margbinal quantities are the same. Always remember to draw this diagram in that way. The MC and MR curves intersect directly below the point of tangency of AR and AC.

will occur when the AR curve moves to a position tangent to the AC curve. At this stage the profit-maximizing firm's position will be that in Figure 21–11. Extranormal profits will have disappeared, but each firm will be operating with excess capacity.

This analysis shows that "competition," as it is usually understood, is not sufficient to bring about maximization of welfare. Wherever market imperfections exist, whether because there are not enough sellers or because sellers differentiate themselves from each other through brands, trademarks, advertising, or similar devices, there is a persistent tendency toward excess capacity and relatively higher prices than necessary. Prices remain above marginal costs, and it is impossible to equate benefits and costs at the margin. This is true even if there are no barriers to entry, sellers act completely independently, and firms try to maximize their profits.

● **Free entry** is a market condition in which there are no barriers to entry of new sellers. This contrasts with **restricted entry**, in which there are barriers to the entry of new sellers.

Selling Costs
The analysis of monopolistic competition is not changed significantly by the use of advertising to create product differentiation and customer loyalty. The same results will prevail, except that the firm's cost curves will be shifted upward by the amount of the selling costs, as shown in Figure 21–12. Shifting the average cost curve upward merely results in a different locus of the price and quantity sold by the firm, whether it is the restricted entry or free entry case. Since costs have risen, the ultimate cost to the buyer will be increased.

We can use Figure 21–12 to return briefly to the discussion of advertising in Chapter 16. There it was pointed out that one of the arguments made on behalf of advertising is that selling costs can so enlarge a firm's sales that it can reduce the price of its product. In

Figure 21-12
Selling Costs Shift Cost Curves Upward

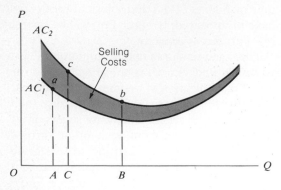

Selling costs shift the *AC* curve upward from *AC₁* to *AC₂*, drawn here to show declining selling costs per unit as *Q* increases.

terms of Figure 21–12, if the selling costs shown were to increase a firm's sales from *OA*

to *OB*, average costs per unit would be lower (*bB*<*aA*) and it would be possible for the seller to lower his price. That outcome, however, depends on the assumption that other firms will not also advertise their competitive brands. If they do, the initial firm's sales might increase a little and then stabilize at *OC*, with higher average costs (*cC*>*aA*) and consequently higher prices to consumers. The attempt to move from *a* to *b* fails because of retaliatory action taken by other firms to protect their own sales. The ultimate outcome is *c*, with higher prices due to the selling costs that are now necessary to sustain sales at *OC*. Note that in all three cases the rivalry of monopolistic competition keeps profits at the normal level.

- **Selling costs** are incurred by sellers who wish to increase sales in markets in which they face a downward sloping demand curve.

Summary

The distinguishing characteristic of all monopoloid markets is a downward sloping demand curve for all sellers. That is, more can be sold only if price is reduced. By contrast, in competitive markets the demand curve for the firm is horizontal: the firm can sell all it wishes at the existing market price.

In the case of pure monopoly, the profit-maximizing monopolist will choose an output and price that provides profits above normal profits, and average costs of production will be higher than the lowest possible production costs. If the monopolist wishes to discourage entry of new firms it will reduce price and increase output, perhaps even to the point at which the extranormal profits disappear. Even in that case, however, production costs will be above the possible minimum.

Monopolistic competition is far more common than pure monopoly, which is about as rare as pure competition. Monopolistic competition with restricted entry leads to results analogous to pure monopoly: high profits, high costs, and restricted output. Free entry eliminates the extranormal profits, but at the expense of even higher costs and enlarged amounts of unused capacity. Selling costs make the situation even worse. Their chief effect is to raise prices to the final buyer even further.

The analysis of monopolistic competition and its variants must be a sobering experience for those who uncritically assume that "competition" answers all economic problems. It doesn't. Even in retailing, the sector of the economy where competition is most prevalent, elements of monopoly are ubiquitous. Almost all retailers face downward sloping demand curves. The result is that the long-run monopolistic competition solution tends to prevail very widely.

Furthermore, the retailer's downward sloping demand curve is largely his or her own creation, aided and abetted by the manufacturer who seeks to distinguish his product by brand names, trademarks, and advertising. Efforts on the part of manufacturers and retailers to gain more than a normal profit bring about a situation in which it is impossible for the economy as a whole to maximize its welfare. Prices end up higher and output lower than those at which maximum benefits are obtained. Prices diverge from marginal costs. The irony of it all is that the extranormal profits whose quest started the process prove to be ephemeral as new sellers appear. Selling costs make the situation even worse: their chief effect is to raise prices to the final buyer even further.

Key Concepts

monopoloid markets   **free entry**
monopoly   **restricted entry**
monopolistic competition **selling costs**

For Discussion

1. In a monopoloid market, price is not equal to marginal cost. How does that affect social welfare?

2. The fundamental differences between competitive and monopoloid firms occur on the demand side rather than on the cost side. Explain.

3. What output and price would a monopolist choose if he wished to maximize his total revenue? Does the length of his time horizon (long run vs. short run) make a difference?

4. How does a monopolist reconcile the conflicting goals of maximizing profit now and avoiding potential competition?

5. What is competitive about monopolistic competition? What is monopolistic?

6. The typical firm in a monopolistically competitive industry exhibits excess capacity. Why?

Chapter 22

Oligopoly: Market Strategy and Pricing Policies

We have seen that monopoloid markets cannot achieve an optimal price and output that enables the economy to maximize consumer satisfactions. Whenever the individual firm faces a demand curve that slopes downward, the ultimate adjustment will bring a price above the lowest point on the firm's average cost curve, often accompanied by extranormal profits and reduced output. Even if free entry eliminates extranormal profits the level of output will differ from the optimal level. All of these results prevail even if "competition" reigns.

In those sectors of the economy dominated by big business, however, oligopoly is the characteristic situation. A limited number of large firms develop market strategies that affect the decisions made by other firms, leading to a complex pattern of both rivalry and live-and-let-live relationships among firms. As we move into the oligopolistic world of big enterprise we are inevitably drawn into consideration of market power, entrenched economic positions, and their implications. Some of these considerations and implications will be explored in greater detail in the sections of this chapter that follow.

Market Strategy: Profits, Security, and Growth

Three objectives dominate the market strategies of large monopoloid firms: profits, security and growth. Profits are, of course, the primary objective, for without profits neither security nor growth is possible. A profitable position must be protected, however, if the profits are to be maintained. The firm's share of the market must be defended against other large firms seeking to enlarge their share of the market, and against newcomers seeking to enter a lucrative field. Security must also be sought against economic change. A firm's position in the market is also threatened by changing consumer tastes and changing technologies, which impel large firms to seek diversification and expansion into new fields. Growth as a goal is also fostered by the need to invest retained earnings and the desire for still larger profits. The three objectives are related: each reinforces the other, and none can be pursued to the exclusion of the other two.

Large firms in monopoloid industries have varying degrees of leeway in adopting market strategies. The number and strength of rival firms and their reaction to another firm's action are important constraints. No single large firm has complete control of the market, so its strategies are limited by the potential or actual rivalry of others. The technology of production and distribution is another constraint. A firm with heavy investment in specialized capital equipment will have different needs from one utilizing large amounts of relatively unskilled labor as its chief input. For one thing, the first will have fewer worries about potential new entrants to its markets than the second. A third constraint is the nature of the market. A firm manufacturing expensive heavy equipment for other large firms will have a market strategy different from that of a firm producing relatively inexpensive consumer products, for example.

Growth of the firm is one of the great goals of big enterprises. Their managements, as we have seen, are strongly motivated by the twin goals of wealth and power, and both are fostered when the firm has a strong growth record. Furthermore, the relatively high profits earned by firms with strong monopoloid positions provide the resources for growth. Large retained earnings are available for investment, and high profits can attract additional funds from the money markets. Finally, the U.S. tax system fosters retention of profits instead of payment of dividends: the relatively low capital gains tax (compared with higher tax rates on incomes earned by many stockholders) causes the stockholders to approve of management policies that stress retention of earnings to promote growth of the firm.

The growth goal is particularly strong during periods in which the economy as a whole is growing relatively rapidly, such as, for example, during the 1950s and 1960s in the United States. During periods of relatively weak growth, like the years following the post-World War II era of rapid expansion that ended around 1970, security of existing positions becomes more important. Thus, in the years after 1970 large firms gave greater emphasis to developing and maintaining a large share of the market for their chief products, often dropping products that had only a small market share and channeling their investments to the areas in which a strong monopoloid position was most feasible. A new mix of profits, security and growth in corporate strategies appeared as economic conditions shifted.

Price Policies and Market Strategies

Widely different pricing policies can emerge from the differences in markets, technology, industrial structure, and the emphasis on growth. It is a little too simple to assume that short-run profit maximization is the firm's goal. One firm may be willing to sacrifice immediate profits in order to grow more rapidly. Another firm may seek to maximize the shareholder's equity per share and sacrifice some growth as well as immediate profits. A third may seek a high degree of stability of output and earnings. All of these strategies may be thought of as maximizing profits in the long run, but each will result in a different pricing policy to fit into a different market strategy.

Several commonly observed pricing policies and accompanying market strategies are characteristic of large oligopolistic firms in American industry. A study of large U.S. firms in the 1950s provides some insight into the usually secret world of corporate strategy.[1] The price leader in the automobile industry, General Motors Corporation, sought a target return on investment, after taxes, of 20 percent. The pricing policy works this way:

1. A standard operating level is selected as the level of output the company prefers.

---

[1]The following discussion of price and market strategies draws heavily on A. D. H. Kaplan, J. B. Dirlam, and R. F. Lanzilotti, *Pricing in Big Business: A Case Approach* (Washington, D.C.: Brookings Institution, 1958).

2. Cost of production per unit, including both variable and fixed costs, is calculated for that standard output.

3. An amount sufficient to achieve aftertax profits on investment of 20 percent is added to that standard cost. This determines the price.

4. The company then seeks to sell the standard output at the determined price.

This policy was highly successful until the industry began to run into problems in the 1970s because of foreign competition and poor management decisions. Until then the target level profits usually were achieved, along with a market share of a little over half of domestic new car sales.

The steel industry's price leader, United States Steel Corporation, built its pricing policy around the goals of *price stability* and *stability of profit margins*. Price stability is important in an industry with very large investment in costly, single-purpose equipment. A steel rolling mill costs over $200,000,000, and it can't be used to do anything but produce rolled steel sheets or strip. If price cutting should start, the selling price could be driven down to levels just equal to the mill's operating costs (labor plus materials inputs) with nothing left over to pay for the large capital investment. No company could long survive in such a situation. Hence the need in the industry for a leader devoted to keeping prices stable at profitable levels. As for profit margins, steel mills last almost indefinitely with proper maintenance, yet technological change goes on. Unless pricing policies protect the profit margins of the older mills, the investment in them will be lost. Newer mills will make larger profits, of course, but it is only natural for the largest firm in the industry to protect itself by setting prices that keep up the value of its older mills. Since most other firms in the industry have similar problems they usually find little to criticize in the leader's actions. In the steel industry this policy ultimately fostered penetration of domestic markets by foreign producers, but for a time it was successful in eliminating price competition from the domestic steel market.

When companies follow the leader in their pricing policies they bask in the shelter of a price umbrella held by the price leader, protecting them from the rigors of competition. Or they may use the umbrella to expand vigorously in a few selected portions of the market, thereby earning better profits than the leader (who protects his leadership position by blanketing all parts of the market). Or they may try to cut costs while accepting the leader's price. Or they may try to develop their own brands within the larger market to obtain an even more protected position. Whatever they do, however, the fact that these other companies accept the leader's price prevents cost benefits from seeping down to the level of the final customer.

Another objective of market strategy and price policy may be to maintain or improve the company's market position. Sears Roebuck and Co. follows such a policy. Its pricing structure seeks to achieve a return on its investment of 15 percent, with a lower limit of 10 percent considered acceptable in relatively poor years. However, it also seeks a growing share of the retail markets in which it participates. The chief technique used to achieve that goal is consistently low prices compared with those of other retailers. The low prices are achieved primarily at the manufacturing level, by either company-owned (or partially owned) plants or contractual buying arrangements with independent companies. By eliminating seasonal swings in output and by operating close to capacity, these "tied" producers are able to cut costs per unit of output below those of most other producers. Elimination of selling costs by the manufacturer (Sears is the customer) also helps cut costs. As a result, Sears is often able to achieve its target level of profits *and* enlarge its relative share of total sales volume.[2]

Finally, we come to new products plus pricing to meet competition. General Foods Corporation is a good example. General Foods has emphasized specialty or novelty food products, such as Jell-O, Postum, and Sanka. Its general pricing rule is "one-third to make, one-third to sell, and one-third for profit." But that type of margin is impossible to maintain over the long haul as imitators and competitors appear, except for a few products whose imitation is difficult. After an initial period of high profits on a new product, prices are cut to meet the competition attracted by the high profits, and prices drift down to more normal levels. The company's policy, however, has been to introduce new specialty food products in a continuous stream, with high initial profit margins and relatively high noncompetitive prices that it expects to reduce slowly as competitors appear.

It should be clear from this brief discussion of prices and market strategies that big enterprises have considerable leeway in setting prices and adjusting them to fit into larger market strategies. These are all "administered prices," freed in some degree and sometimes quite significantly from the market forces of demand and supply.

Administered Prices

Administered prices can be distinguished from prices determined by market forces by two characteristics. They are established by administrative decision of corporate officials as matters of operating policy or business planning.

---

[2]Note the anomaly here. Why enlarge your sales volume while maintaining the rate of profit at a given level? Why doesn't Sears take its cost advantages in rising profit rates and slower growth? No one knows the answer, but apparently the company does not seek maximum profits because management wants a larger share of the market.

In addition, the price administrators have the power to implement or validate their price decisions within more or less wide limits. Administered prices are a characteristic feature of both oligopoly and monopoly.

- **Administered prices** are prices established by business firms as part of the firms' operating strategy, independent of market forces to a greater or lesser degree. These firms are *price makers*. Administered prices are distinguished from prices determined wholly by market forces, which are competitive prices, and are accepted by *price takers*.

The prevailing practice in most administered price sectors of the economy is for the leading or dominant firm to set prices at some given percent markup above the full costs of production and distribution to provide the desired level of profit. Pricing decisions often become dominant from the time an enterprise or product is conceived. For example, when planning a new product a corporation may first determine what customers feel the "appropriate price" should be, and then, with price determined, direct its engineers to design a product to sell at that price while yielding the necessary markups to cover selling costs and corporate profits.

Administered prices, taken together with an industrial structure containing significant monopoloid elements, have three effects. They contribute to an unsatisfactory response of firms to the changing wants of consumers. They lead to efforts to manage consumer wants through advertising and similar sales expenses that raise costs and waste resources. And they promote additional efforts to diminish competition.

Administered prices also react differently from competitive prices to changes in aggregate demand. They tend to be stable and unchanging not only under normal conditions, but also when aggregate demand falls. Oligopolistic firms using administered prices hold their prices steady when sales decline, reducing their output and employment instead of prices. This action puts the main burden of adjustment on workers and their families. It also affects long-run planning of plant capacity and costs by the firms themselves; they plan for plants that can "break even" at relatively low levels of output. Thus, in the steel industry, for example, most steel mills do not start losing money on current operations unless output falls below about 50 percent of plant capacity. The results are that profits are high when output is close to capacity levels, and the industry has significant excess capacity. The typical administered price industry features price stability, substantial layoffs during recessions and depressions, and large unused capacity in normal times.

Administered prices also contribute to inflation. They are part of the inflationary environment of the economy, along with big labor unions and government policy toward growth and employment, that lead the modern economy into slow but steady price increases. The

stability of administered prices keeps them from going down during periods of economic slack, but it is easy for them to rise during inflations. The result is that the economy has a significant sector in which prices tend to rise in the long run.

The Kinked Demand Curve

The idea that administered prices are flexible upward but not downward is supported by a theoretical analysis of the situation faced by the oligopolistic firm. The normal situation faced by such a firm is one in which it can expect other firms in the industry to match any price reductions it may make in order to protect their sales and share of the market. It can also expect other firms not to match an increase in price because of their desire to increase their sales at its expense. These expectations rest on the normal situation of substantial excess production capacity available in the industry. The oligopolistic firm, therefore, has every incentive to hold prices where they are.

Figure 22-1
The Oligopolist's Kinked Demand Curve
(With Unused Plant Capacity in the Industry)

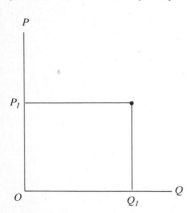

A. At the existing price P_1, the oligopolist sells output Q_1.

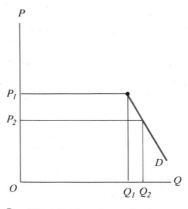

B. If he tried to reduce price in order to sell more, other firms would match his reductions, so that sales would increase only slightly.

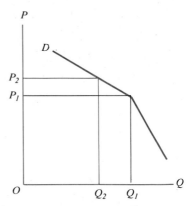

C. An increase in price would bring a large loss in sales, however. Wisdom, therefore,dictates price stability as long as the existing price brings reasonable profits.

Reductions would be matched quickly, so no one firm could gain. But increases would not be matched and the firm trying to raise its prices would lose. These expectations are equivalent to the existence of a kink or bend in the firm's demand curve at the prevailing price, shown in Figure 22-1; hence, the term *kinked demand curve.*

The situation changes, however, if the economy is expanding, excess capacity is negligible, and firms in the industry are operating close to their production capacity. In that situation, no firm has any incentive to cut prices: it would expect other firms not to match its cuts because they would know the price-cutting firm could not sell much more anyway. It would be unable to satisfy the new customers it could attract. On the other hand, there is considerable incentive to increase prices. Since sales are large and growing and capacity operations are the rule, any firm would match price increases in order to get its share of higher profits. In this situation the kink has reversed itself, as in Figure 22-2.

The oligopolistic industry, then, normally tends to sustain the existing prices for its product. But when aggregate demand is rising and begins to push on the capacity to produce in industry after industry, the oligopolistic industry will see its selling prices move up. This situation builds a permanent ratchet type of price increase into the economy; administered prices tend to go up when demand is strong, but do not go down when demand is slack.

The kinked demand curve of an oligopolist has another property of interest to economists: the marginal revenue curve associated with it has a gap, so that the firm would not change its output level even if its marginal costs or demand were to shift substantially. Assume an oligopolistic firm that perceives a kink in its demand curve at the existing price. The mathematical relationship of marginal to average quantities is such that its marginal revenue curve will appear with a gap, as in Figure 22-3.

Figure 22-2
The Oligopolist's Kinked Demand Curve
(At Capacity Operations)

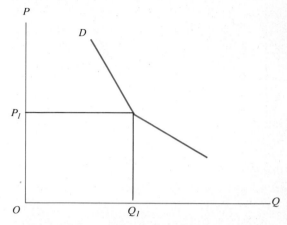

At price P_1 and output Q_1, reduction in price could bring greatly enlarged sales because other firms would not be expected to match the price cut. But why do it, since Q_1 is the firm's capacity output? On the other hand, an increase in price would be eagerly followed by other firms because they know they won't lose many sales. The result: prices go up as everyone follows the leader.

Figure 22-3

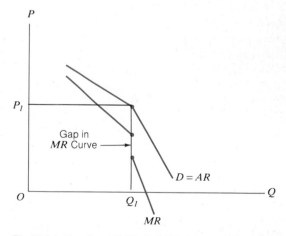

The kink in the oligopolistic demand curve creates a gap in the *MR* curve at the existing quantity of output. Why? Because change in the slope of *AR* is associated mathematically with discontinuity in *MR*.

Figure 22-4

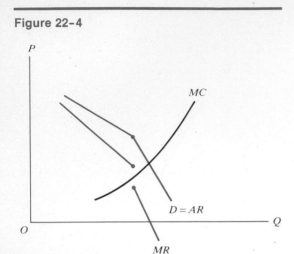

When the oligopolist's *MC* curve passes throuogh the gap in his *MR* curve (which may or may not be the case, but it is highly possible) the firm will have no reason to change its price even if *D* or *MC* changes, so long as *MC* continues to pass through the gap in *MR*.

Now draw the oligopolist's marginal cost curve so that it passes through the gap in his marginal revenue curve (Figure 22–4). In this case, even if the oligopolist were trying to maximize his profits, his price and output would not be changed in response to changes in either marginal costs or demand unless they were large enough to shift the *MC* curve out of the gap in the *MR* curve. This situation is added reason to believe that prices will remain stable while costs or demand conditions change.

- The **kinked demand curve** is the demand curve of the individual firm in oligopolistic markets. It has a "kink" at the existing price caused by the firm's expectations of the actions its rivals are likely to take if the firm changes its price.

Price Leadership

Administered pricing in oligopolistic industries commonly takes the form of price leadership. There are times when economic conditions call for price changes: during inflation, when costs of production change, or when market demand shifts, for example. *Price leadership* arises out of the need to make these changes in an orderly fashion that does not upset the existing market position of the important large firms.

Dominant firms are usually the price leaders in unbalanced oligopolies, simply because no price could be established without their consent. A dominant firm has coercive power to bring to bear upon lesser firms if they should step out of line, so the smaller ones let the giant call the tune. In balanced oligopolies, in which four to six firms have similar shares of the market, price leadership is usually assumed by a firm that the others recognize as particularly well managed and alert to changing market conditions. Sometimes leadership rotates among the large firms in a balanced oligopoly.

- **Price leadership** is the pattern of price setting in many oligopolistic markets in which a single firm sets the price and other firms follow. It promotes "orderly" transition from one price to another and reduces or eliminates competitive pricing practices.

Price leadership is a form of tacit collusion among large firms. The antitrust laws prohibit overt agreements to fix prices, although there appears to be a substantial amount of such illegal action in monopoloid industries. The chief alternative is an informal pattern in which one large firm establishes a price and the others accept it. The purpose is to avoid price competition. This procedure achieves the same results as a price-fixing agreement, but it is not illegal.

A classic example of price leadership is the price of iron ore in the U.S. midwestern states. When the first iron ore ship arrives at Cleveland in the spring of each year, the price of ore is announced by the large iron ore mining company that controls the shipment. That price then becomes the price for all iron ore transactions in the midwest for the year. How is that price determined? Who is consulted?

Why does everyone follow the leader? No one outside the companies knows the answer to those questions. But we do know that there have been no significant deviations from the so-called "Lake Erie price" for iron ore since the last independent mining company was absorbed by one of the large steel firms in the late 1930s.

Price leadership is widespread in the U.S. economy, as one would expect in an economy with many industries dominated by a relatively few firms in each. General Electric dominates pricing for such important household equipment as refrigerators and washing machines. International Harvester calls the tune for farm tractors and other farm machinery. General Motors makes the price levels and price differences in the automotive industry. United States Steel dominates the market for iron ore and basic steel (although in recent years some smaller firms have been taking the lead in pricing some of the lighter steel products). Aluminum Corporation of America administers prices for aluminum and its products. The list could go on almost indefinitely and would include most of the industries dominated by a few firms, together with the basic products and many of the lesser products in those industries.

The price leader looks after its own interests, of course. Its leadership is used to help attain its profit goal, sustain its share of the market, achieve its growth goals, and preserve its position of leadership. Leadership also provides some constraints on the dominant firm that prevent single-minded concentration on its own interests. If a price change is contemplated, the leader must assess the situation to determine whether the other large firms are willing to go along. If they are not, the change may have to be revoked. On the other hand, if the firm is big enough it can impose its will on the others.

Price leaders are not completely isolated from market forces. Changes in costs may enable small firms to cut prices; if this pattern becomes widespread it may be impossible to hold price levels up. A shrinking market or a growing one can make all firms restless. Imports may indicate that domestic prices are too high. When these and other changes occur, however, it is the price leader's task to assess their strength and probable duration, and then to lead the industry to a new level of prices consistent with the changed conditions and profit goals.

Price leadership is designed to preserve order and stability. Under normal conditions, it prevents the price competition that could undermine the profits of all the leading firms in an industry. When economic conditions change, leadership enables the industry to adapt in an orderly fashion that does not threaten anyone's position or profits, and does not open the way to price competition.

PRICE LEADERSHIP: ONE CASE

Price leadership sometimes prevails against the interests of all firms except the price leader. In the mid-1950s, for example, the Venezuelan government was pressuring U.S. Steel for higher royalties from the USS iron ore concessions there, claiming that the world price was high enough for USS to pay more for its mining rights. As part of its counterattack, USS began selling iron ore once more in the U.S. Great Lakes region, which it had not done in over fifteen years, in order to impose a reduced price on Lake Erie iron ore. It was able to do so because it was, and remains, the largest iron ore producer in the region. It was then able to show the Venezuelan government that, with the new market price that prevailed, its iron ore profits were not high enough to allow for higher royalties on the ore it mined in Venezuela. The other U.S. iron ore producers howled in rage, but all they could do was retire to their dens and lick their wounded profits. U.S. Steel, of course, did not reduce the price of steel, so its lower profit on iron ore was recouped in higher profits on steel.

Markup Pricing

Administered prices are closely related to an oligopolistic industry's need for capital. As the economy expands, any individual industry will also grow, creating a need for capital to provide increased output capacity. In oligopolistic industries the price leader normally seeks to establish and maintain a level of prices that enables the major firms to finance necessary expansion. The price is designed to include the following:

1. Full costs of production and distribution, including all fixed and variable costs.
   These are sometimes called *prime costs*.

2. An additional markup designed to cover:
   A. A satisfactory dividend for the stockholders. In economic terms this is roughly equivalent to "normal" profit.
   B. An additional amount for capital investment to provide for expansion.

The markup is usually stated as a percentage of prime costs. For example, in automobile retail sales the markup over wholesale prices to determine the "sticker price" offered to customers was cut to 18–20 percent in 1980, depending on the type of car. Smaller cars had the lower markup, larger cars the higher. The former markup of 20–22 percent had prevailed for many years. It was reduced by General Motors Corporation, the price leader, in reaction to competition from imported cars. At the manufacturing level GM's markup over prime costs is still designed to achieve a profit of 20 percent on invested capital at the desired level of output, but in recent years foreign competition has prevented the company from achieving that level of sales and, consequently, its profit goal. The markup over prime costs is still set with that objective in mind, however.

Markup pricing can be illustrated by a modification of the usual cost-revenue diagram, shown in Figure 22–5.

- **Markup pricing** is a method of pricing in which a seller adds a fixed percentage of cost to the *prime cost* of an item to arrive at a selling price. Prime costs are the full costs of production and distribution, both fixed and variable.

Pricing decisions are made by the price leader, which starts from an estimate of sales and output based on its normal share of the market. This estimate usually ignores short-run fluctuations in sales caused by relatively mild recessions and recoveries, in order to avoid numerous changes in prices. The objective is a price that will be relatively stable. Once this "standard output" is selected, a careful calculation of prime costs per unit of output is made, including all variable and fixed costs of production and distribution. This calculation of prime costs provides an estimate of the minimum revenues necessary to keep the firm operating at the standard output in the short run. An upper level of revenues to which the management aspires is provided by calculation of the amounts required for a satisfactory dividend payment to stockholders plus the capital required for expansion. The markup over prime costs is then calculated to raise total revenues to the desired amount.

This account of the bare bones of the mechanics of markup pricing must be modified by further considerations that will vary from one industry to another. First, the markup may be larger than that necessary merely to provide capital to maintain the leading firm's share of the market. It can be set higher to provide capital for the firm to diversify into other industries. Whether that is possible depends on the nature of demand for the product. If demand is inelastic (an increase in price results in only a small reduction in total sales for the industry), it may be quite possible for a high price to be sustained that enables all of the large firms to become conglomerates. For example: the U.S. petroleum refiners in 1945–1970 were able to expand worldwide and then diversify into chemical, coal and other indus-

Figure 22–5
Markup Pricing

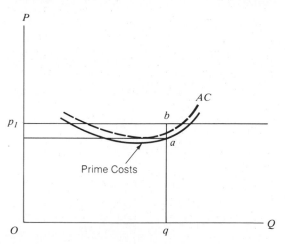

Output and sales of *Oq* represents the price leader's usual share of the market. At that level of output prime costs per unit of output are measured by *aq*. Note that prime costs are less than average costs; the difference is the normal profit the firm expects to pay to stockholders as dividends. The markup, *ab*, is designed to bring in enough revenue to provide those dividends plus additional retained earnings for investment and expansion.

tries on the base of high profits in the U.S. gasoline market.

Second, the markup may be below the level required to provide all of the capital necessary for expansion. In that case the price leader, as well as the other firms in the industry, will have to borrow in the capital markets to finance part of their necessary expansion. This case arises when demand for the product is relatively elastic (an increase in price brings a large decline in total sales for the industry). The price leader must then decide whether a higher price would increase or decrease retained earnings. If the markup is raised from the existing level, bringing the price up, it is quite possible for sales to decline (even if all other firms follow the leader), bringing total revenues down and a reduction in retained earnings.

These two considerations lead to a general

proposition: price leaders try to maximize retained earnings at a level of output that represents their customary share of the market. The markup over prime costs reflects that goal.

Even that goal must be qualified by two other factors. One is possible entry into the industry by other firms. If the markup is increased and prices rise, new firms are encouraged to enter the industry. Furthermore, the high profits to be obtained will help them pay the costs of overcoming the barriers to entry that the industry maintains. Barriers to entry are extremely important both in maintaining an oligopoly and in providing freedom in pricing policies for the price leader.

The second qualification is the possibility of federal government intervention. If the industry's pricing policies are perceived as contrary to the public interest, the industry may have to face (a) taxation, (b) tariff reductions, (c) sale of government stockpiles, (d) qualitative restrictions of a variety of types, such as strict enforcement of environmental or health regulations, (e) antitrust prosecution, or even (f) government ownership. In the hurly-burly of U.S. politics and given the strong influence of business power in the federal government, these actions are seldom taken. Indeed, the historical record shows just the opposite. For example, the high profits of the oil companies in the 1950s and 1960s were supported by federal and state legislation that made possible high markups and large retained earnings for the industry giants. Nevertheless, the constraint of possible government intervention is real, particularly if the industry is obvious and arrogant in its pricing policies. Price leaders learn to slip a velvet glove over the nailed fist.

Markup Pricing and
Profit Maximization
Maximization of retained earnings on the basis of a standard output is not the same as profit maximization. In the first place, the strategy goal is different. The firm is motivated by a long-range goal of expansion for the firm,

within the framework of growth for the economy as a whole and the industry in particular. The markup is designed to achieve the firm's growth targets. Secondly, the firm seeks to protect its share of the market, without threatening other firms in the industry. That consideration defines the standard output. Reduced output would give up sales to other firms, reducing the retained earnings needed to achieve the growth targets. Increased output would probably require price reductions or increased selling costs, both of which would also reduce retained earnings. Enlarged sales would also threaten the market position of other firms, inviting retaliation. Finally, the firm may not have the information necessary to maximize profits—recall the kinked demand curve analysis a few pages back—and may be fearful of the uncertainties involved in an oligopoly when a leading firm upsets the status quo. The essential point is that a modern oligopolistic firm faces a complex decision-making environment that leads it to use markup pricing. Its goals are growth and the retained earnings necessary to achieve its growth targets, plus protection of its present position.

The results in both price and quantity of output differ from those that would be achieved by maximizing profits. For example, picture a price leader in an oligopolistic industry, which uses market pricing to generate the desired level of retained earnings. It has built a plant that achieves its lowest production costs per unit of output at its standard output, which reflects its normal share of the market. This situation is shown in Figure 22–6, which also indicates the firm's demand curve (AR) and the marginal curves (MR, MC) relevant to profit maximization.

The price at which profit is maximized is higher than the markup price in this case, and output is lower. This is the general case, if we assume that the firm tries to design its plant and equipment so that average prime costs are minimized at its standard output.

Note what happens if demand should decline

Figure 22–6
Markup Pricing and Profit Maximization Compared

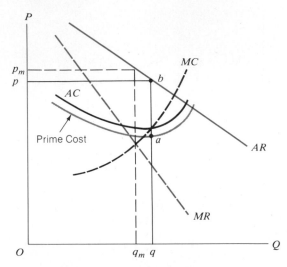

The price leader sets its price by adding markup ab to its prime costs aq at standard output q. Point b is one point on a hypothetical AR curve, which is associated with a marginal revenue curve MR. We can also show the marginal cost curve MC associated with the firm's average cost curve AC, which is prime cost plus dividends (normal profit). The price and quantity at which profit would be maximized (p_m, q_m) are different from these obtained from markup pricing (p, q).

during a recession. The cost curves in Figure 22–6 stay the same, but the revenue curves shift to the left. The profit-maximizing firm would reduce both output and price. You can draw the new revenue curves on Figure 22–6 and see for yourself. But the firm using markup pricing will keep the same price while reducing output. This stability of prices with reduced output replicates the real-life behavior of an oligopoly during recessions.

Markup Pricing and Costs of Production
Markup pricing is an important connecting link between rising costs and stagflation. When costs of production rise for any reason—increased costs of energy, wage rates rising

faster than output per worker, rising taxes, rising interest rates, whatever—prime costs increase. Adding the customary markup means both higher prices and reduced output. Figure 22–7 shows this relationship.

When the customary markup is added to prime costs, selling prices rise. At the higher prices less will be sold, so output will be cut. The result is both higher prices and reduced employment. As this sequence of events is duplicated throughout the oligopolistic sectors of the economy we get in the economy as a whole an upward shift in the aggregate supply curve and the stagflation effect described in Chapters 7 and 14. Markup pricing is one of the elements in the economy that transforms rising costs at the microeconomic level into stagflation in the economy as a whole.

Techniques of Market Control

The effectiveness of administered prices and, in particular, markup pricing, is enhanced by a variety of market practices commonly found in oligopolistic industries. These techniques of market control are designed to achieve cooperation among existing firms or, at the very least, reduce rivalry among them; to keep out newcomers; and to protect the existing pattern of market shares. Price leadership has already been discussed. Other common practices include overt collusion and price fixing, coercion of smaller firms by larger ones, differentiated products and advertising, and barriers to entry. Any one oligopolistic industry will usually have a network of market controls of several types that reinforce and strengthen each other. In the steel industry, for example, there is a strong pattern of price leadership, tacit sharing of markets, repeated cases of price-fixing agreements among firms, and strong barriers to entry via alliances with large banks and insurance companies and control over sources of raw materials. Of the techniques of market control discussed here, only

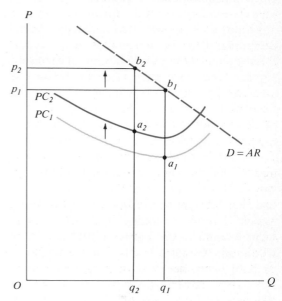

Figure 22–7
Markup Pricing and Costs of Production

An increase in costs pushes prime costs up from PC_1 to PC_2. The firm adds its usual markup, ab_1, which is equal to ab_2, pushing prices up from p_1 to p_2. With no change in demand, output falls from q_1 (the standard output) to q_2.

product differentiation and advertising is insignificant in the steel industry, largely because the shrewd and hard-nosed industrial buyers of steel and steel products are not swayed by the sorts of emotional appeals that are effective with the general public.

Collusion
Collusion among large firms to restrict or eliminate competition is also illegal. Yet it occurs, in spite of the antitrust laws. The benefits are often so attractive that oligopolistic firms tend naturally to be drawn into schemes for fixing prices, dividing markets, and sharing customers. But collusion *is* illegal, and vigorous enforcement of the antitrust laws is the only safeguard against it.

The most widely publicized example of price fixing and market sharing in recent years, and

394 Chapter 22 Oligopoly

probably the largest of all time in terms of money losses to the general public, was the electrical equipment conspiracy of 1955–1960.[3] This case concerned the pricing of electrical apparatus and supplies used by large electrical generating plants, products that had an annual sales volume of over $1.75 billion. The conspiracy involved some very large firms (such as General Electric and Westinghouse) as well as the medium sized and small companies that make up a series of interlocking oligopolies in the heavy electrical equipment industry.

The industry had a long history of price- and market-sharing conspiracies dating back to before World War I. Sixteen conspiracy cases had been brought by the Department of Justice against various groupings of electrical equipment manufacturers between 1911 and 1949, with either General Electric or Westinghouse or both being involved in every case. Trade associations have always been important in the industry, and GE was often a leader in their activities.[4] The industry was dominated by GE ($4 billion of annual sales, one quarter in electrical apparatus) and Westinghouse ($2 billion of annual sales, half in electrical apparatus), with other large companies like Allis-Chalmers ($500 million annual sales) trailing behind.

This particular price-fixing conspiracy was a direct result of the slowdown in national economic growth that occurred in the 1950s. The industry was equipped for the highest levels of production in its history when demand for electrical apparatus fell drastically. The chief suppliers began cutting prices in order to keep their plants busy, only to discover that profits disappeared. This situation triggered a series of secret meetings among executives of the important firms. Decisions taken at these meetings included schemes for selection of the firms that would be low bidders on sales to the federal government, electric utility companies, contractors, and industrial corporations; guidelines to determine the prices each firm would quote; and the share of sales each company would get. For example, sales of power switchgear assemblies to the federal government were divided as follows:

General Electric Co.	39%
Westinghouse Electric Co.	35%
I-T-E Circuit Breaker Co.	11%
Allis-Chalmers Mfg. Co.	8%
Federal Pacific Electric Co.	7%

Contact between the firms included elaborate codes and secrecy to avoid detection. Meetings were held at fashionable hotels, resorts, and clubs, but never at the same location twice. Expense accounts were doctored to conceal the location of meetings. But in spite of the hugger-mugger, the whole affair was uncovered.

The conspiracy was broken by the glare of publicity. The Tennessee Valley Authority, tired of receiving identical bids on electrical equipment, began including information about them in its news releases. Picked up by a Knoxville newspaper, the information set in motion an investigation by the U.S. Senate Subcommittee on Antitrust and Monopoly. Public hearings at Knoxville uncovered more evidence of collusion in bidding, and the Department of Justice began a grand jury investigation in Philadelphia. Just when it seemed that only circumstantial evidence could be developed, one of the conspirators, an executive of one of the smaller companies, confessed

---

[3]The electrical equipment case has been written up several times. See John Fuller, *The Gentlemen Conspirators* (New York: Grove Press, 1962); John Herling, *The Great Price Conspiracy* (Washington, D.C.: Robert B. Luce, Inc., 1962); Richard A. Smith, *Corporations in Crisis* (Garden City, N.Y.: Doubleday & Co., Anchor Books, 1966), Chaps. 5–6; and Clarence C. Walton and Frederick W. Cleveland, Jr., *Corporations on Trial: The Electric Cases* (Belmont, Cal.: Wadsworth Publishing Co., 1964). All are fascinating reading.

[4]Gerard Swope, president of General Electric, proposed in 1932 that industry trade associations take the lead in stabilizing prices and production during the depression. This proposal for "self-government of industry" was later developed into the ill-fated National Recovery Administration (NRA) of the New Deal years. Crucial to NRA were "codes of fair practice" for various industries, the great majority including provision for minimum prices or costs.

everything. He gave names, dates, and full details of the whole sordid business. Brought to trial, there was little the companies could do but confess their guilt. Twenty-nine firms were fined, from $7,500 each for some of the smaller ones up to $437,500 for General Electric. A number of individuals were fined and several were briefly jailed.

One feature of the case was the morality expressed by the principals. Most of the individuals involved seemed to feel that their behavior was only natural in the circumstances, that "everybody did it." Or that they had little choice: the business system led inevitably to such things. The top management of big firms like GE professed abhorrence of the conspiracy and ignorance of the price fixing, and put all of the blame on the lower-rank executives who were actually caught. Even more revealing was the behavior of GE stockholders at the next annual meeting after the trial: "They hooted down the few management critics who called for an impartial investigation and they assailed a complaining union leader with cries of 'Shut up' and 'Throw him out,'" according to the *New York Times*.

Yet Federal Judge J. Cullen Gainey, in his formal statement prior to sentencing, said, "One would be most naive indeed to believe that these violations of the law, so long persisted in, affecting so large a segment of the industry, and finally, involving so many millions upon millions of dollars, were facts unknown to those responsible for the corporation and its conduct." And one of the lawyers defending a GE vice president explained that "what he did was something that he inherited as a young man as a way of life that had been established within the General Electric Company even before he came."

Coercion

The market strategy and price policy of large firms can also include coercion of smaller firms. The objective may be to strengthen the larger company's market, or to protect its share against a too vigorous pygmy that wants to grow. Or a firm may seek to become the only seller in the market, attempting to drive other firms into bankruptcy or mergers.

Example from real life—only the names have been changed to conceal the guilty: two firms supplied crackers to grocers in Metropolis. One was a nationally known giant whose well-advertised brand sold for 30¢ per pound. One was a local firm whose product was priced at 28¢. The price differential resulted in a division of the market highly favorable to the giant. The local firm decided to increase its share by lowering its price to 27¢. The giant immediately imposed a "penalty price," in that one local market of 26¢. The local firm tried to recreate the 2¢ price differential by reducing its price to 24¢. The giant reimposed the "penalty" by pricing its crackers at 23¢. Within a week enthusiastic shoppers were buying crackers at 14¢ a pound, the local firm's management was frantic, and terms of surrender were arranged: prices were established once more at 28¢ for the local firm and 30¢ for the giant. The local firm's president sighed with relief, "Boy, we'll never try *that* again." They didn't. The cracker market in Metropolis has been "orderly" and market shares have gone largely unchanged for the last twenty-five years.

This type of price warfare was used by the old Standard Oil Co. back in the 1880s to build the most famous "trust" of that period, leading directly to passage of the Sherman Antitrust Act of 1890 and the outlawing of predatory price cutting. To give the devil his due, however, Standard Oil always offered to buy out smaller firms at a good price and only drove them to the wall if they refused to sell, which seldom happened. In the cracker case cited above, the "penalty price" was clearly an illegal move on the part of the giant. The small firm *could* have sued for triple damages under provisions of the Sherman Act: the case would have been in the courts for years, and the firm bankrupt in three months.

Almost all forms of coercion of other firms,

particularly the use of prices for that purpose, have been outlawed by the various antitrust laws. Although these practices are illegal, they are occasionally found. One reason for their scarcity in recent years has been the continuing expansion and growth of the economy. It has not been necessary for one firm to challenge another in order to grow. Nevertheless, there are still instances in which price leadership is ineffective and product differentiation and advertising do not suffice, and a firm steps out to challenge others. At those times coercive action is likely to occur.

Another common predatory practice is known as "the squeeze." It occurs in integrated industries like metals manufacturing. The large dominant firm may produce the basic metal as well as finished products made from the metal. It also sells the metal to nonintegrated fabricators. In this situation the dominant firm will sometimes use its market power to hold down the prices of finished products while it raises the price of the basic metal that it sells to other fabricators. All firms will find their profits on fabricated products held down, but the integrated giant will make it up on sales of the basic metal to the other manufacturers, who are caught in a squeeze between high materials prices and low prices for finished products. The squeeze can be employed in such industries as copper, steel, and aluminum to provide high profits for large integrated firms, to keep small firms from growing, or even to drive fabricators into mergers with the large firms on favorable terms.

Differentiated Products and Advertising

Although the oligopolistic firm has strong reasons to support and sustain the existing relationships within its industry, primarily for fear of the reaction of other firms to unsettled conditions, it also has strong reason to build a defensive position for itself as a protection against possible changes. *Product differentiation* achieved by use of brand names, advertising, or styling is the easiest path to follow. If consumers can be induced to buy a firm's product because the name is familiar, because it has certain features that are slightly different from other products, or because of the product's reputation, the firm will be more secure against any attacks on its sales from other companies and may even be able to charge higher prices than other firms charge for similar products.

- **Product differentiation** is a form of rivalry among oligopolistic firms in which essentially similar products are provided with relatively small differences. It is often associated with large selling costs and brand names.

The classic example is aspirin. All aspirin is chemically the same, and is produced in bulk by only two U.S. manufacturers. It is packed into pills with a variety of components to hold it in the pellet form (hence the claims of "speed" of dissolving; but by the time the aspirin gets to the portions of the digestive tract where the body absorbs it, any pill will be dissolved). Yet in spite of the homogeneity of all aspirin, a variety of trade names are publicized. One, Bayer Aspirin, is more expensive than others, largely because of extensive advertising. Bayer also induces retailers to give its product more prominent display by enabling the retailer to earn a higher markup, made possible by the higher price.

Its advertising and other sales efforts enable Bayer to achieve a relatively inelastic demand curve for its brand. This is the fundamental reason for product differentiation of all kinds. It enables the seller of the branded product to raise his price above the others without losing enough customers to reduce his profits. Indeed, he may well enlarge his profits. Figures 22–8 and 22–9 show the relationship between elasticity of demand and product differentiation.

Product differentiation is found widely in oligopolistic markets, particularly those producing goods sold directly to final consumers.

Figure 22-8
Market for the Undifferentiated Product:
Relatively Elastic Demand

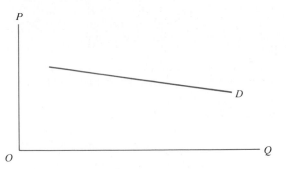

Without brand names, a higher price will bring a large
drop in sales.

Figure 22-9
Market for the Brand Name Product:
Relatively Inelastic Demand

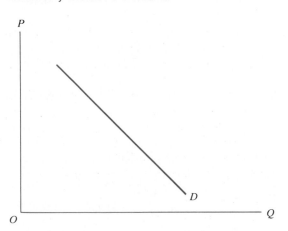

With brand names, a higher price will cause a much
smaller drop in sales.

It introduces an element of rivalry into markets
that lack significant price competition. When
the differentiation goes beyond mere brand
names and introduces qualitative differences, it
brings a larger variety of products for consumers to choose among. On the other hand, it can

bring a great proliferation of seemingly different brands, but all similar in their essential
characteristics, and all requiring large advertising expenses to keep them continually before
the public.

**Nonprice Competition: Selling Costs, Model
Changes, and Keeping Up with the Joneses**
Product differentiation opens the door to several varieties of *nonprice competition.* One is
advertising and other sales efforts. Where differentiation is largely by brand name rather
than in the product itself, oligopolistic firms
may spend large amounts on advertising. The
soap industry spends over 10 percent of its
total revenues on advertising, while the cigarette and whiskey industries spend close to 15
percent of revenues (after excise taxes). The
automobile industry spends only 1–2 percent of
its revenues on advertising, however, because
there is more real difference in the product
than in the other industries cited.

The auto industry uses model changes instead. It is such a tight oligopoly that the
principal source of competition is last year's
models available as used cars. General Motors'
chief competitor this year is General Motors
last year. To forestall as much of that competition as possible, each year's model is restyled,
or has added options, or a former option
becomes standard equipment. The auto firms
try to keep a steady stream of changes coming
every year.

Closely related to model and styling changes
is the much criticized "planned obsolescence"
of some durable consumers' goods. If enough
changes occur in models and styling over a
period of, say, three years, there may be little
demand for well-made products that have a
useful life of five to ten years. There is little
reason, then, to design products to last. A
circular chain of cause and effect is set up:

1. Oligopolistic pricing policies eliminate or
   greatly diminish price competition, leading
   to . . .

2. Product differentiation, which in turn triggers . . .

3. Frequent model and styling changes and large selling expenses. The result is . . .

4. Rapid *market* obsolescence of durable goods, causing manufacturers to produce . . .

5. Shlock.[5]

Yet shlock may be exactly what the public wants. Consumers who spend to keep up with or outpace the Joneses want the latest and fanciest products. Model and styling changes help them use their income to validate claims to social status.[6]

- **Nonprice competition** is competition via selling efforts, model changes, and product differentiation characteristic of oligopolistic competition in the absence of significant price competition

Barriers to New Firms

The patterns of economic concentration that have developed in the U.S. economy are supported and continued by *barriers to entry* of new firms. The chief barriers are product differentiation and their attendant selling costs, and large-scale production with its requirement of large investment in facilities. Other significant barriers include patents and trade secrets, control of raw materials by existing firms, and existing supplier-distributor relationships. To these should be added a variety of government restrictions. Counterbalancing these factors, however, are the continuous economic changes, particularly in consumer preferences and technology, that are at work in a dynamic economy.

- **Barriers to new firms** are conditions or arrangements that hinder the intrusion of new sellers into a market. The chief barriers to entry are large capital requirements, control of patents by existing firms, control of raw materials, and, in many consumer goods markets, product differentiation and high selling expenses.

Product differentiation is a major discouragement to new firms. In industries such as automobiles, whiskey, cigarettes, and gasoline, the existence of well-known brand names, continually publicized by large-scale advertising, contributes to serious disadvantages to new firms. Very large selling expenses may be necessary for entry into the industry, forcing a new firm to incur higher costs per unit than established firms before it can achieve enough market penetration to hold its own against the established firms and the well-known brands. Indeed, the classic study of barriers to entry estimated that the cost disadvantage of new firms in such markets may be as high as 10 to 25 percent.[7]

Product differentiation through brand names and advertising discourages entry of new firms if buyers are ignorant. But if advertising can provide buyers with enough information to know that a new firm's product is as good as or better than existing products, product differentiation can be an aid to entry. This is one reason why informative advertising that stresses a product's characteristics is more socially useful than competitive advertising that makes largely emotional appeals.

The *large amounts of capital* required for

---

[5]A Yiddish word meaning shoddy goods. Rhymes with flock. Sometimes spelled schlok. A store that sells shoddy goods is a shlock-house.

[6]An auto executive friend of the author's put it this way: "We don't make shlock. Besides, that's what the public wants."

[7]Joe S. Bain, *Barriers to New Competition* (Cambridge, Mass.: Harvard University Press, 1956). It is possible that product differentiation can foster the entry of new firms producing specialized products for a sector of the market not well served by existing products. In the automobile industry, for example, American Motors was able to survive in the 1950s by doing that, and the growing popularity of small and sporty foreign cars in recent years was based on the same sort of situation. The giants of the industry moved to occupy the new markets as soon as the venturesome newcomers were beyond the pioneering, exploratory stage, however.

entry into the large-scale mass-production industries are another important barrier to new firms. There have been no large new firms in the basic iron and steel industry since World War II, when government loans financed construction of the Kaiser Steel plant in California. No new firms have entered the automobile industry since mass-production assembly-line methods were widely adopted in the 1920s. Instead, there has been steady attrition of the smaller firms. When the need for large amounts of capital is associated with the cost disadvantages of product differentiation, as in the case of automobiles, the combined barriers become practically insurmountable.

The other important limitations to entry are more subtle. Control over technology through *patents* can help build a large enterprise, while continued development of improvements, modifications, and extensions can prolong its predominance. Domination of the photoduplication industry by Xerox Corporation is a recent example, although its growth was fostered by shrewd and vigorous marketing programs. Patents, however, can also shelter a new firm from appropriation of its technology by already existing giant firms. Xerox itself operated in this shelter during its early growth years; another example is the entry of Polaroid Company as an important participant in the photographic equipment industry.

Control over raw materials is significant in a number of industries. Most metals, sulfur, and fertilizers are examples. One can hardly fault a producer for seeking to acquire the best ore deposits, but restriction of those ores to his own use will give him a preferred position. However, ore deposits are used up in time, new ones are discovered, and in the long run these changes can erode an existing firm's position. This is one reason why producers in industries heavily dependent on supplies of raw materials move toward refining, fabricating, and distribution. The large capital requirements of these vertically integrated firms then

BARRIERS TO ENTRY: LONG-TERM CONTRACTS

In April 1981 U.S. Steel Corporation announced plans to expand production of steel pipe used in the oil industry. The plant would be built and owned by the plant's customers and leased to U.S. Steel for operation. The customers—oil companies and oilfield equipment suppliers, including a U.S. Steel subsidiary—would sign long-term contracts to take the output of the new plant. U.S. Steel says this arrangement is necessary to assure financing of the new facility at reasonable interest rates. That may or may not be the case, but one point is clear: the long-term contracts will cut off competitors or potential competitors of the plant's customers from this source of supply.

become a significant deterrent to other challengers.

Government barriers to entry are found in regulated industries, where licensing is used to restrict entry. Many professional and semiskilled occupations require licensing or certification by a public body. A very wide variety of occupations is included—plumbers, dentists, doctors, lawyers, and beauticians are some common examples. Government licensing is used to restrict entry in some important sectors of the economy, including transportation (air, bus, intercity truck), banking, and public utilities, three economic sectors thoroughly dominated by big enterprises.

Does Oligopoly Work?

This chapter's analysis of prices and market strategy in oligopolistic industries has shown that markets are typically restricted and managed. Markets are only partially free. Competition is highly imperfect. The particular degree of market restriction and limitation of competition will differ from industry to industry and from one sector of the economy to another.

It is also clear that the results of oligopoly are widely different from those ideal outcomes derived from the theory of competitive markets. To the extent that stable administered prices and shares of the market protect firms from the gales of competition, we can expect their internal efficiency to be diminished. In a world of administered prices rivalry takes the form of advertising and sales effort; product differentiation through brand names and model changes; and price leadership. Coercion and collusion are common enough in spite of legal prohibitions. To the extent that lack of competition brings prices above and output below the competitive norm, we can expect a diminution of economic welfare.

But doesn't the economy function effectively in spite of all this? Many would argue that it does, that the entrenched position of dominant firms is continually challenged. Where market control exists and either monopoly profits or economic sluggishness persists, the protected economic position becomes a target for innovators of all kinds. The monopolistic position falls to the attack of new firms, upgrading the whole economic performance of that sector of the economy.

The challenge to entrenched position can come from a variety of sources. Technological innovation is one. New products, new processes, and new materials that promise reduced costs or expanded markets are a direct result of the continuing attack on the economic status quo. When established firms seek to gain control over the innovation process they become part of it themselves and contribute to revitalization of the economy.

One source of challenge to entrenched positions is the market for business enterprises themselves. A firm doing poorly will find the value of its securities falling. Enterprising business executives, spotting the poor performance, can use the financial resources of their own firms to buy control of the laggard, inject new capital and imaginative management, and revive the backward firm. One spectacular historical example is the Union Pacific Railroad: Edward H. Harriman used the resources of the Illinois Central Railroad to gain control of the badly run and dilapidated UP in 1897 and turn it into one of the nation's most profitable lines. A more recent example is the case of Norton Simon, Inc., a recently built conglomerate based on a middle sized food-manufacturing firm whose resources were used to gain control of and revive a number of troubled firms in a variety of industries. The "corporate takeover" is one way the financial markets provide for the entry of new capital and new management even in industries with strong barriers to new firms.

The public may also benefit from competition between giant firms. The "countervailing power" of a giant buyer such as Sears Roebuck or A & P can balance the market power of a giant seller like General Electric or General Foods. The bargaining power of U.S. Steel can mitigate that of the steelworkers' union. A large department store can sell its own line of private brands of manufactured goods. To some extent power will beget power and one center of power will neutralize another, although the danger of collusion between centers of power may require a very watchful economic policeman with strong punitive powers.

Some of the most sophisticated observers of the American economy argue that these elements have made an oligopolistic system a workable one, in spite of its inefficiencies. It works, they argue, because consumers are free to buy what they like; because ambitious people continually seek to gain a share of the advantages held by those established and vested interests that prevail throughout big business; because the elite of big business is a circulating one in which entry of newcomers depends to a large extent on innovative and managerial ability; and because government attacks monopoly through the antitrust laws and regulates firms.

This resolution of the problem is not adequate, however. A system of supercorporations *may* be effective in contributing to rising living standards and accommodating to economic change, but if advertising adjusts consumer preferences to the sales needs of big enterprise, rather than the other way around, the rationality of the system as a whole may be seriously deficient. If one result is heavy reliance on military spending that is in part fostered by a mutuality of interest between big business and big government, then the system as a whole may be destructive rather than constructive. Such an economy does not promote human values, but only the wealth and power of a few.

There are political implications as well. A self-selecting business elite, even an open one, can exert influence on political institutions and press for legislation favorable to its own special interests. Special favors can be obtained through the tax system or through allocation of government expenditures. National policies as a whole can be distorted in favor of the rich and powerful, to the detriment of the general public. The rules of the economic game can be structured to favor the haves at the expense of the have-nots. The political impact of an economy dominated by giant corporations controlled from the top may be far more important than economic issues such as price, quantity of output, profits, and the nature and speed of innovation.

Finally, simple observation tells us that the success of the oligopolistic U.S. economy cannot be taken for granted. As the decade of the 1980s opens the U.S. economy has fallen on hard times, and the oligopolistic sector has been hit hardest of all. The steel industry has difficulty meeting competition in its home market from more modern and efficient foreign producers. The automobile industry faces huge losses because of failure to produce the types of cars in heavy demand by consumers and failure to match the quality standards of foreign manufacturers. The electrical equipment industry is unable to compete effectively with imports of many products. Output per labor hour has been declining in the manufacturing sector as a whole. It is fashionable in U.S. business circles to blame labor unions, inflation, or government interference for this time of troubles, just as you or I seek scapegoats for our own failings. Yet the basic point cannot be evaded: it is in the oligopolistic sector of the economy that these troubles are most severe, and it is the oligopolistic sector that has had the greatest difficulty in resolving them. The argument that oligopoly works is suspect.

Summary

In oligopolistic industries the actions of one firm affect the positions of other firms, leading to a variety of price and market strategies. Some of the more prominent pricing strategies are:

Pricing to achieve a target return on investment.

Price stability and stability of profit margins.

Following prices established by a leader.

Maintaining or improving market position.

Pricing to meet competition, with emphasis on high profits from new products.

All of these strategies involve administered prices established by company policy, with significant freedom from market forces.

Administered prices tend to remain stable, but are flexible upward in times of high aggregate demand and relatively full use of plant capacity. When price adjustments occur they tend to be "orderly," utilizing a variety of patterns of price leadership by dominant firms.

The chief technique used to set prices in oligopolistic industries is markup pricing. Prime costs (full fixed and variable costs) per unit of output at a standard or customary output are the base. A percentage of prime costs is added to the base to arrive at a selling price. The markup over prime costs is designed to maximize retained earnings at the standard output and provide funds for growth of the firm. This goal is not the same as profit maximization.

Administered prices require some form of market control. Price leadership is the most common. Others are coercion of small firms by large firms and collusion among giants. Large firms also maintain their market positions and avoid direct price competition by using advertising and sales effort, product differentiation through trademarks and model changes, and other forms of nonprice competition.

In spite of these characteristics of the modern economy, some economists argue that the final results are not all that bad. The system works, and many people are happy with the results. But in the long run an economy of giant enterprises run from the top by a relatively small business and financial elite has more than purely economic effects. Its political implications can be more significant than its immediate economic effects.

Key Concepts

administered prices	**markup pricing**	**barriers to new firms**
kinked demand curve	**product differentiation**	
price leadership	**nonprice competition**	

For Discussion

1. Why does oligopoly lead to significant losses of economic efficiency?

2. In what ways can administered prices contribute to inflation?

3. Why do prices in an oligopoly tend to remain stable, even when there are changes in costs of production?

4. Explain why maximization of retained earnings on the basis of a standard output yields results in both price and quantity of output different from what would be achieved by maximizing profits.

5. Should an economy dominated by oligopolistic industries be characterized by the phrase "free enterprise"? Explain carefully.

6. Is there a connecting link between relatively high profits in oligopolistic industries, markup pricing to maximize retained earnings, and the trend toward increased oligopoly?

Chapter 23

Big Business and Public Policy

The existence of a high degree of oligopoly and significant amounts of market power create major problems of public policy. Is the economic power of the large corporation a danger in a democratic society? If it is, what remedies are there? In a more restricted sense, what should be done about the purely economic effects of market power? Should monopoly be tolerated? Should it be eliminated wherever possible and prevented from arising elsewhere? If it can't be eliminated or prevented, should it be regulated, and if so by whom, to what ends, and with what instruments? Or is government ownership the only answer where monopoly or great market power exists?

In the United States, public policy toward big business has concentrated almost wholly on the economic effects of business behavior. Policy has sought to do two things:

1. Preserve competition and prevent monopoly through antitrust legislation.

2. Regulate monopolies when it is impractical to eliminate them.

There have been some important exceptions, however, and in some important instances the federal government has fostered and supported monopoloid practices and market control.

Public policy in the United States has given little attention to the larger problems of political and economic power that arise when important sectors of the economy are dominated by large firms. The growth of big business has gone largely unchecked, except where a clear impact on markets and prices is evident.

This chapter will examine these issues: first, antitrust legislation to promote competition, public utility regulation, and government support of private market control. It will then look at the issue of economic power and the problems and dilemmas of nonpolicy in that area.

Maintaining Competition

Prevention of monopoly and promotion of competition are the chief function of the *antitrust laws*. There are three significant pieces of legislation: the Sherman Act (1890), the Clayton Act (1914), and the Federal Trade Commission Act (1914). Two important amendments to the Clayton Act should also be included: the Robinson-Patman Act (1936), which actually restricts competition in retailing; and the Celler-Kefauver Act (1950), which forbids mergers that tend to dominate competition.

- **Antitrust laws** are designed to prevent monopoly and promote competition.

The Sherman Antitrust Act

The Sherman Antitrust Act of 1890 came as a reaction against the many business efforts to control markets, fix prices, and eliminate competition of the early decades of large-scale industrialization in the United States. The spread of a national network of railroads created large regional and national markets in place of the former local markets protected from competition by high transport costs. Concurrently, technological changes were creating industries with high capital costs and expensive, single-purpose equipment. The simultaneous opening of markets to more sellers and the growth of industries requiring sales and price stability, together with the great instability added by recurring business cycles, led to a pervasive movement in industry to control the economic environment. The trust, from which the Sherman Act takes it name, was one such device: competing firms in the same industry would deposit their voting stock with a single board of trustees, which would then have voting control (but not ownership) of the formerly independent firms. A simpler device was the holding company, formed to buy stock control of formerly independent firms. Less effective than either of these devices were varieties of cartels, that is, voluntary agreements among firms to divide markets, fix prices, pool sales revenues for division on a prearranged basis, or limit output. The cartels tended to break down under the stress of depressions and financial crisis, leading to more formal arrangements like trusts and holding companies. These, in turn, led to the great public outcry against monopoly that produced the Sherman Act.

The wording of the Sherman Act is simple and inclusive, and broad enough to require considerable interpretation by the courts:

> Every contract, combination . . . or conspiracy, in restraint of trade or commerce among the several states, or with foreign nations, is declared to be illegal.

and

> Every person who shall monopolize, or attempt to monopolize, or combine or conspire . . . to monopolize any part of the trade or commerce among the several states, or with foreign nations, shall be deemed guilty of a misdemeanor.

Enforcement of the Sherman Act (and the Clayton Act, to be described shortly) is the responsibility of the Antitrust Division of the U.S. Department of Justice, by way of legal prosecution of violators of the law. Injured private parties can also sue violators for triple damages under the Sherman Act.

This broad law, which could have been used to prevent the rise of giant corporations to their present positions of dominance, received its first setback because of failure to enforce it. Enforcement requires a lawsuit brought by the Attorney General of the United States against persons or firms accused of violations. Yet from the beginning the attorney general failed to act, and Richard Olney, a former corporation lawyer who served in the position from 1893 to 1895, thought the law should be repealed and refused to enforce it. When a case was finally brought to the Supreme Court in 1895, involving a sugar industry trust that controlled about 98 percent of the nation's sugar refining capacity, the Court decided that this indeed was a monopoly, but in manufacturing, not commerce, and the Sherman Act did not apply. This interpretation of the law was not reversed until 1899. But by then the gates had been opened to the merger movement of 1895–1901 through which many industries were organized in giant, quasi-monopolistic form.

This reluctance to challenge size and market control continued as a basic attitude until after

World War II. In 1911, two great cases involving Standard Oil and American Tobacco came before the Court, which ordered the dissolution of those firms not because of their monopoly positions (which were indisputable), but because they used their power unreasonably to harass other firms. This famous *"rule of reason"* was applied in the next decades to such firms as Eastman Kodak, United Shoe Machinery Corp., International Harvester, and U.S. Steel, each of which held a near monopoly or overwhelming market dominance in its industry. In each case the courts held that no offense had been committed because the firms had not attacked or attempted to coerce their few rivals. They didn't have to; they achieved dominance during the first merger movement because of the benign neglect of the Department of Justice and the courts, and their size alone was enough to cause rivals to accept their leadership. "Mere size" was not an offense according to the earlier Supreme Court interpretations of the antitrust laws.

- The **"rule of reason"** was the interpretation that only "unreasonable" restraint of trade was prohibited by the Sherman Act.

The "rule of reason" was not significantly modified until 1944. In that year, an antitrust suit against Aluminum Co. of America could not be heard by the Supreme Court because too many of its members had participated in the case as attorneys general to obtain a quorum. The case was heard instead by the federal court in New York under Judge Learned Hand. Hand overturned the rule of reason on the ground that large size in relation to the industry as a whole brought market dominance and the evils of monopoly even if the firm did not consciously exercise its power. Hand held that such monopoly power was prohibited. His rule of thumb was that control of 90 percent of aluminum production "is enough to constitute a monopoly; it is doubtful whether sixty or sixty-four percent would be enough; and cer-

tainly thirty-three percent is not." This landmark decision at last accepted the contention that the word "monopolizing" included high degrees of concentration and the tacit cooperation that accompanies them.

While this long sequence of changing judicial interpretation of "monopoly" has been going on, the courts have consistently outlawed restraint of trade in its many forms. This has included rate agreements between railroads, market sharing, price fixing, collusive bidding on supply contracts, exclusive selling arrangements of several types, and restrictions of output, among many others; the list of prohibited collusive actions is a very long one. The Sherman Act, then, was used consistently to prosecute predatory monopolistic practices, but was not used for over half a century to prevent the development of monopoloid industrial structures.

The Clayton Antitrust Act

The Clayton Antitrust Act (1914) exhibits some of the same limitations as the Sherman Act, and probably for the same reasons. Its prohibitions of predatory action were clear and effectively enforced, but where it sought restrictions on corporate power and size the results were ineffectual.

The act itself was in large part a reaction against the revelations of the 1911 antitrust suits against Standard Oil and American Tobacco, which had shown how a giant corporation could ruthlessly suppress or gobble up its rivals. There was demand for legislation that would outlaw the specific tactics used, and in the 1912 national election campaign the topic of big business and monopolistic practices was one of the main issues. The new President, Woodrow Wilson (trained as an economist, incidentally, although his academic career was spent mainly as a historian and political scientist), immediately sought legislation to prevent repetition of the evils found in petroleum refining and tobacco manufacturing. The Clayton Act was one result.

The specific practices outlawed by the Clayton Act were only four in number. Two related to market practices. Price discrimination was forbidden except when it was the result of real differences in cost or when it was used "in good faith to meet competition." Thus, the practice by Standard Oil of cutting prices in a local market to drive a rival to the wall, while maintaining prices at higher levels in other areas, was henceforth illegal. The act also forbade agreements between supplier and distributor in which the supplier offers one line of goods only if the distributor agrees to also take another (tying contracts), and in which the distributor agrees not to handle the goods of other suppliers (exclusive dealing contracts). These were devices used extensively by American Tobacco. These prohibitions of the Clayton Act have been effectively enforced in subsequent years.

Two other provisions of the Clayton Act tried to deal with the structure of big enterprise, and they proved to be ineffective. One forbade acquisition of competing firms by stock ownership. The other forbade direct interlocking directorates among competing firms.

It was useless to forbid a firm from buying stock control of a competitor if the assets themselves could be bought. Instead of holding companies (like Standard Oil) owning a controlling interest in rival firms, the competitors could merely merge, or the large firm could buy the assets of the smaller. This is exactly what happened in the merger movement of the 1920s.

The loophole in the law was not closed until 1950, when the Celler-Kefauver Act amended this portion of the Clayton Act to forbid any corporate acquisitions whose effect "may be substantially to lessen competition or tend to create a monopoly." This broad language has enabled the Department of Justice to challenge and prevent a number of large mergers. But it still permits the conglomerate mergers across industry lines that have enabled concentration in the economy as a whole to continue to grow.

As for interlocking directorates, prohibition of direct interlocks has merely caused a shift to indirect interlocks as the basis for corporate community-of-interest groupings. Instead of Mr. *A* being on the boards of directors of two steel companies (a direct interlock), *A* will be on the board of Steel Company of America and the Friendly National Bank while his associate, Mr. *B*, is on the board of Friendly National Bank and American Steel Company (an indirect interlock). The direct interlock is prohibited but the indirect interlock is legal. One wonders if *A* and *B* ever talk about the affairs of the steel companies when they meet at the regular board meetings of the Friendly National Bank.

The Federal Trade Commission

When the Clayton Act was passed in 1914, President Wilson had wanted a long list of predatory monopolistic practices outlawed and a commission established to enforce the law. Congress balked, however, and only a few specific practices were named in the Clayton Act. However, the special commission was established by the Federal Trade Commission Act (1914), which also outlawed "unfair methods of competition" in more general terms. The FTC has five members appointed by the President. It is authorized to investigate unfair methods of competition, deceptive practices, monopolistic devices, and practices in restraint of trade, and to prosecute violators of the law. It can issue cease-and-desist orders to halt illegal practices, which the accused can appeal to the courts.

The FTC has never been a strong and vigorous watchdog over the economy, however. Most of its activity has been in the areas of retail trade and small business, protecting consumers against small business and small businesses from each other. Few of its activities have involved big business and the use of market power, except for a campaign in the 1930s against pricing practices in steel and chemicals and another in 1945–1951 against several major oligopolies. Intended as a body with strong powers to initiate action against a wide variety of anticompetitive practices, it has instead taken a largely passive role.

The tendency of the FTC to avoid facing issues raised by the dominance of big business is illustrated by a 1980 decision concerning DuPont Co. The research staff of the FTC had found that DuPont controlled the market for titanium dioxide, which is widely used as the pigment in white paint. The Commission, however, refused to prosecute DuPont, on the ground that the company's market dominance had been obtained by hard, aggressive competition based on production efficiencies. This judgment repudiated the 1944 Alcoa decision and reaffirmed the old "rule of reason" of 1911. Market dominance was legitimized, as long as it is not obtained by predatory action, and, presumably, does not inflict unreasonable damage on the public. The larger issues of whether an economy dominated by large firms is desirable or not was not addressed.

The Robinson-Patman Act

The conflicting attitudes toward big business and competition that prevail in the United States, and that have affected both the administration and legal interpretation of the antitrust laws, are exemplified in the way retail trade has been treated. When chain stores began spreading in the 1920s their impact on independent retailers was blunted by national prosperity. But during the Great Depression of the 1930s, when competitive pressures really began to squeeze, independent retailers sought legislative help. In particular, they objected to the large discounts that chain stores were able to get when they bought in large quantities from manufacturers and other suppliers, claiming that in many instances the cuts were not justified by savings in costs. The result was passage of the Robinson-Patman Act (1936), which tightened the Clayton Act's prohibition on price discrimination that served to lessen or injure competition and specifically outlawed certain business practices that evaded the Clayton Act.

This legislation has been highly controversial. It was designed to reduce the buying advantage of big firms, but as it has been administered the law has sometimes prevented price reductions that could be shown to be based on real savings in cost that result from large-volume sales. This discrimination in favor of small buyers has promoted the survival of higher cost systems of retail distribution. The law also tends to inhibit price cutting when markets turn soft, and has helped to promote the downward rigidity of prices in the modern economy.

Antitrust: Where Do We Go from Here?

The dilemma of antitrust is that it has permitted the development of an economy dominated in large part by big business and has allowed that economy to structure itself in oligopolistic form. At the same time it has outlawed a variety of specific business practices that are the natural mode of behavior of giant firms and oligopolies. Yet the drive toward market control, price stability, and a live-and-let-live attitude is the natural outcome of the oligopolistic structure that antitrust has failed to attack. This paradox has never been resolved. Proponents of vigorous enforcement of the antitrust laws argue, however, that if concentrations of business power can be broken up and the antitrust laws as they now stand are continuously enforced, the economy can be made essentially competitive and kept that way. Break up the large multiplant firms and large conglomerates to give competition a chance, they argue. Little will be lost in productive efficiency, since that is to be found primarily within plants. Much could be gained, however, as price competition is revived and replaces advertising and other forms of nonprice competition. That development would benefit consumers by reducing both prices and costs. In addition, the power of large corporations to influence national policy would be reduced or eliminated. A program to make smaller economic units out of giant ones may be difficult to accomplish, but at least some economists feel that it would greatly ease some of the chief problems of modern industrial capitalism.

Proposals to recreate a competitive economy face huge political obstacles, however. The large enterprises to be broken up are politically powerful. Their securities are owned in substantial amounts by large banks and insurance companies, and by upper income families. They have large numbers of employees. All of these groups could be expected to oppose changes in the existing situation. These political realities make the success of any concerted effort to restructure the economy seem very doubtful.

Government Regulation: Old Style

In some industries government has accepted monopoly as unavoidable or competition as impractical, particularly in public utility services. Without a competitive market to protect the consumer and to force firms to provide adequate services at reasonable prices, administrative regulation has been used as a means of control. An institutionalized form of conflict between regulatory bodies and regulated firms has been established, the results of which are seldom fully satisfactory to anyone. The regulated sector of the economy seems always to be in a state of crisis. The reasons for that condition illuminate many of the basic economic realities of a big business and high technology economy.

The Legal Basis of Regulation

The legal basis for *public utility regulation* is the concept of business firms "affected with the public interest." This means a firm or firms that provide an essential service to the community as a whole, yet so small in number that they could exact a large toll from the community for those services. The legal principle was first defined in the famous case of *Munn v. Illinois* in 1877.

● **Public utility regulation** began as government regulation of industries "affected with the public interests" when preservation of competition was felt to be impractical.

The Illinois legislature passed a law in 1871 for the regulation of grain elevators and warehouses in Chicago, including establishment of maximum rates. One company refused to comply, on the grounds that the law deprived it of property without due process of law and was an unwarranted interference with interstate commerce. In the trial it was shown that nine companies controlled the business, that they met periodically to establish grain storage rates, and that the potential sites for grain elevators were strictly limited; that is, a monopoly prevailed. The trial also showed that grain storage in Chicago was vitally important to both the city's economy and to midwestern farmers. The U.S. Supreme Court upheld the law on the argument that the state's police power could be used to regulate an industry "affected with the public interest," that is, one with a monopoly of an essential public service and therefore in a position from which "a tribute can be exacted from the community," to quote a later case.

Thus public utility regulation was born. For almost sixty years after *Munn v. Illinois*, the courts wrestled with the problem of which industries came under the category of those "affected with the public interest." Finally the problem was given up; in 1934, the U.S. Supreme Court held that the definition was up to the state legislature or Congress. Thereafter it was up to the people, speaking through their elected representatives, to determine the industries to be regulated. The result was a large expansion of government regulation.

The federal government is very largely responsible for regulation of the transportation industries, including railroads, intercity motor transport, airlines, and pipelines; the natural gas industry; and the various communications industries. The federal and state governments share responsibilities for regulation of electric power production, with the greater part of the job being done by state agencies.

The Economic Basis of Regulation

The economic basis for regulation of public utilities, at least in theory, is that competition cannot prevail because one firm could supply the market at lower costs per unit of output than two or more firms. If the market were left unregulated the forces of competition would lead to the survival of only one seller, which as a monopoly would then be able to extract large profits from the community dependent on its services. The situation is sometimes called a "natural" monopoly, since it would result from the normal operation of economic forces. The theoretical analysis is shown in Figure 23–1.

Once regulation of prices begins, however, the regulatory process must be extended very deeply into many aspects of the industry. Methods of accounting must be controlled in order to prevent escalation of costs due to inefficiency, dishonesty, or efforts to evade the intent of regulation. The value of the utility's business assets must be determined in order to set a fair base on which the utility's rate of return on its investment can be estimated. That rate of return, together with the base, will largely determine the rates. Furthermore, the rate structure must be set, because any utility has several types of customers—families, business firms, and so on—each with varying needs and ability to pay. Finally, the quality of service, safety, and efficiency must all be considered. By this time it is obvious that there is not very much a utility does that does not come under the jurisdiction of the appropriate regulatory agency.

Figure 23–1
Natural Monopoly

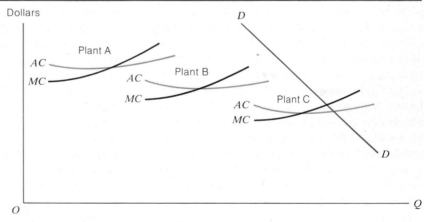

The line *DD* shows the market demand curve for the product, and the three *AC* curves show average costs for plants of three different sizes. As plant size is increased average costs of production are reduced. Since the size of the market is limited relative to the size of the lowest-cost producer, a single supplier would emerge.

   Economies of large-scale production give Plant C a cost advantage over smaller producers. Competition could prevail for a time, but mergers and bankruptcies would soon leave but one firm. Alternatively, firms A and B could agree to share the market and fix prices, but this would mean higher costs of production and economic waste. With only one producer, however, lower costs might not be reflected in lower rates to the public, indicating a need for regulation.

The Permanent Crisis of Regulation

The fact of regulation, however close and detailed, is not the underlying cause of the continuing problem of public-utility regulation. Most of the differences between utility and regulatory body can be resolved, particularly since the utility always has recourse to legal action, if it can show that its rates are kept so low as to constitute deprivation of property. A utility is entitled to "a fair return on a fair value" and both utility and regulatory commission know it, while the courts are there to enforce the rule.

Nor is the problem necessarily that the regulatory commissions tend to be "captured" by the industries they are supposed to regulate, although that has always been an issue. Utility regulation is a complex job, requiring detailed knowledge of both the industry and the law. Appointments to commissions generally go to knowledgeable people, yet where can they be found outside the ranks of lawyers employed by the utilities themselves? Such people tend to have the attitudes and viewpoints of the companies and see issues through the industry's eyes. It is hard to get both knowledge and the consumer's point of view in the same person. The choice is often between lack of competence combined with a consumer viewpoint versus high competence combined with an industry viewpoint. The result is either poor regulation or predominance of the industry viewpoint on the regulatory commissions themselves. In either case the public loses.

The fundamental difficulty lies elsewhere. Efforts to hold the returns to utilities down to the level that would prevail in a competitive market are doomed to failure in an economy in which many, and perhaps most, industries are oligopolistic or monopoloid in nature. The stable prices and substantial profits of the monopoloid sector make it difficut to attract capital to utilities whose rates of profit are kept close to the competitive norm by regulatory bodies. If profits on invested capital in most industrial oligopolies run upwards from 15 percent per year, even a sheltered and regulated monopoly may not be able to get the capital it needs for expansion if its earnings are held to a "mere" 10 percent annually. Indeed, in recent years many regulated firms have tried to use the capital available from profits and depreciation charges to diversify into other and unregulated types of enterprise. Unless checked, this trend can bring significant deterioration of services and failure to expand rapidly enough to meet the needs of an expanding economy.

This economic reality can be stated as a very simple proposition. In an economy in which the chief alternative for the use of capital is investment in monopoloid sectors of the economy, efforts to hold profits in regulated industries to competitive levels bring deterioration of service. Only if something close to oligopolistic profits is allowed can deterioration of service be prevented. If the rest of the economy were strongly competitive, this dilemma could be avoided. It isn't, however, so the regulatory agencies are in the unenviable position of either allowing high rates of return and correspondingly high charges or forcing an increasingly poor quality of service on the public. In practice, this dilemma has sometimes led to both high rates and poor service, particularly in federal regulation of the transportation industries.

The Move to Deregulation

The faults of regulation brought on a concerted move toward deregulation, particularly at the federal level in transportation and natural gas.

Transportation

Deregulation began with airlines. Between 1965 and 1975 the Civil Aeronautics Board, the regulatory agency, began permitting the airlines a small degree of flexibility in setting fares, in the form of family fares, youth fares, late-night fares, and stand-by fares, and competition from charter lines. Then in 1976 the CAB began to allow a great deal more competition in rates and shifted to a more permissive policy in approving applications for new routes. The new policies did not result in any serious problems and brought important advantages to travelers, so in 1978 the agency proposed and Congress passed legislation that would gradually phase out all regulation of airline rates and routes and even abolish the CAB itself in 1985.

The Interstate Commerce Commission, which regulates railroads and motor trucks, was the next agency to move toward deregulation. The ICC was long known as a particularly poor regulatory agency. "The commissioners are not evil men, they're just stupid," observed one critic of policies that led to high costs, excess railroad trackage, inadequate innovation, obsolete facilities and poor service. But a new and vigorous chairman in the late 1970s pushed the agency toward deregulation. Proposals by the ICC enacted by Congress in 1980 gave railroads much greater freedom to raise and lower rates and to abandon lightly used lines, while taking away much of their power to agree among themselves on common, noncompetitive rates.

The ICC also moved in 1980 to deregulate trucking. Companies were given much greater freedom to extend their routes into new areas and compete with existing trucking companies, as well as to set rates. Similar action was taken with respect to passenger transportation by bus.

The Interstate Commerce Commission did not seek the complete elimination of regulation or its own abolition. But it has promoted competition among and between railroads, trucks and barges (water transportation was never regulated to any significant extent) to allow each mode of transportation to define its own sphere of activity by competing with others, while new technologies like that of coal-slurry pipelines add a further competitive dimension to land transportation.

Deregulation of railroads was supported by the railroad companies because it enabled them to compete more effectively with trucking companies, barge lines, and pipelines—and was opposed by firms in those other fields for the same reason. The truckers also opposed deregulation of their industry because it would mean increased competition within the industry. Protected economic positions are not willingly surrendered, and the discipline of competition is a hard one. How far deregulation of land transportation will proceed is a question for the future, but it has begun.

Natural Gas

Deregulation of the price of natural gas at the federal level was closely related to the nation's energy problems and the escalating price of imported oil that began in 1973. The price of natural gas has traditionally been regulated at two levels. Prices to consumers are the responsibility of state regulatory commissions. They have shown wide variations in their behavior, from strong protection of consumers by keeping rates down through a variety of indifference and incompetence to the other extreme of protecting the profits of the gas-distributing utilities. Whatever their behavior, however, prices to the ultimate consumer must dance to the tune played by prices at the wellhead.

The price of natural gas at the wellhead was regulated by the Federal Power Commission, starting in 1954. The FPC did not want the job, but was required to take it on by the U.S. Supreme Court as the result of a suit against Phillips Petroleum Co. by the state of Wisconsin and three midwestern cities. The basic economic problem was that the price of gas began rising as domestic supplies began to dwindle relative to rising demand in a growing economy. Consumers wanted to be protected against increased rates. The FPC succeeded in stabilizing prices to consumers during the 1960s, but that policy gradually brought on new problems. With prices held at relatively low levels, there was little incentive for producers to search for more gas, and a shortage began to build up.

The supply problem became much more acute after 1973, when the price of imported oil was first doubled, doubled again, and then raised once more by the OPEC oil cartel. The FPC was reluctant to allow gas prices to rise, partly because of political pressure to protect consumers and partly because the Commission did not want to endow the owners of gas reserves with large windfall gains in the value of their gas. The Commission compromised by holding down the price of gas from existing wells and allowing higher prices for "new" gas. Very shortly there was a complex system of four different prices and confusion reigned. Finally, a reluctant Congress stepped in to mandate decontrol of the price of natural gas, starting in 1978 and continuing in stages to 1989, when price control is finally to end.

If all of this sounds somewhat weird, it is. With energy prices and costs of production rising by large amounts, natural gas would gradually start disappearing from the market if its price were held to artificially low levels. Adequate availability requires that the price provide profits to the marginal producers of gas equal to those available to marginal producers of other forms of energy. Consumers would have to pay those costs. Yet high prices provide very large profits to the lower cost producers— the so-called "windfall" profits obtained solely because the market price rises. The reluctance of FPC and Congress to embrace the free market solution was based on the fact that price decontrol would result in a large shift of wealth from consumers to producers. The result of these conflicting interests was a policy of gradual deregulation of natural gas.

The "New" Regulation

The "old style" of government regulation was designed to protect the public from the eco-nomic effects of monopoly, including high prices and poor service. The "new" regulation has a different objective. It is designed to protect the environment, the public, and workers from the sometimes destructive impact of modern technology and other undesirable business practices. It is not applied to individual industries like electric power or airplane transportation, but is directed toward all sectors of the economy and applied on a national scale.

State and local governments had shared for many years the regulation of a wide variety of enterprises that could affect the welfare of the public, such as beauty parlors and barbershops, restaurants, liquor stores, as well as the licensing of a number of professionals, such as doctors, psychologists, teachers, and others. Economists have never been licensed or regulated, perhaps because no one could quite figure out what they do, or maybe because they are quite harmless. At the federal level, the Food and Drug Administration, established in 1911, sought to maintain the safety of foods, drugs and certain types of medical devices; and the Federal Trade Commission, established in 1914, was supposed to protect consumers from fraud, unfair practices and deception in sales and advertising.

Beginning in the early 1960s regulation of business designed to protect people and the natural environment was expanded substantially. Five major federal agencies or commissions were established to administer the new regulations. Their titles indicate the areas covered:

Equal Employment Opportunity Commission
Environmental Protection Agency
National Highway Traffic Safety Commission
Occupational Health and Safety Administration
Consumer Product Safety Commission

By the mid-1970s the legislation and administration of the new style of federal regulation was in place.

The fight in Congress against the legislation establishing these new areas of federal regulation was led by the lobbyists and trade associations of big business. Industries like steel, automobiles, and chemicals, largely free of regulation in the past, now found that they had to get government approval for such business decisions as the construction of equipment and factories (to prevent excessive pollution), design of products (such as the safety and fuel requirements of automobiles), packaging (to prevent deception and fraud), methods of hiring (to prevent discrimination), and organization of the workplace (to avoid health and safety problems for workers). The new regulation brought government "bureaucrats" into the decision-making process that had been the exclusive right of management, and it added to costs of production. Advocates of the new legislation argued that it merely shifted costs from the general public to the producers of the "bads" that accompanied production of goods. Indeed, they argued that total costs—private costs to producers plus social costs to the public—would be reduced by stopping the problem at its source rather than making good the damage later. It is almost impossible to reach a judgment on these issues in a purely objective fashion, primarily because the business costs of the new regulations are relatively easy to estimate—cost accounting is a highly developed, if imperfect, discipline—while social costs are almost impossible to measure accurately.

Furthermore, the new regulation applies to almost all business enterprise. The old regulation, by contrast, applied to specific industries, for the most part, so it was difficult to mount unified opposition to it on the part of the business community as a whole. The broad applicability of the new regulation, however, makes it a political target for business enterprise in general. The result has been increased conflict between the business community and the federal government over the desirability and extent of enforcement of much of the new regulation. The basic issue is whether business firms should be allowed to shift some of the costs of production to the public (see Chapter 32).

Government Support of Market Control

The most spectacular case of U.S. government support of private control of markets occurred under the National Industrial Recovery Act of 1933–35. Intended as a means of stabilizing prices and promoting increased production at the depths of the Great Depression of the 1930s, the act suspended the antitrust laws to permit firms to draw up "codes of fair conduct" that had the force of law. Over 550 codes were approved, covering almost all industries. The codes controlled prices, divided markets, controlled terms of sale and distribution channels, and limited capacity to produce, among other aspects of business. A few codes limited output in accordance with estimates of total sales and assigned production quotas to the participating firms. Most of the codes tried to control prices without also controlling output, however, and that proved to be a fatal defect. By the time the U.S. Supreme Court declared the entire scheme unconstitutional in 1935, most of the cartels established under the NRA were breaking up as a result of strong competition for the limited markets available in the depression.

After the death of NRA the federal government continued to support market controls in two branches of the energy industry, bituminous coal and petroleum. In coal, the federal government sought to control prices and output in an industry split among large coal firms, giant steel companies producing coal for their own use as well as for the market, and thousands of small firms fighting to survive the depression and engaging in ruthless price cutting to do so. Federal legislation promoted a cartel-type arrangement among the large producers to control output and prices, supervised by a federal Bituminous Coal Commission, but this scheme failed because of inability to control the thousands of small producers. Only after World War II was a successful system of planned production for the industry devised, but this time it was managed by the union, the United Mine Workers, which controlled output and imposed large wage increases on the industry that largely destroyed the small producers. The giant firms loved it, for only they could afford the huge capital investments necessary to remain competitive as wage rates rose. The number of coal miners fell from almost 1.5 million in 1945 to under 500 thousand in 1965, while industry output was stabilized. The coal companies and the union turned their backs on the displaced workers and the coal mining regions of Appalachia become centers of rural poverty. Today coal mining is dominated by large firms, many now controlled by oil companies, and is part of a much larger oligopolistic energy industry.

Market control in the petroleum industry was even more complicated, and is important for an understanding of the structure and practices that prevail in the 1980s. The federal and state governments combined informally with the industry giants to establish a system of price maintenance and production control that provided high profits to domestic oil producers and limited competition in the refining and sale of gasoline.

First, the domestic market was protected from competition from abroad by federal legislation that restricted and licensed imports of crude oil. Import restrictions helped maintain the domestic price of oil and its refined products above the level of a free market. They also helped prevent the entry of new firms into the refined products sector of the industry by preventing potential competitors from obtaining supplies of low-cost crude oil from abroad.

Second, production of crude oil within the U.S. was limited so as to maintain existing prices. The process operated as follows:

1. Each producing state (except California) had a regulatory commission empowered to set production quotas for that state's oil wells. An Interstate Oil Compact Commission, established by federal law and having the oil-producing states as members, reached agreement on each state's share of current output.

2. The U.S. Bureau of Mines made monthly estimates of consumer demand for gasoline and other petroleum products (based, of course, on existing prices), which were used to establish state production quotas. California did not participate because all its oil was used in the state and more imported, so it did not need production quotas.

3. The quotas were enforced by the federal government. The Connally "Hot Oil" Act (1935) prohibited transportation in interstate commerce of any oil produced above the quotas set by the state commissions.

Third, control of pipelines from oil fields to refineries by the industry giants gave them a strategic advantage over independent companies. A "consent decree"[1] by which independents had access to the pipelines on equal terms confirmed this position legally. It enabled the pipeline owner to earn a profit from transporting his competitor's raw materials; part of the competitor's costs became profits for the owner of the pipeline.

Finally, the integrated oil companies "squeezed" the profits of independent refiners by maintaining relatively narrow margins be-

---

[1]A consent decree is a court order under which a firm or firms accused of violating the antitrust laws agree to a settlement agreeable also to the Department of Justice, without admitting that they were guilty of anything for which they were charged.

tween the price of crude oil and the price of refined products. No one made much on refining gasoline, but the integrated companies made large profits from producing crude oil.

The effect of these practices was to stabilize prices and protect the existing large firms from challenges to their market position. The oil industry charged prices for its products that not only gave it a normal profit, but enough more to provide almost all the capital needed for investment in expanded capacity. The rest came from the tax subsidy provided by large depletion allowances.[2] Few large oil companies had to get new capital by borrowing or issuing new stock.[3] This enabled the existing stockholders to monopolize the full gains from economic growth rather than share those gains with suppliers of new capital. Capital for expansion came from the consumer of gasoline and fuel oil, and from the taxpayer, but the gains went to oil company stockholders.

There was a dual justification for this system: it was supposed to promote conservation of oil supplies and maintain large domestic production as an aid for national defense. But just to state these twin goals is to point out a basic contradiction. Conservation of domestic supplies is antithetical to maintenance of large domestic production. If we really wanted to conserve supplies at home, we would have used imported oil to a far greater extent. As for national defense, it was argued that the U.S. needed large domestic oil production in case foreign supplies are cut off in times of war. Yet government support for private monopoly brought inadequate refining capacity, which is what really counts, while it fostered production

of crude oil, in order to benefit the oil companies.

The energy crisis of 1973–74 changed the situation drastically. National policy shifted to promotion of crude oil production rather than restriction. As for public policy, the general principle illustrated by the example of the oil industry is more widely understood.

○ When a community or a nation becomes dependent on a single company or group of companies for a vitally important product or service, the company or companies can exact a large and sometimes increasing toll from the community as a condition of continuing to provide the product or service.

The large firms of the oil industry were in that position, and the toll was prices high enough to provide all of the capital needed for replacement, for expansion, and for diversification (into chemicals, for example). Now the OPEC nations control the supply, but the earlier system pointed out the way.

Government programs that help fix levels of output and prices exist in other sectors of the economy. Agriculture is the most obvious example, with subsidies that come directly out of government appropriations and are obvious to everyone. The direct subsidies have largely been replaced by federal loans that enable farm enterprises to hold surpluses off the market. The chief beneficiaries are the large agricultural enterprises.

For agricultural industries, the federal government for many years operated a production and import quota system that effectively controlled the output and price of sugar; milk production and marketing is controlled in the "milk sheds" of big cities; and a system of agreements among growers of commodities produced within limited geographical areas, such as fruits, nuts, and some vegetables, is administered by the Department of Agriculture.

---

[2]Depletion allowances allow mining and oil companies a tax deduction as their reserves are used up. Until recently oil producers could continue taking their depletion allowance even after the entire value of their oil was written off.

[3]The inflation of the late 1960s forced the large oil companies to go to the capital markets for new capital on a significant scale for the first time since the 1920s.

The federal government has supported and promoted big enterprise and market control in other ways. Its research program in atomic energy developed an entirely new source of power, and then turned it over for development to the existing regulated monopolies in electric power. Procurement for defense and the military has strongly tended to favor large firms. So did the strategic materials stockpile program, which is now largely phased out. Tax policies providing for rapid amortization of new investment have been of special help to large firms.

In recent years, the federal government has protected the textile and steel industries from competition from abroad by imposing special tariffs on imports. In the more competitive textile industry this form of market control has not caused firms to raise their prices significantly, although less expensive imports were kept out of U.S. markets. In steel, however, which is a relatively tightly controlled oligopoly, the industry took advantage of import restrictions to raise its prices in the U.S. market. Jobs for workers may have been protected, along with corporate profits, but the public paid the cost through higher prices. In the automobile industry, billions of dollars of federal loan guarantees rescued Chrysler Corporation from bankruptcy in 1980, avoiding large losses for the company's stockholders and the financial institutions that held the company's debt.

The federal energy program of the 1980s will also provide large benefits to big enterprise. Hundreds of billions of dollars from the new windfall profits tax imposed on oil production will be channeled into the hands of large corporations to develop the technology and production of alternative energy supplies. The Department of Energy seems to be curiously reluctant to promote the less capital-intensive, relatively small-scale technology of solar energy in favor of mammoth projects for extraction of oil from shale and conversion of coal to gas, and even more reluctant to promote conserva-tion of energy on a large scale. It is hard to escape the conclusion that "the federal government . . . has . . . become one of the principal bulwarks of concentration and monopoly."[4]

Public Ownership

One alternative to an economy based on large corporations grouped informally with each other is public ownership. This "socialistic" alternative has been given little consideration and not much trial in the United States, although one of the most successful publicly owned enterprises in all the world, the Tennessee Valley Authority, is run by the federal government. The TVA precedent is worth exploring further.

First, we should note that public ownership of utilities is quite common at the level of local government. This includes a wide variety of enterprises such as water systems, sewer systems, garbage and trash collection, swimming pools, golf courses, and tennis courts. Most port facilities in large cities like New York or Los Angeles are publicly owned. Even some electric power and telephone services are publicly owned, either by governments or by cooperatives. None need be public; in almost all parts of the country there are private enterprises that operate all of the business activities named above.

Second, there is no reason to believe that a large bureaucratic private corporation need be any more or less efficient than a large bureaucratic public enterprise. Business firms seem to be more efficient than government agencies, most of the time, because their performance

---

[4]Walter Adams and Horace M. Gray, *Monopoly in America: The Government as Promoter* (New York: Macmillan, 1955). Although old and partly out of date, this book is the classic statement of how the federal government promotes market control in the economy.

can be measured in dollars of cost and profit. Most government services are not subject to such simple criteria for purposes of evaluation because their goals are usually more diverse than those of private firms. But where the behavior of government agencies can also be measured with the yardstick of the market, as in the case of TVA or the Port of New York Authority, some highly efficient operations are found. Who would be so brave as to argue that the Penn Central Railroad was more efficient than the Pennsylvania Turnpike Authority or the New York Throughway Authority?

The great drawback to public enterprise is lack of freedom from political interference. Special and often narrow interests are allowed to impinge upon the decision-making process, drawing it away from efficiency considerations and toward political expediency. This was the underlying problem of the Post Office, which may have been even less efficient an organization than the Penn Central Railroad. Both public and private bureaucracies can be highly inefficient.

Third, the government-owned enterprise has a striking advantage that the private corporation does not share; its long-term goals are directly to further the public welfare rather than to further private interests. This pervasive theme influences all of the activities of government-owned enterprises, from selection of management through labor relations to determination of the level and type of services it will provide. A well-run public corporation can achieve goals and objectives that private enterprises are not expected to seek.

"Yardstick" Operations

These remarks would imply that, ideological considerations aside, public ownership of business enterprises, properly structured to eliminate political interference and to provide market tests of efficiency and effectiveness, may be a highly useful alternative to the giant private corporation.

Public ownership need not encompass all of an industry in order for it to be useful. One significant firm in an industry, owned by the public, can provide a working *"yardstick"* against which privately owned firms may be judged. It can also prevent the tight control of a market leader from being effective. Indeed, an industry in which only one firm is publicly owned, competing with several private enterprises, may provide the best environment for good performance for the industry as a whole. Desire on the part of the public firm's management to show that they can do a better job than private enterprise, countered by the private firm's efforts to do well so as not to be nationalized, can provide a healthy discipline for both. This situation has certainly prevailed in the electric power industry ever since the establishment of TVA.[5] Public-private competition has also worked well in railroad transportation in Canada, where half the railway network is publicly owned and half is owned by a single private firm. The private firm is thriving, the public firm is subsidized (its lines run through less densely populated areas) and Canada has noticeably better rail transport services than the U.S., with its regulated private system. Another example is the Bank of North Dakota, a state-owned enterprise established in 1911 to provide easier credit for farmers and now the largest bank in the state.

This "yardstick" approach to improved performance in monopolistic industries, via public-private competition, might well be applied to industrial oligopolies as well as to public utilities and transportation. Why should not the federal government own and operate

---

[5]Competition between public and private firms in the same industry should be on an equal basis, especially with respect to the cost of capital. This has not been true of TVA, which is able to borrow with U.S. Treasury guarantees, thereby obtaining capital at lower cost than private firms. This special advantage should not be continued since it represents a national subsidy for users of electric power in the TVA service area.

one of the large integrated steel companies, one of the large automobile manufacturers, one of the large pharmaceutical firms, one of the chief electrical equipment manufacturers, one of the large oil companies? At the very least, there would be less tacit and overt collusion, for one of the large firms, the public one, would refrain from playing that game. At best, those industries would get a larger dose of competition than any of them have experienced for decades.

• A **"yardstick" firm** is a government owned and operated enterprise in an otherwise private industry. Its objective is to provide a standard against which the performance of private firms in the industry can be judged.

Economic Power and the Large Corporation

The large corporation is more than an organization that produces and distributes goods and services. Its decisions affect the lives of many people: employees, customers, and the general public. The choices available to customers are the result of administrative decisions within corporate organizations. Wage decisions affect the distribution of income. Decisions about levels of output influence the prosperity of many communities. Decisions about location of plants influence the growth or stagnation of local areas. Market strategies affect the prices paid by consumers and influence the sharing of economic gains by stockholders, workers, and customers. In all of these ways, corporate decisions govern various aspects of individual lives and the way of life of communities and the nation. In this broad sense, the large corporation takes on some aspects of government: its decisions affect the way people live and the alternatives open to them.

This aspect of the large corporation is well recognized by corporate executives. Some firms make a conscious effort to be "good corporate citizens." A good deal of the advertising and public relations effort of large corporations is devoted to the theme that the corporation seeks to do things that benefit the community. "Progress is our most important product" was the advertising theme of one of the giant conspirators in the electrical equipment price-fixing case. But when community welfare or equity or other public goals become objectives of corporate policy, one of the long-standing distinctions between the public and private sectors becomes obscured. The private corporation takes on a public aspect. It indeed becomes a private government.

Corporate power is characterized by the independence of corporate management from any well-defined responsibility to anyone. The stockholder typically offers few restraints. Government gives a generally free hand to corporate decisions within a broad legal framework. The chief restraints are the corporate rewards and promotion system, the financial community, and the network of intercorporate relationships. Corporate power is exercised by men who are largely responsible to themselves alone. The essence of the problem, then, is that corporate power is unilaterally used in ways that increasingly affect the public, yet the public has little influence over that power.

The power of the large corporation manifests itself in many ways. It exerts a pervasive influence on life styles and attitudes, illustrated in the mass media by its advertising. A philosophy emphasizing the virtues of materialism, of consuming more, of buying the latest style runs continually through advertising appeals. One reason for its use is its success: it taps some deep and persistent attitudes on the part of the general public. But it also contributes to the persistence of those values.

Politically the large corporation has its greatest leverage at the local and state level. Plant location, expansion, or contraction are powerful levels with which tax concessions, zoning laws, roads, and related matters become items for negotiation between sovereign powers rather than the results of the will of the people. In this contest the corporation has some major advantages: great scope of choice, strong financial resources, knowledgeable management and the best legal talent, while governments at the local and state level are often weak and change frequently.

Finally, the large corporation affects the large society in subtle ways. Business leadership tends to become society's leadership. Business leaders become government administrators, particularly in such federal departments as State, Defense, Commerce, and Interior, and in agencies like the Atomic Energy Commission and the Central Intelligence Agency. Most of the "national security managers" of the last thirty years have been either business executives or lawyers from firms specializing in corporate law. Business leaders take a leading role in charitable organizations and on the boards of trustees of foundations and universities. Indeed, business leadership is usually a necessary prerequisite for leading positions in such organizations. The result: the value system and attitudes necessary for promotion within the large corporation are transferred to many other aspects of American life.

The economic position of the large corporation enables its leaders to shape political action, attitudes, and a whole way of life into its own image. Along the way, some special economic advantages may be obtained for particular corporations. But even if that were not the case, and antitrust laws and utility regulation are attempts to minimize the toll, the significant import of the giant corporation is its tendency to become the dominant force throughout the entire social and economic order. As the trend toward economic concentration continues, the role of large corporations as private governments will also grow, and their political influence will increase.

The significance of big business for present-day America goes beyond the issues of market power and its effect on economic efficiency. The very survival of political democracy is at stake. Dispersal of political power among the many, on which democracy rests, is at odds with concentration of economic power among the few. The growing power of big business must lead us to rethink the question of whether private enterprise in its big business form is compatible with democratic values.

The choices of policy, when reduced to the esentials, come down to three large alternatives.

1. The present policies that have led to a large and growing presence and influence for big enterprise can be continued. They promise more of the same gradual accretion of big-business influence. Radicals claim that down that path lies fascism.

2. Big business can be socialized and brought under government ownership and management. There are two variations of the socialist solution.

   A. One is the centralized variety that involves detailed administrative planning. Conservatives argue that this solution leads directly to authoritarianism.

   B. The second variant is a decentralized system of market socialism as described in Chapter 36. The problem here is that it is largely untried.

3. The third choice is to retain private enterprise but without the giant corporation. Make little ones out of big ones, even at the cost of some inefficiency. Nationalize the few giants that can't be effectively broken up. But get back to more competitive markets.

The first solution is the easiest, for it essentially retains the status quo and keeps us on our present path of development. All of the others are radical solutions, for each represents a substantial break from the existing pattern. Which do we want?

Summary

Public policy toward big business has been a curious mixture. The antitrust laws were a reaction against the rise of big business, but they have not been effective in curbing its growth. The "rule of reason" interpretation of the Sherman Act allowed large firms to continue as long as they did not harass other firms: it gave tacit approval to the live-and-let-live policies that naturally develop in oligopolistic industries. The Clayton Act's provisions directed against bigness were ineffective. The Federal Trade Commission has not taken vigorous action against big business. The Robinson-Patman Act has had the unintended effect of holding back price competition. On the other hand, all of this legislation has permitted strong action against business firms that restrict or eliminate competition by collusion, coercion, or other means.

Regulation of monopoly was developed simultaneously with antitrust policy to cover those sectors of the economy in which competition was thought to be impractical. It has not been an unqualified success either. Quality of service tends to deteriorate unless returns to the regulated industry are equal to those that can be earned elsewhere, and that includes the oligopolistic high-profit industries. At the present time there is widespread agreement that current regulatory practices are unsatisfactory. The alternatives are deregulation and return to competition, public subsidies, or public ownership.

While government policy has been ostensibly one of controlling the growth of big business and regulating monopoly, the federal government has done many things to promote big enterprise. The petroleum industry is perhaps the best example, but there are others as well.

Public policy toward big business is confused. Antitrust policy and regulation are ostensibly intended to protect the public interest, while other government policies foster and succor big enterprise. Public ownership has been used only on a small scale. Meanwhile the economic and political power of big business has become a serious problem that few are willing to face.

Key Concepts

antitrust laws   public utility regulation
"rule of reason"   "yardstick" firm

For Discussion

1. From the public's point of view, what are the advantages and disadvantages of big business?

2. Explain the economic basis for public utility regulation.

3. What are the chief difficulties in regulating public utilities?

4. Explain the pros and cons of public ownership of important industries.

5. Discuss the political ramifications of concentration of economic power.

6. What would be a desirable public policy toward concentration of ownership of energy resources by the large oil companies?

PART 6

DISTRIBUTION OF INCOME AND WEALTH

The economic analysis of the distribution of income is in serious disarray, and the distribution of wealth has been surprisingly ignored in orthodox economic analysis. The following five chapters seek to bring some order into this chaos by bringing together a number of disparate lines of analysis in a new synthesis. We start in Chapter 24 with the theory of marginal productivity, which seeks to explain the earnings of labor and other factors of production solely in terms of market forces. According to this theory, returns to a factor depend on its productivity at the margin.

For a variety of reasons, which are discussed in Chapter 24, market forces cannot fully explain patterns of income distribution. The institutional structure of labor markets is also significant, including conflict between capital and labor; primary, secondary and internal labor markets; racial and sexual discrimination; and the tendency of persistent unemployment to give the upper hand to buyers rather than sellers of labor time. Chapter 25 discusses these issues.

Labor markets are also affected by collective bargaining between unions and management. Chapter 26 shows that bargaining power is one of the key determinants of the division between wages and profits. According to Marxian analysis a healthy capitalist economy will produce a surplus—output greater than that needed to sustain the economy as a functioning enterprise—which is appropriated by the owners of the means of production. How and why that happens, and its implications, is the subject of Chapter 27.

Finally, Chapter 28 examines the persistence of poverty amid affluence, with particular emphasis on why the modern economy generates and reinforces poverty at the same time that concentration of wealth, and the power that goes with it, tends to increase. The chapter closes with an analysis of why a more egalitarian distribution of income is likely to increase net welfare.

While incomes from work are influenced strongly by market forces, the structure of labor markets, and bargaining power, ownership of property and control over the accumulation of capital are crucial for understanding both income distribution and the distribution of wealth.

Chapter 24

The Theory
of Marginal Productivity

For many years the *theory of marginal productivity* was widely accepted as the basis for explaining income distribution in a private-enterprise economy. According to that theory, the earnings of a factor of production depend on its relative scarcity and its productivity at the margin. Put another way, one's earnings depend on one's contribution to total output. An American economist, John Bates Clark, was one of the first to develop that idea into a theory of income distribution. He wrote, in 1899:

> The effective value of any unit of labor is always what the whole society with all its capital produces, minus what it would produce if that unit were to be taken away.

The theory of marginal productivity has serious flaws, however. The chief difficulty is that it is rigorously correct only under perfectly competitive conditions, and even then it requires the assumption that capital and labor are perfectly substitutable for each other. In the quotation above, for example, there is a hidden assumption that the existing capital can be reallocated to all workers after one worker is taken away. Added to these theoretical problems is the fact that empirical tests of the theory have been largely inconclusive. As a result, other approaches sought to fill the theoretical and factual gaps: bargaining theories that brought labor unions into the analysis, exploitation theories like those of Karl Marx, and aggregative theories that sought to relate macroeconomic variables to profit and wage rates.

Nevertheless, the theory of marginal productivity makes a significant contribution to an understanding of the pure market forces that influence the earnings of the factors of production in a private enterprise economy. It is one place to start. So we enter the highly simplified world of perfect competition with its profit-maximizing producers and satisfaction-maximizing consumers, in which capital and labor are perfectly substitutable for each other, and where nothing interferes with the market adjustment process.

- The **theory of marginal productivity** seeks to show that under conditions of perfect competition in the long run, the return to a factor of production is determined by its productivity at the margin.

Demand and Supply in Factor Markets

In a competitive market economy the price of any factor of production is determined by the interaction of demand and supply in the market. Figure 24–1 shows the market for a factor of production with the interaction of demand and supply determining the price (wage) and amount purchased (employment) when the market is in equilibrium.

Changes in the price of factors of production affect the amount used. For example, the United Mine Workers Union succeeded in tripling the wages of miners in the 1940s and 1950s, but at the higher wages employers were unwilling to employ as many workers and wage increases were accompanied by substitution of machinery for men in mining coal. Output of coal remained about the same and wages were much higher, but employment fell from some

Figure 24-2
Wages and Employment in Coal Mining

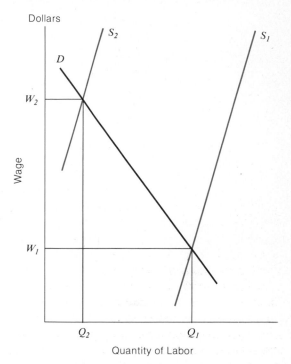

Tripling the wages of coal miners from W_1 to W_2 brought employment down from Q_1 to Q_2, forcing a large reduction in employment in the industry and ultimately a decline in the supply of miners from S_1 to S_2.

1,500,000 men to about 250,000. Workers left the industry and the coal mining areas, and in the long run there was a substantial decline in the supply of coal miners. Figure 24–2 shows what happened.

Another example will show that demand and supply relationships in factor markets can be complex. Real wages in the United States have risen substantially above the level of fifty years ago, even though the labor force grew. The reason for the increase in real wages was that the demand for labor grew more rapidly than the supply. Economic expansion and capital accumulation added to the demand for labor, whose rising incomes contributed further to

Figure 24-1
Price of a Factor of Production in a Competitive Market

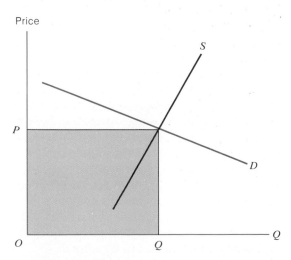

The price of the factor is OP and the number of units employed is OQ. The total income earned by the factor is equal to $OP \times OQ$ (the shaded area).

Figure 24-3
Wages and Employment with Economic
Growth

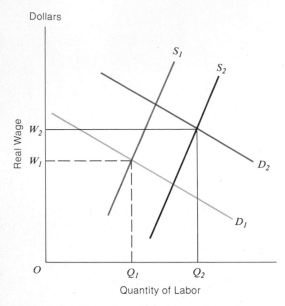

Although wages rose from W_1 to W_2, employment
increased from Q_1 to Q_2. The supply of workers rose from
S_1 to S_2, but an even larger increase in demand from D_1
to D_2 pulled wages up.

the increase in demand. Wages and employment increased together, in contrast to the coal mining case in which wages rose and employment fell. Figure 24–3 shows this example.

These two surprisingly diverse results—reduced employment in one case and larger employment in the other, both associated with higher wages—show that the basic forces of demand and supply can be affected by a wide variety of forces. In these examples the influences were bargaining power and technical change in one case, and economic growth and population changes in the other.

Demand for a Factor of Production

In the theory of marginal productivity, the demand for a factor of production is deter-

mined by its productivity at the margin. Just as the demand for a consumer good is based on its utility at the margin, so the demand for a producer good (any input into the production process) is based on its usefulness at the margin to the user.

Here is an example. A manufacturer of electronic circuits can add another worker to his assembly line at an hourly rate of $4.00. Doing so will increase his total output per hour by 10 units, which are sold for 50¢ each. The manufacturer's revenues will increase by $5 per hour (10 units × 50¢), but his costs will rise only $4 (we assume that there are no other additional costs aside from the added worker). Hiring the additional worker will add $1 to net revenues, and the employer will do so. This is exactly parallel to the decision of a consumer on whether he should or should not buy another unit of a good. In that case the consumer (the buyer) compared costs with utility at the margin. In this case the employer (the buyer) compares costs of an added worker with revenue at the margin.

Marginal Revenue Product
Economists have given the name *marginal revenue product* to the increase in revenue resulting from an increase in employment of a factor of production. In our last example it was the $5 per hour increase in revenue derived from hiring an additional worker.

As an employer adds units of any factor of production to his existing operations he will increase his output, but at a diminishing rate. This is because of the law of diminishing returns: As a variable factor of production is added to a fixed factor, or to a fixed combination of other factors, increases in output will be obtained, but the increases will start diminishing in size at some point. This proposition was explained and illustrated in Chapter 2.

In competitive markets, each unit of output is sold at the market price, irrespective of the amount sold by a single firm. The marginal revenue product is equal to the increase in

Table 24–1
Marginal Productivity in Competitive Firm

Number of Units of Factor A	Number of Units of Output	Marginal Physical Product	Price of Output per Unit	MMP × P	Marginal Revenue Product
100	1000				
101	1010	10	$10	$100	$100
102	1019	9	10	90	90
103	1027	8	10	80	80
104	1034	7	10	70	70
105	1040	6	10	60	60

Table 24–2
Marginal Productivity in Monopoloid Firm

Number of Units of Factor A	Number of Units of Output	Marginal Physical Product	Price of Output per Unit	Total Revenue	Marginal Revenue Product
99	989		$10.05	9939.45	
100	1000	11	10.00	10,000.00	$60.55
101	1010	10	9.95	10,049.50	49.50
102	1019	9	9.90	10,088.10	38.60
103	1027	8	9.85	10,115.95	27.85
104	1034	7	9.80	10,132.20	17.25
105	1040	6	9.75	10,140.00	6.80

output (marginal physical product) multiplied by the price of the product:

$$MRP = MPP \times P$$

It follows that the marginal revenue product will decline in exactly the same pattern as the quantity of the marginal product, as in Table 24–1.

The case of the firm in a monopoloid industry is different. It cannot sell increases in output unless it reduces its price. Its marginal revenue product will reflect not only a declining physical product due to diminishing returns, but also the price reductions required to sell increased output. This means that its marginal revenue product will be below that of an identical competitive firm. Table 24–2 gives an

example of those relationships for a monopoloid firm identical with the competitive firm of the previous table. The difference is that the price at which the output is sold declines for the monopolistic firm.

In both cases the marginal revenue product declines as factors of production are added to the production process. In the case of the competitive firm the falling MRP is the result of diminishing output at the margin. In the case of the monopoloid firm the MRP falls faster because of diminishing output at the margin and a reduced price for the output.

● The **marginal revenue product** is the change in total revenue associated with a change in the quantity of a variable input into the firm's production process.

The Firm's Demand for a Factor of Production

The marginal revenue product schedule will determine the demand of a firm for the factors of production. If the market price of the factor is greater than the *MRP* the firm will not buy or hire an additional unit of the factor. In the examples above, suppose that Factor A is a machine whose cost is $60. The competitive firm will employ 105 machines (*MRP* = $60), but the monopoloid firm will use only 100 machines (*MRP* = $60.55). Figure 24–4 shows the two demand curves for Factor A, using the figures from Tables 24–1 and 24–2.

Equilibrium of the Individual Firm

We can now determine the amount of a factor the firm will hire, on the assumption that it seeks to maximize profit. First, we specify the situation. The firm uses only two factors of production—labor and capital. The prices of both factors are determined by the interaction of demand and supply in competitive markets. Finally, the firm's goal is profit maximization, which is achieved by equalizing costs and revenues at the margin. We shall start with the decision to employ labor, but the analysis will apply to capital as well.

With a fixed amount of capital, the firm will increase its employment of labor until labor's marginal revenue product equals the wage rate. As long at *MRP* is greater than the wage rate, an additional worker can be hired and profits can be increased. A profit-maximizing firm will do just that, up to the point at which *MRP* falls to equal the wage rate. This profit-maximizing situation is shown in Figure 24–5. The profit-maximizing firm will employ *M* workers. Adding more workers up to that point will increase the return to capital. If *M* + 1 workers are employed, however, the added revenue would be less than the cost of the

Figure 24–4
The Firm's Demand Curve for a Factor of Production

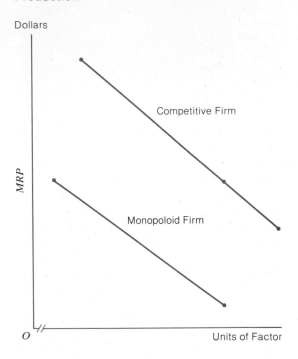

Figure 24–5
Marginal Productivity and Profit Maximization (Labor the Variable Factor)

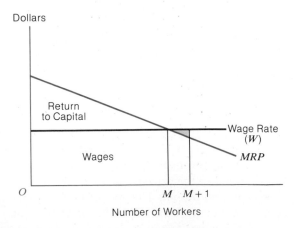

additional worker and the return to capital would be reduced by the shaded area in Figure 24–5.

Exactly the same analysis can be applied to capital and the return paid to it. The firm will increase its use of capital up to the point at which capital's marginal value product is just equal to the payment that must be made for its use. Holding the number of workers constant but adding capital to the enterprise merely reverses the position of the diagram, as shown in Figure 24–6. Increasing the amount of capital with a fixed amount of labor, the firm employs K units of capital. At that point capital's *MRP* equals its cost (given by the rate of interest in the money markets) and a profit-maximizing position has been reached. The areas marked "Return to Capital" in this figure and Figure 24–5 are equal, and so are the areas marked "Wages."

Combining the Factors of Production

Factors of production are not used independently of each other, however. A more expensive factor can be replaced by a less expensive one, to a limited extent in the short run but very widely in the long run. In the short run, with the size of the plant and its process of production fixed, not much substitution of factors can take place. In the long run, a wide variety of plant sizes can be chosen, along with one of the several production processes that are usually known. Whatever the time period, the search for the least-cost combination of factors goes on simultaneously with the effort to push the use of each factor to the point at which $MRP = P$ for the factor.

The *least-cost combination of the factors of production* is achieved when the *MRP* derived from a dollar's worth of one factor is equal to the *MRP* derived from a dollar's worth of any other. If we designate the factors as *a, b, c, . . . , n,* the least-cost combination of the factors is achieved when

$$\frac{MRP_a}{P_a} = \frac{MRP_b}{P_b} = \frac{MRP_c}{P_c} = \cdots = \frac{MRP_n}{P_n}$$

This formulation is analogous to the consumer's utility-maximizing allocation of his income. In this case, a similar principle is involved, except that a producer allocates his limited resources to maximize profit instead of a consumer allocating limited income to maximize satisfactions.

Suppose that a firm does not achieve this least-cost combination of the factors of production, that is,

$$\frac{MRP_a}{P_a} > \frac{MRP_b}{P_b}$$

In this case, the last dollar spent on hiring Factor *a* brings in greater revenue than the last dollar spent on hiring Factor *b*. The firm could raise its profits by using less of Factor *b* and more of Factor *a*. By substituting *a* for *b*, it will eventually move to the least-cost combination of the factors.

There are two basic conditions for profit maximization in the internal operations of a firm that must be simultaneously achieved:

Figure 24–6
Marginal Productivity and Profit Maximization (Capital the Variable Factor)

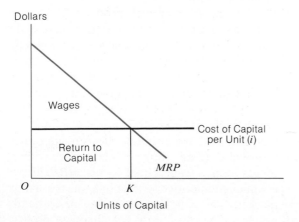

1. $MRP = P$ for each factor of production.

2. $\dfrac{MRP_a}{P_a} = \dfrac{MRP_b}{P_b}$ for all factors of production used in combination.

- The **least-cost combination of the factors of production** is the combination of inputs that minimizes the cost of production for any level of output, such that:

$$\frac{MRP_a}{P_a} = \frac{MRP_b}{P_b} = \frac{MRP_c}{P_c} = \cdots = \frac{MRP_n}{P_n}$$

where $a, b, c, \ldots, n$ are the inputs.

The Demand Curve for a Factor of Production

We can now move from the individual firm's demand for a factor of production to the market demand curve for the factor. For any factor of production, the MRP curve defines the firm's demand for the factor of production. The industry's demand for the factor at any point in time will be the sum of the demands of the individual firms. The total demand for the factor in the economy as a whole will be the sum of all the industry demand curves for the factor. This, of course, brings us back to the original demand curve for the factor, which, together with the supply curve, determines its price and the total income paid to the factor.

Returns to the Factors of Production

Extension of the theory of marginal products from factor prices to the distribution of income in the economy as a whole seems initially to be a simple matter of logic. We can multiply the number of units of each factor by its price to get the total earned by each factor. The next step is to add together the totals for each factor to determine the total amount of income earned by all of the factors. This process will give us total income and the share going to each factor. The analysis is stated in formal terms in the following paragraph.

We are given inputs $a, b, \ldots, n$, each one of which has a price determined by the interaction of demand and supply in the market. Since the demand curve for the factor is its marginal revenue product, $P = MRP$ for each factor. We should then be able to multiply each factor's MRP by the number of units employed, add those sums together, and obtain the total income earned:

$$MRP_a \times N_a + MRP_b \times N_b + \cdots + MRP_n \times N_n = TRP$$

where TRP is the total revenue product.

This proposition embodies a distribution of income among the factors of production in which each factor's share of the total is determined by its marginal revenue product and the number of units of the factor. Since the units of any factor are homogeneous, no one unit can be distinguished from any other and each will get its proportionate share of that factor's portion of the whole; that is, each unit of any factor will receive a return equal to the MRP of that factor. Thus, all units of a particular type and skill level of labor will receive a wage equal to the MRP of that type of labor.

Marginal Productivity and Economic Justice

The theory of marginal productivity is the cornerstone of the argument that economic justice is one of the products of a competitive private enterprise economy. The market mechanism assures any factor of production a return (wage, profit, rent) equal to its contribution to total output at the margin. If a worker, for example, is offered a wage lower than his marginal revenue product, he can go somewhere else, to an employer who will be willing to pay him a wage equal to his MRP, if we assume competitive conditions in the labor market. The employer, on the other hand, motivated by his desire to maximize profits, pushes added employment until $MRP = W$. Both market opportunity and business motivations assure that the wage will equal MRP in a competitive market. Since the same is true of capital and any other factors of production, whatever their quality, no one can exploit anyone else and everyone gets what he deserves. At least, according to the theory.

The economic justice that emerges from the market is a special sort, however. It means inequality rather than equality. Individuals are born different, with different combinations of skills and abilities. These inherited differences will be reflected in differences in productivity and hence in incomes. Individuals also have different experiences in their youth and education that create differences in attitudes, motivations, and skills. These differences will also be reflected in differences in productivity and in income. Even if we leave out of consideration such factors as inherited wealth (and position) and unearned incomes, the concept of economic justice embodied in the theory of marginal productivity is one that is rooted in the values of the marketplace: an individual's income is determined solely by the value placed upon his efforts by the marketplace; a human being is, indeed, worth only as much as he or she is valued in the market.

Is There a Surplus?

One point needs to be cleared up before we go any further. Is all of the value of the economy's output accounted for when each factor of production earns a return equal to its MRP? If it is, the theory of marginal productivity is a satisfactory explanation of income distribution. If it isn't, something is wrong: there may be a surplus or a deficit to fight over.

Karl Marx argued that a private enterprise economy produced *surplus value* that rightfully belonged to workers but was appropriated by owners of capital. He argued that all production is the result of human effort, and that a return to labor was the only justifiable one. Capital was thought of as the result of past

labor effort which had been appropriated by capitalists (owners of capital) who had no right to its earnings since they did not labor for that reward. The attempt of capitalists to enlarge this surplus and appropriate more was seen by Marx as the root of the conflict between labor and capital that would ultimately destroy capitalism.

In the ideological debates engendered by Marxism, the theory of marginal productivity became one part of an answer to Marx. It can be shown that when factors of production are paid according to their marginal revenue product the entire output and income of the economy is accounted for. However, if there is a disparity between the total output of an economy and the earnings postulated by the theory of marginal productivity, the door would be opened to conflict over how a surplus or a deficit would be shared.

We can visualize the problem by returning to the analysis of the individual competitive firm and its decisions to hire the various factors of production. In Figure 24–7 (the same as Figure 24–5) the firm equalizes the wage rate with labor's MRP and employs M workers. The shaded rectangle is the amount of the total output paid to labor, while the upper triangle is the return paid to capital (assuming only two factors of production).

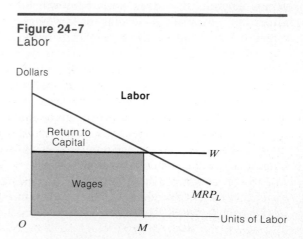

Figure 24–7
Labor

Figure 24-8
Capital

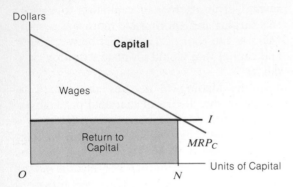

Now turn to Figure 24–8 (the same as Figure 24–6), where the shaded rectangle is the return earned by capital as a result of the firm's decision to employ *N* units of capital, based on a cost of capital set by *I* and an *MRP* schedule for capital as shown. The wages in Figure 24–7 plus the return to capital in Figure 24–8 must add up to the total area under the *MRP* curve in Figure 24–7 if the theory is to be an adequate explanation of the division of income between the two factors. The rectangle of one diagram must equal in area the triangle of the other diagram. If it does not, there will be either an unexplained surplus or an unexplained deficit and potential conflict between the two factors of production.

This may seem like a trivial problem, but its resolution involves some of the fundamental issues of modern society. Is there an inherent conflict within capitalism between labor and capital? Or is it possible to achieve a just division between the two? For a time it appeared as if the economists had an answer.

The answer was provided by a mathematical proof that the entire product will be used up in paying each factor of production a return equal

to its productivity at the margin.[1] The economic analysis underlying the proof is essentially this:

○ In a long-run equilibrium that has no extranormal profits, total revenue equals total costs for each firm. Each factor of production is paid a return equal to its marginal revenue product. The sum of all payments to the factors of production, which is total cost, is therefore equal to the total revenue of the firm. Since this is true for each firm it must also be true for all firms in the economy.

Algebraically:

$$TR = TC = MRP_a \cdot N_a + MRP_b \cdot N_b + \cdots + MRP_n \cdot N_n$$

where

$$TR = \text{total revenue}$$
$$TC = \text{total cost}$$
$$MRP_{a,b,\ldots,n} = \text{marginal revenue product of factors } a, b, \ldots, n$$
$$N_{a,b,\ldots,n} = \text{amount of factors } a, b, \ldots, n$$

Several important conditions are necessary for this proof to be valid. The most obvious one is the assumption that free entry prevails, an assumption necessary for elimination of extranormal profits in the long run. Another condition is the requirement that techniques of production permit easy substitution of one factor of production for another. That assumption is necessary so that if a factor has an *MRP* greater than its market price it can be substituted for other factors of production and its use increased until its *MRP* is equated with its price. This substitutability condition is equiva-

---

[1]One well-known proof uses Euler's theorem, named after a famous eighteenth-century Swiss mathematician who was trying to solve an entirely different problem. Marginal productivity theory was unknown in his day. A good explanation using Euler's theorem is in George Stigler, *Production and Distribution Theories* (New York: Macmillan, 1946), pp. 320–387. An alternate proof, somewhat more elegant mathematically, is given in Paul A. Samuelson, *Foundations of Economic Analysis* (Cambridge, Mass.: Harvard University Press, 1948), pp. 81–87.

lent to the assumption of a long-run equilibrium in which technology and capital are freely substitutable for each other and can adjust readily to economic forces.

The Problem of Capital

The issues raised by the assumption that capital and labor are readily substitutable for each other were fought out among economic theorists in a famous "capital controversy" in the 1960s. One of the results of the argument is considerable loss of credibility for the theory of marginal productivity as an explanation of the distribution of income.

Capital can be thought of as a fund of value that a business firm can shift around from one combination of capital goods plus labor to another combination of the two factors. A machine can be sold and the funds used to hire labor, or workers can be laid off and the funds for wages diverted to purchase of a machine. In that sense, the capital of the enterprise is perfectly malleable. But that is true only at the financial level. Capital as a fund of value produces nothing—only capital goods can do that. And capital goods such as machinery and buildings cannot readily be transformed into labor, or labor into capital goods. A production system with real labor instead of a fund for paying wages and with real capital goods instead of a fund of capital values contains rigidities that prevent easy substitution of one for the other at the margin.

Here is an example. Six workers are digging a ditch, using six shovels. Add a seventh worker. Will the ditch be dug faster? A little, perhaps, but the six shovels cannot suddenly be divided into seven smaller shovels (keeping the total amount of capital constant) to provide each worker a shovel. A slightly faster pace might be maintained, however, if the seventh worker is used to relieve the other six periodically and provide rest periods while keeping the six shovels working. But that is trivial, and does not represent the type of capital-labor substitution implied by the theory of marginal productivity, which would involve spreading the existing capital among the entire work force.

In the short run, then, in an economy that uses capital goods to produce a real output, capital is not simply a fund of value. It is not possible, therefore, easily to substitute capital for labor and labor for capital. One side in the capital controversy argued, however, that in the long run substitution of one factor of production for another can readily be accomplished. Capital goods wear out and must be replaced. At that stage the entire structure of capital goods can be reorganized to fit a changed supply of labor. For example, in our example of workers and shovels, when the six shovels wear out they can be replaced by seven smaller shovels (keeping the amount of capital constant) to accommodate an additional worker (and providing an accurate measure of the marginal product of labor). The assumption of easy substitutability of one factor for another seemed to be rescued. It appeared that in the long run an increase in interest rates relative to wage rates would bring about a smooth substitution of labor for capital—and vice versa if the prices of the two factors moved in the opposite direction.

The critics had the last word, however. They argued that everything depends on the nature of the technological alternatives. Production takes place over time, they pointed out, and in any given technology or production process labor and capital enter at different stages. When that is the case, the rate of interest determines which process is most profitable, and changes in interest rates can lead to switching from one to the other and back again. This "reswitching," as it came to be called, is incompatible with the smooth substitutability of capital and labor for each other postulated by marginal productivity theory.

Here is an example of reswitching. We treat capital as a fund of value, and let labor stand for all inputs into the production process. Postulate a product that can be produced by two different methods. Both require six time periods and both turn out the same amount of product. Method one uses six units of labor in the first time period and one unit of labor in each of the last five. The second method uses two units of labor in each of the first five time periods and eight in the last. Figures 24–9 and 24–10 show the two production processes graphically. Process I will be the least-cost process when interest rates are very low and very high. Process II will be the least-cost process at intermediate levels of interest rates. At very low rates of interest the first method will be used because the firm must invest capital equal to the value of eleven units of labor as against eighteen for the second method. Because interest rates are low, the fact that the value of six wage units is tied up for six time periods at compound interest does not make much difference. At a zero rate of interest it is obvious that method one will be used.

As interest rates rise, however, the cost of the capital invested in six wage units over six time periods becomes increasingly significant. At some point it will be more profitable to switch over to the second production method, in which the large capital investment in labor must be carried for only one time period. As interest rates rise, a switch point will appear—at which point method two is cheaper than method one.

Now comes the interesting point. At very high interest rates method two will become more expensive, because of the larger amount invested in labor costs. Capital becomes very dear at high interest rates, and it will be profitable to switch back to the first production method.

Reflect on what has happened. At low interest rates a production method using little capital overall was most profitable. As interest rates rose, a switch was made to a different method using more capital. This result is contrary to the adjustment process postulated in marginal productivity theory, where higher interest rates are supposed to bring less use of capital. Only when interest rates rose still higher was there a second switch back to the process that used less capital.

To summarize: marginal productivity theory tells us that higher interest rates lead to production processes that economize on the use of capital and vice versa. But when production processes use varying quantities of inputs at

Figure 24–9
Process I

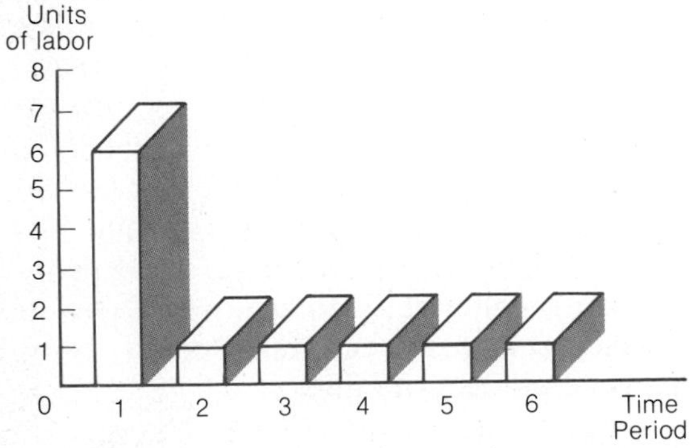

Figure 24–10
Process II

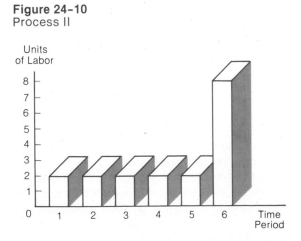

different stages of production, it is quite possible for higher interest rates to bring production processes that utilize more capital rather than less, and vice versa. And this is true even if capital is treated as a fund of value that can be instantaneously shifted from one production process to another.

Return now to the theory of marginal productivity. Let the supply of labor rise relative to the supply of capital, because population grows more rapidly than capital accumulation. The increased supply of labor, relative to the demand for labor, causes wage rates to fall. As wages fall, according to marginal productivity theory, employers will hire more workers, continuing to maximize profits at the level of employment at which the wage rate equals the marginal revenue product of labor ($W = MRP_L$). Relative to labor, a smaller amount of capital will be used in the production process, its marginal revenue product will rise, and at the new employment equilibrium the rate of interest will be equal to the marginal revenue product of capital ($i = MRP_K$). A unit of capital will earn more and a unit of labor less.

Reswitching forced a reconsideration of this simple adjustment process and its conclusions. Even in the long run, it might never take place. A relative decline in wage rates could be quite compatible with relatively less use of labor and relatively more use of capital. Whether a unit of one would earn more or less is problematic. The fundamental logic underlying the theory of marginal productivity was devastated. In 1960 an economist who criticized the theory was considered a far-out oddball by his colleagues. By 1980 it is hard to find one who accepts marginal productivity theory as an explanation of the distribution of income. At best, even its advocates argue that it is only a theory of the demand for labor (or other factors of production): a business firm will hire a factor of production up to the point at which its productivity at the margin equals the price that must be paid for the marginal unit of the factor.

Profit

Profit is an elusive concept. In down-to-earth terms it is simply the surplus of income over costs that accrues to the owners of the enterprise. In payment for what productive service? What does ownership of the enterprise contribute to production of goods and services that should merit payment? We are considering pure ownership here, not the service of management. Management is paid a salary for managerial services, just as workers are paid a wage for labor services. Both can be thought of as a wage or salary for productive services performed.

In the logic of marginal productivity theory, profits disappear altogether in the perfectly competitive economy. There is not even a normal profit, as we have used that concept, in the long-run competitive equilibrium. Competition drives revenues down to a level that just covers payments to labor, capital and land for productive effort. The total value of output is fully exhausted by payments of wages, interest and rent.

This theoretic construction may be an answer to Marx's theory of exploitation, which is explained in Chapter 27, but it is not a realistic concept. Profits are there, and they perform a vital economic function in motivating the market adjustment process. Marginal productivity theory mystifies rather than clarifies the nature of profits.

Profits are indeed a surplus, over and above amounts paid to the factors of production for productive services. They arise from the fact that production takes place over time. A business firm contracts in the present to hire factors of production, agreeing to payment of specified amounts in wages, salaries, interest and rent. It plans to use the factors of production to produce goods for sale in the future—an uncertain future. The firm does not know in advance the exact revenues it will obtain, although it does know in advance the costs it will incur. Costs are determined in the known present, while revenues accrue in the unknown future. The firm, of course, expects revenues to exceed costs, but it has no way of knowing in advance if that will happen.

Suppose the firm expects its income to be less than its costs. It will obviously not carry out the production. Suppose the expectation is that the income will be equal to the outgo, with a 50-50 chance that it will be either greater or less. Half the time a profit would be earned, and half the time there will be an equal loss. No go. In the long run there will be no profit, just as if you were gambling heads or tails on a perfectly balanced coin. Now suppose that income is expected to be greater than outgo by 15 percent, with a 50-50 probability that it will be greater or less. It's not certain, but, if those expectations are fulfilled, in the long run the 15 percent surplus will be obtained. Under those circumstances the production will be undertaken, if the return is large enough to match expected earnings in other uses.

In these pragmatic terms, profits arise from the uncertainty that always prevails in business operations in a private enterprise economy. Only in an economy in which perfect certainty prevailed would there be no need for profits, and we know that such a world does not exist. Profits are indeed a surplus above costs of production.

How large is the surplus? Its size depends on how much uncertainty prevails, and the extent to which decision makers perceive it. There is no economic law, such as the theory of marginal productivity, that determines how large it must be.

Here is the nub of the problem. Some economists argue that profit is a return to entrepreneurs as a return for the service of assuming the burdens of uncertainty. They argue that without entrepreneurship the economy would remain in a static state, unchanging, without growth or progress. Profit is the reward entrepreneurs obtain, over and above payments for managerial services and to capital for its contribution to production, in return for ephemeral but necessary services.[2] At the other extreme is Marx's view that human effort is the sole productive resource and that all returns to owners of capital and land are illegitimate, even though they may be necessary for the functioning of a private enterprise economy. In between is another position: profits are a surplus above necessary direct or prime costs of production, a residual that accrues to owners of business enterprise. The size and division of that surplus is the bone over which the various beasts of the economic jungle contest with each other.

---

[2] Two classics that present this view: Joseph Schumpeter, *The Theory of Economic Development* (1912) and Frank H. Knight, *Risk, Uncertainty and Profit* (1921).

Summary

The price of a factor of production is determined in the market for that factor, and depends on the conditions of supply and demand that prevail.

The demand for any input by the individual firm, when the price of the input is given, depends on the input's marginal revenue product. The profit-maximizing firm will use any input in the quantity at which its price is equal to its marginal revenue product. The profit-maximizing firm will also substitute less expensive factors for more expensive factors until the marginal revenue products per dollar for each are equal to each other. The firm will achieve an internal profit-maximizing equilibrium when

$$MRP = P \quad \text{for each input}$$

and

$$\frac{MRP_a}{P_a} = \frac{MRP_b}{P_b} = \frac{MRP_c}{P_c} = \cdots = \frac{MRP_n}{P_n}$$

where $a, b, c, \ldots, n$ are its inputs.

When the theory of marginal productivity is generalized to a theory of income distribution, it must be limited to the perfectly competitive model in the long run, with a high degree of smooth substitutability among the factors of production. It is only under those conditions that payments to inputs on the basis of their productivity at the margin can be shown to result in full exhaustion of the product. There are two serious deficiencies in the theory, however, that seriously limit its usefulness. One is the problem of capital. The theory doesn't work with real capital goods, but only if capital is thought of as a fund of value. The other is the reality of profits, which are a true surplus above earned income that results from the uncertainties of business operations extending into the unknown future. Nevertheless, the theory explains market forces that are always at work. One of the elements in any general analysis of the distribution of income must be the productivity of factor inputs at the margin as at least a partial explanation of earned income.

Key Concepts

theory of marginal productivity
marginal revenue product

least-cost combination of the factors of production

For Discussion

1. How could the theory of marginal productivity explain the fact that baseball player Reggie Jackson makes more money than the president of the United States? Does such an explanation seem reasonable to you? Why or why not?

2. How would wage rates be affected by an increase in labor productivity resulting from technological progress? Explain.

3. In the hypothetical case of a firm that uses only two factors of production—labor and capital—why is the value of total output equal to the sum of payments to labor and capital—according to the theory of marginal productivity?

4. Discuss: The capitalist who risks his or her capital in an uncertain business venture deserves a reward much as a worker who works eight hours a day deserves a reward.

5. Is the distribution of income according to one's productivity at the margin your idea of economic justice? Explain.

6. What are the chief limitations of the theory of marginal productivity? To what extent do you think this theory can be used to explain patterns of income distribution in the U.S. economy today?

Chapter 25

Labor Markets

The market for labor is far more complex than the theory of marginal productivity implies. In addition to the conceptual difficulties discussed in Chapter 24, it is an oversimplification to conceive of modern labor markets in terms of many individual workers facing many buyers of labor in an essentially competitive economic environment. There is an inherent conflict in the relationship between employer and employee that is not resolved by market determination of wages, even though production requires that capital and labor cooperate with each other. Furthermore, the organization of business enterprise together with the technology of production often creates a pattern of alienation and hostility in the workplace. Labor markets themselves are structured in ways that modify the working of market forces —with "primary" and "secondary" workers, "internal" labor markets in large firms, and discrimination and "crowding" that affect women and minorities. The threat of unemployment always hangs over workers, and such uncontrollable factors as competition from foreign workers increase the uncertainties of the marketplace. The real world is quite different from the simplified view of labor markets presumed by the theory of marginal productivity,

and the results are also different. This chapter examines some of these aspects of labor markets and working life in an effort to arrive at a fuller appreciation of the factors that determine the earnings of workers and the distribution of income and wealth.

Labor and Capital

The relationship between capital and labor contains a fundamental contradiction. On the one hand, the two complement each other in the production process. Both workers and shovels are needed for digging ditches. Furthermore, both labor and capital have an interest in maintaining the economy as a going concern. If economic activity comes to a halt or even slows down significantly, workers lose their incomes and business firms their profits, and the economy fails to produce the things everyone needs. Both capital and labor have an interest in the continued and stable functioning of the economy. Yet labor and capital are separated by the property system. The instruments of production are owned by one group of private owners, usually organized as a business firm. Labor power, on the other hand, is owned by individual workers who, having no other source of livelihood, sell their labor power for a wage.

The exchange of labor power for a wage payment creates an inevitable conflict between labor and capital. The seller would like to receive the highest possible payment, while the buyer would like to pay as little as possible. Furthermore, the buyer would like to get as much output as possible from the labor he hires. This leads to efforts on the part of employers to speed up the pace of work and increase the hours of work. Those efforts are antagonistic to the best interests of the worker, who is, after all, working for someone else's profit. From the worker's point of view, an eight-hour day is better than a nine-hour day, given the daily wage, while the employer would like to have just the opposite.

There are, of course, limits to how much each side can gain at the expense of the other. One limit to wage rates is the market for labor. There is always a prevailing wage, and that makes it difficult for most employers to pay less or workers to get more than market forces dictate. If labor markets were thoroughly competitive on both the buyer's and seller's sides, there would be little leeway for one side to gain immediate advantage over the other. But in the modern economy that is generally not the case. Large employers have an advantage in "bargaining" with individual workers. Furthermore, as we shall show later in this chapter, a variety of market forces combine to create conditions that interfere with the forces of demand and supply in labor markets, and can result in wage rates below the value of labor's marginal product.

One group of market forces works persistently against the interests of workers and to the advantage of employers: persistent unemployment and continuing recruitment of new workers into the labor force. Unemployment comes from two chief sources—inadequate aggregate demand and displacement of workers by machinery. However, workers also face competition from other sources. Young people enter the labor force looking for jobs. Older and experienced workers often leave the labor market entirely when jobs are scarce, only to return quickly when economic activity revives. In addition, in the long history of industrialization new workers were drawn steadily into the labor market from agriculture. This process is still going on but has shifted from the already industrialized nations to less developed areas. The bargaining power of workers in Detroit is reduced by the migration of rural workers to cities in Brazil or Mexico, just as fifty years ago it was affected by a similar rural-urban migration within the United States. On the supply side of the labor market, then, there is persistent downward pressure on wage rates. It was recognition of these market forces that led Karl Marx to argue that, if left alone, market forces will tend to drive wage rates down to what he called the "socially necessary" level of subsistence.

When labor markets are "tight" and workers are fully employed, market forces push wages up simply because employers bid for the available labor. On the other hand, when there is a significant amount of slack in labor markets wages tend to be lower. A rapidly growing economy causes low unemployment rates and tends to pull wages up, while a slowly growing or stagnant economy allows slack to appear in labor markets. The resulting unemployment tends to keep wage rates down. Unfortunately, the usual situation is one of substantial slack, so that employers usually have the upper hand in the wage bargain.

Nevertheless, employers do not have unlimited freedom to lengthen the working day and speed up the pace of work. The physical capabilities of workers are limited by human strength and endurance. Even before physical limits are reached, however, limits are imposed by the antagonisms workers feel when more is demanded of them. Disgruntled workers are less productive than "gruntled" ones, as all employers and supervisors know. Dissatisfied workers have high absence rates and can sabo-tage production lines.[1] Furthermore, workers can get together informally to slow the work pace or formally to organize unions and oppose the boss directly. These actions can be expect-ed long before physical limits of hours and intensity of work are reached.

A private enterprise economy has much space for conflict between labor and capital. Employers need labor, but the employer who does not squeeze his labor as much as possible is likely to lose in the competitive race with employers who do.[2] Workers, on the other hand, need jobs to support themselves and their families, but are continually threatened by unemployment or technological displace-ment and are the ones who get squeezed by employers. A continuing conflict between labor and capital is inherent in these economic relations.

Big Business and the Labor Market

Many large business firms are *dominant buyers of labor* in the markets from which their labor is drawn. Some typical examples are:

1. The textile mill in a small Southern town.

2. The branch manufacturing plant of a giant corporation located in a small Midwestern city.

3. Groups of plants of a large manufacturer located in a small city. General Motors Corporation in Flint, Michigan, for exam-ple.

Let's examine these cases of domination of the labor market by a large firm. Firms in these

---

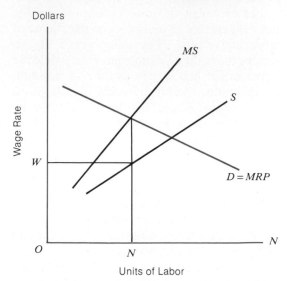

Figure 25–1
The Labor Market with a Dominant Employer

MS is the marginal supply curve for labor. It shows the marginal cost to the employer of employing additional amounts of labor. *S* is the market supply curve of labor, showing the average wage needed to draw forth any given amount of labor. The firm's demand curve for labor is *D*, which is derived from the marginal product of labor.

---

situations know that the supply curve of labor in their locality slopes upward. That is, more labor could be drawn from the local labor market only by raising wage rates. The higher wage would have to be paid to all workers, however, not just the last ones hired. The increase in costs to the employer will equal the wage necessary to hire the marginal worker plus the increase in wages paid to everyone else. Under those conditions the marginal cost of the additional worker is higher than the wage rate, and increases more rapidly. Table 25–1 illustrates this relationship. In this hypo-thetical example, the firm with 100 employees pays a wage of $2.00 per hour. In order to attract an additional worker the hourly wage has to be raised to $2.10. All workers have to be paid that wage, which raises the total wage

---

[1]*Sabotage* is derived from "sabot," the French word for wooden shoe. In the early years of industrialization in nineteenth century France workers would throw a wooden shoe into machinery to get a break from long hours and work speedups.

[2]John Pierpont Morgan (1837–1913): "Any businessman who does not pay his labor the least he can get them for is robbing his stockholders."

Table 25–1
Marginal Labor Cost in Imperfect Markets

No. of Workers	Hourly Wage (Average Cost)	Total Wage Bill	Marginal Cost of Labor
100	$2.00	$200	
101	2.10	212.10	$12.10
102	2.20	224.40	12.30
103	2.30	236.90	12.50
104	2.40	249.60	12.70
105	2.50	262.50	12.90

bill from $200 per hour (100 workers at $2.00 per hour) to $212.10 per hour (101 workers at $2.10 per hour). The marginal cost to the firm is $12.10, although the marginal increase in the hourly wage was only $0.10. Put in geometric terms, the rising supply curve for labor in the market as a whole is accompanied by a *marginal supply curve for labor* that lies above it. These supply conditions are shown in Figure 25–1, along with the demand curve for labor based on labor's marginal revenue product.

The employer who finds himself in the situation shown in Figure 25–1 could maximize his profits by employing *N* workers. At that level of employment the marginal cost of labor, shown by the *MS* curve, equals the marginal revenue product of labor, shown by the demand curve *D*. However, *N* units of labor can be hired at wage *W*, rather than at the higher wage equal to labor's *MRP*. In this case the wage is below the worker's *MRP*, contributing to extranormal profits for the firm—a clear case of exploitation of labor made possible by the firm's dominance of the labor market.

We now can get a better understanding of the role of labor unions and why they are organized. In an economy of big business units with high degrees of market power in the hands of employers it is possible for large firms to press wage rates below the level that would otherwise be set in competitive labor markets.

Even within the framework of marginal productivity theory, those wage rates are "exploitive" in the sense that labor earns less than its marginal revenue product.

It is not surprising to find labor unions emerging in those sectors of the economy in which large firms developed market power in labor markets. The growth of big business brought a preponderance of market power to the buyer of labor in many important sectors of the economy. The reaction on the part of workers was to organize unions to match that power. The idea was stated by Senator Barry Goldwater, who is no friend of union power:

As America turned increasingly, in the latter half of the nineteenth century, from an agricultural nation into an industrial one, and as the size of business enterprises expanded, individual wage earners found themselves at a distinct disadvantage in dealing with their employers over terms of employment. The economic power of the large enterprises, as compared with that of the individual employee, was such that wages and conditions of employment were pretty much what the employer decided they would be. Under these conditions, as a means of increasing their economic power, many employees chose to band together and create a common agent for negotiating with their employers.[3]

---

[3]Barry Goldwater, *The Conscience of a Conservative*, 14th ed. (New York: Manor Books, 1974), pp. 47–48.

- A **dominant buyer of labor** is a firm large enough that its demand for labor affects the wage rate, leading to an upward sloping supply curve for its labor.

- The **marginal supply curve for labor** shows the marginal cost of additional units of labor for a dominant buyer of labor.

Union Objectives and the Conflict with Management

When unions organize in sectors of the economy in which employers would otherwise dominate the labor market, in industries like steel, automobiles, petroleum refining, chemicals, and rubber, they can make large gains for their members. The profits that result from wage rates below labor's marginal revenue product can be captured for labor, in whole or in part. Just as the firm may seek to keep the wage at a level that maximizes the firm's profit, the union seeks to raise the wage to a level at which the firm is making only a normal profit. The difference between the two wage levels gives both sides plenty to fight over. Figure 25–2 illustrates this source of the conflict between union and management. Note also that the conflict between union and management in this case does *not* affect the price of the product, but only the division of the gains. Back in the old days, prior to passage of the National Labor Relations Act, many employers used a wide variety of tactics, including violence, to prevent the organization of unions among their employees. If unions were organized, some employers tried to gain control over them. Their purpose was to maintain the powerful market position that enabled them to keep wages down at or near the level of W_1. Unions, on the other hand, sought to organize workers and use the strength of the union organization to force employers to pay higher wages, pushing wage rates up toward the level of W_2.

A second source of conflict involves the locus of the *MRP* curve. Technological change and substitution of capital for labor can shift it

Figure 25–2
Conflict Between Union and Management

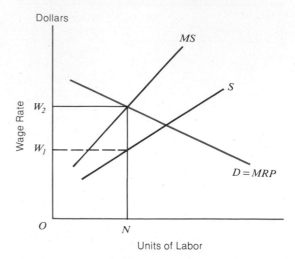

Management seeks to employ N workers at wage W_1 in order to maximize its profits. The union knows, however, that wage W_2 will leave the firm with normal profits when N workers are employed, and seeks to push the wage up to that level. The result is a conflict between the two parties.

upward, widening the gap between W_1 and W_2, and enlarging the potential spoils.

The struggle between labor and management is a real one. In an economy of large firms wage rates are not fully determined by competitive market forces. There is an area of indeterminacy (in Figure 25–2 it is the difference between W_1 and W_2) in which the economic power and bargaining skill of labor and management determine the outcome.

Restricted Entry

Market power is not always on the side of employers. In some professions, particularly those in which workers have significant skills, workers are able to restrict entry and gain higher incomes by reducing the market supply of their skills. Figure 25–3 shows the economic analysis of restricted entry.

Restricted entry is more common than most people appreciate. The classic examples usually given are the craft unions in the construction industry. Entry is restricted in two ways. Unions control the apprenticeship programs that qualify new entrants for union membership (although many present members have bypassed apprenticeships to take skill examinations after learning on the job). Unions in local areas are also able to deny membership to qualified union members from other areas, thereby holding back migration. These restrictions have been used in the past to give favored consideration to relatives and friends of existing members, and to prevent blacks and other minorities from moving into the higher skilled crafts, thereby helping to create a social as well as an economic problem. Now that pressures are being brought on the building-trades unions to provide greater opportunities to minority groups, the members see this development—correctly—as reducing their control over entry and their ability to restrict the supply of workers and as a threat to their economic position.

Workers in the building trades are not the only ones who restrict the supply of labor in their occupations, and labor unions are not the only means for doing so. Workers in a number of public service occupations, such as beauticians and barbers, benefit from similar restrictions on supply through state laws requiring completion of educational programs and passing of tests before people are allowed to practice those occupations. Perhaps the most notorious example is found in the medical profession, in which state and national organizations of doctors, supported by state legislation, set standards for admission to the profession. Members of those associations largely manage and staff the medical schools and determine the numbers of new students admitted. One result of the limited number of doctors this system admits to the profession is a high standard of individual competence. Another result is high incomes for those admitted. The plumber who fixes your kitchen sink and the surgeon who removes your appendix are brothers under the skin; both are beneficiaries of a systematic restriction of entry into their occupations. The plumber does it through his union, the surgeon through his professional organizations.

Restricted entry into many occupations is supported by legislation and regulation by state and local authorities, as we noted in Chapter 22. Much of this regulation is designed to protect the public against incompetent practitioners in such occupations as pharmacist, psychologist, social worker, barber or beautician, and many others. Requirements that workers in those occupations complete approved courses of study, pass examinations, and meet minimal health or ethical standards

Figure 25-3
Labor Market with Workers' Monopolistic Position

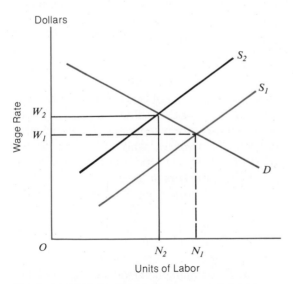

The demand for labor in a particular occupation is shown by *D*. The competitive market supply is shown by S_1. Union organization of workers may bring a restriction of entry into the occupation, shifting the supply curve to S_2. Instead of N_1 number of workers employed at wage W_1, the wage goes up to W_2 and employment falls to N_2.

are designed to screen out incompetents and cheaters. But they also erect barriers to entry that reduce supply and result in higher incomes for those who are able to enter the occupation.

Internal Labor Markets

Internal labor markets within large organizations create further divisions and stratification in labor markets. A large enterprise has a large number of employees working at a variety of levels, with many different skills and a complex pattern of wages and salaries. Any employee must learn how the enterprise functions, the chain of command, what is expected of employees, and the particular skills required for his or her job. Many firms have training programs to teach those things, and much is learned over time just by working there. Whatever the pattern, the firm must bear the costs of training in the specialized skills it needs, and it takes time for workers to reach high performance levels. For that reason, it is usually cheaper for a firm to promote from within than hire from outside. That economic consideration is strengthened by considerations of employee morale and usually by provisions in union contracts requiring reliance on seniority for promotions from within.

The result is creation of an internal labor market within the firm. New employees enter the firm through "ports of entry" at various levels. Unskilled workers are hired for the lower-level jobs that require little education or training. Semiskilled workers may be obtained by promotion from within or hired from outside. Skilled workers are often trained within the firm in apprentice programs. Supervisors and foremen are obtained by promotion within the firm to obtain people who already know the ropes. Many skills are obtained by hiring people who obtained their training outside the firm in educational institutions and who enter through higher ports of entry: accountants, chemists, laboratory technicians, and so on.

Internal labor markets involve a complex system of skill and status ladders that together constitute a hierarchy of employment within the firm. Entry is at the lower levels of each ladder, and there are usually relatively few positions available near the upper reaches of the ladders. For example, a group of white-collar clerks may have a single supervisor for fifty workers, or there may be a single foreman in a production shop with eighty workers. Furthermore, it is often difficult for workers to move from one section of the firm to another. Blue-collar workers don't normally become white-collar workers, and vice versa. To qualify for jobs on higher ladders, a worker must usually leave the firm to obtain the education necessary to reenter at a higher port of entry.

Internal labor markets have three important effects on the labor market. First, access to jobs is limited. A young man or woman who does not succeed in entering the firm at one of its ports of entry will probably be excluded permanently, for the firm tends to promote from within, and next year there will be a new cadre of young workers to hire from. And when layoffs occur the firm usually rehires its former employees when recovery begins. Second, the work force is fractionated into a variety of groups with different interests, attitudes, and points of view. Blue-collar and white-collar workers seldom even see each other and are often separated geographically. Educated employees who enter the higher ports of entry have little interest in or understanding of workers at lower levels. This fractionation of worker interests gives management a freer hand in dealing with its employees, even as it gives up considerable flexibility in hiring and promotion.

Finally, from the economist's point of view, internal labor markets introduce rigidities into the labor market as a whole that interfere with the adjustment of demand and supply. When economic conditions change, internal labor markets react more sluggishly than the "external" sector. For example, employment during a recession is more stable in the internal labor markets as firms try to retain the employees whom the firm has trained and who know how the firm functions. Wages and salaries are also stabilized. When layoffs occur it is the last workers hired who lose their jobs—which helps to explain the higher unemployment rates for young workers and minority groups. On the other hand, when an economic recovery occurs, the laid-off workers are rehired rather than entirely new workers, who find it difficult to penetrate the internal labor market sector.

This relative insulation of internal labor markets from the labor market as a whole causes the bulk of economic adjustments to take place in those sectors of the labor market in which internal labor markets do not prevail—in the so-called "external sector" of the labor market. Fluctuations in employment and unemployment and in wages and salaries are concentrated there. This is the sector of small enterprise, relatively labor-intensive technologies, largely without union organization, and with relatively low wages and salaries.

- **Internal labor markets** are the patterns of training and promotion by which firms fill vacancies in the hierarchy of job skills and status from within.

Discrimination and Labor-Market Crowding

Racial discrimination is usually seen as the chief cause of the high incidence of poverty among racial minorities, and in a general sense that is correct. But discrimination of a voluntary, individualistic nature is less important than the institutionalized discrimination that is built into the structure of labor markets and job opportunities. Relatively few employers are consciously "racist" in their employment policies, but many who seemingly act without prejudice participate in a systematic exclusion of blacks and other minorities from a wide

variety of jobs. Minority groups, including women, are crowded into a relatively small number of occupations in which the excessively large supply of workers serves to keep wage rates down. In other occupations, the supply of workers is correspondingly reduced, bringing higher wages to the white male workers employed in those jobs.

Why don't profit-maximizing employers hire minority workers or women from the low-wage, crowded occupations and employ them in the high-wage, uncrowded occupations, thereby equalizing wages in the two groups? The answer has two parts. First, the existence of institutionalized discrimination that defines certain jobs as male occupations (engineer or dentist, for example), others as female occupations (school teacher or dental technician), others as black (trash collector or cleaning woman). These classifications are not rigid, of course—which often means that a minority worker or woman who breaks into the high-wage sector is paid a substandard wage, which he or she is willing to accept because the alternative employment pays so little. Second, opposition on the part of the white male workers, shown through slowdowns, strikes, or other disruptions, can deter employers from hiring minority workers.

We illustrate the effects of *"crowding"* of minorities and women into a few occupations in Figure 25–4. Start with two occupations requiring identical skills. If blacks are crowded into one, the wage rate in that occupation will be reduced by the large number of workers seeking employment, and, according to the theory of marginal productivity, more will be hired in each establishment. Meanwhile, in the occupations reserved for whites, shown in Figure 25–5, the elimination of workers from the minority group reduces the supply of workers, raises wage rates, and results in higher productivity at the margin.

This analysis clearly shows that it is the white male worker who benefits. He earns more. It makes little or no difference to the employer,

Figure 25–4
"Crowding": Effects on Occupation into Which Minority Group Is Concentrated

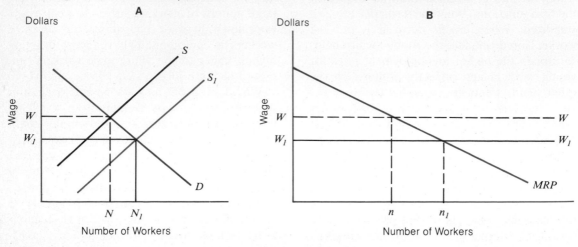

Crowding minority groups into this occupation increases the supply of workers from S to S_1, bringing the wage down from W to W_1 and creating a low-wage occupation. The individual employer pushes his employment up from n to n_1 as a result of the reduced wage, and productivity at the margin is reduced. Total employment rises from N to N_1.

Figure 25-5
"Crowding": Effects on Occupation from Which Minority Group is Excluded

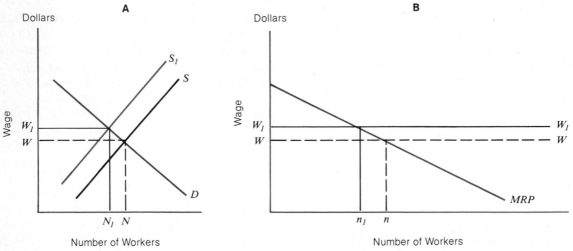

In the uncrowded occupation the reduced supply of labor brings higher wages ($W \rightarrow W_1$) and less employment ($N \rightarrow N_1$) while the individual employer reduces the number he employs at the higher wage ($n \rightarrow n_1$).

who goes about the readjustment of his work force in response to the wage levels he finds in the market. Meanwhile the black or female worker, or any other minority worker, bears the burden in the form of lower earnings. Nor is the level of total employment likely to be affected significantly. Wages in both occupational groups can be expected to move to the levels that will clear the market and provide employment to all willing workers, assuming that the level of aggregate demand is high enough.

There is a social cost, however. It would be possible to move workers from the crowded occupations, where marginal productivity is low, to the uncrowded occupations, where their marginal productivity would be higher. This would bring a net gain of output to the economy as a whole. It would also eliminate the prevailing wage differentials and bring down the earnings of white male workers in those occupations. It is exactly this elimination of differences in marginal productivities for workers with similar skills that would occur in a competitive, color-blind economy, but which does not occur here because of the institutionalized pattern of keeping minority groups and women in a relatively few occupations.

There are additional indirect effects on the economy. Not only are the low-wage occupations and industries overexpanded, but there are other labor market effects:

1. Low wages for minority groups and women reduce incentives to work, resulting in lower labor market participation.

2. More minority-group members move into criminal occupations, where rewards are correspondingly greater.

3. The few minority-group members who are able to get jobs outside the crowded occupations are willing to take lower pay than the majority, because their alternatives are so much poorer.

No individual employer, nor individual worker, need have any personal feelings of animosity toward minority groups, or any "taste for discrimination," as one theory of labor market discrimination phrases it, for the system as a whole to crowd minorities and women into low-paid jobs. The necessary conditions are accepted patterns of behavior or rules of the game that systematically channel those groups into a relatively small number of occupations and exclude them from others.

As far as blacks are concerned, crowding into menial occupations is only the most recent form of coerced labor to which they have been subjected. Slavery was the first; the sharecropping and debt tenure systems in southern agriculture after the Civil War was the second. When that pattern broke up under the combined impact of black migration to the North after 1910 and the technological revolution in agriculture, blacks moved into both southern and northern cities, only to be crowded into menial occupations. As a form of coerced labor, crowding does not have the legal sanctions that preserved slavery or the combination of legal sanctions and social controls that preserved sharecropping and debt tenure in the South for almost a hundred years. Crowding is based on strong pressures from within the labor market, as the recent efforts to provide equal opportunities for blacks and other minority groups indicate. Women are only now beginning to break out of the system.

● **"Crowding"** is the tendency to exclude workers from minority groups and women from many professions and well-paying occupations, forcing them to take jobs in a relatively few menial or low-paying occupations.

Skidding and Bumping

When demand for labor falls during an economic recession, some workers who lose their jobs quickly get other jobs at lower rates of pay, doing work of lesser skill. For example, an engineer laid off by an aerospace firm may take a job selling electrical appliances, or an unemployed assembly-line worker may find a job as a filling station attendant. These moves downward in the hierarchy of jobs are called *skidding*.

When a worker skids to a lower level job he takes the place of another worker who would otherwise obtain that job. This part of the process is called *bumping*. The worker who is bumped often skids to a still lower level job, bumping another worker further downward. At the bottom of the chain, bumped into unemployment, are blacks, Hispanics, poorly educated and poorly skilled workers, young workers seeking to enter the labor force for the first time, and other unfavored groups.

Skidding occurs widely during recessions. A recent study showed that in the 1960s and 1970s, between fifteen and thirty percent of all workers who lost their jobs during recessions skidded to lower-level jobs. The result is relatively large increases in unemployment rates for blacks and young people during recessions and relatively small increases for white male skilled workers. The costs of unemployment tend to be borne most heavily by those who are already in the least favored positions in the labor market.

- **Skidding** occurs when a worker moves down in the hierarchy of jobs.
- **Bumping** occurs when a worker fails to obtain a job because of another worker's skid.

Primary and Secondary Labor Markets

A growing duality is appearing in the modern industrial economy. One sector, called the *primary labor market,* comprises the jobs with relatively high wages and salaries in both blue- and white-collar employment. These jobs require and develop stable and respectful work habits such as getting to work on time and not sassing the boss. Skills are often learned on the job, and "job ladders" enable workers to move up to higher paying jobs as they gain experience and seniority, at least to some extent. In private firms, production jobs in the primary labor market are usually associated with the relatively capital-intensive production methods of such industries as steel, automobiles, machinery, electrical equipment, chemicals, or petroleum refining. Union organization is often strong, and internal labor markets are usually well developed.

There is a substantial degree of labor market segmentation within the primary labor market, however. Many jobs are routinized and require that the worker subordinate himself to rules, authority, and discipline imposed by either supervisors or the technology of mass production, or both. Many production and administrative tasks fall into this category, and a worker will have difficulty in moving out of the "subordinate" to the "independent" sector. The independent sector of the primary labor market comprises jobs that require creativity, problem-solving ability, and individual initiative. These jobs usually require educational credentials and often are highly rewarded.

The *secondary labor market* is qualitatively different from the primary labor market. Jobs often do not require stable work habits; wages are low; turnover and quit rates are high; and employment is often erratic as workers move frequently from one job to another. Promotion ladders are often absent or very short. Many workers in the secondary labor market are black, Hispanic, female, or young. They work chiefly in service industries, but some manufacturing industries are significant employers of low-wage workers from the secondary labor market. The jobs usually require little skill or formal education, and labor-intensive technologies are the rule. Unions are noted mostly for their absence rather than their presence.

Workers in the primary labor market earn more than those in the secondary labor market and the gap seems to be increasing gradually. One reason for the growing disparity between the two sectors is the nature of the technology used. The relatively capital-intensive technology used with primary workers enables productivity to increase relatively rapidly, and the prevalence of unions enables workers to obtain a significant portion of the gains. Secondary workers are employed chiefly in labor-intensive service and manufacturing industries, where productivity gains are low. Lack of union organization makes it difficult for wage gains to be achieved, as well.

The differences tend to be cumulative. Relatively strong wage increases in the primary sector of the labor market encourage increased substitution of machinery for workers, which further increases productivity and enables unions to demand and get wage gains. Employment, however, does not expand rapidly because of the relatively high level of capital investment and substitution of capital for labor. In the secondary labor market, however, low wages encourage continuation of labor-intensive methods of production and discourage substitution of machinery for people, productivity gains are weak or nonexistent, and wages remain low. The result is a persistent tendency for wages in the primary labor market to rise relative to wages in the secondary labor market.

Employment is unstable in the secondary labor market. Jobs are boring and do not pay well; opportunities for advancement are poor. The result is weak attachment to the job by employees, which may be compounded by the availability of unemployment insurance and food stamps to ease periods of unemployment. Employers seem not to mind a casual attitude toward work: they have invested little or nothing in training workers, and substitutes are usually available in large numbers among unemployed members of the secondary labor force. The result is high turnover and movement from job to job.

Instability of employment generates patterns of behavior and attitudes toward both work and bosses that make it difficult for a worker conditioned by participation in the secondary labor market to move easily into the primary labor market. Personnel officers of firms in the primary labor market know that secondary workers readily develop casual attitudes toward work and often have difficulty adapting to the requirements of steady work and discipline that prevail in the primary sector. There is less risk in hiring a young worker who has not learned bad work habits. Because of these factors, it becomes increasingly difficult for workers to move out of the secondary and into the primary labor market.

- The **primary labor market** contains the jobs with relatively high wages and salaries in both blue- and white-collar employment.
- The **secondary labor market** contains the jobs with lower wages and high turnover and quit rates.

International Labor Competition

Labor markets within the United States are now affected strongly by labor markets abroad. Particularly since the mid-1960s, products of American industry have been subjected to competition from goods produced in areas of the world with relatively low labor costs. To some extent that situation always prevailed, but changes in technology, organization and economic development in the years after World War II brought a growing internationalization of economic activity that greatly affects domestic labor markets.

In the industrially advanced countries large international corporations developed techniques of production that substituted physical capital for human capital. The economic force behind this development was the relatively high wage level that labor unions established in collective bargaining, supported by scarcity of skilled labor fostered by heavy government spending on the military and space programs. The effect was that international corporations could export the technology, along with their organization and control, to less-developed countries with an abundant supply of relatively unskilled labor. U. S. corporations began to follow this course from the mid-1960s onward. A variation on the theme in western Europe resulted in labor being imported from nearby less-developed areas in the region of the Mediterranean.

Shifting production to less-developed countries was facilitated by other technological changes in transportation and communication. Jet propulsion permitted rapid travel from corporate headquarters to branch plants. Radio communication via satellite enabled worldwide computer and information systems to function. It became possible to integrate local operations into a worldwide production network controlled from a single center.

In the less-developed countries, economic development drew millions of potential workers into urban centers, where they were available at low wages for employment in branch plants producing for both internal markets and export. Very high rates of unemployment and continuing migration from rural areas keep wage rates low—in real terms, one-half to one-third the level in the advanced industrial nations. Even though skills are often low, the highly capital-intensive technology is able to use relatively unskilled labor profitably.

These developments in the international economy bring the relatively high-wage labor of the industrially developed countries into direct competition with the relatively low-wage labor of less-developed nations. Both can produce much the same product, using similar technologies, for sale in world markets. Competition is particularly strong, or potentially strong, when the final product is relatively expensive compared to transportation costs. For products of that sort, factories can be built anywhere in the world and compete with plants located anywhere else as is the case with electronic components. At the other extreme, it may be profitable to locate branch plants to serve various regions, such as southeast Asia or Latin America, with products that have relatively high transportation costs. Automobile assembly plants are a good example. Almost no product is immune to international competition.

As long as capital is mobile and technology adaptable, the new international competition will affect the labor markets of all countries. Wage rates and the number of jobs in advanced industrial countries are held down by international labor competition. In less-developed countries, programs of economic development rest heavily on relatively low wage rates; public policy takes advantage of the differentials— and often seeks to preserve them. Workers in both areas are affected.

Summary

Labor and capital are continually in conflict with each other over the distribution of income between wages and profits. This inherent conflict is exacerbated by monopoloid elements in labor markets. When a dominant firm is present the wage rate can be held below labor's marginal revenue product, unless workers or-

ganize to use their bargaining power to raise wages. On the other hand, an organized dominant seller of labor can restrict the supply of workers and gain higher wages. Organized economic power influences the distribution of income between wages and profits.

Labor markets have a number of other characteristics that modify the operation of market forces. Internal labor markets within large organizations partially insulate both the organization and its workers from market forces. Discrimination and labor-market crowding prevent large groups of workers from earning decent incomes. Skidding and bumping concentrate the effects of unemployment on the low-wage, already disadvantaged workers. The result is a growing duality in the labor market, dividing it into primary and secondary sectors. Relatively high wages and stability of employment prevail in the primary sector; relatively low wages and instability of employment prevail in the secondary sector. Finally, growing international labor competition tends to keep wages down in the primary sector of the domestic labor market.

The labor market is not a unified, single market in which demand and supply interact neatly to determine wage rates for different types and grades of labor, based on productivity at the margin. Market power has a great deal to do with the outcome. And labor markets are elaborately structured: internal and external, primary and secondary, open and crowded, domestic and international. The institutional structure of labor markets is a major determinant of who gets what.

Key Concepts

dominant buyer of labor	**crowding**	**primary labor market**
marginal supply curve for labor	**skidding**	**secondary labor market**
internal labor markets	**bumping**	

For Discussion

1. If you were a union leader, how would you handle the following dilemma? Your members desire higher wages, but higher wages cause employers to substitute machines for labor or relocate production in low-wage areas.

2. From the consumer's point of view, the price and quality of a commodity are more important than the division of gains between labor and capital. What is the consumer interest in that conflict?

3. Both the American Medical Association (AMA) and the American Bar Association (ABA) seek to protect their members' interests. One difference between the two is that the AMA has considerably greater control over entry into the profession than the ABA. The result is higher average incomes for doctors than for lawyers. Is this result consistent with or contrary to the theory of marginal productivity?

4. Does the economy as a whole suffer because of labor-market crowding?

5. Which groups in the labor market gain and which groups lose because of internal labor markets? because of primary and secondary sectors? because of skidding and bumping? because of crowding? Explain.

Chapter 26

Labor Unions and Collective Bargaining

One of the chief implications of the theory of marginal productivity is that competitive labor markets resolve the conflict between capital and labor. In that analysis, the levels of wages and profits are wholly determined by market forces, and there is no room for quarrels over who gets what. But the world is not that simple. In particular, the economic power of the participants must be taken into account. On the business side power is embodied in the oligopolistic structure of big business. On the workers' side, it is found in their unions. In some occupations workers are able to restrict the labor supply to bring higher wages. But the far more important case is the labor market in which a big enterprise faces a big union to bargain over a division of wages and profits between limits imposed by economic forces. A blend of power relationships and market forces determines wage rates, profits, and the distribution of income. This chapter explains how that happens. It briefly describes the pattern of union organization, examines the historical background of today's labor-management relationships, and analyzes the process of bargaining.

Labor Unions in the United States

The numerical strength of labor unions in the United States is often exaggerated. In 1977 there were a little under 19.5 million union members in a total of about 80 million employed wage and salary workers. Compared with 1960 the number is up from about 15 million and the percent down from about 30 to about 24 percent.

Union membership tends to be concentrated in a few sectors of the economy. Of the union members, three-fourths were in the private sector and one-fourth worked for federal, state, and local governments. Unions are strongest in blue-collar production jobs. About 40 percent of all blue-collar workers were union members, compared with 15 percent of white-collar (administrative and sales) workers and 17 percent of service workers.

Women made up 40.5 percent of the work force—almost 35 million workers—but only about 16 percent (5.3 million) were union members. Almost 30 percent of all men workers were union members. Minority groups are relatively well organized compared to whites.

About 26 percent of all white workers were represented by unions in 1977. The comparable figure for blacks was 33 percent and Hispanics 29 percent.

Government employees are more highly unionized (40 percent) than the private sector (23 percent), but a significant number of teachers who work under union contracts are not members of the unions that represent them.

Unions are particularly strong in transportation, communication and public utilities, representing 52 percent of all workers in those industries. Other sectors with strong unions are manufacturing (38 percent), construction (38 percent) and mining (40 percent). But unions are weak in service industries (22 percent), wholesale and retail trade (12 percent), finance, insurance and real estate (6 percent), and agriculture (4 percent). The most highly organized industries are railroads (83 percent) and the Postal Service (80 percent). The least organized is private household service (under 1 percent).

Although there are over 90 unions with over 25,000 members each, large unions dominate the labor scene. This concentration is understandable, for it takes big, powerful unions to deal with big, powerful corporations and big governments in collective bargaining. The twelve unions with more than 500,000 members have a total membership of almost 11 million, or some 56 percent of all union membership. They are listed in Table 26–1, with their approximate membership in 1977.

If we were to add the next twelve largest unions, the total membership would reach about 15.9 million. Some 82 percent of all union members are accounted for by the two dozen largest unions.

Union membership is geographically concentrated as well. Over 35 percent of all nonagricultural workers are union members in the great industrial states of the northeast, ranging from New England west to Missouri and Minnesota and south to the Ohio and Potomac

Table 26–1
Largest Labor Unions in the United States, 1976

Union	Number of Members (in thousands)
Teamsters	1,889
Automobile workers	1,358
Steelworkers	1,300
Electrical workers	924
Machinists	917
Carpenters	820
State and county workers	750
Retail clerks	699
Laborers	627
Service employees	575
Meat cutters	510
Clothing and textile workers	502
	10,871

Source: AFL-CIO

Rivers. The percentage in the Pacific Coast states is only slightly less. On the other hand the southern, southwestern, mountain and Great Plains states average less than 20 percent union membership.[1]

Types of Unions

Labor unions are typically divided into *craft unions* and *industrial unions,* although the distinctions have become blurred over the years. The carpenters' union (United Brotherhood of Carpenters and Joiners of America) is as close to the concept of the old craft union as any large present-day union. Its members' skills in construction and woodworking distinguish them from other workers in the same industry (plumbers, sheet-metal workers, roofers, and so on). Only those workers who show proficiency in those skills through union-run tests are eligible for membership. The union represents only those workers in dealing with employers.

---

[1]For collectors of trivia, West Virginia is the most heavily unionized state (39 percent of the nonagricultural work force) and South Carolina the least unionized (under 7 percent).

Craft unions are found in industries in which the various skilled trades make up a large portion of the work force. Construction is the classic example. Railroads also had a group of craft unions until recently, when a number of them combined to form a single union in a declining industry. In some industries the craft and the work force are practically identical, as in the case of teachers, barbers, and musicians, and the craft union represents the entire organized work force.

In many of the principal industries of the United States, the work force is composed primarily of semiskilled or unskilled workers, up to 80 and 90 percent in some instances. These are the industries in which industrial unions have been formed: steel, automobiles, mining, electrical equipment, machinery, chemicals, petroleum refining, men's and women's clothing, and others. Unions in these industries are open to all workers regardless of skills, whether they are unskilled laborers, semiskilled assembly-line workers, or skilled craftsmen. The automobile workers' union (United Automobile, Aerospace, and Agricultural Implement Workers of America) is a typical industrial union. The bulk of its membership is made up of workers on the industry's assembly lines, but it also includes lowly sweepers and highly paid tool and die makers. Just like the craft unions, however, the UAW has the fundamental purpose of bringing together into one organization those workers who have close common interests in order to deal more effectively with employers.

- A **craft union** is a union whose membership is restricted to workers in a particular occupation.

- An **industrial union** is open to all workers in an industry, regardless of the workers' occupations.

Union Organization

A large national union with hundreds of thousands of members requires a working structure, just as any large organization does. At the bottom stands the local union, which represents workers in dealing with their direct employer. The local union negotiates with the employer on issues that pertain specifically to the local plant and local workers. It also participates in settling grievances that may arise under the terms of a contract.

At the top is the national union, of which the locals are a part. It often negotiates the basic terms of union contracts that apply to all employers across the nation, or to all workers employed by the same company, as in steel or automobiles. It also assists the local in disputes that the local may get involved with, promotes extension of union organization, and operates union retirement or other welfare programs. In between there may be regional administrative units, depending on whether the activities of the union require it.

Finally, most national unions are affiliated with the AFL-CIO (American Federation of Labor-Congress of Industrial Organizations). The important unions that are not members of the AFL-CIO are the Teamsters and the United Mine Workers. The functions of the *labor federation* are primarily political action and general support for the activities of the national unions that compose the federation. The important functioning units are the national unions and the locals rather than the federation. They do the bargaining, participate in grievance procedures and the establishment of work rules, and collect the dues.

- A **labor federation** is an organization whose membership comprises two or more labor unions. The American Federation of Labor-Congress of Industrial Organizations (AFL-CIO) is the great U.S. labor union federation.

A Little History

1877 was a landmark year in the relationship between capital and labor in the U.S. A major depression that began in 1873 had not yet ended, and the eastern railroads announced a

10 percent reduction in wages—the latest of a series. Workers on the railroads, mostly unorganized, began a walkout. The strike triggered demonstrations and riots in some Maryland and Pennsylvania cities. When the governors of those states called out the militia (forerunner of the National Guard), the untrained troops refused to fire on their neighbors, and the U.S. Army was called on to restore order. In the meantime, railroad workers in Pittsburgh ran the mail trains on their own, and labor leaders in St. Louis took over the city government, imitating the famous Paris Commune of seven years before, until they were ousted by troops. Order was restored after a week of riot and disorder in the cities of the Northeast.

Growing industrialization following the Civil War had spawned a new industrial working class. Except for the textile industry of New England, which employed mostly young women, pre–Civil War manufacturing relied heavily on skilled workers and used a technology in transition from individual craft production to modern machine production. Unions of skilled workers appeared but made little headway against employer opposition and hostile courts. Efforts were made in the 1820s and 1830s to establish local and national federations of craft unions, but most of them did not survive the hard times of the 1840s. Some splinter political parties organized by workers were active in the 1830s, but they, too, were transient. Slavery was the great labor issue of pre-Civil War days, and in a primarily agricultural society it took the form of opposition to slavery on the part of independent farmers in the North, with the support of both workers and business firms whose economic well being depended on prosperous farmers. These groups feared economic competition from an expansionist slave economy in the South.

The Civil War settled the issue of slavery, promoted strong industrial growth, and fixed political power in the hands of northern financial and industrial interests. In the 1860s and 1870s the new technology of railroads, steel, and coal took hold, with its big enterprises (for that time) and large forces of wage workers. The new technology did not require large numbers of skilled workers using modified craft technologies, but large numbers of unskilled employees. Some of these workers came from the natural growth of population and some were eastern farmers forced out of agriculture by the more productive farms of the midwest. The largest numbers were immigrants from Europe. Until restrictions on immigration were imposed in the early 20th century, U.S. industrial growth depended heavily on relatively unskilled workers from Europe. It was this new working class in a growing industrial economy that exploded in 1877.

The *Knights of Labor* came out into the open after the riots. The Knights was a labor union open to all workers and was not restricted to craft workers or any one industry. Organized in 1871, it was a secret organization until 1877, largely because of employer reprisals against known members. It grew quickly after 1877 to a membership of over 700,000 by 1886. Successful strikes against some of the large western and southwestern railroads helped swell its membership, and a nationwide campaign for an 8-hour work day helped gain support from the craft unions. Its membership was largely of unskilled workers who wanted strong and militant programs, but the leadership was too timid or inept to build those sentiments into a strong organization.

The growth of the Knights as a general union challenged the principle of exclusivity of the craft unions of skilled workers. Scarcity of skills in good times enabled craft unions to gain concessions from employers on wages, hours and working conditions that a general union could not get for unskilled workers, who were almost always in abundant supply. So the craft unions kept out the unskilled and represented only the skilled workers. As the Knights of Labor grew, as a union of all workers, the economic advantages of the crafts tended to be lost, and the craft unions took a dim view of the Knights. To protect their interests the major craft unions banded together in 1886 to form the American Federation of Labor (AFL) which emphasized the autonomy of each trade and "business unionism": concentration on wages, hours, and working conditions for their own members. It also rejected the militant, mass action policies of the rank-and-file members of the Knights. Economic advantage triumphed over class solidarity.

Haymarket, 1886

There was one issue on which unskilled and skilled workers could agree: the need for shorter hours—an eight-hour working day. The conflict over this issue came to an armed confrontation in Haymarket Square, Chicago, on May 4, 1886. A strike at the McCormick Reaper Company escalated into a general strike of most workers in Chicago around the issue of the eight-hour day. In a riot at the McCormick plant on May 3 between strikers and strikebreakers the police fired on the strikers and killed several. A protest meeting the next day at Haymarket Square was charged by the police, a bomb was thrown (the first use of dynamite in a civil disturbance), and the police opened fire. Seven policemen were killed and seventy wounded, most by cross-fire from their fellows.

One of the great show trials in American history followed. A group of radicals was rounded up in an atmosphere of hysteria fanned by the press. They were convicted of murder by a jury selected for its antilabor beliefs and sentenced to death or prison by a biased judge who later became the first president of United States Steel Corporation and had the city of Gary, Indiana, named after him. After the usual appeals were rejected by higher courts, four were executed. One committed suicide in prison, and three were pardoned six years later. No one ever found out who threw the bomb, and there was no investi-gation of why the police attacked a peaceful meeting.

The union movement as a whole, and the Knights of Labor in particular, were seriously damaged by Haymarket and its aftermath. Unions were tagged as radical, un-American organizations by much of the press. Local business groups organized vigilantes to wreck union offices and printing shops that printed union or socialist publications, often with the cooperation or benign neglect of local police. Local arrests and trials of radicals or union organizers were common in 1886–88. The Knights of Labor did not survive, withering away to insignificance by the early 1890s, the victim of public hysteria and repression, hard times, and attacks by the AFL, which survived the time of troubles to become the backbone of the union movement from the mid-1890s to the mid-1930s.

Industrial Unions

The AFL did not try to organize the large number of relatively unskilled workers employed by the big mass production industries. Nevertheless, in the 1890s several industrial unions accepting all workers in an industry regardless of skill grew up in the steel, railroad, coal, and nonferrous mining industries. The steel union was broken in the famous Homestead, Pennsylvania, strike in 1892 that featured a pitched battle between workers and a private corps of mercenary soldiers hired by the Carnegie Steel Company, an anarchist attempt to murder the president of the company, and use of the state militia to restore order. The American Railway Union was destroyed in the equally notorious Pullman strike in 1894, in which the U.S. army kept the trains running and a federal court injunction was used to jail the union leaders. One of them was Eugene V. Debs, who, radicalized by the strike and his imprisonment, became the nation's chief socialist political leader in the first three decades of the twentieth century. Court injunctions became a favorite weapon of big business in its attacks on unions after the Pullman strike.

Anthracite, 1902

The United Mine Workers, an industrial union in coal mining, survived and grew. The key event in its early history was a strike in the anthracite coal mines of Pennsylvania in 1902, which forged for the first time a coalition of moderate union leaders, moderate business leaders, and the federal government around a policy of collective bargaining.

The union itself was divided into two factions. The militants favored calling out the bituminous coal miners, who were working under a valid, collectively bargained contract, in order to bring major industries of the country to a halt in support of their fellow workers. The moderates in the union wanted to arbitrate the issues and opposed a sympathy strike by the bituminous coal miners since they had a valid contract.

The business community was divided as well. One group of business leaders—who today would be called "corporate liberals"—favored collective bargaining as a means of avoiding strikes. They were headed by Senator Marcus Hanna of Ohio, a steel, coal and shipping tycoon and Republican Party leader, who a few years earlier had taken the lead in organizing the National Civic Federation, which favored settlement of labor-management disputes by collective bargaining. Hanna was its president, and its vice-president was Samuel Gompers, president of the AFL. Hanna wanted to avoid both strikes and socialism by admitting workers to the gains to be obtained from economic growth. The corporate executives in the anthracite coal companies, on the other hand, were adamantly opposed to unions, refused to deal with union leaders, and would not submit the issues to arbitration. The anthracite mines were big business: anthracite coal was the chief home heating fuel in the eastern cities, and the mines were tightly controlled by a few large

railroads backed by J.P. Morgan, the leading investment banker of the day. Big business in anthracite coal was determined to break mass unionism, just as the steel and railroad corporations had done.

The strike proceeded through the summer of 1902, with a substantial amount of violence as the mining companies brought in strikebreakers protected by the National Guard. However, when the union voted against a sympathy strike by the bituminous coal miners, reaffirming the principle of peaceful settlement of disputes through collective bargaining, public opinion shifted strongly in support of the union. At this point the federal government intervened. President Theodore Roosevelt sent his Secretary of State to speak softly with J.P. Morgan, as if negotiating with a sovereign power, while threatening to use his big stick, government seizure of the mines, unless Morgan agreed to arbitration. Morgan gave in, and the strike was settled on terms established by a government-appointed commission.

For the first time in U.S. history, the federal government had intervened in a labor dispute on the union side. But intervention came only after the union chose collective bargaining over class solidarity. The settlement, furthermore, was a victory for the coalition of moderate labor leaders, moderate corporate executives, and the federal government that sought to develop collective bargaining as an alternative to class warfare. It foreshadowed the accommodation between capital and labor that later brought the labor legislation of the 1930s.

The Industrial Workers of the World

The fourth of the new industrial unions of the 1890s, the Western Federation of Miners, sought to organize the nonferrous metals miners of the mountain states. In the course of a decade of bitter warfare with the mining companies, which were supported by the courts and state governments, the union membership and its leaders were radicalized. They formed the basis of the Industrial Workers of the World (IWW), organized in 1905. Like the old Knights of Labor, the IWW was open to all workers, irrespective of skill or industry. It advocated worker ownership and management of enterprise, which meant abolition of private ownership of productive capital and the end of the wage labor system. Radical change in economic organization was not to be achieved by political action—the "Wobblies" scorned the ballot box as a capitalist device for controlling the working class—but through mass strikes and similar forms of direct economic action. This radical program appealed to unskilled and migrant workers in the west and was also successful with steelworkers and textile workers. The IWW's greatest success was in a bitter strike in the textile mills of Lawrence, Massachusetts, in 1912; its greatest failure came in another textile mill strike in Patterson, New Jersey in 1913. The IWW declined after 1913, but came back strongly during World War I. By 1917 it had some quarter of a million members and was the most rapidly growing union in the country.

The IWW was the culmination of the militant working class radicalism that had begun with the riots of 1877. Mass protest without a program or effective leadership gave rise to the Knights of Labor, which organized the mass protest movement but was in turn destroyed by the repression that followed the Haymarket affair. Mass labor organization surfaced again in the industrial unions of the 1890s, two of which were destroyed by their battles with big business. One gave up class warfare in favor of collective bargaining, aided by the federal government, and one developed by way of class warfare to an American labor radicalism.

The IWW was repressed by the federal government during World War I. The Democratic administration of Woodrow Wilson took a pro-labor stance, which meant support of the collective bargaining philosophy of the AFL. All war contractors were required to agree on wages, hours and working conditions with their employees, which enabled legitimate unions to grow but also caused many employers to organize captive or "company" unions dominated by the management in order to comply formally with the law. This policy of support for unions did not apply to the IWW. In 1917 the U.S. Department of Justice organized a burglary of IWW headquarters in Chicago (a forerunner of Watergate!). Shortly after, IWW offices across the country were raided, its officers arrested, and its assets impounded. Simultaneously, the Post Office refused mailing privileges to IWW publications, and the Immigration Service began deporting Wobblies born abroad. Two great show trials resulted in long jail terms for the IWW leaders. By the end of 1918 the IWW was no longer a significant factor on the labor scene.

The Twenties and Early Thirties

Organized labor had doubled its membership to about 5 million during World War I, but the 1920s and early 1930s saw a steady shrinkage to under 3 million by 1933. The federal government, no longer needing labor peace for military reasons, ended its support of collective bargaining. The National Association of Manufacturers (NAM), which had become the chief spokesman for the anti-union business view, organized a strong drive against unions in 1920—the so-called "American" or "open shop" plan—that gathered force throughout the 1920s. One factor in the shift of business policy toward an active anti-union policy was the suppression of left-wing labor during World War I, which removed any need for business to compromise with the labor union moderates.

The business drive against unions led to a series of armed conflicts. A nationwide steelworkers' strike in 1919–20 involved large-scale use of private armies by the steel companies and retaliatory violence by workers, particularly in Pennsylvania. Martial law and federal troops were introduced in Gary, Indiana, and the National Guard was sent to East Chicago and Indiana Harbor. In 1920 two years of strikes and open warfare began in the bituminous coal mining areas of West Virginia, Pennsylvania, and Illinois. In 1922 New England was the scene of textile mill strikes with sporadic violence. A new wave of violence began in 1928 and continued into the early 1930s, when the usual labor-capital conflicts were exacerbated by the Great Depression. From 1928 through 1934 guerrilla warfare was carried on in the bituminous coal mining areas of West Virginia, Pennsylvania, and Kentucky, most spectacularly in "bloody Harlan" County, Kentucky in 1931. In 1929 and 1930 there was a wave of strikes in the southern textile industry, general mob violence directed against union activity, and deaths from violence in Gastonia and Marion, North Carolina, and Elizabethton, Tennessee. In 1934 the "Battle of Rincon Hill" during a longshoremen's strike in San Francisco resulted in 118 casualties, including 3 dead. Strike-connected violence in Toledo, Ohio, required use of the National Guard. These were only some of the highlights of a decade and a half of class warfare.

Meanwhile, some of the basic elements of an accord between capital and labor began to fall into place. In railroad transportation, a series of federal laws between 1898 and 1934 established the right of workers to organize and provided the framework for collective bargaining between unions and management. The purpose, of course, was to avoid costly railroad strikes. A U.S. Department of Labor was established in 1913, a monument more to the growing political activity of labor unions than to any substantive gains. A system of collective bargaining grew up in the clothing industry after 1910, along with arbitration of labor-management disputes. Restrictions on immigration legislated by the U.S. Congress between 1910 and 1920 strengthened the economic position of workers by diminishing the flow of new workers from abroad into the labor market. Federal legislation against child labor was passed in 1916 and 1919, but both acts were held to be unconstitutional by the U.S. Supreme Court in 1918 and 1922, respectively. An amendment to the U.S. Constitution prohibiting child labor also failed. Nevertheless, several states, particularly Massachusetts, New York and Wisconsin, adopted legislation protecting employed women and children and limiting the age at which children could be employed, and experiments were being made with unemployment insurance and retirement programs that foreshadowed later legislation. Collective bargaining, limits on immigration, and legislation to shield workers from some of the more harmful characteristics of a private enterprise economy were developing as ways of mitigating the sometimes violent class warfare that kept erupting from time to time, Much New Deal legislation of the mid-1930s was in that tradition and helped cement the accord between organized labor and big enterprise that provided a framework for the prosperity and economic growth of the period after World War II.

National Labor Legislation

A national policy designed to promote the peaceful settlement of disputes between labor and management was put into place in the 1930s. Collective bargaining between the two parties was to replace conflict and the unilateral authority of the employer. Such an arrangement implied that workers had to be represented by unions if bargaining was to succeed; and that implied a willingness on the part of employers to accept unions as the workers' representatives and to bargain with them. These were the principles underlying the *National Labor Relations Act* of 1935 (Wagner Act), passed in the middle of the Great Depression of the 1930s.

The National Labor Relations Act was designed to protect the workers' right to organize and prevent employer opposition to union organization. It also required employers to bargain "in good faith" with the legitimate representatives of employees. A National Labor Relations Board (NLRB) was established to enforce the act. It has two chief functions: to manage elections among employees to determine whether a majority wish to be represented by a labor union that would then be certified as the representative of all the employees, and to prevent "unfair labor practices" on the part of employers, such as efforts to prevent organization of unions or refusals to bargain. Under this protective umbrella, and influenced by the tight labor markets of World War II, union membership rose from about 4 million in 1934 to over 15 million in 1948 and to almost 20 million today.

The new national labor policies were not fully accepted. In particular, distrust of collective action remained and was inflamed by nationwide strikes in basic industries after World War II as the economy moved to a new pattern of wages and work hours during the conversion from wartime to a peacetime economy. A reaction set in that brought passage of the *Labor-Management Act* of 1947 (Taft-Hartley Act). This legislation was intended to protect employers, individual workers, and the general public. It restrained certain types of actions by unions as well as employers. It provided individual workers with protections against arbitrary action by unions and set up procedures by which unions could be decertified as bargaining agents when workers no longer wanted them. It protected employers caught in the crossfire of jurisdictional disputes between unions.

The most important part of the Taft-Hartley Act dealt with "national emergency" disputes, or those that imperil the national economy because of their breadth or the essential nature of the service provided. It provides for a "cooling-off period" of 80 days during which efforts to resolve the dispute can be made, and for a vote among employees on whether to accept management's last offer. If that fails, the President can refer the dispute to Congress

with recommendations for resolving it. Even after passage of the Taft-Hartley Act complaints about unions continued. In particular, corruption in some unions, especially in New York and Chicago, and infiltration of unions by underworld elements brought passage of the *Labor-Management Reporting and Disclosure Act* of 1959 (Landrum-Griffin Act). It provided a "bill of rights" for individual union members, established a series of provisions dealing with the financial responsibility of unions, and gave enforcement teeth to protection of the rights of members. It took twenty-five years, but a national system for peaceful settlement of labor disputes was ultimately forged.

- The **National Labor Relations Act** established collective bargaining as the method for settling disputes between labor and management. Passed in 1935, the Wagner Act was amended by the **Labor-Management Act** in 1947 and the **Labor-Management Reporting and Disclosure Act** of 1959.

Collective Bargaining

Collective bargaining is the name given to the process of negotiation that takes place between unions and management. Its goal is a contract between the two parties that embodies their agreement on a wide variety of issues. Among the principal topics that most collective bargaining contracts cover are the following:

Definition of the bargaining unit to which the agreement applies.

Wages, including such items as overtime pay and paid holidays or vacations.

Hours of work.

Grievance procedures that provide ways to settle disputes that might arise under the contract.

Rules for suspension and discharge, and other disciplinary measures.

Rules for seniority.

Payment of union dues if they are to be deducted from workers' paychecks by the employer and paid directly to the union (the "checkoff").

Effective date and termination of the contract.

Looking down this list, one sees most of the topics that define relations between employees and employers. Indeed, the purpose of collective bargaining is to reach agreement on these matters so that productive work can continue without interruption under conditions that are acceptable to both parties.

Wages are usually the chief bone of contention, but there are times when other issues loom large, such as retirement and pension plans, safety conditions within the plant, and hours of work. Most of these other issues are reducible to the money equivalent of wages, however. Their dollar cost to the employer can be estimated, and the employer is usually more concerned about the total cost of wages plus other provisions of the contract than he is about the individual items. As a result, most disagreements in collective bargaining can be resolved once the total "cost of the package" is agreed on.

Bargaining Space and Bargaining Limits
The economics of the situation in which a large union faces a large employer or group of employers establishes economic limits beyond which neither side can be pushed.

○ In the long run, the employers' profits cannot be pushed below those available elsewhere. If they are, the firm can be expected to move its capital.

○ Similarly, wages cannot be pushed below those that draw forth the necessary labor. If they are pushed below that level workers will find jobs elsewhere or remain idle.

These two positions define the *bargaining space* within which unions and management contest with each other for advantage. Within that space agreement is possible. Management tries to keep wages plus the value of other benefits as close as possible to the level just necessary to get adequate supplies of labor. Unions try to raise wages plus the value of other benefits as high as they can without pushing the firm out of business. Thus, there are *bargaining limits,* defined by the economic alternatives open to labor and capital. Figure 26–1 shows the bargaining space and its limits.

The practical limits to the bargaining space are narrower than the limits enforced by economic alternatives. Before the economic limits are reached, one party can be expected to refuse to compromise any further, negotiations will break down, and a strike will occur. The reason is that pushing one party to the economic limit of the bargaining space implies its destruction.

If the union allowed the wage rate to fall to the lower limit and stay there, the union would

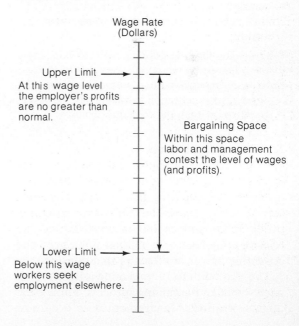

Figure 26–1
Bargaining Limits: Economic

Wage Rate
(Dollars)

Upper Limit
At this wage level the employer's profits are no greater than normal.

Bargaining Space
Within this space labor and management contest the level of wages (and profits).

Lower Limit
Below this wage workers seek employment elsewhere.

have little economic reason for its existence. Workers would do just as well by getting jobs elsewhere. Any self-respecting union would go out on strike before it accepted any such settlement. The minimum it would settle for without a strike would have to be enough above the lower limit of the bargaining space to give members a reason to remain members.

Likewise, the upper limit is seldom achieved. At that limit the firm would do just as well by moving its capital elsewhere. As the limit is approached, the firm's willingness to let its workers go on strike increases and further concessions are harder and harder to get. The union finds that if it wants to settle without a strike, it can't push the employer's profits all the way down to the normal profit level.

These considerations are particularly important when both parties consider their relationship to be a relatively permanent one. If both sides anticipate bargaining with each other in another year, they will have to maintain workable relationships, and that means not pushing the other party to the wall. The practical limits to bargaining are shown in Figure 26–2.

- **Bargaining space** is the area within which an agreement between union and management is possible.
- **Bargaining limits** are the limits of the bargaining space defined by the opportunity cost of the two parties. These are normal profits for the employer. The practical bargaining limits, however, are narrower than the economic limits.

The Bargaining Process

We are now ready to examine the bargaining process itself. We want to determine why some disputes are settled peacefully, and why some lead to strikes; how the bargaining space between labor and capital is divided; and the relative importance of market influences and economic power in effecting that division.

The first point to keep in mind is that neither party in the bargaining process knows the other's position. Management does not know

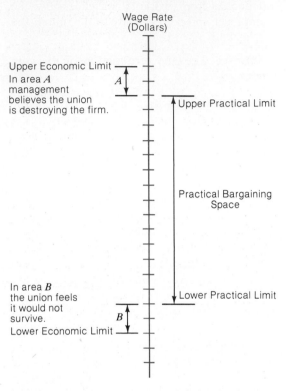

Figure 26–2
Bargaining Limits: Practical

The practical bargaining limits on the right side of the diagram define the area of nonantagonistic conflict: in that area the right of the other party to continue to exist is accepted by both parties.

the minimum for which the union will settle. Nor does the union know the maximum wage increase that management would willingly give. Uncertainty prevails on both sides.

Uncertainty about the other party's position leads each to take extreme positions that are known to be unrealistic. The purpose is to try to discover how far the other party will give in or compromise while giving up as little as possible yourself. Yet these initial positions can't be so extreme as to forfeit all credibility, nor can they be so rigid that the other party feels that no compromise is possible. The union, for example, will make an initial demand that it knows to be greater than the maximum that management can be expected to grant without a strike. Anything less than that maximum means that the union would be gratuitously giving up some of its bargaining space and its potential gains. Having made such a demand, the union's strategy will be to compromise gradually, while trying to learn from management's reactions exactly where its point of maximum concessions is located.

Management, likewise, will make an initial offer that it knows is so low that it lies below the minimum the union would accept without calling a strike. It, too, will then seek to compromise its offer upwards until it can determine where the union's minimum is located.

During the bargaining process each party may try to bluff the other party,[2] compromises will be made on one issue in order to gain advantage on another, and, in the most important part of the whole process, each party will try to learn what the other party's true position is while trying to conceal its own. This is the essential element of bargaining skill. Another important aspect of the process is public opinion, particularly in important and highly visible negotiations, for the ultimate results in major industries are often colored by the attitude of the public and government.

Reaching Agreement— or Failing to Reach Agreement

In the typical bargaining situation an agreement is possible if two conditions are met:

1. The maximum the employer is willing to grant is equal to or greater than the minimum the union is willing to accept.

2. The process of bargaining does not create so much hostility that the parties fail to recognize that there is an area of potential agreement.

We show this overlapping area of potential agreement graphically in Figure 26–3. The range within which the union would be willing to settle (A–B) overlaps the area within which the employer would be willing to settle (M–N).

Once the two parties sense that they have compromised into the area of potential agreement, the bargaining is likely to become intense and difficult. Each side can then gain by being stubborn and trying to get the other side to make the largest compromises. Negotiations can become protracted even though there is little difference between the positions taken by the two parties. This is one reason why many disputes are not settled until the last moment.

On the other hand, it is quite possible that there will be no overlap of union minimum and employer maximum, and no area of potential agreement. This can develop because of real differences between the parties or rigidities on

Figure 26–3
Bargaining: Agreement Is Possible

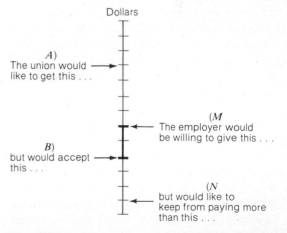

Bargaining can bring about an agreement between M and B, where the positions of labor and management overlap.

---

[2]The bargainer's prayer: "Lord, make me conciliatory but unyielding." A bluff won't work unless it has credibility, which a negotiator may even seek to achieve by putting himself in a position from which he can't retreat. For example, the union may whip up such rank-and-file enthusiasm for a particular point that management knows there can't be much compromise by the union leadership. The management negotiators must then decide whether to give in so that they can continue to deal with that leadership, or fight on that issue and risk getting a tougher union leadership in the future.

either side. Either the union leadership or the union membership may feel that it can't compromise any further. Perhaps other unions have obtained large gains, or the cost of living has risen substantially, or there is an internal struggle for power within the union, or bitter feelings have developed between management and its work force. On the other hand, management may feel that its stockholders (or financial backers) will vote it out if larger concessions are given, or that the federal government may step in to try to keep prices down, or other internal management problems may intervene. In any event, pressures on one or both parties to the bargaining process may keep them from compromising enough to reach an agreement. Under these circumstances a strike is almost sure to occur. This situation is diagramed in Figure 26–4, showing the gap ($M-B$) between management's top offer and the lowest amount the union will accept.

The Strike

Most union-management negotiations result in agreement and a contract acceptable to both parties. Strikes are not particularly frequent. The average union member in the U.S. participates in a strike about once every seven years. When strikes occur, they usually are short: the average union member loses about 2 to 2.5 days of work annually because of strikes.

The economic loss due to strikes is usually negligible. This is true even of the spectacular, long strikes in basic industries. In steel or automobiles, for example, firms build up backlogs of output prior to strikes and work overtime afterwards to catch up. Workers may even come out ahead because of time-and-a-half overtime pay before and after a strike. As for output, little is usually lost, because customers are able to postpone their purchases until after the struck industry is back at work. In a durable goods industry these factors combine to create a situation in which real economic losses, and financial losses to either workers or firms, do not start building up until after a

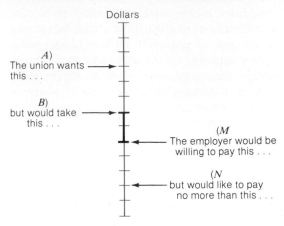

Figure 26–4
Bargaining: Agreement Is Not Possible

The employer's best offer M is below the lowest amount at which the union will settle B. The existence of this gap brings on a strike.

strike has been going on for about eight weeks. That is why strikes in durable goods industries, when they occur, are often long ones. Economic pressure on the contesting parties takes time to build up.

The case is different for industries producing perishables or services. In that case the economic losses start almost immediately. For example, a strike of truckers or railroad workers slows down economic activity generally, affecting equally those industries producing durables, nondurables and services. While output in the durable goods industries would otherwise be made up later (if the transportation strike is relatively short), other industries can't make up the lost output. Generation of income will fall (the multiplier works itself out here), and the entire economy is affected. That is why government usually intervenes to halt widespread strikes in transportation, but usually does not intervene in other industries.

When a strike occurs, who is responsible? The common response is to blame the union. It is, after all, the union that decides it will not continue under the existing situation, or will not accept management's last offer. But this is only the way things appear on the surface. Why not blame management because it didn't accept the union's last offer? When looked at as a problem in bargaining, it quickly becomes apparent that both sides are equally to blame, or equally blameless. Negotiations break down because the bargaining positions of the *two* sides do not overlap and enable an agreement to emerge.[3]

The strike is a test of economic strength. The employer's fixed costs continue even though his operations may not. As financial reserves are used up the costs of continuing the strike mount and a settlement looks more attractive. The maximum wage increase the employer would be willing to give starts to move upward. Similar pressures are felt by the union. Some members can get other jobs temporarily, but they usually don't pay as well; other members can't get other work. Family savings start to disappear, and the union's strike fund declines. Financial stress begins to appear among the rank-and-file union membership and puts pressure on the union leadership. The wage increase for which it will settle moves downward. As the strike continues, then, the gap between the two parties shrinks until a point is reached at which settlement is possible. The function of the strike is to cause the bargaining positions of two parties to shift to an area of potential agreement that did not previously exist.

Mediation, Conciliation, and Arbitration

Third parties can often intervene in disputes between labor and management with good results. Sometimes an agreement is possible during the bargaining stage, but the two parties do not realize it. The negotiations themselves may have created anger and bitterness that

prevent agreement on the economic issues. Under these conditions a third party can help both labor and management understand that an area of potential agreement exists even though neither party has recognized it.

If a strike should occur, it can continue on its own momentum even after economic pressures on the two parties make a settlement possible. Unless they are brought together by a third party the strike may continue long after a settlement is possible.

There are three types of third-party intervention in labor-management disputes:

1. *Mediation* occurs when a third party endeavors to assist the disputants in reaching an agreement on their own. The mediator acts as a middleman who tries to bring the parties together, but he does not actively participate in negotiating a settlement.

2. *Conciliation* occurs when a third party tries actively to work out terms of a settlement with the disputants. The conciliator goes beyond acting merely as a stimulus to negotiation and participates in the effort to find a common ground for agreement.

3. *Arbitration* occurs when a third party makes the decision for the disputants. There are two types of arbitration:
   A. The meaning or applicability of an existing contract may be disputed. Many contracts provide for an arbitrator to decide on interpretation or applicability of the contract if the disputants cannot settle the matter among themselves.
   B. In negotiating a new contract the two parties may agree to have an arbitrator decide on some of the issues rather than fail to agree on a new contract. In some countries, *compulsory arbitration* is provided for some or all disputes.

In the United States third-party intervention

---

[3]It is also possible that there was an overlap but the two parties could not find it. We will return to this problem a little further on in this chapter.

in labor-management disputes is quite common. The federal government and some state governments have mediation and conciliation services that try to settle disputes and avoid strikes. A large number of union contracts provide for arbitration of disputes that arise under the contract. The emphasis, however, is on voluntary agreement between labor and management. Public policy has consistently emphasized that the best interests of labor and management are most effectively furthered if they can agree rather than have a decision imposed upon them from the outside. That is the reason why compulsory arbitration to determine the terms of a contract has never been widely used in the United States.

- **Mediation** is a third party's attempt to assist the participants in a labor dispute in reaching an agreement.
- **Conciliation** is an attempt by a third party to actively work out an agreement in cooperation with the disputants.
- **Arbitration** is the settlement of a dispute by a third party.

Collective bargaining does not work perfectly—few social policies ever do. Agricultural workers are not covered by the legislation, and farm enterprises are not required to bargain with their employees. Some firms continue to try to evade the law: J.P. Stevens and Co., the large textile manufacturing firm, was for many years a notorious corporate outlaw that finally was forced in 1980 to agree to play by the rules. Whether it has truly reformed remains to be seen. Other firms observe the letter of the law while attempting to weaken or eliminate the unions they are required to bargain with. Thus, the textile workers' union in the South and the newspaper reporters' guild were largely eliminated as effective unions in the 1950s by astute employer use of some of the provisions of the Taft-Hartley Act. On the other hand, corruption and infiltration of underworld elements remains a problem in some unions, and the large size of others creates a

gap between the rank-and-file member and policy-making officials. Management of union pension funds remains a problem. But those are the ways of the world; big unions are no more free of corruption, dishonesty, and mismanagement than big business or big government, and there is certainly a great deal more rank-and-file participation than in business enterprise. In spite of these problems, collective bargaining has greatly reduced the direct conflict that formerly characterized American capital-labor relationships.

Mutuality of Interests Between Unions and Management

So far in this chapter we have stressed the conflict of interest between labor and management, and collective bargaining as a means of resolving the conflict. We should not lose sight of the fact that unions and management have common interests as well.

Some writers stress the fact that both labor and capital require each other in order to produce the goods that are needed both by workers and owners of capital. This argument has been made for generations by advocates of a private-enterprise system, and it is true, of course. Labor can't produce much without using capital, and capital must be combined with labor in any production scheme. But physical combination of the two factors in the processes of production does not necessarily require preservation of any one social organization of production, be it socialist or capitalist. Capital and labor can be combined if capital is either privately or publicly owned, and there are many examples to illustrate the point; the Canadian railroad system, TVA and the privately owned electric power companies, or municipal and private water supply systems come immediately to mind.

A more subtle mutuality of interest has grown up between big business and big unions in the contemporary American economy in spite of the contest between the two that is

ARBITRATION: AN EXAMPLE

Disputes that arise under collective bargaining agreements are often resolved by referring them to arbitration by a third party. Here is an actual case, taken from the records of the American Arbitration Association.

The Handicapped Papermaker

Despite a glass eye, and limited vision in the other eye (which was corrected by glasses), Richard J. did very satisfactory work as a machine operator in a paper mill for six years, and he had never suffered an accident in that time. Richard's job was such that if an accident had occurred, it might have been serious, for his machine had sharp knives for cutting cardboard, and they could very easily cut through a careless finger.

In October, 1962, Richard suffered a slight cold, or infection, in his natural eye, and saw the company doctor, and eventually an ophthalmologist, about it. The latter found no occupational disability and recommended that Richard seek private treatment. A report of this examination was given to the insurance company that handled the paper mill's workmen's compensation cover-age. This was the background of a grievance that eventually arose.

It seems that the insurance company sent a safety engineer to the plant who, after an inspection, advised management to transfer Richard to a less hazardous job. Fearful that if it did not comply with this request, it might be held liable for "negligence," the employer transferred Richard to a job management regarded as safer. Unfortunately, it was a job that paid less than Richard had been earning.

On hearing the union's protest, management examined the collective bargaining agreement very closely and relied on a clause that gave the employer the right to demote employees for "good cause." This alone justified the action the company took, the industrial relations director argued.

The union answered that Richard had done his job reasonably well and that an insurance company's recommendation was not binding in an area where only labor and management jointly had decisive power.

This case ultimately went to arbitration by a third party. If you were the arbitrator, what would your decision be? Why?

---

continually played out in collective bargaining. The current pattern of labor-management relations has helped to preserve and stabilize the positions of both big business and big unions. Long-term contracts, industrywide bargaining, grievance procedures, and arbitration, even the process of collective bargaining itself, contribute to the security of both sides.

Corporations gain uniform wage rates throughout the industry. The uniformity eliminates one source of cost differences between firms and facilitates maintenance of common prices in oligopolistic industries. It is easier to prevent price competition if all firms have a similar cost base. Long-term contracts assure large corporations of known wage costs over a period of one to three years, facilitating the planning that gives large firms an advantage over small. Firms are protected against unauthorized strikes and work stoppages that could disrupt production lines. As long as collective bargaining agreements are reached the industry is protected against government intervention in determining wages and working conditions.

Unions as organizations also benefit from the current pattern. Exclusive bargaining agreements protect the union from having its membership raided by other unions. Grievance procedures and arbitration offer a means by which members' discontent is channeled into agreed upon settlement procedures, thereby reducing the pressures of internal discontent that might arise within the union. Even union dues are often collected by the firm and paid directly to the union. Finally, a wise business management will protect a "reasonable" union leadership by seeing to it that the membership of the union obtains economic gains large enough to keep them contented with the union leadership as well as with their jobs.

In recent years this growing mutuality of interest between big union and big business has been disturbed by the process of inflation. As long as the economy expands at a rate fast enough to maintain reasonably full employment, and government fiscal and monetary policies provide the necessary level of total spending, it is tempting for both unions and management to seek gains that promote inflationary price increases. We examined this problem in Chapter 14 and concluded that the structure of the economy made the whole system inflation prone. As long as wage increases plus fringe benefits do not exceed productivity gains, there is no internal cost pressure on the business firm. But it is tempting for unions to try to push for greater gains, particularly in oligopolistic industries in which administered prices can be moved upward. As long as government stands ready to maintain aggregate demand at full-employment levels the burden is shifted to the general public, to the mutual benefit of workers and business firms. Inflation can be a safety valve.

On the other hand, when government imposes fiscal and monetary policies designed to halt rising prices, the conflict between unions and management is intensified. Union members press for wage increases to compensate them for the rapid rise in prices, while management is faced with both rising costs and government pressures to keep prices from going up. Management is unable to provide the wage increases demanded by unions. These conflicting pressures make it more difficult to find areas of potential agreement in collective bargaining, and the mutuality of interest between the two parties tends to disintegrate.

The Blue-Collar Blues
With all of these elements in the larger picture working themselves out through the market

and collective bargaining and the grand strategy of big business–big labor–big government relationships, what is happening to the ordinary Joe and Jane on the assembly line? They have the blues. They may be living well, but affluence bypasses them and their life doesn't get any easier. The job is not very rewarding. During inflation their real income falls. And their total life pattern leaves much to be desired.

An American worker can look forward to doing the same job for an entire working life. Only a limited few move up to supervisory positions. Jobs of higher skill and higher pay are available, and significant numbers of workers move into them by reason of their seniority in lower-ranking jobs. But progress is slow and even the higher-rated jobs are usually routine, unchanging ones.

One result of that pattern is a growing economic squeeze as the worker becomes older. Aside from an occasional or erratic jump to a higher-level job, production workers can expect increases in their real wage approximately equal to the growth of productivity, say 3 to 4 percent annually. But their living expenses rise by 6 percent each year, on the average, according to the U.S. Bureau of Labor Statistics. They marry, have children, buy a home, raise their children and send them to school, buy insurance—these costs rise at about twice their increase in base pay. By the time they reach 45 years of age their budget may be tighter than it was twenty years before. Unless they have been able to move up in the pay scale at their plant they may well be worse off economically than they were when they started their working life. In the next twenty years of their working life the pressures may ease as immediate family obligations are reduced, but other things become important; typically middle-aged workers feel that their retirement pension, life insurance, and health benefits are inadequate.

Lack of satisfactions on the job are also felt by large numbers of workers. Many production jobs are repetitious, boring, and mind-deadening. They do not stimulate the imagination, use the full range of skills people are capable of developing, or promote the development of the individual as a person. Production jobs contain fewer of the elements that make for personal satisfaction than white-collar jobs at the same income level. They are also more dangerous, with injury and disability more common.

Away from the job, the workers' environment brings them into intimate contact with some of the more severe environmental problems of our time. They are likely to live in an urban neighborhood beginning to show signs of decay, located closer to the urban sources of air pollution than others. Crime is likely to be more prevalent in their home neighborhood, along with greater fear of crime. Black workers in the central cities, where almost all of them live, feel this problem more than others.

The effects of the blue-collar blues are being felt in a number of ways. Absenteeism from the job and turnover are high. Closely related to absenteeism are alcoholism and drug addiction, seen by some authorities as means by which workers escape both boredom and the realization that they are caught on a treadmill. Lack of pride in the job leads to sloppy work and defective products. Resentment produces deliberate sabotage of the finished product. Both poor quality of production and sabotage have become problems of increasing concern to production managers in a number of American manufacturing industries.

None of these problems is new. They have been with working people in industrial societies for a hundred years or more. But the point is that they are still with us and have become more significant in recent decades. The inflation *cum* unemployment of the 1970s and early 1980s created enough uncertainty to dampen active protests, but the underlying malaise remains. Economic growth has brought higher standards of living, and most working people are far better off today in many material aspects of their lives than their counterparts of fifty or a hundred years ago. Labor unions have helped bring that about. But what of the psychic aspects of life: the desire to move oneself forward and lead a richer life as one grows older, the urge to do meaningful and self-satisfying things, the desire for a favorable environment? More and more Americans are coming to feel that there will have to be some better answers to those human problems that lie behind the forces of the market, bargaining, and the organization of power. Collective bargaining does not completely solve the problems of workers in a private-enterprise economy, nor does it eliminate conflicts between capital and labor.

The following chapter will examine the Marxist theory of exploitation for further insights into the nature of those conflicts.

Summary

Labor unions are an important force in the U.S. economy, claiming membership of almost one in four employed workers. Unions are strong in sectors of the economy dominated by big business, in government, and in the older industrialized regions. The bulk of union membership is concentrated in a relatively few large unions.

American labor unions are the product of a long history of conflict between labor and capital that was particularly violent from about 1875 to 1935. Labor divided into two groups. The moderates advocated collective bargaining and followed a "job conscious" policy that sought higher wages, shorter hours, and other benefits. The radicals supported socialism and a "class conscious" policy of opposition to capital. Capital also divided into two groups.

Conservatives opposed all labor unions. Moderates accepted the principle of collective bargaining and recognition of unions. The conflict was resolved, at least for a time, by government intervention that supported the moderates on both sides and repressed labor radicalism. The result was an accord between labor and capital, embodied largely in national legislation during the 1930s. This legislation restricted immigration, allowed collective bargaining between labor and management, and provided programs to insure greater economic security for working people.

Collective bargaining brings labor and management representatives together in an effort to reach agreement within the bargaining space created by the economic limits imposed by the opportunity costs of the two parties. Strikes can occur when there is no bargaining space created by those economic limits or if the negotiations themselves create ill-feelings that prevent agreement. The economic strength of the two parties largely determines the duration and outcome of strikes. Some devices designed to strengthen the process by which agreement is reached include mediation, conciliation, and arbitration.

Collective bargaining does not work perfectly, nor has it resolved all the conflicts between capital and labor. Discontent among working people continues; big unions and big business sometimes develop a mutuality of interests. Collective bargaining is a means for managing, but not eliminating, the conflict between labor and capital.

Key Concepts

craft union

industrial union

labor federation

National Labor Relations Act

Labor-Management Act

Labor-Management Reporting and
 Disclosure Act

bargaining space

bargaining limits

mediation

conciliation

arbitration

For Discussion

1. What causes strikes?

2. Should government employees have the right to strike? Under what circumstances? Why or why not? Should teachers have the right to strike? Should police or fire fighters? Should air traffic controllers?

3. What are the alternatives to collective bargaining as a means of reconciling conflicts between labor and management?

4. Should individual workers be required to join a union as a condition of obtaining a particular job or for keeping a job?

5. Should individual workers be required to participate in a company-sponsored retirement plan arrived at through collective bargaining? Should they be required to participate in the federal social-security program?

6. Why not resolve labor-management differences through the free market and prohibit labor unions?

Chapter 27

The Marxist Theory of Exploitation

The root idea in the Marxist analysis of exploitation in a private enterprise economy is that workers are paid a wage less than the value of their output. The difference between the wage and the value of output is appropriated by owners of the means of production. Analysis of why this occurs requires explanation of the labor theory of value, the process of exchange, and the determination of wages. Like Marx, we assume the best possible case for capitalism—a perfectly competitive economy with highly flexible prices, which adjust quickly to a long-run equilibrium. In this best of all possible capitalist worlds the gains made by capitalists generate capital accumulation and economic growth, which, resting on a base of exploitation of labor, generate class conflict and political turmoil.

The Labor Theory of Value

The Marxist theory of exploitation starts with the labor theory of value. This highly controversial theory is essentially very simple. It is based on a proposition about which there is little disagreement: the products and services that satisfy human wants are produced by human effort. That effort takes two forms. One is the direct effort of labor currently employed in production. The other is the past labor embodied in the tools used by currently employed labor. All products and services are produced by some combination of current labor and past labor. The fact that we call the tools by the name "capital" should not obscure their origin in the labor of generations past.

The cost to society of goods and services is the amount of labor time that must be expended on producing them, including both current labor time and the labor time embodied in capital goods used up in production. As Marx pointed out, at any time, given the existing state of technology, there is a *socially necessary labor time* required for production of any commodity that defines the cost of production. As technology improves less labor time is required to produce goods, and the cost to society as a whole is reduced. What this amounts to is the simple proposition that the value of a good depends on its cost of production. Note that this is the same proposition that emerged from the analysis of competitive markets in Chapter 19.

Karl Marx

Karl Marx was born on May 5, 1818 at Trier, Prussia, in the Rhineland area of what is now West Germany. He completed high school in 1835 and entered the University of Bonn, transferred to the University of Berlin in 1836, where he studied law and philosophy, completing his doctoral dissertation in 1841. A brilliant student, he was considered by his professors to be potentially the next great German philosopher; however, his radical political views and atheism precluded a career in either government or university teaching in reactionary Prussia.

Marx wrote articles for the *Rheinische Zeitung,* an opposition newspaper in Cologne from 1841 to 1842, when he became its editor. He met his lifelong friend, supporter, and collaborator, Friedrich Engels (1820–95), son of a wealthy German textile manufacturer, in 1842. Marx became convinced of the economic basis of politics while writing on political events in 1842–43. The *Rheinische Zeitung* was suppressed by the Prussian government in 1843. Marx married his childhood sweetheart, Jenny von Westphalen, the fiery radical daughter of a reactionary Prussian baron, in 1843 and emigrated to Paris. In Paris Marx wrote a number of articles for German emigré publications, collaborated with Engels on a critical study of young German philosophers, *The Holy Family,* began studying economics, and met French socialist leader Pierre Joseph Proudhon (1809–1865) and the great German poet Heinrich Heine (1797–1856). Expelled from France in 1843 at the instigation of the Prussian government Marx moved to Brussels.

In 1846–47 Marx and Engels collaborated on *The German Ideology,* a classic statement of materialist philosophy; Marx wrote *The Poverty of Philosophy,* a vicious attack on the ideas of his friend Proudhon, who never spoke to Marx again. Marx and Engels helped organize and attended the congress of the Communist League in London, 1847. Marx gave a series of lectures in Brussels in 1847, later published as *Wage Labour and Capital,* an early statement of his economic analysis of capitalism. The *Manifesto of the Communist League,* jointly written by Marx and Engels, was published in London in 1848, just before the revolution of 1848–49 on the Continent: "The workers have nothing to lose but their chains. They have a world to win. Workers of all lands, unite." Jenny may have done the translation into English. Marx and Engels established *Neue Rheinische Zeitung* as a radical newspaper in Cologne, 1848–49, until the revolution failed and Prussian authoritarianism was restored.

Marx and his family settled in London in 1849; years of wandering were over. Marx resumed economic studies in the great library of the British Museum, supported in part by Engels, who was in Manchester managing his family's factory until 1870, when he also moved to London. Marx contributed articles to the New York *Daily Tribune,* 1851–1861, some of which were written by Engels but published under Marx's name so Marx could get the pay. A series of strongly stated revolutionary articles appeared under pseudonyms in some leftist English papers in the early 1850s; recent scholarship suggests that Jenny Marx was the author. Two brilliant pamphlets by Marx on French politics, *The Class Struggles in France* (1850) and *The Eighteenth Brumaire of Louis Bonaparte* (1852) are classics of radical political analysis. Marx filled dozens of notebooks with writings on economics, published after his death, including *Theories of Surplus Value* and the *Grundrisse* and published *A Contribution to the Critique of Political Economy,* with a famous preface on the economic basis of history, in 1858. His great work, the first volume of *Capital,* was published in 1867. Meanwhile, the International Working Men's Association (the First International), an association of communist political organizations, was founded in London in 1864. Marx was an active leader and headed the organization for a time, his salary enabling the family to live moderately well until the Association folded in 1871.

Early in the London period and shortly after Jenny gave birth to their fifth child in 1851, Marx fathered a child by a not-too-bright household servant; the child was adopted by another family, with financial assistance from Engels, who took the blame when whispers started going around. Marx continued working on *Capital,* but did not complete the work. Jenny died in 1881, Karl two years later at age 65. The second volume of *Capital,* edited by Engels, appeared in 1885, a third, edited by Karl Kautsky, in 1894.

How does the productivity of land and other natural resources fit into this picture? Are they not productive as well? Indeed they are. Trees can produce fruit without the intervention of human labor, and the fruit has usefulness in satisfying human wants. In the labor theory of value, however, natural resources are taken as an original endowment which regenerates itself through natural processes from one season to the next. As long as no labor must be expended on it, the production costs nothing. On the other hand, if labor must be employed in producing goods from land, a cost is involved, for that labor could be used in other ways to produce other things. For example, if the fertility of land can be maintained only by applying fertilizers to it, there is a real cost to using land: it is the labor time, current and past, used to produce and apply the fertilizer that sustains the natural productivity of the land. The natural fertility of land is free, like air and water, and a price must be paid for its use only if (1) it is privately owned, or (2) labor must be used to sustain its fertility.

Fundamental to all this is the idea that production is a social process. The society as a whole, in this view, is engaged in sustaining and reproducing itself and growing. The process involves the coordinated activities of many millions of people, who use a wide variety of tools that were themselves produced by efforts expended in the past. But it is human labor that makes the process function, and the cost of the output is the socially necessary labor time expended on it.

This fundamental truth can be obscured if we restrict our view to the specifics of the individual business enterprise. The firm must hire labor, pay for its capital, and rent its land. To calculate costs of production, we add up the wages, interest (return to capital), and rent. From this point of view, labor is only one of several factors of production, and labor costs only a portion of total cost. When the factors of production are privately owned, payment of those costs goes to the owners of capital, land, and labor power. The value of the goods produced is then seen as the sum of these payments. From the point of view of the labor theory of value, however, the real cost of production is the human effort—labor power—that must be expended on reproducing and expanding the work force, capital goods, and natural resources.

The labor theory of value is not contrary to the theory of competitive markets as that theory is developed in modern economics and explained in this textbook. Both argue that the relative value of commodities is determined in the long run by costs of production. The chief difference is that the non-Marxist theory of income distribution defines cost of production as payments to the owners of the factors of production, while the Marxist theory argues that all of those payments can be reduced to the human effort devoted to production.

- **Socially necessary labor time** is the labor time required for production of a commodity, using the existing technology and organization.
- The **labor theory of value** holds that in a capitalist economy commodities exchange for each other in ratios determined by the amount of socially necessary labor time embodied in them.

Capitalist Exchange

According to Marx, goods are produced in a capitalist economy by business units that do not themselves use the commodity but sell it at a price that reflects the amount of labor power expended on its production. A privately owned enterprise puts up the capital necessary to hire labor, buy capital goods, and obtain or rent natural resources and land. All of these inputs are purchased at prices that reflect the labor power necessary to produce them. The inputs are then combined in a production process that transforms them into another commodity that is then offered for sale. The output must be sold at a price greater than the cost of inputs in order to provide a profit to the firm.

Without the profit a privately owned firm would have no incentive to produce. The essence of the process is that an initial amount of capital *(M)* becomes a larger amount of capital *(M′)* by first being transformed into a saleable commodity *(C)*:

$$M \rightarrow C \rightarrow M'$$

In a capitalist economy M' is greater than M, generating the gain that motivates production. Marx applied the term *surplus value* to the difference between M and M'.

In the exchange process all goods are bought and sold at their normal value, which, as we have seen, is based on the labor power required for their production. Labor power itself is a commodity, which is sold by workers and purchased by employers at its normal value. As long as competition prevails and coercion is absent, the worker willingly sells his labor power at the prevailing wage, and it is willingly purchased at that wage by the employer. The exchange itself involves no exploitation.

The Subsistence Wage

Wages are determined, in the long run, by the cost of the workers' subsistence. The level of wages must be high enough to enable the work force to reproduce itself in the required numbers and with needed skills, in both the short and long run. If the wage is below this *socially necessary subsistence,* to use Marx's term, a labor shortage will appear and the wage will rise to the required level. If the wage is above the socially necessary level, a labor surplus will drive the wage down to that level. This is the famous subsistence wage theory of Marxist economics.

Subsistence in this analysis means more than merely the minimum input of food, clothing, and shelter necessary for the physical survival of a single worker. It includes the inputs necessary to maintain a family and insure the long-run reproduction of the working population, the cost of education and training, including maintenance during the training period, to assure the needed supply of skills, and any further amounts that historically have become embedded in the customary and accepted standard of living. For example, the wage will have to be high enough to cover the cost of marriages, burials, and other ceremonies associated with the life of a worker's family. The subsistence wage is more than a physical minimum and is determined by a complex interaction of economic, social, and historical forces. There may be economic forces that push it down toward a physical minimum, but there are also social and historical forces that tend to keep it above the level necessary to merely sustain life.

- The **socially necessary subsistence wage** is the wage required for the reproduction of the working population in the quantity and quality needed for the continued functioning of the economy.

Surplus Value

At this point we return to the labor theory of value. The value of a commodity is determined, as we have seen, by the labor power embodied in it, which takes two forms: the labor time used directly in current production and the past labor time embodied in the capital used up in production.

For example, a textile factory may produce 100 square yards of cloth for every 10 hours of current and past labor employed: 100 yards of cloth = 10 hours of labor. Let the cloth sell for $1 per yard, so that the total value is $100. Let depreciation charges equal $10; that is, capital used up in production is equal in value to 10 yards of cloth. This means that 1 hour of current labor is used to replace past labor and 9 hours of current labor is embodied in the product, for a total of 10.

It might appear at first glance that one hour of labor time will have a value of 10 yards of cloth, or $10, but that is not the case. The value of a commodity is determined by the socially necessary labor time required for its production. In the case of labor power, the cost of producing the workers' subsistence determines its value. And, since this is capitalist production, there must be a profit or surplus for the enterprise to motivate its owners. Of the 100 yards of cloth produced with 10 hours of labor, subtract 10 yards to finance replacement of capital goods used up in production. The remaining 90 must be divided between capital and labor, with labor's share determined by the socially necessary cost of subsistence. To complete our example, let's say that comes to $80, or $8 per hour. This leaves $10 for the enterprise. Marx called this portion *surplus value,* to indicate that it is a surplus over the cost of capital plus the wage bill.

The value V of any commodity can be divided into three parts. Marx called them *constant capital c,* the capital goods used up in production; *variable capital v,* the wage bill; and surplus value *s.* So:

$$V = c + v + s$$

In the example used here, measuring these variables in hours of labor time:

$$10 = 1 + 8 + 1$$

Or in money values and market price:

Constant capital c	=	$ 10
Variable capital v	=	80
Surplus value s	=	10
Total value V	=	$100

Constant and variable capital represent the initial capital of the enterprise M prior to the production process, while total value is the capital of the enterprise after production and sale of the output M'. Surplus value is the difference between the two:

$$s = M' - M$$

Two points of clarification should be added to this brief account of the Marxist analysis of surplus value. One concerns the concept of labor power. The unit in which labor power is expressed is hours of labor. But labor has varied skills: in one hour a skilled and experienced worker will be able to produce more than an unskilled and inexperienced worker. This problem is resolved conceptually by defining the unit of labor power as one hour of homogeneous (identical) unskilled labor of average ability. An hour of skilled labor can be thought of as a multiple of the basic unit. There may be difficulties in measurement, but the unit is at least potentially quantifiable and quite usable as an analytic concept.

The second point concerns the division of surplus value into profit, interest, and rent. Surplus value is that portion of the value of output retained by the owner of the enterprise. If the owner borrowed to buy his capital equipment or pay the work force, payment of interest must be made to the lenders. And rent must be paid on land or buildings and equipment if the enterprise does not own them. Thus, surplus value is normally divided into the three different forms of income received by owners of productive resources in a private enterprise economy: interest on borrowed funds, rent on land and buildings, and profit to the owners of producing enterprises. The proportions in which surplus value is divided among interest, rent, and profit will depend on the pattern of ownership and organization at the time. Surplus value is not synonymous with profit. It is the return to owners of the means of production.

Appropriation of surplus value by owners of capital is the essential element in exploitation of labor in a private economy. Labor is paid a wage equal to the value of its labor power. Labor power is used by the buyer, however, to produce goods with a greater market value than the labor power itself. The difference is surplus value: value produced by labor but appropriated by capital.

- **Surplus value** is that portion of the value of a commodity appropriated by the capitalist. It arises from the fact that in capitalist production workers produce goods with a value greater than the value of their labor power.
- **Exploitation** in the capitalist economy is the appropriation by capitalists of a portion of the value created by the labor power of workers.

Increasing Surplus Value by Squeezing Labor

Although in the long run wage rates are determined by impersonal economic forces, as are the prices of final products, business firms can increase the gap between the two and increase surplus value. In the short run—with a given amount and type of capital equipment—surplus value can be increased in several ways:

1. Increase the length of the working day while retaining the same daily wage.

2. Increase the intensity of work, speeding up the production process, to obtain greater output from the purchased labor time.

3. Reduce the wage bill by substituting women and children at lower wages for adult men, who command higher wages.

4. Take advantage of temporary surpluses of labor to pay wages below the socially necessary subsistence level.

Competition among business firms can be expected to force all firms to adopt these methods of increasing surplus value. The firms that are most successful in doing so will survive the competitive wars of the marketplace. The less successful will not survive. As a philosopher friend of the author's put it—he worked on an assembly line at an automobile plant in southeastern Michigan—"All bosses is bastards; if they're not, they don't last very long as bosses."

There are limits to the exploitation of labor using these methods, however. Increased hours of work are limited by the physical endurance of workers. Speedups of the production process are limited by the nature of the technology used, by the resistance of workers, and by the workers' physical endurance. Technological limitations and the physical requirements of jobs limit the extent to which women and children can be used in the workplace. Market forces restrict the ability of a firm to reduce the wage it pays. A combination of factors—market forces, physical endurance, technology, worker resistance—limit the ability of business enterprises to increase the amount of surplus value they extract from the labor power they buy in the marketplace. Nevertheless, competition among firms forces each to use these methods to squeeze as much surplus value as it can out of the labor it hires.

Increasing Surplus Value by Replacing Labor with Capital

Surplus value can also be increased by substituting capital for labor. A new technology that decreases the amount of total capital, $c + v$ (constant plus variable capital), used in production will increase surplus value and raise the rate of profit. Here is an example that builds on the illustration used earlier:

1. Start with the original relationship we used to illustrate the concept of surplus value:

$$V = c + v + s$$
$$10 = 1 + 8 + 1$$

2. In this example 1 hour of past labor plus 9 hours of current labor produce goods with a total value of 10. Leave V at 10 initially, for the selling price of the commodity is determined by the market and is not controlled by the seller. Now have the firm

substitute capital for labor so that total capital ($c + v$) is reduced from 9 to 8. One hour of past labor embodied in capital equipment is substituted for 2 hours of current labor so that c increases from 1 to 2 and v declines from 8 to 6. Surplus value (s) increases:

$$10 = 2 + 6 + 2$$

3. This means that the rate of profit rises, which is what the firm is after. The rate of profit is, of course, the return to the enterprise (s) expressed as a percentage of total capital ($c + v$). In this illustration it rose from the original 11.1 percent (1/9) to 25 percent (2/8).

Not all technological changes that substitute capital for labor will raise the rate of profit. But the firm will be forced by competition to seek out and use those that do. For example, and continuing the illustration we just used, a change in technology that involves $V = 10 = 2 + 7 + 1$ will be rejected by a profit-seeking firm because it provides only the same rate of profit as the original process in which $V = 10 = 1 + 8 + 1$. Both technologies yield a rate of profit of 11.1 percent. Why bother to make the change? To be used, a new technique that substitutes captial for labor must reduce the total capital used ($c + v$) per unit of output.

The process does not end here, however. Other firms will adopt the new technology and increase their profits also. The higher profits in this industry will also attract new firms as capital shifts to places where it will earn the most. Output of the industry's product will rise, its selling price will fall, and the rate of profit will decline. This process will continue until profits in the innovating industry have fallen to equality with profits elsewhere. Ultimately, after full adjustment to a new equilibrium has been achieved, the new uniform rate of profit across industries will be a bit higher than before, say 12½ percent in our continuing illustration.[1]

In our innovating industry, with its new technology fully installed and the long-run equilibrium rate of profit $s/(c + v)$ of 12½ percent, the value equation will be

$$V = c + v + s$$
$$9 = 2 + 6 + 1$$

The long-run adjustment brought a reduction in the value and price of the product from 10 to 9. The capital invested per unit of output fell from 9 to 8. The amount of surplus value remained the same, achieved by arbitrary selection of an equilibrium rate of profit of 12½ percent; we could just as easily have ended up with an increase or decrease in s by selecting a different rate of profit for the illustration. But the capitalist now has one unit of capital available for investment elsewhere while a higher rate of profit prevails all around. We can understand why Marx considered the capitalist economy, when it functioned properly, to be a gigantic machine for the accumulation of capital.

From labor's point of view, however, 7 hours of current labor is now employed rather than

---

[1] Marx thought that substitution of capital for labor would bring about a declining rate of profit after the full economic adjustment took place, but modern mathematical analysis, not available in Marx's day, shows that the long-run equilibrium rate of profit rises when capital is substituted for labor. The rate of profit in a capitalist economy may decline in the long run, perhaps because of class struggle, higher wages to keep workers happy, taxes to support a large military establishment, etc., but not because of substitution of machinery for people in the processes of production. Marx was wrong on that point.

Why does the long-run equilibrium rate of profit rise? In the innovating industry there is an initial increase in the rate of profit, which draws capital from other industries. As capital moves out of the lower profit sectors into the innovating industry, output falls in those sectors, market prices rise, and surplus value increases. Furthermore, when substitution of capital for labor takes place in production of "wage goods"—goods that workers need for their socially necessary subsistence—the price of those goods will fall, bringing down the general wage level and raising surplus value throughout the economy. As these adjustments work their way through the economic system the increases in surplus value are distributed among all industries as rates of profit are equalized at a slightly higher level. A rigorous proof of this proposition, however, requires use of some theorems in matrix algebra developed around 1910, long after Marx's death.

the original 9, even though the amount of surplus value remained the same. The rate at which surplus value is extracted from currently employed labor rose from 1/8 (12.5 percent) to 2/6 initially (or 33.3 percent) but settled at 1/6 (or 16.6 percent) after long-run adjustment. Marx called this ratio the *rate of surplus value,* or the *rate of exploitation.* The basic principle is that substitution of capital for labor increases the exploitation of labor by raising the rate at which surplus value is obtained by capital. This is true even though the wage rate does not fall below the level of socially necessary subsistence.

- The **rate of surplus value,** or **rate of exploitation,** is the ratio of surplus value to the wage bill for currently employed workers (or *s/v*).

The Unemployed

The substitution of capital for labor throws workers out of jobs, creating downward pressure on wage rates. The continual presence of a "reserve army" of unemployed workers, to use Marx's term, keeps wage rates from rising above the socially necessary subsistence level. In the long run, wage rates cannot fall below the level necessary to provide for the reproduction of the working class and the skills needed to operate the production system, while the presence of substantial numbers of unemployed workers will keep wage rates from rising above that level.

In the short run, however, wage rates can fluctuate, rising or falling above or below the long-run socially necessary subsistence level as the economy moves through cycles of prosperity and depression. In hard times wage rates can be pushed down below the socially necessary subsistence wage, particularly for unskilled workers. Conversely, it is quite possible for wages to rise above the socially necessary subsistence level during business cycle upswings, particularly for skilled workers: pros-

perity may bring shortages of labor for at least some sectors of the labor market.

But prosperity also brings high levels of capital investment and introduction of technical changes that substitute machinery for people. Surplus value, channeled into more capital-intensive methods of production, leads to unemployment. In any business cycle upswing there are two forces at work, one tending to push up wage rates, the other pulling down.

The downward pressures are strong even in an upswing. First, a business cycle upswing starts out with substantial unemployment, which must be eliminated before wage rates start to rise. Second, constant capital will be substituted for labor most heavily in those sectors of the economy in which labor shortages develop, which tends to dampen any tendency for wage rates to rise. The displaced workers are then added to the reserve army of unemployed, which tends to push wages down in the other sectors of the economy. Only when a business cycle upswing is rapid and relatively long-lasting would we expect these downward pressures on wage rates to be countered by the forces of expansion, and then only in the later stages of the upswing. One persistent characteristic of an industrial private enterprise economy is continuing downward pressure on wage rates, in good times as well as bad, that keeps wages from rising above the socially necessary subsistence level.[2]

Three Levels of Exploitation

The Marxist analysis of exploitation of labor in a capitalist economy develops three different aspects of exploitation. At one level, exploitation takes place in the face-to-face relationship between the individual worker and employer

---

[2]Labor unions and monopoloid industries can modify this conclusion, bringing greater upward mobility to wage rates, but remember that we are giving capitalism its best shot by assuming competitive markets and absence of market control. More on this a little later in the chapter.

within the business enterprise. The employer is driven by competitive pressures to attempt to lengthen the working day, speed up the production process, and reduce wages. These efforts are limited by forces beyond the control of employers, as we noted. Nevertheless, they create direct conflict between workers and employers. One result of this conflict is joint action by workers: they form unions to increase their economic power and their ability to protect themselves from this form of exploitation.

At the second level, exploitation is the result of the way labor markets function. Wage rates are pushed down by unemployment and by substitution of capital for labor. All workers are affected. In this sense, workers as a class are exploited because the economic system functions to increase surplus value for all capitalists, as a class. This aspect of exploitation leads to class conflict, in addition to the conflict between individual workers or groups of workers and individual employers at the workplace itself. Class conflict leads in turn to class consciousness, as workers come to understand that they are all affected adversely by economic pressures that, in the long run, benefit the owners of productive resources. Political action based on class economic interests follows, for example, government programs designed to reduce unemployment or restrict immigration.

Third, exploitation of labor is systemic in nature, inherent in a private enterprise economy. Labor power owned by workers is transformed into commodities owned by employers, which are sold to provide surplus value for the owners of the means of production, which is then used to increase the wealth of the capitalist class. This process, of course, is what makes capitalism dynamic, providing for economic growth and expansion of the forces of production. But it also increases the wealth of the capitalist class while leaving workers just where they were before. The growing productive wealth of the economy accrues to a small minority, even though the source of that wealth is the labor effort of the great majority.

As one of the old songs of the Left puts it, "They coin our very lifeblood into gold."

This third aspect of exploitation lies deep within the capitalist economy. It cannot be eliminated by collective bargaining between labor and management, or by government programs designed to ease the burden of unemployment. For it is the appropriation of surplus value that is the *raison d'être* of private enterprise and provides the accumulation of wealth that motivates the system. Marx felt that as the working class comes to understand the underlying reality of its role in the economic process of capitalism, fueled by a growing class consciousness, it will reject the economic system that rests on private ownership of the means of production. Exploitation of labor would lead ultimately to socialism.

The Marxist analysis of exploitation is more than purely economic. It leads into an explanation of the changing class structure, ideology, and politics of the industrial private enterprise economy. It helps to explain why that economy continues to be torn by economic and ideological conflict, in spite of economic growth, collective bargaining between unions and management, and ameliorative legislation. To a moral philosopher like Karl Marx, an economic system that uses the creative power of working people to increase the wealth of others could not long survive.

Exploitation and Alienation

The economic conditions that generate exploitation of working people also lead to a pervasive condition of alienation[3] in capitalist society. In Marx's analysis of the capitalist *economy*

---

[3]Marx adopted the term "alienation" from Protestant theology and Hegelian philosophy, where it refers to the separation of people from God, leading to feelings of isolation, powerlessness, and insignificance. Marx, however, gave the concept a materialist foundation, finding the cause of alienation in the conditions of life in capitalist society. This idea has had a powerful impact on modern sociology and psychology. Note that alienation involves both a condition of separation and the psychic effects of that condition.

there is much discussion of exploitation and little of alienation, but both spring from the same roots in the relations of capitalist production. Four relationships lie at the core of the condition.

1. The workers who provide labor power that produces goods do not own or control the means of production they use.

2. Workers must sell their labor power for a wage payment. The worker's labor power becomes the property of the capitalist enterprise.

3. The worker has no control over the product, which is the property of the capitalist enterprise.

4. The surplus value created by labor power becomes the source of increased productive power for the society as a whole, but this increased productive wealth is the property of people other than those who created it.

In brief, then, there is a physical separation, or *alienation*, of worker from tools, worker from labor power, worker from product, and worker from increased wealth. Workers have no part in deciding what to do with the product of their own lives, their labor power. The separation results from both the legal system of private property and the economic process of production and exchange: the labor power owned by workers is transformed into wealth owned by capitalists through the bargain in which labor power is exchanged for a wage payment.

Feelings of powerlessness, of loss of control over one's life, are not imaginary; they are real, rooted in the separation of worker from tools, products, and the decisions about how labor power is to be used. Nor are feelings of isolation imaginary. They originate in the impersonality of market realtionships, in which the human activity of work becomes a commodity to be impersonally bought and sold like other commodities. Through it all, workers are confronted by a world they never made, a world dominated by a capitalist class and capitalist enterprises that hold both wealth and power. Yet the ultimate irony is that this world was made by workers, for their labor power built and sustains it. Workers made the world . . . and lost it.

● **Alienation,** in Marxist theory, is the loss of control that results from separation of workers from ownership of capital, labor power, product, and the economic surplus as a result of capitalist production and exchange.

Exploitation and the Conditions of Labor

One of the misconceptions about Marxist economics held by many, including some otherwise quite respectable and competent economists, is that exploitation of labor must inevitably lead to a declining standard of living for workers. "Increasing immiseration," to use a phrase invented by Joseph Schumpeter, one of the very few informed and sophisticated critics of Marx's economics, is thought by many to be implicit in Marx's analysis of capitalism. Indeed, a line of Marxist theory that grew up after Marx's death gives great emphasis to the idea that capitalism will be destroyed in a revolution brought on very largely by the misery of the masses. This narrowed and modified version of Marx's analysis of capitalism comes out of the later writings of Friedrich Engels, Marx's friend and collaborator, and the ideas of V.I. Lenin and other Soviet writers. Western critics of Marxism have seized on this point to prove that Marx was wrong, citing both data and observation to point out that standards of living for the great bulk of the working class have risen dramatically in the years since Marx wrote, in the mid-19th century.

A more sophisticated Marxist analysis recognizes that living standards for workers, at least in some portions of the capitalist world economy, have risen as a result of imperialism, an accommodation between capital and labor, and changes within capitalism itself.

Twentieth-century Marxists recognize that real wages and standards of living for many workers have risen. They argue that the imperialist exploitation of colonies and economic dominance of less-developed areas enables capitalist enterprises at the center of the industrial world to exploit workers in peripheral areas intensively, often with the cooperation of favored elites in the colonial or economically dependent areas. Intensive exploitation of the peripheral areas allows capitalist interests at the core to maintain their profits and appropriation of surplus value while making concessions to the working class in the home country in the form of higher wages and governmental income support programs. In this view, imperialism is seen as an inevitable outcome of the worldwide spread of the capitalist process of accumulation, as well as a means by which the system maintains its viability.

Meanwhile, it is argued that within the advanced capitalist countries the conflict between labor and capital resulted in a twentieth-century accommodation between the two. Varying from one country to another, the essential elements of the accord between the contestants were:

1. Collective bargaining between labor and management to divide peacefully the gains from economic growth.

2. Government programs to maintain economic growth and high levels of economic activity.

3. Programs to shield workers from economic insecurity, such as unemployment insurance and retirement pensions.

4. Acceptance by workers of the private enterprise economy and control of the workplace by employers.

Labor got relative affluence and increased security. Capital kept control of productive wealth and the process of accumulation. An increased role of government in the economy was an essential element. In the United States these elements of twentieth-century capitalism were instituted largely during the 1930s under the New Deal. In some other countries they appeared earlier: in England and Sweden, for example, in the decade before World War I, although in England the accommodation broke down in the 1920s and was rebuilt in the 1930s. An authoritarian form of the accommodation, imposed by dictatorships using military power and supported by business interests, emerged during the years between World Wars in the fascist regimes of Italy, Japan, and Germany.

In addition, the capitalist mode of production was itself transformed in the twentieth century by fundamental innovations in technology and organization. Twentieth-century capitalism differs substantially from the capitalism of Marx's time:

1. Production, finance, and distribution are much more concentrated and dominated by monopoloid market structures.

2. Industrial technologies provide managers with greatly increased control of the work force on the job.

3. Government's role in the economy is greatly increased, particularly in welfare programs.

4. A large white-collar administrative and technically skilled group of employees has developed that is neither capitalist nor working class in its outlook and loyalties.

One result of these changes, together with the accord between capital and labor mediated by government, was a new burst of growth and prosperity for the capitalist economy after the second World War. In addition, the worldwide rivalry of capitalism with twentieth-century socialism of many varieties (USSR, China, Yugoslavia, some less-developed countries) brought reaffirmation of the capitalist ideology, united with nationalism, to strengthen the psychological appeals of the capitalist system. The authoritarian socialism of the USSR and China added to this renewal of capitalism by identifying it with political democracy.

Karl Marx, writing in the third decade of the nineteenth century, anticipated an early proletarian revolt that would displace capitalism with socialism. He confidently expected to see it in his lifetime. But the capitalist economy proved to be far more resilient than Marx thought it was. The changed capitalism of the 20th century gained new life by expanding worldwide, reaching a political and economic accommodation with the industrial working class, and renewing its ideological appeal. Nevertheless, modern capitalism retained its key element, the private accumulation of wealth out of the labor effort of millions of working people. The fundamental conflict was not eliminated. Whether the capitalist economy will continue, resolving its present difficulties, remains to be seen.

More on Marx's Economics

This brief explanation of the Marxist theory of exploitation is only an introduction and cannot do full justice to the rich and varied analysis of Marx himself. The best introduction to the ideas developed here are found in two pamphlets written by Marx for general readers, *Wage Labor and Capital* and *Value, Price and Profit* (sections 6–14). Beyond those sources, one should read Chapter 25, sections 1–4, of *Capital,* Volume 1, on "The General Law of Capitalist Accumulation." These three items, totaling about 115 pages, will prepare readers for the first volume of *Capital* itself. The first sixty pages of that book, on the theory of value, are tough going, but persist, for the remainder of the volume is enlightening.

Most of the criticism of Marx's economics by mainstream economists is either trivial or wrong, or based on misunderstandings. One major exception is Joseph Schumpeter, *Capitalism, Socialism and Democracy,* Chapters 1–4. A little-known but excellent and well balanced critique is to be found in Fred M. Gottheil, *Marx's Economic Predictions.* Although some parts of the argument are presented in the algebraic logic that modern economists love, the line of argument is clear.

One should also read two pamphlets by V.I. Lenin, *State and Revolution* and *Imperialism: The Highest Stage of Capitalism* to get the flavor of the branch of Marxism that led to authoritarian socialism in the Soviet Union. Edouard Bernstein, *Evolutionary Socialism,* written at the turn of the century, is a classic statement of Marxist democratic socialism. Finally, three important American Marxist writings since World War II deal with the issue of the survivial or demise of capitalism: Paul A. Baran and Paul M. Sweezy, *Monopoly Capital;* Harry Braverman, *Labor and Monopoly Capital;* and James O'Connor, *The Fiscal Crisis of the State.*

Summary

The Marxist theory of exploitation applies to the modern capitalist economy: Workers sell their labor power for a wage that, in the long run, equals the socially necessary subsistence of the worker. Employers use that labor power to produce goods of greater value, appropriating the surplus value for themselves.

Surplus value can be increased in the short

run by lengthening the workday, increasing the intensity of work, employing secondary workers, and driving down the wage rate. But there are limits to these devices for squeezing labor. Surplus value can also be increased by replacing workers with machines. Both methods serve to increase the rate of exploitation, but substituting capital for labor throws workers out of jobs, and the pressure of unemployment keeps wage rates down. There are three levels of exploitation: in the daily operation of business enterprise, in the impersonal functioning of labor markets, and in the transformation of labor power into capitalist wealth via surplus value.

Capitalism also generates alienation. Workers are separated, or alienated, from the tools they use, the product of their labor, the wealth they create, and their own labor power by the system of private property in the means of production.

The effects of these exploitative aspects of capitalism, although inherent in the very nature of the system, have been blunted by a number of developments since Marx's day. Labor unions, political action by workers, government programs to stabilize economic activity and shelter workers from economic insecurity, and imperialist exploitation of colonial areas gave capitalism a new burst of energy in the twentieth century. An informal economic and political accommodation between labor and capital in all of the industrialized nations prevented or delayed the conflicts inherent in exploitation and alienation from tearing the system apart.

Key Concepts

socially necessary labor time	**exploitation**
labor theory of value	**rate of surplus value**
socially necessary subsistence wage	**rate of exploitation**
surplus value	**alienation**

For Discussion

1. Even in a socialist economy, part of the output must be allocated to economic expansion, preventing workers from earning a wage equal to the full value of their output. Wouldn't this be "socialist exploitation"? Discuss.

2. Discuss: Marx's division of capitalist society into only two classes—workers and capitalists—is an oversimplification that largely invalidates his entire analysis.

3. If labor is the only source of value (and surplus value), why do business firms try to replace labor with machinery? Explain.

4. Using the Marxist analysis, how would you answer the argument that profit is a reward for risk taking?

5. Again using the Marxist analysis, how would you refute the theory of marginal productivity?

6. Imperialism provides benefits for workers as well as capitalists in industrialized countries. Explain.

Chapter 28

Poverty and Wealth

The distribution of income in the United States is partly determined by market forces that set upper and lower limits to wages and profits. Within those limits the terms on which the factors of production are rewarded are fixed by the bargaining power of capital and labor where there are formal systems of collective bargaining, or by an informal struggle between capital and labor where there are not. These two related elements, market forces and power, operate within a framework of economic institutions that also influence the distribution of income and wealth. Large enterprises and big unions with their market constraints and internal labor markets lead to favored positions for some; discrimination, crowding, and the process of skidding and bumping push others to the bottom. Finally, the process of capital accumulation brings growing wealth to those who control the means of production. Poverty and wealth are products of market forces, the structure of power, institutional constraints, and the process of capital accumulation.

The folklore of modern capitalism has it differently. Hard work and saving bring affluence, according to that economic ethic, and wealth is the reward for those who produce and invest. As the old rhyme has it, "Early to bed, early to rise, makes a man wealthy, healthy and wise." It also leads to a good credit rating, for as Poor Richard tells us, "The sound of your hammer at five in the morning makes your creditor easy one month longer." In this simplified view, one's income and wealth are due solely to one's own effort—the theory of marginal productivity is an elaborate statement of that proposition—and the poor are responsible for their own fate. You, too, can be rich if you only will.

The picture of the poor as incompetent or improvident is not borne out by modern scholarship. The poor, when they have jobs, work harder and longer hours than workers with more adequate incomes. They have to, for there are usually many other poor workers who would dearly love to take their jobs, even at the low wages paid. Moonlighting—working at two or more jobs—is more common among low-wage workers than among those earning higher wages. Nor do low-wage workers lack skills, although few acquire them in schools or training programs. Their skills are learned on the job, usually by moving from one type of employment to another. In particular, the poor learn quickly the skills required for survival on inadequate incomes. They are excellent money managers. Frivolous expenditures and impulse buying are characteristic of more affluent families, who have "discretionary income" above the amounts necessary for essential consumption. The poor cannot afford the luxury of saving. They tend to live from day to day, spending income immediately, always on the edge of disaster. Poverty is a terrible thing.

Distribution of Income in the United States

In the United States there was a noticeable shift toward greater equality in income distribution between 1929 and 1944. Since 1944 there has been little change in the pattern. Unfortunately, data for the years before 1929 are so poor and sparse that no firm statements can be made about the earlier period.

Table 28–1 shows the data on which these conclusions rest. The distribution of incomes by families and unrelated individuals is broken down by fifths, each fifth containing 20 percent of the income recipients. Thus, the lowest 20 percent of all consumer units received 3.5

percent of personal income in 1929, 4.1 percent in 1935–36, and 4.9 percent in 1944. By 1962, their share fell (not significantly) to 4.6 percent. It was 4.7 percent in 1971 and 4.3 percent in 1978. Meanwhile, the share of the highest 20 percent fell from 54.4 percent in 1929 to 51.7 percent in 1935–36 and 45.8 percent in 1944. Again, there was little change to 1962 and a slight decline to 43 percent in 1971. Between 1971 and 1978, however, there was a small but noticeable move toward greater inequality. The share of the lowest 40 percent of household fell from 15.5 to 14.6 percent of personal income, while the share of the upper 20 percent rose from 43.0 to 43.9 percent. Nevertheless, these shares had not changed much since 1944. The significant changes came during World War II.

The shift toward greater equality of income can be shown graphically by a clever device called the *Lorenz curve,* named after Max Lorenz, the statistician who invented it. It is based on a calculation of the cumulative share of income received. For example, from Table 28–1 we can see that the lowest 20 percent received 3.5 percent of personal income in 1929, the lowest 40 percent received 12.5 percent, the lowest 60 percent received 26.3 per-

Table 28–1

Percentage Distribution of Household Personal Income, Selected Years, 1929–1978

Fifths	1929	1935–1936	1944	1962	1971	1978
Lowest	3.5	4.1	4.9	4.6	4.7	4.3
Second	9.0	9.2	10.9	10.9	10.7	10.3
Third	13.8	14.1	16.2	16.3	16.9	16.9
Fourth	19.3	20.9	22.2	22.7	24.7	24.7
Highest	54.4	51.7	45.8	45.5	43.0	43.9
Total	100	100	100	100	100	100.1
Concentration ratio	0.49	0.47	0.39	0.40	0.38	0.41

Sources: For 1944 and 1962: *Survey of Current Business*, March 1955, p. 20; April 1958, p. 17; and April 1964, p. 8. For 1935–1936: Selma F. Goldsmith et al., "Size Distribution of income Since the Mid-Thirties," *Review of Economics and Statistics*, Vol. 36 (February 1954), p. 9. For 1929: Selma F. Goldsmith, "The Relation of Census Income Distribution Statistics to Other Income Data," in Conference on Research in Income and Wealth, *An Appraisal of the 1950 Census Income Data*, Studies in Income and Wealth, Vol. 23 (New York: Princeton University Press, 1958), p. 92. For 1929 Mrs. Goldsmith gives a figure (12.5 percent) for only the two lowest fifths combined; this percentage was allocated between the two fifths by Alan MacFayden and published in Edward C. Budd (ed.), *Inequality and Poverty*, (New York: W. W. Norton and Co., 1967), p. xii. For 1971 and 1978: U.S. Bureau of the Census, *Current Population Reports*, Series P-60.

Figure 28-1
Lorenz Curves for the Distribution of Family Personal Income

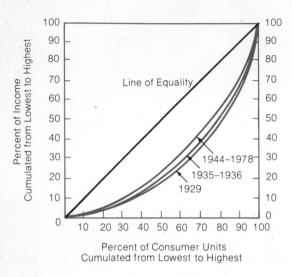

Line of Equality

1944–1978
1935–1936
1929

Percent of Income Cumulated from Lowest to Highest

Percent of Consumer Units
Cumulated from Lowest to Highest

Table 28-2
Distribution of Household Personal Income, Great Britain and India

Fifth	1952 Great Britain After Taxes (Percentage)	1950 India Before Taxes (Percentage)
Lowest	6	7.8
Second	12	9.2
Third	18	11.4
Fourth	22	16.0
Highest	40	55.4
Total	100	99.8

Sources: Harold Lydall and J. B. Lansing, "A Comparison of the Distribution of Personal Income and Wealth in the United States and Great Britain," *The American Economic Review*, March, 1959, p. 48. Simon Kuznets, "Quantitative Aspects of the Economic Growth of Nations," No. 8, "Distribution of Income by Size," *Economic Development and Cultural Change*, January 1963, p. 13.

cent, and so on, until the total of 100 percent received 100 percent of all income. These points can be plotted on a chart to show the Lorenz curve of income distribution. This has

been done in Figure 28–1 for three of the distributions in Table 28–1, those for 1929, 1935–36, and 1971. The straight line drawn diagonally across the chart shows perfect equality of income: 1 percent of the income recipients receives 1 percent of the income, 2 percent receives 2 percent of the income, and so forth. Any deviation downward shows some inequality. Perfect inequality would be shown by a line following the lower and right borders of the chart, a distribution in which 99 percent gets nothing while the richest 1 percent gets all of the income. The degree of inequality can be measured by the area between the line of equality and the actual distribution: the ratio of that area to the total area under the line of equality is called the *concentration ratio,* and is shown on the bottom line of Table 28–1. Note how the U.S. concentration ratio fell from 0.49 in 1929 to 0.39 in 1944, and remained almost exactly the same thereafter. A Lorenz curve for 1944 would be almost identical to the one for 1978.

● A **Lorenz curve** is a graphic representation of inequality in income distribution that shows the cumulative percent of total income obtained by the cumulative percent of income recipients.

International comparisons indicate that patterns of income distribution in the more advanced industrial nations are much the same as in the U.S., even though Great Britain, for example, has a somewhat more equalitarian pattern than the United States. Less developed nations typically show considerably greater *inequality,* however. There tend to be more of the very poor and the very wealthy, with a smaller "middle class." Table 28–2 illustrates these patterns for Great Britain and India.

The Growth of Affluence

Although there has been no significant change in the pattern of income distribution in the

INEQUALITY: LONG-RUN TRENDS

Scholars have begun to examine historical trends in the distribution of income and wealth in the U.S. Data on earned income (wages and salaries) is better than data on wealth, but some broad conclusions are beginning to appear:

1. Among *free* Americans during the colonial period (before 1776) the distribution of income and wealth appears to have been roughly similar to that prevailing today.

2. There was a strong trend toward increased inequality of income and wealth in the four decades before the Civil War, roughly 1820–1860.

3. After the Civil War the trend toward rising inequality stopped, although there was a growth of regional inequality as the southern states fell behind in economic development.

4. A new trend toward greater inequality set in from, roughly, the turn of the century to World War I. During World War I there was a sharp turn toward equality (in earned incomes), but the 1920s saw a move back toward the prewar growth of inequality.

5. Considerable equalization of income and wealth occurred between 1929 and perhaps 1950, with no further changes in the pattern after 1950, when a tendency toward greater inequality was overcome by the effect of taxes and government transfers.

These findings apply primarily to personal income and only secondarily to holdings of wealth. They do not take into consideration the control of wealth by large business firms and the income of governmental units. Even in the case of personal wealth the most recent study (1962) is more than 20 years old.

United States since World War II, the great era of economic growth after the war brought a general upward shift in income levels. The proportion of families living in poverty was more than cut in half between 1950 and 1970. The middle income group remained at about the same relative size, with some of the poor moving into that category while other families became affluent. The affluent group rose dramatically. In recent years, however, the trends changed. The relative economic stagnation of the 1970s stopped the decline in the proportion of families with low incomes while the proportion of families in the affluent category continued to increase.

These trends are shown in Table 28–3, which shows the distribution of family income for selected years between 1950 and 1978, corrected for changes in the price level by use of 1970 dollars. The proportion of relatively poor families (annual income below $10,000) fell from 58 to 24 percent of the total between 1950 and 1978, but the figures for 1970 and 1978 show almost no change. The affluent (annual income of $25,000 or more), however, increased from 6 percent of all families in 1956 to 28 percent in 1978, and their growth seems hardly to have been affected by the slowdown of economic growth of the 1970s.

The Persistence of Poverty

When Jacob Riis wrote *How the Other Half Lives* in 1890 he proposed an antipoverty program that has a curiously modern ring. Included were parks, settlement houses, better schools, improved law enforcement, enforcement of housing laws, building of low-cost housing, and employment programs. He demanded that affluent Americans take a hand in solving the problems of the slums through private charity. With the substitution of public programs for private charity this outline of action could substitute for the antipoverty programs of the 1960s and 1970s. Yet Riis wrote

Table 28–3
Distribution of Family Income for Selected Years, 1950–1978, in 1978 Dollars

| Family Income | Percent of Families | | | | | |
---	1950	1956	1960	1965	1970	1978
Low Income						
Below $10,000	58	45	37	31	25	24
Middle Income						
$10,000–14,999	42*	28	27	23	19	17
$15,000–24,999		21	27	31	33	31
Upper Income						
$25,000 and over		6	9	15	23	28

*$10,000 and above.

Source: U.S. Bureau of the Census, Current Population Reports, Series P-60, No. 20. Figures may not add to 100 because of rounding.

ninety years ago. In the intervening decades the average standard of living in the United States has risen dramatically. Yet the conditions pictured so vividly by Riis were reiterated by Michael Harrington's *The Other America* in 1962 and by more recent studies.

The economy has changed a great deal since the 1890s. The huge immigration from Europe of those days has largely stopped, replaced by a lesser flow from Latin America. A vast shift from rural to urban life took place, and America is now almost wholly an urban society. Within urban areas clearly definable styles of life have emerged, low-income on the one hand and affluent on the other, with clear geographical and life-style separation of the two. We have little hard data for the period before 1930, but the trend during the great prosperity after World War II suggests a great leap upward in family incomes.

Nevertheless, poverty persists. By the early 1970s the proportion of households with incomes below the minimum subsistence poverty level had been reduced to 13 percent, according to U.S. government studies. The proportion below the minimum health and decency level was 30 percent. During the 1970s these proportions remained about the same, increasing just slightly. But the number of poor increased, of course, as population grew.

Who Are the Poor?

The poor are widely distributed throughout the United States. They are found in all regions of the country, in rural and urban areas, among all races and nationality groups, in all types and sizes of family units. Poverty does tend to be concentrated, however. Some regions, like Appalachia, have a great deal of poverty. In urban regions poverty tends to center in the inner city, although there is some evidence that it, too, is becoming suburbanized. Families headed by women have a very high incidence of poverty. People with less education and people with poor health or physical disabilities tend to be poor. There is a great deal of poverty among the aged. And race matters a great deal: a far larger proportion of blacks (and some other racial minorities) are poor, compared with whites. When several of these characteristics are combined, the chances of a family's being poor are greatly increased.

The Bureau of the Census provides limited data on the racial composition of the poor: about one-third are nonwhite (over 90 percent of nonwhites in the U.S. are black). Although blacks make up about one-eighth of the population they comprise about one-third of the poor. Among the white poor are included a large number of Spanish-speaking Americans (Puerto Rican and Mexican-American). About half of all the poor in the United States are from these and other minority groups. To the extent that poverty tends to perpetuate itself from generation to generation, there will continue to be a high incidence of poverty among minority groups. For example, more than half of all nonwhite children are growing up in poverty. With a poor start in life—poor diet, poor education, limited job opportunities—a relatively large percentage of those children will remain poor all of their lives.

Lack of adequate employment opportunities is probably the chief cause of poverty. The bulk of the poor make up a large portion of the so-called "secondary" work force of low-wage and underemployed workers. In normal times some 40 percent of the heads of families below the poverty line are unemployed. Between 25 and 30 percent are employed part-time, and about one-third work at full-time jobs. Contemplate the last fact for a moment: these families are headed by full-time workers who do not earn enough to maintain their families above the poverty line. Although lack of employment is a major cause of poverty, so is full-time employment at low-wage jobs.

Much poverty is associated with families that have only one head, usually a woman. Over 40 percent of all families below the poverty line are headed by a woman, and the proportion has steadily increased in recent years. Looking at the other side of the coin, about one-third of all families headed by women have incomes below the poverty line; among blacks the proportion is over 50 percent. The major source of income for this group is public assistance. There are many reasons for the high incidence of poverty among families headed by women: women with small children tend to stay home to raise their children and do not work; when women work, their wages are relatively low compared with men's; and poor families tend to break up—desertion is the poor man's divorce court. These reasons combine to create large numbers of poor families headed by women.

Large families tend to be poor. The more children the higher is the income needed to get above the poverty threshold. It is also more difficult for the wife to work outside the household. So we find that about 30 percent of all poor families have three or more children, compared with only 17 percent of families above the poverty line.

The aged are another large group among the poor, although in this part of the population the incidence of poverty fell in recent years. The decline of death rates and the inability to compete with younger workers for jobs brought an increasingly serious problem of poverty among the aging. Only one-fourth of those over 65 are in the work force, as compared with two-thirds in 1900. In 1967 about one-third of all poor families were headed by someone over 65 years of age. By 1972, however, the proportion had fallen to a little under 19 percent, because of large increases in social security benefits, widow's benefits, and medical care programs for the aged. This is the only group in the nation for which there has been a significant reduction in poverty in recent years.

Poor health is another characteristic of the

poor. Chronic illnesses and physical disabilities bring reduced incomes, partly because they prevent a person from holding a steady job or even obtaining one. As a result, many persons with poor health are relegated to jobs in the low-wage sector of the economy. In addition, poverty is itself a cause of poor health, since it results in poor diets and poor health care and thereby brings on health problems. The U.S. Department of Labor found in a recent study that workers whose health was excellent earned about 20 percent more than those whose health was classified as fair to poor.

All of these groups of people—minorities, the unemployed or partially employed, low-wage workers, the disabled, people with poor health, the aged, and broken families, have two characteristics in common. They are poor for reasons beyond their own control. And, for a variety of reasons, many are rejected by the economic system from jobs with adequate earnings. When they come up against the test of the marketplace they are denied opportunities, produce too little, or have family responsibilities that take them out of the marketplace. They often become wards of society, subsisting on transfer payments derived from the productive effort of others.

Welfare Payments to the Poor

A great deal of hostility has developed toward the welfare recipient, who is sometimes stereotyped as a southern black woman moving to a northern city that pays relatively high benefits, getting rid of her husband to become eligible for welfare, and having illegitimate children to qualify for higher benefits. The husband, meanwhile, is pictured as lazy, a cheater living illegally on his wife's benefits, while the softhearted welfare worker looks the other way.

Most of this stereotype has been shown to be wrong. Studies indicate that there is probably less cheating among welfare recipients than, for example, among the affluent on their income tax returns. Most welfare families do not have illegitimate children, although illegitima-

cy is high among the poor. The typical welfare family does not stay on welfare indefinitely: the average period is about 1 1/2 years. About half of all welfare families are white. In the broken family, the husband usually left long before the mother went on welfare. Finally, unemployment is by far the chief reason for a family's going on welfare.

Criticism of the welfare system from the social work profession and sociological studies takes a different tack. This line of thought emphasizes the self-perpetuating nature of poverty and the way in which the welfare system worsens the problem. It perpetuates dependency. It keeps family incomes too low to permit children to grow up like others, or to allow normal family efforts of self-help. Administration of the system "shows little regard for them [recipients] as human beings, defeats their attempts to regain self-esteem and self-direction, and tends to prolong the duration of dependency," according to one study of the system in New York.[1] Another expert, Daniel Moynihan, argued that the welfare system "maintains the poverty groups in society in a position of impotent fury. Impotent because the system destroys the potential of individuals to improve themselves. Fury because it claims to be otherwise."[2] The system as a whole institutionalizes poverty. Although no one family may receive welfare payments forever, the system as a whole continues indefinitely, sustaining a group of poor families whose membership may change but whose existence persists.

If these views are correct, the welfare system in the United States must be seen in a new light. While preventing starvation and the extremes of human degradation, it preserves poverty and continues its causes from one

---

[1]Greenleigh Associates, Inc., *Report to the Moorland Commission on Welfare of the Findings of the Study of the Public Assistance Programs and Operations of the State of New York* (1964), p. 3.

[2]Daniel Moynihan, "The Crisis in Welfare," *The Public Interest,* No. 10 (Winter 1968), pp. 3–29.

generation to the next. Indeed, if we were serious about ending poverty, and welfare payments to families now on welfare were increased to levels high enough to move them above the poverty line, the total cost would be approximately doubled.

On the other hand, welfare payments are an important source of income for society's rejects. Significant reductions in welfare payments could well lead to serious social unrest, and that is not politically tolerable either. The resultant equilibrium leads to what might be called "Fusfeld's rule":

○ Welfare payments to the poor are set at that level where the resultant unrest can be held in check by the existing instruments of law and order.

Welfare Payments and Wage Rates

Welfare payments can also become a subsidy for employers of low-wage labor. Consider the case of Mary D., unmarried mother with one child and a second on the way, who is supported by welfare payments. She continues to see her "boyfriend" and they would like to marry, but can't afford it. He works at a filling station earning $3.25 an hour, equivalent to $6,500 a year for full-time employment and well below the poverty line for a family of four. If they got married the welfare payments would stop. In effect, the taxpayer is subsidizing the boyfriend's employer by providing part of the support for the broken family. Although this is only one example, it is common enough on the welfare scene. The most disturbing fact, however, is that most of the current proposals for welfare "reform" include aid for the working poor and requirements that those receiving the aid take jobs if possible. One popular proposal is to supplement the wages of the working poor with payments from government. These proposals, however useful on other grounds, would provide permanent subsidies to employers of low-wage labor and fasten that pattern permanently on the U.S. economy. As long as the taxpayer provides part of the family income through wage supplements, there is a tendency for wages to fall and for part of the burden of supporting the worker and his family to be shifted to the taxpayer.

Analyze the problems as follows: In the market for low-wage, relatively unskilled workers, demand and supply conditions determine the wage and the number of persons employed. Assume, for example, that the equilibrium wage is $2.00 per hour. Now supplement the wage by the equivalent of 20¢ per hour and make the supplement conditional on the worker holding a job. The same number of workers willing to work for a wage of $2.00 per hour will be willing to work for a wage of $1.80 per hour plus a supplement of 20¢ per hour. The same is true of any other wage rate. If the initial wage were $2.20 per hour the same number of workers would be drawn into the labor market by a wage of $2.00 plus a supplement of 20¢. In terms of the supply-demand mechanism, the supply curve for labor shifts downward by the amount of the income supplement. This shift in supply is pictured in Figure 28–2, along with the new equilibrium that results.

Normally, we would expect the income of the individual worker to go up somewhat and the wage rate to go down. If the supply of labor were perfectly elastic (a horizontal line) the wage rate would fall by the amount of the income supplement and the worker's income would not rise at all. At the other extreme a perfectly inelastic supply of labor (a vertical line) would result in no decline in the wage rate and an increase in worker income equal to the supplement. The real world is in between, like Figure 28–2, but a good bet is that the supply of low-wage labor is relatively elastic, because of high unemployment rates in that sector of the labor force and because new entrants to the labor force (young people, rural to urban migrants, immigrants) enter the labor market very heavily through the low-wage sector. If the supply curve for low-wage labor is relative-

Figure 28–2
Wage Supplements and the Wage Rate

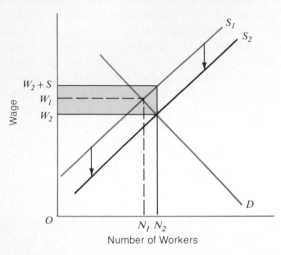

S_1 and D define the initial equilibrium, with wage W_1 and N_1 employment. The wage supplement brings a shift from S_1 to S_2, the vertical distance between the two being equal to the amount of the wage supplement. The new equilibrium brings a wage of W_2 with N_2 employed, but the return to the worker is $W_2 + S$ (wage plus supplement). The cost to the taxpayer is equal to the shaded area, while the employers' wage bill is the rectangle bounded by lines W_2 and N_2.

ly elastic, income supplements for the working poor will bring a relatively large decline in the wage rate and a relatively small increase in the income of the worker. The chief beneficiaries of the public subsidy would appear to be the employers of low-wage workers rather than the workers themselves.

The impact of income supplements on the working poor is sometimes called the "Speenhamland effect," named for a system of welfare payments to poor laborers in England in the late eighteenth and early nineteenth centuries, which caused deterioration of wage rates for the working poor. It brought intensification of poverty and was partly responsible for the degraded position of working people during the early years of industrialization. Similar effects could be expected today from a system of wage supplements that ignores the basic economics of the low-wage labor market.

The Low-Wage Worker
The working poor are full-time employees whose wages do not enable them to earn enough to get above the poverty line. There are more of them than one would suspect. About 7 percent of all employed heads of families earn less than a poverty line income even though they are employed full time throughout the year. About 30 percent of all employed single individuals (not members of a family) are in the same situation. Roughly 8,500,000 working people are in this category of the working poor.

On January 1, 1981, the federal minimum wage increased to $3.25 per hour. At that time almost 12 million workers earned the minimum wage or less (not all jobs are covered by the federal law). A quick calculation shows the annual earnings of a worker earning $3.25 an hour, assuming full-time employment of 40 hours a week for 50 weeks a year (allow for a two-week vacation):

Hours worked per year	2000
Minimum wage per hour	$3.25
Annual income ($3.25 × 2000)	$6500

Those earnings for full-time employment at the minimum wage compare with a poverty threshold income for an urban family of four in 1979 of approximately $7250. No wonder we can speak of the working poor.

Some families are able to supplement these earnings with overtime or second jobs. Others are not, and not all are able to hold jobs employing them for a full 40 hours each week. The hard fact is that the large number of low-wage jobs in our presumably affluent society causes many workers to spend their lives working for seriously inadequate wages.

A very large portion of the low-wage jobs are in service industries rather than production jobs, and there are many entire industries in which the bulk of the workers earn wages that keep them in poverty. Some of the industries in which the average wage is less than the poverty threshold income for a family of four are eating and drinking places, hotels and motels, department stores, miscellaneous retail stores, laundries and dry cleaning establishments, and portions of the furniture and clothing manufacturing industries. Hospitals are another large employer of low-wage workers.

The fact that so much low-wage employment is in service industries means that those who earn higher incomes and buy the services benefit in the form of low living costs. If the service industries paid higher wages, everyone else who bought food services, health and hospital services, laundry and dry-cleaning services, and all the others would have to pay more. Their real incomes would be reduced. This basic economic relationship helps to explain why welfare payments are kept low. If families on welfare received incomes above the poverty line there would be little incentive for others to work in low-wage, dead-end jobs. Higher wages would have to be paid in order to draw enough workers into service industries. That would mean not only higher taxes to pay for the larger welfare payments, but also lower real incomes for the taxpayers because they would be paying more for the services they use.

The existence of low wages in service industries also helps to explain why local governments are reluctant to support antipoverty programs on a large scale, why token programs are all that have been developed. Elimination of poverty on a permanent basis, with the poor actually earning an adequate income, will require turning the low-wage industries into high-wage industries. This, in turn, will raise the price of services, unless significant technological advances can be achieved. Raising the price of services will then raise costs of production in the high-wage industries that are the base of the local economy; wages in those industries will have to go up to compensate workers for the decrease in their real incomes,

and the services used directly by firms in the high-wage industries will cost more. These higher costs will create a competitive disadvantage with other localities and local economic growth will tend to slow down, to the disadvantage of many local economic interests. Just as local economic growth is hampered by high taxes, so it would be hampered by higher wages in the service industries when compared with other localities.

These economic relationships help to explain why it is to the advantage of local economic interests to have their city's poverty program come last with the least. They also help explain the strong drive to force welfare recipients to work in order to be eligible for welfare payments. Additional workers in the low-wage service industries help keep wage rates down. Finally, we must note the close relationship between the low-wage industries and the continuance of poverty. Low-wage employment builds poverty into the basic structure of the present-day American economy. This poverty will not be eradicated by simple programs that skirt the fundamental causes.

The Dynamics of Poverty

Poverty begets poverty. The conditions the poor live in perpetuate their low incomes. This proposition is true even though some individuals may move out of poverty. While that is happening others remain poor and additional people fall into poverty.

Who are the recruits? They come from a wide variety of sources. The technology of an industrial society creates some: those injured or disabled by the hazards of modern life and industrial technology; workers whose skills become obsolete because of technological change; farmers and farm workers displaced by our changing agriculture. The economics of an industrial society creates others: the aged and the young whose level of productivity is low and who are therefore not hired until labor markets become very tight. The educational system creates more: those who drop out of school or are pushed out before they have acquired the skills or credentials necessary for high-wage jobs. Racial attitudes add to the numbers of poor: minority groups are systematically excluded from high-wage jobs and crowded into low-wage employment, pushing earnings there down still more. All of these aspects of the economy tend to create the economic rejects who make up the army of the poor.

Once a family is poor the conditions under which it lives helps to keep it poor. Low incomes mean poor diets and poor housing, which lead to poor health, low productivity, and low incomes. Low incomes lead to poor education and limited educational opportunities, which lead to low skills, poor earnings, and low incomes. Low incomes limit mobility, which in turn limits opportunities and brings reduced earnings. The frustrations and buffetings of poverty lead to discouragement and apathy in many of the poor.

Poverty is characterized by a system of *circular causation with cumulative effects*. The conditions that lead to poverty tend to be perpetu-

ated by poverty itself, creating a vicious circle in which the effects of poverty cumulate to make it extremely difficult for individuals to fight their way out. The circle of causation can be visualized by Figure 28–3, which shows a highly simplified version of the complex social and economic relationships that prevail in the world of the poor.

The systematic nature of poverty and the reinforcement of the conditions of poverty help to explain why poverty persists in an affluent society. When the case is seen in this fashion, the surprising element is that many individuals are able to escape from poverty and move into higher income levels. It is a tribute to the resiliency and initiative of the human being, just as the way in which poverty becomes systematic and self-preserving is an indictment of what might otherwise be an affluent society.

Programs to Alleviate Poverty
Public policy toward poverty has passed through several stages of development. In the days of the laissez-faire state, poverty was seen

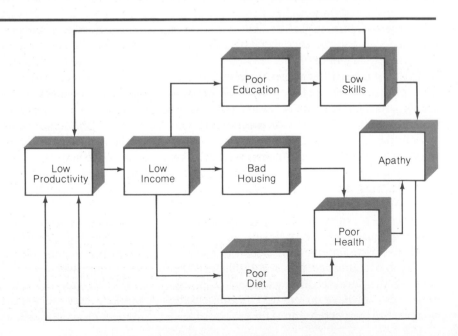

Figure 28–3
Circular Causation
with Cumulative
Effects: The Vicious
Circle
of Poverty

as the responsibility of private charity and local government. As a more positive attitude toward public responsibilities developed during the 1930s opinion shifted and the federal government began to develop programs to alleviate poverty. Chief among these efforts was the social security legislation of the mid- and late 1930s that provided help for the aged and the blind and was later extended to widows and orphans (the origins of AFDC). But whether public or private, these efforts focused on income for the poor rather than on attacking the causes of poverty.

That approach was continued after World War II, supplemented by the Keynesian proposition that full employment and economic growth would gradually move the poor upward to affluence. As the 1950s ran on into the 1960s, the limited gains from that approach became evident at about the same time that the cities exploded into violence in the mid-1960s. New approaches were made necessary by the force of events. One of the new approaches fitted neatly into the Keynesian policies that were directed toward full employment and growth. It was *investment in human capital.* Just as economists were discovering the importance of education, health, and productive skills for economic growth, they simultaneously realized that the poor were badly educated, in poor health, and had limited productive skills. In addition, some argued that the inflationary tradeoff between prices and unemployment might be reduced if the effective labor force could be increased through training programs and elimination of discrimination in employment.

The antipoverty programs of the 1960s were born out of these conditions. The underlying philosophy was that if only the poor could be changed enough, they could earn their way to affluence by themselves. The changes were to be brought about by enlarged expenditures for special programs for the poor: job training, education, health, housing, and related needs. The existing poor were to be upgraded and the

next generation was to be provided with an environment in which poverty could not flourish. And while the poor were being changed, the elimination of racial discrimination in employment, together with full employment, would provide opportunities for the deserving poor to rise. The people who discriminate would also be changed. As for regions of the country in which low incomes were common, their special problems could be met by regional development programs. This philosophy was expressed in a series of important federal legislation: the Area Redevelopment Act (1961), the Manpower Development and Training Act (1962), the Economic Opportunity Act (1964), and the Appalachian Regional Development Act (1965). These laws were supplemented by other programs in the already established education, health, and welfare agencies of the federal government, as the framework for a great antipoverty drive was put together.

The results were not encouraging. The first flaw was inadequate funding. The war in Vietnam and the military-space expenditures of the federal government took funds and resources that could have gone into a large-scale antipoverty program. The second flaw was the ineffectiveness of the programs themselves. Programs designed to upgrade the poor did not always have that effect, or they were successful in only a portion of the cases. Some of that result was expected, but public officials were unprepared for the large proportion of instances in which investment in human capital seemed to have little impact. Even if a great deal more money had been poured into the antipoverty program, it may not have been much more successful. The third was failure to strike at the roots of poverty. Even if individuals could be rehabilitated, there would be little impact on the problem as a whole if others were falling into poverty. Poverty might be reduced if more people moved up and out of poverty than fell into it, but as long as the low-wage industries remained and as long as measured unemployment rates remained above the approximately

2 percent level of frictional unemployment there would be a hard core of poverty that could not be eliminated.

The most important flaw in these programs, however, was failure to realize that poverty had become a systematic part of the nation's economic structure, built into the low-wage industries and supported by crowding of minorities into menial occupations, by ghettoization of the chief minority groups, and by the gains that accrued to the white majority. It is not enough merely to change people when a poverty-ridden sector of the economy prevails and continually reinforces itself.[3]

The Distribution of Wealth

There are few decent studies of the distribution of wealth, and there is no government agency that regularly publishes data on that topic. Good information on holdings of wealth in the United States is almost as hard to find as the facts about income distribution in the USSR. There may be a moral here. The most comprehensive recent study of wealth ownership in the U.S. was done by Robert Lampman of the University of Wisconsin.[4] It brings the data up to 1956. Sponsored by the National Bureau of Economic Research, the study found that the distribution of wealth was considerably more unequal than the distribution of income. Lampman compared the Lorenz curves of gross income of spending units in 1952 with the net worth of spending units in 1953. The striking difference is shown in Figure 28–4. The

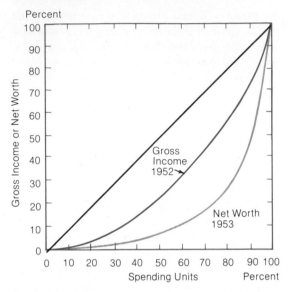

Figure 28–4
Lorenz Curves of Total Money Income and Net Worth Among Spending Units Ranked by Income and Net Worth

(*Source: 1953 Survey of Consumer Finances*, reprinted from *Federal Reserve Bulletin*, 1953. Supplementary Table 5, p. 11.)

personal wealth (net worth) of U.S. adults in 1953 was estimated at $1,120 billion. Its distribution was highly skewed in favor of the wealthy:

1. Half of the adult population at the poorer end of the distribution owned just over 8 percent of the wealth, and two-thirds owned about 18.5 percent.

2. At the other extreme, 1.6 percent of the adult population, at the wealthy end of the scale, owned 27.6 percent of the nation's personal wealth.

Table 28–4, taken from Lampman's book, summarizes the facts as he found them.

A more recent study of wealth holdings in 1962 was carried out under the auspices of the Federal Reserve's Board of Governors. It found a rapid escalation in average holdings of

[3]Three short paperback books from the late 1960s and early 1970s provide a fuller description and appraisal of the antipoverty programs. Oscar Ornati, *Poverty Amid Affluence* (New York: Twentieth Century Fund, 1966); David Hamilton, *A Primer on the Economics of Poverty* (New York: Random House, 1968); and Ben B. Seligman, *Permanent Poverty: An American Syndrome* (Chicago: Quadrangle Books, 1970).

[4]Robert J. Lampman, *The Share of Top Wealth-Holders in National Wealth: 1922–1956* (Princeton, N.J.: Princeton University Press, 1962).

Table 28–4
Estimated Distribution of Total Adult Population by Gross Estate Size, United States, 1953

Gross Estate Size (Dollars)	Number of Persons Aged 20 and Over (Millions)	Percent	Average Estate Size (Dollars)	Total Gross Estate	
				Billion Dollars	Percent
0 to 3,500	51.70	50.0	1,800	93.1	8.3
3,500 to 10,000	19.00	18.4	6,000	114.0	10.2
10,000 to 20,000	21.89	21.2	15,000	328.4	29.3
20,000 to 30,000	6.00	5.8	25,000	150.0	13.4
30,000 to 40,000	2.00	1.9	35,000	70.0	6.3
40,000 to 50,000	0.80	0.8	45,000	36.0	3.2
50,000 to 60,000	0.35	0.3	55,000	19.3	1.7
Total under 60,000	101.74	98.4	7,900	810.8	72.4
60,000 to 70,000	0.18	0.1	61,000	10.5	0.9
60,000 and over	1.66	1.6	186,265	309.2	27.6
All estate sizes	103.40	100.0	10,800	1,120.0	100.0
Median estate size			3,500		

Source: Lampman, *Share of Top Wealth-Holders,* p. 213.

wealth for individuals and families with incomes over $15,000 annually. (A $15,000 income in 1962 would have put one on the edge of the top 5 percent of income recipients.) Table 28–5 shows the figures.

The Federal Reserve study also found that at the top of the wealth pyramid:

1. About 200,000 consumer units with over $500,000 in assets owned over 22 percent of the total wealth reported.

2. The next 500,000 units, holding assets in the $200,000 to $500,000 range, had 13 percent of the wealth.

3. An additional 700,000 units with assets of $100,000 to $200,000 had 8 percent of the wealth.

Together these 1,400,000 consumer units— about 2 percent of the total—held 43 percent of the total assets held by all consumer units in 1962. These findings are somewhat different from Lampman's. The two studies used differ-

ent data and treated the data somewhat differently. They both show the same result, however—the ownership of wealth is distributed in a highly unequal pattern. A relatively small number of people hold a relatively large proportion of the fruits of economic activity.

A second proposition is that the very wealthy inherited a substantial portion of their wealth. The Federal Reserve study showed that the majority of those with high incomes and large assets were the beneficiaries of the accumulation of assets in earlier generations, while those with lower incomes and smaller asset holdings had largely made it themselves. Table 28–6 shows that wealth tends to perpetuate itself. If you haven't already got it it's hard to obtain.

Finally, those who are wealthy have the types of assets that generate more wealth, while those with lower incomes and wealth characteristically own assets that are used up rather than generating more. Assets held in the form of investments and business assets make up by far the largest portion of the assets of the

Table 28–5
Average Amount of Wealth by Income Groups, 1962

Income	Average Amount of Assets
Under $3,000	$ 7,609
$ 3,000– 4,999	10,025
5,000– 7,499	13,207
7,500– 9,999	19,131
10,000–14,999	28,019
15,000–24,999	62,965
25,000–49,999	291,317
50,000–99,999	653,223
100,000 and above	$1,698,021

Source: Dorothy Projector and Gertrude Weiss, *Survey of Financial Characteristics of Consumers,* Federal Reserve Technical Papers, August 1966, p. 110.

Table 28–6
Percent of Families with Substantial Inherited Assets, 1962

Income	Percent with Substantial Inherited Assets
$ 5,000– 7,499	4
10,000–14,999	5
15,000–24,999	6
25,000–49,999	8
50,000–99,999	14
100,000 and above	57

Source: Dorothy Projector and Gertrude Weiss, *Survey of Financial Characteristics of Consumers,* Federal Reserve Technical Papers, August 1966, p. 148

wealthy, bringing in more income that can be reinvested to add further to wealth and income. At the middle-income levels, however, a far larger proportion of assets is held in the form of houses, automobiles, and cash. Table 28–7, adapted from the 1962 Federal Reserve study, shows the difference very clearly.

Is Ownership of Wealth Becoming More Concentrated?

According to Karl Marx, one of the inherent weaknesses of capitalism was a trend toward greater concentration of wealth. Ultimately, Marx predicted, a capitalist economy would face a revolutionary situation brought about, in part, by the polarization of society into two warring camps. According to Marx, these groups would be:

1. A small number of very wealthy capitalist-financiers who would gather into their hands a growing share of the productive resources of the economy. At the same time, competition, the attrition of business cycles, and the results of technological change would make this top group smaller and smaller. Both centralization and concentration of wealth would increase over the years.

2. At the other extreme would be a growing mass of workers whose incomes and wealth would be held down by the presence of unemployment because of business cycles and technological change. Although Marx was willing to concede that the level of life of the working class might be raised, he insisted that, *relative to the wealthy,* the economic position of the worker must worsen.

The growing conflict between the dispossessed and the possessors, Marx argued, would ultimately bring on a social revolution in which the tables would turn, the majority would seize power, and a new social order would be constructed. Crucial to this analysis is the proposition that growing concentration of wealth in the hands of a few is an inherent characteristic of a private-enterprise economy. Is it? The answer is not obvious, although ideologies of left and right continually claim the truth.

Lampman's study found that inequality in ownership of wealth decreased between 1922 and 1956. In 1922, the top 1 percent of all wealth holders owned 32 percent of all personal wealth. In 1953, the proportion had fallen to 25 percent.

The change was not the result of a steady decline, however. In the prosperous, low-

Table 28–7
Asset Holdings by Income Level and Type of Asset, 1962

Income	Total Assets	Percent Held in the Form of		
		Home and Miscellaneous	Liquid Assets	Investment and Business
$10,000– 14,999	$ 28,021	41	16	43
15,000– 24,999	62,966	33	14	53
25,000– 49,999	291,317	30	7	63
50,000–100,000	653,223	9	6	85
Over $100,000	1,698,021	11	3	86

Source: Dorothy Projector and Gertrude Weiss, *Survey of Financial Characteristics of Consumers,* Federal Reserve Technical Papers, August 1966, p. 110.

income-tax twenties (1922–29), the share of the very rich in total personal wealth rose to 38 percent. The early depression years pulled their share down drastically to 30 percent by 1933, but by 1939 their share recovered to 33 percent. World War II, with its changed tax structure and artificial economic environment, brought the share of the very rich down to 26 percent in 1945 and 22 percent in 1949. Then a moderate but steady rise began to the 25 percent level in 1953. Other data cited by Lampman indicate a continuing rise to 1956. These trends are shown graphically in Figure 28–5. No one knows what the trend has been since 1956.[5] But we can make some informed guesses. Periods of consistent peacetime growth in GNP have been associated with a rising share of wealth for the very wealthy. This was true of 1922–29, 1933–38, and 1949–56. If the 1949–1956 trend is projected beyond 1956, the U.S. would have returned to the 1922 figure of 32 percent of personal wealth in the hands of the top 1 percent of wealth holders sometime in the mid-1960s.

These speculations about recent trends in ownership of wealth are partially supported by the study made by the Board of Governors of the Federal Reserve System, which reported that at the end of 1962, 22 percent of personal wealth was held by 200,000 households owning assets worth more than $500,000 each. This is less than four-tenths of 1 percent of all households. This compares with Lampman's figures for 1953 showing that 1 percent of families held 25 percent of personal wealth. While the Lampman and Federal Reserve studies are not strictly comparable, together they suggest that the trend toward greater concentration of wealth has continued in recent years, but at a rather slow pace.

Economic factors affecting the concentration of wealth seem to work both toward and against an increased share for the very wealthy. Most of their assets, such as bonds, common stock, and real estate, produce income. As the economy grows, the earning power of these assets also grows, creating capital gains for their owners. The rest of us hold assets primarily in the form of durable consumer goods: automobiles, houses, and their furnishings, and the like. These assets often are used up over the lifetime of the family and require replacement or maintenance instead of producing income. The assets of the rich usually add to their wealth, while

---

[5]A critique of Lampman's findings found his estimates a little low and confirmed the post-World War II increase in concentration of wealth through 1958. See James D. Smith and Staunton K. Calvert, "Estimating the Wealth of Top Wealth Holders from Estate Tax Returns," in American Statistical Association, *Proceedings of the Business and Economic Statistics Section* (Washington, D.C.: American Statistical Association, 1965), pp. 248–265.

Figure 28-5
Share of Top 1 Percent of Wealth Holders
in Total Personal Wealth, U.S., 1922–1956

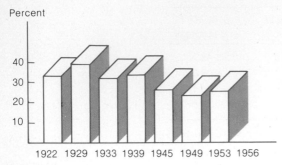

(*Source:* Lampman, *Share of Top Wealth Holders*, p. 202.)

the assets of the middle-class family usually do not. As a result, the rich tend to become richer as their wealth begets greater wealth.

On the other hand, middle-income families add to their wealth by saving from their incomes to a greater extent than the wealthy do. This pattern counters the tendency for the growing wealth of an affluent society to concentrate itself in the hands of those who are already rich. As the total amount of wealth in the economy increases, both groups seem to move ahead at somewhat similar rates. The only ones left behind appear to be the poor, who have neither earning assets nor incomes large enough to generate significant amounts of savings.

The wealthy, however, with a large portion of their assets held as investments, benefit very substantially from rising prices of securities during periods of prosperity with stable prices. But inflation tends to bring down the value of already existing productive assets, for interest rates rise faster than profits, and that keeps the value of securities from rising when prices go up, to the detriment of the wealthy. We would have expected, then, that the wealthy would benefit from the rising stock market, economic

growth, and relatively stable prices of 1945–1965, and that the concentration of wealth would increase in that period. Conversely, we would have expected a change in the late 1960s and early 1970s, when the stock market did not move up consistently and high and rising interest rates prevailed. The logic of the situation would lead us to expect a slower rate of increase in the concentration of wealth in recent years, and perhaps even a decline. Unfortunately there is no data to tell us whether that is correct.

The Great Fortunes

The great accumulations of wealth are not the result of a careful process of saving and investment to increase one's assets. Accumulation in that manner would require many generations to build the sort of fortune that characterizes the holders of great wealth. For example, $10,000 of savings (a large amount for most American families) invested at 8 percent requires thirty years to become $100,000 and sixty years to become $1 million. That's two to three generations. With taxes the time period would be even longer, depending on the tax rate. If health problems arise over the family's life cycle (the typical family has at least one major health emergency costly enough to wipe out the family's savings) no accumulation at all may be possible.

The great fortunes were accumulated much more rapidly, usually within one generation. Classic examples are Cornelius Vanderbilt, John D. Rockefeller, Andrew Carnegie, Edward H. Harriman, and Henry Ford, from an earlier period, and, more recently, John Paul Getty, Howard Hughes, Edwin H. Land, N. Bunker Hunt, Howard Ahmanson, Sherman Fairchild, and others. These fortunes did not arise from a slow process of accumulation based on savings out of income, although a number got a strong start from relatively modest inheritances.

The great fortunes appeared during the rapid growth periods of the long waves in economic activity described in Chapter 4. They developed out of the innovative industries that clustered in the early years of those economic expansions. A relatively small investment in a successful enterprise in one of the rapidly growing industries could generate huge capital gains for the successful entrepreneur and the lucky investors who provided the initial capital. "Getting in on the ground floor," as the saying goes in Wall Street, is the requisite for great wealth—provided the enterprise is in a leading sector at the start of a long period of strong economic growth and is able to succeed and grow. Thus, we are not surprised that a number of new great fortunes developed in the 1945–1965 era of rapid growth, and few, if any, in the period of economic doldrums that followed.

Luck has a great deal to do with the great fortunes. Being there at the right time and place at the right age is most important. Being able to take advantage of the opportunity is also important—for the entrepreneur, but not necessarily for the investor. For example, a number of large fortunes originated among the early investors in Ford Motor Company, even though Henry Ford forced them out of the enterprise just before the really huge gains were made. But those investors did not have to be extraordinarily able; all they had to do was guess correctly. Other investors in other automobile firms at the time were probably just as capable and took just as large a risk, but they happened to bet on the losing horse rather than the winner.

The case of the entrepreneurs is a bit different. They also had to be in the right place at the right time. The U.S. economy in 1945–1950 was a much better environment for generating great fortunes than the same economy in 1930–35 or 1965–70. The entrepreneur also has to have a gambler's instincts, going for the really big gains against very large odds, rather than being satisfied with lesser gains at lower risks. Ability to manage, plan, and execute is also important. These are all personal qualities that

enable successful entrepreneurs to become winners, but whether they contribute significantly to the real growth of the economy is doubtful. The American railroad network would have been built without Vanderbilt, the steel industry without Carnegie, the automobile industry without Ford. The structure of those industries may have been different, but the larger economic development had other sources than those entrepreneurs.

To give a recent example, the savings and loan business in California grew as a result of economic expansion and prosperity after World War II, population growth and shifts, tax incentives for home ownership, and federal credit programs to finance buying of houses. Within that industry Howard Ahmanson built the largest savings and loan association in the country in California from very small beginnings, as well as a great fortune for himself and his heirs. But it is highly doubtful that the state of California has even one more house, or one less, as the result of Ahmanson's efforts.

The mythology, of course, has it that you are better off because Henry Ford became extremely wealthy. A closer look at the situation seems to indicate that, while Ford may have been very smart, he was also very lucky, and that you are better off because of the forces of economic development and change over which Ford had no control and which also enabled Ford to accumulate his wealth.

Inherited Wealth and Unearned Income

Very little is known about the significance of inheritance as the basis for large incomes and great wealth. Surveys of people with high incomes indicate that only about 20 percent of their assets can be attributed to inheritances and their appreciation in value. When people with large assets are surveyed, however, the importance of inheritance turns out to be much greater.[6] Where sociologists have studied the sources of large accumulations of wealth in the United States they have found that

> Nearly all the current large incomes . . . are derived in fact from *old* property accumulations by inheritors.[7]

One study of the very rich found that inheritance was an increasingly important source of wealth. Of the very rich in 1950, 68 percent came from upper-income families and 62 percent had relatives among the very rich of earlier generations. A quarter of a century earlier (1925), 56 percent of the very rich came from upper-income families and only 33 percent had very rich relatives from the previous generation. As for the very rich in 1900, only 39 percent were children of upper-income parents, and 34 percent were known to have inherited fortunes of at least half a million dollars.[8] Apparently it is becoming easier, not more difficult, to transfer wealth from one generation to the next.

Unearned Income

The income provided by inherited wealth is the clearest example of *unearned income* that there is. The individual who receives it does so only because of the accident of birth. Even if he devotes his energies to the management of his assets and busies himself with increasing his wealth, any income above a manager's salary is unearned. A paid manager could do the job equally well and perhaps better. Where assets

of the wealthy are managed by others all of the net income is unearned.

We could put it another way. Even if we were to assume that a bloc of wealth should be held together as an investment, and managed to maximize its earning power after the death of its owner, the maximum amount of resources society needs to pay for that task is the salary of the manager. Any payment above that amount is unearned income for the owner. The benefit derived by the economy as a whole from the use of the capital would be there in any case, whether or not payment is made to the inheritor.

- **Earned income** is received in payment for productive services, such as wages—or royalties to authors of economics textbooks.

- **Unearned income** is received even though no productive service is performed. The dividing line between the two is sometimes blurred.

Passive Wealth

The organization and management of American business enterprise shows a massive dissociation of wealth from active management. We have already noted the large-scale separation of ownership and control in the large corporation that leaves management decisions in the hands of a well-paid bureaucracy. It is the top levels of the business hierarchy that make the decisions determining the growth patterns, production and marketing strategies, and immediate business tactics pursued by large firms. Stockholders have little direct impact on those decisions.

Business decisions are influenced, however, by what happens in financial markets. If poor decisions are made, profits and growth will be poor, the price of the company's stock will reflect the poor showing, and it will be difficult for the firm to attract capital and other resources. In these circumstances the financial managers who make decisions for holders of large wealth will direct their funds toward the more successful firms and away from the less

---

[6]Robin Barlow, Harvey E. Brazer, and James N. Morgan, *Economic Behavior of the Affluent* (Washington, D.C.: The Brookings Institution, 1966), pp. 87–91.

[7]Ferdinand Lundberg, *The Rich and the Super-Rich* (New York: Lyle Stuart, Inc., 1968), p. 132. Lundberg states his case in a florid, muckraking style, but it is hard to argue with his facts. Other scholarly studies bear out Lundberg's conclusion. See E. Digby Baltzell, *An American Business Aristocracy* (Glencoe, Ill.: The Free Press, 1958), and *The Protestant Establishment: Aristocracy and Caste in America* (New York: Random House, 1964); and G. William Domhoff, *Who Rules America?* (Englewood Cliffs, N.J.: Prentice-Hall, 1967).

[8]C. Wright Mills, *The Power Elite* (New York: Oxford University Press, 1956), p. 107.

successful, which is exactly what happens in the money markets anyway.

Perhaps an illustration of what we might do, but don't, will make the point clear. Let us suppose that the United States had taxes that prevented the inheritance of more than $50,000. Mrs. Gotrocks, a wealthy widow, dies and leaves an estate of $50 million, of which all but $50,000 must be paid to the government in taxes. Such an estate will have been invested in a wide variety of assets, such as stocks and bonds, real estate, and so on, which will have to be sold in order to pay the taxes. Sale on the open market will put those assets into the hands of investors of all kinds, individuals as well as corporations, who will continue to manage their investments just as well or as badly as they did before. The real assets whose ownership has been sold continue producing as before, since only their ownership has shifted. Output in the economy has not changed one bit. The real cost to the economy of dispersing the Gotrocks fortune was zero. In this sense the income from inherited wealth is essentially passive. It does not contribute in any significant way to the overall growth of the economy, nor do those who own it significantly influence the decision-making process. The wealth is passive and the income unearned.

The economic analysis of inheritance does not stop here, however. Would these capital assets have been accumulated in the first place if there was no way to pass on the benefits to an heir? Does not the desire to leave a legacy provide incentives for saving that help to promote economic growth? Beyond that, are there not other beneficial economic functions performed by inheritance of wealth?

The Economic Functions of Inheritance

Inheritance of privately owned wealth antedates the development of the modern market economy by thousands of years. Our present patterns of inheritance were taken over from a feudal society dominated by a landed nobility, in which peasant households within manorial villages were the basic economic units. Inheritance performed two very important functions in that type of economic organization:

1. It assured the continuity of a decision-making, governing elite from one generation to the next.

2. It provided for the continuity of viable manors and household units from one generation to the next.

When urban-centered trade and handicraft production developed in the later medieval and early modern period, inheritance played a similar role. It enabled merchant enterprises and handicraft shops to survive as producing and managerial units even though the individual owners might retire or die. In the political sphere it provided for continuity of the national state through succession of rulers by means of family inheritance. It was in this environment that our present law of inheritance was developed. Although much of the detail has changed, the basic legal concepts have remained. Yet the economic (and political) environment has changed. The modern corporation developed as the chief instrument for preserving the continuity of enterprises over time. Although ownership may change as stock changes hands, and although management may change through retirements and promotions, the corporation continues as an economic unit. Merit and personnel development programs have in large part replaced inheritance as the chief source of continuity of management. Securities markets have largely replaced inheritance in creating continuity by providing for a continuous organization in spite of the continuous changing of owners. Where those developments have been held back in some family-controlled corporations, the dominant owners have usually been replaced by professional corporate executives in the making of business decisions. Something similar has happened in the political structure. Political constitutions, both formal and informal, provide for continuity of political units, selection of leadership and administrative cadres, and transfer of power from one generation to the next. The functions of inheritance are now performed better by other economic and social institutions.

Inheritance, however, could perform other functions in a market-oriented economy. It could provide significant incentives for individuals to save and accumulate wealth to pass on to their children, thereby promoting economic growth and expansion. Inherited wealth may also be an important source of savings that promote further economic growth. These are familiar arguments; but they come primarily from those who have wealth to pass on, from those who have received it recently, or from their spokesmen. Such arguments must necessarily be examined for empirical content.

The evidence on these points is scanty, at best. But it tends to show that the motive to pass on wealth to future generations accounts for an insignificant amount of the economy's savings, and that those who hold inherited wealth tend to save less than their share of wealth would imply. The second point can be disposed of first. We have already cited the fact that the very wealthy save proportionately less of their income than middle-income groups do. Lampman found that the top 1 percent of holders of wealth, with some 22–25 percent of all personal wealth in the mid-1950s, were responsible for about 15 percent of personal savings. These figures suggest that a redistribution of wealth away from the top 1 percent of wealth holders would tend to increase total savings.

The argument is as follows: if 75 percent of the wealth (99 percent of all families) does 85 percent of the saving, while 25 percent of the wealth (1 percent of all families) does 15 percent of the saving, and if holding of wealth is functionally related to savings, then a shift of wealth to the top 1 percent will reduce total savings and a shift away from that group will increase total savings. This is, of course, a logical proposition that could be verified only

by trying it out and measuring the results. But the logical deduction from Lampman's data is that concentration of ownership of wealth, as it now exists in the United States, does not contribute significantly to total savings.

But what about the desire to leave a legacy? Is that an important motive for saving? To answer that question we can turn to the so-called "life cycle" analysis of savings.

Savings and the Family Life Cycle
The pattern of savings in a family changes as changes take place in the age and size of the family, and the economic situation in which it finds itself. A young family will tend to live beyond its current income in the early years, partly because its income is relatively low, partly because it must invest in housing and other durable goods at an initially large cost, and partly because the size of the family and its expenses increase as children are born. Debts appear and increase at this stage, or parents may provide financial assistance. As family income grows and equipment expenditures diminish, income moves up relative to spending, and debts are reduced. As debts disappear, positive net savings start to accumulate. At the next stage, children complete their schooling, become economically independent, and move out on their own. The family's expenses fall and net savings grow as the parents start to prepare for retirement. Finally, after retirement the family's earned income usually drops precipitately and past savings are drawn upon quite heavily to sustain the level of living the couple would like to maintain. Ideally, savings would provide maximum utility if they fell to zero at the moment the last of the family unit died, leaving nothing for inheritance. According to this analysis, the life cycle of family savings would resemble Figure 28–6. There is not much room in the family's life cycle for saving to build up a legacy. By the time children are educated and on their own the parents are looking ahead to retirement. When retirement comes, there is not enough income to

Figure 28-6
Life Cycle of Family Savings

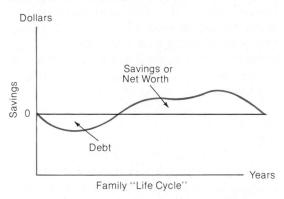

(*Source:* Adapted from James Tobin, "Life Cycle Saving and Balanced Growth" in *Ten Economic Studies in the Tradition of Irving Fisher* (New York: John Wiley and Sons, 1967), p. 241.)

make much saving possible, particularly since patterns of spending and the style of life have been established for some time. For these reasons, the *life cycle analysis of savings* deliberately omits the desire to leave an estate to heirs as a significant element in savings behavior. Instead, it stresses such factors as age, family income, size of family, current spending needs, and provision for old age. Empirical studies based on this approach are highly consistent with the theory. That point is important: if significant factors influencing saving were not included in the theoretical analysis, the observed behavior would differ from the behavior predicted by the theory. The absence of divergence indicates that the desire to leave a legacy is not an important motive for saving. Other evidence supports that conclusion. The Brookings Institution study of affluent Americans, cited earlier in this chapter, found the following reasons for saving among people with incomes over $10,000 per year in 1963:

1. Half said that they saved to accumulate funds for retirement years.

2. One-third saved "for a rainy day," to meet emergencies.

3. Some saved without any ultimate purpose in mind, which might be called the "pack-rat syndrome."

4. A few said they were unable to save it all.

5. A significant group said that they saved in order to leave a bequest. This motive was weakest among the lower range of incomes but grew stronger as incomes rose, presumably because the other, more important motives for saving could be readily satisfied by past savings or out of current income.[9]

- The **life cycle analysis of savings** is based on the assumption that the family needs to maximize its benefits over the life of the family, leading to a changing pattern of saving/spending behavior at different stages of the family life cycle.

Other survey data support these findings: people save, or try to save, primarily to meet emergencies such as illness or unemployment, for retirement or burial expenses, and for education of their children.[10]

It is difficult to escape the conclusion that the desire to leave a legacy to one's children is the least important motive for saving and the one least likely to be missed. On the other hand, some saving is done for that reason. It is done, however, primarily by those with high incomes (over $100,000 annually), and represents a relatively small proportion of total savings. We have already seen that, proportional to their wealth, the very rich save less than the rest of us. The savings on which we rely for economic growth and expansion come instead from the

---

[9]Barlow et al., *Economic Behavior of the Affluent,* pp. 31–33. Some of the very, very wealthy must save because it is impossible to spend their income as fast as it is generated. There is a perhaps apocryphal story about John Paul Getty, the oil multimillionaire, to the effect that he once attempted to give a very lavish party that cost more than the income his assets earned while the party was in progress—and failed!

[10]George Katona, Charles Lininger, and Eva Mueller, *1964 Survey of Consumer Finances* (Ann Arbor, Mich.: Institute for Social Research, The University of Michigan, 1965), pp. 111–112.

voluntary and contractual savings of the far more numerous middle-income groups and business firms, and from the two together through the taxes they pay. Although we do not usually consider the latter to be savings, a part of government revenues is directed toward investment in human capital (education, health, and so on) and in an economic sense represents part of society's savings.

Estate and Gift Taxes

Most industrial nations impose *transfer taxes* on wealth passed from one generation to the next.[11] The United States is no exception. The federal estate tax was introduced in 1916, during World War I, and gift taxes appeared in 1924–25 to prevent evasion of estate taxes. All states except Nevada also levy death duties of some kind.[12]

- A **transfer tax** is a tax levied on wealth passed from one generation to the next including gift and estate taxes.

In 1981, under the Reagan administration, U.S. estate and gift taxes were sharply revised to greatly facilitate the transfer of large accumulations of wealth to future generations. The amount exempted from taxation was raised from about $176,000 to $225,000 in 1982 and in further steps to $600,000 in 1987 and after. The

maximum tax rate on taxable transfers above $5 million was reduced in annual steps from 70 percent (1981) to 50 percent (1985). Tax-free transfers from a deceased spouse to widow or widower were allowed. Together with the existing forest of exemptions and exclusions, these changes, in effect, abolished transfer taxes on all but the very largest of the great fortunes.

There has been only one decent study of the impact of the estate and gift tax on the distribution of wealth in the United States.[13] It showed that it has had little impact on incentives to work and save, and that it checks the tendency of economic inequality to increase. It induces splitting of fortunes within families and promotes the establishment of trusts that tie up property for long periods of time. It also induces the wealthy to put property into tax-exempt foundations and trust funds.

The most obvious characteristic of our inheritance laws is their complexity. The possibilities of reducing estate and gift taxes are so many and varied that armies of lawyers and accountants are kept busy minimizing the effect of estate taxes on the estates of the wealthy. It is safe to say that no area of the tax system offers more ways of legally avoiding tax liability than the state and federal estate and gift taxes. They could have a far greater impact on the concentration of wealth than they now have. Estate and gift taxes have not been used to eliminate the unearned income derived from large holdings of wealth.

Other Types of Unearned Income

The income from inherited wealth is not the only form of unearned income in the American economy. Here are some other types of income that are received without the performance of some economically useful function:

---

[11]The popular term "inheritance taxes" is used by most people in referring to taxes on wealth transfers between generations. The more general term is "taxes on intergenerational transfers of wealth"; the category has several subdivisions: estate taxes levied on the estate of someone who dies; gift taxes levied on gifts, when both the giver and the recipient are still living; inheritance taxes paid by an heir on that portion of an estate he receives. The U.S. tax system includes only estate and gift taxes. They are the ones people refer to when they use the popular term "inheritance taxes."

[12]A few states had death duties even before the federal tax. Others started levying estate taxes in the 1920s. Some states sought to become tax havens for the wealthy by providing immunity against estate and gift taxes. This favored treatment was halted by amending the federal estate tax law to allow estates a credit against the federal estate tax equal to 80 percent of state estate taxes. Since the states could now levy transfer taxes without increasing significantly the liability of their residents, they passed death duties of various kinds, and the interstate competition for wealthy residents suddenly ceased.

---

[13]John A. Brittain, *Inheritance and the Inequality of Wealth* (Washington, D.C.: The Brookings Institution, 1978).

1. Capital gains of some types. The value of many assets goes up because of economic growth in the economy as a whole or in an individual industry. Is this increase earned? For example, the owner of well-located real estate in a growing city discovers that the value of his or her property rises because of rising population and more intensive use of land. This growing wealth is the result of other people's efforts.

2. Income from speculation. Prices of securities and commodities can fluctuate widely, enabling speculators to profit by buying at the low point and selling at the high. When this is done an economic function is performed: prices tend to stabilize. But what about the speculative manipulator or the person with inside information? The first tries to manipulate prices up or down. Our securities laws make these practices illegal, and some of the more flagrant abuses have actually been found out and the perpetrators punished. The insider problem is more insidious. A corporation director may know that his firm is negotiating a large contract with a supplier that will greatly strengthen the supplier's business position. A strategic purchase of the supplier's stock can bring large and rapid "capital gains." Who earned them? Both inside information and manipulation of securities markets contributed significantly to the building of numerous family fortunes in the past.

3. "Windfall" gains. These are unanticipated gains that result from chance or luck. For example: you are a farmer in West Virginia on whose lands a horticulturist discovers a tree bearing a new kind of apple that turns out to be the Golden Delicious. That actually happened. Or oil is discovered on your farm near Tulsa in 1905. That happened, too. The windfall tax on oil attempts to capture for the government a portion of the windfall gains present in the production of crude oil.

4. Monopolistic profits. Gains derived from monopoly are dysfunctional: they harm the economy rather than help. Yet in many sectors of the economy they are widely prevalent. Since monopoly has already been discussed at length, we only mention monopoly profits here. Some of today's very large fortunes, like the Rockefellers', owe much to monopoly.

All of these sources of income have the same basic character. They are over and above the payments that need to be made for useful products and services. No necessary function is performed by the recipients of these payments, in contrast to earned incomes paid in the form of wages and salaries.

Unearned income has another characteristic: it can be very large. Many large American fortunes have had their origins in capital gains from land values, speculative manipulation of securities markets, and monopoly. Our present laws, regulations, and tax structure were not always present, and in earlier periods of greater latitude in business behavior a good case could be made for the proposition that the largest rewards went to those whose behavior was most antisocial. Many of these large accumulations of wealth are still with us, institutionalized in the form of family holdings, trusts, and foundations, and help to explain the present pattern of the distribution of wealth.

Wealth and Economic Power

Wealth brings power. As the motto of the Medici family of Renaissance Florence put it, "money to get power; power to protect the money." Those among us who have large economic resources are able to maintain a larger control over events and the actions of others than people who have fewer resources.

This enlarged control can be achieved in a variety of ways:

1. Since consumer spending helps to determine the allocation of resources, wealth becomes votes in the marketplace to direct resources toward uses desired by the wealthy.

2. Political campaigns are costly. Contributions from the wealthy can be and are used to influence selection of candidates for office and the issues that candidates develop.

3. Use of the media of communication is costly. Wealth can be and is used to influence newspapers, television, and other media through ownership, which provides direct control of editorial policy, or through advertising and purchase of broadcast time.

4. Gifts by wealthy persons to educational institutions, charities, community funds, and other organizations can be and are used to influence the policies of those institutions.

5. Foundations established and controlled by the wealthy can be and are used to influence the policies followed by recipients of grants.

6. The ability of wealthy individuals to make gifts and bequests gives them power over potential recipients, particularly their children and other close relatives.

These are some of the more obvious ways in which wealth can be used to achieve power. Almost everyone can add other ways, or give specific examples, from his own experience.[14]

Unfortunately, empirical studies of just how much power is derived from wealth, and in what kinds of situations, are largely lacking. These are not issues on which statistics are easily collected, or even on which good case studies can readily be developed. Nevertheless, the status of inherited wealth is clear. It performs little or no function in the economy as a whole, whether it be promoting economic growth or maintaining prosperity or improving the efficiency of the economy. Yet to the extent that inherited wealth brings power to those who hold it, it runs counter to the basic precepts of a society that places high values on dispersal of power and equality of treatment among individuals. Those goals are hard enough to achieve without the additional impediment provided by inherited wealth.

In a broader context, the relationship between wealth and power is the strongest argument for greater dispersal of wealth through more effective transfer (inheritance) taxes. To the extent that wealth begets power, and power is used to strengthen and increase holdings of wealth, a nonfunctional and noneconomic relationship affects the way in which the rewards of economic activity are divided in the long run. A society that places high value on economic justice, even if justice is defined in marginal productivity terms of rewards commensurate with contribution to society, should not tolerate the patterns of distribution of wealth characteristic of modern America.

We must recognize, however, that these are value judgments about holdings of wealth, the nature of the good society, and the locus of power. As we all know, those who have received large inheritances can think of many reasons why their unearned wealth is proper, and they can probably find an economist somewhere who will develop an elaborate mathematical analysis to support their case. The whole topic is a wonderful illustration of the proposition that science (economics in this instance) can help us analyze a problem, but that answers to the large and important questions force us to go beyond science if the answers are to be meaningful.

---

[14]Cartoon in the *Wall Street Journal:* an investment counselor to his client, "My job is to increase your capital. You will have to convert it into power yourself."

Redistribution of Income

Income distribution in an economy organized in a system of markets is not wholly determined by market forces. In present-day America such other factors as the structure and organization of power, institutional patterns, the distribution of wealth, and chance also have an impact. We have no way of measuring the relative importance of any of these factors, but one point can be made: many of them can be affected by social policy.

Some examples will illustrate the point. The pattern of income distribution in France as it existed prior to the French Revolution, or in Russia before the Russian Revolution, was sharply changed after those revolutions. In France the locus of power shifted, in large part, from a landed, hereditary aristocracy to a business-oriented middle class. The distribution of income and wealth soon reflected the shift in economic and political power. In Russia, power shifted into the hands of a militant political revolutionary group with a Marxist ideology, and the new structure of power quickly influenced the distribution of economic assets and benefits.

Closer to home, U.S. tax laws help to structure the pattern of income distribution, with such provisions as those concerning rapid depreciation of real estate and tax exemptions for income from state and local government bonds. Although any individual can legally take advantage of them, only some are in a position to do so. They help to create a pattern of income distribution that affects the whole economy. And these tax provisions are clearly the result of a political process that rests on the existing structure of political and economic power. In a differently organized economy they might be entirely absent, and as the economic order changes, these tax provisions will change also.

These considerations lead inevitably into questions of social policy. What would be the economic effects of income redistribution? Would the economy as a whole be better or worse off if income were distributed more equally or less equally? How would redistribution of income affect economic welfare? economic growth? Suppose we were to move from our present pattern, by one means or another; in which direction should we move, toward greater equality or greater inequality?

Income Distribution and Economic Welfare

A more egalitarian distribution of income will probably increase net economic welfare. This basic proposition has emerged from the long and sometimes acrimonious debate on this issue that has gone on among economists over the last half century. Like all general principles, it must be hedged by some important qualifications, and standing by itself it does not carry the argument for the advocates of egalitarianism, but it is nevertheless an important starting point in any discussion of the economics of income distribution.

● A technically correct statement of the proposition, which we can term the **egalitarian rule,** would have to be put this way: If we can assume that the satisfactions derived from income are similar between individuals, an equal distribution is most likely to maximize the welfare derived from any given level of income.

To put it in more homely language, if a dollar is taken from the rich and given to the poor it is more likely that total welfare will be increased than decreased. This proposition rests heavily on the principle of diminishing marginal utility, which can be applied to income just as well as it can be applied to products and services. When an individual obtains a greater income his utility is increased, but the increases in utility diminish in size as incomes go up. This follows from the proposition that an individual will satisfy his most urgent wants first, leaving his less urgent wants for satisfaction later.[15]

The egalitarian rule can be demonstrated by analyzing an economy composed of two groups of individuals, *A* and *B*. The individuals in group *A* have different schedules of the marginal utility of income than those in group *B*. That is, there are different capacities to enjoy (obtain satisfactions from) income. One hundred percent of total income is to be distributed. In Figure 28–7 we compare two individuals, one from each group. Curve *AA* shows the marginal utility, measured vertically, of different amounts of income (measured from the left axis) for Mr. *A*. Curve *BB* is a similar curve for Mr. *B*, but is measured from the right axis. The proportions in which the income can be divided are shown on the horizontal axis. The curves have been drawn so that Mr. *B*'s curve is higher than Mr. *A*'s. If income were distributed in such a way as to maximize welfare, it would be at those levels at which the marginal utilities were equal, or 30 for *A* and 70 for *B*. (You should review the reason for that statement.) But no one knows the location of *AA* and *BB*. For all we know, they might be just the opposite. If that were the case the result would be the 70/30 line on the other side of the diagram, where the marginal utility for one would be much greater than for the other. Since we don't know which person is which we are likely to make as many mistakes as correct decisions.

Now consider an equal, or 50/50, income distribution between the two. Marginal utility

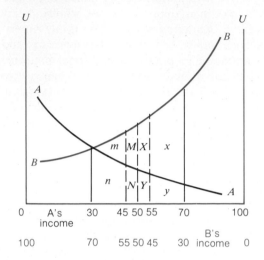

Figure 28–7
Marginal Utility: Two Incomes

will still differ between *A* and *B*. If we move to greater inequality, say 45 for *A* and 55 for *B*, total utility will be increased. *B* will gain *M* + *N*, while *A* will lose only *N*. The net gain is equal to *M*.

But hold on. We don't know where those curves are located. Suppose the move were in the opposite direction, to 55 for *A* and 45 for *B*. Then there would be a net loss of utility. *B* would lose *X* + *Y* and *A* would gain only *Y*, for a net loss of *X*.

Since the likelihood of a net gain is the same as the likelihood of a net loss (we have no way of knowing where an individual's utility curve is located), it would appear that the losses would balance the gains. That is true of numbers, but not for utility. For each pair that balance—loss against gain and gain against loss—the net loss is greater than net gain. That is shown in Figure 28–7 where *X* (the net loss) is larger than *M* (the net gain). Even though the probability of a gain is equal to the probability of a loss, the size of the probable loss is greater than the size of the probable gain. In an

---

[15]There are two exceptions to the rule of diminishing marginal utility of income. First, experience with large incomes may educate one in the enjoyment of luxuries. Taking a dollar from an experienced wealthy spender and giving it to a *nouveau riche* may not increase total welfare. Second, expenditures may be complementary and the utilities more than additive. For example, a successful man may buy a sports car and then get himself a mistress, which he might not be able to do without the sports car, and the combined utilities may be greater than if the two were separable. These exceptions, however, mean only that a shift to greater equality of income should be accomplished gradually so that the poor can learn how to spend money effectively, and that it should be substantial and widespread so that the general benefits overcome the relatively few special cases.

economy with a very large number of *A*s and *B*s we can expect an equal number of gains and losses, but each loss will be greater than each gain, adding up to a net loss in total utility for each step we take toward a less equal income distribution. This exercise shows that if we start from an equal distribution and move toward an unequal one, the likely losses in utility will be larger than the gains. It would be better to stay with the equal distribution.

Now work it out in the other direction. Start with a 70/30 distribution of income and move to a 45/55 distribution. In that case the *B*s will lose *m* + *n* and gain *x* + *y,* which is larger. The *A*s will lose *y* and gain *n,* and the gains here are greater than the losses. Moving to a 50/50 distribution will increase the net gains still more.

The conclusion is inescapable. If we wish to achieve the income distribution most likely to maximize the utility derived from a society's current income (or output), the income (or output) should be divided on an egalitarian basis. This proposition is subject to two qualifications, one theoretical and one practical.

First, it assumes that satisfactions are comparable between individuals, that is, that the benefits or utility derived by Mr. White from the uses to which he puts his income are qualitatively similar to those obtained by Mr. Black from the use of his income. Utility is utility, irrespective of the person who obtains it. This is clearly an assumption, for there is no way of proving scientifically that it is either true or untrue. But this common-sense assumption is one that most people would be willing to make.

Consider the counterassumption, that *A*'s utility is qualitatively different from *B*'s. This is also a proposition that cannot be proven. More important, it implies that the psychological makeup of each person is qualitatively different from that of all other individuals. While there may be some who are willing to support such an extreme view of human individuality, it is not consistent with the regularities in human behavior documented by the findings of modern sociology and psychology. Faced by comparable stimuli, any group of people (from the same cultural background) tend to respond in similar ways. Indeed, this tendency is the basis of order rather than chaos in the social system, and is one of the foundations of the institutions and rules on which any organized social system is based.[16]

The second qualification is related to savings and economic growth. It is often argued that an egalitarian distribution of income implies a lower rate of savings than a more unequal distribution. The affluent save a larger proportion of their income than the poor. Taking a dollar from the rich and giving it to the poor may have the effect of reducing savings in the economy and thereby reducing the potential rate of economic growth. Since economic growth is one way of bringing greater affluence, the goal of maximizing welfare derived from the existing level of income and output may clash with the goal of raising the level of income and output.

Income Distribution and Economic Growth

The distribution of income can affect economic growth patterns in two different ways, through savings patterns and through incentives. The way income is distributed does not determine either, but is one factor that influences both.

First, patterns of savings. We already know that an economy in which savings are a large portion of current income will have a higher growth potential than an economy that saves less. Savings represent resources and output not used for consumption, making them available for investment or other uses. An economy

---

[16]This digression was necessary because some economists feel that the assumption of comparable utility is not proper in a scientific analysis, and that economists, *as economists,* should therefore be silent on the question of the desirability of income equality. But as a practical matter, most economists who take that position agree that in the real world the assumption of comparability can be made.

that saves 25 percent of its income will have a potentially more rapid rate of growth than a similar economy that saves only 20 percent of its income.

We also know that savings come largely from the upper- and upper-middle-income families. Data on income and savings show that in recent decades in the U.S.:

1. The upper 10 percent of income-receiving units accounted for about 75 percent of total personal savings.

2. One hundred percent of personal savings is accounted for by the top 40 percent of income recipients.

3. The bottom 60 percent of income recipients dissaved as much as it saved.

This information suggests that a larger volume of savings would be made available for economic growth if income were shifted into the hands of upper-income groups.

That inference is not correct, however. The great bulk of all personal savings is used for purchase of housing and durable goods. Some studies show that as much as 99 percent of all savings out of personal income are used for those purposes. Others indicate that the proportion is about 95 percent. What, then, are the sources of investment in new plant and equipment that increases the economy's capacity to produce? The answer: business savings. About 85 percent (or more, according to some studies) of all business investment in new plant and equipment comes from retained earnings of business enterprises. Accumulation of capital has been institutionalized within the business firm, and does not depend on a large flow of savings from personal incomes. Economic growth in the modern private enterprise economy requires prosperous and profitable business firms, not large personal savings.

When seen from this perspective, redistribution of income from the affluent to the poor might be expected primarily to change the structure of consumer demand. Fewer luxurious houses in the suburbs and three-car garages filled with fancy cars; more food, clothing and other consumables. Fewer luxury resort hotels; increased camping in national parks. Business investment would shift from production of durable goods and housing toward items of more immediate consumption, to meet the wants of the less affluent. But as long as aggregate demand remains high—and it might rise somewhat if the less affluent have a lower propensity to save than the more affluent—business profits and business savings will be high and resources will be available for economic growth.

An equally important consideration is the role played by government. Prosperous economic growth can be promoted by wise use of fiscal and monetary policy. If a more rapid rate of growth is desirable, taxes on personal income and consumption can be used to reduce spending on personal wants, and the funds can be used for investment in more rapid expansion of the capacity to produce. The United States uses this process to provide funds for military purposes and to finance a substantial investment in human capital via public expenditures on education and medical care. A number of countries in western Europe use taxes to finance a significant amount of industrial investment.

Income Distribution and Incentives

The relationship between economic incentives and income distribution is not well understood. Evidence is very scanty on the relationship between monetary rewards and the length and intensity of work.

The folklore of our society is clear on these matters. It emphasizes the incentive effects of income distribution; an equalitarian distribution of income is said to destroy incentives. Why should one work hard when his rewards will be only as large as those going to someone who is lazy? This question implies its own answer: the hard work and striving for success that lead to economic growth require unequal rewards. Income inequality is necessary to achieve the growth that society wants, according to the conventional widsom.

Facts and folklore are sometimes inconsistent. In this case, it is by no means clear that monetary incentives are as important in motivating people as our folklore would have it. For example, *Fortune* asked, "What Makes the Boss Work?" and came up with the answer that patterns of behavior among executives cannot be adequately explained by income incentives. Rather, the boss seemed to be motivated by a large number of things connected with his status and power. A study of *Economic Behavior of the Affluent* published by the Brookings Institution in 1966 found that decisions by high-income individuals about how much to work were dictated by the demands of the job and by health, rather than by taxes or other pecuniary considerations. A larger study of *Productive Americans* published by the University of Michigan's Institute for Social Research found that people with low hourly earnings worked longer hours than those with higher earnings. Limited rewards apparently stimulated greater effort in a drive to achieve acceptable living standards.

With respect to taxes, two counterbalancing tendencies are at work. One is the inhibiting effect of taxes. If 50 percent of the additional income earned from work effort must be paid out in taxes, an individual may decide it is not worth the candle and go fishing. Countering that effect is the tendency of someone seeking specific high-income goals to work even harder if half of his marginal increases in income are taken in taxes. The important point is that both effects are felt, and the present state of knowledge cannot indicate which one is the stronger, at current rates and levels of taxation. We do know, however, that a series of Harvard studies in the 1950s could find no significant impact of taxes on the level of business investment or the incentives of business management.

Finally, one firm conclusion is that the shift toward equality in income distribution that occurred in the United States between 1935 and 1945 seems not to have had an inhibiting effect on either incentives or economic growth. In all fairness, we must recognize that no one knows, on the basis of either fact or theory, whether a similar shift in the future would either promote or diminish work incentives.

Income Differentials as a Rationing Device

Most people think of income differences as incentives only for the recipients. Thus, if we want people to work hard, we feel that they must be rewarded for past efforts and have opportunities to earn more in the future. A structure of rewards and opportunities is necessary to promote attitudes leading to hard work and maximum effort.

The theory of marginal productivity is itself a reflection of the economic forces underlying such a system of rewards and incentives. It shows that a competitive market economy will produce, by itself, a system of differential rewards based on differences in productivity for the various classes and types of labor effort. A doctor will earn more than a sailor, and a scientist more than a janitor, because the market values their products more at the margin.

Income differentials also serve a rationing function. A business manager, for instance, will not put a physicist to work sweeping floors when research scientists must be paid $48,000 a year and janitors $8,000. The physicist will be put to work in the laboratory, where he will produce at least $48,000 worth of research. Scarce skills, with high levels of productivity, will have high earnings (and high cost). They will be used where their high costs pay off, and that will be in their most efficient uses.

This is one reason for wide differences in earned incomes in the Soviet Union. Scarcity of skilled scientists and engineers requires that they be used where they are the most productive. Placing high costs on their use by paying them high salaries is one way that economic planners get administrators to economize on the use of these skilled people. A more egalitarian pattern of wages would lead to waste of those scarce resources on less productive activities that could be carried out with less skilled and more plentiful types of labor.

Income differentials are an important source of economic efficiency, not necessarily because of the incentives they give to workers, but because of the incentives they give to managers. Executives are constantly striving to substitute less costly for more costly factors of production. A wage and salary schedule in which differences are based on marginal productivities enables them to do so. The result is greater efficiency in resource allocation.

In contrast, by removing some of the penalties for inefficiency, an egalitarian system of rewards offers less incentive to managers to operate efficiently. This is an important point. Even if a nation should decide that, as a matter of social policy, income after taxes should be equalized, it would still be desirable to have incomes before taxes accord with marginal productivities, if only to get managers to economize on expensive workers.

Income Redistribution and Social Policy

This discussion has come to some important conclusions that are quite different from the conventional wisdom. We found some compelling reasons to favor more egalitarian patterns of income distribution than those that now prevail. We found no strong reason to feel that greater equality would significantly affect either the rate of economic growth or work incentives. We did find, however, that income differentials for earned incomes were a desirable prod toward efficient allocation of resources. We are led to an interesting social policy. Wherever possible, market forces should be allowed to determine income differentials for earned income. Beyond that, further moves toward egalitarianism, which are desirable on welfare-maximizing grounds, can be achieved by income transfers through government. These welfare gains need not reduce economic growth if reasonable fiscal and monetary policies are followed. There need be no tradeoff between growth and equity.

Summary

Income distribution patterns in the United States have remained largely unchanged since the end of World War II. Although average incomes have risen, the pattern of distribution as shown by a Lorenz curve has not changed. In the 1970s, however, the decline in the proportion of poor families stopped. Poverty has remained at about 12 percent of all households. The poor are characterized by high unemployment rates, disabilities, poor health, old age, broken families, and racial minority status. Welfare payments have tended to preserve poverty while making it more bearable

for the poor who receive them. Finally, a very large portion of the poor hold full-time jobs in low-wage industries from which they earn less than the income needed to put them above the poverty classification. The economic system creates conditions that serve to preserve and perpetuate poverty, in a pattern of circular causation with cumulative effects. Programs to alleviate poverty have been unsuccessful in part because they have not recognized the systemic nature of the problem. They have tended to treat symptoms rather than causes.

Wealth is more unequally distributed than

income. There is some indication that the distribution of wealth is becoming more unequal, although the trend is by no means clear. A few very wealthy people have a great deal of wealth, however; middle-income groups maintain their proportionate share through savings, while many at the bottom have very little.

Most of the great holdings of wealth originated in rapid accumulations in one lifetime and were largely inherited by their present owners, and the income obtained is largely unearned. Inheritance performs little useful function in the modern economy, since the continutiy of economic units and their management is assured by other social institutions. The desire to leave an inheritance is one of the least important motives for saving. Income from inheritance performs no economic function and there would be little if any economic loss if inheritance of large amounts of wealth were ended. Nevertheless, recent changes in the U.S. inheritance tax laws facilitated the passing on of large accumulations of wealth to the next generation.

If we wish to maximize the likelihood that welfare will be maximized, more equal distribution rather than less should be sought. Higher incomes should be reduced and lower income increased. Doing so would probably have little impact on economic growth or work incentives, contrary to the generally accepted view. Income differentials from earned incomes are an important incentive for management of enterprises to economize on expensive inputs, however. This consideration means that income redistribution by transfer payments after earned income is received is a more desirable method of redistributing income than a policy of equalizing earnings.

Key Concepts

Lorenz curve	**life cycle analysis of savings**
earned income	**transfer tax**
unearned income	**egalitarian rule**

For Discussion

1. How would the American economy be affected if the disparities in incomes that now exist were reduced by half? if they were eliminated entirely?

2. Would the methods used to achieve those goals make a difference in the outcomes? Explain.

3. Alleviating poverty and reducing unemployment among the poor may be conflicting goals. Explain.

4. Fusfeld's rule is that welfare payments to the poor are set at the lowest level consistent with an acceptably low level of civil disorder. This cost-benefit formula suggests that ethical considerations do not significantly influence poverty programs. Discuss.

5. Discuss the pros and cons of high transfer (inheritance) taxes on large accumulations of wealth.

6. Discuss the argument that high personal income taxes on large incomes reduce the funds available for investment and thereby hamper rapid economic growth.

PART 7

GOVERNMENT AND THE ECONOMY

Big government is a key element in the modern economy. Earlier parts of this book dealt with both macro- and microeconomic aspects of the role of government. We turn now to some further aspects of the public sector.

Chapter 29 documents the growth of government expenditures, but its chief focus is on public goods—the products and services provided by the public sector—and the processes by which social choices are made. Chapter 30 analyzes the taxes that provide the funds that pay for public goods. The underlying questions are the traditional issues of public finance: efficiency and equity. Here, however, they are embedded in a matrix of political economy issues, particularly class conflict and rivalry among special interests for control over decisions on taxes and spending.

Three chapters follow that deal with issues in the public sector of particular importance at the present time. Chapter 31 discusses the political economy of war and defense. Chapter 32 analyzes problems of pollution and the environment. Chapter 33 treats the political economy of energy. Social choices are of major significance in all of these areas. The discussions focus on the basic economics of the problems, the various groups and classes whose interests are involved, and how the various policy alternatives affect those interests.

In general, the art of government consists in taking as much money as possible from one class of citizens to give it to another.

Voltaire (François Marie Arouet),
Philosophical Dictionary (1764)

The subjects of every state ought to contribute towards the support of the government, as nearly as possible, . . . in proportion to the revenue which they respectively enjoy under the protection of the state.

Adam Smith, *An Inquiry into the Nature and Causes of the Wealth of Nations* (1776)

When war comes it is difficult to gather money as well as to take up arms; and it is hard to say which task presents the greater problem.

Giovanni Botero, *The Reason of State* (1589)

Do you not know with what lack of wisdom the world is governed?

Axel Gustafson Oxenstierna, letter (1648),
commenting on his son's criticism of Oxenstierna's
policies as prime minister of Sweden

Chapter 29

The Public Sector

The role of government in the twentieth-century American economy is large and expanding. We have already examined some of the important functions of the federal government in establishing a framework wherein the modern economy can flourish. Some of the more important are promotion of economic growth; maintenance of high levels of aggregate demand, including management of the monetary system; maintenance of competition and regulation of monopoly; resolution of labor-management conflicts; socialization of the risks of a private-enterprise market economy; and promotion of equity in distribution of income.

In addition to these functions, governments continue to perform their essential and traditional functions. They carry out the daily housekeeping tasks necessary in any community, such as fire and police protection, sanitary and sewer services, and others. Government is also responsible for national defense and international relations, essential functions in a political system of national states.

At a more fundamental level, government is responsible for the reproduction of the economic order. The legal system, including police and courts, defines and protects private property and enforces contracts. The educational system provides young people with the skills, special training, and attitudes needed by a business-oriented economy. Military and foreign policy are oriented toward extension of national economic interests and opposition to the foes of capitalism. Much of the governmental activity in the U.S. seeks the reproduction of the U.S. style of capitalism, just as government in the U.S.S.R. is devoted to preserving and strengthening the Soviet brand of socialism.

The importance of a government function is not always measurable by its cost. For example, military and international affairs account for about one-third of the expenditures of all governments in the United States. The resolution of conflicts, however, which may be an even more important function, costs very little. Maintenance of a legal and operational framework for collective bargaining is a very minor budget item, and consumer protection (related to the customer-seller conflict) is only a little more costly. Nevertheless, governments must raise money to carry on their operations and they must allocate their revenues to particular purposes. In doing so, the economy feels an impact in three different ways:

1. The amount of government expenditures affects the level of economic activity.

2. Taxation and expenditures affect the distribution of income. It is impossible to devise a tax system that falls with equal impact upon all. It is also impossible to spend government funds in a manner that affects everyone equally.

3. Governments provide services and products that would not normally be provided by the private sector of a market- and profit-oriented economy.

The Growth of Government Expenditures

Government spending in the United States has grown considerably more rapidly than the economy as a whole. From the beginning of the twentieth century to the late 1970s, spending by all governments in the United States—federal, state, and local—rose from under $2 billion (in 1902) to about $140 billion (in 1979), corrected for changes in the price level. This is a multiplication of 70 times. Over the same period, GNP increased about 23 times, or only about one-third as fast.[1]

Government employment has risen significantly faster than employment in the private sector. Civilian employment by all governments rose from a little over 1,000,000 persons in 1900 to about 15,600,000 in 1979, a fifteenfold increase. In the same period total employment outside the public sector rose from

27,000,000 to 73,866,000, an increase of a little over 2.7 times.

The trend of growth in government spending does not seem to be affected by political ideologies. It has gone on equally under Republican and Democratic national administrations at the federal level. On the other hand, federal spending has been affected by major wars. Large wartime increases in spending are not balanced by equally large postwar reductions. Instead, a new plateau is reached, which is moved upward by the next war to a still higher level.[2]

The growth in spending has taken place at all levels of government. Federal spending has grown most rapidly, state spending next, and local government least of all. Yet even local government spending grew from about $900 million in 1902 to $128 billion in 1979. The shift in the locus of government spending is shown by the fact that prior to World War I local governments spent more than the state and federal governments combined. By the mid-1930s the upswing in federal spending had reversed the picture: Washington was spending as much as all other governments together. During World War II, federal spending rose to about ten times the spending of all state and local governments. By the late 1970s the share of government spending by the federal government was almost double that of state and local governments at 64 percent of the total. If the various revenue-sharing programs are allocated to state and local governments, however, the federal share of total government spending is reduced to about 55 percent. Table 29–1 gives the figures that illustrate these changes and Table 29–2 shows the breakdown by type of government.

[1]Some notes on this comparison: the figures are corrected for changes in prices. See Table 29–1, Note, for the way in which the correction was made: The GNP figure for 1902 is only a rough estimate, since data back that far are not very accurate. The government spending figures include transfer payments; GNP does not. This is the most serious difficulty with the comparison.

[2]The two authoritative studies of these phenomena are Solomon Fabricant, *The Trend of Government Activity in the United States Since 1900* (New York: National Bureau of Economic Research, 1952); and M. Slade Kendrick, *A Century and a Half of Federal Expenditures* (New York: National Bureau of Economic Research, Occasional Paper No. 48, 1955).

Table 29–1
Federal, State, and Local Spending, Selected Fiscal Years, 1902–1973

Year	Total	Federal	State	Local	Percentage Federal
		(Billions of Dollars)			
1902	1.7	0.6	0.2	0.9	35
1913	3.2	1.0	0.4	1.9	31
1936	16.8	9.2	3.1	4.4	55
1944	109.9	100.5	4.1	5.4	91
1979	832.4	535.7	168.6	128.1	64

Notes: Figures for each year may not add to total because of rounding.
   A rough estimate of how these figures would be affected by correcting for changes in the price level can be made by using the old consumer price index based on 1937–1939 = 100. On that basis, the 1909 dollar was worth $1.62 and the 1979 dollar 17 cents. The corrected increase in total government spending, 1902–1979, would be from about $2 billion to about $140 billion. The federal proportion of the total would not be changed, of course.

Table 29–2
Government Expenditure by Level of Government, 1979

	Amount (millions of dollars)	Percent
Federal	535.7	64.4
State	168.6	20.2
Local	128.1	15.4
Total	832.4	100.0

Types of Public Spending

Government spending has focused on services that normally are not provided by the private sector. A breakdown of government expenditures for any recent year makes that situation evident. Table 29–3 shows the pattern for 1979. Half of all government spending is for investment in human capital, and on social insurance and public welfare. Table 29–3 minimizes the spending for national defense, however. Much government debt was incurred by the federal government in fighting recent wars. Significant sums spent on the military are listed in some of the other categories, such as social insurance (veterans benefits), general administration, and part of the spending on development of the economy. If all military and military-related spending were included in the national defense and international relations category, the total would be at least $175 billion rather than $128.5 billion, and the proportion of all government spending going for those purposes would amount to at least 20 percent of all government spending.

The proportion of these expenditures made by federal, state, and local governments is quite irregular. The federal government has exclusive responsibility for military and international affairs. It also spends substantial amounts on social insurance and secondarily on community services (primarily the postal services). The functions of state governments center on highways, hospitals, and schools. Local governments concentrate on education and community services.

One last point: the proportion of government expenditures on general administration is only 2 percent. This does not include administration of programs in the various functional categories, but covers only general governmental costs. We should also note that the federal government's general administrative costs are

Table 29–3
Government Expenditures: Federal, State, and Local, 1979

Service		Amount (Billions of Dollars)	Percentage
Community services (post office, utilities, prisons, sanitation, fire, police, libraries, etc.)		93.2	11
National defense and international relations		128.5	15
Expenditures on human capital		174.6	21
Education	129.4		
Health	37.2		
Housing and urban development	8.0		
Social insurance and public welfare		241.7	29
Development of the economy		70.5	8
Transportation	36.0		
Natural resources	30.3		
Space research	4.2		
Interest on debt		61.8	8
Other		36.5	4
General administration		25.2	3
Total		832.4	99

Note: Figures do not add to totals because of rounding.

only about 1 percent of total expenditures, while state and local governments spend about 4 percent on general administration. These figures tell us little about "efficiency," but they probably indicate a higher degree of central or executive control at the state and local level than at the federal.

Government spending on income transfers is now a subject of volatile political debate. Some government transfer payments, such as social security, unemployment insurance, workers' compensation, and Medicare, replace loss of income due to events beyond the recipient's control. Programs like Aid to Families with Dependent Children, Medicaid, and food stamps, however, provide economic support for those with little other income. The effect of government transfer programs on the patterns of income distribution has been to considerably lessen the incidence of poverty.

The Theory of Public Goods

Whatever level of government provides the services, government services differ in some important ways from goods produced in the private sector. Two principles are involved: the nonexclusion principle and the zero marginal cost principle. Together they help to explain why some facilities and services are provided publicly while others remain in the private sector.

The *nonexclusion principle* is the simplest. Some services are enjoyed by everyone. No one can be excluded from the benefits. Since no one can be excluded it is impossible to charge a price for their use. The classic example is a lighthouse on a dangerous and rocky shore. Once established and sending out its beacon of light, its signal can be seen by all ships. No ship can be excluded from its benefits. If all can use the light, no one would be willing to pay for it voluntarily, and no ship can be charged a fee. Since a price cannot be charged, no private enterprise could be induced to establish a lighthouse and, if it is to be built at all, public auspices are necessary. In contrast, an ordinary product like bread, or circuses, can be provided by the private sector because those who don't pay can be excluded from enjoying the product.

Many public services involve the nonexclusion principle. National defense is one. Everyone benefits from protection against the Red Meanies, no one can be excluded, no fee can be charged only to the users, and all must pay. So if you are wondering why you have to pay taxes to support the National Guard, or the FBI, or the CIA, credit it to the nonexclusion principle.

Education is only partially subject to the nonexclusion principle. Individuals can certainly be excluded from its direct benefits, a fee could be charged, and it would be possible for the private sector to provide educational services. The nonexclusion principle enters because of the secondary effects of education: the entire society benefits from increased education and all participants in the social order share in the benefits. We find, as a result, that even public colleges charge tuition, but students are also subsidized by public funds. At the elementary and secondary level, however, the secondary effects are so important to a democratic society that education is free.

Many public services have a mixed private-public character, like education. Some examples are port facilities in a large city, recreation facilities for the poor, and sanitation and sewage facilities. These services are usually provided through public agencies and sometimes by a combination of public and private efforts. The public activity arises because the private sector will provide a level of services based only on charges for the immediate benefits. Since secondary benefits accrue to all, a public

interest in a higher level of service develops and public services are provided.[3]

- The **nonexclusion principle** holds that some goods have to be supplied by a public agency because no price can be charged for them, since no one can be excluded from using them.

The second basis for public services is the *zero marginal cost principle.* There are some services for which the cost of one more user is nil. If welfare is to be maximized, marginal cost should equal price. Since $MC = 0$, no charge should be made, and if no charge is made the service won't be provided by the private sector. The classic example is a highway bridge. Users could be excluded and a toll charged that would pay for all costs plus a normal profit. Private enterprise would be quite feasible. But the marginal cost of one more automobile crossing the bridge is zero or very close to it. If net benefits from use of the bridge are to be maximized there should be no toll.

A specific example is the great Mackinac Bridge connecting the upper and lower peninsulas of Michigan. A toll is charged that is intended to cover costs of operation, maintenance, and retirement of the bonds issued to finance construction. The only subsidy involved initially was low interest rates on the bonds because of a state guarantee.[4] Otherwise, the bridge might as well be operated

---

[3] Economists today sometimes distinguish between pure *social wants* (those fully subject to the nonexclusion principle) and *merit wants* (those for which the public desires a higher level of output than that provided privately). Richard Musgrave makes that distinction in *The Theory of Public Finance* (New York: McGraw-Hill, 1959), pp. 9–14. The economist who originally developed these ideas, John Stuart Mill, in *Principles of Political Economy* (1849), recognized that "merit wants" were like other social wants, but based on secondary rather than direct benefits.

[4] The toll is not high enough; the bridge loses money and must be subsidized directly. Incidentally, when this $100,000,000 monument to the annual slaughter of the upper peninsular deer herd was first built, it was painted to show up as blue and gold (University of Michigan colors) in the daytime and green and white (Michigan State University colors) under artificial light at night. Such is the politics of public services, about which more shortly.

Figure 29-1
Economics of Toll Bridges

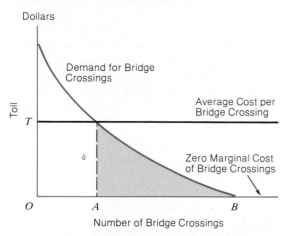

The toll limits the number of crossings to *OA*, leading to a loss in total welfare equal to the shaded area. Welfare would be maximized with crossings equal to *OB*, at which level *P = MC*.

privately. But there is public pressure for a free bridge, and rightly so. The marginal cost of bridge crossings is nil, and if benefits are maximized the toll would be reduced to zero so that it equals marginal costs. Figure 29–1 shows the principle in graphic form.

To summarize, public services in a private-enterprise economy tend to follow the old folklore maxim that government should do those things private enterprise cannot do (the nonexclusion principle) or cannot do so well (the zero marginal cost principle). In one way or another, the great bulk of government services involves the nonexclusion and zero-marginal-cost principles.

● The **zero marginal cost principle** is the principle that public agencies should supply some goods free in order to maximize consumer welfare, since the goods in question have no marginal cost.

Public Services and the Political Process

The nature of public services is such that a price cannot easily be justified for them. Either the nonexclusion principle prevails for direct or indirect benefits, or the zero marginal cost principle is present. This being the case, the market mechanism cannot readily be used to organize production and allocate output. Instead, political processes are used to determine the level of output, the extent of service, and the price (or tax), if any, that will be charged.

Measurability of Benefits
This aspect of public services creates difficulties that are not present in the private sector. The chief problem is lack of measurability of the benefits involved. In the private sector both benefits and costs can be reduced to dollars and cents. As we have seen, in competitive markets both the real costs of production and the real benefits to consumers are reflected in prices and costs, and the adjustment process tends to maximize net benefits.

The public sector does not function within this neat framework. Costs can be calculated, just as in the private sector, and voters are often very sensitive to their level. But benefits are not often measurable, particularly at the margin, because price signals are not given to the decision makers. With no prices attached to public services, it is impossible to obtain an accurate measure of the benefits obtained by those who use public services.

For example, a city provides young people recreational services paid for from taxes levied on taxpayers who generally do not use the services. An accurate decision on the extent of recreational services to be provided would involve equating the marginal benefits to users with the marginal costs to taxpayers. The users' marginal benefits cannot be measured directly because no price is charged (in this example). The taxpayer's marginal costs cannot be measured because one normally does not pay a recreation services tax but a general property or sales tax out of which the costs of recreational facilities are paid. Furthermore, any one taxpayer may not use the services at all. When that happens, a transfer of real income is made from that taxpayer to the user of the services.

One apparent way out of this dilemma is to charge a fee for the services to be paid by the actual user. The direct marginal benefits could then be equated with marginal costs. This is only an apparent solution, however. The indirect benefits of recreation programs for youth accrue to the community as a whole, like education, and all participate in the benefits. No one can be excluded. It is a public good. In addition, a fee may exclude exactly those young people for whom recreation services provide the greatest benefits to the community as a whole. No, a fee does not solve the problem. The result is that benefits cannot be easily measured, nor can those individuals who benefit the most be identified.

Lack of measurability of the benefits throws the decision-making process into the political arena. Once there it is subject to such political processes as

1. Logrolling, or "you vote for my project and I'll vote for yours." (A variant is "you support mine or I'll vote against yours.")

2. Consensus, that is, compromising until majority support can be obtained.

3. Lobbying, or political pressure from organized interests to achieve their goals.

4. Bribery, or payment to the politician because it is the cheapest way to get what you want.

Whether a rational decision emerges from these processes is difficult to determine. It may or may not. Since marginal benefits cannot be measured there is no way to tell.

Those Who Pay the Taxes May Not Benefit

A second basic problem with public services is the fact, already briefly noted, that their costs are borne generally by all taxpayers while their benefits may accrue more to some than to others. In the private sector this problem is avoided by the price system: if you want something, you pay for it; if you don't want it, you don't pay. In the public sector the problem is different: you pay for the service whether you want it or not. This element in the situation has important political repercussions. It leads to logrolling. It leads to compromises in which programs are modified so as to provide benefits to enough people to get the measure adopted. It brings efforts to shift costs to the general taxpayer while benefits go to a few via subsidy or subsidy-like programs. These processes may or may not bring desirable results. Since we have no good way of measuring benefits at the margin, we cannot tell.

Emotional Appeals and Ideology

All of this uncertainty and difficulty leads to a third important problem in the political process that provides public goods. The absence of firm quantitative guidelines leads to use of emotional appeals and ideological criteria for programs of public services that can often obscure the economic reality beneath them. The emotions aroused by such recent issues as comprehensive medical insurance, guaranteed annual incomes, and large military expenditures illustrate the problem.

These factors bring the public economy inevitably into the political arena. There is no escape. Especially in the modern world, in which public wants have been expanding over the last seventy years and have become important elements in the level of production and the flow of income and strongly affect the uses to which resources are put, the functioning of the political economy is an integral part of the economy as a whole. The nature of public wants makes it so.

The Theory of Social Choice

The political nature of social choice raises a new problem: is it possible to make rational social choices within a democratic framework? Can a democratic society make those decisions in the public sector that maximize social welfare, or will the decisions represent the special interests of organized groups and an economic elite? These questions have always been important, but they take on great relevance to economics as the economic functions of government expand and government spending increases.

Classical and Pluralist Theories of Democracy

The "classical" theory of democracy prevailed at the time of the American Revolution and was the philosophy behind the U.S. Constitution. In that theory each voter was seen as a distinct individual seeking to maximize his own welfare. He would vote for representatives who, responsible to the electorate, would reflect the views of a majority of the voters. Choices made by individuals could be added up to achieve welfare-maximizing decisions for society as a whole. If social welfare were not maximized the decision would quickly be changed. Any minority could be protected by a "bill of rights" to guarantee individual freedoms, and by a philosophy of government that minimized government's role in everyday affairs.

- The **classical theory of democracy** is that representative government reflecting majority opinion will tend to move social policy toward maximization of social benefits.

The classical theory of democracy rested on the same assumptions about people and society as the economic theory of competition and private enterprise—an atomized social order composed of welfare-maximizing individuals.

In today's world of big business, big labor, and big government, of cohesive economic interest groups, it was modified to become the "pluralist" theory of democracy. This theory recognized that government reflected the interests of organized groups, and only indirectly the welfare-maximizing decisions of individuals. Political coalitions are built among groups that represent the interests of their individual members. Politicians compete for the support of various organizations and voting blocs, trading proposed legislation or opposition to legislation for votes in an effort to maximize their political support. Compromise and coalitions that reflect the interests of the complex elements comprising a modern industrial society emerge through this political process. Politics turns conflict into agreement. In essence, the pluralist theory interposed self-interested groups and voting blocs between the individual and his political representative. The groups and blocs reflected free choices of individuals and in turn influenced political decisions that brought satisfactory compromises.

- **Pluralism** is the theory that compromise among voluntarily organized interest groups will lead to maximum social benefits.

Critiques of Pluralism

Pluralist theory has been strongly criticized. Three chief lines have been taken. One is the "elite" theory, which sees representative democracy as the politics of an economy dominated by big business and led by an elite of top business management, wealthy families, and financial interests. That group is allied with military leadership, accommodates itself to the leadership of big labor, and dominates the educational system. As long as it provides full employment and rising living standards to the great majority of people the leadership of the elite is not challenged and it is free to pursue its goals of wealth and power. Recent events have given considerable credence to this view.

The second critique of pluralism comes from an economic analysis of the formation of groups and group action. Mancur Olson, of the University of Maryland, showed that small groups with concrete economic interests can readily form and take collective action. Each member of the group perceives that his support is necessary for the group to succeed in obtaining gains for its members. Without that support, the group as a whole is significantly weakened. Gains for any one individual become possible only if all participate. But a large group is quite different, even when it has a common interest. Any one individual can stay out of the group and still benefit from group action. Gains can be obtained without incurring costs. Olson concludes that it is relatively easy for small special-interest groups to organize for political action to achieve economic gains, but it is difficult for the general public interest to be expressed.

Olson's analysis leads into a third critique of pluralist theory. It is argued that a modern industrial society is characterized not by a unified economic elite, but by a variety of economically powerful elites that maintain privileged positions in each sector of the economic and social order. Social choices reflect compromises among the interests of powerful elite groups rather than the interests of the many. One can argue that government policy toward medical care, for example, accommodates itself to the leadership of the "medical-industrial complex." In this view a pluralism of elites lies behind social choices.[5]

[5]These summaries of classical and pluralist theories and their critiques are simplified in the interest of brevity and contrast. There is an important literature on all of these topics. The classical theory of democracy: Joseph Schumpeter, *Capitalism, Socialism, and Democracy* (New York: Harper and Brothers, 1942), Chap. 21. Pluralism: Robert Dahl, *Who Governs?* (New Haven, Conn.: Yale University Press, 1961); *Pluralist Democracy in the United States* (Chicago: Rand McNally, 1967); and Anthony Downs, *An Economic Theory of Democracy* (New York: Harper and Brothers, 1957). The three critiques of pluralism: C. Wright Mills, *The Power Elite* (New York: Oxford University Press, 1956); Mancur Olson, *The Logic of Collective Action: Public Goods and the Theory of Groups* (Cambridge, Mass.: Harvard University Press, 1965); and Andrew S. McFarland, *Power and Leadership in Pluralist Systems* (Stanford, Calif.: Stanford University Press, 1969).

The Marxist Theory of the State

In Marxist political theory the state reflects the underlying economic system and the structure of social classes. In a capitalist society, private ownership and control of the means of production and the process of capital accumulation provide the economic power that enables the capitalist class to dominate government. Either directly or indirectly, the apparatus of the state is used in the interest of the capitalist class—to protect and extend the capitalist economic system. There may be bitter conflicts among capitalist interest groups to control the state for the advantage of one group or another, but on basic issues, such as preservation of capitalism and opposition to those who would change the economic system itself, the opposing capitalist interests can agree. Marx viewed the modern capitalist state as alienated social power that rightfully should lie with the many rather than the few.

• The **Marxist theory of the state** is that state power is controlled by those classes or groups that control the forces of production and the accumulation of capital.

At one extreme, this approach to the role of the state leads to complete rejection of political democracy as developed in the United States and western Europe. Lenin, for example, scorned "bourgeois democracy" as the "dictatorship of the bourgeoisie" over the working class. Lenin looked forward to a "dictatorship of the proletariat" through seizure of power by a "vanguard party" of the working class during the revolution against capitalism. The new regime would build a socialist and ultimately classless society in which true democracy could flourish.

Democratic socialists, on the other hand, see the development of political democracy, political rights, and individual freedoms as a positive step. They would use these political instruments as the means by which socialism would triumph through a peaceful, ballot-box revolution. Socialism would bring social control over the means of production and the accumulation of capital, using and improving the democratic political institutions pioneered in the capitalist era.

These brief paragraphs can only introduce the chief ideas of the classic Marxist analysis of the state and its two chief variants.[6] But they have one fundamental idea in common. In a capitalist society, politics reflects basic class conflicts, which are irreconcilable by their very nature. These conflicts are transposed to the political arena, where they cannot be reconciled by compromise or consensus, except on relatively superficial matters that skirt the basic issues. In the end, those who control the forces of production and the process of capital accumulation will call the tune.

Arrow's General Impossibility Theorem

At a different level in the debate over the political economy of social choice is the *general impossibility theorem* developed by Kenneth Arrow. His point: it is not possible for rational social choices to be made in a democratic fashion when widely different value systems prevail. Differing value systems prevent rational individual choices from being added to each other to determine a rational social choice. This is a crucial problem in the theory of social choice; it is worth examining in some detail.

Assume a variety of social policies from among which society must choose by majority vote. The social choices, based on individual preferences, should enable them to be ranked. One ranking might be like this:

A is preferred to *B*
B is preferred to *C*

It follows that *A* is also preferred to *C*. That is, the rankings are "transitive": *A* dominates *B*, *B* dominates *C*, so *A* must also dominate *C*. A rational decision should have that property.

Now assume that there are three political parties of equal size (or any three groups within the decision-making process). Each one has a rational (transitive) ranking of preferences. But the values and goals of the groups differ, thereby creating three different rankings of the alternatives, as follows: Group I prefers *A* over *B*, *B* over *C*, and therefore *A* over *C*. Group II's ordering is *B, C, A*, while Group III prefers *C, A, B* in that order.

	Political Party or Group		
	I	II	III
1st choice	A	B	C
2nd choice	B	C	A
3rd choice	C	A	B

Under these conditions a majority vote or coalition of parties cannot come to a firm decision. Suppose the choice were between alternatives *A* and *B*. Groups I and III prefer *A* to *B*. They will outvote Group II and select alternative *A*. But Group II, which prefers *C* over *A*, then forms a coalition with Group III, which also prefers *C* to *A*, and alternative *C* is chosen by a 2 to 1 vote. Now it is Group I's turn. It prefers *B* to *C*, as does Group II, and they combine to outvote Group III and select alternative *B*. Which gets us back to the beginning, to a comparison of *A* and *B* out of which comes selection of policy *A*. No firm decision is possible.

The problem is that rational (transitive) choices made by an individual or a group can lead to intransitive rankings of choices by the larger social group and inability to arrive at a firm majority decision. Any conclusive choice would require the imposition of authority from outside the voting procedure, and whatever choice is made a *majority* would prefer a

---

[6]Two pamphlets by Marx use political events in France in the nineteenth century to develop his theory of the state, *The Eighteenth Brumaire of Louis Bonaparte* and *The Civil War in France*. Lenin's views are presented in *State and Revolution*. The classic statement of democratic socialism is Edouard Bernstein, *Evolutionary Socialism*.

different one. A democratic decision is impossible.

Although this may seem highly theoretical, it may well typify real-world situations. For example, for policies *A, B,* and *C* substitute expenditures for public schools, parochial schools, and busing of minorities, and for Groups I, II, and III substitute white Protestants, white Catholics, and blacks, and we are right in the middle of a current policy dilemma.

Further work on the impossibility theorem has restricted its applicability somewhat. We know that aggregation of individual choices to achieve a stable social decision is possible if the number of discrete individuals is large and they do not tend to cluster in groups based on differing value systems. Under those conditions the "cyclical voting" of Arrow's paradox either disappears or occurs to only a trivial extent. Rational social decisions can be made under the conditions assumed by the classical theory of democracy, including the existence of a large number of individual voters.

It is also true that if the policy alternatives are divisible a viable social choice can be made, even if the number of voters or groups of voters is small. Take a case of government appropriations for military spending, with the total divided among army, navy and air force. If an initial proposal cannot gain acceptance, taking a little from one to split among the other two may achieve majority approval. The general principle is that the larger the range of choices and the larger the number of voters the greater is the likelihood of a firm social choice. On the other hand, if there are a limited number of parties or groups (but more than two) and their goals and values are widely different, a simple majority vote may not lead to an effective social choice.

We return to the original question. Is it possible to make rational social choices within a democratic framework? The answer: In a society with a high degree of conflict between economic interest groups, with haves and have nots in a world of rich nations and poor nations, rational social choices based on a majority or a consensus may not be possible. It is a sobering thought, and Arrow well merits his 1973 Nobel Prize in economics for calling attention to the dilemma.[7]

- The **general impossibility theorem** is the principle that there is no way to aggregate preferences when goals and values differ among a limited number of (but more than two) individuals or groups.

Social Costs and Social Benefits

The economic issues involved in the provision of public goods are just as complex as the political-ideological issues. Economic analysis, however, simplifies the problem to a comparison of marginal costs and marginal benefits in order to determine the optimal social gain. Just as a rational individual would maximize his or her welfare by equalizing costs and benefits at the margin, so a rational government would maximize net gains to the community by equalizing marginal social benefits and marginal social costs.

There are three aspects to the *principle of optimal social gain.* First, no project should be undertaken unless the gains exceed the cost. Once past this minimum test, a search should be made for the method of implementation that provides the greatest net gain to the community. Finally, the size of the project or program should be increased until benefits at the margin just equal costs at the margin. Up to that point the net welfare of the community increases; beyond that point net welfare diminishes.

The basic analytic principle applies marginal analysis to public decision making. Any public program provides benefits. But like any good,

---

[7]For further reading: Kenneth J. Arrow, *Social Choice and Individual Values,* 2nd ed. (New Haven, Conn.: Yale University Press, 1963); and Gordon Tullock, "The General Irrelevance of the General Impossibility Theorem," *Quarterly Journal of Economics,* Vol. 81, No. 2 (May 1967), pp. 256–270.

Figure 29-2
The Principle of Optimal Social Gain

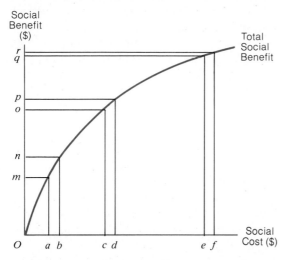

The curve of increasing total social benefit shows diminishing marginal returns as the program expands. With a small program, a given increase in cost (*ab*) provides a large marginal gain in benefits (*mn*). As the program expands, a level is reached at which the increase in cost (*cd*) is just equal to the increase in marginal benefits (*op*). Beyond point *d*, increases in costs (*ef*) bring marginal benefits (*gr*) smaller than the increase in costs. Point *d* is the optimal level of spending.

marginal benefits tend to diminish as the quantity of the good increases. If we are able to estimate the money value of the benefits, we can compare benefits at the margin with marginal increases in money costs. At some point the marginal benefits will equal marginal costs, giving us the optimal level of the public program that maximizes net benefits to the community. Figure 29–2 provides a graphic illustration of this principle of optimal social gain.

There are numerous problems raised by this simple principle. How are social benefits and costs measured? Can all of them be reduced to monetary measures? If not, what other measures are to be used? Decisions must be made by the present generation that will affect future generations, yet there are no ways to measure costs or benefits for them. Finally, benefits may

accrue to some, while costs may be borne by others, involving a shift in the distribution of real income. We know of no way to resolve these problems fully.

Nevertheless, public decisions must be made, and several techniques for doing so have been developed. Their purpose is to provide a rational way of approaching the problem, based on the principle of optimum social gain.

● The **principle of optimal social gain** is that net social benefits are maximized when marginal social costs and marginal social gains associated with a public good are equalized.

Nonmarket Decision Making

In recent years important advances in public-sector decision making have been achieved. Managers seek to introduce a higher degree of rationality into problems of social choice by identifying goals, specifying alternatives, and analyzing benefits and costs. These nonmarket decision-making techniques are still in the early stages of development, but they offer the promise of more efficiency and less politics. The most important are program budgeting, cost-benefit analysis, and systems analysis. They are not a solution to the problem of rational decision making in a democratic framework, but once decisions are made they help provide more reasonable ways to achieve the goals.

Program Budgeting

One method for organizing the decision-making process is *program budgeting*. The first step is to specify the *goals* that a particular agency or department of government seeks to achieve, together with a *target date* for their achievement and *criteria* by which their achievement can be judged. In the ideal case all the goals would be quantified, that is, stated in measurable terms: so many hydrogen bombs produced, a given percent reduction in air pollution in a specified area, a given reduction in the unemployment rate, or others. The second step is to list the various *programs* that could achieve the goals. The programs could be quite different from each other and involve rather widely different alternatives. Some programs may bring results rapidly and others slowly, and this may require some flexibility in the target date set in the original goals. Some programs may achieve the goals more fully than others, and this will introduce flexibility into the goals themselves. The third step is to calculate or estimate the costs of the alternative programs, and their benefits, in order to determine which program is best. There are several ways in which this step can be accomplished. One is by use of cost-benefit analysis, which will be explained presently. Finally, a budget is constructed which expresses the chosen program in terms of monetary appropriations and the uses that will be made of them.

Program budgeting is essentially a logical approach to planning by rational people. Goals are selected, alternatives are enumerated, costs and benefits are calculated, and an operating plan is constructed. Its essential element and the characteristic that is new is the application of economic analysis to complex problems, achieved by comparing the costs and benefits associated with the various alternatives. Program budgeting does not solve the Arrow problem, however. It assumes that a decision has been made, and seeks the most efficient way to achieve the goal.

- **Program budgeting** is a method for determining government budgets in which goals, alternative programs, and cost-benefit comparisons are related to each other and expressed in terms of expenditures.

Cost-Benefit Analysis

Efficient implementation of policy goals requires maximization of benefits relative to costs. The method for doing this is called *cost-benefit analysis.* Here is an example. A flood control project is planned for a small valley. Four alternative programs are possible, each with different costs and effects. Which one should be chosen, if any? A cost-benefit analysis compares the estimated damages in an average year with no flood protection and with the four proposed flood protection schemes.[8] For each alternative the annual cost (mostly the cost of the capital) and the estimated reduction in flood damage are calculated. The figures are shown in Table 29–4. In each case the annual benefit exceeds the annual cost. But Plan C is best. Its superiority can be seen if we examine the incremental costs and benefits involved in moving from the less to the more costly plans,[9] as shown in Table 29–5.

Plan C costs $8,000 more than Plan B, but its benefits are $9,000 greater. The increase in benefits from moving from Plan B to Plan C are greater than the increase in costs by $1,000. But moving from Plan C to Plan D brings a $12,000 increase in costs in exchange for only a $7,000 increase in benefits. It's not worth it. A marginal analysis is used to select the plan for which the increase in benefits is equated with the increase in costs, as closely as possible, to maximize net benefits.

- **Cost-benefit analysis** compares marginal benefits and costs to determine the net benefits of a particular policy or program.

Some Limitations of Cost-Benefit Analysis

One of the difficult parts of any cost-benefit analysis is determining what to include in the costs and the benefits, particularly when there is no simple market price that can be attached to them.

---

[8]The example is taken from Otto Eckstein, *Public Finance* (Englewood Cliffs, N.J.: Prentice-Hall, 1964).

[9]We use the term "incremental" rather than "marginal" for a technical reason. The term "marginal" applies to increases in benefits per dollar of increase in annual costs. That calculation can't be made because the alternatives involve large jumps or increments. The same principles are involved, however.

Table 29–4
Cost-Benefit Analysis: Alternative Flood Control Projects

Plan	Annual Cost	Average Annual Damage	Benefit (Reduction of Damage)
No protection	0	$38,000	0
A—Levees	$ 3,000	32,000	$ 6,000
B—Small reservoir	10,000	22,000	16,000
C—Medium reservoir	18,000	13,000	25,000
D—Large reservoir	30,000	6,000	32,000

Table 29–5
Cost-Benefit Analysis: Incremental Costs and Incremental Benefits

Plan	Incremental Cost	Incremental Benefit
No protection	0	0
A—Levees	$ 3,000	$ 6,000
B—Small reservoir	7,000	10,000
C—Medium reservoir	8,000	9,000
D—Large reservoir	12,000	7,000

Whose costs and whose benefits are to be included in a cost-benefit analysis? The money cost of constructing a reservoir for a flood control project can be readily estimated. The reservoir may have a variety of side effects, however. For example, during flood periods it may be full, but much of the time it may be largely empty, leaving mudflats or swampy areas that are either unsightly or harmful to the nearby residents. None of these costs will be borne by the downriver townspeople who are protected from the floods and get the benefits, but they may be heavily felt by upriver farm families.

One problem is that some costs, such as those borne by the upriver farmers, are not readily measurable. That being the case, such costs are likely to be ignored in a simple cost-benefit analysis. They shouldn't be, but they often are. For example, how does one put a dollar value on the psychological costs borne by parents whose children's health was permanently damaged by pollution at the Love Canal? One way out of this dilemma is to include a sophisticated list of all costs and benefits, unmeasurable as well as measurable. "Shadow prices" based on reasonable and informed estimates of what the prices might be if they were determined in the market can then be given to the unmeasurable costs and benefits. That, of course, is better than nothing, but it sometimes involves heroic assumptions about relative values that may differ widely between individuals.

A second problem is that most government projects or programs involve a redistribution of income between economic interests. Pure cost-benefit analysis ignores that problem and leaves the decision to the political process. That is not a full solution. We have already seen that, on welfare grounds, a more equal distribution of income is more desirable than a less equal distribution. A project that can be justified on the basis of a cost-benefit analysis may move the real distribution of income (after costs and benefits) toward greater inequality. Yet the income distribution effects of a program or project are seldom included in cost-benefit estimates.

The difficulties of cost-benefit analysis limit its usefulness. It can be used to evaluate specific programs when decisions have already been made about goals and about the desirability of a general objective. But cost-benefit analysis is of limited use in making those prior decisions. In flood control schemes, for example, the side effects, income distribution effects, and other largely unmeasurable effects must be considered in determining that a flood control policy is desirable. Cost-benefit analysis can help in making the decision by showing that the direct and measurable benefits exceed the direct and measurable costs, and it can help identify the other considerations that enter into the decision. Once the decision to develop flood control programs is made it can also help determine which ones are economically sound (direct benefits exceed direct costs). But even in those more restricted decisions cost-benefit analysis does not resolve all of the problems that arise because of difficulties in measuring full costs and benefits.

Systems Analysis

A broader approach is provided by *systems analysis,* which examines the component parts of policy formulation, including the intangible elements that enter into the decision-making process. Systems analysis provides a method of identifying the essential features of highly complex problems. It can generate "models" of the system under analysis that can be used for simulation of the actual operation of the system in order to determine the expected results of alternative programs. Simulation is a substitute for actual trials and can turn up defects in proposed programs that lead to improvements while projects are still in the planning stage. As an approach to problem solving and decision making, systems analysis has been used in a variety of military, engineering, and business applications, and is beginning to be used to analyze problems of social choice in the governmental process.

The essential elements of systems analysis are: specifying the end products or outputs, analyzing the process by which they can be obtained, and identifying the necessary inputs. When those tasks are completed, evaluation of alternatives by cost-benefit analysis can lead to selection of the best method for achieving the goals. Systems analysis is the general method that identifies the ways in which goals can be achieved; cost-benefit analysis compares them in order to select the one with the greatest net benefits; a program budget expresses the decision in operational terms.

Planning in the Public Economy

The methods of nonmarket decision making that have been sketched here are substitutes for the automatic decision-making system embodied in market relationships, which works effectively when costs and benefits accrue to individual economic units and price tags can be applied to them. When public goods are involved, however, the market system does not work effectively and other methods have to be used. The political process has been the predominant method used in the past and it is still very widely used in making social choices. Its great defect is very heavy reliance on power and influence rather than rational analysis of all of the alternatives. As the role of government has expanded, more rational methods of planning have emerged, such as systems analysis, cost-benefit analysis and program budgeting. Sophisticated economic planning based on those techniques is the next stage in the development of the public economy, whose growth over the last half century or more has been so spectacular.

The Problems Ahead

When the newer methods of nonmarket decision making are seen as sophisticated methods of planning, they raise further problems at a higher level of complexity. They imply a centralization of decision making in the hands of expert analysts whose skills and access to information place them in a strategic position to control events affecting the lives of millions. Even if the experts themselves do not occupy the seats of power they will serve those who do. Better methods for making nonmarket decisions enable a center of administrative power to operate more efficiently, which is exactly their purpose. They suggest an economy and society with greater central control rather than less. One has visions of *Dr. Strangelove* and the system losing control over its power to destroy; of the final scene in Karel Capek's play, *R. U. R.,* in which robots advance downstage to attack the audience; of the final incident in *1984* when the protagonist, just released from a reeducation camp, feels an uncontrollable surge of love upon seeing Big Brother's picture thrown upon the screen; of *Catch 22* and the essential irrationality of rational systems.

Yet there is another aspect of nonmarket decision making with exactly the opposite implications. Systems analysis not only identifies goals, it also identifies the constraints within which the system must function. If those constraints entail a given distribution of income or structure of power or ownership or productive resources, the systems analysis of alternatives will identify the constraints and analyze the way in which they limit the possible choices. The results may then be used to raise questions about whether the constraints themselves should not be changed in order to move toward a more desirable set of alternatives. These considerations suggest that once the rational analysis of alternatives is started it can become revolutionary in nature. The systems approach to management, which starts as an effort to increase efficiency, can lead to recognition of the need for fundamental changes in the structure and operation of the economy.

Summary

Governments perform a wide variety of functions in the present economy that create the environment in which economic activity is carried on. Beyond those functions, government expenditures affect the level of economic activity; taxes and government spending affect the distribution of income; and governments produce goods and services in substantial amounts.

Spending by all levels of government has increased more rapidly than the economy as a whole has expanded in this century, concentrating on services that are not normally provided by the private sector, such as national defense and education.

Two principles characterize production of goods and services by governments. One is that prices cannot be attached to some goods because no one can be excluded from consuming them; they must be produced by government or not at all. The other is that some goods have no marginal costs; if welfare is to be maximized they will be supplied free by a public agency.

These principles do not take politics out of the public economy. Government actions are heavily influenced by the economic and political power of special interest groups of all kinds. Indeed, Kenneth Arrow's general impossibility theorem indicates there is good reason to doubt that a society with a multiplicity of goals and values can make rational decisions by a democratic process. Once decisions are made, however, the principle of optimal social gain enables economic analysis to provide a rational basis for implementation. Efforts have been made in recent years to apply several new types of nonmarket decision-making methods to the decisions made within governments, including program budgeting, cost-benefit analysis, and systems analysis. Some of them are promising steps toward more rational management, but we are a long way from solving the intricate problems of rational social choice.

Key Concepts

nonexclusion principle
zero marginal cost principle
classical theory of democracy

pluralism
Marxist theory of the state
general impossibility theorem

principle of optimal social gain
program budgeting
cost-benefit analysis

For Discussion

1. Discuss the argument that big government can be reduced by providing much of the services performed by government through the private market system.

2. How would you apply the principle of cost-benefit analysis to the defense budget?

3. The federal government helped rescue Chrysler Corporation from bankruptcy through loan guarantees that cost no money to taxpayers. Is such an action justified? Explain.

4. Should users of waterways maintained at the expense of taxpayers be required to pay a user's fee, or should use of the waterways remain free? Explain.

5. College students are subsidized by contributions to the cost of their education by public funds and public gifts. Why should not college students be expected to pay the full cost of their education?

6. Discuss: Political democracy will not work when there is no shared set of values.

Chapter 30

Taxation

Like the weather, everyone complains about taxes but no one does anything about them. One reason, perhaps, is that our tax system is terribly complicated and difficult to understand. A cynic could point out that one reason for the complications might be to keep the average voter from understanding the system so he won't know what to do about it. Any tax system is a reflection of the political and economic power structure of the social order. Taxes have to be paid by some, while others can avoid them. The result is a continuous struggle for advantage by individuals and groups to get the benefit of government services while other people pay the costs. Taxes affect economic growth, the distribution of income, and the allocation of resources. They involve concepts of equity and justice. Yet these larger issues are often lost sight of in the continuous struggle for advantage that goes on behind the scenes.

Taxes and the Conflict of Interests

Conflict and tension are continuous within any system of taxation. First, there is tension between the government that levies the tax and the taxpayer who pays it. Governments need money, so the first requirement is to get it. But not many people like to pay taxes, so the second requirement is to get it as painlessly as possible. This leads to the two principles of taxation as seen by the bureaucrat:

1. A good tax is one that raises money.
2. The best tax does it without the taxpayer knowing he is paying it.

It follows from these principles that any tax system will be full of hidden taxes, taxes that can be shifted from the person who pays to others who don't realize they are bearing the real burden, and taxes that are levied because they yield revenues now even though the long-run effects may be bad.

Nevertheless, most governments that rely heavily on tax revenues, as practically all do, are continually starved for revenues. Taxpayers are reluctant to vote for new or higher taxes; they seek to evade payment wherever possible and try to shift the burden onto others.

This leads to the second fundamental conflict, that between interest groups. Farmers try to have taxes paid by business. Business wants taxes paid by consumers. The rich want to tax the poor and the poor the rich. Polluters want the general public to bear the cost of antipollution devices. Shipping companies want the public to bear the cost of harbor development. And so on, ad infinitum. Innumerable pressure groups want to get the benefits from government expenditures while others pay the cost. A variation on this theme is exemption from taxes. Interest groups seek to pay less than their share of the cost of government through special tax privileges.

These considerations lead to the two principles of taxation as seen by the taxpayer:

1. A lower tax is better than a higher tax.

2. If we have to have taxes, it is best if someone else pays them.

Finally, trying to stand above this hurly-burly is the economist, who analyzes taxes in terms of their effects on economic welfare via the allocation of resources, on the distribution of income and the equity of the tax burden, and on economic growth and incentives. Most of the time no one listens.

Yet our tax system, federal, state, and local, is the outcome of all of these conflicting forces and the political power that special interests are able to mobilize. The wonder is that it makes as much sense as it does. This situation creates an understandable feedback. If taxpay-

ers view the tax system as full of favored or sheltered positions for some and undue burdens for others, their opposition is increased, which reinforces the tax bureaucrat's attitude, and the whole system moves further from the economist's goals of equity and rationality.

Types of Taxes

Now that we have paid our respects to the basic irrationality of the tax system, we should examine its size and structure. In 1979 total tax receipts and other charges collected by the federal, state, and local governments were more than $955 billion. Naturally it was the largest amount collected in any one year up to that time. The total is larger now, and so is the amount per person. Around the turn of the century the total was about $1.6 billion (about $17 per capita). As late as 1940 the total was only $16.5 billion and the per capita amount was $102.77. Price levels have risen, of course, but we still buy a lot more government than we used to.

The chief federal taxes are the personal and corporate income taxes. Together they are responsible for about 62 percent of all federal tax receipts. The bulk of the remaining federal tax revenues come from employment taxes and taxes on commodities (excise taxes). States and local governments also use income taxes, but

Table 30–1
Tax Revenues by Type of Tax, 1979

	Federal	State and Local	Total
	(Billions of Dollars)		
Individual income tax	$217.8	$ 36.9	$254.7
Corporate income tax	65.7	12.1	77.8
Excise and sales taxes	26.7	27.7	54.4
Property taxes		65.0	65.0
Other taxes	8.7	17.3	26.0
Total	318.9	159.0	477.9

their chief revenues (63 percent of their total revenue) come from sales taxes and taxes on property. Table 30–1 breaks down the total by chief types of tax.

Our next step is to take a closer look at the major taxes that provide the great bulk of government revenues in the United States. In doing so, we shall examine a number of features of the tax system associated particularly with each type of tax:

1. The individual income tax and the concepts of progressive, proportional, and regressive taxes.

2. Excise and sales taxes and the question of who actually pays a tax and bears its burden.

3. Property taxes and the relationship of taxes to urban development and special economic interests.

4. The corporate income tax and problems of determining the full economic effects of a tax.

In the discussions that follow one point will become clear: the tax system raises revenues, but it also has important effects on the relative economic positions of rich and poor, business and consumer, and special interests and the general public. At times it is hard to tell whether the good guys are winning or losing.

The Personal Income Tax: Progressivity

All taxes are controversial, and the personal income tax is perhaps the most controversial of all. At the very least, it is the one under the most constant attack. The attack comes mostly from the conservative (that is, wealthier) side of the political spectrum, for the key fact about the personal income tax is that at the federal level it is moderately "progressive," and even

Table 30–2
Progressive Tax

Income	Percentage of Income Paid in Taxes	Amount of Tax
$ 5,000	10	$ 500
10,000	15	1,500
15,000	20	3,000

Table 30–3
Proportional Tax

Income	Percentage of Income Paid in Taxes	Amount of Tax
$ 5,000	10	$ 500
10,000	10	1,000
15,000	10	1,500

state or local income taxes either are progressive or could be made progressive.

A *progressive tax* is one that takes a larger proportion of income in taxes, the higher the income. Table 30–2 is an example. The key to whether a tax is progressive or not lies in the increasing percentage of income paid in taxes, not in the amount paid.

For example, the tax rates in Table 30–3 are an example of a *proportional tax,* in which the percent of income paid in taxes remains the same irrespective of income. In this case the amount of the tax rises as income increases, but the ratio of tax to income remains constant at 10 percent.

A *regressive tax* is the opposite of the progressive tax. In this case the percentage of income paid in taxes declines as income rises, as in Table 30–4. Note that in this latter example the amount of tax still rises as income rises, but not very much. The distinguishing feature of the regressive tax is the declining proportion of taxes to income in the middle column, however. If the tax is steeply regressive, it is even possible that the amounts shown in the last column could also decline.

Table 30–4
Regressive Tax

Income	Percentage of Income Paid in Taxes	Amount of Tax
$ 5,000	10	$500
10,000	8	800
15,000	6	900

- A **progressive tax** takes an increasing percentage of income in taxes as incomes rise.

- A **proportional tax** takes the same percentage of income in taxes as incomes rise.

- A **regressive tax** takes a decreasing percentage of income in taxes as incomes rise.

Many state or local income taxes are designed as proportional taxes. For example, a local income tax may require payments equal to 2 percent of total income.[1] The federal income tax is designed to be progressive, however. This design is modified by a huge number of exemptions and modifications that enable the few people with very high incomes to pay smaller proportions of their income in taxes than many people with lower incomes. Let's look at this very highly controversial situation.

The progressiveness of the federal income tax is built into the basic rates charged. These rates are modified by deductions and exemptions open to all taxpayers, which depend upon the number of persons in the household. Table 30–5 is an example of the progressiveness of the system as illustrated by the tax liability of a married couple filing a joint return and taking the standard deduction for the years 1980 (before the 1981 tax legislation) and 1984 (after the new legislation). Tax liabilities were reduced for all income levels but the larger

reductions, in both dollars and percent, were for the higher incomes. The changes were scheduled to take effect in stages over the 1980-1984 period.

The progressiveness of the basic system has been strongly modified by provisions that enable persons with higher incomes to avoid some of the tax liabilities they would otherwise incur. Some of the more important are:

1. Certain types of income do not have to be reported for tax purposes or can be offset by "losses" or "costs." These include
   A. Income earned as interest on state and local bonds.
   B. Losses on business activities.
   C. Depletion allowances on natural resources (such as oil) and large depreciation charges on income-producing real estate (up to 20 percent annually in some instances) can be deducted from earned income for income tax purposes.
   While many of these provisions make sense for ordinary business activities, they provide large loopholes for tax avoidance.

2. "Capital gains" are taxed at a flat rate of 28 percent, irrespective of an individual's

---

[1]Most state and local income taxes allow some exemptions, and people with higher incomes are usually better able to avoid paying taxes on part of their income than people with lower incomes. In practice, this makes most state and local income taxes somewhat regressive.

Table 30–5
Federal Personal Income Tax, 1980 and 1984

Taxable Income	1980 Tax		1984 Tax	
	Dollars	Percent	Dollars	Percent
$ 15,000	$ 2,055	13.7	$ 1,581	10.5
25,000	4,633	18.5	3,565	14.3
35,000	8,088	23.1	6,218	17.8
50,000	14,778	29.6	11,368	22.7
75,000	27,778	37.0	21,468	28.6
100,000	41,998	42.0	32,400	32.4
150,000	73,528	49.0	56,524	37.7
200,000	107,032	53.5	81,400	40.7

*For incomes of $5,000 or less, the optional standard deduction was used; above that, deductions were assumed to be 10% of income.

income. This allows for substantially reduced taxes on income from increased values of securities and other assets. It also enables corporation executives to be paid in part by capital gains rather than salaries, through stock option plans. The greatest benefits accrue to families with incomes over $75,000 annually.

3. "Income splitting" (filing of separate returns by husband and wife) enables families to move downward to lower tax brackets.

There are many similar loopholes in the tax system, some created originally in order to provide tax privileges for special economic interests and now all but impossible to remove. They are all regressive in nature, because they usually apply to income other than earned salaries or wages. The rationale for most of them is that they are designed to encourage capital investment, increase initiative, or subsidize activities important to the national interest. As such, they embody the "trickle down" theory of economic benefits: encouraging capital and promoting the interests of the wealthy stimulates economic growth and thereby benefits everyone. The cost, however, is a distortion of the tax system that fosters a particular pattern of income distribution that may well be far from the best.

Tax loopholes allow a few large incomes to avoid all taxes. In most years there are several hundred individual returns reporting adjusted gross incomes of $100,000 or more, and a few over $1 million that pay no federal income tax at all. One should remember, too, that these incomes include only the income that must be reported and not necessarily all of the income received.

One regressive aspect of the federal personal income tax is the individual exemption. As of 1980, a taxpayer was allowed to reduce his or her taxable income by $1,000 for each dependent. On the surface it seems as if this affects everyone equally, but it doesn't. It allows the richer person in a higher tax bracket to reduce tax payments by more than the poorer person in a lower tax bracket. For example, if you have a taxable income of $35,000, one personal exemption reduces your tax by $490. But if your taxable income is $9,000, the personal exemption saves you only $210. That happens because the tax rate on income in the $35,000 range is 49 percent, while the rate is only 21 percent on income in the $9,000 bracket. The basic principle is that when the tax rates are progressive with each increase in income, as ours are, any flat exemption that applies to everyone makes the system less progressive. Thus, an income tax exemption for families with children in college, a widely supported proposal, would benefit Mrs. Gotrocks more than Mr. Steelworker or Mr. Blackman. Perhaps it would make more sense to abolish the present personal exemptions and use the additional revenue for a federal scholarship program based on need.

The net result of these and other provisions of the federal income tax law is to make the whole system far less progressive than the nominal rates would suggest. Average tax rates at all income levels are below 30 percent and no one pays a tax above 50 percent of his income, however large that income might be. Indeed, effective tax rates tend to decline somewhat for incomes above $150,000 annually. Figure 30–1 shows the situation as it prevailed in 1973, giving the nominal rates and actual rates. Nominal rates were above actual rates, with a wider gap at higher incomes.

The Pros and Cons of Progressive Taxation
Supporters of progressive taxation start with an underlying bias against income inequality on ethical grounds. It can be argued that every participant in the economic life of a society makes his contribution to that society and that continuation of the society requires each person's participation. All should, therefore, be treated equally. Contributions may be unequal because individual abilities differ, but the dif-

Figure 30-1
Nominal and Actual
Federal Income Tax
Rates, 1973

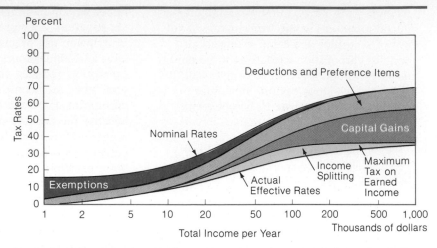

The horizontal scale is a logarithmic or ratio scale, so that a straight line on the chart represents a constant rate of change. The total income shown on the horizontal scale does not include income unreported for tax purposes—such as interest on state and local bonds.

(*Source:* Joseph A. Pechman, *Federal Tax Policy* (Washington: Brookings Institution, 1966), p. 66.)

ferences in abilities may rest on factors over which the individual has little control, such as heredity, the influence of the socialization process in the early ages, and access to the education system. Since differences in contribution to society are usually not the result of individual choices, in this view, there is no ethical basis for differences in reward. The ethical argument is supplemented by the argument that the wealthy can afford to pay a larger percentage of their income than the poor because their welfare will be less strongly affected.

Finally, there is the political argument. Large inequalities of income (and wealth) put greater political power in the hands of the rich. This power can be used to change the rules of the game and direct more wealth and power to the wealthy until the whole social fabric becomes dominated by an oligarchy of the wealthy few. A progressive tax system is one way in which this sort of development can be held in check.

The opponents of progressive taxation respond chiefly on economic grounds, stressing the incentive effects of progressive taxes. It seems to many a matter of common sense that if the government takes away a sizable percentage of increases in income, people will work less. This effect will reduce the production potential of the economy by making leisure more attractive relative to work. On the other hand, it is equally sensible to argue that a modest reduction in incomes will stimulate more work in order to maintain incomes at the former level. Attempts to measure these conflicting effects of taxes on work effort have been inconclusive: some work harder, others work less, and the net effect seems to be very small—at present tax rates.

Opponents also argue that in the long run progressive taxation will reduce the supply of capital by reducing savings. They argue that people with high incomes save a larger proportion of their incomes than people with lower incomes, causing a progressive personal income tax to reduce the flow of savings available for investment and economic growth.

The heart of the debate remains on the plane

of values, however. If one views the social order as composed of discrete individuals who exercise free choice among alternatives, the arguments for progressive taxation do not make much sense. People should be rewarded for their efforts because they choose to make those efforts. They could choose not to, and society as a whole would suffer. Social justice, in this view, is that an individual ought to get what he earns. On the other hand, if one views the social order as a cooperative effort in which individual actions are determined by one's heredity, background, and place in the world, there is a strong presumption that rewards ought to be more or less equal. In this view, earnings are the result less of individual choice and more of forces beyond individual control, and adjusting those earnings will not significantly affect the size of the pie.

Arguments such as these can only be settled in the political arena. There the argument that the rich can afford to pay at a higher rate than the poor has carried the day. This implies acceptance of the argument that a more egalitarian distribution of income tends to increase aggregate welfare, as long as total output is not significantly affected.

Two Conflicting Principles of Equity

The argument over progressive income taxes involves a fundamental disagreement over the question of how to achieve equity in taxation. One side would apply the ability-to-pay principle. The other side emphasizes the benefit principle.

The *benefit principle* is the older one. Taxes are levied to pay for public goods and services that benefit those who use them. One principle of equity is that the users should pay the cost of the services. This principle might be applied easily when those who benefit from a public service can be readily identified, such as the users of water from a publicly owned water supply system. But it is extremely difficult or impossible to apply to true public goods char-

acterized by the nonexclusion principle, as explained in the last chapter. The problem is that water can be priced and supplied by a private firm perhaps as well as by a public agency, and market principles of pricing can be applied to it; but what does one do about the costs of operating the lighthouse on a rocky shore whose services can't be priced?

The same sort of problem arises for the other type of public good, the one whose marginal costs are nil and welfare maximization dictates that it be supplied free. If it isn't priced, the users can't be required to pay for it.

Advocates of the benefit principle are forced to fall back on the assumption that for most public goods the benefits are about the same for each person, so the tax burden should be borne equally. Or that benefits are proportional to income, so that taxes should be proportional rather than progressive or regressive. Or that benefits are linked to property ownership and taxes should be based on the value of property. At the very least, what started out as an apparently simple rule ends up in a maze of uncertainty.

The *ability-to-pay principle* is more widely accepted today, but its rationale also is widely questioned. It is based on the principle of diminishing marginal utility, and is related to the idea that a more egalitarian distribution of income produces greater social welfare than a less egalitarian one. In its simplest form, it holds that the rich should pay proportionately more taxes than the poor because they are richer and can afford it. A dollar taken in taxes from the rich man reduces his satisfactions less than a dollar taken from a poor man. In that sense the rich man can afford to give up the tax dollar more readily than the poor man.

We have already examined the logic behind this argument in Chapter 28 and found that it has a great deal of validity but is correct only in terms of probabilities and requires the assumption that the utilities or satisfactions of the poor and the rich be comparable. Many economists argue that this assumption cannot be proven and is highly unscientific.

The ability-to-pay principle has a broad plausibility, however, when applied to the two extremes of the distribution of income. Dollars can be used to provide a vacation in Acapulco for Mrs. Gotrocks' daughter, or food for the children of a poor rural family in Appalachia. Whatever the comparability of utilities, one's first reaction is to feed the kids.

The ability-to-pay principle also has some administrative justification: taxes can be collected only from people with the income to pay. Tax officials from time immemorial have tried to apply that simple rule. It means that those with higher incomes must bear the larger burden because they are the only ones who have the money.

Even if the ability-to-pay principle is accepted—because of its logic, or its common-sense plausibility, or its administrative feasibility—the problem of equity is not resolved. How much progressivity should be introduced into the tax system? Isn't a proportional tax enough, since the rich pay a larger dollar amount than the poor? Indeed, that is true even for some regressive taxes. These kinds of questions are not answered by the general principle.

The search for concrete standards of equity in taxation is doomed to failure. Neither the benefit principle nor the ability-to-pay principle provide definitive answers. The solution to the problem is inevitably thrown into the political arena, where the resolution of the problem depends in large part on the relative strength and power of contesting interests.

- The **benefit principle** of taxation is that taxes should be based on the amount of benefits that individuals receive from government services.

- The **ability-to-pay principle** of taxation holds that taxes should be based on ability to pay because a marginal tax dollar is allegedly less useful to a rich person than a poor one.

Excise and Sales Taxes: Incidence

An excise tax is a tax on the production or sale of an individual commodity, such as alcoholic beverages or tobacco products. A sales tax differs in that it is a tax on sales of all commodities (unless some are specifically exempted). Excise taxes have an ancient history. They include such classic taxes as those on salt or matches that have been famous throughout history. The notorious tax on tea levied in the American colonies by the British government, which led to the Boston Tea Party of 1773, was essentially an excise tax levied in the form of a tax on importation of tea.

An excise tax such as the tax on whiskey or

Figure 30–2
Effect of an Excise Tax

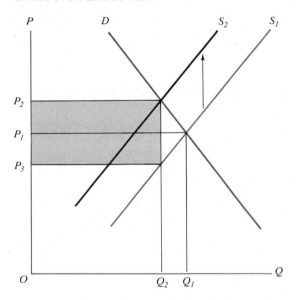

Starting with D and S, the market is in equilibrium at price P_1 and output Q_1. An excise tax is imposed, raising costs to the producers and shifting the supply curve upward by the amount of the tax, to a new supply curve S_2. A higher price P_2 now prevails, along with reduced output Q_2. The difference between P_2 and P_3 is the amount of the tax, and the government's total revenue from the tax is the shaded area.

Figure 30–3
Excise Tax with Elastic and Inelastic Demand

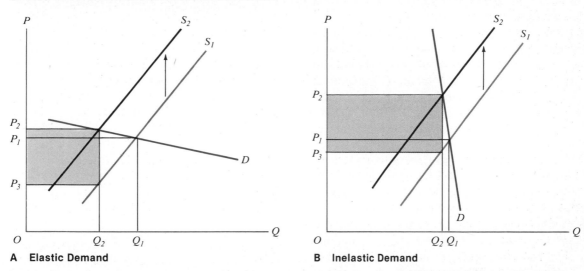

A Elastic Demand

B Inelastic Demand

In **A**, where the taxed product has an elastic demand, the excise tax brings a large decrease in *Q* and a small rise in *P*. Total receipts are relatively small and the incidence of the tax falls largely on the producer. In **B**, where the taxed product has an inelastic demand, there is a large increase in *P* and a small drop in *Q*. The burden of the tax has been shifted very largely to the buyer, and tax receipts are relatively large.

cigarettes, which is paid directly to the government by the manufacturer, is partly shifted to the consumer in the form of higher prices. A portion of the burden of the tax is borne by the producer, however. Figure 30–2 shows what happens in the simple case of a competitive industry whose product is taxed. In this case the producer was able to shift a portion of the burden of the tax forward to the consumer. The *incidence* of the tax—the final resting place of the full tax burden—was partly on the consumer and partly on the producer.

The extent to which the incidence of a tax can be shifted to the consumer depends very largely on the elasticity of demand for the product taxed. Where demand is elastic an excise tax will bring a large reduction in sales and most of the burden will be borne by the producer. The opposite is true where demand is inelastic: sales will not fall significantly and

the burden is shifted largely to the consumer. Figure 30–3 shows why. These diagrams help to explain why excise taxes are levied only on certain commodities: on necessities that people must buy, on luxuries for which price is an insignificant element in the decision to buy, or on "big ticket" items like automobiles, for which the tax is a small percentage of the selling price. These are the items for which demand is relatively inelastic.

Sales taxes differ somewhat from excise taxes in that they are collected from the consumer at the point of sale. They are usually levied as a fixed percentage of the sales price, and usually apply to all commodities. Most sales taxes in the United States are levied by state and local governments. Since they apply to all commodities and are borne by consumers, sales taxes have the great political advantage of not arousing the opposition of important business interests. They also are borne most heavily by lower income groups and do not arouse the opposition of the wealthy. This also has political advantages.

Sales taxes are one of the most regressive elements in the U.S. tax system. The reason for their regressiveness is that people with lower incomes spend a larger proportion of their income and save less than people with higher incomes. A larger proportion of their income is therefore subject to the tax. For example, a study in Illinois in the 1950s showed that poor families with incomes of $1,000–$2,000 annually spent 80 percent of their income on taxed commodities, while families with incomes above $10,000 spent only 45 percent on goods subject to the sales tax. This regressive feature of the sales tax is sometimes modified by exempting food and medicine from the tax, but while popular with the poor this exemption is not admired by financial officials because it reduces revenues very substantially.

● The **tax incidence** is the locus of the ultimate tax burden. When one economic unit is able to compensate for its tax payment at the expense of another, we say that *shifting* of the incidence occurs.

The Property Tax: Special Interests and Urban Development

Property taxes are the mainstay of public revenues for local governments, including school districts and a wide variety of other local government units. They are under greater local control than any other tax, yet they are more poorly administered, more unfairly levied, and have more evil effects than any other tax.

Why, then, are they so widely used? Briefly, because they bring in revenue, and local governments need revenue. Land and buildings can't run away and hide when the tax assessor comes around, and can always be seized if the tax isn't paid. Furthermore, it is very difficult to shift property taxes to someone else. The

Figure 30-4
Who Pays the Property Tax on Rental Property? Before the Tax

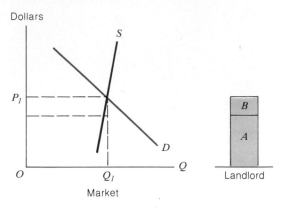

The rental payment P_1 is determined by supply and demand in the market. The owner's profit B is the difference between total revenues $A + B$ and the owner's costs A.

homeowner, of course, bears the burden himself. Owners of rental property are able to shift the tax to renters in the long run but not in the short run. In the short run, housing rents are determined by the supply of and demand for rental housing and property taxes must be paid out of the landlord's revenues. In the long run, reduced returns from higher taxes influence the supply of property available for rent and the burden shifts to the renter while the landlord's profits return to normal. Thus the renter is affected in the same way as the homeowner. How this happens is shown in Figures 30–4 through 30–6. As for farmers and owners of business and commercial property, they are unable to shift the property tax to others. It adds to their costs, but selling prices are determined by supply and demand in the market. It is only because costs affect supply in the long run that property taxes can shift the allocation of resources somewhat if they bear more heavily on one industry than another. In short, property taxes are a good source of revenue; they cannot be avoided and usually cannot be shifted to others.

Figure 30–5
Who Pays the Property Tax on Rental
Property? After the Tax: The Short Run

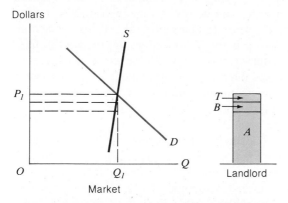

The imposition of a property tax does not change demand
and supply in the market, so the price and total revenue
are unchanged. The owner's profits B are reduced by the
amount of the tax, T.

Figure 30–6
Who Pays the Property Tax on Rental
Property? After the Tax: The Long Run

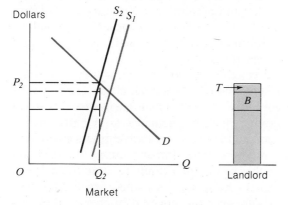

In the long run, reduced profits relative to earnings on
other investments reduce the supply of rental housing
from S_1 to S_2, rents go up to P_2 and the owner's profits
B return to normal. Because there are fewer rental units,
total profits of all owners are reduced even though profits
per unit recover to where they were before. The full
impact of the tax is now felt by the renter, while the individual owner is just as well off as he was before. (B in this
figure is just as large as B in Figure 30–4.)

Nevertheless, property taxes have had a
very serious impact on urban development and
are an important reason why slums and deteriorating housing are a feature of the urban
scene. Property taxes are levied on the assessed value of property, including improvements. Since improvements are taxed, owners
and landlords are discouraged from maintaining their property adequately. If we wanted to
encourage good housing, we should tax land
but not its improvements.

Perhaps an even more harmful aspect of
property taxes is the almost universal practice
of taxing undeveloped land at very low rates
while developed property is taxed at much
higher rates. In most localities this practice is
forbidden by law, but it is nevertheless
achieved by setting a taxable value on undeveloped land at levels much below its market
value while assessing developed property at
levels much closer to its market value. This
practice enables speculators to buy and hold
land for future gains at very little cost to
themselves. Builders then find that the price of
land is higher and home buyers have to pay
more for their houses. Because prices are
higher, there is less building, contributing to
our persistent housing shortage. Builders move
further out beyond developed areas to build,
leaping over the speculative tracts and leaving
them as irregular weed-filled areas of urban
sprawl. As a result, streets are extended and
cost more, sewer and other utility lines are
longer and more expensive, and the fiscal
strain on local governments is increased. The
fiscal strain is compounded, of course, by low
tax yields on the underassessed and undertaxed
open lands.

By contrast, if undeveloped land were properly taxed, speculative land could not be held
so easily for long periods, the demand for land
would be reduced by cutting down the practice
of holding it for increased prices, and the price
of land would be lower. The cost of housing
would thereby be reduced, there would be less
urban sprawl, and costs of urban services

would be lower. One side effect would be to bring about a more centralized urban development and hence more open space in the long run. Government revenues would be greater, both from higher taxes on underdeveloped land and greater revenues from improvements, and more funds would be available for urban planning and other city services.

All of this has been known in detail for a hundred years, ever since the American economist Henry George (1839–1897) published his pamphlet *Our Land and Land Policy* in 1871. Yet perverse property tax policies remain. Why? The reason, apparently, has been the dominant role of real estate interests in local governments and farmers in state legislatures. Low taxes on land bring an increased demand for land and thereby raise its price, benefiting all those whose assets are held in land at the expense of everyone else. While few economists today would accept George's view that a single tax on land alone would solve most of our economic problems, few would not agree that the inequitable (and sometimes corrupt) administration of the property tax exaggerates our already difficult urban problems.

The Corporate Income Tax: Economic Impact of Taxes

The corporation income tax is levied by the federal government on the earnings of corporations. It appears simple. The first $25,000 of corporate profits is taxed at a rate of 22 percent. Everything over that pays 46 percent. The reason for the difference is to aid small firms as compared with larger ones.

But now everything becomes *very* complicated. In order to determine profits, a firm must deduct costs from revenues, with the difference being the amount taxed. This gives firms every incentive to overstate costs and understate revenues. Since most firms pay the 46 percent rate, they can provide expense accounts and bonuses for executives, raising costs and having

about half of the actual expense offset by reduced taxes. Advertising, in effect, costs only 46 percent of the total bill, with Uncle Sam paying the remainder. Depreciation charges can be set at very high figures, reducing corporate taxes in the short run: a machine that lasts ten years can be depreciated in five, reducing taxes now at the expense of higher taxes later (this is equivalent to a short-term loan from the federal government). In these and other ways the allocation of resources is distorted.

The corporate income tax brings about a form of double taxation. The corporation's profits are taxed. It then pays dividends out of its after-tax income. Those dividends become part of the taxable income of individuals who pay the personal income tax. Two taxes are paid on the same income. In addition to the inequities involved, this situation provides incentives for the corporation to spend more for expansion instead of paying larger dividends. The expansion creates capital gains for the stockholders, who can then sell their stock and be taxed at a rate of only 28 percent on the gains instead of 46 percent on the corporate profits and perhaps 20–35 percent on the dividends. This process encourages the growth of big business, not for economic reasons, but as a device for tax avoidance.

Even the question of who pays the corporate income tax is not clear. The easy answer is the corporation itself. Since an income tax is on profit, which is calculated after costs are accounted for, it does not affect prices charged to consumers. The firm maximizes its profit on the basis of market conditions and the tax then comes off the top. But when firms have some control over the prices they charge, they can anticipate the corporate income tax and try to gain profits after taxes that are as large as profits before taxes. In setting prices, the tax on profits becomes an implicit cost, is embodied in selling prices, and is thereby passed on to the consumer. There is some indirect evidence that this is what happens: rates of profit are lower today than they were in the days before the corporate income tax, but they aren't 46 percent lower. If the corporation bore the entire burden of the tax, they would be. Apparently a combination of adjustments has occurred. Costs are probably overstated somewhat, firms are using more of their earnings to finance expansion, and some of the corporate income tax has probably been shifted to consumers in the form of higher prices. The convention among economists is that half of the corporate income tax is shifted to consumers—then they can be only half wrong, at most.

These considerations indicate that the corporate income tax has had a variety of influences on resource allocation, the distribution of income, the structure of industry, and the burden of taxation. Yet no one knows exactly how or to what extent. It is this last point that is most important: here is an important tax whose impact is largely unknown and subject to wide speculation. Since it brings in large revenues and can't be shown to be significantly harmful (although it may be; we just don't know), it answers the Treasury officials' prayer for a productive tax whose burdens are largely hidden.

The impact of the corporate income tax has been greatly reduced over the last quarter century, however. The rate of the tax was reduced from 52 percent to 50 percent in 1964, to 48 percent in 1965, and to 46 percent in 1979. The purpose of these reductions was to stimulate business investment. Other changes in tax laws enabled corporations to depreciate their capital equipment more rapidly than the assets actually wore out (1954), thereby allowing firms to overstate their costs for tax purposes. Even more rapid depreciation was permitted in 1962, 1971, and 1981 for various types of capital assets. In addition, since 1962 corporations have been allowed to take credits against their tax liabilities for the purchase of new equipment. There is now a veritable forest of tax exemptions and credits that have reduced the effective corporate income tax rate from its

statutory level of 46 percent to an average of about 28 percent. Some corporations pay more than the average and others less, depending on the extent to which they can take advantage of the various allowances and credits.

Further legislation in 1981 liberalized even further the system of investment credits and depreciation allowances, while keeping the statutory level at 46 percent, as part of the Reagan administration's program of encouraging business investment. The effect of this legislation would reduce the effective level of the corporate income tax to about 14 percent by 1986, which would be a 50 percent reduction from the 1980 effective rate.

The corporate income tax is gradually disappearing. In 1950 it provided about 25 percent of all federal tax revenues, in 1980 only 10 percent, and the share will continue to fall under present legislation. But the method of reducing the tax using a variety of tax credits and depreciation allowances gives favored treatment to some forms of investment compared to others, thereby distorting the economic system as a whole. The best solution would appear to be repeal of the corporate income tax altogether, which would make the entire system of tax credits and depreciation allowances irrelevant.

Corporate income could still be taxed as if it were the personal income of stockholders, with the tax on both dividend income and corporate retained earnings withheld at the source in the same manner as withholding income taxes on wages. In this way the double taxation inherent in corporate and personal income taxes could be eliminated while continuing to tax incomes earned by individuals through stock ownership.

Neutrality in Taxation

Most economists would agree that taxes should influence the pattern of production as little as possible. This view is consistent with the proposition that the private sector tends to adapt to consumer demand in a welfare-maximizing pattern. Taxes, it is argued, should distort the pattern as little as possible.

For example, a general sales tax that is levied equally on all commodities is superior to an excise tax, which is levied only on a few commodities. The excise tax increases the price of the goods on which it is levied and consumers tend to buy less of those goods than they otherwise would. This distortion of consumer behavior is greater than would be created by a sales tax of equal amount that does not discriminate against some commodities.

Even a sales tax would distort the choice between spending and saving to some extent, so it is not completely neutral. Neither is an income tax, which may have some impact on the choice between work and leisure. For some taxes, like the corporate income tax, so little is definitely known about its incidence that its *tax neutrality* is very hard to assess. Indeed, no tax is completely neutral with respect to the allocation of resources, and some distortion is inevitable. We must think in terms of degrees of neutrality. The principle of neutrality is abridged if the tax applies to some people, commodities, or situations and not to others, or if incidence can be shifted. The broader the base of the tax and the fewer the possibilities for shifting its incidence the more neutral it will be.

- **Tax neutrality** occurs when taxes do not affect any decision in the private sector. Complete neutrality is impossible.

Does the United States Have a Progressive Tax System?

When all aspects of the whole tax system in the United States are taken into account and their incidence estimated according to the best current knowledge, the U.S. tax system shows up as largely a system of proportional taxation that is highly regressive for the lowest 5 percent of income recipients and progressive for the upper 4 percent. Those are the findings of the most recent authoritative study by economists Joseph A. Pechman and Benjamin A. Okner of the Brookings Institution.[2] Pechman and Okner studied the tax system in 1966, including taxes levied by all levels of government. They made estimates of tax incidence and shifting to arrive at two different results, one based on the "most progressive" and one on the "least progressive" assumptions, in order to determine the limits within which the tax system fell. The conclusions were surprisingly alike. Only families at the very top and bottom of the income distribution pay more than 25 percent of their incomes in taxes, and in the range between those two extremes the tax system does very little to alter the pattern of income distribution. Figure 30–7 provides a summary of the chief findings.

Pechman and Okner found that homeowners pay lower taxes than renters, rural families less than city families, and married couples less than single persons. So if you want to minimize your taxes you should marry and buy a house in the country.

They also studied the differences between taxes paid on property income, such as rent, interest, and dividends, and those paid on income from work. Their conclusions on this point depended strongly on the assumptions about the shifting of tax incidence. If much shifting occurs, income from property is taxed at about 21 percent and income from work at 17 percent. If shifting does not take place, the tax rate on property income is 33 percent while it stays at 17 percent for labor income.

---

[2]Joseph A. Pechman and Benjamin A. Okner, *Who Bears the Tax Burden?* (Washington, D.C.: The Brookings Institution, 1974).

Figure 30-7
Effective Tax Rates by
Population Percentile,
1966

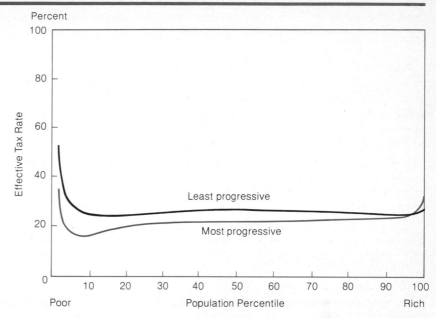

The Pechman-Okner study shows that the effective tax rate (taxes as a percent of income) remains nearly the same except for the very poor and the very rich at either end of the income distribution.

The Net Distribution of Burdens and Benefits

Government budgets not only take away income in the form of taxes, they also provide benefits in the form of expenditures. It is possible to estimate the net effects of government budgets by supplementing tax burdens with expenditure benefits. The task is not an easy one and some heroic assumptions have to be made. For example, how should the benefits from general government expenditures such as police protection and national defense be allocated? Should they be distributed to each family equally, or according to income? As for taxes, how shall the burdens of the corporate income tax be allocated, to the stockholder or the customers, and in what proportions? These and other problems make any estimates of redistribution of income through government budgets a difficult and controversial task.

Nevertheless, two worthwhile estimates of this sort have been made, and their results are summarized in Table 30–6, which shows the redistribution of incomes after taxes and benefits from government spending. Both were based on sophisticated (but somewhat different) assumptions about the burdens of the various sorts of taxes and the distribution of benefits from government spending. The results show a strikingly similar pattern existing in the late 1930s, the mid-1940s, and 1960. There is a net redistribution in favor of the poor and against the upper-middle and upper income groups, while there is little change in the net incomes of lower-middle income families. As of 1960, the poorer one-third of all families had higher incomes, while the affluent upper 15 percent had lower incomes. The majority in the middle showed little impact from government budgets. When allowance is made for changing price levels and for the

Table 30–6
Redistribution of Incomes Through Government Budgets

Income of Consumer Unit	Redistributed Income as a Percentage of Original Income		
	1938–1939	1946–1947	1960
Under $1,000	123.2	173.4 ⎱	⎰ 155.1
$1,000–1,999	100.9	122.4 ⎰	
2,000–2,999	96.5	111.1	144.4
3,000–3,999	96.7	106.6	118.5
4,000–4,999	98.0	98.5	98.7
5,000–7,499	100.9	92.6	97.1
7,500–9,999	80.8 ⎰	78.6	101.7
$10,000 and over			86.8

Source: Data for 1938–1939 and 1946–1947 is from John H. Adler, "The Fiscal System, the Distribution of Income and Public Welfare," in Kenyon E. Poole (ed.), *Fiscal Policies and the American Economy* (New York: Prentice-Hall, 1951), p. 396. Data for 1960 is from W. Irwin Gillespie, "Effect of Public Expenditures on the Distribution of Income," in Richard A. Musgrave (ed.), *Essays in Fiscal Federalism* (Washington: Brookings Institution, 1965), p. 162.

somewhat different methodologies of the two estimates, there has been remarkably little change over the years.

Two further points should be made about Table 30–6. The redistribution of income toward the poor, which it shows, would be changed if general government expenditures were allocated differently. Table 30–6 is based on the assumption that those expenditures are equally beneficial to each person. One could argue, however, that the protection aspects of government, particularly police and fire protection and national defense, are more valuable to the rich than the poor. The benefits from those expenditures could be allocated according to income, and this would reduce the redistribution of income from the affluent to the poor, leaving the middle income groups largely unaffected. If the allocation of these benefits were done according to holdings of wealth the picture would be even more different.[3] If one wished to argue the best possible case for the welfare-maximizing effects of gov-

ernment budgets, one would use the data in Table 30–6.

The Overall Picture

Taxes and budgets reflect the prevailing ideology and the structure of economic power. The economist can do little more than analyze their impact in terms of burdens and benefits. The analysis involves the theory of tax incidence (who pays the tax and in what form) and the shifting of tax burdens (whether the real effects are felt by the person who actually pays the money or by someone else). This chapter has shown how the analysis can be done and some of the results. Perhaps the single most important conclusion is that the tax system of the United States is far from an ideal one. This result is modified by the distribution of benefits from expenditures, but whether the system as a whole tends to redistribute incomes from the rich to the poor remains largely an open question. If we take seriously the proposition that a poor family will gain more welfare from an additional dollar than an affluent family will lose by giving up a dollar, then we must be

---

[3]We have no idea of how different it would be. This type of estimate has never been made—illustrating some of the ideological preconceptions of contemporary economics.

highly critical of the U.S. tax system and sceptical about the net benefits from government budgets as a whole.

The tax system is equally deficient with respect to economic stability and growth. Little consideration is given to the effects of taxes on these important questions. An important tax, the corporate income tax, is maintained even though its macroeconomic effects are largely unknown and its effect on the corporate structure may well be to strengthen giant enterprise. The property tax as it is now structured and administered has clearly detrimental effects on patterns of urban development, yet it continues as is because it is such a good producer of revenues. The loopholes and exemptions present in the federal income tax are there largely because of pressures from special economic interests.

It would be possible to devise a tax system to promote equity in income distribution, sustain prosperity, and promote economic growth. A tax system of that sort would be quite different from the present one.

Tax Policies of the Reagan Administration

The complexities of tax policy are well illustrated by the tax legislation of 1981.

First, there was a general reduction in personal income tax rates averaging about 25 percent. The purpose of this change is to stimulate economic activity by increasing the after-tax incomes of consumers at all levels. The administration expects that the increase in economic activity will be strong enough to raise government revenues by more than the tax reduction, thereby contributing to a reduced budget deficit. No one can tell in advance if that will happen, but a similar program worked in the early 1960s under somewhat different economic conditions. Administration spokespersons talk about a balanced budget by the 1984 or 1985 fiscal year.

A substantial portion of the tax reduction will be recaptured by "bracket creep." As incomes rise because of inflation, individual taxpayers move up into tax brackets where the tax rate is higher. The Treasury estimates that by 1984 more than 85 percent of the tax reduction will have been eliminated by bracket creep. The reduction is designed to have only a temporary stimulating effect on the economy. In 1985 and after, however, the legislation will "index" the personal income tax system—rates will be adjusted to compensate for inflation—in order to eliminate bracket creep.

Second, several changes were made that were designed or intended as stimuli to savings. These provisions were of great benefit to the wealthy. The administration expected larger savings by the wealthy to flow into investment, thereby increasing employment and output. The increase in output was expected to reduce inflation. To achieve these goals, the tax rate reductions were greater for upper-income families than for lower-income families. The reductions for taxable incomes below $50,000 per year ranged between 20 and 30 percent. For incomes above $50,000 the reductions ranged upward to 50 percent.

In addition, a number of changes were made in taxation of oil wells, leased equipment, and other investments that will provide new opportunities for the rich to shelter income from taxes. Estate and gift taxes were liberalized to free from taxation all but the very largest inheritances. Provisions for tax-exempt individual retirement plans were substantially liberalized. These changes in the law were designed to benefit primarily those with incomes of $50,000 or more each year.

Third, taxes on business enterprise were reduced. Existing capital equipment can be depreciated for tax purposes more rapidly, in three, five, or ten years, depending on the type of equipment, and buildings can be depreciated in fifteen years. Tax credits for new investment were increased. The corporate profits tax on the first $50,000 of profit was reduced as an aid to small firms, but the tax rate on profits above $50,000 was kept at 46 percent. However, the new depreciation rules and investment tax credits are expected to cut the effective corporate income tax rate in half, from an average of about 28 percent in 1980 to about 14 percent five years later.

Most individual taxpayers will end up in about the same position from which they began, as far as immediate effects of these tax changes are concerned. Tax liabilities will be reduced in 1982-83, but bracket creep will eliminate most of those gains by 1984. The relatively affluent will gain substantially, however, and business tax liabilities will be significantly reduced.

Investment should be stimulated by the 1981 tax changes. Most investment in new plant and equipment is financed out of business savings, which should increase because of the reduction in the effective rate of the corporate income tax. The economy's propensity to save should also increase, because of the increased after-tax income of the affluent. These two changes will make it more difficult for the economy to sustain high levels of output and employment. Increases in output capacity will be promoted by the stimulus to investment. But a higher propensity to save reduces the multiplier. The purchasing power created by new investment will be reduced below present ratios. Before 1981 the purchasing power generated by new investment was, in most circumstances, not great enough to absorb the output made possible by the new investment—this was the basic problem that gave rise to Keynesian economic policy—and continuing automation of production techniques makes the problem worse. The new tax structure worsens the situation even more. For the same reason, however, the economy will be less prone to inflation caused by excessive aggregate demand. How large these effects will be is almost impossible to predict.

The tax changes of 1981 show how important tax policy can be. The pattern of income distribution will be changed in favor of the affluent. The distribution of wealth will change in favor of large agglomerations of wealth. Business enterprise will benefit from lower taxes. All this legislation is designed to give private enterprise capitalism in the United States a new lease on life. But these benefits for the few will entail costs for the economy as a whole. The ability of the economy to sustain high levels of employment and output will be weakened. The great dilemma of the private enterprise economy is left unsolved: how to maintain a balance between aggregate supply and aggregate demand at high levels of income and output.

Summary

Any tax system involves the interplay of widely divergent economic interests, and the outcome is normally a hodgepodge of compromises arising out of conflict between government, taxpayers, and organized economic interest groups.

In the United States the most important taxes are the individual and corporate income taxes, excise and sales taxes, property taxes, and employment taxes.

The federal individual income tax has progressive base rates, but income splitting, deductions, exemptions, and special treatment for capital gains make it much less progressive, and even somewhat regressive at very high incomes. Arguments for and against progressive taxation rest ultimately on value judgments. Although the ability-to-pay principle argues that the rich are better able to pay taxes than the poor, it does not provide any guidelines to the degree of progressiveness that is desirable. The benefit principle holds, by contrast, that taxes should be paid by those who benefit from public services, but it is extremely difficult to apply in practice.

Excise and sales taxes are strong revenue producers. Excises are generally levied only on commodities with inelastic demand, which limits their usefulness. They are generally shifted to the final buyer of the taxed commodity and no pretense of fairness is made. Sales taxes are widely used by state and local governments, imparting a strong trend toward regressiveness to the tax system as a whole.

Property taxes, used widely by local governments, are usually not shiftable, except that in the case of rental property they are shifted to the renter in the long run. The administration of property taxes is almost uniformly poor, and they have been one reason for our present urban problems.

As for the corporate income tax, little is definitely known about its incidence and shifting, except that, as a double tax, it tends to promote the growth of big business by encouraging investment of retained earnings by business firms rather than payment of higher dividends to stockholders. In recent years the corporate income tax has been gradually reduced by a variety of allowances and credits. It should probably be abolished altogether.

In 1981 changes in federal tax legislation show how complex the goals of tax policy can be. They provided large benefits to the affluent and to business enterprise, while weakening the ability of the economy to sustain high levels of economic activity.

Taking all taxes together, the U.S. has a generally proportional tax structure, modified by rather limited progressivity in the upper incomes and regressivity in the lower. When government benefits are allocated to recipients, the combination of taxes and benefits redistributes real income in a progressive fashion; but there are doubts about that conclusion because of the way studies allocated benefits.

Key Concepts

progressive tax	**benefit principle**	**tax incidence**
proportional tax	**ability-to-pay principle**	**tax neutrality**
regressive tax		

For Discussion

1. Economists tell us that the excise tax on cigarettes is borne primarily by smokers rather than by the tobacco companies. Explain.

2. In what ways would the American economy be changed if the federal personal income tax were proportional instead of progressive?

3. In what ways would the economy be changed if the personal income tax were more progressive?

4. What are the pros and cons of replacing the personal income tax with a rational sales tax?

5. Should retired people with no children in the public schools be required to pay a property tax to help finance the school system? Explain.

6. What about families without children in school but with wage or salary income: should they be required to pay school taxes?

Chapter *31*

The Economics of War and Defense

Military spending requires that resources be shifted from civilian to military uses.

Output of both consumer and investment goods is reduced, sacrificing both current consumption and economic growth.

During active warfare the conversion to military production is done on a large scale, but it must be accomplished with minimum damage to production incentives. The strains imposed on the economy are almost sure to bring problems of inflation. Under these conditions a modern nation will move to economic planning and production allocations and a variety of other administrative economic controls.

A limited war brings similar problems but on a smaller scale. Solutions to the economic problem are more difficult, however, largely because the psychological environment does not permit full use of wartime mobilization methods.

The economy devoted heavily to military production but not actively at war has another dimension. It provides jobs and security for many people and develops a psychological and political environment conducive to its continuation, even though much productive effort produces no economic benefits. The jobs created in military production become important for maintenance of prosperity, and shifting to greater emphasis on civilian production becomes difficult. This chapter examines these problems of a wartime economy, and a militarized economy.

The Basic Economic Problem in Wartime

When a nation mobilizes it shifts its resources from civilian or peacetime uses to military or wartime uses. That is the *basic economic problem in wartime.* All other problems, like financing the war and keeping prices under control, are secondary and derive from the problem of how to shift to producing swords and away from producing plowshares.

The problem can be visualized in the simple terms of the production possibilities frontier. When an economy at full employment wishes to produce more military goods it can do so only by reducing production of civilian goods, as shown in Figure 31–1. Only when a country has significant amounts of unused capacity can it have more of both military and civilian goods. This was the position of the United States entering World War II. The high levels of unemployment of the Great Depression still prevailed, the economy was operating inside its production possibilities frontier, and for almost two years the enlarged wartime spending pushed up both civilian and military output. By the end of 1943, the classic wartime problem prevailed, as illustrated in Figure 31–2. Output was shifted from civilian to military products once full production was reached.

When a war lasts a long time, investment is also channeled into military production. This distorts the production possibilities of the economy by increasing military production capacity by larger amounts than civilian goods capacity. Figure 31–3 shows the distortion.

- The **basic economic problem in wartime** is how to shift the use of resources from civilian (peacetime) uses to military (wartime) uses.

Wartime Mobilization

The *wartime mobilization* of personnel and resources for the armed forces and military production is usually accomplished by use of nonmarket means. Men are drafted. Materials for production are controlled by administrative allocations. Personnel and materials for civilian production are restricted. A system of allocative planning run by a war production bureaucracy is evolved. This was the pattern that started in World War I and was developed on a large scale in World War II. It was not used during the limited wars in Asia (1953–55 and 1962–73), largely because the economic conversion to war was limited.

This need not be the pattern of wartime mobilization. It would be theoretically possible to rely fully on the market mechanism. The government could enter the market and bid away from the private sector all of the resources and labor power needed for war production. The added spending would be inflationary, however, unless taxes were raised by more than the increased government spending,

Figure 31–1
The Wartime Economic Problem

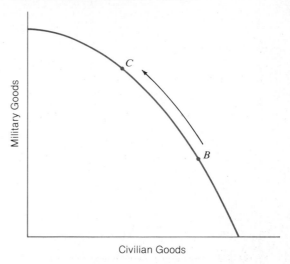

How to move from peacetime output *B* to wartime output *C*.

Figure 31–2
The U.S. in World War II

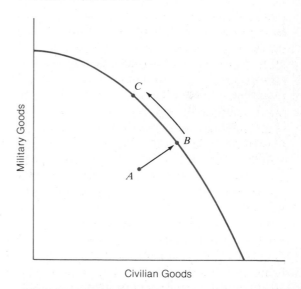

The economy moved from depression *A* to full employment *B* under the impact of war. It then moved along its production possibilities frontier to a full wartime economy *C*.

Figure 31-3
Investment in Wartime

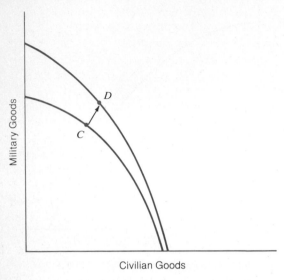

Planning of investment in wartime enlarges production capacity for military goods more rapidly than for civilian goods. The economy can then move from *C* to *D* (or some other point on the outer curve).

largely unrecorded chapters of history is the opposition that has prevailed in all nations to all wars, even when the patriotic response has seemed to be overwhelming. It is important then that wartime planners minimize the sacrifices required in wartime. This means that as we shall see when we examine the problem of wartime inflation presently.

Why, then, does a modern nation move to planning, allocations, and labor controls under the stress of war? The answer, apparently, lies in the area of incentives. If people were taxed heavily, even in wartime, public support of the war would be damaged. Every war creates a variety of reactions, from enthusiastic support to lukewarm acceptance, to doubts, to unspoken opposition, to overt opposition. The costlier the war, the more people can be expected to oppose it, and the shorter the period of enthusiasm on the part of supporters. One of the

taxes cannot be raised high enough to reduce demand for civilian goods so as to free all of the resources required for the desired production of military goods. In addition, higher incomes act as an incentive to draw additional workers into the work force and to get all workers to work harder. Patriotic appeals are used for these purposes, but patriotism plus cash works better. If taxes wiped out workers' income gains these incentive effects would be reduced.

Reliance on monetary incentives has its limitations, however. It can't very well be applied to the armed forces. The wage necessary to get soldiers to give up their lives may be very high, running the expenses of the war up to astronomical levels. These costs can be shifted away from taxpayers to nonvoting youths by drafting them into the armed forces, providing them with patriotic appeals supported by the threat of prison or death for desertion, and marching them off to war. The absence of monetary incentives, however, requires that military operations based on labor acquired in this fashion be organized on the basis of discipline, threat, and command.

If the major costs of the war are borne by drafted youths, it seems unfair for the civilian sector to be allowed to profit excessively. Burdens must be partially equalized, at the very least, or opposition to the war will escalate. Taxes, wage controls, and profit limitations become inevitable. But since those devices reduce incentives, they also reduce the ability of the government to obtain the necessary shift in use of resources through the market mechanism. Planning is used instead.

In this fashion the policy compromise inherent in a war economy is evolved. Economic burdens on the civilian population must be held in check in order to maintain incentives and avoid an early appearance of "war weariness." The ensuing effort to keep the cost of the war down leads to use of a military draft. This creates equity problems, so the civilian sector is asked to do its share by paying higher taxes and making other voluntary sacrifices. But this policy conflicts with the incentives and "war weariness" constraints. Incomes are therefore allowed to rise, taxes are inadequate to finance the war fully, and production planning and controls are used to mobilize resources. In the process, a problem of inflation is created, which must be held in check by further economic controls.[1]

- **Wartime mobilization** uses planning, allocations, and labor controls to provide resources for wartime use by the military.

War and Inflation

Inflation accompanies wars. In theory this need not be so, but the pragmatic compromises inherent in a wartime economy make it inevitable. An economy straining to produce beyond its capacity requires a safety valve. Inflation provides it (see Figure 4–8 on p. 86).

Wartime inflation is caused by excessive aggregate demand. Like any inflation, it can start even before full employment is reached. The situation is complicated, however, by the fact that products are diverted from civilian markets into the military sector. Even if demand were held down by taxes, the diversion of goods would be enough to cause inflationary price increases. This point is not obvious, and it requires some further explanation.

Imagine a peacetime economy at full employment with stable prices. Now send that economy to war, adding more government spending. But have the government raise taxes to pay the entire costs of the war. Allocations shift production from civilian to military goods, while payment is made out of the increased taxes. One might suppose that the inflation problem would be solved, since both incomes and civilian production are reduced by equal amounts. That is not so. An increase in government spending balanced by an equal increase in tax revenues will raise total spending by the amount of the increase in the government budget (remember the balanced-budget multiplier). Aggregate demand will increase beyond the full-employment level and prices will rise. In order to avoid inflation taxes would have to be large enough to not only pay the costs of the war, but also to eliminate the increase in aggregate demand. A budget surplus is called for, large enough to reduce consumer spending by an amount equal to the diversion of resources from the civilian to the military sectors. Taxes would have to be high enough to both eliminate the increase in aggregate demand and reduce consumer incomes by the same proportion that output of civilian goods is reduced. These two requirements add up to a budget surplus. But who ever heard of a wartime budget surplus? Any government that tried it would be accused of failing to pursue the war fully. In wartime it is politically impossible to raise taxes enough to prevent inflation.

Another alternative is to reduce the propensity to consume with war bond sales drives. This has the psychological advantage of seeming to help supply the armies, but its true purpose is to reduce inflationary pressures. War bond sales performed this function in both world wars.

A third alternative is price controls and rationing. If they are effective they will leave excess purchasing power in the hands of consumers because the limited supply of goods available at fixed prices will not absorb all of the wartime purchasing power. Savings will pile up in banks and the bond drives will sop up some more. It also helps if some sectors of the economy are left unregulated to help take the

---

[1]The wartime economic problem is never presented to the public in these terms. War is not a time for rationality, but for emotion. A rational analysis would lay bare all of the irrationality involved. Wartime policy makers don't seem to think in these terms, either. They are pragmatic people with problems to solve. They find their way to solutions for the economic problems of war based on their perception of the current situation, as they balance incentives and attitudes against the need for mobilization of resources in ways that fit everyday events. In this way, wartime management of the economy develops in somewhat different fashion with each war, even though the basic economic issues and problems are similar.

pressure off the more important regulated sectors. Nightclubs, gambling, and prostitution are the usual areas left uncontrolled, as long as their prosperity and rising prices do not absorb too much labor.

In spite of all the remedies and safety valves, prices are almost sure to rise anyway. The fundamental economic imbalance caused by excess aggregate demand remains. At best, wartime price controls and rationing can only postpone the inflationary pressures until after the war by preventing consumers from spending and forcing them to save during the war.

Limited Wars

The wartime economy described to this point is based on the experiences of World Wars I and II. We shall not see their like again. World War III will be different: minutes instead of years. The economic problems of World War III are to be found instead in the arms race and limited wars leading up to it and the reconstruction (if any) that will follow. Nevertheless, the fundamental economic problems remain even with limited wars, albeit on a reduced scale. Resources must be allocated to the military and away from civilian uses, and inflationary pressures must be accommodated.

The example of the war in Vietnam is instructive. As the war began to escalate in 1965, the economy was approaching the level just below full employment at which prices could be expected to start rising. A larger number of young men were drafted into the armed forces and military spending rose. Mobilization of increased resources for military use was starting, but a basic policy decision was made to avoid as much as possible such devices as tax increases, production allocations, and price controls. The national administration tried to act as if the economy could have more swords without reducing the number of plowshares, to avoid causing even more political opposition to the war than already existed. The economic

strategy was to bid away resources from the private sector by increased government spending. But since tax increases were to be minor at best, the result was a $26 billion deficit in the federal budget in the 1968 fiscal year.

The inflation of the late 1960s followed. Not only was GNP increased by the multiplied effect of the deficit, but the resources available for civilian uses had been diminished.

A new administration in 1968 tried to adapt, but went only part way. The avowed strategy was to end the war (or reduce its intensity) so that military expenditures might be leveled off (no one seriously contemplated a large reduction), thereby eliminating the main cause of inflation. In the meantime the administration sought to restructure the federal budget by reducing spending on nonmilitary items. Reallocation of resources was to take place within the federal sector. Like the previous administration, the basic policy decision was to leave the private sector untouched by production allocations and price controls.

The new administration also had to deal with the problem of inflation it had inherited from the economic policies of the previous administration. Rather than use price, wage, and profit controls, it used a tight monetary policy administered through the Federal Reserve System, and brought on the recession of 1970. Efforts to stimulate the economy and get unemployment rates down before the 1972 presidential election then led to the disastrous inflation followed by recession of the early 1970s. Unwillingness on the part of two successive adminstrations to accept the economic policy implications of limited war was at the root of the problem.

The economic strategy adopted during the Vietnam War was a failure. Three successive administrations knew that mobilization of additional resources for the military was necessary. But public opposition to the war brought a decision to avoid increased taxes and wartime economic controls. Resources were to be mobilized by higher government expenditures, and that meant inflation. Some effort was made to reduce government spending on non-military budget items, but not much could be accomplished along that line because it, too, raised opposition to the war. A tight monetary policy was used to reduce demand in the private sector, but that strategy also had limited effect: increased federal spending plus tight money brought the threat of financial crisis, forcing temporary abandonment of the tight money policy. Eventually, a half-hearted effort at price controls was made. All efforts at economic constraint were largely abandoned in 1972, however, to make way for a presidential reelection drive, and the economy was abandoned to escalating inflation. One lesson from this experience is perhaps that a nation should not try to fight an unpopular war. A more important lesson is that even limited wars require fiscal control and taxes in order to mobilize resources for military purposes.

The Militarized Economy

Most Americans are unaware of how much the American economy has become a *militarized economy*. Professor Seymour Melman of Columbia University estimated that in 1969 about 20 percent of the U.S. civilian labor force was directly or indirectly employed as a result of military spending. This included 1.1 million civilians employed by the Department of Defense, 3.4 million persons serving in the armed forces, and 3.4 million workers directly employed on war contracts. In addition, about 10 million persons were employed as a result of the purchasing power created by the primary employment listed above. This makes a total of about 18 millions jobs out of a total employment of about 80.5 million (including the armed forces).

A more normal picture might be obtained by looking at the U.S. economy after the end of the Vietnam war. In 1977, based on data published by the U.S. Departments of De-

fense, Commerce, and Labor, we find that 9 percent of total employment in the U.S. was attributable to military contracts, either directly on defense contracts or indirectly by firms supplying defense contractors. This is certainly an underestimate, for it does not include employment in firms further back in the supply line than those directly supplying military contractors. Employees of the Department of Defense and persons in the armed forces are not included, nor is the indirect employment generated by defense jobs. Inclusion of these jobs would at least double the estimate. Even in peacetime, then, Melman's estimate that military spending supported about 20 percent of the civilian labor force may be close to the mark.

There is a high degree of geographic concentration of military production. More than half is accounted for by just seven states: Massachusetts, Connecticut, New York, and New Jersey in the Northeast, Texas in the Southwest, and California and Washington on the Pacific Coast. In California over 20 percent of all manufacturing employment is on defense contracts, either directly or indirectly. In some states defense contracts are the primary economic base: in Utah almost half of all employment (not just manufacturing) is attributable to military spending.

Military production is also highly concentrated in a relatively few large corporations. The hundred largest defense contractors supply about two-thirds of military supplies contracted for by the Department of Defense, and the ten largest account for about 30 percent of the total. This is out of a total of 15,000 to 20,000 prime contractors. Much of the actual production is subcontracted to other firms, and by subcontractors to still more firms. But this serves to draw large numbers of firms into the web of military production while it eases the administrative problem for the Department of Defense by reducing significantly the number of firms it must deal with directly.

Close connections are maintained between

the large military contractors and the Department of Defense. Some are informal: many retired military officers of high rank are hired by large defense contractors, and some of the chief procurement officers of the Department of Defense are recruited from defense contractors. At more formal levels, the Department of Defense has established an Industrial Advisory Council, whose chief function is to help plan future defense-systems technology. Its membership is composed of representatives of the federal government and the large military contractors. Thus the contractors help to plan the very system on which they will be bidding (competitively) in the near future; their advantage over newcomers should be obvious.

A significant portion of the capital equipment used by military contractors is supplied by the federal government. Estimates of the total vary widely, ranging upward to $60 billion; official figures are not available. The private firms are allowed to make a profit on this capital, just as if it belonged to them. Some have illegally used it in producing for civilian markets, according to congressional investigations, but the firms still manage to get more contracts. Indeed, the symbiotic relationship between the Department of Defense and its primary contractors has caused such a proliferation of rules, procedures, and regulations that the big defense contractors take on increasingly the aspect of government arsenals and the procurement arm of the Department becomes more and more like a giant producing enterprise.

A high concentration of technically skilled persons are employed in the military sector. According to Melman, in 1970 more than half of the nation's research and development budgets, and R & D employment, were devoted to research for the military, and one out of five engineers worked either for the military or on military contracts.

Economists are only now coming to understand the long-run impact of this "brain drain"

on the national economy as a whole. It has the direct effect of reducing the skilled labor available to the private sector, thereby hindering improvements in technology and increased productivity. The indirect effects are even more significant. Recent studies show that the international competitiveness of U.S. exports of manufactured goods has been damaged severely by high costs of skilled labor and technicians engendered by the rapid escalation of demand for that type of labor resulting from military spending.

Finally, military spending does not result in increased employment. Contrary to popular belief, employment would rise and unemployment fall if the federal government reduced its spending for military purposes. The reason is that military spending is considerably more capital intensive than consumer spending. The amount of military spending that employs one worker would, if spent on consumer goods, employ about 1.25 workers. A reduction of military spending by 25 percent, accompanied by a tax reduction of equal amount, could cut the unemployment rate to about half its 1980 level.

Concentration of military production locally, industrially, and occupationally makes conversion from military to civilian production quite difficult. If government spending were shifted strongly from military needs to social; for example, education, health, and housing, different workers would be employed, in different localities. Fewer highly technical skills would be required, production would shift to less highly capital-intensive industries, and the locus of output would shift. All of these conversions would create significant structural changes in the economy, the work force, and the educational system. Although the level of aggregate demand could be maintained at high employment levels the transitional problems would still be great.

Realization of this fact has created a widespread pattern of support for military spending and sharp competition for military production contracts, not only by corporations but also by public officials and union leaders. There is competition for new contracts both to promote expansion and to maintain existing jobs and the economic interests dependent upon them.

A political feedback is established. When jobs in military production become important, Congress tends to support military appropriations, as senators and members of Congress respond to the economic interests of their states and districts. These economic interests are fostered by the Department of Defense and by military contractors themselves. The Department maintains a corps of "political liaison" employees larger in number than the U.S. Senate and House of Representatives combined. This lobbying effort is supplemented by that of the large military contractors and their trade associations. Labor union officials have also helped bring pressure on senators and representatives when large contracts or installations were at stake.

When military production becomes important to an economy to the extent that it has in the United States, with perhaps one in five or six employed persons dependent on military spending for his or her job and status in society, a group of strong economic interests develop around continuation of the policies that require large military expenditures. Wide general support for those policies can be expected to develop, which in turn makes possible the continuation of heavy military emphasis in the economy. Even though it may be quite feasible to organize the economy around a different emphasis, such a transition becomes increasingly difficult. The great danger of militarization of the economy is that it can expand beyond the real need for it and continue longer than necessary.

- **A militarized economy** is dependent upon military production for the maintenance of prosperity and full employment.

The Military-Industrial-Academic Complex

President Dwight D. Eisenhower, in a speech to the nation on January 17, 1961, first used the term "military-industrial complex" to describe the "conjunction of an immense military establishment and a large arms industry" whose influence is felt throughout the entire nation. "Our toil, resources, and livelihood are all involved, so is the very structure of our society," he said, cautioning that the nation must be on guard against unwarranted influence in the councils of government exercised by the military-industrial complex. But Eisenhower went on to draw in the universities, calling attention to "the prospect of domination of the nation's scholars by federal employment, project allocations, and the power of money."[2]

This *military-industrial-academic complex* can be best defined as "a natural coalition of interest groups with an economic, political, and professional stake in defense and space."[3] It includes the military officers whose responsibility is to assure preponderance of U.S. military power over actual or potential enemies. It includes large international corporations whose business interests abroad are fostered by a strong U.S. military position in the world. It includes large business firms with defense contracts. It includes the union whose members depend heavily on jobs in military production. It includes local businessmen in areas where military production is an important support for the local economy. It includes the congressman concerned about the prosperity of his district, and about campaign contributions from local business and labor. It includes the university that does scientific research related to weapons, participates in overseas assistance programs, and receives funds for support of gradu-

---

[2]Address by President Dwight D. Eisenhower to the nation by television and radio, Jan. 17, 1961. Published in U.S. Department of State, *Bulletin*, Vol. 44, Feb. 6, 1961.

[3]Walter Adams, "The Military-Industrial Complex and the New Industrial State," *American Economic Review,* Vol. 58, No. 2 (May 1968), p. 655.

ate students in a variety of fields associated with military, space, and international programs of the federal government.

● The **military-industrial-academic complex** is a coalition of interest groups with a strong economic, political, and professional stake in military expenditures.

The Military and Social Choice

The influence of the military-industrial-academic complex over national policy is far more important than economic efficiency, for it involves the social preferences that determine the mix of military and civilian production in the economy as a whole. Even if the military procurement system were highly efficient, producing high-quality weapons systems at minimum costs, the problem of national goals and their translation into economic terms would remain.

Civilian Control

Military leaders are undoubtedly correct when they argue that ultimate responsibility for public policy decisions rests with the President and Congress. The military may be very persuasive, and may be supported by lobbyists from big defense contractors, but the final decisions about budgets and programs are made by the national security managers, those political figures, administrators, and civil servants who hold top positions in the Department of Defense, State Department, Atomic Energy Commission, Central Intelligence Agency, and related agencies of government. They are the men who devise the strategies and defense systems Congress is subsequently asked to fund.

The national security managers, however, are drawn very heavily from the ranks of big business, large financial institutions, and the law firms that serve the business and financial community. A study sponsored by the Brook-

ings Institution showed that 86 percent of the civilian heads of the military departments of the federal government were either business executives or lawyers with a business practice. A study by Gabriel Kolko showed that 60 percent of top foreign-policy decision makers came from big business, the investment sector, and the law. Another study by Richard Barnet showed that 70 out of 91 civilians in top national defense positions had backgrounds in big business or high finance. Perhaps this situation is only natural, for administrators with experience in handling large organizations are needed in the national defense portion of the public sector, and they can be found more readily in big business than elsewhere. But the result is that the national security managers are drawn largely from the business elite and have the viewpoints that dominate that group. Few have ever held elected political positions, which means that their views have never been tested against those of the general electorate. Finally, the policies and viewpoints that the national security managers bring to their jobs undoubtedly are similar to those of the military leadership and the large defense contractors. It is not enough to argue that civilians make the final decisions. The U.S. political economy has evolved in such a way that those chosen to make strategic decisions about military and international affairs are drawn from the sector of the economy that benefits directly from not only large military expenditures, but also a predominant position for the U.S. in world affairs. They share the values that lead to large expenditures on military and military-related programs.

Special Interests

Large expenditures on the military designed to maintain U.S. military power and national influence give rise to special economic interests that profit from such policies. The aerospace industry, the petroleum industry, the electronics industry, and much of the nation's research and development effort are directly or indirectly supported by military spending. These industries must also be financed, and a variety of financial institutions have become involved with their continued prosperity. The interests of large international corporations and financial institutions are also protected by U.S. military strength.

Public Opinion

A militarized economy affects all Americans. The jobs and economic security of some are directly created by military spending, and for others indirectly. The economic payoff is widespread. Only when that payoff stopped after 1965 or 1966, with escalation of the Southeast Asia war and its attendant military draft, higher taxes, and inflation, did public opposition to the war become important. As long as the economic costs could be held to low levels while jobs and prosperity continued, there was not a great deal of antiwar sentiment. Viewed in this fashion, the military-industrial-academic complex is seen only as that sector of the economy that has the most obvious interest in continuance of military production. Economic benefits to many others flow from the same source. Government decisions in the national security area reflect these interests. In a militarized economy the economic interests of the majority are promoted by high levels of military spending.

A Corporate State?

This chapter has ended on a pessimistic note, implying that for the foreseeable future the American economy will retain its strong emphasis on military and military-related spending, not because a few special interests benefit but because much of the economy has come to depend on it.

But beyond that immediate point there is a far more significant one. An economy in which government plays an important role develops feedbacks from public policy to the economy and back again to public policy. These relationships may be mutually supportive, such as, for example, those between big business and big government explored in Chapter 23 and those described in this chapter's discussion of the military-industrial-academic complex. A new political economy is emerging out of these relationships. The economic role of government is vastly expanded over a half-century ago. Big business has grown in significance, strengthening the position of a managerial and financial elite. The entire economy has developed a military emphasis. And all three of these elements, big government, big business, and the military, now operate in a mutually supportive, symbiotic manner. Each tends to strengthen the other. These may well be the outlines of a peculiarly American *corporate state* analogous to the economic base of European and Japanese fascisms in the period between World Wars I and II. In the U.S., however, the political structure is not authoritarian and terror is not generally used as a political weapon. Rather, the American corporate state rests upon the mass support provided by high levels of employment and growing affluence, combined with the psychological appeals of nationalism and world power. The economics of war and defense open up a seriously troubling vision of the future.

- The **corporate state** is a society in which big government, big business, the military, and their leadership operate in a mutually supportive manner, unifying the concentrated political, economic, and military power of the modern state.

Summary

Military production requires that resources used for military purposes not be used to produce either consumer or investment goods. Accomplishing such a shift of resources in wartime requires a system of economic planning to sustain economic incentives and avoid inflation. Limited wars have the same problems as full-scale war, but to a lesser degree. When a war is unpopular, like the Vietnam war, the controls and taxes necessary to avoid serious economic dislocations are politically difficult to apply, and both political and inflation problems are likely to multiply.

In the modern economy, preparation for war and sustenance of large military-related programs develop a strong dependence on the military sector. The militarized economy tends to develop vested interests in continuing the military emphasis, interests that have been termed the military-industrial-academic complex. A broad base of support for continued large military spending is created that makes a shift away from the militarized economy difficult to accomplish. Diversion of resources is large and permanent.

In the United States the presence of a large military-industrial complex brings together the political power of big government with the economic power of big business to support a policy of military strength oriented toward world power. It creates the specter of a corporate state oriented toward the goal of world power and corporate wealth, supported by the many whose affluence depends heavily on military production and using the psychological appeals of nationalism and domination.

Key Concepts

basic economic problem in wartime

wartime mobilization

militarized economy

military-industrial-academic complex

corporate state

For Discussion

1. Explain the economic costs of mobilizing resources for military purposes.

2. Why does inflation occur during wartime?

3. Is military spending during peacetime less inflationary and does it have lower economic costs than during wartime? Explain.

4. Discuss: In the long run, the most significant effect of large military expenditures is the creation of economic and political interests in maintaining a militarist posture.

5. Discuss: The basic dilemma of U.S. military policy is that the measures taken to strengthen U.S. military power weaken the economic base of that power.

6. What would be the advantages and disadvantages of a unilateral reduction of U.S. military spending without a prior agreement with the USSR to do the same?

Chapter 32

Pollution and the Environment

One of the pressing current problems of the public economy is preservation of the environmental framework of economic activity. Air, water, and land are essential to the maintenance of life, yet they are also parts of the economic system. In particular, they are used as reservoirs for the disposal of wastes. This use can spoil their function in the ecological system. In this chapter we examine the potential incompatibility of the economic and ecological systems, together with the efforts now being made to bring the two systems into greater compatibility.

Open Systems and Closed Systems

As the industrial economy spread to all parts of the world over the past two hundred years, pulling all the peoples of the continents and all of the world's resources into its orbit, we have gradually become aware of the limited resources available for human use. Until the last half of the twentieth century people were able to move into relatively unoccupied territories and find new resources as inputs for the industrial economy. Indeed, that can still be done, for all of the mineral resources have not been

opened up, all of the oil has not been discovered, virgin forests are still to be found, and unused agricultural land is still available. Although unused resources are no longer as plentiful as they were in the past, when natural resources are used up in one area, others are still to be found, and an advancing technology continues to find substitutes. Exhaustible resources may mean diminishing returns or higher costs, but they don't bring disaster.

The outputs from the production system are never used up, but in the long run, however, inputs are limited and production can only change their form. Matter cannot be destroyed. It is only transformed. Except for the energy that continuously enters the earth's atmosphere from the sun, people must live with only those resources that are now available on the earth. The economic system may continue to transform inputs into outputs and waste products, but in the long run the outputs and wastes must become part of the inputs. The natural world is a *closed system,* in which there is a continuous processing of inputs to become outputs that must be recycled as inputs once more.

By contrast, an *open system* continually draws inputs from sources other than the sys-

Figure 32–1
Open and Closed Systems

A.   Simple Open System

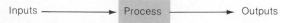

An open system requires continual supplies of new inputs
to continue functioning.

B.   Simple Closed System

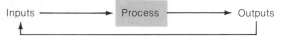

A closed system uses its own output to continue
functioning.

tem's outputs. The outputs are then distributed independently of the inputs. An open system emphasizes the level of production, the amount of the output. A closed system emphasizes the continuation of the process as an end in itself. The fundamental differences between the two are shown in Figure 32–1.

In the short run, the economy is an open system. Production of goods and services draws inputs of resources and labor from the ecological and human systems enveloping the economy. *Residuals* (or wastes) are usually disposed of by diluting the reservoirs of air, water, and land. Those reservoirs are beginning to fill up, however. The natural regenerative forces that break down wastes and recycle waste materials are unable to function as rapidly as new wastes are dumped into the reservoirs. Some of the wastes are harmful products that do not exist in nature or are produced in such large quantities that the natural environment may never be able to absorb them fully. In other instances, natural substances are concentrated in amount so that they become local problems: mercury is a problem not because it is produced by man, but because it is concentrated by man out of a natural environment in which mercury is highly dispersed.

The ecological system is closed, however, for

natural resources can only be changed in form and not destroyed. As the production system of modern society has grown in size and spread more widely, the damaging effects of its waste disposal processes have escalated. We now realize that production of goods and services is only a subsystem within a larger general system of relationships that encompasses both people and their environment. We live in a closed system in which there is no choice, in the long run, but to recycle all outputs and wastes back through the system as a whole.

- A **closed system** uses its own outputs as its inputs and does not rely on anything outside the system itself either as a source of inputs or as a means of using outputs.

- An **open system** draws inputs from outside the system itself, and outputs are disposed of outside the system.

- **Residuals** are the unusable outputs of a system.

The Effects of Pollution

Waste discharges lead to economic costs in a variety of ways. These feedback effects of environmental pollution decrease the production possibilities of the economy by:

1. Reducing the productivity of labor and land.

2. Reducing the available supplies of land, capital, and labor.

Pollution also affects the utility level of consumers by creating disutilities that consumers must bear. Much of the discussion of the costs of pollution has concerned the effect on consumers: the reduced utility obtained from the production of goods and services plus waste because of the deterioration in quality of air, water, and land. But the impact on production possibilities may be even more important, since the wealth of human beings and the level of production itself is involved. Reducing environmental pollution can enable people to live better lives because they are wealthier, may enable output to be increased, and can reduce the disutilities created by waste.

Pollution and Health
Several studies show that air pollution increases death rates, illness, and physical disability. A 1962 study estimated that a 50 percent reduction in air pollution levels in major U.S. urban areas would save over $2 billion annually in lost time from work because of illness, disability, and premature death plus medical care costs for treatment of pollution-induced illness. A study of Buffalo, New York, showed increased hospitalization for asthma and eczema of children under 15 years of age as air pollution rose where they live. Urban auto commuters and people who live near major expressways and other traffic arteries breathe in relatively heavy doses of lead from auto exhaust emissions, at levels that many medical authorities feel can ultimately have physical effects. Most authorities also agree that low-income families are most affected by air pollution, because they are concentrated in the central city and industrial areas where air pollution is greatest.

The workplace is another source of environmental pollution, affecting production workers most heavily. Workers in mining and manufacturing industries are most likely to face health problems because of environmental pollution. Coal miners get "black lung" that disables at a relatively early age; workers in asbestos products plants are subject to a particularly serious problem of asbestos poisoning; lung cancer and tuberculosis rates are high among smelter workers, who are exposed to sulfur dioxide fumes; the incidence of cancer is high among workers in coke plants, who are exposed to fumes containing cancer-causing benzopyrene.

The case of polychlorinated biphenyls (PCBs) recently received a good deal of publicity. PCBs are chemicals used in electrical insulation, heat-exchange and hydraulic systems, plastics, automobile tires, and some fabrics. Workers in chemical plants producing PCBs are subject to a severe skin disease, chloracne, which causes pustules to break out over the body. The chemical can be carried home on workers' clothes, sometimes causing chloracne among their wives and children. PCBs are often contained in products that are eventually junked and burned; the PCBs are carried into the smoke and deposited in the bodies of sanitation workers, who do not develop chloracne but who can develop other physical disabilities as a result.

All of these health effects of environmental pollution add to the amount of health care society must provide. Time spent at work is reduced. To the extent that death rates are increased or workers retire early for health reasons the labor force is reduced. Environmental pollution, therefore, leads to a smaller work force that works less and requires more labor and resources devoted to its health care. And on top of all that is the pain and suffering caused by ill health and disability.

Pollution and Natural Resources
Environmental pollution can lower the quality of water supplies and the productivity of forests, fisheries, and land. Mercury discharged from chemical plants became concentrated in fish in Lake St. Clair, near Detroit, in 1969, and large amounts of contaminated fish had to be destroyed and commercial fishing halted. Shad used to be plentiful in eastern seaboard rivers, but pollution greatly reduced their numbers and almost eliminated them as a commercial fish. Oyster beds in Chesapeake Bay and on the Atlantic seacoast of the U.S. have been greatly depleted because of pollution.

Synthetic insecticides used by farmers affect the environment in several ways. Washed into streams and lakes, they enter drinking water and can accumulate in the human body to toxic levels after a time. These chemicals enter the food chain and are ingested by fish, poultry, and mammals, where they also can accumulate to dangerous levels when people eat the fish, poultry, or meat.

Forests can be detrimentally affected by air pollutants. The smog of Los Angeles has killed off pine trees in the surrounding mountains, destroying some of the vegetation that reduces the water runoff from heavy rains and increasing the danger of floods and mud slides. "Acid rain" caused by the burning of coal and oil with high sulfur content in England and Germany affects the growth of forests in Scandinavia.

These environmental effects can reduce the availability of any plant or animal resource. The fundamental principle is that the equilibrium population of a species is reduced when its natural environment becomes less favorable to its survival. The more favorable the environment the larger the equilibrium population that can be harvested by humans and the larger the annual harvest that can be obtained without reducing the population supplying the harvest. As the environment is degraded by pollution the equilibrium population of the organism is reduced and the potential annual harvest falls. Production can be temporarily maintained at prepollution levels, but that only depletes the natural population at a faster rate.

Pollution and Environmental Services

Environmental pollution also affects the intangible environmental services provided by natural resources. These are essential functions performed by the natural environment that make possible other productive activity, such as insect pollination of agricultural crops, soil stabilization and flood control by trees and other vegetation, creation of soil by fungi and other microorganisms, natural checks on pests that might attack crops, oxidation of organic wastes, and climate regulation by natural meteorological systems. We often ignore the regulation of the natural environment by nature itself, but that environmental service is highly important.

Ignoring or abusing natural environmental services can have important consequences. A small example is Trout Creek Pass in the Colorado mountains. When the first railroad was built through the pass in 1879 the surrounding mountains were covered with trees, which were largely cut down in the next decade to fuel the smelters of Leadville and other mining centers of Colorado, and to provide mine props for underground mines. After the mountains were denuded of trees, floods and washouts forced continual relocation and ultimate abandonment of the railroads through the pass. Today the floor of Trout Creek Pass is some thirty feet above the level of a hundred years ago, filled with rocks and debris, while its western entrance is approached over a fan-shaped delta of washout from floods.

A much more important case is the problem of pest control in agriculture. Chemical attacks on pests foster the emergence of strains of pests resistant to the chemicals, requiring increased dosages and new chemicals to keep them in check. Meanwhile, the natural enemies of the pests are greatly depleted, since the chemicals attack friend and foe alike. In the Central Valley of California, for example, DDT was first used for mosquito control in 1946, but within three years a DDT-resistant mosquito appeared and by 1951 the use of DDT was phased out, to be succeeded in turn by a series of ever more powerful chemicals—malathion, ethyl parathion, methyl parathion, and fenthion—each in turn failing as resistant strains of mosquitos developed. By the late 1960s nothing worked and the control problem was worse than in 1946 because some of the natural enemies of mosquitos were depleted by the harmful effects of the antimosquito chemicals.

One endangered environmental service is insect pollination of agricultural crops. Most farm crops are pollinated by a relatively small number of insects. Yet insecticides kill the pollinators as well as insect pests that destroy or reduce crops. Continued use of pesticides may enlarge the crop by killing pests, but it may also greatly increase the cost of production if pollination must be done artificially because the natural pollinators have been killed.

One of the most important of all environmental services is weather control and maintenance of climatic conditions. Environmental pollution can affect that function: continued increases of carbon dioxide and particulates may affect the radiation of heat or absorption of the sun's rays by the earth's atmosphere, and thereby the earth's weather. As increased energy use releases heat into the atmosphere there may be a gradual heating up of the air that leads to great climatic changes. Scientists disagree about the possible significance of these developments and on the extent to which they may occur. In that area our hard knowledge of the environmental effects of pollution is scant and, perhaps for that reason, most frightening. Yet in the long run it could be the most significant of all, for very small changes in temperature could have drastic consequences on the earth's livability.

Environmental services are freely available to all productive enterprises. They are a public good in the classic sense that no one can be denied their use so no price can be placed upon them. They are not subject to property rights and are not bought and sold on markets. Yet they are essential to the economic process. Any program for preservation of the natural environment will have to give high priority to preservation of environmental services.

Accumulation of Pollutants

We usually think of environmental pollution as directly related to the amount of waste currently discharged. That is only part of the story, however. Two other factors are important: the stock of the pollutant that accumulated in the past, and the rate at which the pollutant decays and becomes part of the natural environment once more. Furthermore, some pollutants become more concentrated over time because they enter the food chain, and dangerous pollution can grow even after the current flow of wastes has stopped.

The rate at which pollutants convert to forms that are not harmful varies widely. Some last only a few days while others last indefinitely. For example, sulfurous gases turn into diluted sulfuric acid in the air, which is then precipitated to the ground within a few days. On the other hand, some iodine isotopes emitted during the reprocessing of nuclear fuels persist almost infinitely (fortunately they emit only low-energy radiation—but it builds up because the isotopes do not degrade).

A striking case of environmental problems created by an accumulated stock of pollutants is the oxidation of organic wastes by bacterial agents; in more ordinary language, the problem of sewage. Oxidation of organic material in water is ordinarily both rapid and complete. But if the discharge of organic material per day into a watercourse is too large the amount of oxygen necessary for decomposition of the wastes will exceed the amount in the water. When that happens the oxygen is used up, organic matter accumulates, and smelly gases like methane and hydrogen sulfide are formed. When that happens the natural process of oxidation can begin again only if the waste emission is reduced to a level that allows natural aeration processes to add oxygen to the water over a period of time, or if the water flow is increased. In the meantime the watercourse is an open sewer.

The time sequence is important in this case. For a while there is no problem at all as organic wastes are dumped into the watercourse, because oxidation takes place quickly and completely. But increased waste emissions cause the oxygen in the water to be used up. *Suddenly* the biodegrading process slows down, and the undegraded stock of wastes in the water rises rapidly. The change can take place almost from one day to the next. In economic terms, there are no costs from the waste discharges for a time, even though the discharges grow rapidly. Suddenly the costs are high. Once that threshold is reached even a very low rate of waste discharge will maintain the pollution level and the high costs.

The policy implication of these facts is that the stock of certain pollutants in the environment has to be monitored and their current emissions limited so as to keep the stocks within tolerable bounds. These measures may have to be taken even though current costs from the pollutant may be negligible or absent. Once the threshold of pollution is reached and pollution costs are significant it may not be possible to avoid large human costs and high costs of pollution abatement.

Externalities

Pollution is an example of an economic phenomenon that economists have labeled *externalities*. Externalities are costs (or benefits) that do not accrue to the economic unit that creates them. We have met externalities before in discussions of the public economy. One aspect of some public goods is that part of their benefit is obtained by economic units other than those who acquire the goods. For example, students obtain an education in publicly supported colleges and universities and get economic benefits from it. The community as a whole also benefits in a variety of ways from having a larger number of educated citizens. These latter benefits are externalities, sometimes called "spillover effects" or "neighborhood effects." They accrue to people other than the direct consumers of the goods.

Pollution creates external costs rather than external benefits. Goods are produced and sold to consumers, but if the producer does not have to pay for use of air, water, or land to dispose of the wastes from production, the costs of waste disposal are not included in the price of the goods. Yet inconveniences or losses may be created for other people by the process of waste disposal if it pollutes resources that the other people wish to use.

For example, a papermill may deposit effluent into a river far upstream from any other user of the river's water. The natural cleansing action of water flow brings the purity of the water back to its original state before any communities downstream take water out for human consumption. In this case there are no external costs, except perhaps for those fishermen who no longer find fish in the stream just below the mill. However, let a second papermill be established on the river, or perhaps a third and fourth. By the time the water gets downstream to the towns below it is no longer usable in its natural state and must be purified before being used by the townspeople. Now there are external costs which must be borne by others than those who use the paper.

The external costs involved in this illustration are the costs of purifying the water downstream so that it will be fit to use. Resources that could be used to produce other things must be devoted to water purification. These costs should properly be included in accounting for the total costs of producing paper in the mills upstream. The total costs, therefore, include two separate items:

1. *Internal costs* incurred by the papermills themselves, including the value of those raw materials and productive services used by the producing companies. These costs are borne by the producer.

2. *External costs* incurred by the downstream communities, including the value of the resources used to restore the purity of the water. These costs are paid by others.

External costs result in a misallocation of resources. Where external costs exist, the costs of production of the economic unit that decides on levels of output and prices are lower than they would be if all costs were internal. Competition will tend in the long run to push selling prices down to levels that just cover average internal costs. The competitive price will be below average total costs by an amount equal to average external costs. The lower costs will tend to bring forth larger output of the good in question. When competition prevails, any good whose production involves external costs will tend to be overproduced and underpriced in comparison with goods whose production does not involve external costs.

When monopoloid conditions prevail external costs may have little impact on price and output. However, they offer an opportunity for higher monopolistic profits and/or a larger share of the market for monopoloid business firms.

External costs have a further important characteristic: they involve involuntary exchange transactions. External costs are imposed on people and not incurred voluntarily. Internal costs, on the other hand, are incurred willingly by economic units that seek to gain from the transactions they engage in. But when an asphalt plant, for example, fills the air with smoke, it imposes costs that others have to bear whether they like it or not.

We can understand now why pollution of the environment is such a prominent feature of the modern economy. Any individual economic unit can benefit from pollution created by disposal of its wastes. Its costs are reduced. Its price can be lowered and either its sales can be greater (in the competitive case) or its profits can be enlarged (in the monopoloid case). Furthermore, the external costs created by its actions must be involuntarily accepted by other economic units. External costs, by reducing costs to the producing unit, enable it to obtain economic gains at the expense of others. Exploitation of the natural environment really means exploitation of other people.

- **Externalities** are costs or benefits that do not accrue to the economic unit that creates them.
- **Internal costs** are costs of production that are directly paid by an economic unit.
- **External costs** are costs of production that are shifted by an economic unit to others.

External Costs and Private Property

If all resources were privately owned, including air and water, and property rights were fully enforceable in courts of law, external costs would become internal costs. The owners of environmental resources that were being polluted could sue for damages or charge for the use of their property. For example, the owner of a lake polluted by a paper mill could obtain damages from the paper company, get an injunction against continuing pollution, or charge the company for the privilege of using the lake as a dump for its chemicals. These added costs for the paper mill would shift the costs of pollution from the owner of the lake to the firm itself.

Unfortunately, however, some resources, including air and water, are not owned by anyone. No one has property rights in them that could be protected by law, so no one cares to protect them. As one observer commented, if General Motors Corporation owned the Mississippi River, the company would jolly well charge for use of the river and preserve it as an income-producing property. But, since no one owns the air and the water, no one has a direct economic interest in preserving them.

Air and water are a "commons" available to the entire community. The existence of this environmental commons enables any individual enterprise to externalize some of its costs by using the commons as a charge-free dump.

The problem is complicated by the fact that pollution caused by any single user of the commons may be insignificant, but as the number of users increases, the costs can become significant. Automobile exhaust emissions are the classic example. No one automobile emits enough exhaust to bother anyone, except perhaps some very old cars that function inefficiently. Yet many automobiles together create highly uncomfortable and even dangerous amounts of exhaust-laden smog. The cost of pollution attributable to any single automobile owner is nil, but the cost attributable to all taken together may be great.

These characteristics of the natural environment make pollution a public problem, taking it out of the private economic sector. The environmental commons is a public good, because no one has property rights in it; and the pollution caused by a single user of the commons may be nil, while the total can be great.

Technology and Pollution

Most of the pollution problems of the United States are of recent origin. They became apparent or worsened in the period of great economic growth following 1945. The first major incidents of smog in Los Angeles occurred in 1942 and 1943. This first radioactive pollution from atomic weapons occurred in 1945. DDT was first produced during World War II. A series of discoveries in physics and chemistry in the 1930s gave us nuclear physics and chemical synthesis of new organic compounds such as detergents, synthetic rubber, and new synthetic fabrics. Advances in biology led to great increases in agricultural production through the use of pesticides, herbicides, and large doses of nitrogen fertilizer. In many instances the new technologies were ecologically harmful, polluting air, water, land, and living things. In some instances the new synthetics, never before existing in nature, have an almost infinite life and can be considered permanent, nondegradable sources of pollution. Radioactive wastes from production of nuclear weapons and nuclear power are only one of the most widely publicized examples. The new technologies that helped trigger the great era of recent economic growth were one of the chief causes of environmental degradation.

Profits and Pollution

New technologies replace the old for one reason alone: they are more profitable. The higher profits are due to one or both of two condi-

tions: costs of production are reduced and/or consumers prefer a new or improved product. If, in addition, part of the costs of production can be externalized, the new technology has an additional advantage. Thus, in the thirty years after World War II, soap lost some 80 percent of the cleanser market to detergents. Part of the reason was that the environmental costs of producing detergents were avoided by the producing firms, providing a cost advantage over soap, which has almost no environmental impact. If the environmental costs of detergents had been internalized, its cost advantage over soap would have been less or perhaps even nonexistent. Similarly, plastic clothes displaced cotton and wool, partly because of cost advantages derived from externalizing environmental costs in the production of plastics. Decisions on these matters are made by business firms on the basis of profits derived from comparison of revenues and internal costs only. Pollution is profitable.

Can We Solve the Problem of Pollution?

Three solutions to the problem of the environment have been widely discussed. All three have been tried, and all found to be only partial solutions with severe limitations. The three methods are subsidies, regulation, and effluent charges.

Subsidies
One strategy for reducing water pollution is to subsidize construction of municipal water treatment plants. The federal government will provide up to 55 percent of the cost of construction (but not operation) of local waste treatment plants. Lesser subsidies are available to industrial plants. Some plants are connected to municipal sewer systems and can benefit from subsidies to the local government. The subsidies have to be supplemented with enforcement by means of establishment of standards, court orders, and fines, for even with a

subsidy it is cheaper just to dump untreated wastes into a lake or stream.

The consensus among experts is that the subsidy system has not worked effectively. Federal appropriations have lagged, and local governments hold up their expenditures until federal funds become available. Enforcement proceedings are costly and time-consuming, and the political power of large firms has effectively hindered enforcement. A number of waste-treatment plants constructed under the program have not operated efficiently and have failed to accomplish the tasks for which they were presumably designed.

Other subsidies apply to business firms, chiefly through accelerated depreciation and investment tax credits for pollution abatement investments. Business firms are provided with subsidies and tax cuts in exchange for less pollution, with the general taxpayer paying the bill. The general public bears the costs of environmental protection instead of the costs of pollution.

Regulation

In recent years the environment protection strategy has shifted to regulation. Under the Environmental Policy Act (1969) a Council on Environmental Quality modeled after the Council of Economic Advisors was established. In 1970 a federal government reorganization established the Environmental Protection Agency (EPA) as part of the executive branch of the government. The EPA combines all of the pollution control and related research activities of the federal government that were formerly scattered and isolated in various federal agencies. These administrative changes were supplemented by legislation in 1970 to require maintenance of air quality standards and their enforcement by the federal government. Proposals were placed before Congress to extend and strengthen the Refuse Act of 1899, which was until recently an unenforced law requiring business firms to obtain licenses to discharge wastes into navigable streams.

A new era in pollution control began. Regulations established standards for noise pollution by cars and aircraft. Restrictions were placed on dumping refuse into water and the air. Environmental impact studies were required for large private and public construction projects. The initial thrust of regulation was to establish uniform standards for all sources of pollution, but in recent years more flexibility has been introduced. It may be possible for a firm to emit more of one pollutant if it reduces emissions of others, meanwhile staying within an overall limit, depending on the arrangement the firm can make with the pollution control agency.

The management of the pollution control program is being led by the federal government, while enforcement is divided between federal and state authorities. Mobile sources of air pollution are regulated federally, while stationary sources are regulated by the states. Water quality standards are regulated primarily by federal agencies, with some assistance from the states.

Many economists, however, are skeptical of the results of regulation when strong economic interests are at stake. The history of regulation in other areas of the economy is not good: regulation tends to be more expensive than economic incentives; it creates a regulatory bureaucracy; the bureaucracy tends to be captured by those whom it regulates; legal challenges lead to protection of property rights rather than the public interest. All of these dangers are present in regulation of environmental standards. The problem is compounded by the fact that our knowledge of environmental relationships and our technological capabilities are limited. Economists might be pardoned if they yearn longingly for the use of economic incentives, for they are known to be effective.

Economic Incentives

The most commonly proposed economic incentives are effluent charges. An *effluent charge* is essentially a tax on a producer of waste requiring him to pay a fee for every unit of harmful waste dumped into the water or air. For example, a municipality that discharges untreated sewage into Lake Erie may have to pay a charge of $10 for each 1,000 gallons of discharge. If the sewage is treated to remove 90 percent of the pollutants the charge may be reduced to $1. If all of the pollutants are removed, the charge might be eliminated altogether. By varying the amount of the charge, any desired level of water purity might be achieved. If absolutely no discharge of pollutants is desired, the authorities could enact an outright ban, just as governments prohibit use of certain drugs. But short of complete prohibition, reduction of pollution to any desired level can be achieved by establishing the proper charge.

● **Effluent charges** are a fee levied by a public agency on a producer of waste for each unit of harmful waste discharged.

The idea behind effluent charges is to internalize costs that heretofore were external. Imposing additional costs on users of the environmental commons will cause them to economize on the use of that resource by diminishing their wastes. In doing so, costs of production to the firm are raised to levels closer to real costs and in the long run the misallocation of resources is reduced.

The success of effluent charges in reducing pollution would depend on the standards set by the administrative agency charged with managing them. The simplest technique is a variation of cost-benefit analysis that compares the marginal cost of pollution abatement to the polluter with the marginal cost of pollution to the community.

Figure 32–2 shows the fundamentals of the concept. Curve *A* is essentially a demand curve for pollution abatement. It shows the costs to the community, at the margin, of any given level of pollution from the effluent of an industrial plant. It indicates the price per unit of

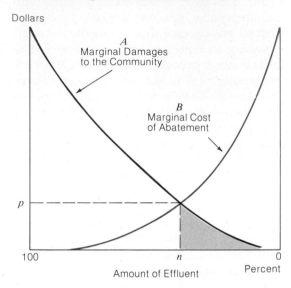

Figure 32–2
Effluent Charges to Reduce Pollution

Curve *A* shows the marginal damages to the community of the pollution caused by an industrial plant. Very high when no effort is made to reduce pollution, the costs to the community fall to zero before all of the effluent is eliminated. Curve *B* shows the marginal cost of eliminating pollution at the source by reducing the effluent. Note that total elimination is very costly and may not be possible, but (as in the typical case) some effluent can be eliminated at little or no cost if the firm's engineers will only put their minds to it; costs rise very steeply, however, as total elimination of pollutants is approached.

effluent a rational community would be willing to pay for pollution abatement for any given discharge of effluent. Curve *B* shows the marginal cost to the industrial firm of reducing pollution.

In this simple case the optimal level of pollution abatement would occur by levying an effluent charge equal to *p*. With a charge at that level it would pay the firm to reduce its effluent to level *n*. At lower levels of effluent discharge the firm's marginal cost of pollution abatement would exceed the effluent fee and clearly would be unprofitable. At abatement levels greater than *n* the firm could save money by reducing its effluent, since its marginal abatement costs would be less than the effluent fee.

The solution shown in Figure 32–2 would not eliminate all losses due to pollution. Those losses that remain are shown by the shaded area, but they are relatively small compared to the losses that have been eliminated (shown by the unshaded area under curve *A*). Note, however, that all damages due to pollution could be eliminated if the effluent charge *p* were set high enough. Such action would raise the marginal costs of abatement to levels well above marginal benefits to the community. Although a charge that high might satisfy the conservation purist, it goes beyond economic rationality to a different set of values. If the polluter were a public agency, such as the community's sewage treatment plant, the community would be wise to set the effluent charge

Figure 32–4
Raising Effluent Charges

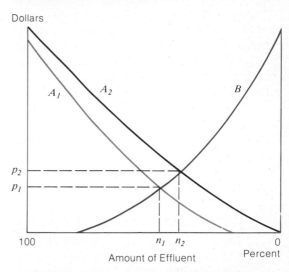

Increased demand for pollution abatement requires higher effluent fees to achieve the new goals. Greater demand for pollution abatement means that the marginal costs of pollution to the community have risen, in the opinion of its citizens, from A_1 to A_2. An optimal abatement program would raise the effluent charge from p_1 to p_2 in order to reduce the effluent from n_1 to n_2.

Figure 32–3
Reducing Effluent Charges

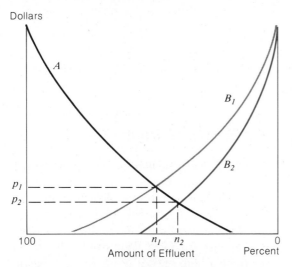

Reduced costs of pollution abatement permit lower effluent charges to eliminate more pollution. Reduction of marginal abatement costs from B_1 to B_2 enables the effluent charges to be lowered from p_1 to p_2, while reducing the effluent from n_1 to n_2.

at *p*, thereby equalizing its benefits and costs at the margin.

Advances in pollution abatement can be made, with reduced effluent charges, if technological advances reduce the cost of abatement. On the other hand, if community attitudes change toward a demand for less pollution, which is equivalent to shifting the curve of marginal damages upward, a higher level of effluent charges will be required. These extensions of the analysis are shown in Figures 32–3 and 32–4.

This analysis of effluent charges must be qualified, however, by the very great difficulties encountered in estimating the damages to the community caused by pollution. Everything said earlier about accumulation of pollutants is relevant here, particularly the fact that some pollutants have a threshold below which costs are very small and above which they are high. An added problem is that the polluter is probably bringing to bear upon the pollution control agency all the pressure he can to get them to minimize their estimate of damages. When this is added to the difficulty of estimating dollar amounts where prices are not available, it should not surprise us that the estimates of damage probably will tend toward the low side.

Effluent charges have several advantages, however. They provide a strong economic incentive to voluntary action by private economic interests to protect the environmental commons. They achieve that goal with a minimum amount of regulation and legal action for enforcement. If effluent charges are administered properly, business firms are encouraged to find lower-cost methods of pollution abatement that can then be followed by reduced charges. Finally, by internalizing at least some external costs, effluent charges make possible a more efficient allocation of resources in the long run.

If effluent charges have such great advantages, why were they considered and rejected when the recent environmental legislation was passed? The congressional hearings have the answer. Business interests opposed effluent charges because they would add another operating cost. Apparently they felt that regulation would be less costly to them. Representatives of municipal governments opposed effluent charges because local governments would have to pay for discharging untreated sewage. On the other hand, the federal program to subsidize local sewage treatment plants adds to their revenues. Conservationists appeared not to understand how effluent charges would work, calling them "a license to pollute"—as if regulation is not!—and did not realize the incentive they would provide to business firms and municipalities to reduce their emission of pollutants voluntarily. Perhaps underneath the conservationists' position was the realization that effluent charges would bring use of the environmental commons more fully into the price system, moving away from the principle of free public use.

THE MARKET FOR POLLUTION RIGHTS

Starting in 1978 the federal government, together with a number of states, began to encourage the purchase and sale of "rights" to pollute the air. The overall level of air pollution for an area is established by the state regulatory agency. A firm that reduces its air pollution obtains "emission credits," which may be bought by another firm to offset increased pollution from plant expansion or new construction. The two firms negotiate the purchase price and other details. The trading of pollution rights enables the selling firm to reduce the cost of pollution controls, the buying firm is able to expand its operations, and the state agency keeps the overall level of pollution within desired limits.

Here are some examples of the process at work. An automobile company in Pennsylvania signed a long-term contract to buy steel from a nearby steel manufacturer in exchange for enough emission credits to enable a new auto assembly plant to be built. A paper mill was built in Oregon after the company bought emission credits from a local dry cleaning plant and another company that had gone out of business. A national market in emission rights is slowly developing.

The Question of Equity

The poor and the near-poor bear more of the burden of pollution than the rich. They are not able to avoid air pollution or noise pollution by moving to the suburbs as readily as middle- or upper-income families. This problem is particularly intense for racial minorities. The urban poor show a high incidence of chronic respiratory conditions such as asthma and emphysema. The air they usually breathe is contaminated by automobile exhaust emissions. Industrial workers are often subject to high degrees of pollution on the job, including high temperatures, toxic gases and fumes, noise, dust, and high humidity. In addition, they often live near the factories that belch smoke and fumes into the atmosphere they and their families breathe.

Meanwhile, the plant manager works in an air-conditioned office, lives in an air-conditioned home in the suburbs, and travels between the two in an air-conditioned car. His company's public relations man is very likely to point out that elimination of pollution can raise costs and threaten the employment of the company's workers. Meanwhile the company's profits are derived, in part, from production methods that involve environmental pollution.

The benefits of pollution control are likely to accrue chiefly to low-income families and to production workers. Those groups, however, are also likely to bear the larger burden of the costs of pollution abatement. Effluent charges are analogous to an excise tax. They are levied on the production of products and services. Like any excise tax, they add to production costs and in the long run are embodied in the sales price of the product or service. And, like any excise tax, effluent charges are regressive. The poor spend a larger proportion of their income than the rich, pay the same prices for the same goods as the rich, and would end up paying a larger proportion of their income in higher prices caused by effluent charges. The same is true of any costs of pollution abatement incurred by business firms under regulatory restrictions. The costs will be passed on to consumers by price increases, which will be most burdensome to low-income families.

The Long Run

Even problems of equity recede into relative insignificance when we consider the longer-range relationships between economy and environment. None of the policies with respect to protection of the environment that have emerged in the last few years provides anything more than a temporary solution at best. Subsidies, regulation, and even effluent fees remain largely within the framework of an open production system. Inputs remain independent of outputs and wastes are still to be disposed of outside the production system itself. The technological framework remains largely the same. Yet if pollution is to be reduced and the environmental commons preserved, the material substances now called pollutants will have to be transformed into either benign or useful substances. They can't be made to just disappear. They must be recycled back into the production processes of the economy or into the ecological system. Instead of being destructive or harmful, they must be changed to useful and life-supporting substances.

Closed production systems imply goals and priorities different from those associated with open production systems. One high-priority goal in a closed system is the maintenance of the system itself. Continuation of production rather than expansion of production becomes the keynote of the system. Preservation of the capital stock becomes more important than increasing the capital stock. Maintenance of a steady state becomes more important than growth. In such a system, waste is recycled rather than disposed of, because recycling is necessary for the viability of the system.

We are a long way from a closed production system. The implications of such a system for economic motivations, the property system, population policy, and governmental institutions are enormous. Our current environmental problems are pushing us in that direction. We move reluctantly, however, as indicated by the shift toward regulation as national policy, instead of a set of incentives built into the system. Nevertheless, in the long run there is no way to bring the production system into harmony with the ecological system without recycling wastes and turning outputs into inputs. We have to move toward a closed production system.

Summary

The modern economy has an open production system in which inputs are transformed into outputs. Part of the output is waste that is disposed of by dumping it into the environmental commons of air, water, and land. The resultant pollution threatens to overwhelm the ecological system that supports life.

In economic analysis pollution is an externality: a cost not borne by the producer. Using the environmental commons as a reservoir for waste disposal, economic units are able to shift some of their production costs to others. These external costs are forced upon others against their wishes, and result in misallocation of resources. Yet there are strong incentives in our economy impelling producers to use the environmental commons in this fashion.

Subsidies to municipalities and, to a lesser extent, to producers have been used to alleviate the problem but have not had much success. Recently we have turned to regulation of polluters by federal and state governments as the problem worsened. The economic path to a solution—use of effluent charges to provide incentives to reduce discharge of wastes—has been largely rejected at this stage, although it is probably the most promising in the short run. Effluent charges do not adequately deal with problems of equity, however, and in the long run more fundamental solutions will have to be found that move toward a closed rather than an open production system.

Key Concepts

closed system	**internal costs**
open system	**external costs**
residuals	**effluent charge**
externalities	

For Discussion

1. Is economic growth (higher standards of living) incompatible with environmental protection and preservation?

2. Should U.S. policy require American firms to internalize the costs of pollution when they must compete with foreign firms that externalize those costs?

3. Compare the advantages and disadvantages of effluent charges and regulatory limits as means of controlling pollution. Which do you prefer? Why?

4. Should the federal government provide subsidies as an incentive to local governments to reduce pollution? Why not use effluent charges?

5. Would a socialist economy have less of a pollution problem than a capitalist economy?

Chapter 33

The Economics of Energy

The current energy problem derives from a complex intermingling of three factors. One is the economics of an exhaustible resource whose costs of production rise in the long run. In that situation very large amounts of unearned income are available for those able to seize it. Another is the complex political economy of oil. The industry is dominated by a few international oil companies that control transportation, refining, and distribution, and by a group of producer nations that manipulates output and prices. Each seeks to maximize their share of the unearned income. In addition, the industry is caught up in a world struggle for power between the U.S. and the USSR and the political struggle between haves and have-nots within both the oil-producing regions and the oil-importing countries. Finally, there are alternative sources of energy for a more viable energy future based on renewable resources. This chapter seeks to disentangle these various aspects of the energy problem.

The Economics of Exhaustible Resources

Oil is an exhaustible resource. Although use increases with economic growth, the quantity in the ground is finite. It will be used up at some time in the future, and alternate sources of energy will have to be developed. Most of the public discussion of the energy problem has centered on these supply and demand issues.

But an exhaustible resource has another important characteristic. Costs of production rise as the resource is exploited. For example, in a mine, the minerals nearest the surface are taken out first. As the mine goes deeper more capital must be invested to extend the shaft or the slope and more time is required to haul the product to the surface. All of this costs money, and as the mine goes deeper, costs of production rise. Soon it becomes more profitable to open a new mine that taps mineral deposits closer to the surface, even if the mineral content is lower than in the deeper mine. The same is true of oil. A shallow oil pool close to the surface from which the oil flows naturally will be opened before a deeper pool that requires pumping, for example.

Two factors can modify this general rule of rising costs of production for exhaustible resources. One is discovery of a rich new source, cheap to exploit, that was not known before. Thus, when the Spindletop well came in, in 1901 in East Texas, it alone produced an amount of oil equal to about 50 percent of annual oil production in the entire world prior to 1901, at about one-tenth the cost per barrel. That level of output from the Spindletop gusher lasted only a few weeks, but it transformed the world oil market and was the basis for the growth of one of today's giant oil companies, Texaco.

Technological change is the second factor that can overcome rising costs of production for exhaustible resources. Improved production techniques can reduce costs. In most mining industries, as in oil, there is a continuing race between the increasing returns from technical change and the decreasing returns from exploitation of the resource.

There is a corollary to the basic rule that costs of production rise as an exhaustible resource is exploited: the price rises as production increases. As demand grows, the higher cost units are brought into production. Initially production costs are low, but they rise as producers start to exploit their higher cost reserves. The price, therefore, must rise to compensate the marginal producer for its higher costs. As a result, the long-run supply curve for the industry slopes upward.

This is a key concept when dealing with the economics of exhaustible resources. Let the price of a barrel of oil equal $30. At that price, any oil well that can produce oil for a total cost plus normal profit of $30 or less will be brought into production. Any well with cost plus normal profit over $30 will be shut down. At the margin will be the well or wells for which cost plus normal profit exactly equals $30. The market price will be equal to the cost plus normal profit of the marginal producer.

We can now show what the market for an exhaustible resource is like. Figure 33–1 shows the long-run supply curve S_L, assuming no discoveries of new, low-cost supplies and no cost-cutting technical changes. Given the demand for the resource at any given time D, a market price p will be established that covers the cost of production plus normal profit for

Figure 33-1
The Market for an Exhaustible Resource

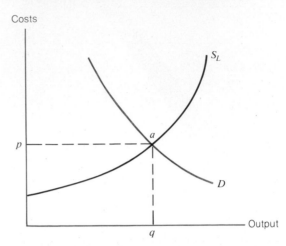

The long-run supply curve S_L rises because costs of production per unit rise at the margin as output increases. With demand curve D the quantity produced is q; the price is p. Cost of production plus normal profit for the marginal unit of output is aq, which is equal to the market price p.

the marginal producer, at the quantity at which the demand and supply curves cross q.

Keep this point in mind as the first key to understanding the political economy of energy. The price of any exhaustible resource, including oil, will tend to equal the cost of production plus a normal profit for the marginal producer. Even if the price is controlled or fixed by governments or a combination of producers, unless there are production controls, output will be pushed to the level at which the marginal producer earns a normal profit above costs of production. Only some form of production control can keep this basic economic relationship from developing.

Competing Sources of Energy
The economy is supplied by several different fuels, including oil, natural gas, coal, hydroelectric power, and nuclear power. In recent years in the U.S. the proportions have been approximately those shown in Table 33–1.

Table 33–1
U.S. Energy Consumption

Fuel	Percent of Total
Petroleum	50
Natural Gas	25
Coal	18
Nuclear	4
Hydroelectric	3
Total	100

All of these sources of energy have the characteristic of exhaustible resources: production costs at the margin rise in the long run as demand increases.

All fuels produce the same product, energy. Energy is measured by the British Thermal Unit (BTU), which is the amount of energy required to raise the temperature of one pound of water one degree Fahrenheit. Buyers of fuels buy BTUs. If the cost of BTUs is higher when obtained from one fuel, buyers will substitute others that cost less. Supplies and price will then adjust, leading to equal prices per BTU for the various souces of energy.

Take the competitive case first. If the price per BTU is higher for oil than for natural gas, users will shift from the more expensive oil to the less expensive gas. The reduced demand for oil will cause output to fall. At the reduced output, production cost plus normal profit at the margin will be lower, and price will fall. With an increase in demand for natural gas, however, a higher output means higher production costs plus normal profit at the margin and a rising price. The shift from oil to natural gas will continue as long as production cost plus normal profit per BTU is higher for oil than for natural gas. It will stop, and the market will stabilize, when production cost plus normal profit per BTU is equalized for the two fuels.

The principle holds even if the price of oil is fixed by monopoly or by agreement among sellers. In that case the price of oil will remain high instead of falling and an even larger shift to natural gas will occur. The result will be an energy glut, as producers of both oil and natural gas push output to the level at which the selling price is equal to the cost of production plus normal profit per BTU at the margin. This is exactly the process that caused the oil glut of 1980–81. OPEC doubled the price of oil in 1978–79 and a worldwide economic recession began in 1980. Demand for all forms of energy leveled off, while the high price for oil stimulated additional production of all fuels, including oil, as well as increased production of other sources of energy. The resulting surplus of oil on the world market forced price reductions as the market moved toward equalization of demand and supply.

We arrive then at two related economic principles applicable to any exhaustible resource.

1. Selling prices move toward equality with cost of production plus normal profit at the margin.
2. In the case of competing exhaustible resources, such as different fuels producing energy, selling prices per unit of output tend toward equality. Therefore, production costs plus normal profit per unit of output at the margin also tend toward equality.

These principles apply when competitive conditions exist in the market. They can be modified by control over price and output by producers and sellers, of course. But even OPEC control of the oil market is unable completely to control competition among producers of the various forms of energy and insulate oil production and prices from the effects of these market adjustment processes.

Unearned Income from an Exhaustible Resource

The presence of a rising long-run supply curve enables the owners of exhaustible resources to obtain large unearned incomes. For the marginal producer the selling price is just equal to the cost of production plus a normal profit. Costs of production for all other producers are lower, yet the selling price is the same. They make extranormal profits, an unearned income.

The unearned income is shown in Figure 33–2. The total revenue of the sellers is the rectangle $A + B$. Total cost of production plus normal profit is the area under the long-run supply curve S_L, or area A. The difference between the two, area B, is the unearned income.

Why is that income unearned? Earned income is the income paid to factors of production for productive services. We include in that category all the costs of production plus a normal profit, recognizing that this definition would not satisfy the Marxist definition of earned and unearned income. Another way of looking at it is to recognize that if the unearned income were taxed away or confiscated, the producers would still be earning a normal profit and would remain in production. Some economists call it an *economic rent* because it is a payment to the owners of a resource in excess of the necessary costs of production.

● **Economic rent** is a payment to the owners of a resource in excess of the necessary costs of production.

This is the case with oil, as with all exhaustible resources. As economic growth causes demand for oil to increase, price and output rise. The higher price is required to bring forth the increased output, for costs of production at the margin rise. The higher price enriches the owners of the existing oil wells, for their costs do not rise even though the price of the product goes up. The result is great wealth from oil. The "windfall profits tax" on oil production is designed to capture some of those economic rents for the government.

The greatest wealth goes to those who own the oil in the ground and the right to produce it. This led to the use of mineral leases that pay royalties to the owner of the land. An oil lease might call for payment of an initial lump sum plus a royalty payment of 50¢ per barrel. When the price of oil rises the leaseholder will gain the entire increase in economic rent. Or the royalty might be set at 12.5 percent of the selling price. In this case seven-eighths of any increase in economic rent will go to the leaseholder and one-eighth to the landowner. Of course, the land might produce no oil at all, in which case the leaseholder will lose the original investment in the lump sum payment for the lease and the cost of drilling a dry well.

These sorts of financial arrangements developed early in the industry. The major oil companies negotiated this type of lease with the countries bordering the Persian Gulf, and elsewhere overseas, when they began moving into those areas. For example, the famous D'Arcy concession for exploration and produc-

Figure 33-2
Unearned Income from an Exhaustible Resource

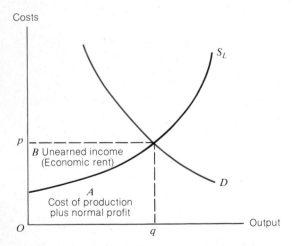

At any given level of output, Oq in this case, total revenues $A + B$ exceed the necessary costs of production A by an amount equal to B. B is unearned income, which is sometimes called economic rent.

tion of oil covering 500,000 square miles of Persia (later Iran) in 1901 was obtained by a payment of £20,000 in cash, £20,000 in company stock, 15 percent of annual net profits, and a rent of £1,800 per year.

In the rapid growth era of the oil industry—to about 1965—the unearned income of owners of oil was less significant than the profits that could be made from refining and distribution. New low-cost supplies were periodically discovered and developed in various parts of the world: the Gulf Coast, Oklahoma, Southern California, East Texas, and West Texas, to name some of the great producing areas within the U.S., and Venezuela, Mexico, Indonesia, Iran, Iraq, Saudi Arabia, Kuwait, and Libya, in other parts of the world. Each discovery brought the world price of oil down, and periodic gluts of oil on world markets were one of the industry's problems. The great oil companies jockeyed for control of oil production to feed their refineries, rather than for the unearned income to be derived from ownership. But by the 1960s, new sources of oil were becoming harder to find, costs of production at the margin were rising, and the inexorable economics of exhaustible resources began to dominate the counteracting forces of new oil discovery and technical change.

At this point the rulers of the oil-producing countries realized that if they took back ownership of the oil and raised the price, the unearned income could be greatly increased and they would get it all. OPEC was born.

The Oil Business
(pronounced "erl bidnes")

In world markets outside the United States the oil industry is dominated by seven major corporations. Prior to the rise of OPEC in the 1970s the "seven majors" controlled 98 percent of oil production outside the U.S. Five are American-based corporations: Exxon (formerly Standard Oil Company of New Jersey),

Mobil (formerly Standard Oil Company of New York), Standard Oil Company of California (known as Socal), Texaco, and Gulf. The first three were part of the original Standard Oil Company, which was broken up by antitrust prosecution in 1911. Texaco and Gulf got their start in the first decade of this century out of the great oil discoveries of that period in Texas and Oklahoma. The other two of the seven majors are British Petroleum, which is dominated by British capital, and Royal Dutch Shell, which is controlled by Dutch and British interests. Both have large operations within the United States. Royal Dutch Shell built up its own operations in the U.S. chiefly after World War I. British Petroleum moved into U.S. markets in the 1960s.

Prior to the first World War, Standard Oil and Royal Dutch Shell contested for—shared is a better word—dominance in the world market. They controlled the bulk of production and developed elaborate transportation, refining, and distribution facilities. Entry of competitors was largely forestalled by this elaborate vertical integration. If an independent obtained production facilities, it had no place to get its oil refined and no distribution facilities to market the product. Texaco needed fifteen years to gain a significant share in the world market, and even Royal Dutch Shell, with huge financial resources, required two decades to crack the U.S. market on a significant scale.

The oil industry in the United States today is an unbalanced oligopoly. The largest, Exxon, has twice the sales of the second largest firm, Mobil. These two firms, together with Texaco, Gulf, Amoco, Shell, and Standard of California, are the industry price leaders in the domestic market. Price leadership in any region rests with the firm that has the largest refining capacity and distribution network in the area. The role of the price leader is to adjust prices for gasoline and fuel oil up or down as market demand and supply change, thereby avoiding competition that might unsettle the customary share of the market enjoyed by the various sellers. The industry is also populated by some two dozen other large companies, but these firms are not part of the inner circle that dominates domestic markets.

The United States was the world's largest producer outside the Soviet bloc until it was supplanted by Saudi Arabia in the 1960s. Domestic needs were met from domestic production, with a substantial amount for export to other parts of the world until the late 1940s. In 1948 the U.S. imported more oil than it exported for the first time and has been a net importer ever since. Domestic production continued to increase until a peak was reached in 1970 of 11.3 million barrels a day. By 1979 U.S. production was 10.2 million barrels a day, which figure includes Alaska. Consumption, however, continued to rise through 1978, when 18.4 million barrels a day were used. By 1980 the U.S. was importing some 48 percent of its oil.

Oil and World Power

Oil became a major element in the world balance of military and political power in the decade before World War I, when the world's navies converted from coal to oil. When oil was discovered in Persia in 1908 by a British-owned company, the Anglo-Persian (later Anglo-Iranian) Oil Company, the British government sent a detachment of troops from India to protect the operation and in 1911 obtained a controlling interest in the producing company in exchange for a contract to buy oil for its navy. After the war Britain obtained a League of Nations mandate over Mesopotamia (later Iraq) and sought to gain complete control over the rich oil resources there. However, complex diplomatic maneuvering and political pressure forced the British to allot part ownership to the French government and several of the American companies. These interests were brought together to form Iraq Petroleum Co., which had a monopoly in the Iraq oil fields.

The United States government got into the scramble for world oil early in the 1920s, but not as a direct owner. It was content to press the interests of private U.S. corporations. At the end of World War I over 80 percent of world demand for oil was satisfied by exports from the U.S. and producing areas controlled by U.S. corporations in Mexico. But demand was large enough to create a temporary shortage, and U.S. output had temporarily levelled off. Fears that the world was running out of oil brought a drive by the U.S. government to assist U.S. companies in gaining control over foreign sources of supply. One result was the compromise in Mesopotamia, noted above, that gained U.S. participation there. A second result was the start of close cooperation between the federal government and the U.S. oil majors that continues to this day.

The world oil shortage of the 1920s was soon replaced by a glut, however, with major discoveries between 1928 and 1932 in Texas, Louisiana, and California heightened by a large decline in demand brought on by the Great Depression of the 1930s. In the U.S. domestic economy, the industry developed its system of price leadership, along with production controls organized in cooperation with the federal and state governments as described earlier in Chapter 23. Internationally, two agreements in 1928 between the major companies sought to stabilize world oil prices—with full approval of their governments that amounted almost to international treaties. The "red line" agreement among the companies and nations involved in Iraqi oil postponed development of oil production in Arabia and the Persian Gulf in order to stabilize production, and the "as is" agreement pledged the major companies to respect each other's shares of the world market. Nevertheless, Gulf Oil jointly with Iraq Petroleum gained a concession in Kuwait, then a British protectorate. Gulf was assisted by negotiations between the U.S. and Britain led by Andrew W. Mellon, who wore two hats: U.S. Ambassador to Britain and chief stockholder in Gulf. Then in the early 1930s Socal (Standard Oil of California) moved overseas through a Canadian subsidiary, getting a concession for oil development in Bahrain, a Persian Gulf island that was also a British protectorate. It also outbid the other majors in 1938 for a large concession in eastern Saudi Arabia, which turned out to be the richest of all. Socal got a half interest in Texaco's marketing facilities in Asia and Australia-New Zealand and sold a half interest in its Saudi Arabian venture to Texaco. By the start of World War II the U.S. majors, with a strong assist from the U.S. State Department, were well established in the Middle East, controlling 42 percent of the reserves, where only twenty years before the British were dominant.

U.S. Oil Diplomacy in the Mideast

During and after World War II, the American oil companies and the U.S. government moved to supplant British oil interests and political dominance in the Middle East and the Persian Gulf. The Saudi Arabian government was in financial trouble early in the 1940s, because the war greatly reduced the flow of pilgrims to Mecca. Furthermore, oil production was reduced after the Japanese conquest of southeast Asia cut off sales by Socal and Texaco in that region. The U.S. government filled the void with financial assistance to Saudi Arabia, which brought the royal family firmly to support U.S. interests. Such legalized bribes had long been used by the British in that area.

After the war Britain was forced by economic difficulties to reduce its military commitments throughout the world, including the entire area from the eastern Mediterranean through the Middle East-Persian Gulf to India. The British Empire was on the wane. Not so for the U.S., however. Fearful of a military and political vacuum that could be exploited by the USSR, the U.S. government began to replace the British. Economic and military aid was given to Greece and Turkey starting in the late 1940s to shore up those countries against

Soviet penetration. The U.S. Sixth Fleet was stationed in the eastern Mediterranean as the British pulled their ships out, acting as both a defense against and a threat to the USSR, depending on whether one was behind or in front of the guns. The fleet also protected the flow of oil from the Mideast to large markets in Europe. The Western European allies of the U.S. strongly supported U.S. policy because Mideast oil was now essential to their domestic economies, and the U.S. taxpayer paid for the protection provided by the Sixth Fleet. It was a more subtle form of bribe.

U.S. Mideast policy also embraced a program to assure control of Mideast oil by U.S. capital. There were two potential threats. One was the rise of nationalist movements opposed both to the venal and authoritarian governments of the region and to control of oil by foreign interests. The nationalist movements, particularly in Iran and Iraq, had a radical political program in the late 1940s and 1950s and were supported by the USSR. The answer to this threat was U.S. military aid, economic assistance, and diplomatic support for the existing governments. The purpose was to enable them to hold the line against both Soviet influence and the threat of nationalization of the oil industry.

The second threat was a growing demand by those very governments for a larger share in oil profits. These demands had to be met, from the viewpoint of the U.S. government, partly to meet the financial needs of the Mideast governments, and partly to respond to the growing nationalist sentiment. The oil companies did not want to share their gains, of course, and a potential conflict was developing in the neat *menàge a trois* that had been devised. Not to worry. A way was found to shift the burden to the U.S. taxpayer. The device was pioneered in Venezuela in 1948 and introduced to the Mideast in 1950 in Saudi Arabia. Payments by the companies were increased to 50 percent of profits. Instead of being called a royalty it was called an income tax. Simultaneously, the U.S. corporate income tax was revised to allow U.S. firms operating abroad to deduct income tax payments to foreign countries from their U.S. tax liabilities. By means of this creative accounting procedure, payments to ruling families and governments in the Mideast were more than doubled, and the U.S. oil companies practically ceased to pay income taxes to the U.S. government, not only from their foreign operations, but from their domestic business as well.

If all of this sounds as if it were from the script of a sensational Hollywood extravaganza, remember that the makers of oil policy in this period in both the State and Defense Departments were chiefly former oil company executives, or oil company executives-to-be, or lawyers and bankers whose firms had close ties to the oil industry. In addition, Congressmen and Senators from the oil-producing states formed a strong and cohesive bloc in Congress, supported by campaign contributions from the oil companies. It was democracy at work during the era of the great barbecue.

The U.S. Takeover in Iran

The nationalist movement in Iran was not bought off as easily as in the other Mideast oil areas. In 1946 Iran was a major bone of contention between the U.S. and Britain on one side and the USSR on the other. The USSR caved in after U.S. spokesmen pointed out that the U.S. had atomic weapons and the USSR did not—a lesson the Kremlin never forgot. Both the USSR and Britain agreed to withdraw troops that had occupied Iran during World War II, a Soviet-dominated independence movement in northwest Iran was ended, and strikes by communist-dominated unions in the Iranian and Iraqi oil fields were halted, in exchange for representation in the Iranian government for the Tudeh (communist) Party. The Anglo-Iranian Oil Company remained a British firm, however, with a monopoly of Iranian production. Soviet demands for oil concessions in the north were turned down by the Iranian

parliament. By 1947 the first crisis was over; the USSR had pulled back under pressure; and the Shah of Iran, supported by U.S. aid, held a shaky throne.

The nationalist movement was still strong, however. Agitation for nationalization of the Anglo-Iranian concession and properties began in 1949, and could not be bought off by an offer of the new 50-50 split of profits then in vogue. In 1951 the parliament nationalized the oil industry and Mohammed Mossadeq, the nationalist leader with left leanings, became prime minister. Armed intervention by the British was vetoed by the U.S., which feared a Russian invasion from the north. The major oil companies came to the rescue of Anglo-Iranian, however, by organizing a boycott of Iranian oil. With no market, oil production in Iran plummeted to almost nothing. The ensuing economic crisis threatened a leftward shift in Iranian politics. Mossadeq introduced legislation to increase taxes on the rich and end feudal payments in rural areas; the Shah fled for his life to the French Riviera; and the U.S. Central Intelligence Agency helped put together a coalition of Iranian military leaders, landowners, and others to seize power, get rid of Mossadeq and bring back the Shah. This second crisis was ended by imposing on Iran the beginnings of the repressive authoritarianism that the Shah gradually built up in the 1950s and 1960s, financed by large amounts of U.S. economic aid and enforced by U.S. military assistance—a bulwark against the Soviet Union.

But the camel had its nose in the tent. Iranian oil remained nationalized, although control of production remained with the consortium of companies that operated the properties through the reorganized and renamed Iranian Petroleum Company. The British demanded compensation, however, and got it through purchase of a 40 percent share by a syndicate of U.S. oil companies, which involved tiny shares for eight independent producers that were included at the insistence of the U.S. government. This introduced a second camel's nose into the tent. The independents learned about the large profits in Mideast oil, sought concessions elsewhere in the years to come, and ultimately undermined control of production by the seven majors.

The Great Barbecue, 1948–1960

For a dozen years the international oil companies made extraordinary profits. They controlled 98 percent of world oil production outside the U.S., the USSR and Eastern Europe, and Mexico (which nationalized its oil industry in the 1930s). They also controlled over 40 percent of U.S. production. A system of joint ventures made them informal partners in most world markets. They had long-term contracts to supply each other with oil where a company might have an imbalance between production capacity and refining and marketing capacity. World markets were divided, and market shares were respected by potential rivals along the lines of the "as is" agreement of 1928. Sources of supply were protected by royalty or profit-sharing agreements with governments in producing regions, and were bolstered by U.S. economic and military aid, as well as by the general protective umbrella of U.S. world power.

Costs of production were low: 16 cents per barrel at the margin in Saudi Arabia, 51 cents in Venezuela, and $1.73 in the U.S., according to a Chase Manhattan Bank study in the early 1960s. But world prices were set at levels high enough to make U.S. production profitable. Persian Gulf oil was priced at $1.75 to $2.22 per barrel at the Mideast shipping terminals. Exact records are not available on company profits, but even after sharing 50-50 with the governments involved, the company profits were enormous: 75 cents to $1 of unearned income per barrel of Saudi Arabian oil, for example.

It couldn't last. Independent oil companies were attracted by the huge gains, and governments in the producing areas wanted a larger share of the profits. EMI, the government-owned oil company in Italy, obtained a concession in Iran by giving up 75 percent of the profits; Getty Oil got into the neutral zone between Kuwait and Saudi Arabia; Occidental Oil opened up Libya; production rose in Egypt, Algeria, and other areas not controlled by the international majors. Throughout the world, new sources of production began coming on line in response to high prices. A growing glut of oil began to appear in the late 1950s, brought about by the pricing policies of the international oil cartel. The companies were able to raise prices to a new high level in 1957, but in 1959 and again in 1960 prices were reduced to dispose of growing inventories.

The price reductions of 1959 were a threat to U.S. oil production, for domestic costs of production at the margin were now a bit higher than the cost of imported Mideast oil. This situation benefited the international majors, for they could enlarge the market for their very profitable Mideast crude oil. But they also pumped over 40 percent of domestic U.S. production. To that extent, they were competing with themselves. Independent U.S. producers would be hard hit by imports, however, and they were an important political influence that could not be ignored. Independent domestic refiners, on the other hand, would be benefited by lower prices on imported crude oil. The majors, with profits from their own domestic production to protect and unwilling to promote the interests of the independent refiners, joined the independent crude oil producers to push through Congress a law imposing import quotas on foreign crude oil supplies. Beginning in 1959 a license from the federal government to import crude oil was necessary. Control of prices and production within the U.S. was now protected from the surplus in world markets.

The ruling families and governments in the Mideast producing areas were badly damaged by the price reductions of 1959 and 1960, for their incomes were sharply reduced. The income was needed to pay for expensive economic development projects and welfare programs designed to maintain political stability. This issue became increasingly significant later in the 1960s as world inflation began to escalate. In addition, there was growing criticism from radical and nationalist groups about national destinies being controlled by foreign corporations accountable to no one. It was true. The governments of the Mideast oil areas were furious because the oil companies had neither consulted with them or informed them in advance that the price cuts were coming.

At this point, in 1960, five governments joined together to form the Organization of Petroleum Exporting Countries (OPEC), Saudi Arabia, Kuwait, Iraq, Iran, and Venezuela. Membership later expanded to include thirteen countries.

Interlude: the 1960s
Although the end of the great barbecue for the seven majors was already foreshadowed in 1960 by their inability to control production by the independents and by the formation of OPEC, political instability in the Mideast enabled them to maintain effective control over world oil production and prices for another dozen years. The radical-nationalist political movement had already overthrown King Farouk in Egypt (1953) and President Nasser was in power by 1956. In 1958 a radical-nationalist party gained power in Iraq, Syria followed in 1963, and Libya in 1969. These governments supported the Palestine Liberation Organization and were supported by the USSR. On the other side of the political spectrum were the right-authoritarian regimes supported by the U.S. and Britain in Iran, Saudi Arabia, and the Persian Gulf sheikdoms. During the 1960s these two factions contested for power in the region. In 1962 a left-nationalist coup in Yemen brought conflict between Saudi Arabia and Egypt and led to a struggle for power within the Saudi royal family that was not resolved until a final purge of dissidents in 1969. Throughout the decade the efforts of the radical-nationalists to confront the oil companies were opposed by Saudi Arabia, Iran, and the sheikdoms as part of the political struggles between right and left. One area of disagreement was the demand by the left-nationalists that oil revenues be used for the benefit of all Arabs, not just the ruling cliques. Ultimately the right bloc led by Saudi Arabia gained the upper hand, not through its own efforts, but because of the defeat of Egypt and Syria in the 1967 war against Israel. The balance of power also shifted away from the militant left with the death of Nasser in 1970.

These political events seemed to indicate that the tide in the Mideast was running in favor of U.S. hegemony and the interests of the oil companies. But appearances were deceiving. OPEC had learned a great deal about how the oil companies were managing the oil industry for greater profits and how oil could be used as a pawn in international politics. OPEC also learned an important lesson from the 1967 war, when there was an unsuccessful attempt to embargo oil shipments to Europe and the U.S. The embargo failed because the oil companies simply supplied their markets from other sources where there was unused production capacity, including the U.S. Furthermore, the oil glut continued through the 1960s. By 1969 prices reached a low of $1.00 to $1.20 per barrel in the Persian Gulf. Algeria and Libya became large oil exporters in the 1960s, with production primarily by independent companies whose output could not be controlled by the seven majors. But by 1970, the year in which U.S. domestic production peaked, output in Algeria, Libya, and Kuwait also began to reach capacity production. Saudi Arabia and Iran were the only producing areas with substantial ability to increase output. This was the key to control of production and prices. Until 1970 the seven majors could always discipline an obstreperous nation by limiting output there and increasing production elsewhere. By 1970 they were no longer able to do so.

The seven majors, together with a number of independents, seem to have anticipated the coming shift from oil abundance to oil scarcity. During the 1960s they diversified their activities and became energy companies rather than chiefly oil companies. This move was made primarily in the U.S., where other energy resources are great and where political stability (which meant protection for private enterprise) was assured. Always strong in natural gas production, which is usually found with crude oil, oil companies acquired by merger and purchase companies that produced over 50 percent of U.S. coal and owned over half of U.S. coal reserves. Most also positioned themselves in uranium refining and processing to gain a foothold in nuclear energy. Several gained control over oil shale and tar sand leases, in the synthetic fuels section of the energy industry. Exploration for new sources of oil in the U.S. culminated in opening up the large Alaskan oil and gas fields in the 1970s. But the chief source of new production for the majors in the U.S., particularly in the 1970s, was through acquisition of independent producers rather than exploration and discovery. Losing dominance in the international oil market to OPEC, the companies used the large profits from the great barbecue of the 1960s to stake out dominant positions in alternative sources of energy and gain even stronger positions in U.S. oil and gas production.

OPEC Gains Control

The balance of power in world oil markets shifted to the producing nations in 1970. An accident triggered the change. A Syrian bulldozer operator severed a pipeline connecting the Iraqi oil fields with their Mediterranean shipping port. The Suez Canal had already been closed in 1967 because of the Israel-Arab war. The resulting shortage of oil in Europe could not be overcome by increased U.S. output, which was already at capacity. The new left-nationalist dictator in Libya, Colonel Kadaffi, seized this opportunity to demand large increases in revenues from a vulnerable independent, Occidental Oil, which had no other source of oil to supply its profitable European markets. Occidental gave in, and the shift in power was obvious to both the Mideast countries and the oil companies.

Early in 1971, at a conference in Teheran between OPEC and the oil companies, new agreements were reached that provided for larger participation in profits for the producing countries and a 50¢ per barrel increase in the price of Persian Gulf oil. This was followed by nationalization of the oil industry in Algeria, Libya, and Iraq in 1971 and 1972.

Meanwhile, demand for oil continued to increase in world markets. The Vietnam war was reaching its peak, a business cycle upswing was in progress, and the U.S. lifted its import quotas. The world oil market had shifted, in about three years, from substantial oversupply and excess production capacity, to severe tightness. By 1973 only Saudi Arabia had surplus production capacity, and even Saudi production was at 97 percent of capacity output.

At this point, in 1973, the third Arab-Israeli war broke out, temporarily uniting the Mideast governments, in spite of the persistent quarrel between left-nationalists and right-authoritarians. OPEC responded to U.S. military aid to Israel by cutting output and declaring a boycott on oil sales to the U.S. and a number of other nations. The oil panic was on, with gasoline and fuel oil shortages within the U.S. Frantic bidding for available oil in the world market drove prices to a high of $22.60 per barrel by December 1973. But the war ended; the boycott was halted; and oil prices stabilized at a new and substantially higher level. The average price of oil imported into the U.S. had risen from $2.57 in 1972 to $11.01 in 1974.

Five years of relative stability in oil prices followed. By 1978 the average price per barrel of oil imports into the U.S. had risen only to $13.29, and the increase from the 1974 level lagged behind the rate of inflation. Slowed economic growth in the world economy decreased the rate of growth in demand for oil. New sources of oil were opened up in the North Sea and Alaska, and these supplies were not controlled by OPEC. Production of oil by the members of OPEC was a bit less in 1978 than in 1974.

But the great increase in oil revenues in the Mideast in those years increased political destabilization there. Oil revenues were used for huge economic development expenditures. Even applying the general rule of one-third for graft, one-third wasted, and one-third for development, the impact was tremendous: inflation, rapid urbanization, destruction of traditional industries and commercial patterns, immigration of foreign laborers and technical-managerial personnel, growing inequality of income and wealth. The first impact was felt in Iran in 1978: revolution against the Shah that brought a cutoff in oil exports in the winter of 1978–79. This coincided with a business cycle upturn in the industrial nations and a large increase in demand for oil. OPEC took advantage of the situation to increase the price of oil rapidly. In 1979 and 1980 Saudi Arabia raised the price of its oil to $25 per barrel, and other countries to $32 to $35. These were contract prices, but prices on the open market rose even higher, to over $40 per barrel.

Beneath the Surface

In the early 1980s the OPEC nations seem to be in control. Huge amounts of unearned income due to high prices and low costs of production shift perhaps as much as $100 billion per year of the world's wealth to the OPEC countries. With control of the supply of Mideast oil they are able to increase or decrease production in amounts large enough to determine the world price of oil, particularly since production elsewhere is at capacity lev-

els. World demand for oil, as for all forms of energy, continues to rise, in spite of relative stagnation in the world economy. Having displaced the seven major oil companies, OPEC seems to be in the catbird seat.

Appearances may be deceiving. A new slump in world economic activity began in 1980, diminishing demand for oil. Demand also fell because of the doubling of oil prices in 1978–79. Prices were now high enough to induce a large shift to other sources of energy on a large scale, a shift that had been prepared technologically and psychologically by the energy uncertainty after 1973. The new high prices also made production of other forms of energy more profitable, and output of coal, natural gas, and other fuels rose. In all of the fossil fuel industries, output continued to be pushed up to the levels at which marginal cost plus a normal profit equalled the new and much higher price made possible by oil price increases. Even if world demand for energy moved up with a business cycle upturn, an energy glut at existing prices was foreseeable.

Yet the OPEC nations are committed to maintaining a high oil price and increasing output at the same time. Expensive development programs anticipate the day when the oil runs out. Large social welfare expenditures are needed to satisfy popular demand for higher living standards. Rising imports caused by higher incomes have to be paid for, and oil income is the only source. Yet in most of the OPEC countries oil production peaked in the late 1970s, particularly in such left-nationalist countries as Libya, Algeria, and Iraq. High prices and large oil revenues continue to be needed for internal political reasons, but high prices plus large output is an economic contradiction that cannot long be maintained in the face of a worldwide shift to other sources of energy and increased oil production not controlled by OPEC.

The rulers of Saudi Arabia seem to understand the problem, and they are also concerned about the internal political destabilization oil wealth can bring. So in 1978 and 1979 Saudi

Arabia tried unsuccessfully to moderate the rise in oil prices. Unable to convince fellow OPEC members, Saudi Arabia persistently increased oil production, helping to cause the new oil glut of 1981 that began to pull world oil prices down from 1979 levels.

The immediate future would seem to be dominated by production and price trends more favorable to oil buyers and users. Increased demand for oil will continue to be moderated by substitution of other forms of energy. High energy prices will continue to stimulate greater output of alternative energy sources. Internal political and economic pressures should continue to push the less developed oil-producing areas of the Mideast, Africa, and Latin America to maintain high levels of output. There may even be a semipermanent oil glut, as some forecasters are predicting, that will keep oil prices relatively stable.

These prospects could change overnight, of course, because of political changes in the notoriously unstable Mideast oil-producing region. War and/or revolution could be triggered by significant losses in oil income, brought on by lower prices for oil, and that could change the energy situation almost overnight.

Optimism should also be qualified by the fact that the bulk of the alternative energy supplies in the U.S. are controlled by the great energy conglomerates, which are entrenching themselves even more securely with each successive merger or acquisition. Energy "independence" may mean merely going back to dependence on domestic energy oligopolies.

Energy Alternatives

The earlier parts of this chapter made two chief points about the energy situation of the U.S. and the world. First, exhaustible sources of energy such as oil, coal and natural gas are subject to rising costs of production at the margin. Reliance on them in the future means higher energy costs, unless large amounts of new low-cost supplies are discovered. Exhaust-

ible resources also bring large unearned incomes, or economic rents, to their owners. Second, the chief fossil fuels are controlled by a very few: oil by OPEC, and much of the others by the great energy conglomerates. Control of fossil fuels by a few means that, as use increases and prices rise, an increasing amount of wealth will be transferred by the many to the few, by people who receive earned income to those who levy a toll of economic rent on energy users.

Alternatives to the present sources of energy should be evaluated with both of these points in mind. Renewable sources of energy are not subject to rising costs and do not bring unearned incomes (unless they are monopolized). The two renewable sources of energy available now are certain types of nuclear energy and solar power. Each has strong and weak points, advantages and disadvantages.

Solar Energy

In many respects, solar energy is the most desirable long-run alternative. It is safe for both people and the environment. It does not entail the risks present in production of nuclear energy, disposal of nuclear wastes, or the possible use of nuclear materials for military purposes. As the technology of solar energy production advances and as costs of fossil fuels rise, solar energy is becoming economically practical in an increasing number of uses. Over the long run it may turn out to be relatively inexpensive, flexible in its uses, and capable of a highly decentralized pattern of production.

Solar energy is available in many forms. Electricity can be generated in photovoltaic, or solar electric, cells. They convert sunlight into electric power and store it, much like a battery. At the present time they are not efficient enough to produce significant amounts of electricity at costs lower than other sources of electrical energy. But a technological breakthrough could come at any time, according to researchers involved in their development. Solar energy can also produce heat in so-called "passive" applications, such as heating a house by sunlight that heats bricks, stone, water or air, with the heat being transferred and distributed through the house by a variety of means. Wind is also a form of solar energy, for winds are caused by differential heating of the atmosphere by the sun. Windmills tap that source. Electricity can also be generated from the oceans, using the difference in water temperature between the upper layers warmed by the sun and the cold lower layers. Hydroelectric power is also based on solar energy through the evaporation of water by heat from the sun and the water cycle that eventually brings it back to the oceans. Wood provides solar energy in solid form. Plants use the sun to transform carbon dioxide and water into carbohydrates.

One of the most promising uses of solar energy is production of liquid and gaseous fuels from agricultural products and animal wastes. Grains and sugary plants can be used to produce alcohol for use as a liquid fuel. The chief by-product is a protein-rich animal feed. Manure from the animals then becomes the raw material for production of methane gas, which is similar to natural gas. This restructuring of agriculture need not reduce production of food, for in the Midwest much of the existing grain production is used directly for livestock production. Introducing alcohol as an intermediate product and methane as an end product could be accomplished with no reduction in food output. Another potentially large source of fuel is methane produced from artificially grown seaweed in warm coastal areas and from garbage and sewage in urban areas. Several estimates of fuel production from these sources indicate that they could supply 50 to 90 percent of present U.S. consumption levels of natural gas and liquid fuels used for transportation.

Hydrogen is probably the most useful transportation fuel in the energy future. It can be burned in internal combustion engines, and produces no pollutants. Hydrogen is produced from water, using electric power, and turns back into water when burned. In the future either solar or nuclear energy could be used to produce the electricity.

Solar energy is much less capital-intensive than nuclear energy, requiring less capital and more labor and land per unit of energy produced. This means that relatively small production units can be spread out more widely, closer to the point of use, saving transportation costs. For example, a small array of photovoltaic cells on the roof of a house can produce electricity per square foot of exposure just as efficiently as a huge array at a central power plant, and will avoid the cost of transmission from the central plant. Economies of large-scale production will not dominate an energy future based on solar energy.

The political and institutional effects of this characteristic of solar energy are important. Sources of energy could be decentralized in relatively small operations. Sources of capital would not be a large barrier to entry into energy production. Centralized control over capital accumulation by either government or private industry would therefore be unnecessary. The political effect of these economic conditions could be enormous: solar energy could reverse the trend toward central control over the economy that has been fostered by the economics and technology of fossil fuels.

Technology remains a barrier to use of solar energy, but it is less important than most people think. The bulk of the technology is already available, particularly for conversion of vegetable materials, sewage, manure, and human wastes into liquid and gaseous fuels. Electricity from voltaic cells is not yet economically feasible, but may be within a very short time as technical advances are made. The transition to solar energy has already begun on a small scale in some lesser applications. But as that movement spreads, as energy prices rise, and if significant funds can be allocated to research and development, an accelerated transition to solar energy is a prospect.

Nuclear Energy
A power plant using nuclear energy produces heat to boil water that produces steam to run an electrical generator. The heat is produced in

a nuclear reactor that splits atoms of enriched uranium ore, which process produces heat and spent nuclear fuels. This process has five serious flaws. The cost of construction is high and the operating plants have had continuing problems in maintaining operations at efficient levels. These economic problems have kept costs per unit of energy higher than those in coal-fired power plants in the U.S., where the cost of mining and transporting coal is relatively low. In Europe, where coal is more expensive, nuclear power has less of an economic disadvantage.

A second flaw is that uranium, the fuel, is both expensive to mine and process, and very limited in supply. It is an exhaustible resource subject to increasing costs of production at the margin and ultimate exhaustion of supplies. A second stage in development of nuclear energy could eliminate this problem, however. The breeder reactor (which uses plutonium rather than uranium as a fuel) can produce more nuclear fuel than it uses. Several breeder reactors are in use in Europe, but none yet in the United States. A third stage, fusion reactors that use nuclear fusion rather than fission, are true producers of power based on renewable energy sources: they would use the same process at work in the sun itself. The technology of controllable nuclear fusion is still in the relatively distant future, however. Oil resources will run out before nuclear fusion is a practical alternative, unless very large oil discoveries are made.

The third flaw in nuclear energy is the problem of disposal of nuclear wastes, some of which remain dangerous for 100,000 to 200,000 years. This problem has not been solved and there seems to be no possibility for solution in the foreseeable future. Breeder reactors have less of a waste disposal problem than fission reactors and nuclear fusion would, presumably, have little or none.

The possibility of a nuclear accident that could have disastrous consequences is the fourth flaw. All forms of nuclear power have this problem. The 1979 near-disaster at the Three Mile Island nuclear power plant near Harrisburg, Pennsylvania, was started by the failure of a single pump and compounded by human error on the part of inadequately trained personnel. A disaster was averted only because other people who knew what they were doing were mobilized from elsewhere, along with special equipment brought in from the atomic laboratory at Oak Ridge, Tennessee. At all levels of production from uranium mining and enrichment, to the power plants themselves, to disposal of wastes, nuclear energy entails serious hazards.

Finally, there are security problems. Nuclear fuels can be used to make nuclear weapons. The world has not yet been able to reduce the national rivalries and antagonisms that can lead to nuclear warfare. The bombing of an Iraqi nuclear energy laboratory by Israeli warplanes in 1981 brought this problem to the fore.

Nevertheless, nuclear power remains a possible source of renewable energy supplies—if it can compete economically with other sources, and if safety, waste disposal, and security problems can be resolved. In its present form, however, nuclear energy is not the answer.

Nuclear energy, even if it were safe, secure, economically viable, and renewable, would require very large accumulations of capital for large producing units. An electrical generating plant based on heating water in large vessels has inherent economies of large-scale production. The size of the market and the increasing cost of distributing electricity from a central source are the chief economic limits to plant size. Nuclear energy, therefore, may be best adapted to production of electricity for relatively large and densely populated urban areas. These aspects of nuclear energy would call for centralized processes of capital accumulation by big government, big business, and big financial institutions, as well as relatively few large enterprises in control of energy production. Where solar energy would promote decentralization of economic and political power, nuclear energy would be a base for centralization.

Nuclear energy has another drawback. In the transition period large amounts of resources would be required for development because of the highly capital-intensive nature of production and distribution. These investment expenditures would divert resources either from consumption and living standards or from other investment uses, and probably both. Solar energy, which uses a less capital-intensive technology, would cause a lesser diversion of capital from other uses.

Conservation

An energy system based on renewable resources can provide a stable price for energy, because the increasing costs of exhaustible resources would be eliminated. In the transition period, however, which may last fifty years or more, exhaustible fossil fuels such as oil, natural gas, and coal will still be needed. But their use will be phased out as supplies diminish, costs rise, and the economic incentive to shift to solar or nuclear energy increases. In addition, increasing energy costs, relative to prices of other goods, will stimulate a reduction in energy use. Energy conservation is achieved voluntarily for economic reasons. There can be severe technological limits on energy conservation in the short run, but economic incentives are a great stimulus to both changes in technologies and life styles.

In the days of cheap energy, such as the period of rapid economic growth between World War II and the Vietnam War, energy use rose at about the same rate as economic activity. A one percent increase in GNP in the U.S. was accompanied by approximately a one percent increase in energy use. By the late 1970s the ratio had changed under the impact of high energy prices. A one percent increase in GNP was accompanied by approximately a 0.8 percent increase in energy use. Some estimates are even lower. In a stable energy supply future based on renewable energy sources, it might appear that such conservation will not be necessary. Indeed, without the pressure of

rising costs and prices the incentive for energy conservation may well be reduced or eliminated. That is not the case, however.

Use of energy releases heat into the atmosphere, but the atmosphere traps a portion of the heat, prevents it from radiating into space, and can cause the temperature of the atmosphere to increase. Carbon dioxide in the air increases that effect. Burning of fossil fuels and the reduction in forest areas has increased the proportion of carbon dioxide in the earth's atmosphere in the last hundred years of industrial growth, leading some authorities to predict a long-range warming trend that could make the earth almost uninhabitable in another hundred years. This "greenhouse effect" may soon be irreversible unless the increase in energy use is halted, in this view. Other authorities argue that increased pollution from burning fossil fuels screens out enough radiation from the sun to prevent any significant increase in the temperature of the earth's atmosphere. The debate over the greenhouse effect has been inconclusive, but in the last five years a consensus has started to appear among scientists to the effect that it is a serious problem.

In an energy future without fossil fuels, reduced output of carbon dioxide as a by-product of much production of energy may negate the greenhouse effect. But another problem will remain, heat. All use of energy releases heat into the atmosphere, while it is simultaneously being radiated into space from the upper atmosphere. Will enough be released to compensate for the heat created by economic activity? Here, again, scientists are not sure. The preponderance of opinion is that increased economic activity will result in a very slow but persistent rise in the temperature of the earth's atmosphere, even without rising levels of carbon dioxide.

The need for energy conservation will not be eliminated in a solar energy future, but the individual incentives for conservation may be reduced greatly by two factors. First, rising energy costs may be largely eliminated. Second, the costs of increased energy use would be largely social, in the form of atmospheric temperature changes and climatic change. Solutions to the problem will require social choices and decisions to develop energy-saving technology and to limit energy use. These decisions will have to be made world-wide, for the earth's atmosphere is a world resource. In the long run, a viable energy future seems to require, if not an international government, some international supervision or control of energy production.

Summary

Oil, like all fossil fuels, is an exhaustible or nonrenewable resource. These resources are subject to rising costs of production at the margin. As supplies are used up, or as demand increases, rising prices are required to draw forth the marginal output. The difference between costs of production and selling price for producers with lower costs than the marginal producers leads to economic rents, or unearned income.

Around 1970 a number of changes in the industry and in world politics enabled the governments of the Mideast oil-producing nations and Venezuela to gain control over production and prices. They used that control to raise prices and shift a much-enlarged unearned income to themselves.

The chief alternatives for an energy future based on renewable resources are solar energy and nuclear breeder reactors. Solar energy has large advantages: a currently available technology, relatively low capital intensity of production, safety with little or no pollution, and the possibility of small-scale and decentralized production patterns. Breeder reactors, on the other hand, are still in the early stages of technological development and could not produce significant amounts of energy for several decades in the future. They are highly capital-intensive, have significant safety and pollution problems, and would form the base for a more highly centralized economy and society.

Solar energy also has the advantage that it is more compatible with the need to limit overall energy use to levels that will not cause the temperature of the earth's atmosphere to rise. The greatest advantage of solar energy, however, is that it can provide the economic base for more highly decentralized patterns of economic and political power.

Key Concept

economic rent

For Discussion

1. Why does an exhaustible resource have an upward-sloping long-run supply curve?
2. Does the windfall profits tax on unearned income from oil production reduce the incentive to develop greater production of oil? Explain.
3. Explain why the OPEC increases in the price of oil stimulated rapid development of other sources of energy.
4. Discuss: The present world energy situation is in large part the outcome of a worldwide struggle for wealth and power.

PART 8

SOCIALISM

One of the continuing conflicts that troubles the modern world concerns alternatives to the capitalist mode of organizing economic activity. The chief alternative is socialism. But the socialist movement itself has developed along three different lines. In western Europe it was largely diverted from the goal of social ownership of the means of production and social control of the economic surplus to income equalization via the tax system and provision of a variety of welfare services by government. Although some important sectors of industry were nationalized when socialist parties gained office, the bulk of industry, trade and finance were left in private hands. The class structure of society was left largely unchanged. This hybrid pattern has been alternatively called welfare socialism or welfare capitalism.

The second type of socialism developed in the Soviet Union and was later imposed on most of Eastern Europe. The Russian revolution of 1917 displaced the old order. In the period between the two World Wars a new political-economic order developed in which the forces of production were collectivized—government ownership of industry, trade, and finance, with agriculture were organized chiefly in collective farms—but control over the means of production and the economic surplus was highly centralized in the government administrative structure. A new social organization of production developed, with a managerial-administrative-political bureaucracy in control of state power. Government ownership of productive resources, with control by the Communist party, the central administration, the police forces, and the military became the institutional framework of the new political-economic order. The Soviet system is often called authoritarian socialism. State collectivism is a more apt term, however, for the socialist emphasis on a classless society, democracy, and equal income distribution is not found in the USSR.

The third development of socialism remains a promise rather than a reality. It emphasizes decentralization of both economic and political power to workers, farmers, and other producers through workers' management and use of the market to achieve economic coordination. It is a truly revolutionary doctrine, for drastic economic and political changes would have to occur in both the U.S. and the USSR, to achieve this ideal.

These are the larger issues at stake in Part 8. Chapter 34 examines socialism and its ideology, and discusses some of the key issues of economic organization, political power, class structure, and problems of transition that socialists must deal with. Chapter 35 describes and evaluates the system of central planning used in the USSR. Chapter 36 turns to market socialism and workers' management as the chief alternative to capitalism.

Chapter 34

Socialism

Socialism differs from capitalism in two respects.[1] The first concerns property relations, the second, ideology. This chapter deals both with the differences between the two systems and some of the forms they take in the contemporary world. The discussion emphasizes the various forms that economic organization can take, laying out the chief alternatives to capitalism that are feasible in the latter part of the twentieth century.

The Socialist Ideology

Socialism is rooted in three ideals: equality, brotherhood, and cooperation. These principles embody a humanistic ethic essential to the achievement of a humane society, in the view of most socialists.

The principle of equality is based on the belief that in basic human qualities all persons are the same and of equal value, and that artificial distinctions should not be made among them. Any socialist would agree that people differ in intelligence, ability, interests, and desires. Most would also agree that any society needs incentives to motivate people and help organize productive effort, and that any incentive system may lead to differences in earnings. But socialists also place heavy emphasis on equal treatment, equal opportunity, and elimination of artificial differences in income or privilege. They take a dim view of inheritance, dislike private schools that provide special educational opportunities for the wealthy, and protest any manifestations of rank and privilege.

This viewpoint runs deep in the heritage of western culture. Judaic-Christian theology tells us that all people are the same in the eyes of God. This viewpoint has cropped out whenever people have protested against the organized inequality of their time. For example, the theme song of the peasants who marched on London in 1381 was

---

[1] The term *socialism* was invented by Pierre Leroux (1798–1871), a French reformer and journalist, who intended the word to be the antithesis of *individualism* and not the general name for an ideology and social movement that it became. Karl Marx (1818–1883) was the first to apply the name *capitalism* to the private-enterprise, market-oriented, industrial economy of the nineteenth century. He chose that word to emphasize the fact that owners of capital and workers were different people who performed different functions in the economy and therefore made up two distinct social classes of opposing interests. He called it capitalism to indicate the dominance of the capitalist class and the crucial importance of capital accumulation in the economy. One measure of the debt owed to Marx by modern social scientists is the fact that all use his descriptive term, although many define it differently.

When Adam delved and Eve span,
Who was then the gentleman?

Similar sentiments motivated the American and French Revolutions:

We hold these Truths to be self-evident,
That all Men are created equal . . .

Liberté, egalité, fraternité.

The socialist wishes to apply that ethical ideal to the economy and to political and social organization. The result is emphasis on more equal patterns of income distribution, the ending of great holdings of wealth, and the elimination of economic privileges. Some would call it a "classless society."

A second ethical principle of socialism is belief in the brotherhood of people, manifested in concern for those who are in need. This ideal is closely related to the belief that the relationship of the individual to the social group is the most important social tie. Socialists believe that there is a collective responsibility for the alleviation of individual distress, for if the individual cannot function well, the effectiveness of the group as a whole is diminished. Socialists are eager to establish a welfare floor below which no individual is allowed to fall. They look with favor on the social service and welfare philosophy that sides with the less fortunate and those in need. Social action against deprivation and poverty is high on the agenda of socialism.

A third socialist ideal is belief in the concept of cooperation. This aspect of socialism rejects competition, individualism, and rivalry in favor of group action, full participation by all in the decision-making process, and collective responsibility for the welfare of society. In its extreme form this ideal can be reduced to the proposition that people ought to work for the social good, and not for their own gain. In more moderate form, many socialists argue that people feel happier and work harder when they work for goals that go beyond personal material benefits. At the very least, most socialists would like to organize the incentive system so that rewards go heavily to those who work for the social good, and not just for their individual gain.

The socialist principle of cooperation presents some well-recognized difficulties. The first stems from the proposition that people are both individuals and social beings. Their motivations are also dual. The socialist would argue that a private-enterprise, capitalist society accentuates only one side of human nature while almost ignoring the other. The result is distortion of the human psyche and development of the social evils of aggression, conflict, and materialism. Socialists argue that shifting the structure of society toward cooperative behavior patterns, with a different type of motivational pattern, would enlarge the values of human experience and lead the individual to a fuller and more rewarding life in which both personal and social goals can be more fully achieved.

The second difficulty arises from the nature of social groups. They may not express the cooperative ideal of brotherhood in their relationships with others. Their goals as groups may be selfish, restrictive, and harmful. Internally, they may be intolerant of dissent and demand conformity. The human drive toward gregariousness and commonality may lead to narrowness of attitude and outlook rather than openness.

The cooperative ideal, then, is fraught with dangers on two sides. On the one hand, the socialist would bring it to birth out of an individualistic society. This involves a transformation of individual goals and motives and cannot be done merely by changing the ownership and top management of a giant firm from private to public. And on the other hand, the organizational structure of a socialist society must continually guard against the narrowness and special interests of groups themselves as it seeks a broad and far-reaching concept of brotherhood and cooperation.

● **Socialism** is an economic system based on social ownership of the means of production, in which the values of equality, brotherhood, and cooperation strongly influence social policy. The capitalist's definition of socialism: tyranny.

The Socialist Critique of Capitalism

At the heart of the socialist critique of capitalism is strong emphasis on the effect of capitalism on people. People are prevented from achieving their full potential as human beings by the poverty that persists in a capitalist economy, by boring and repetitive jobs that reduce work to nothingness, and by a system in which control is held by a few. The organization and technology that place authority in the hands of bosses separate workers from control over their daily working lives. Any meaningful relationship between people and their most important activity is destroyed. Meanwhile, the emphasis on acquisition of wealth turns every person against everyone else. Winning dominates personal behavior in an atmosphere of insecurity and hostility that is opposed to the human need for affiliation and also for community.

At the national level, capitalism brings about the economic dominance of giant corporations, large financial institutions, and great accumulations of wealth. An economic elite of people and organizations controls society's productive wealth, just as a landed aristocracy controlled the forces of production during the feudal era. Control of productive wealth brings political control as well, and the economic elite dominates government, in spite of democratic forms.

Internationally, capitalist economic rivalries lead to great wars as business interests are translated into national interests. In the twentieth century the great wars have usually involved strong economic motives, from the Boer War at the turn of the century (British control over the resources of South Africa) to

World War I (the German challenge to British economic and political hegemony) to World War II (German economic and political domination of Europe; Japanese dominance in Asia) to Vietnam (U.S. efforts to contain the spread of communism). In each case the economic interests and rivalries of the great powers were among the underlying causes of the conflicts.

The international spread of capitalism, one of the sources of national rivalries, has led to economic dominance of less-developed areas by the more advanced capitalist center. An additional cause of conflict and unsettled international politics is created by the economic and political relations between center and periphery.

At the root of the problem lies the essential element of capitalism, private ownership of the means of production. The productive effort of millions is used to build up the wealth and power of an economic elite. The economic and political life of society comes to be dominated by a group of giant corporations managed by a small corps of managerial elite. The social order is divided into a great mass of people alienated from control of their own lives, and a small group who hold effective power.

Socialists recognize that capitalism released tremendous energy and advanced the forces of production as the economy was freed from the restrictive effects of the feudal system of the Middle Ages and its outgrowth, the aristocratic society of the sixteenth and seventeenth centuries. But just as the feudal organization of the European economy, in its early years, also released great forces of production—as indicated by the growth of population, extension of cultivation, the Crusades, the growth of cities and trade, and the era of the discoveries—only to become ossified and stagnant and a barrier to further human advancement, so capitalism is also reaching a period in which great wealth and monopoloid structures interfere with further progress. Socialists argue that tremendous vitality, innovation, and originality bottled up within the working class could lead to further great advances in civilization if those forces could be freed from an economic system that constrains them, just as capitalism freed the innovating middle class of an earlier era from the restrictions of feudal society. One goal of a socialist society is release of those great human energies.

● **Capitalism** is an economic system based on private ownership of the means of production, individualistic motivations and goals, and coordination of economic activity chiefly or wholly through a system of markets. The socialist's definition of capitalism: tyranny.

Property Relationships Under Socialism

Social ownership of the means of production distinguishes socialist property relationships from those of capitalism.

A capitalist economy is founded on a wide recognition of the right of private ownership of the means of production. Ownership may take a variety of forms, such as individual proprietorships, partnerships, and corporations. The owners have unrestricted rights to buy, sell, or exchange their property. A pure capitalist economy would have no restrictions on these rights of ownership and purchase and sale of the means of production.

A socialist economy substitutes ownership by society as a whole, or by workers as a group, for private ownership. Here again, the forms of ownership may vary widely, ranging from ownership of entire industries by the national government, to ownership of public utilities such as water systems by local governments, to ownership of a factory by those who work there, to communal life like that of the Israeli kibbutz. The fundamental idea, however, is that an individual participates in the ownership of the means of production because of his membership in a group rather than because of his legal ties to property itself. The individual

is a member of the group; the group owns the means of production.

A socialist economy does not require the elimination of private property altogether. Personal property would remain. On the Israeli kibbutz, for example, land, machinery, and other productive resources are owned by the kibbutz, which also provides housing for its members. Clothing, furniture, and other personal effects are privately owned. Many socialists argue that productive resources using personal or family labor should remain private and that only large enterprises employing a substantial number of people should be socially owned.

Social ownerhsip of productive resources is the element that distinguishes socialism most significantly from capitalism. Under capitalism, ownership of the means of production is a direct, legally defined relationship between people and things. The farmer, for instance, has the right to use tools and land because they are his. In a kibbutz, however, a farmer has those rights because he is a member of a commune that owns the tools and land. If he were to leave the commune he would give up his rights in them. The group rather than the individual is the significant producing unit of society and the economy.

Although basic concepts of property relationships are fundamentally different under socialism and capitalism, it would be hard to find a real-life economic system that is purely socialist or purely capitalist. The only known economies are mixtures, although a clear emphasis on one or the other may be found. Private ownership of property clearly predominates in the United States and a capitalist emphasis is obvious. But there are elements of social ownership. The federal government owns and operates the Tennessee Valley Authority. Many local agencies own and operate public utility firms. Full freedom of the marketplace is restricted by regulation of the securities exchanges, antitrust laws, and regulation of industries "affected with the public interest," to give only a few examples. Capitalism in the United States is mixed with many elements of socialist property relationships.

Other mixed economies are found in other countries. In England a number of basic industries, such as banks, transportation, communications, coal mining, and the steel industry, are socially owned. Other sectors of the economy are privately owned. Even in the Soviet Union there are elements of private ownership of the means of production. Some of the livestock and implements on collective farms are private property, and handicraft manufacturing with employment of limited amounts of hired labor is permitted.

Many socialists used to think of their system primarily in terms of government ownership of the means of production. Karl Marx, for example, defined socialism as "nationalization of the means of production, distribution, and exchange," believing that ownership of the means of production determined the nature of society as a whole and the behavior of the people involved. He felt that people could be transformed by restructuring the economic environment, and that government ownership was the path to that goal.

Modern socialists are less rigid. Norman Thomas (1884–1968), a great American socialist leader of the first half of the twentieth century, believed that government should own natural resources, the banking and credit system, and giant monopoloid business firms, and that there should be a significant amount of economic planning. But he also believed that the remainder of the economy could stay in private hands and remain under the influence of competitive market forces. Other socialists advocate government ownership only when it can be shown to be more efficient than private ownership, or is necessary to eliminate the political influence of big business. It would be quite possible to have a mixed socialist economy in which social ownership of the means of production dominates, but private ownership remains significant.

Socialism and Economic Planning

A socialist economy based on ideals of equality and cooperation, in which private enterprises either did not exist or did not dominate economic activity, would have to find its own methods of allocating resources, determining levels of output, and distributing the product. Rejecting the capitalist, market-oriented solution as based on individual and not social goals, the socialist movement initially stressed economic planning.

Economic planning shows many faces. Even an economy based on private ownership of the means of production, like the capitalistic United States, has a government that seeks to plan the level of aggregate demand, the level of prices, and the rate of economic growth. We have shown in the early parts of this book how it is done and the economic analysis on which this type of planning is based.

A far more interesting problem, however, is how an economy of publicly or socially owned enterprises will or can operate. What are the managerial and allocative alternatives? Briefly, they are two:

1. A socialist economy can be organized on the basis of a central authority that determines goals, draws up plans, creates incentives to promote their achievement, and supervises their accomplishment. This type of planning directed from the top is characteristic of large bureaucratic enterprises everywhere, from General Motors Corporation to the USSR. It is examined in the next chapter.

2. A second style of planning is based on the market mechanism, and is sometimes called *market socialism*. Here the central planners are concerned chiefly with the amount and direction of investment. Individual enterprises are socially owned, and their activities are coordinated by a market system. This approach seeks to

achieve a decentralized pattern of decision making that cannot be achieved in either the centralized planned economy or the monopoloid capitalist economy. Several eastern European countries, including Yugoslavia, are trying out various aspects of market socialism (see Chapter 36).

The important point is that economic planning is an important feature of the policies of all advanced nations. The question is no longer whether planning can work, but what type of planning is most desirable. Aggregative economic planning to promote economic stability and growth is used extensively in nonsocialist countries like the United States, Japan, and Germany. The USSR uses a system of centralized, detailed planning. Market socialism is largely untried, although the beginnings of experiments are seen. It may turn out to be the only effective alternative to the economy of large bureaucratic organizations characteristic of the United States and the Soviet Union.

Socialism and the State

The socialist movement has taken three different views about the role of the state in a socialist society. They can be labeled the Marxist, the anarchist, and the democratic socialist positions. The Marxist would use the state to create and manage a socialist society. This has, in fact, been done in the USSR. The Marxist view is that government is the arm of the social class that dominates the economy. In a capitalist economy the property-owning classes hold the reins of power. Their rule can be overthrown only when a revolutionary party representing the working class seizes power and uses the instruments of state control to dispossess the capitalists, nationalize the economy, and build a socialist society. The authority of the state would be used to remake the social order. This was the script followed by the Russian Revolution and the Soviet Communist Party.

The ultimate goal is claimed to be an abundant economy and a classless society in which the coercive power of the state is allowed to wither away, but the USSR developed in another fashion.

The Russian revolution of 1917–18 was itself one of the reasons for the political authoritarianism of Soviet communism. The Russian government prior to the revolution was highly centralized, with a large bureaucracy responsible to the Czar and his ministers. It tried to repress the political movements seeking change, which forced them to go underground and develop a highly centralized revolutionary organization. There was no tradition of parliamentary government within which to seek change or to take authority when the ability of the state to govern broke down under the impact of World War I. There was an initial attempt to organize a parliamentary government, but it was unable to govern effectively. Instead, the highly centralized Bolsheviks were able to seize power and reestablish central authority. A conscious choice was made by V.I. Lenin, the Bolshevik leader, to place power in the hands of the Communist Party rather than the soviets (organizations of workers and others that had sprung up as local governing bodies).

Once in power, the Communist Party drove the nation to modernization, economic growth and international power. The methods were authoritarian in the extreme. The Leninist theme of the 1920s was "dictatorship of the proletariat" (proletariat = working class) led by its "vanguard," the Communist party, which was quite different from the revolutionary theme of 1917, "All power to the soviets." The costs in human suffering were tremendous, but there were benefits in the form of higher standards of living as well. Soviet authoritarianism also brought a greatly enlarged economic base for national power that enabled the USSR to emerge as one of the victors in World War II. Indeed, without Soviet authoritarianism we might all be under the thumb of

German Nazism today: the decisive battles of World War II were fought at Moscow, on the plains of central Russia, and Stalingrad and were won by the Russians with little help from anyone else.

Socialism in the USSR took an authoritarian path, partly as the result of events and conditions special to that country, and partly because of choices made by the leadership. Once on the path to central authority a pattern of hierarchal organization under central control continued to develop in both economic administration and the organization of political power. Special privileges and economic affluence for those at the top are only outward manifestations of the authoritarianism of the Soviet system.

At the other pole of the socialist movement, the anarchist would do away with the state altogether. Anarchists see the state as the chief source of oppression and the chief support of capitalism. They also see a bureaucratic *state collectivism* like the USSR as equally oppressive. An anarchist revolution would do away with the political apparatus of government. In its place the anarchist would substitute collectives of workers who own and manage the enterprises in which they work. At one extreme are anarchists who believe that this is all the public administration any society requires, but most see the need for governmental functions and economic planning through elected representatives of the collectives.[2] All anarchists agree, however, on the need for control from below and full participatory democracy.

- **State collectivism** is the economic system that developed in the USSR after the 1917 revolution. It is based on government ownership of the means of production and a centralized system of authority, planning, and control. It is defined as tyranny by both capitalists and socialists.

---

[2]Political organization based on worker representatives elected by economic units is called *syndicalism*. It has been represented in the United States by the IWW (Industrial Workers of the World), founded in 1905, and the Socialist Labor Party, which developed a Marxist version of a syndicalist workers' government under the leadership of Daniel de Leon (1852–1914).

Democratic socialism is far more pragmatic. As developed in England, Scandinavia, and other countries of western Europe when labor parties were in power, it put its greatest stress on the welfare and egalitarian aspects of socialism, on cooperative enterprises, and on maintenance of traditional democratic practices in government. The result has been a mixture of policies and programs that vary widely from one country to another. England and the Scandinavian countries, for example, have tax systems that seek to prevent the accumulation of large fortunes and great agglomerations of economic power. In England some basic industries were nationalized, while in Sweden emphasis is on consumer cooperatives; yet in both countries an avowedly socialist regime allowed 85–90 percent of economic activity to remain in private hands. Most western European countries have very extensive welfare and social insurance programs that have largely succeeded in eliminating poverty. All except England were successful in reducing unemployment rates to very low frictional levels and keeping them there most of the time, until the relative economic stagnation of the 1970s began. Ironically, France made the greatest strides toward a planned economy even before a socialist regime was elected in 1981. Many variations on democratic socialism emerged, with various mixtures of the welfare state, levelling of incomes, public ownership, cooperatives, and economic planning. The one common element is the use of parliamentary democracy to move toward socialist goals. The state, in this development is a democratic instrument through which the general public determines both goals and the speed of their attainment. Democratic socialists believe that public opinion must be changed to accept the socialist ideals and program, which can then be instituted by government action arrived at through democratic procedures. They reject the "dictatorship of the proletariat" of Lenin's path to socialism in favor of a slower and less complete transformation of society that would preserve and use democratic procedures.

- **Democratic socialism** is an economic system of social ownership of the means of production, egalitarian distribution of income and wealth, and social-welfare programs that is achieved by democratic political procedures.

Socialism and Social Classes

In socialist theory, classes are defined in relation to property in the means of production. The capitalist class owns the means of production and hires workers. The working class works for wages and does not own the means of production. Ownership of the means of production enables one class to dominate and exploit another. Hence the basic conflict within capitalist society between the capitalist class (and its managerial allies) and the working class. Exploitation and conflict rest on the class structure of society, which is derived in turn from ownership of the means of production.

In a socialist society, classes in that sense disappear. Private ownership and control of the means of production and the economic surplus becomes social ownership and control. Without private ownership and control of capital, the class distinctions of capitalist society no longer exist. Socialism means a classless society. This was the classic theory of socialism as it appeared in the nineteenth century.

With the development of capitalism in the twentieth century, however, the class structure of modern society changed significantly. The most important change was the emergence of a variety of economic groups that could not readily be identified with either the capitalist or working classes. Government administrative employees are one. They do not view themselves as members of the working class; they earn annual salaries; and their jobs are protected by various civil service protections. White-collar administrative persons in private enterprises are in a similar position. Within that group there is a tendency for those at upper levels to identify with capitalist or business interests, while those at lower levels tend to identify with workers. But the ties are not strong. Both groups comprise people whose relationship to property in the means of production is ambiguous. Their political commitment tends toward leaders who promise affluence and security. Demagogues like Hitler and Mussolini were able to recruit strong support from these groups for the authoritarian capitalist regimes we call fascist.

These groups, or social classes (for they also are defined in relation to ownership of the means of production), will not disappear with socialization of the means of production. Rather, the public and private administrative hierarchies become unified when large enterprises are nationalized and controlled by a central public administration. The socialist goal remains the establishment of a classless society, but that can no longer be thought of simply as a working class society, with workers controlling the means of production. The modern development of the forces of production, including organization and technology, requires a large administrative cadre. What is to prevent the upper levels of the administrative stratum from moving to power as a new dominant class after the means of production have been socialized? This was the path taken in the USSR as its state collectivism developed after the revolution.

Reconstructing society along socialist lines requires more than nationalization of the means of production, distribution, and finance. Specific programs for worker control and for decentralization of economic power are required. That is why the development of market socialism and workers' management, which we discuss in Chapter 36, are so important. Economic planning, the organization and role of state power, and the structure of social classes are interrelated issues that socialists must wrestle with as they seek to build a just society in this complex modern world. Simple nationalization of the means of production, or some other form of social ownership and control, will not by itself usher in what could be considered a worker's utopia.

The Path to Socialism

The transition from capitalism to socialism will affect the way in which a socialist society resolves the economic, political, and social issues we have discussed. Goals are not independent of means. As the philosopher Schopenhauer teaches, ethical goals cannot be achieved by unethical means; any attempt to do so mortally compromises the goals.[3] For the socialist, this doctrine means that if a democratic socialism is to be achieved, democratic methods must be used.

A distinction is often made between revolution and evolution in the transition to socialism. Democratic socialists have argued that a gradual evolution through education, development of a popular majority, and passage of legislation through democratic political institutions, is the proper way to achieve a democratic socialist society. More radical groups, particularly communist parties, argue that the evolutionary path to socialism will not work, partly because it is difficult for people to develop a socialist point of view within a capitalist society, and partly because the capitalist state will use police and military force against the socialist movement. Seizure of political power and use of that power to transform the economy and society, while simultaneously repressing the forces of counterrevolution, are the means to be used.

The issues are clear, but the solutions are not. In western Europe and North America, where civil liberties and democratic political institutions are accepted parts of political life,

---

[3]Arthur Schopenhauer (1788–1860), German philosopher whose great treatise *The World as Will and Idea* (1819) developed the idea that feelings and emotion rooted in the inner self are superior to reason as a way of understanding the world.

a democratic transition to socialism by way of a majority vote may well be feasible. France took that path in 1981.

On the other hand, a society without a tradition of democratic institutions and ideas, but with a history of authoritarian control and political repression, has little in the way of a democratic tradition on which to build. Russia before 1917 was a nation of that sort, and China before its continuing revolution that began in 1911. So is much of Central America, where the revolutionary drama is being enacted today. An evolutionary and democratic transition to socialism may be impossible in societies of that sort in a very large part of today's world.

Revolutions need not generate authoritarian regimes. The American Revolution did not, although cynics might attribute that result to the fact that it merely substituted a domestic elite committed to a freely operating economy for a foreign elite that followed a policy of colonial exploitation. Both the French and Russian revolutions began as great popular uprisings against an exploitive aristocracy supported by an authoritarian state, and both developed into revolutionary authoritarian regimes. But it is quite possible for a revolution to be both popularly based and democratic in its outlook rather than centralized and authoritarian: the Polish rebellion of 1979–81, which continues to escalate as this is written, is of that sort. The very fact that it is directed against a highly centralized political and economic system seems to push its leadership to emphasize a mass-based decision-making process and decentralization of authority. Socialists everywhere await the outcome of the Polish revolution with great expectations, for it may show the way to transformation of state collectivism into democratic socialism.

Summary

Socialism and capitalism differ most clearly in ownership of the means of production. The one stresses social ownership, the other private. The socialist ideology also stresses the ideals of equality, brotherhood and cooperation, in opposition to the individualism of capitalism. Although socialists recognize that capitalism at one time represented a great advance in releasing and developing the productive forces of human society, they argue that it is now a hindrance, limiting human development, holding back economic growth through the effects of big business and great wealth, and leading to wars and domestic conflict.

Socialism itself has problems, however. The extent and organization of the economy, types of economic decision making, and the role of the state are three of the chief issues on which socialists do not agree. Whether it is possible in the modern world to achieve a classless society is also in doubt. The USSR stands as a warning to socialists everywhere, for the initial socialist thrust of the Russian revolution was transformed as the Soviet Union developed an authoritarian state collectivism that is neither socialist nor capitalist.

Men make their own history, but not always in the way they think they will.

Karl Marx, *The Eighteenth Brumaire of Louis Bonaparte* (1851)

Key Concepts

socialism   state collectivism

capitalism   democratic socialism

For Discussion

1. If socialism is so desirable, why has it not already superseded capitalism?

2. Explain the basic principles of property ownership in a socialist economy.

3. How and why would incentives in a socialist economy differ from those in a capitalist economy?

4. Can the ideal of a classless society be achieved, even in a socialist system?

5. How would democracy in a socialist society differ from democracy under capitalism (a) according to socialists and (b) in the view of the defenders of capitalism?

6. Is some form of socialism a viable alternative to capitalism in the United States?

Chapter 35

Central Planning and Socialism: The Case of the Soviet Union

The Soviet economy is only one variant of socialism. Even in the early 1920s, however, it had begun its evolution into today's state collectivism. Industrial enterprises are owned by the government, together with most of the marketing system and all of the financial, transportation, and communications sectors. Agriculture is largely organized into collective farms. Although most of the land is held and worked collectively with individual families holding small private plots, state-owned farms can also be found. A system of production planning has been established to manage this vast network of enterprises. Control is largely from the center, requiring an elaborate network of administrative agencies. This chapter will examine the Soviet economy as a case study of central planning in an economy based on state enterprise. The chief emphasis is on the use of central planning as an alternative to a system of markets in coordinating the activities of economic units.

Basic Decisions in Planning

Before any plan for allocation and use of resources can be made, economic planners must make several fundamental decisions that will strongly limit, or in some instances determine, the way resources are to be used. These decisions include determination of:

1. The long-run goals.

2. The speed with which those goals can be achieved.

3. How resources can be mobilized to achieve the goals.

Only then can the planners turn their attention to the problems of planning how resources are actually to be used, the levels of output desired, and the techniques of administration.

Long-Run Goals in the USSR

In the Soviet Union there was a great debate over long-run goals and the speed of their attainment prior to the start of the first *Five-Year Plan* in 1928. The decisions made at that time have not been significantly altered, although in recent years some modifications have been made and discussion of long-run goals has occasionally occurred. In public, that is. We don't know much about the closed discussions taking place at the highest decision levels of Soviet planning and policy formulation.

The discussion of the late 1920s focused on the problem of economic growth. The Soviet economy by then had recovered to approximately the pre-World War I levels of output, after a sequence of war, revolution, and inflation that had seen a tranformation from the old imperial, aristocratic government to the early stages of state collectivism. The economy remained backward, however. Agriculture still dominated the economy, and its technology was preindustrial. Heavy industry was small and centered in only a few parts of the country. Many consumer goods—shoes, for example—were still produced by handicraft methods instead of by machine. Illiteracy was still strong. The country remained largely a rural, peasant society.

Yet the leadership was committed to an ideology, the Marxist variation of socialism, which looked to the industrial working class as the builder of a new social order on a world-wide-scale. At the same time, the Soviet Union as the self-proclaimed bearer of world revolution faced a hostile world committed to the preservation of a capitalist, private enterprise economy. Finally, the security of the regime at home was by no means certain: the proportion of the Soviet people strongly committed to the new ideology was probably a minority even as late as 1928. This was particularly true among the peasantry.

The policy discussions of the late 1920s emphasized the problem of backwardness in a hostile world and embodied, in addition, a struggle for political power that saw the emergence of Joseph Stalin to predominance over his chief rival, Leon Trotsky. The policies that emerged from the debate and the struggle were these:

1. A socialist society based on an industrial working class had to be built by transforming a rural, agricultural nation into an urban, industrial one. This view was a fundamental policy inherited from the leader of the revolution, V. I. Lenin.

2. The new society had to be protected against the expected counterattack of a hostile capitalist world. In 1930 Stalin predicted that the USSR had ten years to prepare—a prophetic vision.

3. The spread of socialism could best be achieved by demonstrating its superiority over capitalism to the workers of the world, especially in achieving economic growth and industrial expansion.

These considerations all pointed in the direction of rapid, large-scale industrialization. Economic growth became the primary goal of economic policy—to build a socialist society, to protect it from its enemies, and to promote its spread. Even though the Soviet mode of production was evolving away from socialism, it continued to state its goals in terms of socialist ideology.

- A **Five-Year Plan** is the production plan for a five-year period that states the goals the Soviet economy tries to achieve.

Speed of Attainment

Decisions about the rate of economic growth in the Soviet economy are made at the top levels of government and the Communist Party. They are expressed in the Five-Year Plans, which provide the economic goals the system seeks. For example, the Five-Year Plan for the 1981–85 years calls for percentage increases over the five years as shown in Table 35–1. The plan itself is much more detailed, but these figures illustrate the pattern of goal setting.

The goals of the Five-Year Plans are selected with regard to the resources available to achieve them. Planning always starts from an existing position and the path projected into the future is constrained by the resources that can be mobilized and the effectiveness with which they can be used. Soviet planners have tended to select goals that strain the upper limits of the economy, "taut" planning as they call it, which does not allow for any slack. As a result, their goals are not always achieved.

Table 35-1
Soviet Five-Year Plan, 1981-85

	Planned Increase (percent)
National Income	18-20
Total Industrial Production	26-28
Electric Power	21*
Steel	16*
Machines and Metals Manufacturing	40
Agricultural Output	12-14
Productive Fixed Capital	26-28
Consumer Goods	27-29
Per Capita Real Income	16-18
Retail Trade	22-25
Average monthly wage	13-16
Collective farmers' income from the communal sector of collective farms	20-22

*The draft plan published in *Pravda* and *Izvestia* on December 2, 1980 gives production targets rather than percentage increases. The percentage figures listed here are estimates made by the author.

The plans give indications of policy goals and decisions about the planned speed of attainment. In the eleventh five-year plan for 1981, for example, the overall growth goal is quite modest, only about 3.7 percent per year for national income. An effort is being made to increase incentives for agricultural production: the planned growth of collective farmers' income from the communal sector of the collective farms is projected at about 4 percent annually, as compared with increases in the average monthly wage for industrial workers of only about 3.5 percent annually. And consumer goods production is planned to grow at about the same rate as capital goods, even though agricultural production has a much lower planned rate of increase.

The Five-Year Plans are not operational programs used to guide the decisions of individual enterprises. Annual plans perform that function. The annual plans provide specific targets that important sectors of the economy and principal industries are expected to achieve. They are than broken down into operating plans for each productive unit. They act as a bridge between the goals expressed in the Five-Year Plans and the daily operations of each economic unit. Later on in this chapter we shall have more to say about how the annual plans are drawn up and used.

At any rate, the Soviet economy has consistently sustained high rates of economic growth since the first Five-Year Plan started in 1928. With the exception of 1937-1950, when preparation for World War II, the war itself, and the aftermath of the war greatly slowed down economic growth, the economy of the Soviet Union sustained growth rates well above 5 percent annually through 1970 (Table 35-2).

This good track record, sustained over a long period of time, has not been maintained so well in recent years. The speed of Soviet growth slowed considerably in the 1970s to under 4 percent annually. Economic growth in the USSR no longer exceeds that of many other advanced nations, although it is still faster than in the United States. For example, in 1965-1970 both France (5.8 percent) and Japan (12.0 percent) had more rapid growth in GNP than the Soviet Union.

The Soviet slowdown in growth, together with more rapid growth in some other industrial countries, triggered within the USSR another important discussion of economic policy, together with the start of some economic reforms. The reforms have been oriented toward achievement of greater efficiency, however, rather than basic changes in policy. There has been little change in the official doctrine that rapid economic growth is the cornerstone of Soviet economic policy.

Rapid economic growth had its costs, however. Other important goals had to be compromised or sacrificed: consumer goods, for example. Every ton of steel used to produce automobiles or refrigerators is one ton less for railroad rails or electrical generators. Each bushel of wheat used at home is one bushel less for sale abroad, the revenue then being available to buy foreign machinery.

Table 35–2
Average Annual Growth Rates of Soviet GNP
1928–1965

Period	Estimated Average Annual Percent Increase
1928–1937	8.3
1937–1950	2.4
1950–1970	6.0
1950–1955	6.9
1955–1960	6.0
1960–1965	5.0
1965–1970	5.7
1971–1978	3.7

Note: All percentage rates of growth for the Soviet economy are approximations. The difficulties involved in the calculations are enormous. The estimates for 1928–1978 are simplified and adapted from calculations in Stanley H. Cohn, *Economic Development in the Soviet Union* (Lexington, Mass.: D. C. Heath and Co., 1969), Chap. 7, which has been reprinted in Morris Bornstein and Daniel R. Fusfeld, *The Soviet Economy: A Book of Readings* (Homewood, Ill.: Richard D. Irwin, Inc., 1974) with data for the 1965–1970 period added by Professor Cohn. Data for 1971–78 are from Herbert Block, "Soviet Economic Performance in a Global Context," *Soviet Economy in a Time of Change* (Washington, D.C.: U.S. Government Printing Office, 1979), Vol. 1, pp. 110–40.

Or working conditions. One hour cut from the work week is an hour less for production. Every absentee worker means that much less output. Every worker moving from one job to another, requiring training or adaptation to the new job, means lost output.

Or distribution of income. Scarce skills, like those of engineers or plant managers, scientists and economic planners, have to be priced high to encourage people to acquire those skills and to push management into using them efficiently. Plentiful unskilled labor can be priced correspondingly cheaper. Considerations of economic efficiency call for substantial inequalities of earned incomes in a nation pushing for high growth rates.

Or labor discipline. A taut economy in which labor is fully utilized encourages workers to move from one job to another, seeking a better slot. In addition, restrictions on output of consumer goods reduce an important work incentive that can only be partially replaced by wage differentials. As a result of high labor turnover (moving from job to job), absenteeism, and shirking on the job, negative incentives to work began to appear in the late 1930s and were not eliminated until the 1950s. These included fines and reduced pay for absenteeism or failure to produce up to the assigned norms, restrictions on quitting a job to take another, and loss of housing or fringe benefits if a worker quit his job. Some still remain in mild forms. The extremes of repression in the USSR, such as forced labor camps, were used primarily for political purposes and to eliminate real or fancied threats to the internal security of the regime. They were present in the Soviet system from the early 1920s, but were greatly expanded during the 1930s as part of the transition to authoritarian state collectivism, serving both to reduce dissent and establish firmly the authority of the Communist Party and the administrative apparatus.

Mobilizing Economic Resources

The Soviet Union has used a variety of approaches to the problem of mobilizing resources to achieve its growth goals. First, it sought to use all of the available labor. This meant elimination of the unemployment that still existed as the era of planning began, drawing women into the labor force on a large scale, and moving the increase in population from rural to urban locations and drawing it into industrial production. Or, put another way, the growth of the economy could be increased by adding to the labor available for industrial production from those three sources. More labor inputs could bring greater industrial output. This portion of the growth strategy resulted in some interesting changes in policy toward hours of work, retirement, and related matters. As long as substantial increases in total labor effort could be obtained, policy was directed toward shorter hours and improved retirement plans. Once the sources of additional labor began to diminish significantly (by the mid- and late 1930s), and the pre-World War II arms race began, reductions in the work week stopped and pension plans were no longer improved. Even today the Soviet planners are reluctant to move toward those human goals in the face of the need for additional labor to sustain economic growth. In recent years, when population growth has been slow short-ages of labor have been one reason for slowed economic growth.

Agriculture

Agricultural resources were also mobilized to achieve the growth goals. Farm products were needed to feed the growing industrial work force in the cities and its supporting services, to provide industrial raw materials, and for export to pay for imports of machinery. If agriculture were to do its part its output would have to be increased without using more labor time. This goal could only be achieved by large-scale mechanization of the still primitive Soviet peasant farming system. At the same time, the planners felt that it was necessary to draw any increases in farm output into the growth process, and not allow them to be used to raise farmers' standards of living.

These considerations led to collectivization of Soviet agriculture during the early 1930s. By a combination of exhortation and force, peas-ant agriculture was ended. In its place a system of large-scale farming units was developed— the collective farms—which were, in theory, owned and run by the farmers themselves. In fact, they were managed by a combination of Communist Party and government officials and integrated into the system of national plan-ning. The collective farms were supplemented by a network of government-owned machine-tractor stations that provided the equipment for mechanized production methods.

The Russian peasants largely opposed these measures and fought back with a combination of passive resistance and sabotage that was ruthlessly suppressed. The result was one of the great human tragedies of our time: several million Russian peasants literally starved to death during the winters of 1931–33. A side effect was the slaughter of millions of head of livestock, leaving the USSR with a deficiency of meat and dairy products that is still felt by the Soviet consumer.

Nevertheless, the government largely achieved its agricultural goals. Agricultural production was increased by perhaps as much as 50 percent (experts differ on this figure) with no increase in agricultural labor. A system of payments for the services of the machine-tractor stations, plus a system of government procurement, succeeded in channeling the en-tire increase of output into government hands. Finally, the farm population remained station-ary, freeing the population increase for the urban-industrial sector of the economy.

Agriculture has remained a problem for the Soviet economy, however. There was little increase in farm output between the late 1930s and the late 1950s until a big effort to increase acreage was made by bringing lands in central Asia into production. A substantial increase was recorded, but by the early 1960s stagnation once more set in. The problem seems to be inadequate incentives and inadequate invest-ment in agriculture, together with unwilling-ness on the part of planners to channel addi-tional resources into farming instead of industry.

Agriculture remains a problem in the USSR. The government has persistently channeled resources into heavy industry and production for the military. Competition with the United States for world power requires diversion of huge amounts of resources and manpower di-rectly into military production. Agriculture, which produces consumer goods for the most part, has been slighted. Investment in agricul-ture lagged, and, as a result, so did production. Furthermore, a very large portion of invest-ment in agriculture comes from the retained earnings of collective and state farms, which reduces payments to the farmers themselves and diminishes incentives. Productivity lags on the collectives while farmers work their private plots intensively to produce for sale on the farmers' markets in the cities. With agricultural production relatively stagnant—there had been no significant increase in the last 20 years—and population growing, a nation that was formerly a great grain exporter is now a large importer.

Capital Accumulation and the Turnover Tax

Capital was also mobilized for economic growth. The chief device used for that purpose has been the turnover tax, which is deliberately used to reduce consumer purchasing power. The Soviet turnover tax is analogous to a sales tax, except that it is levied on producing units at the time an item enters the channels of trade, rather than being paid by consumers on retail purchases. For example, a steel mill will pay a turnover tax on each ton of steel sold to a government procurement agency, or a sugar refinery on each pound of sugar sold to a

wholesale distribution enterprise, and so forth. The Soviet *turnover tax* is not uniform for all commodities, but varies considerably. On producers' goods, like steel, it is quite low or even nominal, and is used primarily for control purposes: the State Bank collects the turnover tax and audits the books of each enterprise for that purpose; in so doing it also checks up on how well the enterprise has fulfilled its production plans. The turnover tax on consumers' goods is often quite high, however, and performs a vital function for the economy. By raising prices to consumers it limits the amount of goods they can buy, thereby freeing resources for investment purposes. At the same time, it provides large revenues to the government for investment and military purposes. In effect, the turnover tax forces consumers to save (in a real sense) while they continue to spend as much of their income as they wish. The function of the turnover tax in forcing consumers to save is illustrated in Figure 35–1.

Figure 35-1
The Soviet Turnover Tax as a Source of Savings

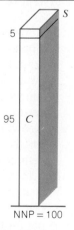

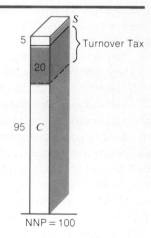

A. Hypothetical Soviet NNP Without the Turnover Tax. Money and real NNP = $C + S$, where $C = 95$ and $S = 5$. With consumers' sovereignty, only a small proportion of NNP would be available for investment $S = I = 5$.

B. Soviet NNP With the Turnover Tax. Money NNP = $C + S$, where $C = 95$ and $S = 5$, just as before. But production of C is reduced from 95 to 75 while its price is kept at 95 by turnover tax of 20: real NNP = 75 + 25. The *resources* available for investment are raised from 5 to 25, and investment is financed out of savings (5) and the turnover tax (20).

Figure 35-2
Soviet Prices: Use of
the Turnover Tax to
Clear the Market

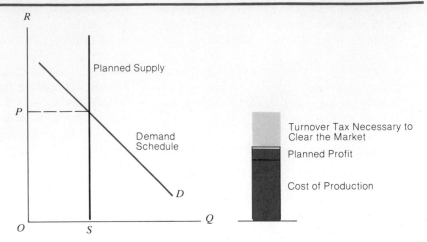

Soviet planners restrict supply of consumer goods in order to make resources available
for investment and the military. This requires price *P* to clear the market and avoid
rationing and price controls, which would be awkward and difficult to enforce. Result:
imposition of a turnover tax just large enough to make up the difference between prices
and costs plus planned profit.

The turnover tax also performs an important function in the price system. All Soviet prices have three component parts: production costs, planned profit, and turnover tax. Production costs are self-explanatory. Planned profit provides for some capital accumulation, for bonuses, and for some fringe benefits to workers. The turnover tax, as part of its use in diverting resources to investment and military purposes, is used to raise the selling price to one that will clear the market at existing levels of output and demand. Because output of consumer goods is deliberately restricted in order to maximize production of investment and military goods, cost of production plus planned profits do not equal the price that would clear the market. Figure 35–2 makes this point clear.

If the Soviet planners wished to adjust output levels to the wants of consumers, they could increase output and bring prices down to levels that just covered costs plus planned profit. Prices at those levels would be analogous to the long-run equilibrium prices of the competitive market, just covering full production costs including a "normal" profit. But the larger output necessary to achieve those price levels would reduce the resources available for investment and the military. Even the pricing system reflects the goals of the planners.

In the early years of its rapid growth the Soviet Union was able to draw on additional resources that hitherto had been unused or only partially used. They included unused labor as well as the increase in agricultural production derived from the transition from peasant to collective farming. But the stimulus to growth from these sources was soon exhausted. The Soviet Union now finds itself dependent primarily on capital accumulation and the normal growth of the work force to provide increased output. In this respect the USSR is in the same position as other industrial nations. The turnover tax and voluntary savings have become the chief means by which resources are mobilized.

- The **turnover tax** is a Soviet tax on commodities at the time they first enter the channels of trade. It has two purposes: it raises prices so that markets are cleared (usually) and limits consumption to make resources available for investment.

The Process of Planning

Once goals are defined, the speed of attainment is decided, and methods are developed for mobilizing resources, the process of deciding what should be produced and in what quantities is a relatively simple but often arduous job. This is the task assigned to the annual production plans.

Soviet planning starts with "leading links." These are the important basic industries whose performance is essential for achievement of the year's goals, such as fuel, power, steel, grain production, and perhaps some other industries. A balance sheet will be drawn up for a leading link, steel, for example, that shows the resources expected to be available and the uses to which they will be put. In very simplified form, it would resemble Table 35–3.

In the final plan these estimates of resources and uses will have to balance each other, in total. One key element in the planning process is adjusting the various quantities to achieve a balance. Doing so will tell the planners where expansion can take place, or where it must take place in order to avoid bottlenecks. On the uses side of the balance sheet, the amounts used in other industries tie the leading-link industry to other sectors of the economy, defining the resources available to them. This enables the planning agencies to develop *balanced estimates,* as they are called, for those industries as well. On the resources side of the balance sheet for the leading-link industries, production estimates enable the planners to determine the inputs needed, including raw materials and semifinished products from supply industries. These estimates enable the planners to make balanced estimates for the industries producing inputs as well as those using outputs.

● **Balanced estimates** are the industry balances of resources and uses that make up the annual production plan in the USSR.

Table 35–3
Simplified Materials Balance

Resources	Uses
Stocks on hand at the start of the year	Used in production
Production from existing plants	Used in other industries
Production from new plants	Exports
Imports	Stocks on hand at the end of the year

A financial plan is also worked out, to provide the short- and long-term credit and payments necessary to carry out the production plans and their corollary input plans. A special plan is also developed for expansion and construction of new facilities. These four segments —production, input, expansion, and financial plans—make up the comprehensive annual plan.

The final plans, usually completed after two to three trials, result in a system of balanced estimates for each significant industry or product, all linked forward and backward to other industries. This huge job requires a large planning bureaucracy, although in recent years the use of computers has greatly speeded up the process and reduced the labor needed.

The balanced interindustry planning is done by a central agency, the GOSPLAN, or State Planning Commission, but does not become official until it is approved by the Council of Ministers, which is the top policy-making agency of government analogous to our Cabinet.

Much of the input into the planning process is provided by the producing enterprises themselves and intermediate administrative agencies. Prior to the beginning of a year, the government announces the projected increase in output to be embodied in the economic plan for the coming year. Each enterprise is then expected to produce a plan for its operations that helps achieve those goals. Its draft plan is sent to the next higher administrative unit, where the plans for a number of enterprises are coordinated and summarized and then sent further up the administrative hierarchy, until a ministry for an entire industry is able to submit a draft plan to the State Planning Commission. The draft plans are used as the basis for the complete set of balanced estimates for the economy as a whole drawn up by GOSPLAN.

Once the national plan is drawn up, with balances for each industry, it is then broken down by the ministries into plans for each industrial subdivision, which in turn develops plans for each plant or group of plants under its jurisdiction.

The plan, then, embodies the goals of national policy as determined by the Council of Ministers, the abilities and desires of local plant managers as developed in the draft plans, and the need for coordination and balance provided by GOSPLAN. In varying degrees, all of these elements influence the final plan.

The plan guides the operation of the individual unit. It can be specific in great detail, giving little leeway to the plant manager in deciding how the goals can be best achieved. This was the case until 1965, when a series of reforms were instituted to promote efficiency by giving greater responsibility to management at the local level. Under the reforms the following items are included in the operating plan for the individual enterprise.

Total output

The main assortment of products

Total wages

Amount and rate of profit. This planned profit is used by the enterprise for
bonuses and other incentives and workers' benefits, and as a source of capital
for expansion

Payments into and allocations from the state budget

Capital investment

Utilization of capacity

Introduction of new technology

Supplies of inputs

If this list seems highly detailed, it nevertheless represents a significant reduction in specifications from the earlier system. A number of Soviet economists have argued for even greater latitude for managerial decisions as a means of increasing efficiency and raising output. The present pattern represents a compromise between two styles of planning, one emphasizing central control and the other advocating decentralization.

Making the Plan Work

Devising a balanced plan is one problem. Keeping the economy operating along the lines of that balance is a larger problem. If one industry overproduces while another underproduces, stocks will pile up unused in one area while shortages, bottlenecks, and unmet production quotas spread in other areas. A close watch must be kept, requiring rapid and accurate reporting of actual production levels from plants to higher administrative agencies. This information must then be used to identify imbalances immediately so that steps can be taken to eliminate them.

For this purpose the Soviet planners have devised "synthetic indices." A synthetic index indicates the relationship between planned production in two related industries. For example, coal is used in producing steel. Let us assume that the plan calls for production of 500 million tons of coal and 100 million tons of steel. The ratio between them is 5 to 1, a "synthetic index" representing the balance existing in the plan. Now let us suppose that in the first quarter of the year the index, based on actual production statistics, is 5.2 to 1. This can mean one or both of two things. Coal production may be running ahead of schedule, which

Table 35–4
Monthly Earnings of Selected Groups of Salaried and Wage Earners, USSR, 1970

Occupation	Monthly Earnings (in Rubles)
Scientist (academician)	800–1,500
Minister (head of Government ministry or department)	700
Opera star	500–2,000
Professor (science)	600–1,000
Professor (medicine)	400– 600
Docent (assistant professor)	300– 500
Manager of enterprise or establishment	100–1,000
Engineer	90– 200
Physician, staff	90– 170
Teacher, high school	80– 137
Teacher, primary school	80– 137
Technician	80– 200
Worker, skilled	100– 250
Worker, semiskilled	70– 90
Worker, unskilled	60– 70

Note: The official tourist exchange rate is 1 ruble for $1.11.
Source: Edmund Nash, "Purchasing Power of Workers in the Soviet Union," *Monthly Labor Review,* Vol. 94, No. 5 (May 1971), pp. 39–45.

means that more will be available to raise output in other industries using coal as a raw material. Or steel production may be falling behind, in which case it will have to be brought up to planned levels unless adjustments can be made in the industries that use steel as an input. The synthetic index gives early warning of these problems and tells the planners where to look for difficulties and where the adjustments will have to be made.

Plans have to be continually revised. Even the best balanced plan will develop imbalances as it is carried out. Changes in inventories give the planners time to identify the imbalances and correct them. They can change the plan while it is in operation, which is where balance is important, to maintain a balanced economy as well as a balanced plan.

Incentives

The Soviet Union has established a system of varied incentives designed to promote achieve-

ment of its goals and fulfillment of plans. Plant managers, their subordinates, and rank-and-file workers receive bonuses for achieving or exceeding planned levels of output, paid for out of the enterprise's revenues. Promotions go to those who perform particularly well, while demotions are meted out to those who fail.

The wage and salary system provides incentives in the form of steeply progressive increases as an individual moves up the ladder from one job to another. Information on these matters is not easy to find for the USSR, since a regime professing the goal of equality is naturally defensive about inequality, but Table 35–4 gives some monthly wages and salaries in 1970.

These wage differentials tell us much. A high-salaried professional earns 12 to 24 times the income of a low-salaried employee, a differential substantially greater than those prevailing in the U.S. for earned income. These differentials provide incentives for people to acquire the skills necessary to qualify for higher paying jobs and to work hard to get into those jobs. The greater the differences, the greater this incentive effect. There is a variation on this theme. Higher earnings are provided in geographical areas where skills are in short supply: earnings in the "far north" are 50–100 percent above other parts of the country. Wage differentials also provide incentives to management to use little of the high-cost skills, substituting lower-wage employees wherever possible. Here again, the greater the differential, the greater the incentive to economize.

Contrary to misconceptions held by many people, labor is not directed by the central planners in the USSR. Choice of occupation is freely made, and so is choice of job. Soviet planners rely on market forces to obtain the necessary workers and give them incentives to acquire the needed skills. There are some minor modifications of the principle of freedom of choice of occupation, just as there are in the U.S. economy, but the market principle dominates the process by which labor is allocated among its various uses.

The Soviet Union also uses "socialist incentives." These are primarily psychological rather than material in nature, stressing patriotism and achievement of national goals. At times they have been quite effective, especially in the early years of the planned economy (1928–1935) and during World War II (1939–1945). Their effectiveness seems to have diminished considerably in recent years.

We have already mentioned that negative incentives to work and labor direction, which began to appear in the late 1930s, were strongly developed during World War II and lasted into the 1950s. They involved such labor legislation as the following:

1. The amount of social insurance benefits was tied to the length of time a worker was employed in one plant.

2. Permission of the employer had to be obtained if a worker wished to quit his job.

3. Workers trained in certain special skills had to work in jobs assigned to them by the government for a period of time.

These forms of labor direction are gone, for the most part—a result of the reaction against Stalinism. But some persist. Where industrial plants operate retail stores or housing developments, a worker's privileges in those units will cease if he quits his job. Recent legislation prevents a worker who quits his job several times during a year from using the government employment service to get another, an obvious effort to cut down on labor turnover. Workers must carry employment books that list their past employment and contain ratings by their employers. University and technical school graduates are subject to placement in government assigned jobs for a period of time; however, their education is free and they receive living allowances while in school. While these measures are not onerous, they do represent departures from full reliance on the market mechanism for allocation of labor and provision of incentives.

Prices in the USSR

Prices in the USSR play a significant part in the guidance of economic activity. Their role, however, is different from that in a capitalist economy, or even in a "market socialist" economy as described in the following chapter. Prices in the Soviet Union are not a significant determinant of resource allocation and production. Rather, they are used by the planning authorities as one instrument to be used in achieving their planning goals.

Resource allocation is determined within the annual plan in physical terms. Nevertheless, the planners have to express complex input and output targets in value terms in order to have a common measure for dissimilar units of materials, labor, capital, and finished products. The plan, therefore, contains both goals and costs stated in terms of money value. Those money values are the prices at which goods are exchanged, both between enterprises and in final sales to consumers.

When prices are used in that fashion it is important that they reflect real costs of production. That is a requirement for the efficient operation of the economy. Suppose, for example, that one ton of coal requires for its production ten units of composite labor and capital, and one barrel of oil requires five units. A price ratio of two oil to one coal would reflect relative real costs. Now suppose that the prices established by the planners were set at 1:1 instead of 2:1. The coal is artificially cheap in money terms, and planners or managers seeking to minimize money costs of production would tend to substitute coal for oil. But they would be substituting a good that cost two units of labor and capital for one that cost only one unit of labor and capital, and they would continue doing so far beyond the point that minimizes real costs. Only when the money prices are in the same proportion as real costs will the substitution of one for the other tend toward the optimum proportion and not go beyond it in either direction.

For that reason, the Soviet planners try to set prices for raw materials and intermediate products as close as possible to actual costs of production. They do not always succeed, and the result is some inefficiency in planning. But the planners are aware of the problem and continually seek relative prices that reflect relative real costs.

Prices of final consumption goods are priced differently, however. There the turnover tax is used to clear the market for most consumer goods at levels that keep buying down so that the desired amount of capital investment and military spending can take place.

Finally, prices are used to compensate partially for the unequal income distribution pattern created by the wage system. Wages (the price of labor) are used to allocate labor and to provide incentives to both workers and em-

ployers. The resultant inequality is partially offset by a broad program of free or very low-cost health and education services financed from general government revenues; by charging low rents for housing and allocating housing space administratively; and by fixing relatively low prices for mass consumption goods and relatively high prices for luxury goods, which is accomplished by setting different turnover tax rates.

Consumption in the USSR

The tradeoff between consumption and investment is well understood by Soviet planners, and they have made no secret of their preference for the latter. More investment means more rapid economic growth and more resources with which to build for the future.

There is a more subtle tradeoff between growth and living standards, however. People cannot be expected to work hard without receiving rewards in the form of a better life. Those rewards have to be provided if the continued effort is to be forthcoming. The Soviet Union has begun to feel the effects of that principle, so in recent years planning has begun to shift its emphasis away from present investment for future gains and toward present benefits.

After 1950 both consumption per person and real wages (wages corrected for price changes) have risen steadily and rapidly. There was rapid growth during the 1950s, a sharp slowdown during the 1960s when Soviet economic growth slowed down, and a renewed upsurge after 1965. The two Five-Year Plans after 1965 called for continuation of the trend toward higher standards of living, but economic difficulties in the 1970s forced those plans to be scaled down, and improvements in living standards have largely stopped. The present five-year plan calls for resumption in the growth of real income per person, however. Soviet citizens are eating better and are better clothed than earlier generations, although the supply of housing remains tight and the economy has not yet entered the era of mass consumption of personal services or large-scale use of automobiles. Differences between urban and rural areas remain (as they do in almost all countries) but are being reduced.

The most striking changes have taken place in communal consumption. Heavy government expenditures are made on education, health care, and support of the aged. The Soviet government reports that in 1970 the value of free consumer services and other benefits amounted to a little over one-third of average earnings per person. If that estimate is correct, about one-fourth of all consumption has been "socialized."

The Efficiency of Soviet Planning

Soviet planning has a number of serious deficiencies. The emphasis on quantity of output from each production unit often causes plant managers to use inefficient methods of production, pile up inventories of materials, and sometimes produce unneeded goods. Costs of production are difficult to judge accurately in a system in which prices tend to remain fixed for long periods of time. Inadequate provision is made for the cost of capital, leading to a tendency toward overly capital-intensive methods of production.

A particularly important drawback has been slowness in applying technological advances that have been adopted in western Europe and the United States at a much more rapid pace, particularly in electronics and computer sciences. The result has been relatively slow increases in productivity that have contributed significantly to the slowdown of economic growth in recent years.

From the point of view of the Soviet consumer, the chief deficiency of planning has been failure to give adequate attention to consumer preferences. The assortment and quality of consumer goods made available in the stores is the end product of planners' decisions rather than consumers themselves. Inadequate supplies of some goods, shortages of others, frequent poor quality, and high prices have combined to bring a continuous barrage of criticism. The economic reforms of the late 1960s attempted to ease the problem by giving enterprise managers greater flexibility and by putting greater stress on profitability as a criterion for judging the performance of management. These reforms were designed to make enterprises more responsive to consumer wants, and some success was achieved. A fundamental conflict is involved, however, between the "planner's sovereignty" that would continue to push for rapid economic expansion and the "consumer's sovereignty" characteristic of a market-oriented economy.

Nevertheless, the Soviet planners have been successful in transforming a backward economy and society into an advanced one. They have also been successful in mobilizing the nation's resources to achieve very ambitious rates of economic growth and to match U.S. military strength. Perhaps their very successes have helped produce some of the problems the planning system now faces. Driving a relatively backward economy from the top, and driving it hard, may have been necessary to bring modernization and rapid growth. But a larger, more complex economy, and a far more sophisticated urban population, probably requires another type of driving force, one stressing individual motivations more and central directives less. The Soviet Union has been grappling with that problem in recent years. Changes in planning have featured reforms toward decentralization, elimination of much of the repression of the Stalin years, and growing attention to production of consumer goods. Indeed, some Soviet writers feel that easing of the driving force from the top is one reason for the slowdown in growth, and they are reluctant to advocate greater reforms.

In whatever way these issues may be resolved in the future, the Soviet Union has shown that economic planning can work. But the Soviet style of planning, run by a large and powerful bureaucracy and denying the basic tenets of consumer sovereignty, does not have a great deal of appeal in western Europe or the United States. Socialists, in particular, have sought other approaches.

Trouble in Paradise

In spite of its undoubted economic successes, the Soviet Union has not turned out to be the ideal workers' state. There are signs of a pervasive social malaise: high rates of absenteeism among workers, widespread drunkenness and growing alcoholism, a surprising rise of infant mortality and health problems, a persistent conflict between intellectuals and the government. There is a large and growing underground economy that bypasses the system of planned production and distribution.

Corruption and favoritism seem to be endemic in the administration of economy and government. The one-party government and structured elections have depoliticized the great bulk of the population. These problems are different from the French malaise, English sickness, Scandinavian despondency, Italian violence, or American alienation—everyone seems to be afflicted with something—and poverty like that of southern Asia is absent.

But something is wrong. Many socialists feel that the basic flaw is centralized authority and failure to develop everyday rank-and-file participation in decision making. Central authority is antithetical to a successful socialist society. The Soviet Union has shown that a planned economy can work and that it can achieve great goals. But when the goals are those of an elite leadership and not those of the general public a high degree of compulsion is necessary, which, in the long run, is self-defeating. Socialists outside the USSR are looking for something better than the state collectivism of which Soviet planning is part.

Summary

Any planned economy must determine its long-run goals, speed of attainment, and how to mobilize its resources. The ideological goal of the Soviet leaders was the building of a socialist society. In economic terms this goal was translated into a continuing drive for high rates of economic growth. The strategy was to use centralized planning to push the economy forward as rapidly as possible. Rapid growth was achieved, but with several important costs: living standards were kept low, required work effort was kept at high levels, inequality of earned incomes was retained, and some forms of negative incentives to work and labor direction were introduced. In the process, the centralized administration and power of state collectivism were established.

Resources of all kinds were mobilized for economic growth. Labor power resources were utilized more fully by eliminating unemployment, drawing women into the labor force, and drawing farmers into urban jobs. Collectivization and mechanization of agriculture raised the agricultural surplus, which was moved almost wholly into government hands to be used to promote industrialization. Capital was made available by holding consumption down via the turnover tax.

The process of planning operates through annual production plans supplemented by plans for inputs, expansion, and financing. The annual plans feature balanced estimates for all important industries, and these are tied together into a complex plan for the entire economy.

The national plan is divided into operating plans for each economic unit. This cumbersome method has worked satisfactorily, but with some difficulty. Implementation of the Soviet plans often requires modification and revision, but that should be expected of any plan.

The incentive system is tied to achievement of plans. Freedom of occupational choice is preserved by use of wage differentials designed to provide incentives to workers to select those occupations and localities where they are needed, and to provide signals to management to promote economy in the use of scarce skills.

Planning in the USSR has important flaws, and reforms are being made to provide plant managers with greater freedom of action. But planning has worked, and the goals given to the planners have been largely achieved. Nevertheless, the system has serious flaws that are rooted in the centralized system of decision making reinforced by the police and military power of the state.

Key Concepts

Five-Year Plan
turnover tax
balanced estimates

For Discussion

1. Is the Soviet economy less efficient than the U.S. economy? In what ways? In what respects is it more efficient?

2. How does the speed of attainment of planned goals affect the methods used to achieve the goals? Does Soviet experience throw any light on that question?

3. How is the turnover tax in the USSR used to divert resources from consumption to investment and military spending?

4. How is labor allocated to various uses in the Soviet economy?

5. The Soviet Union combines political authoritarianism with centralized economic planning. Could the latter function effectively without the former?

6. In what ways does the Soviet Union depart from the goals of the socialist ideology described in the previous chapter? How has it moved toward achieving these goals?

Chapter 36

Market Socialism and Workers' Management

One of the most compelling arguments of the advocates of socialism is that a socialist economy can use the principle of self-adjusting markets to avoid central planning, orient itself toward satisfaction of consumer wants, and operate efficiently. Furthermore, the development of techniques of workers' management makes possible a new regime of democracy in the workplace. This chapter will examine the theory of market socialism, so called, and describe the emergence of workers' management in Yugoslavia.

Prices and Welfare Maximization

Our analysis in earlier chapters showed that a competitive market economy tends to maximize the welfare derived from any given level of output, given the existing pattern of income distribution and assuming that prices reflect full production costs. The argument also assumes that consumers seek to maximize their satisfactions and producers their gains. The market equilibrium that optimizes the use of resources has these characteristics:

1. Prices clear the market, so that supply equals demand at the existing price $(S = D)$.

2. Prices equal costs of production at the margin $(P = MC)$.

3. Costs of production per unit are minimized $(P = AC$ at the lowest point on the AC curve).

We now take up the question of whether the welfare-maximizing market equilibrium can be achieved only in a private economy. Is private enterprise a necessary condition for welfare maximization? Or can it also be achieved when the means of production are socially owned? Indeed, may it be possible to come closer to the optimum results under socialism?

Market Socialism: Basic Concepts

Market socialism seeks to use self-adjusting markets to determine the pattern of production and the allocation of resources, while retaining other aspects of socialism such as social ownership of the means of production and an equalitarian pattern of income distribution. Use of the market mechanism would enable the economy to respond flexibly to consumer wants and provide for wide freedom of occupational choice. At the same time, the central government would retain control over macroeconomic policy to determine the level of investment and sustain full employment and the desired rate of economic growth. Social ownership of the means of production and distribution by the central government, cooperatives, or workers' organizations would eliminate private control of resources, enabling the pattern of income distribution to be based almost wholly on earned income. Yet even with social ownership of the means of production, consumer sovereignty would dominate the allocation of resources through the reliance of the economy on the market system for production decisions.

In short, market socialism seeks to retain the attractive aspects of the socialist ideology without resorting to planners' sovereignty and its inevitable compulsions, for which the Soviet Union has been so strongly criticized. The question is, Can it work?

● **Market socialism** is an economic system in which the activities of socially owned enterprises are coordinated through freely functioning market forces.

The Role of Planning in Market Socialism

Market socialism would retain a central planning commission for the nation as a whole. The function of central planning is restricted, however, to two major economic tasks:

1. Determination of the aggregate level of economic activity and the rate of growth of the economy. Fiscal and monetary policies similar to those used in any contemporary economy would be the chief policy instruments. Maintenance of a particular

rate of economic growth, however, may require that the central government use its taxing powers to accumulate capital for that purpose. As we shall see in a moment, the uses to which the capital is put would be determined by the allocative forces of the market.

2. Determination of prices. Planners would have the job of setting prices for all inputs and outputs of the economy. This includes the products turned out by all economic units and also the raw material and semifinished units they use as inputs. It would also include wage rates and salaries for labor inputs and interest rates charged for capital. Everything involved in the production and distribution of goods and services would have a price.

Setting Prices
The basic rule for the setting of prices by the central planners is simple but very important:

○ Prices must be set at levels that clear the market.

This means that the planners must set prices at which supply and demand are equal. Both shortages and surpluses are to be avoided by adjusting prices to eliminate them.

The logic behind this rule for price setting is the theory of competitive markets: When the market is cleared, both sellers and buyers are satisfied. The marginal benefits to the buyer derived from the last unit purchased are just equal to the marginal costs to the producer. This is the first condition for the system as a whole to reach a welfare optimum.

Prices that clear the market can readily be achieved by trial and error. Suppose, for example, the price of a product set by the central planning commission results in shortages in the market, as in Figure 36–1. This situation will tell the planners that the first condition for optimum use of resources is not being met, and that the price is too low. On the other hand,

Figure 36-1
Shortages Under Market Socialism

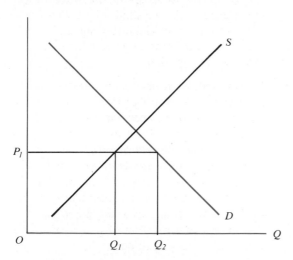

At price P_1 the producing units are willing to supply quantity Q_1, but consumers wish to buy quantity Q_2. The result is bare shelves in the stores, inadequate inventories and customers lining up to buy when new shipments come in. The planners know from these signs that they should raise the price in order to clear the market.

Figure 36-2
Surpluses Under Market Socialism

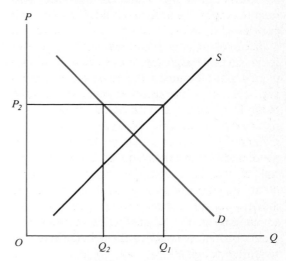

At price P_2, the producing units will supply quantity Q_1, while buyers will take only quantity Q_2. The difference represents unsold output, telling the planners that price should be reduced.

Figure 36-3
Clearing the Market Under Market Socialism

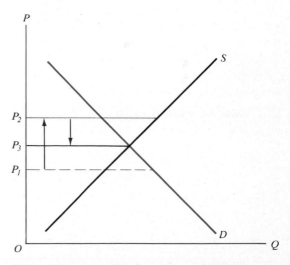

Starting from a price (P_1) set too low, the planners may overshoot the mark and raise the price too much to P_2. Growing amounts of unsold output quickly cause them to move down again until they reach the equilibrium price at P_3.

suppose that the planners find unsold goods piling up on the shelves and inventories rising, as in Figure 36–2. This is their signal to bring prices down. By a process of successive approximations, probably assisted by computers and economic forecasts, the central planning commission can arrive at a price that clears the market, leaving no unsold surplus and creating no shortages. Figure 36–3 shows what the adjustment process might be like.

There are striking similarities between price setting under market socialism and in the competitive model. The results are similar, the causes of the price movements are similar, and the trial-and-error process of successive approximations are similar. In one case the mechanism works automatically—and is perhaps subject to large shocks and wide fluctuations. In the other case the mechanism is managed, would probably avoid some of the price shifts of the competitive model, and may well function more smoothly if the central planners and plant managers are alert. If they are not, surpluses and shortages could last for long periods of time.

Price setting in an economy based on market socialism is a large job, however, requiring a managerial bureaucracy of some scope, particularly in a large and complex economy. But the planning system that limits itself to planning of prices will inevitably be smaller and more manageable than one that seeks to also plan production inputs and outputs. The results may well be worth the extra resources devoted to planning, since the practical alternatives in the modern world apparently are the planners' sovereignty of the Soviet Union or the quasi-monopolistic economy of the United States or western Europe.[1]

Another approach would do away with planning of prices altogether. This is done in Yugoslavia, where prices are determined by market forces alone, in an open economy very heavily influenced by the international economy. The advantage of this system is that there is no need for a large planning bureaucracy. The chief disadvantages are that the economy is subjected to price fluctuations, including inflation, that may be generated abroad, while it is also subject to monopoloid price control within portions of the domestic economy not strongly affected by exports and imports. More on these issues in the Yugoslav economy later in this chapter.

Adjustment of the Producing Unit

A market socialist economy cannot limit itself only to the setting of prices. It must also provide incentives to the management of socialist enterprises that lead to responses that

maximize efficiency. The basic principle here is also simple but vitally important:

○ Management of enterprises must be motivated to maximize the profits of producing units.

This means that rewards and incentive systems must be based on profit levels, and adequate indicators and measures of profit must be developed, just as in a private-enterprise economy.

This operating rule is necessary to satisfy the second and third criteria of welfare maximization:

○ Prices must equal costs of production at the margin ($P = MC$).
○ Costs of production per unit must be minimized ($P = AC$ at the lowest point on the AC curve).

Incentive systems of this sort are not difficult to devise. Large corporations are quite able to do it, and the socialist systems of eastern Europe have moved a long way in the same direction. Even the Soviet Union has taken some steps toward the same goal. The chief problem is not the incentives and rewards themselves, that is, high salaries, bonuses, and public recognition for success, but the devising of accurate measures of costs and accurate indicators of profit.

Under the assumption that these problems can be largely resolved, as many American corporations have already shown, the enterprise managers must then be given a great deal of latitude in making decisions about which inputs to use, which outputs to schedule, and the best ways to combine inputs in the process of production. The better the reward systems and the freer the management, the closer the enterprise will come to maximizing profits, and the closer the enterprise and the industry will come to achieving the criteria of welfare maximization.

Any plant manager who seeks to maximize

---

[1]Some advocates of market socialism argue that price planners under market socialism would probably be fewer in number than the people engaged in advertising and marketing in present-day America, whose services would no longer be needed under market socialism.

profits when his selling price is given will have a horizontal demand curve for his output, just as in the case of pure competition. As a price taker, he will try to move toward that level of output at which his selling price equals his marginal cost. His supply curve is his marginal cost curve. The enterprise in a market socialist economy will tend toward the competitive equilibrium. In Figure 36–4 the first stage of the profit-maximizing solution is achieved. But not the second stage, which minimizes costs per unit of output. How is that brought about under market socialism?

In the first place, this enterprise could add to its profits by building another plant. Since its profits are above normal it will have every incentive to borrow the capital necessary to do so, subject to the price placed on loanable funds. Secondly, other enterprises will discover the profit opportunities available and will also have strong incentives to build additional plants or enter this type of production. Just as in a private competitive industry, the incentive of profits will bring additional capital and enterprise into this industry.

The result will be similar to that achieved by the competitive model. As output rises, supplies coming on the market are increased, surpluses start to appear, and the central planning commission brings the price down. This process can be expected to continue until the industry as a whole has reached its equilibrium size and expansion stops, shown in Figure 36–5.

This result may be slow in coming under market socialism if the producing enterprise is in a monopolistic position. For example, if it is a large automobile manufacturer in a relatively small nation without significant foreign markets, the management may become lazy, allow inefficiences to creep in, and permit the cost structure slowly to drift upward. It may still operate in the short run at the output that equates price with marginal costs, and appear to be maximizing profits, but it is not trying to push average costs downward.

Figure 36-4
Equilibrium of the Enterprise in Market Socialism, I

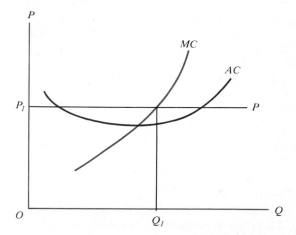

With the price P_1 established by the central planning commission and not under the control of the enterprise manager, the level of output Q_1 at which profits are maximized, $P = MC$, is set.

Figure 36-5
Equilibrium of the Firm in Market Socialism, II

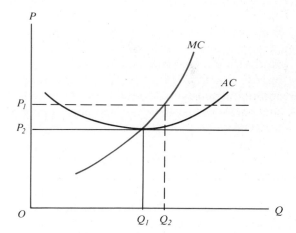

As new plants are established in response to the high profits made at price P_1 the central planning commission brings the price down toward P_2 in order to keep the market cleared. Ultimately, the individual enterprises will be operating at price P_2 and output Q_2, at which point price equals marginal cost at the lowest point on the average cost curve.

For these reasons a market socialist economy may find it wise to provide incentives for management to bring costs of production down. It may encourage competition within enterprises for the managerial positions, or allow imports from other countries to discipline monopolistic industries. Even market socialism can have problems of monopoly if the size of the market, in combination with the best available technology, gives enterprises a monopolistic position. Indeed, this problem has already appeared in some of the eastern European countries now moving toward market socialism.

In spite of these problems of application in practice, there is no theoretical or analytical reason why market socialism cannot achieve a close approximation to the optimal long-run adjustment of the competitive market economy. Its chief advantage is that firms are price takers, making it possible to achieve the cost-minimizing and optimal output levels of the purely competitive model.

Wages and Salaries

Payments to workers under market socialism would also be designed to clear the market. Wages and salaries would be set by the central planning commission to equate the demand for labor with the available supply. For example, suppose a new shipyard is being established, requiring a substantial number of electricians in an area where they are in short supply. Wages would be set at levels high enough to draw electricians from other areas or to draw unskilled workers into appropriate training programs. Just like the trial-and-error process for product pricing, the pricing of labor services will seek to establish a market equilibrium.

Capital

The same is true of capital. Funds for investment can be made available from two sources. One is the earnings of the enterprise itself, which would be available for expansion. The more profitable enterprises would be the ones with the greatest resources for expansion, just as in the competitive market economy.

The second source of investment funds is the capital market, in the socialist economy dominated by state-owned banks. These banks would be reservoirs for the voluntary savings of individuals, and some would also dispense government-owned funds. Whatever the source, loans would be available to any enterprise at interest rates established by the central planning commission at levels designed to clear the money markets.

Just as in a private economy, the supply of funds available to enterprises and consumers could be managed with stable growth at full employment as the goal. Together with the demand for funds, this supply would establish the rate of interest that would balance demand and supply in the money markets. One task of the central planning commission would be continually to seek that level by trial-and-error adjustments of the interest rate.

This method of allocating capital would function effectively if the supply of funds were based solely on the voluntary savings of individuals and enterprises. It would also function effectively if voluntary savings were supplemented by a political decision, presumably arrived at democratically, to add additional savings through taxes or borrowing by the central government, designed to raise the level of capital accumulation and reduce aggregate consumption levels. The important point to remember is that the market mechanism would be used to ration investment funds among all those who would like them, with the amount available going only to those enterprises willing and able to pay the going price.

Market Socialism as an Alternative Future

The two dominant economic systems today are the "managed capitalism" of western Europe and the United States, and the state collectivism of the Soviet Union. Market socialism provides a third alternative. It combines the concepts of the self-adjusting market economy that are derived from capitalism with the equalitarianism of the socialist ideal. By vesting ownership of the means of production in the public rather than private individuals it eliminates the large disparities of wealth and the economic-political power of big business that are characteristic of capitalism. By eliminating the centralized administrative planning of the Soviet system, market socialism makes possible a democratic dispersal of power. Yet it would provide for an effective management of economic affairs that may well be superior to either capitalism with big business or socialism with a planning bureaucracy.

Economic Equality

One of the chief advantages of market socialism is its ability to avoid the inequalities of income that arise in a capitalist economy through private ownership of the means of production and distribution. Almost all income would be earned income from wages and salaries. Differences in earned incomes may be large from one individual to the next, but the greater differences created in a private economy through accumulation of profits, interest, and rent, and by the unearned income resulting from ownership of great wealth, would be greatly reduced or eliminated entirely.

An economic system based on social ownership of the means of production need not provide payments to private individuals for use of resources. Instead, those payments could be retained by the community as a whole and used to achieve social rather than individual goals. Income from work would be the basis of the distribution of income. In a private-enterprise economy, by contrast, the distribution of income is based on income from property as well as income from work. Since ownership of property is highly unequal, a significant amount of inequality is built into the income

distribution pattern. This factor could be largely eliminated in a social economy, enabling the economy as a whole to move toward a more equalitarian distribution of income.

A socialist economy probably cannot achieve full income equality, at least initially, and full equality may not be desirable. The need for management and technical expertise may require continuing income differentials based on the type of work performed, although some socialists argue that in the long run even those differentials could be eliminated. Market socialism can also avoid the type of inequality generated in the state collectivist economy of the Soviet Union, where the privileged position of the party and state bureaucracy enables the upper administrative levels to obtain high incomes. In those economies control over economic resources has led to a new form of social stratification based on position within the hierarchy of economic and political control. Decentralization of a country's economic power can reduce or eliminate that source of unearned income.

Economic Efficiency

Advocates of market socialism point out that their system can come closest to approximating the welfare-maximizing equilibrium of the competitive market economy. Since prices are established by the central planning commission, they cannot be used by monopoloid firms to create more-than-normal profits and to gain special economic advantages. The individual enterprise must take the price as given and adjust its operations to that already established amount.

By contrast, the big enterprise in a capitalist economy can gain considerable influence over the market because of its size. To a greater or lesser extent, depending on circumstances, the big enterprise can set its own prices—to its own benefit and to the detriment of the public. These sources of private gain at the expense of the public would not exist under market socialism. The result is a closer approximation to the economic efficiency of a competitive market system.

Much of the inefficiency of a private economy could be eliminated. A large amount of information would be available to the central planning commission. It could be made available to all interested enterprises to minimize overexpansion of a particular industry, for example. Similarly, control over the pricing process could dampen down erratic or excessive swings in prices caused in a private economy by the incorrect expectations or overenthusiasm of individuals or speculators. The advocates of market socialism may be right. A well-managed pricing system may be more effective than a freely functioning one, particularly if it avoids monopolistic controls by producers.

Decentralization of Decision Making
One of the great advantages of market socialism is decentralized decision making. Only prices and the level of aggregate demand would be determined by central planners. All other decisions would be made at the level of the producing enterprise. Consumers would be free to exercise their choices in spending their incomes. Workers would be free to choose their occupation and employment. All of this is possible because the market is used as the coordinating mechanism, enabling decisions to rest with the enterprise, the consumer, and the worker. Even price decisions would reflect impersonal market forces.

Decentralized decisions provide a sharp contrast with Soviet planning, with its heavy emphasis on control from the top and administrative allocation of resources. Although the recent trend in the USSR has been toward greater reliance on signals from the market, the basic principle of centralized administrative planning and resource allocation remains. A complex bureaucracy manages economic affairs for a powerful national state.

Market socialism could reverse the trend toward bureaucracy, which is also to be found in the large corporation of present-day capitalism, and provide a larger scope for individual action. If one of the problems of modern humanity is the conflict between individual goals and those of large organizations, market socialism offers one possible path toward a solution.

Decentralization of economic decisions can open the way to effective patterns of workers' management. The full promise of socialism cannot be achieved as long as workers do not have effective control over their own working lives. Yet in both the centrally managed Soviet economy and the large corporation of modern capitalism there is little opportunity for grass-roots or "shop-floor" democracy. In a system of market socialism, however, management by workers themselves is possible.

Individual Freedoms
Market socialism provides a mechanism by which economic freedoms can be reconciled with social ownership of the means of production. It retains the principles of consumer sovereignty and freedom of choice of occupation. It makes possible greater equality in income distribution than under private-enterprise capitalism, together with wide participation in decision making by those most closely affected by the decisions. It enables rational and efficient decisions to emerge from a complex set of economic relationships without resort to the constraints and compulsion of centralized production planning. The contrast between the decentralized economy inherent in the theory of market socialism and centralized planning as it developed in the Soviet Union is particularly striking. Finally, decentralized decision making permits a shift of authority from the top of bureaucratic organizations to the rank-and-file worker. It may be that some form of market socialism will be the key to a more humane and responsive economic and social order.

Yugoslavia: Market Socialism, Workers' Self-Management, and Central Planning

Market socialism has never been adopted on a full-scale basis anywhere, but for more than twenty years the Yugoslav economy has been moving toward greater reliance upon it, combined with a large dose of workers' self-management as well as a significant amount of central planning.

Yugoslavia came into the orbit of the Soviet Union after World War II and initially emulated the central planning of the USSR. But in 1948 the Yugoslav leadership successfully resisted efforts to make the country subservient to the USSR and was "expelled" from the international Communist movement. The leadership reevaluated central planning, decided it was part of an authoritarian pattern incompatible with the humanist goals of socialism, and set out to build a new system based on workers' self-management and decentralized economic power.

There were several significant constraints on Yugoslav policy, however. First, the nation was undeveloped economically, and the leadership decided on a program of industrialization via large investment expenditures. Second, Yugoslavia is a country composed of various national groups—Serbs, Croats, Macedonians, Slovenes, Albanians, and more—requiring considerable attention to the more undeveloped areas within the country for political reasons, regardless of economic criteria. Third, the regime was too insecure politically to alienate the peasantry by collectivization of agriculture Soviet-style, so it quickly reverted to private enterprise in farming. Finally, as a relatively small country trying to industrialize it had to wrestle with the problem of market dominance by one or several enterprises in individual industries. For all of these reasons the move toward market socialism and away from central planning has been incomplete.

Several factors supported a new approach to socialism in Yugoslavia. First, World War II brought a fundamental change in the class structure of the country. When the German armies were driven out the landowning and business elite went with them, to avoid the victorious Communist Party. The country was without a capitalist class capable of mounting significant opposition to reconstruction of the economic order. Second, Yugoslavia was freed from the Nazis by a native revolutionary movement, not by Soviet forces. A national leadership, both triumphant and capable, was in charge. Third, when the break with the Soviet Union came in 1948, there was a general understanding among all the nationality, religious, and regional groups that unless they made their system work, the Russians were likely to take over. This general feeling, highly pervasive throughout the country to this day and requiring little government propaganda to reinforce it, brought a unity of effort that overcame other divisive forces. Fourth, the single-party political system provided a unified leadership that cut across other divisions. As the Yugoslav *bon mot* puts it: "We are a nation of five nationalities, four languages, three religions, two races—and one party."

Throughout the 1950s and well into the 1960s a large degree of central control of the economy was maintained, largely to generate and manage investment funds for purposes of expansion. Nevertheless, much progress was made toward decentralization. Workers' management was begun in 1950 and by 1952 was largely in operation throughout the economy. Agriculture had been collectivized prior to 1948, but in 1953 decollectivization began and was quickly accomplished. A high degree of central control over the economy was maintained. A large share of GNP was collected in taxes for purposes of investment, which, together with a significant volume of foreign aid, enabled output to grow by 8–9 percent annually. In addition, price and wage controls were instituted in order to check an inflation that was stimulated in part by rapid growth and in part by price increases by worker-managed firms whose employees wanted higher wages. Nevertheless, controls over wages, prices, and investment were relaxed in 1961 and, in spite of continued inflation, reduced very substantially in 1966. By the late 1960s not only were most enterprise decisions controlled by workers, including prices of finished goods, but even investment decisions were made in large part by individual enterprises using their own earnings or borrowed funds. Yugoslavia had converted from a nation with Soviet-like central planning in the late 1940s to a new type of market socialism with workers' management and some elements of central planning.

Ownership and Control of the Means of Production

Yugoslavia is committed to social ownership of the means of production, but not to centralized, bureaucratic management. An enterprise is publicly owned, but it is managed by the people who work at it.[2] A workers' council of 15 to several hundred members is elected as a representative body to decide basic issues of management policy, such as prices, hiring management, distribution of the income of the enterprise, marketing, labor productivity, expansion, and similar matters. Because the council is too large for close attention to management, a three- to eleven-person board is delegated authority to make decisions, much as an executive committee or a board of directors. This management board selects the top management of the enterprise, in cooperation with the local government and the trade association for the industry, subject to approval by the workers' council.

Workers have an interest in how well the

enterprise functions, for they are the claimants to the residual income after all other payments are made. There is a minimum wage that all enterprises must meet and an established wage scale for all enterprises. The enterprise must meet all costs of production, and is required to pay taxes, make interest payments on its debt, and set aside reserves. Net income above all of those payments is then shared among the workers through bonuses. Enterprises have a large degree of freedom in determining just how the residual income will be divided.

Agriculture, meanwhile, is organized largely on an individual farm basis, although there are some cooperatives and state farms. Individual farms are limited in size to 10 hectares (1 hectare = 2.471 acres) and are privately owned.

The Role of the Market

The market is the coordinating mechanism of the Yugoslav economy. Prices are determined by the interplay of supply and demand. Decisions of individual enterprises are based on production costs and prices of finished products, motivated by the desire of workers to maximize their income and maintain their jobs. Those basic principles are modified by various government actions that affect individual firms: taxes, depreciation policy, wage level policies and minimum wage laws, foreign exchange controls and tariffs, price supports for farm products, and control over interest rates. Most of these controls are closely related to management of the rate of economic growth and investment policy, which remain under central direction.

The Yugoslav economy differs from the theory of market socialism, however, in one fundamental respect. Prices are not determined by a central planning board, with individual enterprises being price takers who then seek to maximize their profits. Prices are set by enterprises themselves. The chief reason seems to be the Yugoslav belief that a system of admin-

---

[2]Enterprises employing fewer than six persons can be privately owned, leaving a place in the economy for family enterprises. Less than 2 percent of all employed persons work in this small private nonagricultural sector.

istered prices is too cumbersome, while market-determined prices can achieve essentially the same result with less time lag and fewer disparities between actual prices and those that clear the market.

Unfortunately, that makes the economy vulnerable to monopoloid pricing practices, particularly since a developing economy may have relatively few individual enterprises in some industries. For example, distribution of petroleum products in Yugoslavia is dominated by enterprises that have divided up the country into regional monopolies, encouraged by local authorities who wish to protect local industries. This conflict between the desire to decentralize economic decisions and the need to maintain competitive prices has not been fully resolved in the Yugoslav economy.

In one respect the absence of a system of price administration is an advantage. Domestic products must compete with imported goods, and exports must compete in world markets. The openness of the economy provides competition that disciplines domestic producers to remain competitive by keeping costs of production down, developing new products and processes, and exploiting whatever economic advantages they may have. The government fosters these effects of the market by trying to reduce import tariffs from their formerly high levels, although that policy is restrained by the need to keep imports down as standards of living rise and as demand for imported goods rises. The basic policy, however, is to allow enterprises to set their own prices, competing with both domestic and foreign firms, and to maximize the efficiency effects of price competition.

Central Planning

The chief element of central planning in the Yugoslav system is control over the aggregate level of investment. The central government controls the rate of investment and the rate of economic growth. Here is how it works.

A decision is made on the desirable growth rate and the investment necessary to achieve it. The required investment funds come from consumer savings and retained earnings of enterprises, plus the tax revenues of the central government. Each enterprise pays taxes for the support of the social security system, for general government expenses, and for contributions to "social investment funds." The central government funnels the latter revenues plus consumer savings into the banking system and establishes interest rates at which enterprises borrow investment funds. In a pure system of market socialism, all investment would be based on enterprise earnings plus borrowings at the established interest rate. But the Yugoslav government adds direction to economic development by allocating some funds to particular economic sectors and geographic areas and by making direct government investments. The individual enterprise, however, decides for itself on its investment policy, based on the cost of borrowing and the expected rate of return.

The central government, in addition, levies high taxes in order to accumulate investment funds, follows expansionary monetary and fiscal policies to stimulate investment, and has strict rules governing the distribution of income by enterprises. The result has been high rates of investment (22–30 percent of GNP) and relatively low rates of consumption (under 50 percent of GNP). Yugoslavia has shown that a decentralized economy with aggregative economic controls can achieve high rates of capital accumulation and economic growth.

Decision Making: An Example

With a complex pattern of workers' management, market socialism, and central planning, in a one-party socialist state, decision making can be quite complex. Here is an example based on an actual case of a manufacturing enterprise in Bosnia. The firm supplies a large share of the national market for dies, bits, and other cutting and shaping parts for power-driven machine tools, and some 25 percent of its output is exported. A large expansion was planned in the early 1970s, to double output with a 25 percent increase in employment, with fully half of the increased output to be sold abroad. Note that output would increase faster than labor costs; profits would rise, given the world price of the products. The decision to expand was made by the management council and approved by the larger workers' council, based on detailed plans drawn up by the management. Behind that decision lay other pressures. The government of the Serbo-Croatian Republic (one of five republics) wanted to increase the number of industrial jobs in a backward, largely agricultural region and was willing to provide some of the capital in the form of a low-interest, long-term loan. The federal government was also willing to provide a low-cost loan from its regional development funds. These public funds came from government tax revenues. The workers also wanted to create additional jobs, for many of their children, relatives, and friends would be employed either directly in the new plant or indirectly as the result of increased economic activity in the area.

The local government was also drawn into the decision, for it had to approve the location of the new plant, provide for expanded housing for the workers, and construct needed schools, roads, sewers, and other public facilities out of its tax revenues. With governments at all levels involved, the League of Communists (the name of the Yugoslav communist party) was also involved in the decision making, from the start in the enterprise and at all levels of government administration. Indeed, the original impetus for the project may well have come from the party. Whatever its origin, the decision for expansion involved a complex interaction between management, workers, party, local government, and regional and central planners.

The financing of the project was almost as complex. Twenty percent of the funds came from the retained earnings of the enterprise itself. Thirty percent was in the form of loans from the Republic and national governments at interest rates about half of the going market rate. Ten percent of the capital was in the form of a loan from the International Bank for Reconstruction and Development, an international lending agency, with an interest rate slightly below market rates. The remaining 40 percent of the capital was in the form of a long-term loan, at market interest rates, from a syndicate of private banks in western Europe. This loan was conditional upon the firm arranging for all the other sources of capital. The last two loans, from the International Bank and the private banks, were particularly important. The firm had to show those organizations that it would be able to compete in world markets and make a profit. The discipline of the market was at work in raising capital, just as it would be later in selling the products.

Socialism in Yugoslavia: An Appraisal

The Yugoslav economy is an interesting mix of market socialism, workers' management, and central planning. An overview indicates that the system is working relatively well. Central planning has been effective in mobilizing capital for economic growth and regional development. Living standards have risen, particularly in the cities. Yugoslavia is one of the more successful of the developing countries. The economy is shifting from agriculture to industry. Yugoslavia still has several serious economic problems, however, including inflation, unemployment, and poverty.

Nevertheless, socialists all over the world are watching the Yugoslav economy eagerly. Its mixture or workers' management, market socialism, and economic planning may point to a "third way" that avoids the pitfalls of both the state collectivism of the USSR and the monopoly capitalism of the U.S.

Summary

The theory of market socialism shows how an economy in which the means of production are socially owned can function through a decentralized system of decision making in which consumer sovereignty prevails and freedom of occupational choice is retained. Central planning is restricted to maintenance of high levels of aggregate demand and price planning by a central agency.

The price-making rule is that prices must clear the market. This makes the individual enterprise a price taker in the same sense as the firm in the purely competitive model of self-adjusting markets. Plant managers respond to the price established by the central planning agency on the basis of a profit-maximizing rule supplemented by a system of incentives and rewards. Consumers are free to choose what they want to buy, and thereby signal producers about what to produce. Workers are free to take any job available. Capital is allocated through the price mechanism. The result should be a strong tendency to achieve the welfare-maximizing equilibrium of the purely competitive model.

There is no economy based wholly on market socialism. Yugoslavia, however, has a mixed system of market socialism and workers' management, but with important elements of private enterprise (agriculture) and central planning of aggregate investment and economic growth. Although that system functions successfully, it has problems, too, just as any real economy has. Nevertheless, it may provide a "third way" that avoids the extremes of both monopoly capitalism and state collectivism.

Key Concept

market socialism

For Discussion

1. What are the advantages and disadvantages of the Yugoslav system of unplanned prices?
2. Would the Soviet economy function more effectively if it were converted to a system of market socialism? Explain.
3. Would the U.S. economy function more effectively if it were converted to a system of market socialism? Explain.
4. Discuss the advantages and disadvantages of market socialism.
5. How would the amount and direction of capital accumulation be determined in a market-socialist economy?
6. Would a market-socialist economy continue to need fiscal and monetary policies designed to achieve high levels of output and employment? Explain.

PART 9

THE INTERNATIONAL ECONOMY

The world economy is increasingly becoming a single economic unit. Individual national economies are developing closer linkages through trade, capital investment, and financial institutions. Multinational corporations spread their activities across national boundaries and the Eurobank system carries on international banking activities based very heavily on the U.S. dollar.

The economic basis for international trade is explained in Chapter 37, with emphasis on the advantages of specialization and trade. This chapter also shows why protection of individual industries against foreign competition usually makes the ordinary person poorer. Chapter 38 explains the financial aspects of international trade and investment, including a nation's balance of payments and the value of its currency in international financial markets, along with the relationship between these financial matters and the struggle for advantage and power among nations.

Finally, Chapter 39 takes up the problem of economic development in the third world. It compares the recent economic development patterns of various parts of the world, explains the reasons for the self-reinforcing poverty of much of the third world, and compares the capitalist development strategy with the socialist strategy in China and a third strategy designed to avoid limitations of the other two.

> If two countries which traded together attempted . . . to produce for themselves what they now import from one another, . . . the two together would not obtain from their industry so great a quantity of commodities, as when each employs itself in producing, both for itself and for the other, the things in which its labour is relatively most efficient.
>
> John Stuart Mill, *Principles of Political Economy* (1848)

> The industrially more developed country presents to the less developed country a picture of the latter's future.
>
> Karl Marx, *Capital* (1867)

Chapter 37

International Trade in Theory and Practice

Upon learning that you have progressed this far in your studies of economics without becoming overly discouraged, your rich and eccentric uncle, whom you have not seen since Christmas of the year you were eight years old and who has been engaged in trading milk and whiskey with the Indians of the upper Amazon, endows you with exactly $1,000,000, provided that you use it in international trade between England and the United States, dealing in milk and whiskey, of which he is very fond. Puzzled, you inquire into the situation and discover that the prevailing prices and shipping costs are those shown in Table 37–1.

Your uncle glances at these figures and remarks gleefully, "Aha! You'll make a fortune!"

"How?" you respond. "Don't I have to know the exchange rate between English and American currency?"

"What an idiot," responds your uncle. "You have no more intelligence than an eight-year-old. Didn't they teach you *anything* in your economics course? I think I'll take my million and visit Las Vegas."

"Wait," you respond in an agonized voice. "I'll figure it out."

The first thing you notice is that milk is cheap in England, compared with the United States. You can buy ten gallons of milk there for what one gallon of whiskey would cost. In the United States milk is more expensive: it is equivalent to one-fifth gallon of whiskey rather than one-tenth.

Just the opposite is true of whiskey. It is relatively cheap in the U.S. and relatively expensive in England. In the U.S. you would have to give up only five gallons of milk to get one gallon of whiskey, while in England the exchange would be ten for one.

These relative prices can be easily compared, as shown in Table 37–2. This was the relationship your uncle saw at a glance: whiskey is cheap in the U.S. while milk is cheap in England *relative to the price of other things*. Put

Table 37–1
Prices of Milk and Whiskey in England and U.S.

	In England	In U.S.
Milk	1s/gal	$1/gal
Whiskey	£1/gal (= 10s)	$5/gal

Note: Shipping costs between the U.S. and England for both milk and whiskey are 1¢ per gal.

Table 37–2
Relative Prices of Milk and Whiskey

	In England	In U.S.
Milk (in gallons of whiskey)	0.1	0.2
Whiskey (in gallons of milk)	10.0	5.0

another way, English milk is relatively cheap and English whiskey relatively expensive *compared with their prices in the U.S.* Correspondingly, U.S. milk is expensive and whiskey cheap *compared with their prices in England.*

This information is all one needs. "Buy cheap and sell dear," you murmur as you reach for the telephone to set the following transactions in motion:

1. Buy 200,000 gal of whiskey in the U.S., at $5/gal for. $1,000,000

2. Ship it to England, where you sell it for 10s/gal, a total of £200,000
Shipping costs, to be settled later, are $2,000.

3. Buy 2,000,000 gal of milk in England at 1s/gal, for £200,000

4. Ship it to the U.S. by refrigerated tankship, where you sell it for $1/gal. You receive $2,000,000
Shipping costs at this stage are $20,000.

Settling your accounts, you end up by almost doubling your original $1,000,000:

Cash on hand when transactions end
. . . . $2,000,000

Cash on hand at start 1,000,000

Shipping costs 22,000

Telephone calls. 0.40

Net gain . . . . $ 977,999.60

At this point you call in your eight-year-old brother, explain the simple transactions to

him, and leave him in charge of the original $1,000,000. Reaching for the telephone, you call your uncle, "About that trip to Las Vegas. . . ."

The Flow of Trade and Factors of Production

These transactions have set in motion a flow of trade between the two nations. The U.S. exports whiskey and imports milk, while England exports milk and imports whiskey. At the root of this trade are international differences in price relationships. These price relationships are, in turn, based on differences in costs of production within the individual countries. The 1 to 5 ratio between the prices of milk and whiskey in the U.S., that is, the relatively costly milk and cheap whiskey, is the outcome of all of the economic forces within the country that bring prices to approximate the long-run average costs of production for each commodity, modified by whatever monopoloid industrial structures that may prevail. The same is true of the 1 to 10 ratio in England.

This is a key point in the analysis. As we shall see in a moment, the flow of trade causes adjustments in relative prices within trading countries, and these in turn set in motion the long-run market adjustment process that brings prices into accord with long-run costs of production. Relative prices within any nation will then reflect the real economic relationships that exist within the nation—real costs, real benefits, and net welfare.

Much depends on the availability (and the price) of the factors of production. In the United States land is relatively plentiful, labor is scarce, and capital is abundant. This makes land and capital relatively inexpensive and labor relatively costly. Capital-intensive products that use relatively large amounts of capital and little labor will be relatively inexpensive in the U.S. and will be the sort of item exported, like farm and industrial machinery, electrical equipment, and so on. We also export agricultural products like wheat, which use large amounts of both land and capital in production. On the other hand, labor-intensive products will be relatively expensive in the U.S. and these items will be high on our list of imports.

A tropical country, on the other hand, which has much labor and land but little capital, will tend to export labor- and land-intensive products such as rubber, cocoa, or bananas while it imports capital-intensive products from countries like the U.S. and the industrial nations of Europe.

Scarcity relationships between the factors of production vary from region to region and from country to country. No two are exactly the same. Four main divisions of the world economy can be distinguished, based on the relative scarcity or abundance of the factors of production within the divisions. They are shown in Table 37–3.

Each area exports characteristic products based on its particular endowment of the factors of production. Hong Kong, for example, which like Japan has very plentiful labor, much capital, and very little land, exports highly labor-intensive products of industry, such as textiles and clothing. Malaysia, however, with plentiful land and labor and little capital, exports land- and labor-intensive plantation products such as rubber. The list could go on indefinitely.

These relationships among the factors of production change with time. Although the natural resources of an area remain the same, except as technology enables their utilization to change, population growth and capital accumulation change the pattern of relative scarcities. For example, a hundred years ago the United States was a typical developing Great Plains nation, with an abundance of land relative to labor and capital. Its principal exports were land-intensive commodities such as wheat and cotton. With growth of population and a very high rate of capital accumulation, the relative scarcities changed. The U.S. became an industrial nation in which capital was relatively abundant and labor the scarcest factor of production. The principal exports were capital-intensive industrial products.

Finally, after World War II the international trade position of the U.S. economy changed still further. As other nations caught up in accumulation of physical capital U.S. exports began to shift toward goods embodying human capital more heavily. After 1950 U.S. exports of manufactured goods were relatively more intensive in the services of human capital, as compared to physical capital and unskilled labor, while U.S. imports were more intensive in the use of physical capital and unskilled labor relative to human capital. The great U.S. investments in education and science resulted in exports that embodied those relatively plentiful elements of human capital more intensively. Even U.S. agricultural exports reflect the

Table 37–3
Relative Scarcity of Factors of Production

Main International Trade Areas of the World	Labor	Capital	Land
Western Europe	Scarce	Plentiful	Scarce
Great Plains areas			
Mature (U.S.)	Scarce	Plentiful	Plentiful
Developing (Australia,			
Canada, . . .)	Scarce	Scarce	Plentiful
Tropics	Plentiful	Scarce	Plentiful
Japan	Plentiful	Plentiful	Scarce

heavy emphasis on scientific agriculture, combined with large amounts of physical capital and extensive use of land.

These changes continue, in the rest of the world as well as in the U.S., at varying rates of speed. The pattern of world trade reflects those changes, subtly and slowly. The result is a continuous ebb and flow in the composition of any one nation's imports and exports.

Equalization of Relative Prices

The relative price ratios used in our little tale about trade in whiskey and milk are only the beginning. They cannot be maintained. The flow of trade itself will cause them to change and ultimately be brought into equality with each other. The only difference between the relative price ratios will be accounted for by transportation costs. The process is another example of how a system of self-adjusting markets function under the impact of buyers and sellers who seek to maximize their gains.

Return to the example. Prior to the flow of trade between the two countries, the price of milk in the U.S. was $1 per gallon and whiskey $5 per gallon. Trade brought exports of whiskey and imports of milk. The additional supply of milk coming into domestic markets will drive its price down below $1, while the export demand for whiskey will push its price above $5. The 1/5 ratio of their prices will start going down toward the 1/10 ratio prevailing in England.

Just the opposite events occur in England. The original price of whiskey (10 shillings per gallon) will fall because imports raise the supply available, while the price of milk (1 shilling per gallon) will rise because of the export demand. The original 1/10 ratio of their prices will rise toward the 1/5 ratio prevailing in the U.S.

Somewhere in between the two original ratios the two will meet, pushed toward that point by milk exports from England and whis-

Table 37–4
Prices of Milk and Whiskey After Trade

	In England	In U.S.
Milk	1s 1d/gal	90¢/gal
Whiskey	8s 8d/gal	$7.20/gal

key exports from the U.S. Trade between the two nations will continue to increase until the equality of relative prices is established, and the equality will be maintained by one specific level of trade. Any deviation from equality will set in motion a change in the level of trade that will bring the system back to its equilibrium.

This is brought out forcefully to you upon your return from Las Vegas, where you lost all your gains at the gaming tables. Your brother meets you at the door furiously, claiming that you deceived him; he followed your directions and ended up with no profit at all. He didn't even cover his shipping costs. Mystified, you look at the prices prevailing when he bought and sold and discover that they were those shown in Table 37–4.

You realize then that the trading you did the day before you turned over the business to your brother was just enough to bring the price ratios in *both* countries to just 1/8.

"You haven't done anything since?" you ask him carefully.

"No," he replies.

At this point you make a few discreet telephone calls, discover that prices have gone back to their original levels, and once more set the original transactions in motion. Only this time you plan to pass up Las Vegas.

The Long-Run Adjustment

Changes in domestic prices set in motion by the flow of trade between countries have the same effects on output as any changes in prices. For industries in which prices rise, profits are increased and resources are attracted to them. Where prices fall, however, profits decline and resources move out. Output rises in the former and declines in the latter until profits in the two are equalized and the long-run equilibrium is reached. Monopoloid influences and other market imperfections or restrictions may set limits beyond which the adjustments cannot go, but the tendency is always there.

In our whiskey-milk illustration, for example, international trade reduces the price of milk in the U.S. and increases the price of whiskey. Production of milk in the U.S. will decline and production of whiskey will rise until the producers in both industries are once more earning just a normal profit. The opposite trend will take place in England, where the price movements are in the opposite direction, but a new long-run equilibrium also will be established there.

These changes can be visualized as shifts along the production possibilities frontier in both countries, as shown in Figure 37–1.

The Gains from Trade

International trade enables both parties to gain from the exchange, in the sense that each country can have more goods than without trade. Without trade a nation will have to use large amounts of resources to produce high-cost items. With trade it can specialize in the things it does efficiently while trading with other countries to obtain its other needs. In the process, it can have more of everything.

Look at the whiskey-milk example we have been using. Before the trading operations began the price of milk in the U.S. was $1 per gallon and whiskey $5 per gallon. For another 5 gallons of milk to be obtained, resources would have to be shifted from whiskey production, requiring a 1 gallon reduction in whiskey out-

Figure 37-1
International Trade Brings a Shift Along the Production Possibilities Frontier

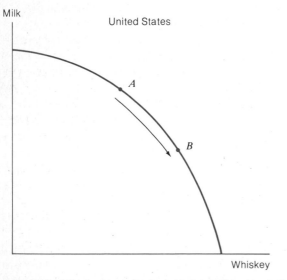 

As a result of the long run adjustment to international trade the U.S. produces more whiskey and less milk, while England produces more milk and less whiskey.

Figure 37-2
International Trade Enables Nations to Move Beyond the Production Possibilities Frontier

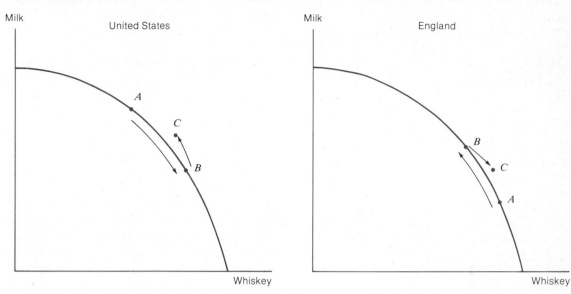

Specialization induced by international trade enables each nation to move from *A* to *B*. It trades part of its increased output of the specialized product for other goods that it can get on favorable terms in the international economy, ending up outside its domestic production possibilities frontier.

put. But if that gallon of whiskey were exported and sold in England, the proceeds would buy 10 gallons of milk. The net gain is exactly 5 gallons of milk, with no change in the amount of whiskey available for domestic use.

The same is true for England. For another gallon of whiskey to be obtained from domestic production, output of milk would have to be cut by 10 gallons. But with trade, that added gallon of whiskey could be obtained by exporting only 5 gallons of milk to the U.S. Here also there is a net gain of 5 gallons of milk.

At the end of the process of long-run adjustment, the gains at the margin are smaller, because the relative price ratios have been equalized at 1/8. At that ratio, 1 gallon of whiskey exported from the U.S. will bring 8 gallons of milk in England. This is a net gain of 3 gallons of milk when compared with producing it domestically, without trade, at a 1/5 ratio.

Correspondingly, in England 8 gallons of

domestic milk can be traded for 1 gallon of imported whiskey. This is a net gain of 2 gallons of milk, for without trade an additional gallon of whiskey could be obtained only by reducing output of milk by 10 gallons.

For the world economy as a whole there has been a net gain of 5 gallons of milk as a result of that last marginal trade. The gain was divided, with 3 gallons going to U.S. consumers and 2 gallons to English consumers. There is nothing magic about the source of those gains; they come from the specialization of each nation in the production it does most efficiently.

The gains from trade can be graphically shown in relation to the production possibilities frontier. They enable both parties to trade to move *beyond* the production possibilities frontier and have more than they would be able to produce on their own. This is shown in Figure 37–2.

In our whiskey-milk example the gains from trade accruing to the U.S. are pictured in

Figure 37-3
U.S. Gains from Whiskey-Milk Trade with England

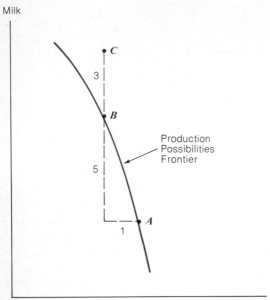

By producing more milk at home, the U.S. could get 5 gal of milk by reducing whiskey production by 1 gal. Alternatively, it can trade 1 gal of whiskey and get 8 gal of imported milk, for a net gain of 3 gal of milk. Instead of moving from A to B on the production possibilities frontier, it can move from A to C. At C it will have as much whiskey as at B, plus 3 gal of milk more than it would have at B.

Figure 37–3 to show the move beyond the domestic production possibilities frontier in detail.

The Terms of Trade

The division of the gains from international trade depends on the equilibrium price relationships established by the flow of trade. Those relationships are called the terms of trade. They may be favorable to countries specializing in capital-intensive exports if there is a general shortage of capital in the world economy. They may be favorable to land-extensive exports if there is a general lack of food or other products of agriculture, as there usually is during big wars. Furthermore, the terms of trade may shift as the world economy develops and changes; the introduction of synthetic rubber worsened the trading position of nations specializing in natural rubber exports, for example.

To pin this idea down, note in our whiskey-milk example that the 1/8 equilibrium price ratio between milk and whiskey established by trade between England and the U.S. left 60 percent of the gains with the U.S. and 40 percent with England. If the ratio had ended up less favorably to the whiskey exporter, say 1/7, the proportions would have been reversed. The total gain from trade would remain at 5 gallons, but the U.S. would gain only 2 gallons instead of 3.

The terms of trade between primary products (raw materials and foodstuffs) and manufactured goods are particularly important to the less developed countries, especially those that export the former and import the latter. A nation that exports raw materials and foodstuffs sells commodities whose prices fluctuate widely, and whose output can be a glut on the market for extended periods of time. When a country's exports are dominated by one or two such commodities, its whole economy will feel the repercussions of wide price swings and prolonged depression. Neither condition is good for economic development.

Some long-run changes in the terms of trade in the world economy may be in the making. The worldwide growth of population is beginning to press upon food supplies, to the benefit of food-exporting areas. The United States should be an important beneficiary of this development: the world's richest and most productive agricultural region is the U.S. Midwest, and it is the world's largest exporter of agricultural products. Another development is less favorable to the U.S. trading position.

World industrial expansion is pressing on the supply of minerals and fuels, pushing up their relative prices and benefiting their producers. Many third world countries are important exporters of minerals and fuels, although the bulk of the resources are owned by corporate giants based in the United States, Europe, and Japan. Many knowledgeable observers predict a movement in third world countries to gain control over those resources and to take action to raise the price at which the resources are sold, following the lead of the Arab nations and their oil. Finally, industrialization in some third world countries is reducing their dependence on imports of manufactured goods from the more advanced countries. As this trend continues, the trading advantages of manufacturers in the industrialized nations could diminish and the terms of trade could shift in favor of the industrializing sectors of the third world. Taken together, these long-run changes in agriculture, resources, and manufacturing mean that terms of trade throughout the world economy are changing, and the place of the third world countries is also shifting.

The International Economy

We have just sketched in nontechnical terms the basic propositions on which international economic relationships are founded. A brief summary is in order, because the matter is somewhat complex and was treated in highly compact fashion.

1. International trade is based on relative scarcities of the various factors of production, which vary from region to region and from country to country.

2. These relative scarcities would lead to different relative prices within countries if there were no trade.

3. Those different relative prices offer opportunities for private gain if trade is allowed, however, leading to a flow of trade between areas and nations.

4. The flow of trade sets in motion a long-run adjustment within the domestic economies of the trading nations that brings about greater specialization in export commodities.

5. Specialization is the source of real gains from trade that are divided among the trading nations according to the terms of trade that develop out of the national-international economic equilibrium.

These basic propositions lead to a fundamental policy proposition: international trade leads to increased output. As long as trade is free and unrestricted, following the profit-maximizing pattern of a competitive economy, it brings gains to both parties to the exchange. Under those conditions more trade is better than less. Any restrictions such as tariffs, quotas, exclusive trading rights, and other barriers to imports and exports reduce the amount of trade, reduce the gains, and leave everyone worse off.

The Principle of Comparative Advantage

The theoretical analysis of the basis for international trade is called the principle of *comparative advantage*. A nation has a comparative advantage in production of a commodity if its opportunity cost of producing the commodity is lower than that of a second nation. A corollary of that principle applies specifically to the case of two nations and two commodities: if a nation has a comparative advantage in one commodity the other nation *must* have a comparative advantage in the other.

Our whiskey-milk example was an illustration of the principle. The opportunity cost of producing a gallon of whiskey in the U.S. was 5 gallons of milk. In England the opportunity cost was 10 gallons of milk. We say, then, that the U.S. has a comparative advantage in whiskey production.

Looking at England, we see that the opportunity cost of producing milk is 0.1 gallon of whiskey. In the U.S. it is 0.2 gallon of whiskey. England has a comparative advantage in milk production.

All of this merely repeats the basic principle, but it is important for the reader to know the terminology used by economists and to have a careful statement of the theoretical principle.

- A nation has a **comparative advantage** in production of a good if its opportunity cost of producing it is less than another country's opportunity cost of producing the same good.

Absolute Advantage

At this point the student must be warned against one of the most common misconceptions about international trade, one very widely held. It is this: a nation exports those things that it produces more cheaply than other nations, and imports those things produced more cheaply elsewhere. The example usually given is something like bananas in Guatemala. It takes little land, labor, and capital to produce bananas in Guatemala, while if they were produced in hothouses in the U.S., it would require much more land, labor, and capital. *Therefore,* the argument runs, the U.S. imports bananas from Guatemala. The argument sounds plausible, and we are all familiar with it; indeed, we were all taught it by the teachers and geography books we had in elementary school.

Well, there's no help for it: you'll just have to unlearn it, because it's wrong.

In this chapter the principle was never stated that way. If we were to translate the case of Guatemalan bananas properly into the principle of comparative advantage, it might turn out this way: the cost of producing bananas in Guatemala is less, *relative to the cost of producing other things,* than it is in the U.S. The direct

comparison of physical costs of production between the two nations must never be made.

A little reflection and some specific examples will show why this is so. Example: it takes less land, labor, and capital to grow wheat in the Mohawk Valley of New York, or in tidewater Virginia, than it does in North Dakota or Kansas. In fact, tidewater Virginia is known for some of the highest wheat yields per acre in the world, much higher than the wheat-growing areas of the Midwest. Why, then, is no wheat grown there? Because other crops are *more* profitable. The opportunity costs of producing wheat are too high. The area produces peanuts instead and Smithfield hams from hogs fed on peanuts.

Another example: your rich uncle may be a better typist than his secretary, but it would be foolish for him to do his own typing. He can earn perhaps $500 per day as a businessman, while he can hire a typist for $40 per day. He won't give up $500 in order to save $40, even though he could do more typing than the secretary in one day.

When lower real costs of production exist, an *absolute advantage* prevails. This is true of wheat production in tidewater Virginia or your uncle's typing skills. A nation has an absolute advantage in production of a commodity if for a given amount of effort, it can produce more of the commodity than another nation. Yet it is quite possible for a nation with an absolute advantage in a commodity to specialize in other things while the nation with an absolute disadvantage in that commodity specializes in producing it and exporting it. Like Kansas wheat or your uncle's typist.

Take our whiskey-milk example, for instance. Suppose the U.S. had an absolute advantage over England in production of both whiskey and milk. That is, suppose it could produce both commodities at lower cost in units of land-labor-capital than England, as indicated in Table 37–5. *Yet this makes no difference to the flow of trade.* The original price ratios on which your profit-making series

Table 37–5
U.S. Has an Absolute Advantage in Production of Both Milk and Whiskey

	U.S.		England	
	Price	Units of Cost	Price	Units of Cost
Milk	$1/gal	5	1s/gal	10
Whiskey	$5/gal	25	£1/gal	100

of trades was based have not changed, and the profit-making behavior of business managers will not have changed. The original flow of trade set in motion by the price relationship will develop. Indeed, turn the situation around and give England an absolute advantage in both commodities. The flow of trade will continue just as before.

International trade is based on comparative advantages, not absolute advantages. It may appear at times that absolute advantages are important, for a nation with an absolute advantage in a product may also have a comparative advantage in it. But it is the comparative advantage that is significant.

Don't be trapped by the following question, a favorite on economics examinations:

> True or false: a nation will specialize in production of goods that it can produce at lower cost than other nations.

That statement is false. It would be true only if the phrase "relative to other products" is inserted after "at lower cost." Or if the phrase "opportunity cost" were to replace the word "cost."

- A nation has an **absolute advantage** in producing a good if its cost in terms of units of land, labor, and capital is less than another country's.

Some Qualifications

The astute reader of this chapter will already have identified several assumptions in the analysis that should be made explicit. First is the assumption of full employment. The illustrations of the production possibilities frontier were all based on the proposition that without trade a nation would produce along the frontier and not within it. Trade would not bring unemployment.

This assumption may not be correct in the real world. A nation may export capital-intensive products and import labor-intensive ones, making it more difficult to maintain full employment at home. A shift in relative costs may create difficult employment problems in some areas or industries if international markets are suddenly lost. The resulting unemployment may more than offset the gains from trade.

Two points can be made in defense of the full-employment assumption. First, macroeconomic policies can keep any economy at or close to full employment with any pattern of world trade that may prevail. Second, special employment, education, and development programs can ease the transition of labor from an industry with declining exports. In the long run, the gains from trade can be expected to prevail. There is a second important assumption in the theory: market prices within individual countries reflect the real relative scarcities that prevail. This assumption may also be untrue:

1. Monopolies and market control may distort scarcity relationships in favor of the owners of monopolized resources or firms.

2. Governments may subsidize export industries to increase domestic employment.

3. Producers may not bear the full costs of production (pollution, social insurance, and so on), enabling them to obtain lower relative costs than foreign competitors.

All of these potential distortions are serious. By preventing relative prices from fully reflecting relative scarcities, they prevent the welfare-maximizing level of trade (and sometimes direction of trade) from developing. Their most significant effect, however, is in distorting the distribution of the gains from trade *within* a nation, in favor of monopolists or favored industries or producers in general.

The Special Economic Position of the United States

The American economy has a unique advantage in the development of new products that is unmatched anywhere else in the world. A large domestic market of over 200 million people with a high average income provides conditions favorable for marketing new or improved products. A flourishing educational system creates the skilled labor force necessary to produce new products. Finally, investment in research and development provides the technological basis for innovation. Innovation prospers under these conditions and attracts capital from a large pool of retained earnings and savings. Innovations of all kinds tend to originate in the U.S. economy and spread to other parts of the world, not because Americans are more innovative than other people, but because the forces of production tend to foster innovation and people take advantage of their opportunities.

New products pass through a cycle of development as they find their place in the consumer's pattern of demand. A foreign market was probably present from the start, particularly among the more affluent in foreign countries. But the foreign market expands and becomes large enough for foreign production to replace imports from the United States. At the same time, standardization of production takes place in the U.S. economy as firms seek to cut costs through mass production. Mechanization breaks down complex labor skills into their component parts, and less skilled labor replaces the highly skilled workers who were needed in the early stages of innovation and growth. At this point in the development of the industry, U.S. producers begin to lose their comparative advantage to foreign producers. The advantage created by relatively abundant human capital in the U.S. is lost as the changing technology of production uses labor of lesser skills, and the advantage shifts to nations with relatively abundant unskilled labor.

According to this theory of *product cycles,* the U.S. economy has a comparative advantage in new products for relatively affluent consumers, and for products that use highly skilled labor in the initial stages of development. Innovation continues, however, to a second stage during which production techniques are simplified and foreign markets expand. In this stage the U.S. comparative advantage declines, and firms in the U.S. industry find themselves in difficulty. Examples include such diverse industries as steel products, automobiles, electrical equipment and electronic components, pharmaceutical and chemical products, and various types of machinery. In the end, a third stage can develop in which imports from abroad penetrate the U.S. market and U.S. production declines.

The source of U.S. advantages in international trade rest on engineering and scientific talents and skilled labor, together with a large and affluent domestic market. Anything that interferes with or modifies those advantages will damage the economy. For example, starting in the 1950s and continuing through the 1970s much of the U.S. comparative advantage in international trade was lost as a result of the cold war military buildup, space exploration, and the Vietnam War. Large increases in government spending for those purposes drew skilled labor, engineers and scientists from the private sector. Wages and salaries for people with highly developed skills were bid upward, and they become relatively scarce rather than relatively plentiful. As that trend developed, costs of production in the U.S. rose relative to costs of production overseas for the manufactured products in which the U.S. had a comparative advantage. American manufacturing industries began to feel the impact of reduced foreign sales and foreign penetration of the U.S. market.

This "demand reversal," as it has come to be called by economists, was the indirect result of the U.S. effort to maintain world political and military hegemony. The irony is that it undermined the economic base of that hegemony. As Pogo put it, "We have met the enemy and they are us."[1]

We cannot afford to ignore the basic forces of production. America's place in the world economy rests heavily on allocation of a large portion of our economic surplus to science, engineering, education, and innovation. That is the path the U.S. took to affluence. Without those expenditures there is no way to sustain the affluent American standard of living. Diversion of resources into economically wasteful expenditures such as military spending is the long-run path to the poorhouse.

- A **product cycle** is the series of stages in the development of an innovation resulting in growth and then decline of exports followed by rising imports.

The Movement Toward Free Trade

From the mid-1930s into the 1960s the United States led a worldwide movement to reduce tariffs and other barriers to world trade. In recent years, however, the trade liberalization movement has slowed down both here and abroad. In the late 1960s the United States began to swing away from its policy commitment to freer trade and started a move toward greater protection for domestic industry. At the present time the philosophy of *free trade* is fighting a delaying action against a revived protectionism, both in the United States and elsewhere.

The heyday of U.S. tariff *protection* was the 1920s. Back in the days when a President could say, "The business of America is business," the tariff acts of 1921 and 1922 and the Smoot-Hawley Act of 1930 moved tariffs to their highest levels in the nation's history. The New Deal turned this policy around. The Trade Agreements Act of 1934 enabled the President to negotiate tariff reductions with other countries, with the same benefits to be made available to other trading nations. Some progress was made prior to World War II, but this was a period of economic nationalism throughout the world and the U.S. policy ran against the tide.

The world situation changed after World War II. Problems of reconstruction were so great that twenty-two important trading nations set aside their special national interests to sign the General Agreement on Tariffs and Trade (GATT). This agreement established a general code for commercial policy: all nations were to be treated alike, and discriminatory treatment was barred. In addition, quantitative restrictions such as important quotas were prohibited (except under special circumstances). The most important result of GATT's establishment, however, was a series of general tariff reductions.

U.S. tariffs were greatly reduced. In 1934 the average U.S. tariff duty was 48 percent of the value of the imported item. By 1970 it was about 8 percent. Similar patterns prevail among the other GATT nations. By 1970, tariffs had reached their lowest levels in this century. The freeing of world trade after World War II was a very important factor in

---

[1]"The enemy is within the gates; it is with our own luxury, our own folly, our own criminality that we have to contend," Marcus Tullius Cicero, 63 B.C.

the expansion of world trade and helped sustain the great era of economic growth that followed World War II.

- **Free trade** is a policy in which tariffs and other barriers to trade are absent.

- **Protection** is a policy of protecting domestic industries from foreign competition using tariffs and other restrictions.

Economic Blocs

Concurrent with the move toward freer world trade, regional economic groups of nations have formed. The chief *"blocs"* are:

1. The Soviet–East European group.

2. The European "Common Market."

3. The European Free Trade Association.

There are other economic groupings as well. The Latin American countries have taken some steps toward common international trade policies, and the nations formerly part of the empires belonging to France and Great Britain maintain special economic ties with those countries.

Economic integration proceeded in Europe along with the GATT tariff reductions. In 1957 the Treaty of Rome established the European Economic Community (EEC) of six nations— France, West Germany, Italy, Belgium, Netherlands, and Luxembourg. These countries agreed to remove tariffs and other trade barriers among themselves; to allow free movement of labor, capital, and business enterprise within the community; to establish common policies toward agriculture, transport, and business practices; to harmonize their monetary and fiscal policies; and to adopt a uniform external tariff on trade with the outside world. Despite problems of transition, the move toward a single western European economy has been successful. Measures designed to lead to a common monetary system have begun. A European *common market,* the name given to the emerging European economy, appeared.

Seven European nations that for a variety of reasons did not join in the Treaty of Rome formed a looser economic federation in 1960 called the European Free Trade Association (EFTA). This "outer seven," as they were called, included Great Britain, Norway, Sweden, Denmark, Austria, Switzerland, and Portugal. The members of this group also reduced tariffs among themselves, but have not moved toward a common external tariff. The main purpose of EFTA is to protect its members from adverse economic effects of the common market set up by the "inner six" EEC countries. Denmark joined the Common Market in 1973 and Great Britain in 1975, and the "Outer Seven" became the "Outer Five."

The Soviet–East European bloc was far more political in its origins. It was formed in 1949 as a response both to the recovery of western Europe under the U.S.-sponsored Marshall Plan for economic assistance and to the increasing conflicts between East and West during the Cold War. It is called the Council of Economic Mutual Assistance (CEMA) or COMECON. Initially it stressed trade agreements between the USSR and the eastern European countries (which were highly favorable to the USSR); but during the 1950s emphasis shifted toward investment and economic development designed to create complementary production, enlarged trade, and closer economic cooperation. For example, the USSR and four East European nations joined to develop Soviet phosphate deposits, which will provide fertilizers to be exported to eastern Europe. Czechoslovakia provided financing for electric power stations that feed power into a six-nation electric power grid. Natural gas from the USSR is used in eastern Europe, shipped in pipelines built from pipe made in the eastern European countries.

Growth of these and other economic blocs are a paradox. Internally they provide for reduced tariffs and elimination of other barriers to trade. But if they sustain barriers to trade with other countries, even at reduced tariffs, they can become a threat by diverting trade to internal producers and away from those outside the bloc. If firms within the European Common Market supply a larger share of Common Market needs, producers in the outer five will supply a smaller share because of the Common Market tariffs against outsiders. This can cause a shift in resource allocation away from lower-cost producers outside the Common Market to higher-cost producers inside. It was fear of this "trade diversion effect" that led to formation of the European Free Trade Association among the countries that did not join the Common Market.

The Shift Toward Economic Nationalism

The existence of strong economic blocs and the slowing down of the movement toward free trade combined with increased world tensions in the late 1960s to start a move toward greater trade restrictions. The worldwide inflation of the 1960s and 1970s made many nations concerned about their openness to unfavorable economic developments imported from abroad. Worries about stability of the international financial system contributed to feelings that nations should protect their own interests. The threat of rapid technological change and the spread of international corporations added to the uneasiness.

In the United States, for example, inflation raised costs of production for several products subject to sharp competition from foreign producers. Shoes, textiles, clothing, automobiles, and certain types of electrical equipment were faced with rising imports from the Far East. Steel produced in Europe and Japan began to penetrate U.S. markets. Electrical equipment such as transistors and television sets produced in Japan and other Asian countries came to dominate U.S. markets in the 1970s, and by 1980 imported automobiles accounted for over 25 percent of U.S. sales. Meanwhile, the European Common Market worked out a program of agricultural subsidies combined with tariffs

and import restrictions designed to protect its farmers. West Germany developed a system of subsidies for domestic producers to promote sales abroad. Japan has long had a network of legislation intended to limit foreign penetration of its home market. It was clear by 1970 that a battle was forming between the advocates of free trade and the concept of one big international economy and the proponents of special economic interests and *economic nationalism.*

- An **economic bloc** is a group of countries that acts as a unit in some or all aspects of international economic affairs.
- **Economic nationalism** is the philosophy that a nation's economic policies should be designed to strengthen national interests.

The Philosophy of Economic Nationalism

Restrictions on foreign trade are rooted in attitudes of patriotism and nationalism that put national or local interests at very high levels of priority, and that look on foreigners with fear and suspicion. In a world of sovereign national states it is commonly assumed that benefits to one nation mean less for the others—that there is a limited amount of employment or trade available in the world and that one nation's advantage is another's disadvantage. This belief flies in the face of the theory of comparative advantage, which shows that economic cooperation through trade leads to more for all.

There is nevertheless a modicum of validity to the ideas of the economic nationalists. *At any given level of world trade,* the division of the gain from trade depends on the terms of trade. It may be possible for a nation to gain at the expense of others by so manipulating prices and the flow of trade as to move the terms of trade in its favor. A large portion of the bargaining and jockeying among nations involves this principle. The difficulty is that two or more can play the same game. The long-run result is a series of restrictions on trade that move all the participants to lower levels of real welfare. Temporary advantages are destroyed by retaliation that leaves everyone worse off.

What a nation can do to improve its position in world trade is to promote lower costs of production at home by investing in transportation facilities, promoting capital accumulation and technological advances, and improving the health, education, and efficiency of its work force. Achieving those goals will enable it to cut production costs in the long run. Its exports will be more attractive to foreign buyers and its position in world trade will be strengthened. To achieve the maximum benefits, however, it will have to trade freely with others and take advantage of international specialization. Such action will shift some of the benefits of the nation's improved efficiency to others and the gains will be worldwide.

The economic nationalist, on the other hand, argues that imports take jobs away from domestic workers. They also reduce profits made by domestic producers and thereby slow down capital accumulation. Exports, on the other hand, provide employment and promote profits, leading to a stronger domestic economy. Furthermore, new industries may be hampered by having to compete with imports from firmly established foreign producers. Finally, some industries are essential to national defense and should be sheltered from foreign competition. These arguments, however plausible they may seem, are *all* fallacious. Even the last two, which have some validity, cannot justify barriers against trade.

Keeping Out Imports: The Methods

There are seven methods generally used to keep imports from entering domestic markets. A tax on imports is the most common. The *tariff,* as it is called, is usually a specified percentage of the market value of the item. By raising the selling price to the ultimate consum-

er, tariffs reduce the quantity consumers are willing to buy and leave a larger share of the market to domestic producers. They also enable domestic producers to sell their output at higher prices. If the domestic industry is competitive it will have a larger number of producers, after the long-run adjustment. If there are significant monopoloid elements in the domestic industry, the profits will be higher.

Imposing a *quota* is a second way to reduce imports. Quotas limit the amount of a product that may be imported, and directly reduce the supply available for sale in domestic markets. The United States has import quotas on sugar, for example, in order to benefit high-cost producers within the country.

Internal excise taxes are another method. For example, the U.S. excise tax on diamonds raises their sale price, reduces the quantity purchased, and results in smaller imports. The purpose of this tax is to raise revenues, not to protect domestic producers, but its effect is to reduce imports when there is little or no domestic production.

Administrative and public health *rules* are used to keep out contagious diseases and insects harmful to agriculture. They are sometimes enforced as a means of protecting domestic producers. *Government purchasing* is very often used to favor domestic industry over foreign, as when the U.S. government pursues "Buy American" policies.

Systems of *import permits* are often used by developing countries to limit imports generally, and to channel them to necessary products. A country may not have enough foreign currency plus gold to pay for all that its citizens wish to import. It uses import permits to limit the total amount its citizens can spend abroad and particularly to cut down on buying luxuries. Finally, a nation may require that foreign trade be carried on by *government agencies.* This is the practice of the Soviet Union, the East European countries and China, but some non-Communist countries (Egypt, Burma) use the same method.

- A **tariff** is a tax on imports.
- A **quota** is a limit on the quantity of a good that can be imported (or exported).

Keeping Out Imports: The Rationale

Most of the pleas for import restrictions make little sense—except to the workers and business firms in the industries affected. Here are the chief arguments.

Protection defends a high standard of living. This general statement is usually made as a self-evident proposition without further elaboration. Yet there is hardly anything better for a nation's standard of living than cheap imports. Light from the sun is free: should we board up all our windows and expand our electric light production? Will this raise living standards? Domestic living standards will be raised by low-cost imports in exactly the same way that they would be raised by a new and lower-cost production method at home.

A variation on that theme is the argument that *protection defends high-wage workers against low-wage foreign competition.* This issue is more complex. First, we know that low-cost imports produced by low-wage labor raise real incomes for everyone. Protecting the economic position of high-wage workers reduces the real incomes of everyone else. Second, the dollars earned by foreign producers from their sales in the U.S. find their way back by way of purchases of U.S. goods. This means that U.S. workers will be employed in producing those exports. As long as the U.S. exports goods that use relatively large proportions of human capital, where we have a comparative advantage in world trade, U.S. wages will remain high. Third, restrictions on imports cause other nations to impose restrictions on U.S. exports. This hurts, and shifts the burden to other sectors of the labor force. To sum up, restricting imports to protect workers in one sector of the economy hurts all consumers of the imported goods and, if foreign countries retaliate, will also hurt workers in export industries.

These conclusions depend, however, on our ability to maintain full employment at home. For example, when low-cost imports of textiles and clothing start coming into the U.S., domestic production and employment in those industries may well fall. It would be nice if the effect were gradual, workers were retrained for higher skilled jobs, and jobs were available at full-employment levels. Those three conditions may not be met, however. Under those circumstances an import tariff or quota might be justified as a temporary measure to ease the transition and give workers, firms, and the national government time to adapt to the new conditions. The problem here is that the tariff may not be temporary and the adaptation might never occur.

In the long run, there are three ways to protect the standard of living and prosperity of an economy that is freely open to world trade. First, a high rate of capital accumulation, replacing older capital equipment rapidly, maintains productive efficiency and rapid increases in productivity. Second, investment in human capital—health, education, scientific research—pays off in the skills required for high incomes in an age of advanced technologies. Third, competition in the domestic economy is necessary for international competitiveness. Monopoloid economic structures provide a protected position for business firms and reduce their incentive to keep up with the rest of the world. When these three principles are not implemented, any nation's economy can get into difficulties, and the industries most heavily affected will start crying for help in the form of import restrictions.

Another argument of the economic nationalists is that *protection is justified as a means of equalizing the competitive position of domestic producers.* Foreign manufacturers may have "unfair" advantages if their workers are not unionized, if their workers get pensions through public rather than private social insurance programs, and so on and on. These advantages should be neutralized by tariffs, runs the argument, so that competition can then be carried on fairly and evenly. This seemingly valid argument, which appeals to our feelings of sportsmanship and fair play, has little to recommend it. If foreigners wish to subsidize their exports, our standards of living are raised. Why should we hurt ourselves by applying a tax that merely serves to raise the prices of what we buy? The assumption is, of course, that we are smart enough to maintain full employment at home by use of proper domestic economic policies. Under those conditions, the "fair competition" argument makes no sense.

It begins to carry weight during depressions. When unemployment is high, any nation may be tempted to export some of its unemployment by encouraging its producers to "dump" exports abroad at unprofitable prices, while sustaining prices at home. This can be done by export subsidies and import tariffs and quotas, and was quite common during the depression of the 1930s. Once started, however, these policies bring retaliation by other countries, who are also affected by the depression. They raise tariffs and impose quotas as well. The result is fewer jobs and higher unemployment in both countries. "Beggar thy neighbor" policies would work if the neighbor would only stand still for them. He won't, however, and everyone is worse off.

A variation on this theme may occur if a single industry in one country has overproduced and dumps surplus output in other countries, to the detriment of employment and profits in that industry in the importing countries. Macroeconomic policies designed to keep aggregate demand at full-employment levels are not flexible enough to handle that problem, and counterpolicies may be called for. The problem here is that domestic special interests may try to keep out low-cost goods that reflect long-run comparative advantages by arguing that the low prices represent unfair "dumping" at prices below production costs.

Another form of unfair competition may occur if a monopoly or cartel deliberately sets out to destroy producers in other countries by selling at prices below production costs. After the local producers are gone the price of the product is then raised to monopolistic levels. In cases like that retaliatory quotas or tariffs may well be justified.

These exceptions to the general rule against trade restrictions have to be carefully applied. It is very easy to use tariffs to eliminate comparative advantages under the theory that competitive conditions are being equalized. It is not enough to show that foreign producers have lower costs. Those lower costs are reflections of comparative advantage in most cases. Where they are artificially created by public policy, and are relatively permanent, we should take full advantage of the subsidy by buying as great a quantity of the subsidized products as we can. Only if there is *temporary* selling below cost to accommodate business errors or to generate a monopoly position are countermeasures justified.

We now come to two arguments for protection of domestic industry that have partial validity, the *national defense* and *infant industries* arguments. In both cases, however, protection by tariffs, quotas, or other trade restrictions is the more expensive method of achieving the desired goals. Direct subsidies are the cheaper way.

The national defense argument is that *protection is required for the survival of industries for national defense.* During time of war it may be necessary to produce highly complex instruments, like watches or computers, requiring skills that cannot be developed overnight. A permanent supply of labor and scientific skills must be maintained, and the only way to do it is by sustaining domestic producers during times of peace. This point is well taken, but it does not follow that trade restrictions are the best way to achieve the goal.

The problem is that tariffs and other trade restrictions raise the price of a product irrespective of whether it is imported or produced at home. While the consumer pays a higher price for both the imported and the domestically produced goods, the domestic manufacturers get the benefit only from the higher price of the latter. A direct subsidy, on the other hand, would have to pay only the equivalent of the benefit to the domestic producers, and would therefore be less costly than a tariff.

One might wonder why subsidies are not used instead of tariffs. There are two reasons. Tariffs are a hidden tax, while subsidies are obvious. It is easier for special interests to get away with a hidden tax than to be continually in the public gaze while slurping at the trough of public revenues. Furthermore, a tariff bears most heavily on consumers (which means low-income families more than high-income families), while taxes to pay for a subsidy would come primarily from the progressive federal income tax. A tariff is a means by which the poor can be made to bear more of the burden than the rich.

The *infant industries* argument is related to the much larger problem of economic development. It holds that protection is needed to enable new industries to survive against the competition of established producers abroad. The protection need only be temporary, however, until the domestic industry is mature enough to withstand foreign competition. Comparative advantages are derived from more than the natural endowments of different nations. They change as the labor force grows, capital is accumulated, and income levels change. The development of commerce and industry involves a learning process in which labor and business enterprise develop skills that reduce costs. And expansion of industry may bring long-run cost reductions because of the development of peripheral services in other sectors of the economy. Yet if an industry is fully exposed to foreign competition, it may never be able to grow enough to take advantage of the learning process and external economies, and the whole process of economic development may be aborted. Tariffs or import

quotas may not only protect the domestic producers, they may also encourage foreign firms to leap over the barriers by establishing manufacturing plants within the tariff walls, thereby attracting foreign capital for economic development.

This argument has great appeal in developing countries. Indeed, its greatest supporters were found in Germany and the United States during the nineteenth century, and appear in many of today's developing nations. One must note, however, that vigilance is required to assure that the tariffs really are temporary. The danger is a political one: a truly infant industry doesn't have the political clout to get tariff protection, yet by the time it has grown enough to be politically strong it probably doesn't need the tariff. In addition, just as in the case of the national defense argument for protection, direct subsidies are a cheaper method of achieving the same goals. In the case of a truly underdeveloped country, however, the fastest path to economic growth may be through squeezing the living standards of the poor a little further in order to free resources for development. If the nation is sure that the benefits do not go to the wealthy but are channeled into economic growth, a tariff that protects infant industries may well be an effective device to stimulate economic development.

The Internationalist Outlook

Knowledge of the basic economics of international trade inevitably pushes one toward the view that the world economy is a seamless web in which the advantages of one nation both contribute to and depend on the welfare of other nations. A peaceful world in which trade between nations results in greater welfare for all is one of the great visions that is opened up. The ties between nations that are created by trade can promote world peace; if it can be shown that the material interests of people

JOHN STUART MILL ON FREE TRADE

But the economical advantages of commerce are surpassed in importance by those of its effects which are intellectual and moral. It is hardly possible to overrate the value, in the present low state of human improvement, of placing human beings in contact with persons dissimilar to themselves, and with modes of thought and action unlike those with which they are familiar. Commerce is now, what war once was, the principal source of this contact. Commercial adventures from more advanced countries have generally been the first civilizers of barbarians. And commerce is the purpose of the far greater part of the communication which takes place between civilized nations. Such communication has always been, and is peculiarly in the present age, one of the primary sources of progress. To human beings, who, as hitherto educated, can scarcely cultivate even a good quality without running it into a fault, it is indispensable to be perpetually comparing their own notions and customs with the experience and example of persons in different circumstances from themselves: and there is

no nation which does not need to borrow from others, not merely particular arts or practices, but essential points of character in which its own type is inferior. Finally, commerce first taught nations to see with good will the wealth and prosperity of one another. Before, the patriot, unless sufficiently advanced in culture to feel the world his country, wished all countries weak, poor, and ill-governed, but his own: he now sees in their wealth and progress a direct source of wealth and progress to his own country. It is commerce which is rapidly rendering war obsolete, by strengthening and multiplying the personal interests which are in natural opposition to it. And it may be said without exaggeration that the great extent and rapid increase of international trade, in being the principal guarantee of the peace of the world, is the great permanent security for the uninterrupted progress of the ideas, the institutions, and the character of the human race.

From John Stuart Mill, *Principles of Political Economy*, Book III, Chapter XVII (1848).

depend on peaceful continuation of international economic relations, a strong force for world peace is created.

Free world trade is a fragile thing, however. Exclusive control over key raw materials may give the business enterprises of one nation an advantage over those of another. Special interests may demand special privileges in domestic markets and may be politically strong enough to obtain them. Working people may fear loss of jobs. Militarism and nationalism may create the ideological base that makes possible a move toward economic nationalism. Unsettled political conditions in the world, such as a continuing crisis in the Middle East or long-standing international antagonisms, may encourage nationalist economic policies. These uncertainties and hostilities can open the way to economic policies that exacerbate existing difficulties, with subsequent retaliation and a

heightening of world tensions, suspicions, and hostilities. International economic policies can add to the threat system that makes the condition of man in the modern world poorer than it might be.

The free trade, internationalist outlook rests on the proposition that trade takes place among equals, as, for example, between a large American steel company and a large German chemical corporation. That assumption of trade among equals is often unrealistic. It is modified by the existence of international corporate giants that deal with small firms in various countries. It is modified by selective protectionist measures, such as U.S. controls over imports of steel products that seek to keep prices up for the benefit of U.S. producers. It is modified by government subsidies to exporters in the advanced industrial countries, such as those the German government provides for its major heavy industries. It is modified by international cartels that raise prices artificially, such as the oil cartel run by the Organization of Petroleum Exporting Countries. Business firms and nations able to organize and maintain these special advantages can shift the terms of trade in their favor and against those firms and countries that are unable to do so. In particular, the rich industrial nations tend to be in strong bargaining positions and the poor third world countries in weak positions. The oil cartel is an exception to the general rule. Although free international trade among equals is clearly beneficial to all, it is an ideal that is extremely difficult to achieve in a world characterized by unequal agglomerations of political and economic power.

Summary

Relative scarcities of the factors of production vary from country to country. They are the basis of international trade. Without trade they lead to differences in relative prices of final goods which, in turn, would bring traders into operation to take advantage of the different relative prices and make a profit through trade.

The flow of trade starts a process of adjustment in the trading nations that leads to increased specialization in production of goods for export. The adjustment involves both relative prices and resource shifts into the export industries. One result of the flow of trade is a tendency toward a worldwide general equilibrium in which relative prices are equalized between nations.

Specialization provides gains from trade which are divided among the trading nations according to the terms of trade that develop out of the national-international equilibrium.

The fundamental policy proposition derived from the analysis of international trade is that free and unrestricted trade brings gains to both parties. As long as a nation is able to maintain full employment, more trade is better than less.

Nevertheless, the movement toward free trade that dominated world trade policy for twenty years after World War II began to give way to moves toward economic nationalism as the great postwar economic expansion ebbed. Barriers to trade such as tariffs, quotas, and other impediments to imports, which diminish trade and reduce the benefits from trade, began to appear once more. These restrictions are usually justified by arguments that the entire economy of a nation will benefit from trade restrictions, but all of those rationales fly in the face of the analysis that free trade benefits a nation. They are all arguments for special advantages for private economic interests that must ultimately be paid for by the general public. Indeed, outright subsidies are generally less costly than trade restrictions.

Protectionist arguments make some sense only in the case of underdeveloped countries trying to develop industry. Industrial development may lead to comparative advantages in strong export industries, but the development may not occur unless those industries are protected initially. Even that protectionist argument would lead only to relatively temporary trade barriers, however. In the long run, a free trade policy among equal trading partners is beneficial to everyone. But in the modern world traders are often unequal, and the gains from trade can lie very heavily with the strong rather than the weak.

Key Concepts

comparative advantage	free trade	economic nationalism
absolute advantage	protection	tariff
product cycle	economic bloc	quota

For Discussion

1. Explain why patterns of world trade are determined largely by the opportunity costs of production among nations.

2. Suppose the boss can type faster and more efficiently than his or her secretary. Should the boss do the typing? Explain.

3. Show how the flow of world trade tends to equalize opportunity costs of production among nations.

4. What determines how the gains from trade are divided among trading nations? Explain.

5. Should the United States impose higher tariffs on imported automobiles to protect the jobs of U.S. autoworkers?

6. Should the United States reduce tariffs on imported automobiles to benefit U.S. consumers?

Chapter 38

The Balance of Payments and Exchange Rates Between Currencies

The international trade whose sources were examined in the previous chapter also have financial aspects. They are explained in this chapter. We start with a brief look at the place of the U.S. economy in world trade and investment. This leads to an explanation of the U.S. balance of international payments and its impact on both the domestic and the world economies. The balance of payments affects exchange rates among currencies, which are examined next: the system of fixed exchange rates of 1944–1970, its breakup in the late 1960s and early 1970s, and the system of flexible, but managed, exchange rates that now prevails. In the course of this discussion a great deal will be said about the political economy of the international financial system as nations jockey for economic and political advantage.

The United States in the World Economy

The United States is the most important single participant in world trade, accounting for about 17 percent of world exports and imports. We also provide about half of all the world's savings—because of our affluence and large population—which also makes us the largest source of funds for international investment. This economic position makes the U.S. dollar the most important of the world's currencies and gives it a key place in the international financial system. West Germany and Japan are beginning to challenge U.S. leadership in world trade as their exports and imports grow, although they are far behind the U.S. in foreign investments. As their role in world trade increases, U.S. predominance declines, however, and we can expect a gradual shift in world trade and financial patterns as these trends continue.

World trade is growing in significance for the U.S. economy. In 1980 U.S. exports were equal in value to 7 percent of GNP, up from only 3 percent a decade earlier. This proportion remains low when compared with other important developed economies. The countries of western Europe (West Germany, France, United Kingdom, Italy), as well as Japan and Canada, sell some 10 to 15 percent of their GNP abroad.

International Trade and Employment

An important segment of employment in the U.S. economy now depends on international trade. Studies by several U.S. government agencies estimate that about 4.6 million workers were employed in export-related jobs in 1980, up from 3.5 million in 1973 and double the amount in 1965. About 16 percent of all jobs in manufacturing involve an export product, more than double the percentage in 1965.

Much more attention has been given recently to the effect of imports on unemployment, particularly in the automobile and steel industries. The same studies cited above indicate that imports of manufactured goods resulted in about 2.6 million fewer jobs in 1980, up from 1.8 million in 1970. The loss of employment due to imports is approximately equal to the increase in employment in export industries during that period.

These estimates indicate a standoff. While some workers may lose jobs because of increased imports, others gain employment by producing exports. They may well be different workers, in different industries, in different parts of the country, and economic readjustments may be painful. But there is no evidence that the growing participation of the U.S. economy in world trade over the last decade has had a significant effect on employment and unemployment as a whole.

The U.S. and International Investment

The United States is the largest supplier of capital to the international economy. United States private foreign investments as of 1979 were estimated by the Department of Commerce at about $435 billion. That figure is surely an underestimate, however. It represents the "book value" of foreign investments, which usually means their cost at the time they were acquired rather than their present value. The total increased by almost $57 billion in 1979.

We do not have comparable figures for other major nations, although we know that private foreign investment in the U.S. reached a total of $258 billion in 1979. A recent estimate made by the author, based on available data that unfortunately leaves much to be desired, is that U.S. private foreign investment in the nonsocialist countries amounts to about 60–65 percent of all private foreign investment in those countries. The estimate includes private foreign investment in the U.S.

The Dollar as a Key Currency

The dominant position of the United States in today's world economy has come about primarily because of U.S. economic growth and the large annual savings created by a hard-working, thrifty, acquisitive, and success-oriented people. The very size of the U.S. national income means that U.S. imports will be large. Its advanced technology assures large exports. Large amounts of savings create a spillover into international investment. All of this adds up to a position of dominance in the international economy with respect to both trade and investment. Contributing to the strong U.S. position was the historical fact of two great world wars, in which the trade and investment positions of the major western European nations were seriously eroded: Britain, France, and Germany lost ground during the wars while the U.S. forged ahead in technology, capacity to produce, and international investments. But those changes merely hastened a development that would have come anyway.

Any nation whose trade and capital exports dominate the world economy will take on added importance in the international financial system. This is true of the United States at the present time. Since U.S. exports and imports are the largest in the world, foreign business firms, banks, and central banks find it highly convenient to hold bank accounts in New York banks. Their dollar accounts can readily be used to carry out the many and varied types of transactions required in international trade; and other firms and banks are willing to accept dollars because they know that the dollars can be used when they have to make payments. In this fashion the dollar became a sort of international money, which is generally acceptable in making payments in many international transactions.

The British pound was in a similar position in the years before 1914, for largely the same reason, and it still retains some of its importance as a form of international money because trade among the former nations of the British Empire remains important. The West German mark is becoming more significant as an international money, too, also for the same reasons; West German trade and capital exports are important elements in the world economy.

The dollar is the most important *key currency,* however. About 75–80 percent of all deposits in the Eurobank system are in dollars. The price of oil in world markets is denominated in dollars. The world's central banks hold a large portion of their monetary reserves in U.S. dollars: $160 billion in 1979. Just as the U.S. is the most important unit in world trade, so the U.S. dollar is the most important currency.

- A **key currency** is one in which many nations hold a portion of their international monetary reserves.

The Balance of Payments

Trade, investment, and other transactions lead to a huge volume of transactions between the United States and other countries. Just like the many transactions a family engages in, they all must be settled, and payments must equal income. Debt may increase or decrease if credit is extended, but even those transactions are balanced by the debtor's promise to pay, which the creditor takes in exchange for the funds advanced to the debtor. So it is in international finance as well. Payment in one direction is in exchange for something else going in the opposite direction. The accounts balance at all times. That is why economists call it the *balance of international payments.*

- The **balance of international payments** is a formal accounting statement of all of the payments made between a nation and the rest of the world.

We start an examination of the balance of payments with the U.S. *balance of trade,* which is the difference between exports and imports. In 1979 U.S. business firms sold to foreigners the following list of goods, which comprised our exports:

Manufactured goods	$116.6 billion
Raw materials and fuels	$28.2 billion
Food products	$24.2 billion
Miscellaneous	$13.1 billion
Total	$182.1 billion

In the same year we bought from foreign firms the following imports:

Manufactured goods	$112.2 billion
Raw materials and fuels	$71.5 billion
Food products	$17.7 billion
Miscellaneous	$10.1 billion
Total	$211.5 billion

Comparing the totals shows a net deficit of $29.4 billion. Our income from sales to foreigners was $182.1 billion, while we bought goods worth $211.5 billion.

This "unfavorable" balance of trade, as it is called, was due largely to imports of crude oil, which amounted to $60 billion in 1979. We sold more manufactured goods abroad than we bought (+$4.4 billion), more food products than we bought (+$6.5 billion), and more miscellaneous goods (+$3.0 billion). The overall deficit arose in the raw materials and fuel category (−$43.3 billion).

- The **balance of trade** is that portion of a nation's balance of international payments that reflects trade in goods and services only. It does not include governmental transactions or capital inflow or outflow.

These figures for the balance of trade do not include military transactions. Each year the U.S. government makes grants to various foreign countries to pay for military equipment. These grants are, like imports, payments to foreigners and represent a debit item in the balance of payments. At the same time the U.S. government sells military goods to foreign nations. Like exports, they produce revenue and are a credit item. In 1979 these military transactions produced a net debit of $1.3 billion. Added to the deficit in the balance of trade, the total negative balance becomes $30.7 billion.

There is more to the international economy than purchase and sale of merchandise. Services of various kinds are also exchanged, including transportation, travel, payment of royalties and fees, and a variety of other items. The U.S. generally has a negative balance on travel and transportation (−$2.7 billion in 1979) and a positive balance on other services (+$5.8 billion in 1979). In 1979 we earned more than we paid for services by $3.1 billion. These earnings reduced the negative balance overall from $30.7 billion to $27.6 billion.

Now we come to income from investments. Each year individuals and business firms earn income from investments in other countries. In 1979 those earnings for the U.S. came to $66.0 billion. Foreign firms and individuals also earned income on their investments in the U.S. These payments to foreigners, like purchases of imported goods, represent a debit item in the overall balance of payments. They amounted to −$33.5 billion in 1979. For the U.S. as a whole, then, our net investment income was +$32.5 billion. Investment income puts our running total for the balance of payments in the black at last. The previous figure was a negative balance of $27.6 billion. The positive balance for investment income moves the running total to +$4.9 billion.

We are not finished, however. Some additional financial transfers must be included. Such items as the wages sent home by foreign-ers working in the U.S., social security payments to retired Americans living abroad, and other transfer payments are made. This item is almost always a debit item for the U.S., and amounted to −$5.7 billion in 1979. Our running total is negative once again, −$0.8 billion.

This figure is called the balance on current account. The phrase *current account* is used because it shows the credits and debits that are part of the daily international payments, summed over a year, that result from the normal course of international transactions. We summarize it here.

	Balance:
Merchandise trade	−$29.4 billion
Military transactions	−$1.3 billion
Services	+$3.1 billion
Income from investments	+$32.5 billion
Transfer payments	−$5.7 billion
Total	−$0.8 billion

Two additional types of payments must now be considered, in what is called the capital account. The first is international investment. Americans can add to or dispose of investments in other countries, and foreigners can do the same in the U.S. American investments in foreign countries are a purchase of foreign assets, and, like imports, represent a payment made to foreigners. They are a debit item in the balance of payments. Foreign investment in the U.S. is just the opposite. It is a purchase of assets in the U.S., and, like exports, is a credit item in the balance of payments.

In 1979, U.S. interests acquired $60.6 billion of foreign assets. Private investment accounted for $56.8 billion and the government acquired $3.8 billion. Foreign investment in the U.S. was considerably less, totaling $51.8 billion. The balance on the capital account was therefore −$8.8 billion:

U.S. investment abroad	−$60.6 billion
Foreign investments in the U.S.	$51.8 billion
Balance	−$8.8 billion

Adding the capital account balance to the current account balance gives the amount that must be financed. In 1979 it was −$9.6 billion:

Current account balance	−$0.8 billion
Capital account balance	−$8.8 billion
Balance	−$9.6 billion

In other words, taking all of these payments into account, the U.S. owed $9.6 billion to foreigners at the end of the year.

Financing the deficit is done through the world's central banks, acting for their governments. The monetary authorities of the various nations hold financial assets, or reserves, by which they settle payments among themselves. These assets include currencies of other nations, gold, and reserves in the International Monetary Fund (IMF). The latter includes special drawing rights (SDRs), which are created periodically by the IMF in order to enlarge international monetary reserves.

Settlement of the 1979 deficit for the U.S. required that $9.6 billion be paid to foreign monetary authorities out of U.S. reserves. This is exactly what a family would do if it spent more than it received—it would pay its creditors out of its savings.

In the case of the U.S. in 1979, however, just the opposite happened. U.S. official reserve assets increased by $1.1 billion. This was an increase in U.S.-owned foreign assets, so it was a debit in the balance of payments accounts. Furthermore, foreign central banks sold dollar assets from their reserve accounts to the extent of $14.2 billion. This was equivalent to a U.S. purchase of foreign-owned assets, and, like imports or investment abroad, was a debit item in the balance of payments. On the other side of the ledger, the IMF increased the amount of SDRs, and the U.S. share was $1.1 billion. Nevertheless, the official settlement transactions that are supposed to offset the deficit actually made it larger by $14.2 billion, bringing it to a total of −$23.8 billion, rounding the figures.

Table 38–1
U.S. Balance of International Payments, 1979 (billions of dollars)

		Balance
Current Account		
Goods and services		−27.6
Exports and imports	−29.4	
Military transactions	− 1.3	
Services	+ 3.1	
Investment income		+32.5
Transfer payments		− 5.7
Capital Account		
Foreign investment		− 8.8
Official settlement		
transactions		−14.2
Errors and omissions		+23.8
		− 0.0

What Happened?

A statistical discrepancy happened. We know that the account should balance, just like your personal checkbook. If it doesn't, there must be errors or omissions, like in my checkbook. So the unexplained difference is accounted for by adding a final line to the balance of payments, labeled errors and omissions, which creates the final balance. In 1979, it was, of course, $23.8 billion.[1] By way of summary, the entire U.S. balance of payments for 1979 is given in abbreviated form in Table 38–1.

Why was there such a large errors and omissions item in 1979? It was more than twice the size of any in the past. Part may be the result of inadequate data gathering. Part may reflect a growing international drug traffic. Part may reflect illegal transactions designed to evade U.S. tax laws.

In 1981 congressional hearings revealed that in the late 1970s the U.S. government reached

---

[1] I used to spend hours trying to reconcile my checkbook with my monthly bank statement and never found an error on the part of the bank. Then I studied the balance of international payments. Now all I do is reconcile the two sums by an "errors and omissions" entry, saving untold hours. Who says it doesn't pay to study economics?

a secret agreement with Saudi Arabia, Kuwait, and the United Arab Emirates not to reveal the amounts of their investments in the U.S. economy. A large amount of the errors and omissions item may represent foreign investment that should properly be included in the capital account.

The International Financial System, 1945–1970

For twenty-five years after World War II the international financial system was based on a set of relationships between gold, the dollar, and other currencies established at an international conference at Bretton Woods, New Hampshire, in 1944. The essential elements of the Bretton Woods agreement were these:

1. The United States undertook to maintain the price of gold at $35 an ounce, agreeing to buy and sell gold at that price in official transactions with other governments.

2. Monetary authorities in other countries agreed to maintain a fixed rate of exchange between their currencies and the dollar by buying and selling dollars in their respective exchange markets as demand and supply conditions changed.

3. The *International Monetary Fund* (IMF) was established. Each member nation provided a portion of the Fund's capital in the form of gold or currencies convertible into gold. The purpose of the Fund was to promote stability in the international financial system, primarily by providing reserves to central banks if they had difficulty in stabilizing the value of their nation's currency.

Under this system the value of the dollar was tied to gold through its convertibility into gold at the U.S. Treasury, and other nations' currencies were tied to the dollar by the maintenance of a fixed rate of exchange.

The rate of exchange between the dollar and other countries was maintained by the monetary authorities of other countries and not by the U.S. Treasury or the Federal Reserve System. Each nation's central bank was responsible for keeping the value of its currency within 1 percent of its "par" value. Its par resulted from the definition of the currency in terms of gold. For example, the gold content of the dollar, as defined by U.S. law, was four times the gold content of the franc, as defined by French law. This made one dollar equal to four francs, or one franc equal to 25 cents. The French government, through its central bank, had to keep the value of the franc, as it was bought and sold on the foreign exchange market, within a range of 24¾ cents and 25¼ cents. To do so, it would buy francs whenever the price fell toward 24¾ cents and sell francs when the price rose toward 25¼ cents. Under normal conditions these stabilizing operations were sufficient to contain short-run fluctuations in a currency's price within the required bounds of 1 percent of par value and thereby maintain a system of *fixed exchange rates*.

- The **International Monetary Fund** is an organization formed in 1944 to hold a portion of the international monetary reserves of national monetary authorities. It acts as a central transfer agency for settlement of international accounts between nations and can lend to central banks that need assistance in meeting temporary imbalances in their payments.

- **Fixed exchange rates** are rates of exchange between two or more currencies established by agreement between the countries involved, which agree to maintain fluctuations of exchange rates within limits agreed upon in advance.

Monetary Reserves

A commitment to stabilize the value of a currency in the manner established by the Bretton Woods agreement implies that a central bank must hold reserves of gold or dollars or both. If dollars are to be sold in order to raise the price of one's own currency the central bank must hold dollars, or must have gold to sell to the U.S. Treasury in exchange for dollars. Without sufficient reserves a nation might have to restrict imports or subsidize exports in an effort to equate the demand and supply of foreign currencies, and that would restrict and hinder international trade. Reserves of dollars or gold or both were necessary, along with a nation's account at the International Monetary Fund.

As a result, the dollar became the "key currency" of the world financial system. Foreign central banks were eager to acquire and hold dollars, at least until they felt that their reserves were large enough to take care of emergencies. Gold, of course, was desirable too, but international trade after World War II expanded more rapidly than the gold supply. As for the IMF, reserves there originated in the form of dollars and gold, too (until 1970, when Special Drawing Rights were created), and those monetary reserves were also limited in amount. Thus, as the 1950s moved on into the 1960s a larger and larger portion of *international monetary reserves* was held in the form of dollars. Where did those dollars come from? They came from deficits in the U.S. balance of payments. U.S. private investment abroad, together with U.S. government military expenditures and foreign aid programs, created an outward flow of dollars greater than the amount of dollars earned by a favorable balance of trade. The U.S. as a whole spent more than it earned in the international economy, and the extra dollars were absorbed into the reserves of the world's central banks.

The growth of reserves enabled the system of stable exchange rates to be maintained through the 1950s and 1960s. International trade expanded, trade restrictions and tariffs were reduced, and private investment funds were able to flow relatively freely into international investments. It was, in many ways, a golden era for the international economy.

• **International monetary reserves** are funds held by central banks or other monetary authorities to settle international payments among themselves. They include gold, key currencies, and accounts at the International Monetary Fund.

Special Drawing Rights

The need to provide the international financial system with increased reserves other than dollars led in 1967 to an agreement to create a new international financial asset at the International Monetary Fund. The new asset is called *Special Drawing Rights* (SDRs). They are reserve assets created by the Fund for its members, in proportion to their initial allocation of contributions to the Fund. They are available for use in settling international balances with another member of the Fund. The purpose is to enlarge the total of reserve assets, supplementing gold, key currencies, and IMF reserve positions (which originally came from gold and convertible currencies). The first allocation of SDRs on January 1, 1970, created new international reserves equal to $3.4 billion. Two more allocations of about $3 billion each took place on January 1, 1971, and January 1, 1972, for a total of about $9.5 billion in the first round. This represented an increase in world monetary reserves of about 13 percent over the 1969 level. A second round of increases in SDRs is currently taking place, amounting to about $4.5 billion in both 1979 and 1980.

SDRs are only a small addition to the international financial system at the present time, but they point the way toward the future. They are a step toward a system of international reserves based neither on gold nor a key currency like the dollar, but on an artificial reserve asset created solely for use as a reserve. They will make possible a planned increase in international reserves to complement and facilitate increases in international trade. Their use also makes the IMF into something like a central bank for central banks, able to create monetary reserves when needed. We are a long way from a system that manages international reserves in the same way as a central bank manages the reserves of a nation's banking system, but one small step in that direction has been taken.

● **Special Drawing Rights** are an international reserve asset at the International Monetary Fund created by agreement among Fund members.

The System Weakens

During the 1950s and the 1960s, the U.S. continued to supply dollars to the world economy through large balance of payments deficits. We shall examine the source of those deficits presently, along with some of the problems they created and reasons why they could not continue. Here, however, we examine their impact on the world financial system.

First, as holdings of dollars by foreign central banks increased to levels above those necessary for international reserves, foreign monetary authorities began to exchange dollars for gold at the U.S. Treasury. Gold reserves held by the U.S. began to decline.

Second, confidence in the ability of the U.S. to redeem dollars for gold began to fall as potential claims against the dollar increased and U.S. gold reserves fell. Both knowledgeable financial experts and speculators began to suspect that the U.S. might be forced to increase the price of gold in terms of dollars. That action would both increase the dollar value of the U.S. gold stock and reduce foreign demand for gold by raising its price. In essence, the situation was one in which the demand for gold relative to dollars was expected to rise, ultimately forcing a reluctant U.S. Treasury to raise the price of gold in response to the forces of the market. That is what "devaluation of the dollar" meant in the system established at Bretton Woods. Speculators could expect to profit if they bought gold at the low price and sold it at a higher price later.

These expectations, rooted as they were in economic reality, generated a speculative demand for gold. The first crisis came in 1960,

when speculative buying drove the price of gold on the London gold market to $40 an ounce. That event caused the central banks of the major trading nations to establish a "gold pool" designed to stabilize the price of gold at $35 an ounce. Gold was sold from official reserves to the private market whenever the demand for gold pushed the price above the official level of $35.

The gold pool operated successfully, but with growing difficulty, until March 1968. Continued U.S. balance of payments deficits pushed unwanted dollars into the world financial system, expectations of dollar devaluation grew stronger, private buying of gold increased, and the gold pool found that gold sold from official reserves was steadily moving into the hands of hoarders and speculators. By 1968 the gold pool gave up its impossible task: on March 15 the London gold market was closed for two weeks and reopened to a "two-tier" gold market. The official price of gold remained at $35 an ounce, but only for official transactions between governments and national monetary authorities. The price of gold on the private market was allowed to find its own level, fluctuating upward in response to demand and supply to over $100 an ounce in 1973. With prices in the private market above the official price any new production of gold went into the hands of speculators rather than official reserves.

A growing imbalance plagued the system. As world trade grew, the volume of monetary reserves needed by central banks increased: the larger the amount of trade, the larger the possible imbalance in a nation's balance of payments, and consequently the larger the need for reserves. Those growing reserves were provided by dollars, gold, and IMF reserves, but after the two-tier price for gold appeared in 1968 no more gold moved into reserves. Only dollars (and to some extent strong currencies readily convertible into dollars, like the German mark) were available for increased reserves after March 1968. But the rising proportion of reserve dollars to gold meant that the convertibility of the dollar into gold was threatened. That, in turn, led to an increased speculative demand for gold, a rising gold price, and a growing loss of confidence in the dollar. Yet if the source of the problem, the U.S. payments deficit, were eliminated the additional reserves needed by the system would not be available. The international financial system was slowly destroying itself, fed by a continuing hemorrhage of U.S. dollars into the world money markets.

The System Breaks Down

In the years 1950–1970 the United States earned a total of $742.3 billion from exports, investment income, payments from foreign governments, foreign investment in the United States, and other sources. In the same period we spent abroad a total of $773.9 billion. The difference, $31.6 billion, was the total deficit in the U.S. balance of payments for that twenty-one year period, an average of about $1.5 billion annually. This continually increasing supply of dollars was more than could be absorbed by the normal needs of international trade, creating a growing disequilibrium in world money markets.

On the one hand, the increasing supply of dollars tended to push the value of the dollar down. On the other hand, its value relative to other currencies was fixed by the Bretton Woods agreements. Its par value could be sustained only if the monetary authorities intervened to buy dollars, and that was the responsibility of foreign central banks. Under the Bretton Woods agreements the monetary authorities of each major nation were responsible for maintaining the fixed exchange rate between the dollar and their currency. Figure 38–1 shows the disequilibrium.

In Figure 38–1, D_1 is the normal demand for U.S. dollars in international trade. S_1 is the supply that would sustain the fixed exchange rate, p_1, established by the Bretton Woods agreements. The quantity of dollars consistent with that exchange rate is q_1.

The enlarged supply of U.S. dollars in world money markets caused by the U.S. balance of payments deficit is represented by S_2. The value of the dollar would fall to p_2 if there were no intervention by central banks, and the quantity supplied would equal q_2.

But the Bretton Woods agreements required foreign central banks to maintain the price of the U.S. dollar at p_1. To do this they had to buy dollars equal in amount to ab, increasing demand to D_2. Note that this action draws even more dollars into the international money markets, increasing the quantity supplied to q_3. That is, the artificially high value of the dollar encouraged U.S. corporations to buy foreign assets and U.S. citizens to travel abroad, increasing the U.S. balance of payments deficit even further.

Purchase of U.S. dollars by foreign central

Figure 38-1
International Monetary Disequilibrium

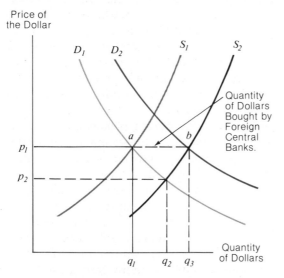

The initial equilibrium (S_1 and D_1) was broken by large U.S. balance of payments deficits that increased the supply of dollars to S_2. The value of the dollar, p_1, could be maintained as long as foreign central banks acquired ab amount of dollars.

banks had two bad effects. First, it caused inflation in the world economy. Purchases of U.S. dollars by foreign central banks were just like open market operations. They increased the reserves of banking systems in foreign countries, fostering a multiple expansion of demand deposits. The resultant monetary ease added to the already mounting inflationary pressures of the 1960s.

Second, purchase of dollars meant a transfer of real assets to U.S. industrial corporations and banks. The dollars were held by Americans, who exchanged them for foreign currencies and used those currencies to buy foreign assets. In effect, foreign central banks were financing a gradual takeover of their economies by U.S. international corporations.

The U.S. government also benefited, paying for part of its military activity overseas with dollars provided by foreign central banks. Up to the mid-1960s there was little objection to this outcome, because U.S. military expenditures abroad were chiefly directed toward protecting Western Europe and Japan from the USSR. But by the late 1960s the war in Vietnam came to absorb the bulk of U.S. overseas military expenditures, and it also caused a huge jump in the U.S. balance of payments deficit to over $30 billion a year. The major European nations found themselves helping to pay the real costs of an unpopular war, in exchange for depreciating dollars, while contributing to escalating inflation.

At this conjuncture the system broke down. A U.S. balance of payments deficit of $30 billion in 1971 caused a great "run" on the dollar. Private holders of dollars throughout the world expected the huge deficit to force a devaluation of the dollar, or, what was the same thing, an increase in the official dollar price of gold from the existing price of $35 per ounce. This would automatically increase the value of other currencies relative to the dollar. So speculators began to sell dollars for other currencies. The amounts were so great that foreign central banks decided they could no

longer stop the flow by buying dollars, so they stopped doing so. Official devaluation of the dollar was now inevitable.

Devaluation of the Dollar

Currency devaluation means simply that the value of that currency is officially reduced, relative to other currencies. When a currency is defined in terms of gold, devaluation is accomplished by raising the price paid for gold. When a currency is valued in terms of another currency, the price of the other currency is increased. Devaluation is different from *depreciation*. Depreciation occurs when the value of a currency is established by demand and supply on the foreign exchange markets and its price falls relative to other currencies. In 1971–73 the dollar was devalued twice and then its value was allowed to depreciate as its price fell on the foreign exchange market.

Currency revaluation is just the opposite. The value is raised relative to other currencies —by reducing the price paid for gold, or reducing the price paid for other currencies. Allowing the price to rise on the free market is called *appreciation*. For example, while the dollar was being devalued in the early 1970s, the German mark was revalued upward, reflecting a German balance of payments surplus; then its value appreciated as the price of the dollar fell further.

Between August 1971 and February 1973 the dollar was twice devalued officially. But that did not end the crisis, for U.S. inflation continued to accelerate, and U.S. balance of payments deficits continued to grow. Finally, in March 1973 the U.S. Treasury announced that the value of the dollar relative to other currencies would be allowed to "float" in response to market forces. The era of fixed exchange rates was over.

The value of the dollar would henceforth be determined by demand and supply in the foreign exchange markets, except to the extent that the U.S. government might temporarily intervene to smooth out short-term fluctuations. Any intervention would be carried out by the Federal Reserve System, which would buy or sell dollars on the foreign exchange market in New York. Foreign central banks were released from their obligations to absorb the outward flow of dollars created by U.S. payments deficits. Instead, those dollars would drive down the value of the dollar on the free market until the payments deficit was eliminated. Further devaluation of the dollar would not occur because of formal action by monetary authorities, but the value of the dollar would appreciate or depreciate as its price fluctuated in the free market.

- **Currency devaluation** is a change in the definition of a currency in terms of gold (or other currencies), in which the price of gold (or other currencies) is raised. This reduces the value of the currency.

- **Currency depreciation** is a fall in the value of a currency on the foreign exchange market. This differs from devaluation in that the definition of the currency in terms of gold does not change, but its price in terms of other currencies declines. Depreciation occurs when exchange rates are flexible.

- **Currency revaluation** occurs when the currency is increased in value by reducing the price of gold (or other currencies).

- **Currency appreciation** occurs when the market price of a currency rises.

Flexible Exchange Rates

Exchange rates between individual currencies are now free to move in response to market forces. Instead of payments deficits and surpluses a nation's currency will depreciate or appreciate in value. The change in exchange rates should be reflected in changes in trade balances to keep the international financial system relatively stable. Fixed exchange rates have been abandoned, except for currency relationships within the European Common Market.

Supply, Demand, and Exchange Rates

In a system of *flexible* (or "floating") *exchange rates* the terms of exchange between currencies are determined by the supply and demand for the currencies on the foreign exchange market. Prices of foreign currencies, in terms of dollars, are set by market forces and not by monetary authorities. For example, the exchange rate between the American dollar and the British pound in December 1971 was $2.60 = £1. In May 1974, after much instability in the international money markets, the dollar had appreciated in value relative to the pound, and the ratio stood at $2.40 = £1. Where in December 1971 Americans had to give up $2.60 to obtain £1, in May 1974 the cost of £1 was only $2.40.

With respect to the German mark, however, the dollar depreciated in value from 31¢ in December 1971 to 41¢ in May 1974. That is, in December 1971 you could obtain 1M for 31¢, but in May 1974 it cost 41¢. The mark went up in value relative to the dollar.

- With **flexible exchange rates,** the ratio of exchange between currencies is allowed to fluctuate in response to supply and demand in the foreign exchange market.

These two examples are characteristic of a system of flexible exchange rates that move in response to demand and supply of currencies. The demand for British pounds by Americans is determined by U.S. demand for British goods, securities, travel services, and anything else British that Americans want to buy. The available supply of pounds is determined by the British demand for American goods, services, and investments. The British buy from us, making a supply of pounds available; we buy from them, creating a demand for pounds. The price of pounds, in terms of dollars, is determined by the interaction of the two market forces of demand and supply. Figure 38–2 shows the result.

Flexible exchange rates will move freely upward or downward in response both to daily fluctuations in demand and supply and basic

Figure 38-2
Market Determination of the $/£ Exchange Rate, I

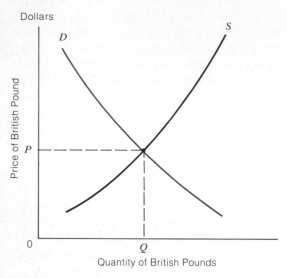

The dollar price of the pound is determined by the interaction of demand and supply in the market for foreign exchange. It will vary from day to day in response to market forces, reflecting the flow of trade and investments between the two countries that lies behind the demand and supply curves.

shifts in flows of trade and investment. For example, suppose the demand for pounds increases because Americans start to buy more English goods. There is no change in the British demand for American goods, and hence in the supply schedule of British pounds. The dollar price of pounds will rise until the demand and supply of pounds is once more equated. Underneath this price shift, however, is a change in the pattern of trade. British purchases of U.S. goods have increased in amount because a decline in the value of the dollar made U.S. goods cheaper for Britishers, and the quantity of pounds available to Americans increased to match the increased American demand for British pounds. The dollar depreciated in value relative to the pound until a new balance of trade developed where the dollar and pound were once more in equilibri-

um. Figure 38–3 shows what happens in the foreign exchange market in such a case.

A U.S. balance of payments deficit could not exist with fully flexible exchange rates. If U.S. government spending and private investment abroad created a demand for foreign currencies greater than the supply made available by existing trade flows at prevailing exchange rates, the value of the dollar would depreciate until a balance of demand and supply in the foreign exchange market was achieved. As the value of the dollar fell U.S. demand for foreign goods and investments would decline because their dollar price would rise, and the amount of foreign currencies demanded by Americans would be reduced. Simultaneously, a cheaper dollar would increase foreign demand for U.S. goods and make larger amounts of foreign currencies available to Americans. A decline in the value of the dollar would prevent any disparity in the balance of payments from even arising.

Purchasing Power Parity
In the long run, freely flexible exchange rates tend to reflect relative price levels in the various countries of the world. The "par value" of a currency will be determined by the domestic price level and not by either an agreement among nations or the "gold content" of the currency. If the U.S. price level were to rise by 10 percent relative to prices in the rest of the world, the value of the dollar on the foreign exchange market would depreciate in value by 10 percent, other things remaining the same. Here is an example of *purchasing power parity*.

Start out with the U.S. and Canadian dollars at equality, so that $1 U.S. = $1 C. A U.S. citizen traveling in Canada could use his dollars freely in buying at Canadian prices (Canadians normally accept U.S. dollars in retail trade). Now have U.S. prices rise by 10 percent while Canadian prices remain the same. The U.S. dollars obtained by Canadians will be worth 10 percent less than before, in terms of what they can buy, and Canadians will start demanding

Figure 38-3
Market Determination of the $/£ Exchange Rate, II

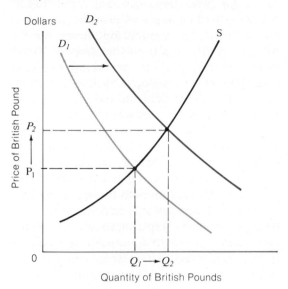

Quantity of British Pounds

The market equilibrium of Figure 38-2 (P_1Q_1) is disturbed by an increased demand for pounds ($D_1 \longrightarrow D_2$) because Americans buy more English goods and investments. The price of pounds will rise ($P_1 \longrightarrow P_2$), making U.S. goods more attractive to Britishers because the relative price of U.S. goods falls. The British buy more U.S. goods and the quantity of pounds available to Americans rises ($Q_1 \longrightarrow Q_2$). A new equilibrium exchange rate is established at P_2Q_2, where $S = D_2$.

10 percent more for dollars spent in Canada. An American will have to pay $1.10 U.S. for a Canadian product priced at $1.00 in Canada. The exchange rate will have shifted from $1 U.S. = $1 C. to $1.10 U.S. = $1 C. After all, the dollar lost 10 percent of its real value at home; it will also lose 10 percent of its real value in other countries.

The principle that exchange rates shift in response to relative changes in price levels when exchange rates are flexible is rigorously correct only if other things remain the same (full employment, no shifts in technology and costs of production, no crop failures or changes in consumption patterns, etc.). Exchange rates reflect real costs of production, consumer tastes, availability of resources, and other factors that influence patterns of world trade as well as price levels. Flexible exchange rates will continue to respond to changes that affect the world pattern of costs and output. But they will also reflect domestic price levels in the various countries of the world.

● **Purchasing power parity** means that, with flexible exchange rates, the normal relationship between currencies ("par value") will depend on relative price levels among countries.

Advantages and Disadvantages of Flexible Exchange Rates
Flexible exchange rates have some definite advantages over the old system of fixed exchange rates. They promote automatic adjustments in the balance of payments that prevent the sort of disequilibrium created in the Bretton Woods system described earlier in this chapter. Balance-of-payments difficulties tend to be self-correcting. On the other hand, the effects of the self-correcting mechanism on a nation's domestic economy may not be desirable on both economic and political grounds.

With flexible exchange rates, a persistent deficit in a nation's balance of payments will cause the value of its currency to fall relative to others. The decline in the value of its currency will bring an increase in exports and a decrease in imports, reducing and ultimately eliminating the balance-of-payments deficit. As the payments deficit is reduced the value of its currency will gradually be stabilized. An equilibrium will be reached when the nation's international payments balance.

The adjustment also works in the other direction. A surplus in the balance of payments causes a nation's currency to appreciate in value. As it appreciates, exports will fall and imports rise, eliminating the surplus and moving toward a new equilibrium.

These adjustments are not instantaneous, but work themselves out over a period of time.

They also cause employment to rise (when the currency depreciates in value) or decline (when the value of the currency appreciates). This relationship adds another element of instability to the domestic economy and complicates the problems involved in using monetary and fiscal policies to promote high levels of employment and stable prices. The effect of fiscal and monetary policies on the balance of payments and currency exchange rates limits the freedom of monetary and fiscal policy.

Flexible exchange rates also introduce an additional element of uncertainty and risk into international economic relationships. An exporter will ship goods now and receive payment a few months later, for example. If his currency appreciates in value in the meantime he will obtain some windfall profits. But if it depreciates he can be saddled with unexpected losses. Traders can overcome these difficulties by "hedging" on the "forward" market for foreign exchange, as we shall see in a moment, but long-term investors cannot because there is no forward market for long-term currency obligations.

Hedging

Trade risks from flexible exchange rates can be greatly reduced by hedging. It works this way. A U.S. importer orders some German beer and agrees to pay for it in marks when it is delivered two months later. His expected profit is based on current prices. Now suppose that the dollar depreciates in value by 10 percent over the next two months and he has to pay 10 percent more dollars for his beer. There go his profits!

What to do?

At the time the importer buys the beer he can buy German marks for delivery two months later. Then, at the time he pays for the beer and loses 10 percent, he sells the marks he paid for two months earlier, and makes 10 percent on that deal because he bought low and sold high. Who is the chap he dealt with in the German marks deal? He could be an exporter who is in exactly the opposite situation from our importer, or he could be a speculator (who guessed wrong this time). If the dollar had appreciated in value instead of falling, the importer would still have come out with his profits intact. In that case he would make a windfall profit on his beer and have an equal loss on his hedging deal. Hedging, then, can eliminate the additional risks to trade that result from flexible exchange rates.

Investment Risks

Unfortunately, it is difficult to make hedging deals of this sort for long-term investments. Long-term forward markets for foreign currencies are just nonexistent, and investors must become, to some extent, speculators in foreign currencies. For example, suppose an American corporation invests $100,000 in a French subsidiary when the dollar is worth four francs (1 fr = 25¢). The value of its investment is 400,000 francs. Now let the value of the dollar appreciate relative to the franc so that it is worth five francs (1 fr = 20¢). The value of the investment bought for 400,000 francs is now only $80,000. Without any action on its part, the U.S. firm has lost $20,000, even though the French investment may show a profit in its operations.

Conversely, let the value of the dollar depreciate so that it is worth only three francs (1 fr = 33¢). The original investment of 400,000 francs is now worth $132,000. A windfall gain is obtained.

The possibility of these windfall gains and losses increases the uncertainty attached to international investment, making it more speculative. The added uncertainties and risks are sure to discourage some portion of the investments that would be made if exchange rates were fixed. So there was some logic to the Bretton Woods system, after all. Fixed exchange rates are more favorable to international capital investment than flexible ones.

Managed Exchange Rates

We can expect some intervention in foreign exchange markets even when flexible exchange rates are the rule. A central bank may try to smooth out fluctuations in the value of its currency that normally occur from day to day, particularly when a long-term shift from one level to another is taking place. Groups of nations may try to keep relatively stable or even fixed rates among themselves while allowing their currencies as a group to fluctuate against others. For example, the European Common Market countries seek to maintain a fixed relationship between their currencies, within a band 2¼ percent wide, while allowing the entire group of currencies to float vis-à-vis the dollar and the rest of the world. Any worldwide system of flexible exchange rates will develop those types of modifications.

There are good reasons for governments to modify a system of flexible exchange rates. Some of the important reasons include:

1. When the value of your currency rises relative to that of other countries, your exports become more expensive to foreign buyers. For example, even if there is no change in domestic prices, if foreigners have to pay more of their currency to get your currency, they will pay more for your goods. Your exports will fall and your citizens will lose their jobs. Normally, then, any government will try to avoid substantial increases in the value of its currency in world financial markets.

2. Conversely, when the value of your currency falls, your nation's exports will become more attractive to foreigners and domestic employment will be stimulated. This relationship causes a government, on the one hand, to try to keep the value of its currency relatively low, and, on the other hand, to counteract actions by other governments to keep the values of *their* currencies low.

The temptation among nations to gain advantages by manipulating foreign exchange rates is often strong. This is particularly true for nations that export substantial portions of their national output, such as the countries of Western Europe. But what one country can do, others can also. The result is usually that no country can get away with such policies for very long. Point and counterpoint lead to foreign exchange instability and a general decline in trade for all. To avoid this competition, in relatively good times nations and their central banks generally try to intervene in foreign exchange markets to stabilize exchange rate relationships, smoothing out temporary fluctuations that might increase the uncertainties of foreign trade. When times get hard, however, stabilization policies tend to break down as each nation seeks to gain trade advantages over others.

The Dollar and the Price of Oil

The price of oil in world markets is quoted in dollars. When other nations import oil they must pay in dollars, or in the equivalent value of their own currencies. This means that when the value of the U.S. dollar rises relative to other currencies the cost of oil for other oil-importing nations rises also, even if the quoted oil price is unchanged. Conversely, when the value of the U.S. dollar falls their oil costs also fall. A 10 percent increase in the value of the U.S. dollar relative to the French franc, for example, will raise the cost of oil imported into France by 10 percent, even if the quoted dollar price of the oil does not change.

This relationship creates problems for other nations. A tight money policy in the U.S., which raises interest rates here, will attract investment funds from other countries. The increased demand for U.S. dollars in the international money markets will tend to drive up the price of the dollar. Costs of oil will rise in other oil-importing countries with the usual unhappy results for the economy, increased inflation and reduced employment. Inflation will result from increased energy costs, and employment will fall because higher prices bring smaller export sales. These effects can be countered by foreign central banks. Tight money policies can be used to raise interest rates, thereby stopping the flow of capital to the U.S. and halting the rise in value of the U.S. dollar. But that policy dampens economic activity and increases unemployment directly. It is not an attractive policy alternative: either deflation and unemployment or inflation and unemployment.

Similarly, a favorable balance of payments for the U.S. economy, in which payments into the U.S. economy exceed U.S. payments abroad, will cause the value of the U.S. dollar to rise. The effects on other oil-importing countries will be the same as those just described.

These considerations mean that domestic economic policy within the U.S. and American participation in the flow of world trade and payments have a significant effect on the domestic economies and economic policies of all other nations. Much of the monetary policy of foreign central banks, particularly in western Europe, is directed toward coping with the effects of U.S. domestic economic policy on their domestic economies, transmitted by the balance of payments and exchange rates among world currencies.

Summary

Any nation's position in the world economy affects its international balance of payments. The U.S. balance of payments, therefore, reflects the large volume of U.S. merchandise trade, including large imports of oil, and the dominance of the U.S. in the flow of international investment funds. The importance of these international aspects of the U.S. economy has made the U.S. dollar one of the world's key currencies.

In the U.S. balance of payments, large oil imports create an unfavorable balance of trade, but a small net credit for services and very large earnings from investment more than counterbalance the debit balance on merchandise trade. U.S. investment abroad, however, usually creates an overall deficit in the balance of payments, which is usually increased by military spending abroad by the U.S. government. These usual relationships were modified since the 1970s by very large credits that somehow evaded the record keepers, so that the accounts were balanced by large reductions in dollar reserves held by foreign monetary authorities.

The international financial system established in 1944 was one of fixed exchange rates between currencies. The U.S. maintained a fixed dollar price of gold, other currencies were defined in gold, and the resultant par values were maintained within a narrow band of fluctuation by foreign central banks. The system was weakened, however, by a persistent U.S. balance of payments deficit. That deficit enabled international corporations based in the U.S. to acquire foreign assets cheaply and the U.S. government to shift part of the real costs of the Vietnam war to foreigners, and financing the deficit helped create worldwide inflationary pressures. The system of fixed exchange rates broke down under these pressures and was replaced in 1973 by a system of flexible exchange rates.

At the present time exchange rates move up and down in response to market forces of demand and supply. Short-run fluctuations aside, currencies will reflect changes in their purchasing power in their domestic economies. The chief advantage of flexible exchange rates is that they help to bring about automatic adjustments in a nation's balance of payments. However, they limit a nation's ability to use fiscal and monetary policies to stabilize its domestic economy. They also increase the risks of international trade and investment. These disadvantages have led nations to manage exchange rates. The world now has a more-or-less managed system of more-or-less flexible exchange rates.

The U.S. dollar remains a key currency, however. In particular, its use by OPEC in setting the price of oil forces any oil-importing nation to try to stabilize the exchange rate between its currency and the dollar. A great deal of the monetary policy of the major oil-importing nations in recent years has been related to this aspect of the U.S. dollar as a key currency.

Key Concepts

key currency
balance of international payments
balance of trade
International Monetary Fund
fixed exchange rates

international monetary reserves
Special Drawing Rights
currency devaluation
currency depreciation

currency revaluation
currency appreciation
flexible exchange rates
purchasing power parity

For Discussion

1. If a nation's international payments must always balance, with payments equaling receipts, where do the advantages of international trade come from?

2. Why is the dollar the world's most important key currency?

3. What causes a nation's currency to depreciate in value? What causes it to appreciate in value?

4. Explain the self-correcting mechanism that brings currency appreciation or deprecia-

tion to a halt when exchange rates are flexible.

5. Why do nations try to manage or control the value of their currencies?

6. How has the large increase in the price of oil in the 1970s affected the U.S. balance of payments? How has it affected the role of the dollar as a key currency?

Chapter 39

Economic Development

Whatever the trade and financial problems of the international economy may be, its greatest human and economic problem is the poverty of the third world. These are the poor countries, concerned with their own problems of poverty, backwardness, and underdevelopment. This chapter examines their economic condition and the reasons for it; their policies for promoting economic development; and their progress or lack of it. The objective is to understand better why the world is divided into rich and poor nations and some of the consequences of that division.

Three Worlds

We speak of a *third world*.[1] It comprises all of Latin America and Africa, Asia other than the Soviet Union and Japan, and the island areas of the southwest Pacific other than Australia and New Zealand. To a traveller from the U.S., the chief distinguishing feature of the

third world is its poverty. In 1977 over two *billion* people lived in countries with a GNP per person of less than $500—about half of the world's population. Another billion lived in countries with a per capita GNP between $500 and $3000. Less than a billion persons lived in the more affluent countries with a GNP per person of over $3000.[2] By this reckoning, almost 80 percent of the world population lives in the poor countries of the third world.

The developed countries of North America and western Europe stand in sharp contrast. They are the industrial areas with a technologically advanced agriculture as well, modern health and medical facilities, literate populations and well-developed educational systems, good communications and transport. They generate about 80 percent of the world's savings (a rough estimate). Table 39–1 lists those with over 10 million population in 1977, their GNP per person in 1977, and their relatively modest average annual growth rates of GNP per person between 1970 and 1977.

The noncapitalist countries of the USSR and

---

[1]The phrase "third world" became popular in the 1950s, when U.S. political strategists began to speak of the need to gain the support of less-developed countries in the cold war rivalry between the U.S. and the USSR.

[2]The data are from the *1979 World Bank Atlas* (Washington: World Bank, n.d.), pp. 4–6.

eastern Europe are by no means as affluent as the developed private enterprise economies. But their economic growth has been more rapid. Table 39–2 shows data for the nations in this group with over 10 million population.

The third world of less developed nations can be divided into several groups. One group comprises the oil-rich countries that have taken advantage of their strategic position in the world oil economy to raise their living standards. These countries are no longer poor, but they are rich islands in a sea of poverty: none has as many as 10 million people.

The poor countries of the third world can be subdivided into those whose economic development is enabling them to catch up—slowly—with the developed nations, and those falling further behind. The dividing line is growth of GNP per person of 2.5 percent annually. A growth rate above that figure enables a country to catch up; below it a nation falls further behind. Some in the latter group have negative growth rates of GNP per person. These nations are becoming poorer in absolute terms and not merely relative to the developed countries.

Included in the countries falling further behind are all of those in Africa south of the Sahara, except for several small countries (Togo, Lesotho) and a populous one, Nigeria (80 million people; growth of GNP per person, 1970–77 = 4.4 percent annually). Nigeria exports oil in large amounts. But all of Africa south of the Sahara has only about 350 million people.

Another area of the world is also falling further behind the developed countries, the Indian subcontinent, which has a total population of about 850 million. One of the world's poorest areas, it also has some of the lowest rates of economic growth. Table 39–3 tells its sad story.

The countries of the western rim of the Pacific Ocean stand in sharp contrast to those of the Indian subcontinent. This entire area has sustained strong economic growth, in spite of large and relatively rapidly growing popula-

Table 39–1
Developed Countries

Country	GNP per person, 1977 (U.S. dollars)	Average Annual Growth of GNP per person, 1970–77 (percent)
United States	8,750	2.0
West Germany	8,620	2.2
Canada	8,350	3.4
Netherlands	7,710	2.2
France	7,500	3.1
Australia	7,290	1.6
Japan	6,510	3.6
United Kingdom	4,540	1.6
Italy	3,530	2.0
Spain	3,260	3.6

Table 39–2
The Soviet Union and Eastern Europe

Country	GNP per person, 1977 (U.S. dollars)	Average Annual Growth of GNP per person, 1970–1977 (percent)
East Germany	5,070	4.9
Czechoslovakia	4,240	4.3
U.S.S.R.	3,330	4.4
Poland	3,290	6.3
Hungary	3,100	5.1
Romania	1,530	9.9
Yugoslavia	2,100	5.1

tions, low living standards, and much political turmoil. The population, including China but not Japan, is estimated at about 1¼ billion. Compare its story, shown in Table 39–4, with the previous table showing data for south-central Asia. GNP per person is significantly greater—because of the more rapid growth rates in the next column. A quarter of a

Table 39–3
The Indian Subcontinent

Country	GNP per person, 1977 (U.S. dollars)	Average Annual Growth of GNP per person, 1970–77 (percent)
Pakistan	200	0.8
India	160	1.1
Sri Lanka	160	1.3
Burma	140	1.3
Nepal	110	2.4
Bangladesh	80	−0.2

Table 39–4
Countries of the West Pacific Rim

Country	GNP per person, 1977 (U.S. dollars)	Average Annual Growth of GNP per person, 1970–77 (percent)
Taiwan	1,180	5.5
South Korea	980	7.6
Malaysia	970	4.9
North Korea	680	5.3
Philippines	460	3.7
Thailand	430	4.1
China	410	4.5
Indonesia	320	5.7
Vietnam	n.a.	n.a.
Singapore	2,820	6.6
Hong Kong	2,620	5.8

century ago, the figures for GNP per person were largely similar. Table 39–4 also includes Hong Kong and Singapore, which, although relatively small in population, act as commercial and financial centers for much of the region.

The nations of the Near East and North Africa are also growing more rapidly than the developed countries. Their living standards are relatively low, but their growth rates are relatively high. Some of this growth is financed by oil exports, but even the countries without large oil production have strong growth rates. This is an area of significant political instability, however, which can cause the pattern of growth to change rapidly. Table 39–5 shows data for the countries in this area with over 10 million people, plus Israel and Saudi Arabia.

Latin American shows a mixed pattern. One country, Venezuela, has grown relatively rapidly in the past because of oil exports. A second, Mexico, may be moving in the same direction but was growing slowly in the past. Colombia has had a respectable growth rate, but Chile's growth has been negative and Argentina's slow. Brazil, however, has been booming. If Brazil's growth continues in the next quarter century as it has in the past twenty-five years, it will become an economic giant. Table 39–6 indicates this mixed pattern, with respect to nations with over 10 million people, plus three smaller countries of some interest.

We can summarize. The countries of the western rim of the Pacific are developing rapidly. North Africa and the oil-rich areas of the Near East are also developing well. But south-central Asia, most of Africa, and much of Latin America are falling behind the developed countries, except for a few striking exceptions, such as Nigeria, Brazil, and a few other countries. Meanwhile, of course, the developed countries of North America and western Europe have entered a period of slowed growth, or relative stagnation. The planned economies of the USSR and eastern Europe are catching up to them.

The Nature of the Third World

The third world is poor. Its economic structure tends to reinforce its poverty and limit economic development. Population problems con-

Table 39–5
Nations of the Near East and North Africa

Country	GNP per person, 1977 (U.S. dollars)	Average Annual Growth of GNP per person, 1970–77 (percent)
Iraq	1,570	7.1
Algeria	1,140	2.1
Turkey	1,110	4.5
Tunisia	840	6.5
Morocco	610	4.2
Egypt	340	5.2
Iran	n.a.	n.a.
Israel	3,760	2.0
Saudi Arabia	7,230	13.0

Table 39–6
Latin America

Country	GNP per person, 1977 (U.S. dollars)	Average Annual Growth of GNP per person, 1970–77 (percent)
Venezuela	2,630	3.2
Argentina	1,870	1.8
Brazil	1,410	6.7
Chile	1,250	−1.8
Mexico	1,160	1.2
Colombia	760	3.8
Puerto Rico	2,450	0.1
Cuba	750	−1.2*
El Salvador	590	2.1

*Cuba is a special case. The sugar crop was a disaster in 1977. If 1977 is excluded, Cuba's growth rate for GNP per capita would be about 4 percent annually in the 1970s.

tribute to both poverty and underdevelopment and hinder modernization. But the chief barrier to economic growth is a dynamic pattern of self-reinforcing underdevelopment rooted in the way in which the forces and relations of production are organized, and an historical background of economic and political dependence. We will examine these issues as a prelude to a discussion of economic development strategies and policies.

Making Ends Meet on Less Than $500 a Year
It is sometimes difficult for affluent Americans to grasp the economics of poverty-stricken peasant societies. For example, how is it possible for a farm family to earn under $500 a year? It's easy. In Bangladesh (formerly East Pakistan), for example, half of the farmers have less than 3 acres of land, which yields an average of about 1000 pounds of rice per acre, with the rice selling for about 10¢ per pound. There you are:

$$3 \text{ acres} \times 1000 \text{ lbs/acre} \times 10¢/\text{lb} = \$300$$

The rice is used for seed for the next crop year and for food for the farmer and his family. And in those areas there are almost no opportunites for jobs to supplement the rice crop.

But how can people subsist on that? It's hard, and many can't. In Kenya (GNP per capita = $290 in 1977), for example, a family of four eats six pounds of yams or cereal per day—day after day. It is filling, but less nutritious than many other foods. This basic food is supplemented by a few ounces of beef or fish, some beans, okra, pepper, and milk. The family spends money on only a few items, such as salt, oil, soap, firewood, kerosene, and matches. Occasionally there will be a large purchase: a lantern, some clothes. And that's all. There isn't any money for anything else.

In economies like these, with millions on the knife-edge of subsistence, loss of a crop due to weather or war or sickness means only one thing—death from starvation or from illness brought on by inadequate food.

Characteristics of Poor Countries
Although poor countries differ markedly from each other, and any generalizations about them must be qualified by the great variety

they exhibit, they differ as a group from the advanced countries in several important respects. The "typical" poor or underdeveloped country

1. Has a relatively large portion of its resources devoted to primary production—agriculture, mining, fishing—and a relatively small proportion devoted to manufacturing.

2. Has a rapidly growing population.

3. Has substantial amounts of unused or underused resources.

4. Has an economically backward population, with high illiteracy rates and relatively low average levels of educational attainment.

5. Lacks adequate capital for the development of its human and natural resources.

6. Has an export orientation in those sectors of the economy that have been developed.

Food and raw materials dominate the economies of poor countries. In the third world of Asia, Africa, and Latin America, two-thirds to four-fifths of the population work in agriculture. Two forms of organization dominate. In some areas, plantations of large size concentrate on cash crops for export: rubber, cotton, tea, coffee, sugar, bananas, cocoa, sisal, and others. In other areas peasant cultivation on small plots is devoted primarily to subsistence agriculture, although some peasant farming is oriented toward cash crops for the market also. In both patterns there is a high density of population relative to land, productivity is low, and methods of production are backward when compared with the highly capital-intensive agriculture of the more advanced nations. Agriculture need not lead to low incomes and backwardness; the high incomes prevailing in the advanced agricultural areas of New Zealand and Australia attest to that fact. It is the backward technology, small amounts of land

per person, and large populations of the poor countries that help keep them poor.

Some poor countries are heavy producers of minerals. The third world accounts for a high proportion of world production of aluminum, copper, tin, manganese, chromium, tungsten, nitrates, and petroleum. Most large mining enterprises are not locally owned, but are owned by foreign companies. Capital must come from abroad, along with managerial and technical skills, while the mineral products are exported. Labor is drawn from the local population at the low wages established by market forces in a poor country.

Shortages of capital keep the economy undeveloped. Although estimates on these matters are subject to wide error, the amount of capital per person in advanced countries is probably about 10 times the level in poor countries. Furthermore, in poor countries capital accumulation through savings is low, because incomes are low and the great majority of people must spend all or almost all of their incomes for consumption. In a consideration of the third world as a whole, savings are probably in the range of 5 to 10 percent of national income. This low proportion of savings is, in many countries, hardly enough to maintain a constant amount of capital per person, particularly where there are high rates of population growth. A significant portion of the saving is done by the wealthy, income distribution being even more unequal than in the more affluent countries, and much of those savings are invested in real estate or in the advanced countries rather than in domestic industry. The limited savings are not used as effectively as they might be.

Where economic development does take place in poor countries, it tends to be heavily oriented toward foreign trade. The typical pattern is for exports to be dominated by a few primary products, like coffee in Colombia, bananas in Guatemala, rubber and tin in Malaya, tea in Sri Lanka, copper and other minerals in Zaire. Foreign capital is invested in those industries, the transportation system is oriented toward exporting them, and financial institutions are heavily involved in financing of exports. Imports, on the other hand, are often dominated by luxuries, like automobiles, which are imported by the relatively few rich, and manufactured goods which might be produced domestically if the economy were more highly developed.

The Population Problem

Population growth in the third world is much more rapid than in the developed countries. In the last twenty years population grew in the poor countries at about 2.5 percent annually and the rate was increasing until recently. In the developed countries the rate of population growth has averaged about 1 percent and is falling. This is the chief reason why there is a growing gap between the living standards of the rich and the poor nations. Unless population growth can be brought under control, the gap will increase and huge numbers of people will remain poor.

Patterns of Population Growth
The population of the world has not always grown rapidly. Until about two hundred years ago world population grew slowly to a level of about 750 million to 800 million people. Technology changed little and living standards remained low for the vast majority in a world devoted primarily to agriculture. Population grew only when the cultivated area devoted to agriculture expanded or where improved agricultural techniques were developed, such as in western Europe.

In the second half of the nineteenth century, the world's population began to grow far more rapidly than ever before. New lands were opened up to agriculture in great areas like the United States, Canada, Argentina, and Australia. New and highly productive food crops, like potatoes and sweet potatoes, corn, cassa-

va, and peanuts, came into wide use. More scientific techniques stressing seed selection and fertilizers spread widely. New methods of transportation, the railroad and steamship, reduced costs of shipping food into population centers. These factors enabled the populations of Europe and North America to grow rapidly, until the spread of birth control techniques slowed down the growth after the 1870s.

Meanwhile, the populations of Africa and Asia began to increase, slowly at first and then more rapidly as the technology developed in Europe and North America began to spread to those areas. Particularly after World War II, modern public health measures were widely introduced. Food supplies continued to increase and better standards of nutrition were more widely maintained. The result was a rapid fall in death rates while birth rates continued high in almost all parts of the third world. Today the world's population is about 4.5 billion, or almost six times its size two hundred years ago, and it continues to rise. Population experts say that it could double in the next fifty years, with the great bulk of the increase coming in the poor nations.

Policies of Population Control
Population control has not been high on the agenda for action in the third world until the last fifteen years. Prior to World War II the explosive population growth of recent decades had not yet appeared and in much of the colonial areas there was not much incentive for colonial powers to take action. Then, in the years up to 1960 most of the third world was preoccupied with gaining independence and trying to start down the path toward industrial growth. It was only in the 1960s that it became evident that significant increases in living standards could be achieved only if population control was developed along with industrial expansion.

Recognition of a problem and development of policies to solve it do not necessarily coincide, and this has been true of population control. Methods that work in the advanced countries, such as contraceptive pills and intra-uterine devices, have had much less success in poorer countries. Widespread use of abortion, successful in Japan, has not been readily adaptable to other countries. China has successfully reduced the rate of population growth to about half the rate of increase in output by raising the age of marriage to the late 20s or later, but other LDCs (less developed countries) have not been able to follow that lead.

Experts recognize many reasons for the difficulties encountered in spreading family planning techniques widely in poor countries, but three fundamental ones stand out:

1. Diffusion of information is difficult in populations with low literacy rates.

2. Large families are advantageous in peasant agriculture because they provide more productive effort.

3. The breakdown of traditional social controls that results from urbanization and the appearance of massive slums.

Very few LDCs have been able to overcome these obstacles to limitation of population. Indeed, the economic development policies of many LDCs help to create population problems rather than alleviate them.

Population pressures are related directly to the conditions in agriculture and labor markets. Birth rates are high and death rates have been cut by importation of modern medical and public health measures. With low productivity in agriculture and a relatively small amount of land per farmer, the amount of food production per person is low. These relationships create the ideal conditions for the population trap discussed earlier in this book. Improved agricultural productivity triggered by improved technology or land reform can set in motion a more rapid increase in population than in output, keeping incomes low and preserving the backwardness of the population

and the economy indefinitely. The result is a population with a large proportion of young people who have to be supported by a relatively small proportion of people of working age who are underemployed because the amount of land per worker is so small.

Despite population pressures, most poor countries have large amounts of unused resources. This may seem to be a paradox, but it is nevertheless true. Large reserves of minerals, petroleum, and natural gas are available, along with underdeveloped forest resources and hydroelectric power sites. "Cultivable wasteland" is found in large amounts throughout Asia, Africa, and Latin America. Irrigation could provide large increases in the area of arable land through many parts of Asia and North Africa. These opportunities remain untapped, partly because of lack of capital and partly because market demand is weak in poor parts of the world.

Population pressures on the land set in motion large migration to cities. Some of the largest and most rapidly growing urban areas of the world are in poor countries, where cities of almost endless slums develop. Lack of industrial employment—because purchasing power is low—makes for high unemployment rates as well as political unrest. The political unrest, in turn, inhibits economic development by creating higher risks for capital.

Marginal Populations

Buenaventura, a city of about 125,000 people, is the largest port on the Pacific coast of Colombia. Oil tankers and freighters take the enormous riches of its hinterland—oil, coffee, sugar, cotton, even frozen shrimp—into the commerce of the world. Near the wharves are busy offices of private firms and government agencies. The government is spending money on improving the port. Between 1970 and 1980, U.S. economic aid to Colombia amounted to over $1 billion, and private U.S. interests invested another $1 billion. Yet the city is poverty-ridden. The paved streets end a few blocks behind the Catholic Church, which faces a row of bars, cafés, and brothels. There the slums begin, a wilderness of wooden and sheetmetal shacks, ragged children, and skinny dogs, receding into swamp and jungle. Some say that 75 percent of the population is unemployed (that's right: 75 percent) and that the chief occupations are theft and prostitution. Those who work earn the low wages found in areas with very high unemployment rates. Ninety percent of the population is black, descendants of slaves brought in many years ago. Students at Del Valle University in Cali, a hundred miles inland from Buenaventura, agitate against "gringo imperialism" and study Marx.

Marginal populations like that of Buenaventura are characteristic of the cities of the less-developed countries. High birth rates prevail in rural areas, and people are driven by poverty and starvation into the cities. There they crowd into makeshift shacks constructed from discarded packing crates and other urban jetsam. Jobs are scarce and wages terribly low even when a job can be obtained. In these slums birth rates are just as high as in rural areas, and perhaps higher. With no place in either agriculture or industry, these people exist on the margin of the economy and on the edge of subsistence. No one knows what to do about this situation, except perhaps the police and armies whose task it is to pacify or suppress these potentially explosive populations.

The Dynamics of Underdevelopment

The characteristics of poor countries are closely related to each other in a system of *circular causation with cumulative effects*. Each element in the syndrome of underdevelopment helps to create and reinforce the other elements. The effect is an accumulation of forces that are strong enough to keep the economy poor and underdeveloped. Just as there is a vicious circle of poverty in an affluent society like the United States, there are *vicious circles of underdevelopment* in the third world.

Consider the situation in a poor country. An underdeveloped country with a backward population has low output per person. This low productivity causes low incomes, which in turn lead to low levels of purchasing power and small savings. Inadequate purchasing power provides little economic incentive to expand investment, and investment funds are inadequate anyway, because of low savings. Low levels of investment continue the pattern of underdevelopment and economic backwardness, completing the circle of causation and continuing the process by which the country remains poor. We show the pattern schematically in Figure 39–1.

Within this broad framework other relationships reinforce the pattern of underdevelopment. Low incomes have the same effects on productivity as in advanced countries. They lead to poor diets, poor health, and inadequate education, which reinforce low productivity and pass it on to the succeeding generation. An economically backward population is unable to develop and fully use the natural resources available, much of which lie idle. Lack of education and low rates of literacy mitigate against population control programs, so that the population tends to rise rapidly if there are gains in output, thereby keeping the population poor and backward. And through it all runs the larger social and economic problem of the nation as a whole: a low rate of savings means that the resources available to change things are meager, even if there were the will to do so.

- **Circular causation with cumulative effects** is a system characteristic of poor countries in which each element in the syndrome of underdevelopment helps to create and reinforce the other elements.

Colonialism and Economic Development

The heritage of colonialism is part of the reason for underdevelopment in poor coun-

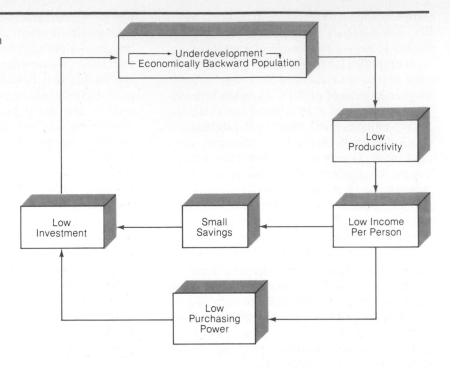

Figure 39-1
Circular Causation with
Cumulative Effects:
The Vicious Circle of
Underdevelopment

tries. Although political colonialism was largely ended for the third world in the twenty years following World War II, the economic effects of dependency have not been eradicated. And, in some respects, the present economic relationships of the poor countries with the affluent nations continue patterns from the colonial era that inhibit development.

The colonial era before World War II often brought *enclaves* of modernized economic sectors within a traditional economy. In the modernized sector, the population was literate, worked for wages or engaged in commerce, and had learned to use some forms of modern technology, such as railroads, automobiles, electric power, clocks, and simple machines. In the traditional sector, the population was largely illiterate and engaged in subsistence agriculture. They were unused to wage labor and accustomed to a preindustrial technology. The contrast was usually between urban and rural economies, but the underlying difference

was between the beginnings of an industrial society and an existing preindustrial one.

The *enclaves of modernization,* however, were generally oriented toward production for export. They originated from foreign capital attracted by the economic opportunites found in international trade. Important markets were abroad rather than at home and a large local demand was not the source of development. Typical examples were the sugar of Cuba, coffee of Brazil, oil of the Middle East, rubber of Malaya, and many others. Tied into the metropolitan economy of North America and western Europe, modernized enclaves in the poor countries were essentially extensions of the advanced economies rather than independent centers of economic development.

The existence of modernized enclaves tended to hinder progress and further development of other parts of the colonial economy. Profits went to the owners of the capital, and they were largely foreigners. Resources of all kinds